British Constitution

Made Simple

The Made Simple series
has been created
especially for self-education
but can equally well
be used as
an aid to group study.
However complex the subject,
the reader is taken
step by step,
clearly and methodically,
through the course. Each volume
has been prepared by experts,
taking account of
modern educational requirements,
to ensure the most
effective way of
acquiring knowledge.

In the same series

British Constitution

Made Simple

Colin F. Padfield, LLB, DPA(Lond)
Revised by Tony Byrne, BA, BSc(Econ)

MADE SIMPLE
BOOKS

HEINEMANN : London

Made and printed in Great Britain
by Richard Clay Ltd, Bungay, Suffolk
for the publishers Heinemann Professional Publishing Ltd,
22 Bedford Square, London WC1B 3HH

First edition 1972
Second edition 1975
Third edition 1976
Fourth edition 1977
Reprinted 1979
Fifth edition 1981
Sixth edition 1983
Reprinted 1985
Seventh edition 1987

British Library Cataloguing in Publication Data

Padfield, Colin F.
    British constitution made simple.—7th ed.—
    (Made simple books)
    1. Civics, British
    I. Title   II. Byrne, A.   III. Series
    320.441   JN906

ISBN 0 434 98609 7

Preface

This book covers the elements of the British constitution. While the text is primarily designed for students preparing for the General Certificate of Education at 'O' and 'A' levels of the various examination boards, the ground covered also makes it suitable reading for professional examinations in local and central government and in public administration generally.

Additionally, the book will be particularly helpful for student accountants and for all those training for professional positions such as company secretaries, hospital administrators, estate agents, surveyors, and many others.

For the general reader the book provides a thorough background to the political constitution under which we live and a comprehensive, up-to-date insight into its workings.

In short, it is a book about citizenship which gives the layman a clear and concise understanding of his rights, benefits, duties, and responsibilities. As such, it should provide interesting and valuable reading for all of us privileged to be members of a great democracy.

COLIN PADFIELD

Tribute

Colin Padfield died suddenly and tragically in December, 1978. He had an acknowledged gift for writing and communicating with people. He was about to retire early from his post as a lecturer at the Somerset College of Arts and Technology in order to devote his time entirely to writing. This was not to be, and we have lost a warm, able and stimulating friend and teacher.

TONY BYRNE

Preface to Seventh Edition

Much has happened and much has changed since the last edition of this book (1983)—in the fields of Local Government, police powers, the Public Corporations, for example. Such developments have been detailed in this new edition, down to July 1987.

The date itself is significant as the final revisions for this new edition coincided with the General Election of June (11th) 1987. I have therefore taken this opportunity to provide an analysis of the election and its actual or potential consequences. This is partly to bring the figures up to date; and partly to enable the reader to judge how far, if at all, Britain's system of government is changing, for a General Election provides a 'flash photo' of the political system. Though it only focuses on one (important) area of the system, it does help to confirm or confute alleged changes or trends.

In 1987, the Conservatives won a remarkable victory—greater in some ways than that of 1983. It was remarkable in the first place because it was a victory by a Government which had presided over an economy with 3 million unemployed. Secondly, though it had only 42 per cent of the vote, it secured a large Parliamentary majority (of 101, excluding the Speaker). But it was also remarkable because the Prime Minister, Mrs Thatcher, won a third successive term of office (last achieved 160 years ago). She has also become the longest serving Prime Minister since Asquith; as she herself has said, she has become 'a bit of an institution'.

Her longevity, her style and her policy orientation have given rise to new political phenomenon: 'Thatcherism'.

Following the Conservatives' victory over Labour in 1979, Margaret Thatcher declared herself to be a 'conviction' politician: having definite principles and goals, and sticking to them without wavering. Under the banner of a 'resolute approach', her Government has sought to eschew what it felt was a slow drift towards Socialism—the product of post-war political compromise or consenus (often known as 'Butskellism' or 'Heathsonism'). Trade Unions have been reformed, State industries have been privatised, market forces have replaced much state planning or intervention, and above all, a 'monetarist' (or deflationary) economic policy has been pursued with a view to reducing or re-allocating public (State) expenditure, curbing inflation, improving efficiency and renewing economic growth.

Many criticise this approach as unreasonable and uncaring (even as un-political). Even within her own Conservative party there are critics of what they see as a too uncompromising or doctrinaire style of government. These doubters have been dubbed 'wets'. Needless to say they have lost position within current corridors of power: the principle of collective responsibility has been invoked to bring about the dismissal of some dissenters (such as Norman St John-Stevas and Sir Ian Gilmour in 1981). Others have lost, or failed to gain, favour for similar lack of faith or commitment, including Francis Pym, James Prior, Geoffrey Rippon and ex-Prime Minister Edward Heath.

When Mrs Thatcher came to power in 1979, the Labour Party itself became more radical and moved to the Left—in terms of policy and in terms of organisation and procedures. This was partly because it felt it had lost the election because it had not been sufficiently Socialist in substance and appeal; and partly because it was felt that it had failed to use its period in office (1974–9) for sufficiently Socialist purposes. This party too contained critics of the consensus ('Butskellite') approach; some even talked of 'extra-Parliamentary action' to counter the power of the Government.

The so-called 'centre-ground' of British politics seemed to be vacant in 1979. The Liberals hoped to capture this, together with the new (1981) Social Democratic Party comprising 60,000 first-time party members and led by a faction of politicians from the Labour Party. Their aim was to 'break the mould' of British politics by replacing the two-party, adversarial approach, and going beyond consensus to actual coalition government. After the 1983 election, the Liberals and SDP created a firm Alliance and achieved some notable by-election successes, as well as steadily building representation in local councils (the Alliance now has over 1,000 councillors). Political commentators could foresee the emergence of a real third force, with consequences for 'hung' or balanced Parliaments, coalition governments, the politicisation of the Queen etc.

The 1987 election has put paid to this speculation. The immediate results were as follows:

	Votes (million)	%	Seats	%
Conservatives	13.7	42.3	375	57.7
Labour	10.0	30.8	229	35.2
Alliance	7.3	22.6	22	3.4
Others	1.4	4.3	24	3.7

There are many possible explanations for the Conservatives' victory: (i) the popularity of its policies (sale of council houses, improved economic performance, lower taxes, increased shareholding (or 'popular capitalism'); (ii) a general perception of competence to govern; (iii) the unpopularity or uncertainty of the opposition parties' policies (especially unilateral nuclear disarmament); (iv) the divided nature of the opposition i.e. Labour and Alliance, who collectively polled more votes than the government itself; (v) the widespread perception of the Labour Party being actually or potentially dominated by the hard (or Militant) Left (a perception perhaps encouraged by the press).

Underlying all this has been the fundamental change in the socio-economic composition of Britain. The restructuring (or 'de-industrialisation') of the economy away from traditional industries (especially in the North) together with the development of newer industries in the South (reflected in the population drift southwards) and from inner cities to sub-urbs and small towns, has tended to reduce the working class. And trade union membership is down by a third from over 12 million in 1979: there are now just as many shareholders. Further, about two thirds of households are now owner-occupiers. Overall it is estimated that about 40 per cent of the population is now 'middle class' in terms of income, job and life style. Coupled with a decline in the public (State) sector component, all this has meant a decline in the traditional bases of support for Labour, as the following table shows:

Percentage votes for the parties, June 1987

	Managerial/ Professional	Clerical	Skilled	Semi-/Un-skilled	Trade Union Member	Owner-occupiers	Council tenants
Conservative	57	51	40	33	30	50	22
Labour	14	21	36	48	42	23	56
Alliance	26	26	22	20	26	25	19

Consequently Labour is seeking to broaden its appeal by reassessing its policies 'in terms of the realities and opportunities of the 1990s'. It aims to make itself more relevant by adapting to social change and appealing to the 'haves' as well as the 'have-nots' (though if it goes too far here Mrs Thatcher will have achieved her 1986 quest to 'rid Britain of Socialism'). It is also planning to alter the selection of candidates to 'one member one vote' (allegedly to remove the excessive influence of small 'hard Left' groups in constituency parties).

Many supporters of the Alliance believe its salvation lies in the uni-fication of its two parties into the Liberal Democratic party. But the leader of the SDP (David Owen) sought to resist the move.

Thus the party system is again under change, having moved from a potentially multi-party to a dominant party situation. This might cause the opposition parties to enter into an electoral pact, which would itself entail a commitment to constitutional reform (e.g. PR voting). However, the present government may itself have to consider constitutional change (i.e. devolution) in view of its now poor representation (down to only 10 seats out of 72) in Scotland (to say nothing of the continuing problem of Ulster). Any such developments will be chartered in the next edition.

TONY BYRNE
Taunton, July 1987

Acknowledgements

I must thank first my colleagues, Tony Byrne and Barrie Foster, both specialists in this field, who read the typescript, criticised it and provided me with valuable source material. In addition, Barrie Foster prepared Appendix Two on study and examination technique, while Russell Pearce, another colleague, also gave me much valuable material.

Ann Fulton and Felix Bourne, students of mine, read and checked the proofs and made useful comments. My wife provided constant encouragement and was of great assistance in arranging the material into chapters and in checking the typescript as it progressed.

I must mention especially David Platt and Margaret Anderson of *Made Simple Books*, who guided the book from its inception to its completion, contributing generous help and comments. I owe them a heavy debt.

I also acknowledge help received from the Clerk of the House of Commons, Sir Barnett Cocks, KCB, OBE, for providing various forms; from the Rt. Hon. Edward du Cann, PC, MP, who also gave me source material; and from various civil servants in numerous Ministries who gave me much help and advice.

Finally, I am indebted to the Controller of HM Stationery Office for permission to reproduce various documents in the book; to the Field Enterprises Education Corporation, Chicago, Illinois, USA for permission to reproduce the illustration on page 103, and, finally, to the Associated Examining Board and the Schools Examination Board, University of London, for permission to reproduce specimen examination questions at Appendix Three.

Any errors and omissions in the book are entirely my own.

COLIN PADFIELD

Contents

British Prime Ministers, Governments and General Elections

Name	Party	Date	Election
Spencer Perceval	Tory	6 December 1809	1818
Earl of Liverpool	Tory	16 June 1812	1820
George Canning	Tory	30 April 1827	1826
Viscount Goderich	Tory	8 September 1827	
Duke of Wellington	Tory	26 January 1828	1830
Earl Grey	Whig	24 November 1830	1831
Viscount Melbourne	Whig	13 July 1834	1832
Sir Robert Peel	Tory	26 December 1834	1835
Viscount Melbourne	Whig	18 March 1835	1837
Sir Robert Peel	Tory	6 September 1841	1841
Lord John Russell	Whig	6 July 1846	1847
Earl of Derby	Tory	28 February 1852	1852
Earl of Aberdeen	Peelite	28 December 1852	
Viscount Palmerston	Liberal	10 February 1855	
Earl of Derby	Conservative	25 February 1858	
Viscount Palmerston	Liberal	18 June 1859	1859
Earl Russell	Liberal	6 November 1865	1865
Earl of Derby	Conservative	6 July 1866	
Benjamin Disraeli	Conservative	27 February 1868	
W. E. Gladstone	Liberal	9 December 1868	1868
Benjamin Disraeli	Conservative	21 February 1874	1874
W. E. Gladstone	Liberal	28 April 1880	1880
Marquess of Salisbury	Conservative	24 June 1885	1885
W. E. Gladstone	Liberal	6 February 1886	1886
Marquess of Salisbury	Conservative	3 August 1886	
W. E. Gladstone	Liberal	18 August 1892	1892
Earl of Rosebery	Liberal	3 March 1894	1895
Marquess of Salisbury	Conservative	2 July 1895	1900
A. J. Balfour	Conservative	12 July 1902	
Sir H. Campbell-Bannerman	Liberal	5 December 1905	1906
H. H. Asquith	Liberal	8 April 1908	1910
H. H. Asquith	Coalition	26 May 1915	1910
D. Lloyd-George	Coalition	7 December 1916	1918
A. Bonar Law	Conservative	23 October 1922	1922
Stanley Baldwin	Conservative	22 May 1923	1923
J. Ramsay MacDonald	Labour	22 January 1924	1924
Stanley Baldwin	Conservative	4 November 1924	
J. Ramsay MacDonald	Labour	8 June 1929	1929
J. Ramsay MacDonald	Coalition	25 August 1931	1931
Stanley Baldwin	Coalition	7 June 1935	1935
Neville Chamberlain	Coalition	28 May 1937	
Winston S. Churchill	Coalition	11 May 1940	
Winston S. Churchill	Conservative	23 May 1945	1945
Clement R. Attlee	Labour	26 July 1945	1950
Sir Winston S. Churchill	Conservative	26 October 1951	1951
Sir Anthony Eden	Conservative	6 April 1955	1955
Harold Macmillan	Conservative	13 January 1957	1959
Sir Alec Douglas-Home	Conservative	19 October 1963	1964
Harold Wilson	Labour	16 October 1964	1966
Edward Heath	Conservative	19 June 1970	1970
Harold Wilson	Labour	4 March 1974	1974 (Feb)
James Callaghan	Labour	5 April 1976	1974 (Oct)
Margaret Thatcher	Conservative	4 May 1979	1979
Margaret Thatcher	Conservative	5 June 1983	1983
Margaret Thatcher	Conservative	11 May 1987	1987

1
The Nature of the Constitution

Introduction

The form or structure of the Government of a society becomes its constitution. The constitution determines the distribution and exercise of the sovereign power within that political society or state. (Professor A. V. Dicey 1835–1922, a learned constitutional lawyer.)

Man is by nature a social being. In early times he formed clans or tribes for the protection and survival of himself and the group of which he was a member. Once a group, clan, or tribe is formed, **rules** are necessary to regulate the relationships of man with man and to ensure **order** and **peace** within the group. A **constitution** may thus be defined as 'the system or body of fundamental principles according to which a nation, state, or body politic is constituted and governed' (*The Shorter Oxford English Dictionary*).

A society cannot exist without such rules. The earliest records show that a King, chief, or leader is chosen or appointed, a council of elders or wise men is formed to assist the King or leader and a **Government** comes into being. In every known form of human society there exists some form of government.

The same basic procedure occurs today, when a group of people wishes to form a football club, an arts group, or a scientific society or similar body. First of all, the members usually arrange a meeting, appoint a committee, choose a chairman, name the officers of the committee—a secretary and treasurer—and then proceed to draw up the rules of the club. These rules usually define the purpose of the club, the powers and duties of the chairman, the committee, the officers, and the individual members. In all essentials a **constitution** is made for that particular group or society.

Obviously a nation or a state is a much more complex body than a small club or society, and each nation or state varies in its constitution. Types of constitutions are discussed further in this book, particularly the British constitution which is, in a sense, unique with its own particular form and procedure. It has, for example, taken over a thousand years to grow and evolve.

It will assist a student to grasp the idea of a political constitution if he remembers his own physical constitution with its skeleton, trunk, limbs, and vital organs such as the brain and the heart. He has a physical structure and framework, and he is able to function as a conscious living person, capable of reasoning and making decisions on which to act.

If we look at Professor Dicey's definition at the start of this chapter we note his reference to 'form or structure' of a Government on the one hand, and the 'distribution and exercise' of **sovereign power** on the other. The phrase 'sovereign power' means for our purposes the highest power in the state, i.e. the power vested in Parliament together with the Cabinet who are charged with the heavy and important duty of governing our lives. In medieval times the 'sovereign power' was vested in the Monarch. In the dictionary definition of 'constitution' we note that emphasis is on the 'system or body of fundamental principles' by which a state is governed. In truth, most definitions of a 'constitution' can be criticised, but for our purposes the above definition serves to pin-point the essentials.

What is a State?

A state is an independent political society situated within defined limits whose subjects are bound together with ties of mutual protection and assistance. Belgium, Denmark, France, Italy, Great Britain, Spain, the United States of America, Venezuela, and so on, are all states and are sometimes called 'nation-states'.

The main functions of a state are:

(*a*) to repel external aggression; and
(*b*) to maintain law and order within its territories.

These are the two basic functions of a state. We are all aware that there are many more duties carried out by a modern civilised state, such as the provision of welfare services, poor relief, health services, unemployment relief, and educational services. The extent of these services is determined by the wealth of the nation, the wish of the people, and by other factors.

Within a state there is a sovereign power or Government. This sovereign power may be one person, e.g. a King, a dictator, or leader, or a body of persons, like a **Council**, a **Parliament**, or a **Congress** having supreme authority. Subjects of a state owe a duty of allegiance to the sovereign power in the state of which they are members.

A nation may be united by race or language but this is not necessarily so. For example, Switzerland and the USA are each composed of different races and there is a diversity of speech within each of these states. The unity which most often binds a nation together is **territorial unity**; that is the occupation by a group of people of a defined geographical area. We may say, therefore, that people who dwell in the same area and are subject to the same laws, are citizens of the same nation or state.

Types of State

There are two main types of states: (i) **Federal**, and (ii) **Unitary**. The reason why the citizens of a state adopt one or the other of these forms is as a result of the historic development of each state or the wishes of its citizens.

(i) Federal States

A Federal State is a group of constituent units (States or Territories) which aims to reconcile national unity and power with the maintenance of individual State rights. Here power is divided between (i) a National Government which, in matters of common concern, e.g. defence, is supreme over the whole country; and (ii) State Governments which are supreme in those matters left to them, e.g. State schools. For the citizens living under Federal authorities there are in fact two sets of laws: (i) Federal Law, and (ii) State Law. The main examples of Federal States are: the United States of America, Australia, Canada, West Germany and Switzerland.

The USA became federated because, following the War of Independence, the thirteen States then in existence were too weak individually to carry on the work of government. They joined together as equals for the common convenience. Though they gave certain powers to the Federal Government, each State preserved its own independence by reserving to itself certain well-defined powers.

Those powers which are usually yielded to a Federal Government are those dealing with (i) national defence; (ii) foreign policy; (iii) the control of international trade, through customs duties and tariffs, and similar matters. Powers of a purely local character are reserved to the State Governments.

In Switzerland the cantons (subdivisions of the country) desired unity in matters of common concern such as defence and tariffs. Nevertheless, German, French, and Italian-speaking sections each wished to preserve some measure of individuality.

Federalism means the distribution of the force of the State among a number of co-ordinate bodies each originating in and controlled by the constitution (A. V. Dicey, *Law of the Constitution*).

(ii) Unitary States

In this type of state, power is **concentrated** in one body and the departments of government are **centralised** in one institution. The United Kingdom is a Unitary State. The Norman kings in the eleventh and twelfth centuries set up a strong central government (the *Curia Regis* and the Great Council). They gradually established control over the whole kingdom and created out of the customary laws the common law of England. Thus was built up a solid structure of government, a national Parliament and a legal system.

Unitarianism, in short, means the concentration of the strength of the State in the hands of one visible sovereign power be that Parliament or Czar (A. V. Dicey, *Law of the Constitution*).

The United Kingdom

The British constitution is the constitution of the United Kingdom of Great Britain and Northern Ireland, and consists of (i) England and Wales, (ii) Scotland, and (iii) Northern Ireland.

Scotland was at one time a separate State, but by the *Act of Union* in 1707, England and Scotland were united and became the **United Kingdom of Great Britain**. Since 1603, both Scotland and England have shared the same Monarch. Moreover, although Scotland and England both had at one time separate Parliaments, the Parliament at Westminster in London now legislates for the whole of the United Kingdom.

For fifty years, Northern Ireland had a separate Parliament at Stormont (Belfast) and an Executive Government. The Northern Ireland Parliament consisted of (i) the Monarch, (ii) a House of Commons of fifty-two elected members, and (iii) a Senate composed of two ex-officio Senators and twenty-four Senators elected by members of the House of Commons at Westminster. The Stormont Parliament was entitled to legislate on certain internal matters only.

All this was temporarily suspended in 1972 following a period of civil unrest. Northern Ireland is now under direct rule by the Secretary of State for Northern Ireland, who is responsible to Parliament in London. In April 1982, the Secretary of State introduced a plan to give 'rolling devolution' to the province. Under this scheme, an elected assembly of seventy-eight members, with deliberative and consultative functions, would gradually acquire executive powers as these received majority support, i.e. with a vote of at least 70 per cent in favour within the assembly. (It was dissolved in 1986.) Then in November 1985 an Agreement was signed by the Prime Ministers of Britain and Eire (Southern Ireland) under which the Irish Government may put forward views on aspects of Ulster affairs (especially security and administration of justice).

Fig. 1. The United Kingdom of Great Britain and Northern Ireland (Ulster)

Local Government

The system of local government in the United Kingdom does *not* make the British Constitution a Federation. Local authorities derive their powers from Parliament (the central legislature) and these are not rightly comparable with those of the individual States of a true Federation. The feature of a State which exists within a Federation is that of **sovereignty** which is what a local authority does not possess or claim. In reality in the United Kingdom a local authority has no separate Legislature, Executive or Judiciary. The United Kingdom local authorities are the creatures of the central Parliament which can, at will, extend or reduce their powers or even determine their size and existence (as the recent abolition of the Greater London Council has shown: see p. 326).

British Commonwealth

The Commonwealth is not a Federation for there is no central Government, no common defence force or judiciary and no rigid obligations or commitments between the members. Nevertheless all the members of the Commonwealth have a broad community of interests, and they are bound together by a common sense of ideals and a common interest in the maintenance of peace, freedom, and security. The Queen's legislative power in the Parliaments of the Commonwealth is a formality. As it has been said— 'She reigns though she does not rule'. The Queen, as personal Head of the Commonwealth, does provide the element of continuity in administration and her personal influence over the whole group is, of course, very great.

Types of Constitution

Constitutions may be divided into two main classes: (i) **rigid**, and (ii) **flexible**, although both types of political constitutions are of course equally concerned with the distribution of the powers of government between the various organs of both central and local Government.

(i) Rigid Constitutions

A rigid constitution may be defined as one which cannot readily be amended. This does not mean, of course, that it cannot ever be amended, but that any amendments that are found to be necessary may only be made by means of a **special process** provided by the constitution for that purpose.

When a community 'starts from scratch', as it were, an attempt is made by the founders to define as clearly as possible and to make secure the relationship of the various organs of government: the Executive, the Legislature, and the Judiciary. The constitution so framed assumes the character of **fundamental law**. Any other law, whether passed by the central Government of a State or local government, derives from the constitution and is subject to the constitution, i.e. is subordinate to the fundamental law.

Some states attempt to embody these principles in a single document (or a small group of documents) called 'the constitution'. In it will be found the necessary rules and principles for the creation of a **Legislature**, an **Executive** and a **Judiciary**, the election of a **President** or a **Prime Minister** and **principles for the conduct of citizens defining rights and duties**.

The best example of a **written** constitution in this sense is that of the

USA formed in 1787. With its preamble extracted from the *Declaration of Independence* 1776 it is a document of some 12 pages and is freely available for anyone to read and study. The *Constitution of the United States* is the **source of government** authority. It is the **fundamental law** of the land, defines the limits of the sphere of action of the National Government and assigns to its three branches—Executive, Legislature, and Judiciary—specific duties and responsibilities.

In composing such a document the founders of a rigid type of constitution are faced with a very difficult task. They realise that by the very nature of things, by the nature of life itself, change must occur. Nevertheless, the founders who formulate the fundamental laws of the constitution do not want their constitution lightly upset or altered. Any change which is found desirable and necessary must follow a special process. This process is in the nature of a safeguard and usually has four objects:

(i) That the constitution should be changed only after due deliberation.
(ii) That the people themselves should have an opportunity to express their views on a proposed change (e.g. by a referendum if need be).
(iii) In a federal system, the respective powers of central and local (or national and State) Governments should not be changed by one party only, e.g. the central Government alone.
(iv) The protection of minorities in language, religion, race, etc.

Most countries today have written constitutions. These include Australia, Belgium, France, East Germany, West Germany, the USA, and the USSR. Many former British colonies such as Nigeria, Kenya, and Aden also have written constitutions.

(ii) Flexible Constitutions

A flexible constitution is one which can be readily amended without any special procedure.

Britain has no formal constitution in the sense here described. There is no written booklet comparable to that described before. There are, of course, constitutional rules and principles, and some are contained in statutes such as the *Magna Carta* (1215); the *Bill of Rights* (1689); the *Parliament Acts* (1911 and 1949); and the *Peerage Act* (1963). No attempt has been made by Parliament to codify or set down separately (as is the case with the USA) the constitutional laws and customs by which Great Britain is, in fact, governed. In theory this does appear to be a weakness, as there would seem to be inadequate safeguards to prevent the arbitrary seizure of political power. But this is not necessarily so and may be advantageous. The constitutional history of Great Britain does not show a long line of dictatorships. Rather, it shows growth of individual rights and liberties based not so much on law but on the **ideas** of traditional freedoms and traditional practices (conventions), which have developed organically.

The British Constitution is nevertheless a reality. It has lasted longer than most, has been the model for many new countries, and has been an inspiration to many peoples scattered all over the world. If asked of what does the British Constitution comprise, we may reply that it embraces laws, customs, and conventions all hammered out, as it were, on the *hard anvil of experience*.

Thus no **special** legal procedure need be followed to amend the British Constitution. This is a notable feature of those constitutions which are unwritten and have not been formally codified. This remark is a generalisation only. New Zealand has a 'written' constitution, but it is also flexible since it can be amended by a simple majority vote of its Parliament.

Although Parliament may alter our constitution by the passing of a statute in the ordinary way, we should at the same time note that important constitutional changes are brought about only after considerable discussion and patient examination of the proposals. The *Parliament Acts* (1911 and 1949), for example, were not passed into law until a full discussion had taken place both in Parliament and outside, i.e. in the Press and by the general public.

It is increasingly felt by responsible politicians that proposals for constitutional change should be preceded by a general election giving a mandate to a Government to effect the change, or by referendum.

Constitutional Structure

In any scheme of government we find there are three essential types of activity which must be carried out:

(i) Making laws = The Legislature.
(ii) Executing laws = The Executive.
(iii) Adjudicating when disputes occur = The Judiciary.

We may recall that the Anglo-Saxon and the early Norman Kings personally ruled their Kingdoms and performed all three functions. Naturally they required staff to advise them on their duties and, of course, staff to execute their commands. The Anglo-Saxon Kings had the **Witan** (group of elders or wise men); and the Norman Kings had the *Curia Regis* and the Great Council to assist them in their rule. The Chancellor was the Secretary of State for all departments. He was chief executive officer. But it is interesting to note that the King sometimes sat with his judges at the Bench (as it was called), and dispensed Royal justice to his subjects. This Royal court of the early English common law subsequently became known as the Court of King's Bench simply because the King himself used to adjudicate with the judges at the Bench. The Monarch was and still is 'the fountain of justice' and the Queen today is technically present in all her Courts of Law.

The distribution of the functions of government in the British Constitution is as follows:

(i) The Legislature

This means the law-making body (*lex, legis* = law, L). In other words it is 'The Queen (or King) in Parliament'. Laws are made by the **House of Commons** and the **House of Lords** with the assent of **the Queen**.

Some laws of a minor or subsidiary character are also made by subordinate bodies, e.g. Ministers, local authorities, public corporations, and similar bodies to whom power to do so has been delegated by Parliament (see p. 286).

(ii) The Executive

Laws are executed or put into effect by HM Government or other agencies specially appointed to do so. The nominal head of the Government is HM The Queen, but in practice actual responsibility rests with the Prime Minister who heads the Cabinet which makes the policy by which the State is to be governed. Most members of the Cabinet are senior Ministers in charge of Departments of Government. These, with the whole of the Civil Service, the local authorities and public corporations carry out, or administer, the laws made by the Legislature (see p. 127).

(iii) The Judiciary

This branch of government includes the whole range of HM judges and magistrates engaged in the task of punishing offenders and settling disputes. The courts range from the House of Lords, the final Court of Appeal in the country, to magistrates' courts. The courts as a whole deal with civil and criminal cases. A fuller description of the English legal system can be found on page 213.

Sources of the British Constitution

Although we do not have a written constitution we may note that many of the sources of the British Constitution are found in documents. There are, for example: (i) **statutes**, which are printed and published; (ii) **legal cases** recorded in Law Reports; (iii) political **conventions** which are described in books and journals; and (iv) opinions of constitutional lawyers, political thinkers and historians which are contained in **treatises** describing constitutional rights and duties and practices.

(i) Statutes

There are numerous statutes containing provisions about the Constitution. Nevertheless it is true that only a small part of the total scheme of government is prescribed by statute law e.g. the existence of the House of Lords is not founded on statute, and neither was the House of Commons created by statute. The Cabinet too was not created by law and owes its existence to convention. These are the most important institutions of government.

The following statutes should be specially noted:

Magna Carta, 1215. The King promised to refrain from imposing any feudal tax save by the consent of the Common Council of the Realm. The Charter also contained the provision: 'To no man will we deny or delay right or justice.'

The *Petition of Right Act, 1628.* This laid down the important principle that there should be no taxation without the consent of Parliament, and that no one may be imprisoned without lawful cause.

The *Bill of Rights, 1689.* This affirmed very important principles of constitutional liberties e.g. Parliamentary debates should be free from interference; so too should the election of MPs. Parliaments should be held frequently; the executive alone cannot suspend laws.

The *Act of Settlement, 1701.* This established the independence of the judges and regulated the succession to the Crown of England.

The *Parliament Act, 1911* and *1949.* These curbed the power of the House of Lords to amend and delay Bills sent up to that House from the Commons.

The *Peerage Act, 1963*. This allowed the renunciation of hereditary titles of peers.
The *Race Relations Act, 1968*. This aimed to prohibit prejudice on account of race, colour or ethnic origin.
The *Representation of the People Act, 1969*. This gave the vote to persons of 18 years of age.
The *European Communities Act, 1972*. (See p. 24.)

In addition to the above there are many more statutes which originate, alter, or abridge the rights and duties of institutions, groups of persons, or individuals, but lack of space forbids their inclusion here (e.g. see p. 24).

(ii) Case Law

Case law is judge-made law. Its importance lies in the fact that the judgements of the highest courts in the land bind all lower courts in similar cases. Most of the disputes dealt with by judges in the past have been private civil cases between man and man, but some cases have determined constitutional rights and liberties. These cases enshrine the law, and since they will be followed and applied by succeeding judges and magistrates we may say that the cases are an important source of constitutional law.

Examples are numerous, but we may note here the following important decisions:

The *Case of Proclamations, 1611*, which held that the King by his Proclamation cannot create any offence which was not an offence before.
Stockdale v. *Hansard, 1839*. The mere resolution of the House of Commons does not alter the law of the land.
Bowles v. *Bank of England, 1913*, which denied the right to levy a tax merely on the resolution of the House of Commons.
A.-G. v. *Wilts. United Dairies, 1922*. The Executive may not impose a charge on a citizen unless Parliament expressly so authorises.
Thomas v. *Sawkins, 1936*, which held that police are entitled to enter a public meeting (even if that meeting is held on private premises) if the police have reasonable suspicion that a breach of the peace is likely to occur.
Christie v. *Leachinsky, 1947*. A person who is arrested by the police must be informed of the charge or crime of which he is suspected.

(iii) Conventions

Conventions are rules of political practice which the courts of law do not recognise. They are not laws and cannot, therefore, be enforced as such. Nevertheless they are an important source of constitutional law.

In our everyday life in a family, club, a class of students, or society generally there are certain unwritten rules which gradually form in the course of time and are observed. A breach of an unwritten rule (or convention) will disturb the working of a group or society and ultimately, if the breach continues, may cause a breakdown. In political life, and in the actual business of government, conventions gradually evolve and are consistently observed. These conventions also ensure the smooth working of the constitution.

We shall consider these conventions more closely later in our study when we deal with the constituent parts of government, e.g. HM The Queen, the House of Commons, the House of Lords, the Cabinet and other important bodies. But here we must observe that in practice conventions are very important. For example, our system of Cabinet government rests entirely on convention. So too does the choice of a Prime Minister, the selection of Cabinet members and the collective responsibility of the Cabinet. These are but a few of the matters in which convention plays a great part.

If, as we have observed, a convention is not law how can it be enforced? The sanction (or force) behind a convention is indirect rather than direct. Breach of a political convention does not result directly in a fine or other punishment in the courts of law. Let us take the following well-known convention: 'Parliament must meet at least once a year.' If Parliament does not meet, several laws will be broken. The *Army and Air Force Act, 1961*, would expire, for this Act must be renewed annually by means of an Order in Council which is subject to affirmative resolution in each House. In other words each House must specifically resolve that the Order be approved. If Parliament does not meet in accordance with the convention the standing Army could not legally be maintained for the defence of the realm. All military discipline would as a consequence cease to exist in the absence of **legal** power to enforce it. A further result would be that the *Finance Act* (an annual Act) could not be passed to enable the collection of revenue, and the appropriation to the various items of public expenditure. Such are the consequences if Parliament does not meet once a year as is required by convention. In effect there would be a breakdown of government, and eventually the law itself would be broken, as described above.

Political conventions include a great deal that is based on custom and expediency. The sanction behind these conventions is ultimately public opinion.

Once established a political convention may form the basis of a law. Thus conventions are a source of law. The following statutes merely embody in written form principles which were previously conventions: the *Statute of Westminster, 1931* (HM The Queen is Head of the Commonwealth; the Commonwealth is a free association of equal and independent states) and the *Ministers of the Crown Act, 1937* (the existence of the Prime Minister and his salary). Some examples of conventions are:

(*a*) *The Monarch.* The Queen will exercise the Royal Prerogative (with a few exceptions) only on the advice of a Minister of the Crown.

The Queen must assent to all Bills properly passed through Parliament.

The Queen must invite the leader of the political party having a majority in the House of Commons to form a Ministry. The person so invited is known as the Prime Minister. Other Ministers of the Crown are appointed on the advice of the Prime Minister.

The Queen must act on Cabinet advice.

The Queen dissolves Parliament at the request of a Government which ceases to command a majority in the House of Commons or is defeated in that House on a major issue.

(*b*) *Parliament generally.* In cases of conflict between the two Houses the Lords shall yield to the Commons. (This convention was given statutory recognition in the *Parliament Acts, 1911 and 1949*.)

The Government must not flout the generally expressed wishes of Parliament.

The business of the House of Commons is arranged between the Prime Minister and the Leader of the Opposition.

Parliamentary committees are miniatures of the House of Commons as regards party representation in them (see p. 74).

(c) *United Kingdom and the Dominions.* The United Kingdom Parliament will not legislate for a Dominion except at its request and with its consent.

Governors-General are appointed by the Crown and act on the advice of the Dominion Prime Minister.

(*iv*) *Treatises*

Text writers of authority sometimes express their opinions on important constitutional problems. Those opinions do not have the force of law, but sometimes they may assist a judge in a legal case to reach the right decision, particularly where the point is obscure or two constitutional principles are difficult to reconcile. In so far as the opinions are adopted by a court they are a source of constitutional law.

Political philosophers and thinkers affect public and parliamentary opinion. By their writings they may initiate new ideas on legislation, the form or institutions by which government is carried on. We may instance: John Locke (1632–1704), Montesquieu (1689–1755); Blackstone (1723–80); Jeremy Bentham (1748–1832); Edmund Burke (1729–97); A. V. Dicey (1835–1922); J. S. Mill (1806–73); Erskine May (1815–86) the author of *Parliamentary Practice.* All have contributed insights and source material by their writings and have affected our own Constitution and those overseas.

The Separation of Powers

The doctrine of the separation of powers is particularly associated with Montesquieu, the French liberal philosopher, who visited this country and studied the English Constitution which he much admired. His book *L'Esprit des Lois* published in 1748 had wide currency throughout Europe. Put simply, the doctrine is that the three functions of government (legislative, executive, and judicial) should be discharged by separate bodies and that to prevent misgovernment no two of the functions should be entrusted to the same hands. If, for example, the power of making laws were exercised by the same persons as those who execute or interpret them, the result would be tyranny.

The separation of the three institutions (Legislature, Executive, and Judiciary) should enable each to act as a check on the others. Each body should be staffed by its own personnel, and no one person should be a member of any of the other two powers or institutions.

Montesquieu wrote:

When the legislative and executive powers are united in the same person, or in the same body ... there can be no liberty; because apprehensions may arise, lest the same Monarch or Senate should enact tyrannical laws, to execute them in a tyrannical manner.

Again, there is no liberty if the judicial power be not separated from the legislative and executive. Were it joined with the legislative, the life and liberty of the subject would be exposed to arbitrary control; for the judge would then be the legislator.

Were it joined to the executive power, the judge might behave with violence and oppression.

There would be an end of everything were the same man, or the same body, whether of the nobles or of the people, to exercise those three powers, that of enacting laws, executing public resolutions, and trying the causes of individuals.

The germ of the idea was not new. Aristotle had referred to it; John Locke (1632–1704), the English liberal philosopher, also postulated the doctrine in his *Second Treatise on Civil Government*; and Blackstone in his *Commentaries on the Laws of England* (1765) referred to the importance of mutual checks on governmental power and of an independent judiciary in the English Constitution.

The Separation of Powers in Britain Today

The doctrine of the separation of powers does not apply **completely** to the British Constitution, as the functions of the following often overlap:

The Sovereign. The Queen is head of the Administration (Executive), head of the Judiciary and an integral part of the Legislature. The Monarch's constitutional position is unique (see p. 121).

The Lord Chancellor. He is a member of the Cabinet, President (Speaker) of the House of Lords, and head of the Judiciary under the Crown. The three powers are joined in his office and are exercised by the same individual (see p. 244).

The Cabinet. This is the centre of the executive power in the State. It is composed of Ministers who must, by convention, be members of one or other of the Houses of Parliament. A strict application of the doctrine would exclude all Ministers of the Crown (the Executive) from membership of the Legislature. Under the British Constitution the Cabinet and the Legislature are closely and continuously associated, and the relationship

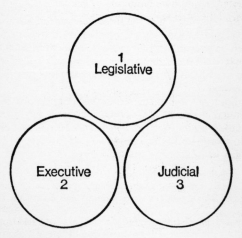

Fig. 2. The separation of powers

may be described as a **partnership** in government, rather than a separation. This, however, is subject to the control vested in Parliament in outvoting the party in power and thus ensuring the discontinuance of the Executive in office and the dissolution of Parliament.

Ministers. Ministers, who in fact constitute the Executive, are frequently empowered by the Legislature to perform (under the authority of statute) legislative duties in the framing of delegated legislation (see p. 286). Moreover certain statutes empower Ministers to perform judicial or quasi-judicial functions which show an encroachment on the essential tasks of the judiciary (see p. 290).

The House of Lords. The Upper House is at one and the same time a constituent part of the Legislature, the final Court of Appeal for all civil and criminal cases and may adjudicate upon, and punish, breach of its privileges or contempt of the House.

The House of Commons. Primarily a legislative and deliberative body, it is the dominant part of the Legislature, but it may also act in a judicial capacity for breach of any of its privileges and for contempt of the House.

The Judiciary. The independence of the Judiciary is an important characteristic of the British Constitution (*Act of Settlement, 1701*). Nevertheless this independence and separation cannot be complete in practice, for in the last resort judges are removable from office on an address from both Houses of Parliament. Further the Rules of the Supreme Court (detailing how an action shall proceed) are made by the judges of the High Court and Court of Appeal under authority of statute. Moreover, we shall see later (p. 215) that the common law of England was largely judge-made out of the customs of the people. Judges continue to develop the common law by their decisions, and they fulfil the statute law by their interpretation and administration of the law. To that extent, therefore, the judges exercise an indirect power of 'legislating' in the sense of making new rules. Moreover, some of the functions of the judges are administrative in substance, e.g. an order made for the guardianship of an infant, supervision of bankruptcy proceedings, and liquidation of companies.

Conclusion. In the strict sense of the doctrine of the separation of powers,

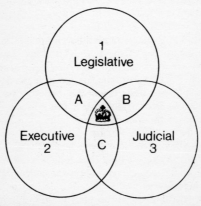

Fig. 3. No complete separation of powers

we may say that the theory has no true application. Nevertheless, the doctrine has assisted in forming essential and fundamental ideas concerning the development of the British Constitution. In particular, the independence of the Judiciary is of the greatest import. Parliament does not, for instance, discuss matters which are *sub judice* (i.e. under consideration by a judge at that moment), nor do Ministers of the Crown interfere with the discretion of a judge in any civil or criminal case—but see p. 25, q. 12.

The British experience, therefore, may be said to be that it has distributed the power of the State among various bodies of which the Legislature, Executive, and Judiciary are the main, and that the various bodies act as *checks and balances* to prevent despotism and to ensure that liberty (within the law) and effective government can be simultaneously achieved.

The Separation of Powers in the United States of America

The doctrine of the separation of powers had a deep effect on the thinking of the 'founding fathers' of the USA in the drawing up of the Constitution of 1787. This well-known document provides the most clear example of a practical separation of the three fundamental powers.

The first three Articles of the American Constitution are important in this respect. Article I vests the federal legislative power in the Congress of the USA (Congress comprises (i) a Senate, and (ii) a House of Representatives); Article II states that the executive power is vested in the President who shall hold office during a term of four years. Article III vests the judicial power in the Supreme Court of the United States of America.

These three powers seem to have been intended to be mutually exclusive. For example, no member of one branch of government may be a member of either of the others as well. The President of the USA is not, and cannot be, a member of Congress (the Legislature). Any member of Congress who wishes to become President of the USA must resign from that body before accepting the Presidency (Gerald Ford resigned from Congress in 1975 on becoming President). The President may, or may not be, a member of the political party with a majority in Congress.

The *checks and balances* which are necessary to maintain equilibrium are written into the Constitution of the USA. Thus the President may veto legislation of Congress, and such veto may only be over-ridden by a two-thirds majority in the Senate before the legislation may come into effect (as happened for example, in 1986 when the Senate over-rode President Reagan's veto on sanctions on trade with South Africa).

With the exception of the Vice-President (who ex officio presides over the Senate) no member of the Government (the Executive) may also be a member of Congress. The President (who heads the Executive) appoints judges to office in the Supreme Court (the Judiciary). This last body is of great importance in that it has overriding power under the Constitution to declare Acts of Congress (or of any State legislature) or the actions of a President to be illegal (or unconstitutional) if they should transgress the provisions of the Constitution itself.

The Rule of Law (or Supremacy of Law)

The Rule of Law is one of the fundamental characteristics of the British Constitution. But, like the word 'constitution' it is difficult to define.

The origin of the Rule of Law is found in Greek and Roman thought. Broadly it was considered that over and above all man-made law (sometimes called 'positive' law) there is a universal law which applies to all men everywhere and at all times.

Bracton, a judge in the reign of Henry III, wrote:

> The King himself should not be subject to any man but to God and the law makes the King.

This universal law (or **natural law** as it was sometimes called) was attributable to God. In the seventeenth century, L. C. J. Coke identified natural law with the **common law of England** which he described as 'the perfection of reason'. Since human reason was given by God, the principles of natural law were deducible by man by the use of his reason.

During the conflict between the King and Parliament in the seventeenth century Coke claimed that the common law was above the King and the Executive (i.e. the King's Ministers). In the struggle for power between the King and Parliament, Coke with other common law judges formed an alliance with Parliament. The Parliamentary forces won the struggle, and finally the supremacy of Parliament over the King and all other bodies was assured by the *Bill of Rights, 1689*.

The doctrine of the Rule of Law (as understood by Coke) had now to be reconciled if possible with the other important doctrine of the **supremacy of Parliament** (or sovereignty of Parliament). Either the law was supreme or Parliament was supreme. The outcome of this contention was the adoption of the theory or principle that the common law was subject to such changes as the King *in Parliament* might make from time to time. Henceforward the law now regarded as supreme was the common law *and* statute law, i.e. the whole of English law.

The important effect of the doctrine was to prevent or preclude any **arbitrary** action of the Crown in person (i.e. the Monarch) or, indeed, of members of the Government acting as servants of the Crown.

Broadly, therefore, today the Rule of Law is the principle that the process of government is bound up with the law and that the law is supreme. A Government in power must act **according to law**, i.e. within the law. For example, a Home Secretary cannot forcibly enter my house unless he has lawful power so to do; neither may he arrest me unless he has lawful power so to act. The law gives me remedies if my rights are infringed. The Rule of Law may, therefore, be said to prevail when the exercise of all forms of public authority (central government authorities, local authorities, police, and other bodies) is subject to review by the ordinary courts of law to which all citizens have equal access.

The Rule of Law may perhaps best be grasped by contrasting it with its opposite, i.e. the arbitrary (uncertain, unpredictable) use of authority against any person or property, unchecked by any other power or body. This state of affairs leads straight to despotism or anarchy. Most reasonable people prefer order and peace to the confusion and misery of anarchy.

Professor A. V. Dicey, in his work *The Law of the Constitution* (1885), gave three meanings of the Rule of Law thus:

(i) Absence of Arbitrary Power or Supremacy of the Law

It means in the first place, the absolute supremacy or predominance of regular law as opposed to the influence of arbitrary power, and excludes the existence of arbitrariness of prerogative, or even wide discretionary authority on the part of the Government . . . a man may be punished for a breach of law, but he can be punished for nothing else.

(ii) Equality before the Law

The Rule of Law means again, equality before the law or the equal subjection of all classes to the ordinary law of the land administered by the ordinary law courts.

(iii) The Constitution is the Result of the Ordinary Law of the Land

The Rule of Law means with us the law of the constitution, the rules which in foreign countries naturally form part of a constitutional code, are not the source but the consequence of the rights of the individuals, as defined and enforced by the courts; that, in short, the principles of private law have with us been by the action of the courts and Parliament so extended as to determine the position of the Crown and of its servants; thus the constitution is the result of the ordinary law of the land (see p. 17).

Is the Rule of Law Valid Today?

However valid the Rule of Law may have been in Dicey's lifetime (some critics deny its truth even for that period) the doctrine has been subject to criticism in the light of modern developments, particularly in the last thirty years.

We shall take each of the main rules in order:

(i) Absence of Arbitrary Power. Today Ministers (and other executive bodies) are sometimes given wide discretionary powers by statute. Thus, a Minister may be empowered by law 'to act as he thinks fit' or 'if he is satisfied'. Such words as 'if necessary', 'requisite', or 'expedient' abound in statutes implementing new services. There is, therefore, discretionary power bestowed by Parliament which is openly and avowedly used even under the 'regular law'. Such discretionary power is sometimes abused, and it is immaterial whether the power is derived from the 'regular law' or not.

During emergencies such as war, much wider powers are given by law to the Executive. For example, the Home Secretary was empowered under *Regulation 18B of the Defence (General) Regulations, 1939*, to imprison any person, 'if he had reasonable cause to believe such person to be of hostile origin or associations'. One person, Liversedge, was detained without trial under *Regulation 18B* and sued the Home Secretary for false imprisonment. It was held by the House of Lords that the court could not inquire into the grounds for the detention; it was a matter for the executive discretion of the Home Secretary in the circumstances of war. Accordingly the imprisonment was lawful. IRA terrorism has given rise to similar powers (see p. 267).

Difficulty arises as to the meaning of 'regular law'. It is understood that Dicey meant the **common law** and the **statute law**, as it then existed. Today, however, much of the legislation is **delegated legislation**, i.e. rules, orders, or statutory instruments made by Ministers and other bodies and not directly by Parliament. Although such legislation is made under powers conferred by statute, Parliament has little control over the making of such legislation (see p. 289). Many citizens frequently find themselves subject to rules not made by Parliament but by the Executive. These rules hardly existed in Dicey's time.

Certain members of society are subject to special rules in their professions. Thus, solicitors, barristers, doctors, midwives, nurses, members of the armed forces, and the police are all subject to special rules, breach of which renders a member of any of the professions named liable to special punishment, such as fines, deprivation of livelihood, or expulsion. Such rules apply to particular classes of people in the community who are treated differently from ordinary citizens. In any case the special rules cannot be treated as part of the 'regular law'.

(*ii*) *Equality before the Law.* However attractive this formula may be, there are obvious exceptions to it. HM The Queen cannot be sued personally in her own courts ('The Queen can do no wrong'). The *Crown Proceedings Act, 1947* (see p. 171) has not affected the personal immunity of the Sovereign.

Certain members of society are obviously exempt from the general law. A child in arms is inevitably treated differently from adult members of society. Children under 10 years cannot in this country be convicted of crime, and those between 10 and 14 only in special circumstances.

More important is the number of officials who have greater legal powers than those possessed by the ordinary citizen. The police, public health inspectors, factory inspectors, medical officers of health, inspectors of weights and measures, customs officers, and so on, all possess special powers. Some may forcibly enter private premises to inspect or take possession of property; some may be empowered to arrest; and some may prosecute for certain special offences. Although these rights are conferred by law they do, in fact, place the officials mentioned in a special position. To that extent there is no 'equality before the law'.

Foreign sovereigns, ambassadors, High Commissioners, and diplomats enjoy a special immunity from civil and criminal law of the country to which they are officially posted. These constitute a further exception to the principle of 'equality before the law'.

Judges of the High Court enjoy immunity from liability for acts done within their official jurisdiction. This judicial freedom and independence is essential for the proper administration of justice. Nevertheless, judges (and indeed magistrates) provide a further exception to the rule.

(*iii*) *The Constitution—the result of the Ordinary Law of the land.* We have noted that many countries have written constitutions. In particular we have mentioned the USA. Most modern states adopt written constitutions. We have mentioned already that the constitutions usually provide clauses defining the rights and duties of citizens (see The *Bill of Rights* which constituted the first ten Amendments to the American Constitution). When, therefore, any person unlawfully invades the rights of person or property of a citizen he may consult the constitutional provisions, decide that the invasion is unlawful and sue the offender before the law courts.

Dicey states: 'with us the constitution is the consequence of the rights of the individual as defined in the Courts of Law'. The British Constitution is unwritten: it is the product of the operation of the ordinary law of the land. The legal rights and duties of a British subject are generally found in the common law (there are, of course, certain rules contained in particular statutes). The broad rule of the common law is that no one may interfere with or invade my person or property unless he has lawful power so to do. Otherwise he commits a wrong (contrary to the common law) for which I may sue. There is no guaranteed constitutional rule in writing to this effect; it is merely the rule of the common law which has been hammered out over the centuries by the judges. Any citizen may, therefore, ascertain his rights from the legal cases decided in the past and from statutes.

There are, therefore, no fundamental and guaranteed rights enshrined in some sacred constitutional code or statute.

How secure are the rules of common law in this respect? Under the doctrine of Parliamentary supremacy we have seen that Parliament can make and unmake law to any extent it pleases. It can, therefore, revoke all or any rights of person or property which we may have, and it may do this at any time it pleases. That is theory. In practice it would be unthinkable. The true safeguard against abuse of executive power lies in the vigilance of an informed electorate, a free Press, the responsibility of the Government to Parliament and of Parliament to the electorate, and an independent judiciary.

As has been said: 'The test of a free country is to examine the status of the body that corresponds to Her Majesty's Opposition' (per Sir Ivor Jennings). All we need to note here is that the traditional freedoms which we know in this country are the result (or consequence) of the operation of the common law and are not enshrined in a written form in a constitution. It is impossible to say whether one or the other is the more secure; the only true safeguard lies in the will and spirit of the people to preserve the freedoms they now enjoy.

The Rise of Parliament

To understand the British Constitution one must look at the history of Parliament and its rise to power. We recall that the British Constitution has evolved over the course of 900 years into its present form which is that of a democracy with a **constitutional Monarch** at its head. By this we mean that although the supreme power in the State lies in the hands of the people, and the representatives they elect, the formal head of the State is the Queen whose actual powers are restricted by constitutional laws, customs and conventions.

The word 'Parliament' meant a talk, and was originally applied in the thirteenth century to the after-dinner gossip of monks in their cloisters which, incidentally, was condemned as unedifying. The word was also used to describe solemn conferences such as that in 1245 between Louis IX of France and Pope Innocent IV. It then came into use for the national assemblies in England after the middle of the thirteenth century.

The Kings of England were once powerful figures who claimed to rule their lands by divine right. A Monarch cannot, however, rule a kingdom by himself. The Anglo-Saxon kings were assisted by the **Witenagemot**, an assembly of the wisest of men in the kingdom, to give counsel (**rede**) to the Monarch. Even in those times it was an English custom that in important matters such as the interpretation of laws, the King ought not to act alone but should first obtain the advice and consent of the wisest of his people. Custom also required that he hold 'deep speech' with the **Witan**, or council of wise men, two or three times a year. After listening to the speeches of the leaders, the assembly gave a vote for or against a proposition by clashing their arms against their shields.

The Anglo-Saxon Witan appears to have been a small aristocratic body of variable composition with great powers. F. W. Maitland stated:

It can elect Kings and depose them; the King and Witan legislate; it is with the counsel and consent of the Witan that the King publishes laws; the King and Witan nominate the ealdormen and bishops, make grants of the public lands, impose taxes, decide on peace and war and form a tribunal of last resort for causes criminal and civil. It is a supreme legislative, governmental and judicial assembly.

Here, we may note, was a free assembly of men who, though not elected, were representative of all parts of the country. They came from the **shires** (later called 'counties') and smaller units into which the country was divided. The **ealdormen** were important local figures; the **sheriff** was the King's outpost officer who represented the King's interests and presided in the shire court to do justice and administer the laws. The sheriff was an important powerful figure and his office survived the Conquest.

After the arrival of the **Normans** in 1066 we find a great change took place. The Norman Kings possessed orderly minds and were efficient administrators. They unified the kingdom, administered the local English customs and laws and introduced *feudalism*. Under this system the King made grants of land to his nobles and followers in return for a promise of allegiance, active help in time of war and the payment of feudal dues. The nobles who held their land directly from the King also made subgrants of land to their tenants, again in return for allegiance and the payment of feudal dues. The lord on his part promised protection and justice. William I went further and ordained that all landholders owed a duty of allegiance to him as King. This qualified the immediate allegiance which a landholder owed to his immediate overlord. Thus loyalty to the King was the supreme and universal duty of all English freemen (or **freeholders**, as they were called). This form of feudalism introduced from the continent made for greater unity and cohesion within the kingdom.

The Witan disappeared with the Anglo-Saxon Kings. William I and his successors held **Great Councils** instead. These were assemblies of the King's tenants in chief (i.e. the nobles and others who held their lands directly from the King). 'Thrice a year,' we are told, 'King William wore his crown every year he was in England; at Easter he wore it at Winchester, at Pentecost at Westminster, and at Christmas at Gloucester, and at these times all the men of England were with him—archbishops, bishops and abbots, earls, thegns, and knights.'

During the thirteenth century the 'Councils' began to be called 'Parliaments'. The barons were thus, on occasion, summoned by the King to attend a 'Parliament'. They were the aristocracy and did not represent all the classes of England. The knights and the burgesses (i.e. citizens) in the medieval boroughs were not represented, and these were growing wealthier and more important.

In 1265 **Simon De Montfort** summoned representatives of the 'commons', i.e. the commoners, which included the knights from the counties and two elected burgesses from the independent towns or boroughs with Royal Charters. In 1295 the so-called **Model Parliament** of Edward I was summoned which included barons (the nobility), knights, burgesses, senior clergy, and lower clergy. All were summoned on the principle that 'what touches all should be approved by all'.

Fig. 4. Witan: Great Council: Parliament

These groups of people, comprising the three estates of the Realm (**the Lords Spiritual**, **the Lords Temporal** and **the Commons**) were summoned by the King to Westminster to some of the Parliaments, particularly when the King required extra money to carry on government or to engage in wars or crusades.

The foregathering of all classes in the country was a big step forward. In the first half of the fourteenth century the practice developed whereby the Lords and the Commons met separately from each other in private assemblies or gatherings to discuss their answers to the King who called them to his presence. These answers were given to the King *in Parliament*.

Most of the discussions or debates took place in these private meetings of the Lords and the Commons. From some time in the middle of the fourteenth century the Commons elected a speaker who presided over the meetings. He acted also as a channel of communication with the King. When the King demanded money from the Commons, the latter began submitting to the King petitions or 'bills' requesting a change in the law of the land. During this time the vital principle of **grievances before supply** was established. When the King asked for financial aid from his people, the Commons chose the moment to strike a bargain with him regarding the redress of grievances which were brought to his notice in Parliament in the form of petitions.

From the time of Henry V (1413–22) a Bill so presented was enacted in the form the Commons desired. Nevertheless for some time afterwards both the Sovereign and the Lords considered they could tamper with or alter the text extensively without obtaining the approval of the Commons. It was not until the reign of Henry VII (1485–1509) that the practice was established of sending up petitions (apart from Private Bills) to the King in the form of statutes to which the King could either assent or dissent.

The Tudor and Stuart Period

The sixteenth and seventeenth centuries witnessed a great constitutional struggle between the Monarchs on the one hand and Parliament on the other. Henry VIII was the most absolute of Monarchs; Elizabeth I, his daughter, avoided a head-on conflict and ruled through Parliament for her own purposes. Charles I was aristocratic and wished to claim **prerogative rights** which Parliament and, eventually, the common law judges opposed. These prerogative powers included the right to issue ordinances and proclamations, the right to tax, and the right to exercise dispensing and suspending powers, i.e. the right to grant immunity or dispensation to any person he liked or to suspend the operation of laws which had properly been enacted.

James II (1685–8) claimed to rule the country by **divine right**, used arbitrary methods which alienated the Crown's supporters and openly defied Parliament itself. In the *Bloodless Revolution* (or *Glorious Revolution* as it is sometimes called) Parliament finally resisted the King in 1688, and James II thereupon fled to France. William III and Mary (1689–1702) were invited to accede to the throne of England, and Parliament thereupon secured the passing of the *Bill of Rights* in 1689, one of the most important constitutional documents. The Bill at long last ensured the ultimate supremacy of Parliament. One of its most important effects was that henceforward the King would be definitely below Parliament and, indeed, owed his position to Parliamentary vote. Executive government depended upon Parliament for the laws it administered and the funds of money which the Executive required for the purpose of government. We must remember that the Monarch continued to play a leading part for some time as head of the Executive, until the emergence of a Prime Minister and a Cabinet.

The Eighteenth Century

George I (1714–27) and George II (1727–60) could neither speak nor understand English with ease and were less interested in the affairs of England than those of Hanover. Both left the affairs of actual government in the hands of their Ministers. As a result we see the emergence of the office of **Prime Minister** (the first was **Sir Robert Walpole**) and of the Cabinet system of government which continues to this day. George III (1760–1820) tried unsuccessfully to re-establish royal power by using the **pocket boroughs** to create a party of King's friends in the House of Commons.

During the eighteenth century the Sovereign began to summon Parliament regularly. The *Mutiny Act* was passed which legalised a standing army for a year at a time, so that Parliament had to be called or summoned at least once a year. By the *Septennial Act, 1716*, Parliament's life was extended from three to seven years which made for greater continuity.

The main task of Parliament, however, was to consolidate the victory of 1689. There was party strife in Parliament, and there was a war with France to contend with. Further, although Parliament had secured supremacy, there was still considerable legal power left with the King and this had to be reconciled with the power of Parliament itself. The solution was found in new institutions within Parliament, in particular the growth of political parties, the office of Prime Minister and the Cabinet.

Reform Act, 1832

This Act is important because it gave political sovereignty to the electorate. Parliament reformed the corrupt system of pocket boroughs whereby constituencies with small electorates returned as their member of Parliament a nominee of a local magnate. The next hundred years saw the introduction of the **secret ballot**, and the eventual extension of the franchise to all adult persons.

Democracy and Britain

Democracy is the most difficult of all forms of government. How far we have gone along the path to its achievement will be seen in the succeeding chapters which deal with its essential features. But first let us look at the concept of democracy in relation to Britain and other countries.

The word democracy comes from *demos* (Greek) meaning people, and *kratos* (Greek) meaning power. Democracy can be of two kinds: (i) **direct** and (ii) **indirect**.

(i) Direct Democracy

Direct democracy was best observed in classical Greece when it was possible to assemble practically all the citizens in one place, as in the city-states of that time, e.g. Athens. The wise men in those city-states proposed legislation and the measures were put to the citizens who expressed their wishes in the form of a **plebiscite**. A plebiscite is a direct vote of the whole nation, or of the people of a district, on a special point; or an ascertainment of general opinion on a matter. It is, in effect, a referendum.

(ii) Indirect Democracy

This is more suited to modern nation-states which we find in the world today. Indirect democracy is practised through representative institutions such as Parliament. In the seventeenth century England achieved that situation through the events leading up to the *Glorious Revolution* when James II fled the country and Parliament assumed sovereignty, thus replacing the despotic rule of the Monarchs of the preceding centuries. Most civilised nations achieved or aspired to democratic institutions by 1850.

Democracy in the sense in which we use the term today in Western Europe, the British Commonwealth, and the USA, is based on certain doctrines. The first is the theory of the **separation of powers** (see p. 12) which involves the following: (i) legislation is made by a freely elected Parliament; (ii) executive power is vested in a Government responsible to the Legislature (Parliament); and (iii) an independent Judiciary. This doctrine implies that there is a free choice at regular intervals between two or more political parties. In the United Kingdom this takes place at least every five years. Elections are held to enable the electorate (the people) to choose or reject one or more parties. If there is only a single list of members of one party we are not using the word 'democracy' in the Western sense here understood.

We may say, therefore, that the separation of powers and free elections are essential characteristics. The other important feature of Western democracy (as in the United Kingdom) is the **Rule of Law** (see p. 15). You will recall that this means in essence that one is free from arrest unless one offends the law. One is free **within** the law. There is no discretionary power vested in a Minister or the police, for example, to arrest for vague 'political' crimes which are unknown to the law. The Rule of Law presupposes that there is equality before the law. There are certain immunities (e.g. the Crown, certain ambassadors, etc.), but as a broad proposition it represents a bulwark of democracy. We also have courts of law where justice is administered openly and fairly. There are no secret courts. We have freedom of opinion and speech, again within the law. We can, of course, alter the law from time to time, and we do so. But Parliament examines all legislation to ensure that it is good and suitable for the nation as a whole.

The word 'democracy' embraces all the above. It is difficult to describe: it is complex and it is the most difficult of systems to operate. But it is fitted with many *checks and balances* against the abuse of power, and it happens to be the best form of Government which the enlightened thought of man can devise. Abraham Lincoln expressed it thus: 'Government of the people, by the people and for the people.'

The expression 'rule of the people' is understood very differently in the USSR, China, Bulgaria, and Outer Mongolia. There is no doctrine of the separation of powers; no free elections; no rule of law; and freedom of opinion, speech, and association are not generally accepted. Yet the supporters of these regimes regard them as 'democratic'. Private ownership of the means of production is regarded as 'undemocratic'. State ownership and central planning for the increase of national wealth are the accepted beliefs of the Communist idea. The Communist Governments believe that the subordination of every interest and activity to the State ensures that the common good prevails over private interests. Ironically, this compares with the pre-nineteenth century aristocratic view of freedom as 'right behaviour': to be truly free people should live according to certain standards, which few (i.e. the aristocratic elite) alone could discern and were duty-bound to sustain.

Sovereignty

Sovereignty is the supreme power within a State. That supreme power in the United Kingdom is Parliament. Sir Edward Coke said, 'The power and jurisdiction of Parliament is so transcendent and absolute, that it cannot be confined, either for causes or persons, within any bounds.'

In theory the sovereignty of Parliament is absolute. It is not, for example, subordinate to any other body or group inside the United Kingdom or outside. No Parliament, it is said, can bind its successors in power, for Parliament can **make** and **unmake** laws to any extent.

In practice, the 'sovereignty' is a number of rights any one of which can be abstracted. The Crown makes treaties with other countries. The agreements give rights and impose duties (the duties or obligations detract from the concept of sovereignty). Moreover the United Kingdom is a member of international organisations and bodies, e.g. NATO, the Western European Union (WEU), the International Monetary Fund (IMF).

Although it is true that the supremacy of Parliament means that no Parliament can bind its successors in power, in practice the treaties solemnly entered into by previous Governments are honoured by the successors in power and membership of the international organisations is continued. Nevertheless, while it is unusual for Parliament to pass legislation which is retrospective (or retroactive), this does occur from time to time (e.g. to deal with tax evasion cases). But it is generally felt to be distasteful and undesirable, and, in general, unconstitutional; thus, it always gives rise to considerable Parliamentary controversy (e.g. the Burmah Oil case and the *War Damage Act, 1965*).

Sovereignty and the EEC

The ultimate aim of the *Treaty of Rome* (*1958*) is to achieve **economic and political unity**. The Treaty of Rome is intended to be of unlimited duration. Opponents of Britain's accession fear the loss of Parliament's authority. They point to the legislation imposed by the community, which is binding on all member States and means a loss of sovereignty. The supporters of the EEC reply that there is no loss or surrender of sovereignty, but a 'pooling' of sovereignty by all concerned. In renouncing some of our sovereignty we receive in return a share of the sovereignty renounced by other members.

The question resolves into whether we believe in international co-operation or not. If we do, then organization is essential and rules are needed to achieve the economic and political benefits foreseen. In framing the rules for the European Community the British Parliament will contribute its part, but it will also be obliged to follow the rules imposed by the supranational authority. On 1 January 1973 the United Kingdom joined the EEC (*European Communities Act, 1972*). And under the *European Communities (Amendment) Act, 1986* the union of member states was enhanced such that EEC institutions (legislative, executive and judicial) take greater precedence over those of each state. But it may nevertheless be argued that the British Parliament retains its sovereignty in that it could pass a Bill to withdraw Britain from membership of the EEC.

UK sovereignty is perhaps being eroded more stealthily. This can occur in two related ways. First, where there are 'offset' arrangements, under which UK firms are awarded contracts to carry out work on behalf of other countries e.g. UK firms helping to produce American Trident missiles and SDI (or 'starwars') equipment. While this may produce trade and employment for Britain, it also brings certain conditions such that the firms become subject to US laws (because of the sophisticated nature of the technology involved). Similarly, US laws may be brought to bear on British firms which have bought US equipment (e.g. to ensure that it is not re-sold without approval).

Quite separate from the EEC, but of related interest is Britain's being a signatory to the **European Convention on Human Rights** (1950) which is monitored by the European Commission on Human Rights (a body of jurists). Individuals have the right to bring petitions to the *European Court of Human Rights* in Strasbourg (not to be confused with the *European Court of Justice*, in Luxembourg, which enforces EEC laws) and a number of British citizens have done so in recent years. As a result, Britain (especially the Home Office) has been found in breach of the Convention in a number of ways including: internment and interrogation of suspects in Ulster, birching young offenders in the Isle of Man, caning in schools, immigration controls, non-payment of invalid care allowance to married women, inadequate compensation for nationalisation and interference with prisoners' mail. While the Convention is not technically part of English law, the British Government is bound by international law to recognise such judgements. Thus the *Mental Health Amendment Act* and the *Employment Act* of 1982 (which improve patients' appeal procedures and restrict trade union 'closed shop' arrangements) are, at least in part, a response to recent rulings of the Court. In this respect, Britons can lay claim to a Bill of Rights—though some would urge the UK to establish its own 'domestic' Bill of Rights to give easier access by British citizens (see p. 378).

Exercises

1. Define a 'constitution'.
2. Define a State and indicate its main functions.
3. Distinguish between a Unitary State and a Federal State.
4. Of which countries is the United Kingdom composed?
5. Some States are said to have rigid constitutions while others are described as flexible constitutions. What is meant by these descriptions?
6. What do we mean by (i) The Legislature; (ii) The Executive; and (iii) The Judiciary?
7. What do we mean by 'the sources' of the British Constitution?
8. What is meant by the doctrine of 'the separation of powers'? Has it any validity today?
9. The Rule of Law (or supremacy of law). Has this doctrine any validity today?
10. Give a short account of the rise of Parliament from Norman times to the early nineteenth century.
11. Why do anarchists seek to live in society without government? How feasible is such an idea?
12. In 1982, the Prime Minister criticised a judge's sentencing in a rape case and declared that in future such cases would only be tried by senior judges. Comment on this in relation to the concept of the separation of powers.

2
Elections and the Party System

The Electoral System

The United Kingdom is divided into constituencies, each of which contains an average of 60,000—70,000 electors. Each constituency returns one member to Parliament as its political representative in Westminster.

All persons, over the age of 18 years, have the right to vote. The actual qualifications and disqualifications are dealt with later.

This voting franchise, 'one man one vote', as it is frequently expressed, is fundamental to our democracy and the British Constitution. We enjoy the privilege of voting for the candidate we prefer; we have secret ballots; an electoral procedure which is fair and just; and an absence of corruption in its administration. All these electoral rights and benefits have been won, step by step, over the past 150 years.

Development of the Franchise

The House of Lords originally contained the aristocratic nobles and barons, and was the predominant chamber until the time of Elizabeth I (1558–1603). The Lords were summoned to the House by writ of summons and duly took their seats. They have at no time in history been elected by the people, and therefore this chamber cannot be described as truly democratic. That position remains substantially the same today.

The House of Commons contained originally in the thirteenth century the knights from the shires and the burgesses from the boroughs. Together these two groups of representatives made up the Commons. At the beginning of the reign of Elizabeth I, two members were elected from each county and two burgesses were elected for each Borough to attend Parliament. These men were squires or landowners from the counties, and landowners of influence and power or members of the middle class from the boroughs.

In the counties of England and Wales the right to vote for a member was laid down in the fifteenth century and was limited to males only having a clear income of 40 shillings per year. The franchise was based on wealth. In the boroughs this rule did not apply; the voting franchise varied from borough to borough, but here also the vote was generally limited to those persons with landed interests which resulted in a small electorate. In 1800 only three persons out of every 100 possessed the vote. That could not be described as just or democratic.

In the eighteenth and nineteenth centuries the rich landowners exercised considerable influence over the electorate. Many county members of Parliament were simply the nominees of the wealthy aristocrats. Some villages or hamlets with only a handful of residents returned a member to Parliament. They became known as **rotten** or **pocket boroughs**. Bribery, corruption, and intimidation of voters were common features of the electoral system of the day. Monarchs used the opportunity to persuade powerful landowners to return to Parliament those members upon whom the King could rely to manipulate the Commons to further his own ends. The members who lent themselves became known as 'King's Friends'.

In the early nineteenth century, however, the industrial revolution effected a great change in the country: coal- and iron-mining increased greatly, railways were constructed, and factories were erected on, or near, the great coalfields in the Midlands and the North of England. Large towns, e.g. Manchester, Leeds, Sheffield, and Birmingham, sprang up. None had proper representation in Parliament. Yet at the same time small hamlets such as Old Sarum (Wiltshire) with six voters, returned two members to Parliament; and Okehampton, Devon, a small town, sent to Parliament as many members as the whole of Yorkshire.

From the industrial revolution emerged a much larger and wealthier middle class who condemned the inefficient political system that excluded them from political power. After considerable agitation and struggle, during which riots broke out in most of the large towns, the *Reform Act, 1832*, was passed. This laid down the foundation for a remodelled franchise. All reforms of the electoral system after this important Act followed as natural steps in the process towards universal franchise which exists today.

The stages are noted as follows in more detail:

The Reform Act, 1832

(i) This Act disqualified fifty-six small boroughs from returning members to Parliament, and thirty other boroughs were deprived of all but one member;

(ii) The seats taken from boroughs in (i) above, were transferred to the growing industrial centres—Birmingham, Manchester, and the County of Yorkshire.

In addition to the above, the Act laid down for the boroughs a uniform **occupation franchise** for any male who occupied as (*a*) owner or (*b*) tenant, any house, shop or other building of an annual unfurnished value of £10.

The county franchise was extended to long leaseholders and copyholders (i.e. those who held their lands by right of a copy of the rolls in the Court manor) of property of the annual value of £10, to all male leaseholders who held land for terms of not less than twenty years and to occupiers of property of £50 annual rental.

The Act produced 215,000 new voters, mainly of the middle class, making a total voting population of 500,000.

Representation of the People Act, 1867

This made for another redistribution of seats. Some forty-five boroughs, each with a population of less than 10,000, lost one member to the new large towns. The Act reduced the property qualification of the leaseholder and copyholder to £5, and introduced as an additional qualification the occupation of a tenement (premises) of a minimum rateable value of £12. In the boroughs the working man was enfranchised, i.e. if he was a male householder occupying for one year a separate dwelling house and paying the poor rate, or a lodger who occupied for a period of one year lodgings of unfurnished value of £10. The total number of voters reached 2,000,000.

Ballot Act, 1872

This Act introduced the vital principle of the **secret ballot** and made intimidation of voters an offence.

Representation of the People Act, 1884

This Act (i) extended the householder and 'lodger' franchise to the counties (bringing the counties into line with the boroughs under the 1867 Act above). (ii) In the counties and the boroughs gave the vote to any person occupying any land or tenement of a clear annual value of £10. (iii) Gave the vote to any servant (e.g. a gardener) living separately from his employer, i.e. not living in the house of his employer as would a butler or a valet.

The main effect of this Act was to give the vote to the working man in the county. The total number of voters now reached 5,000,000.

Redistribution of Seats Act, 1885

This Act also redistributed seats to provide more equal electoral areas on

(1) Presiding Officer checking name of voter
(2) Clerk issuing Voting Slip
(3) Voter receiving ballot paper
(4) Voter in polling booth
(5) Voter in polling booth
(6) Voter putting slip in Ballot Box (locked)
(7) Police Officer preserving law and order

Fig. 5. A polling station

the basis of one MP for every 50,000 of population. The cause of this was the influx of new inhabitants from the rural areas to the Northern and Midland towns. Some 134 seats were taken from boroughs with small populations, and these seats were allocated to the large towns insufficiently represented in Parliament. The number of MPs increased to 670.

Representation of the People Act, 1918

Under this Act (i) The voting qualification was laid down as six months' residence or occupation of business premises. (ii) The vote was given to any woman over 30 years, provided she or her husband was qualified to vote at local government elections. (iii) Disqualification for the receipt of poor relief was abolished. (iv) All Parliamentary elections must be held on the same day; and no elector may vote in more than two constituencies. (v) Any Parliamentary candidate must deposit £150 with a Returning Officer. This sum was forfeit if the candidate did not poll one-eighth (12.5 per cent) of the total votes cast. (vi) Seats were redistributed on the basis of one MP to every 70,000 of population.

Representation of the People Act, 1928

This introduced a uniform franchise for men and women of 21 years and over provided they were qualified by: (i) Residence for qualifying period of three months. (ii) Occupation of land or premises for business purposes of annual value of £10 or more for three months. (iii) Being the spouse of an occupier of land as at (ii) above. (iv) Being a graduate of a British university.

Representation of the People Act, 1948

The main provisions (i) Abolished the business premises' qualification to vote (see (ii) above). (ii) Abolished the graduate vote (see (iv) above).

Representation of the People Act, 1969

Under this Act (i) The voting age for Parliamentary and local elections fell to 18. (ii) The non-resident qualifications for voting at local government elections and the property qualifications for candidates at local government elections were abolished. (iii) Polling hours on election days were extended to 10 p.m. (starting at 7 a.m.). (iv) Political descriptions (maximum six words) were allowed on ballot paper. (A central register of political descriptions is kept.)

With regard to this last point, over eighty different party labels have been used since 1945. The lowering of the voting age in 1969 added some 2,500,000 voters to the register.

Representation of the People Act, 1985

Under this Act (i) British citizens resident abroad may vote (for up to five years after departure). (ii) Holiday-makers may use postal voting. (iii) the deposit was increased from £150 to £500. (iv) The 'threshold' for loss of deposit was lowered to 5 per cent (from 12.5 per cent (see above)).

Owing to inflation, the limits on election expenditure have to be

revised periodically. Currently (1987) a candidate for a Parliamentary
election may spend up to £3,370 plus 3.8p for every entry in the electoral
register in a County constituency or 2.9p for every entry in a Borough
constituency. This limit aims to equalise opportunities.

The Voters

In order to qualify for voting, a person must be aged at least eighteen, be a
United Kingdom (or Commonwealth or Irish) citizen, and have his name
on the electoral register (which is compiled every twelve months). However,
certain people are **disqualified**: these include Peers (i.e. Lords); felons (i.e.
those serving a prison or borstal sentence of one year or more); persons
of unsound mind (i.e. as patients in psychiatric hospital); persons convicted
of corrupt or illegal electoral practices (the latter are disqualified for five
years).

Most people vote in person, i.e. by presenting themselves at the polling
station. However, certain electors are allowed to vote by **post** or by
proxy—for example, British soldiers abroad, people who are sick or who
have recently moved house. Whatever form the voting takes, its **secrecy**
is protected.

Table 1. Electorate and populations

Year	Total electorate	Population aged 20 and over	Electorate as % of population aged 20 and over
1831	438,000	10,207,000	4.4
1832	720,784	10,207,000	7.1
1864	1,130,372	13,051,816	9.0
1868	2,231,030	13,625,658	16.4
1883	2,955,190	16,426,233	18.0
1886	4,965,618	17,394,014	28.5
1914	7,483,165	24,969,241	30.0
1921	19,984,037	26,846,785	74.0
1931	29,175,608	30,096,135	96.9
1946	34,320,351	34,516,000	99.3
1949	33,545,221	34,981,000	95.9
1959	34,523,000	37,211,000	92.9
1964	35,003,000	36,372,000	96.2
1979	41,769,000	42,100,000 (over 18)	99.0
1983	42,197,344	41,300,000 (over 18)	102.0
1987	43,181,321	41,464,000 (over 18)	104.0

Criticism of the Electoral System

The candidate at a Parliamentary election who receives most votes wins
the election and becomes the Member of Parliament for the Constituency.
Whether he wins by 1 vote or 10,000 it does not matter: the candidate with
the most votes gets in. This is the **simple majority** system. In effect the

election has the appearance of a race past the winning post, and the 'winner takes all'. This system has merit: it is simple, quick and decisive. But there are criticisms such as the following.

MPs with Minority of Votes

Let us suppose that in the Camford constituency there are three candidates: Raymond Redd (Lab.), Basil Blew (Con.), and Leslie Liberty (Lib.). The election vote may reveal the following result:

Raymond Redd (Lab.)	26,000
Basil Blew (Con.)	24,000
Leslie Liberty (Lib.)	10,000
	60,000

Mr Redd (Lab.), the successful candidate, has the support of 26,000 voters. But most of the voters, i.e. 34,000 (24,000 (Con.) and 10,000 (Lib.)) voted against Mr Redd. In effect, therefore, a member is returned to Parliament on a minority of the total number of voters in that constituency. This may be looked upon as a weakness if we accept the principle that an MP ought to have the support of the majority of the voters in his constituency. This criticism does not apply in contests between two parties only, i.e. where there is a 'straight fight' between two contestants. For example:

Raymond Redd (Lab.)	36,000
Basil Blew (Con.)	24,000
	60,000

The Distorted Reflection of Public Opinion

The present electoral system is said to be 'unfair' to minority parties. The House of Commons is composed of those members who attract most votes in their constituencies. The leader of the party returning most members to Parliament forms HM Government. If we look at the election results of the country as a whole we may say that the House of Commons constituted in the usual way does not represent the true balance of feeling in the country.

This is best seen by Table 2 below. See p. vi for 1987 figures.

Table 2. Percentage of MPs per Party and percentage of votes cast

Party	Feb. 1974		Oct. 1974		1979		1983	
	No. of MPs (%)	Total votes cast (%)	No. of MPs (%)	Total votes cast (%)	No. of MPs (%)	Total votes cast (%)	No. of MPs (%)	Total votes cast (%)
Con.	47	38	44	36	53	44	61	42
Lab.	47	37	50	39	42	37	32	28
SD/Lib.	2	19	2	18	2	14	3·5	25
Turnout	78.7%		72.8%		76.0%		73.0%	

These figures show the difference in the **feeling of the voters** throughout the country, and the **actual party representation** in the House of Commons. Thus the Conservatives took office in 1979 and 1983 but polled only 44 and 42 per cent respectively of the votes cast. The majority of people, therefore, did not vote for the party which assumed power. Rarely are governments elected by 50 per cent or more of the vote. (Conservatives were so in 1901, 1931 and 1935.)

In the election of 1983, the Liberal/Social Democrat Alliance obtained 7.7 million votes (25 per cent), but gained a mere 23 seats (3.5 per cent) of the total 650 MPs. The Conservative Party obtained 12.9 million votes (42 per cent) and 397 seats. Labour obtained 8.4 million votes (28 per cent) and 209 seats. The Conservatives' majority over all parties was 144 seats Occasionally the distortion is such that the Government takes power although it received less votes than the Opposition (as in February 1974 when Labour took office). See p. vi for 1987 figures.

Reform of the Electoral System

For the past seventy years our electoral system has been the subject of many official inquiries such as the Speaker's conferences of 1968, 1974 and 1978. This recommended against the introduction of a new system, and neither major party is sympathetic to change here. But the SDP–Liberal Alliance is pledged to a radical reform if they accede to power.

No system, however, is perfect, and it is fitting here to consider the alternative suggested forms of electoral representation.

The Second Ballot

This system is based on the principle that a successful candidate must obtain an **absolute majority** of the votes cast so that there will be no minority MPs. Let us suppose there are three candidates, A, B and C. The result of the contest is:

A polls	25,000 votes
B polls	20,000 votes
C polls	10,000 votes

A second ballot is held. Candidate C is eliminated since he obtained the lowest vote. At the second ballot A and B only are the contestants. The contest now resolves itself into a straight fight. Either A or B will be the winner. In the second vote the 10,000 votes could of course be distributed between the two. It is more than likely that A will win, but not necessarily so, since the 10,000 votes cast for C may be given to B who would then have 30,000 (20,000 + 10,000).

Whilst the second ballot eliminates minority MPs it would not increase the representation of minority *parties* to any great extent. The holding of a second ballot is also tedious, and can be inconvenient to the public.

The Alternative Vote

This procedure is similar to the second ballot, but the election is carried out at one election. Voters under this system mark on the voting slips the numbers 1, 2, or 3 against the candidates' names in order of preference. The first count is taken on first choices. Let us suppose Candidate *A* has 25,000 with a '1' against his name; Candidate *B* has 20,000 with a '1', and Candidate *C* has 10,000 similarly marked. If no candidate has an absolute majority on first preferences (i.e. polls more than half of the total number of votes in the constituency), the candidate with the lowest number of votes (i.e. *C*) is eliminated from the contest. The votes cast for *C* are distributed to the remaining candidates (*A* and *B*) on the basis of second preference. One of these contestants will win the election on the basis of the majority of votes. In the event of a tie at an election a recount can be asked for and, if another tie results, the issue can be decided by the spin of a coin.

Proportional Representation (PR)

The principle of proportional representation is based on the idea that each party should obtain representation in proportion to the number of votes cast for it. To operate the system the country would be divided into large constituencies, or the whole country could be regarded as one large constituency in which each party would be represented in proportion to the votes it secured. Generally it is assumed that the country would be divided into large constituencies.

Each constituency would return a number of MPs to the House of Commons. Each party then puts up several candidates. The elector would vote for the candidates in order of preference, marking his voting slip in numerical order. Any candidate who obtains a certain quota of first preferences would be immediately elected. His surplus votes would be distributed to other candidates according to the second preferences expressed on the voting slips. Again, any candidate then obtaining the quota would be returned, and a similar distribution of his surplus votes would take place. Quota equals (number of voters + 1) ÷ (seats + 1).

Example. Let us assume that three seats are available to a large constituency and that there are five candidates contesting the election. Let us also assume that a quota of 40,000 votes are needed for the election of any candidate. The result on first preferences could then be:

Attlee	50,000
Burke	40,000
Churchill	30,000
Disraeli	20,000
Gladstone	10,000

Attlee and Burke are both elected for each has acquired the necessary quota. But the election so far has not given to Churchill, Disraeli, or Gladstone the requisite number, viz. 40,000. The next step in the process is to take the excess of Attlee's votes, i.e. 10,000, and to divide these according to the second preference marked on them. The result might then be:

Attlee	40,000
Burke	45,000
Churchill	35,000
Disraeli	20,000
Gladstone	10,000

We note that Churchill, Disraeli, and Gladstone have not acquired the necessary quota. The next step is to take the surplus votes of Burke (i.e. 5,000). These are distributed among Churchill, Disraeli, and Gladstone. If this distribution does not produce the desired result the candidate with the fewest votes is eliminated from the contest and his votes (let us say Gladstone's) are redistributed according to the next choice. The process is repeated until a candidate gets the quota of 40,000, when he is declared elected to join Attlee and Burke. This is known as the 'Single Transferable Vote' (STV).

The *advantages* of proportional representation are first, that it gives a greater opportunity to minority parties to obtain seats in the House. (The Liberal/Social Democratic Alliance Parties support proportional representation because of the discrepancy between the total number of votes cast throughout the country and the actual number of Alliance MPs elected.) Secondly, if there is a range of candidates of varying abilities the electors are given a choice for particular individuals. Moreover, if there are within a party (let us say the Labour Party) certain members belonging to opposing factions, e.g. Left Wing and Right Wing, an elector would be able to express his preferences for the faction within the party which he (the elector) supports.

The *disadvantages* of PR are said to be (*a*) It is complicated and confusing to the electors. (*b*) It is unlikely to produce better government. Many small parties could arise, so that it would be rare for one political party to obtain a majority of seats overall. This would lead to a coalition (grouping of parties to form a government) which produces weak and unstable governments. (*c*) The link between an MP and his constituents would be broken since the small area, with a single MP, would disappear in the large constituencies with more than one member.

Most European countries have adopted some form of PR (including Eire and, for local EEC elections, Ulster). But it has never aroused deep enthusiasm in mainland Britain. Also, in modern times political power is usually monopolised between the two main political parties who are quite satisfied with the present system, arguing that it gives voters a clear choice and secures responsible (or accountable) government. However, Britain may be required to adopt a PR system for the next EEC elections (1988), and furthermore, a Marplan opinion poll in 1982 showed a large majority (62 per cent) to be in favour of PR in British elections.

In practice, the electoral system may be adapting itself organically through the recent development of 'tactical voting' i.e. where electors vote for the candidate/party most likely to defeat the candidate/party they least wish to win. Thus if the aim is to defeat a Conservative Government, Labour and Alliance parties may develop a strategy whereby they urge voting support for one or other of their parties in those constituencies where they are lying second to the Conservative incumbent. 17 per cent voted thus in 1987.

Development of the Party System

Edmund Burke (1729–97), defined a political party as:

a body of men united for promoting, by their joint endeavours, the national interest upon some particular principle in which they are all agreed.

This definition is clear and memorable. It shows us also that the modern idea of party political organisation had taken root before the end of the eighteenth century. In the following pages we sketch in broad outline the history of the influential parties which have shaped the destiny of the Constitution.

History

The earliest Parliaments had no party system in anything like the form we have today. Members were called by the Monarch to attend upon him at Westminster mainly to allow him to obtain grants of money or to gain practical support in the government of the country. His primary functions as Monarch in the early days were to maintain peace and good order at home and to preserve the kingdom from foreign aggression.

In the reign of **Charles I** there was a division in Parliament between the supporters of the Monarch, called the **Royalists**, and his opponents, the **Roundheads**. In the Civil War, Charles I was executed in 1649, and **Cromwell** (1599–1658) became a virtual dictator until the **Restoration** in 1660 and the accession of **Charles II**.

Right until the end of the seventeenth century the principal Officers of State were chosen by and responsible to the Monarch—not to Parliament or the nation at large. This was a matter within the Royal Prerogative. The officers appointed sometimes acted in concert with one another, but more often they acted independently. The fall from power or resignation of one officer did not necessarily or automatically involve the resignation of the others. Each Officer of State was liable to be dismissed by the Sovereign at any time.

Towards the end of Charles II's reign (1660–85) the Exclusion Bill debates in Parliament (1679–80) were notable in that they gave rise to the birth of two parties in the political life of the nation. These two parties became known as **Whigs** and **Tories**. These names were given by each party to the other, more as terms of reproach, but they were subsequently accepted by each as its label. Later in the 1830s the two parties changed their names again: Whigs became **Liberals**, and Tories became **Conservatives**.

Originally, the Whigs in the late seventeenth century represented the rising merchant class and the new middle class. The Tories represented the landed aristocracy and the squirearchy (country gentry). There was no clear definition of political aim or philosophy. Whigs and Tories were groups, each of which was influenced by royal power and patronage and by the religious questions of the period.

In 1693 a change took place. Both **William III** and **Mary** (1689–1702), found that mixed ministries of Whigs and Tories would not work. The mixture was incompatible with the growth of the political parties now forming definite ideas and policies of their own. The Whigs wished to limit the power of the Royal Prerogative, to extend religious freedom to Protestants, and to favour the monied interests (in London and the provinces) as opposed to the landed gentry, who were the main supporters of the Tories.

In 1693 **William III** was advised by the Earl of Sunderland to select a Ministry from the political party which enjoyed a majority in the House of Commons. The first united Ministry (of the same political party) was appointed in 1696 from the Whigs. The Ministry so formed included Russell (the Admiral), Somers (Advocate), Lord Wharton, and Charles Montague, who afterwards became **Chancellor of the Exchequer**. This group of Ministers became known as the **Junto**. It was made up of a small section which met in secret apart from the main body of Ministers. It attracted some suspicion: people frowned upon the separation into groups or cliques, for they had been dangerous in the past. Nevertheless, the Ministry so formed continued, though it was looked upon as a novelty in the political life of the nation.

The Junto was the forerunner of the modern **Cabinet**. In due time it accepted the principle of a common aim and the joint responsibility of Ministers. If there were internal disagreement in the group this would involve a change of personnel (e.g. where one or two members resigned) or the resignation of the whole body of Ministers. This, of course, happens today.

George I (1714–27), the first of the Hanoverian Kings, could not speak English well. His unfamiliarity with the language was a handicap and he was disinclined to attend and preside at meetings of his Ministers whose business he did not fully understand. The King's absence led to the appearance of a **Prime Minister** who presided over the group in the King's place. **Robert Walpole** (1676–1745), a Whig, acquired the position first in 1721 and retained office without interruption for almost twenty-one years.

In the eighteenth century both parties, Whigs and Tories, were united by family and local ties rather than by a unity of political aims or philosophy. There was no effective party discipline, and there was no Opposition Party in the sense in which it operates in Parliament today, for the simple reason that it was not organised.

The Growth of the Liberals

In about 1830 the old party of the Whigs became known as Liberals. This name also was given to the Party by its opponents, and implied laxity of political principles. Gradually, however, the name was accepted by the Party itself to manifest its claims to be pioneers and champions of political, economic and social reform and progressive legislation.

In 1836 the **Reform Club** was founded as a centre and meeting place for Liberal MPs and sympathisers outside Parliament. In 1861 a **National Liberal Registration Association** was founded, and Liberal Associations sprang up throughout the country. These associations organised lists of local voters after the *Reform Act, 1832*. In 1877 a **National Liberal Federation** was established with Headquarters in London.

During the second part of the nineteenth century the Liberal Party under **W. E. Gladstone** (1809–98) (the founder of modern Liberalism) was in power for long periods. However, during the **Irish Home Rule** crisis of 1886, a group known as **Liberal Unionists** seceded from the Party because of disagreement (the group later on joined the Conservatives). This division within the Party was maintained during the first quarter of the twentieth century. Then a further split occurred into **National Liberals** and **Independ-**

ent Liberals. This further weakened the Party with the result that only fifty-nine Liberal MPs were returned to Parliament at the general election of 1929. After the 1945 election the number was reduced to twelve, and after the 1950 election it was further reduced to nine. In the 1951, 1955, 1959 and 1970 elections the number of Liberal MPs fell to six, reflecting the great change which has come over the Party since its heyday in the nineteenth century. In the elections of 1974, the Liberals won 14 seats (February) and 13 seats (October), fell back to 11 MPs in the 1979 election, but rose to 17 seats in 1983 and 1987. It now has 150,000 members.

The Conservative Party

At the same time as the Whigs changed their name to Liberal we find the Tory Party assuming the name 'Conservative'. This name was reputedly invented by one J. W. Croker in 1830 and became generally adopted at the time of the passing of the *Reform Act, 1832*, to demonstrate the leading principle of the party, namely the preservation of the national institutions.

In 1832 the Tories founded the **Carlton Club** which was the centre and meeting place of the Tory MPs and their followers and adherents outside Parliament.

After the *Irish Home Rule Bill of 1886* (as noted above) certain dissentient Liberals (Liberal Unionists) entered into a compact with the Conservatives. Eventually, in 1912, this group united with the Conservatives under the title National Unionist Association of Conservative and Liberal Unionist Organisations and after 1924 as the **National Union of Conservative and Unionist Associations**. The members became known as 'Unionists'. The name Conservative is the more popular one by which the Party and its members are today referred to.

Edmund Burke (1729–97) and **Benjamin Disraeli** (1804–81) (first Earl of Beaconsfield) exercised most influence on Conservative political theories. Disraeli, Prime Minister from 1874–80, is commonly regarded as the founder of modern Conservatism. One of his aims was to harmonise the 'two nations' (the rich and the poor), an aim which he combined with progressive social reform e.g. health, housing, working hours, unions.

After 1945 the Conservative Party has modified its policy to accord with modern times and generally a more equitable spread of wealth. The party's industrial policy seeks to reconcile the need for central direction with its traditional encouragement of individual and private enterprise which has sometimes been named 'welfare capitalism'.

The Conservative Party has been in office for over half of the post-war period—viz. 1951–64, 1970–74 and since 1979.

The Labour Party

The Labour Party has grown to power over the last hundred years. It is distinguished from the other parties in that it sprang up outside Parliament and was limited, until it could operate politically through the enlargement of the franchise. The Liberals and the Tories were groups of MPs who formed parties within Parliament. Moreover, it may be said that the Labour Party originally represented the working classes. Its present membership has broadened to include others, including many of the middle classes (see p. 203).

The main beliefs of the Party are socialist and are said to derive from about 1834 when **Robert Owen**, a social reformer, established his 'village of co-operation' at New Lanark. He was followed by **Charles Kingsley** (1819–75), priest and writer, and others who established **Christian Socialism**. These were followed by **William Morris**, **John Burns**, and other reformers who were passionately concerned with social justice.

Towards the close of the nineteenth century three socialist organisations were formed:

(i) The Social Democratic Federation (1881) based on Marxist ideas.

(ii) The Fabian Society (1883) (see below).

(iii) The Independent Labour Party (1893–1900).

At about the same time **Trade Unions** were recognised by law (*Trade Union Act, 1871*). These were combinations of workmen and were vitally concerned with the improvement of the wages, welfare, and conditions of employment of the working classes. The Trade Unions allied themselves to the Labour Party, in sympathy with their aims.

Fabianism was the system of beliefs of certain notable intellectuals (Sidney and Beatrice Webb, Graham Wallas, H. G. Wells, G. B. Shaw, to name only some) who held that social change could be brought about by **gradual parliamentary means**. The Fabian Society collaborated with the Labour Party, the trade unions, and the Co-operative Movement, and was concerned with political education of men and their representative organisations.

The British Labour Party believes in peaceful and constitutional change to socialism by democratic methods based on popular support and consent. The party believes also in a planned economy and public (i.e. State) ownership of certain vital industries. This State-ownership of important industries was largely brought about by the Labour Government of 1945–51 which also introduced the National Health Service and a comprehensive system of social security, creating, in effect, a **'Welfare State'**.

The Parliamentary Labour Party

The first appearance of Labour candidates at a general election was in 1892 when there were twenty-seven candidates standing as Labour or Liberal–Labour. At the general election of 1895 there were twelve successful candidates, and at the election of 1900 there were eleven.

In 1900 under Keir Hardie the **Labour Representative Committee** was set up to establish a unified Labour Group in Parliament with its own **Whips**, its own policy and a willingness to co-operate with any party which might be engaged in promoting legislation in the direct interest of labour (i.e. the working classes of the country at the time). In 1906 the LRC became known as the **Labour Party**.

In 1918 some 74 members were returned to Parliament. This number was almost doubled in 1922, and in 1929 some 287 members were returned. In 1931 there were 65, but from then on it has gradually increased its members until, in 1945, after the Second World War, there were some 396 Members in Parliament representing the Labour Party with its greatest ever majority. In 1966 Labour returned 363 members, again with a sufficient majority to form a Government. It was defeated in 1970 but regained office 1974–9.

Minor Parties

The Social Democratic Party (SDP) This party was created in 1981 largely in reaction to radical policy and organisational developments in the Labour Party. It believes in the EEC, the 'social market' and 'mixed' economy and *multi*-lateral nuclear disarmament. It had 6 MPs elected in the 1983 election but only 5 in 1987.

The Scottish Nationalist Party (SNP) This was formed in 1928. Its first success was in 1945 when one MP was returned for Motherwell. In November 1967 Mrs W. Ewing was successful in a by-election at Hamilton. In February 1974 seven Members were elected; in October 1974 it was eleven. But they fell to two in the elections of 1979/1983 and 3 in 1987.

Welsh Nationalist Party (Plaid Cymru) Founded in 1925 this party has fought elections continuously since then, and in a by-election at Carmarthen in 1966 Mr G. Evans became the first Party candidate to be returned to Parliament. In February 1974 two Members were elected; in October 1974 it was three, in 1979 and 1983 it fell to two. It was there in 1987.

In mainland Britain there is also the **Green Party** (formerly the Ecology Party), concerned with conservation and environmental issues. It has no MPs.

Northern Ireland contains three main parties with MPs. These are the **Official Ulster Unionists**, who are Protestant and Loyalist. They have 9 MPs, led by James Molyneaux; the **Social Democratic and Labour Party** who are mainly Catholic, led by John Hume, with 3 MPs; and the **Democratic Unionists**, Protestant loyalists led by Revd. Ian Paisley, with 3 MPs. There is also 1 **Ulster Popular Unions** MP James Kilfedder and 1 **Sinn Fein** (the political wing of the IRA) but this MP, Gerry Adams, has not taken his seat in Westminster.

The Government and Opposition Parties

The Party system of Government in this country is the practice of placing the exercise of the executive authority of the State in the hands of Ministers who are Members of Parliament and belong to one political party whose members have gained a majority of the Parliamentary seats at a general election.

Immediately the result of a general election is known, the leader of the dominant party selects his Cabinet. He chooses members from his own party in either House (Lords or Commons). A wise leader will select the most able members with whom he is in political agreement. Together they will form a united team. The 'Administration', as it is sometimes called, thereupon conducts the business of governing the country and its affairs as efficiently as it can.

The essential feature, however, is the **duality** of the parties: (i) The Government, formed from the majority party, and (ii) the Opposition, comprising the major defeated party. The Leader of the Opposition (who is paid £48,000 p.a.) forms a 'Shadow Cabinet' (of about 15: see p. 80) ready to take over the reins of government at any time if need be.

There are, of course, usually more than two parties in Parliament. Today at a general election both major parties (Conservative and Labour) contest most constituencies. The Liberal and Social Democratic parties, usually in 'Alliance', fight as many constituency seats as they can: in 1987 they collectively fielded some 633 candidates. Many contests are therefore 'three-cornered' affairs. Sometimes there are more candidates, perhaps from a Nationalist party or the Green Party. And apart from many fringe parties (perhaps fighting over a local issue) there are still a few Independents. All the seats are therefore contested these days (compared to the past e.g. in 1859 one third of the seats were not fought). But in the end, there are usually just two main parties: (i) the Government and (ii) the Opposition.

The Opposition is only slightly less important in the Constitution than the Government, because it may 'if the balance of party power shifts become or be willing to follow Her Majesty's Ministers' (Sir Courtenay Ilbert). On the same theme Walter Bagehot (1826–77) wrote:

> The House of Commons lives in a state of perpetual choice; at any moment it can choose a ruler or dismiss a ruler. And therefore party is inherent in it, is bone of its bone, and breath of its breath.

Coalitions

Where no party obtains an overall majority (i.e. has more MPs than all other parties put together) a difficult position arises. In the 1920s we had three parties: a major party (the Conservative), and two minor parties—Liberal and Labour. In these circumstances an Administration can only be formed if a major party (with many, but not an absolute majority of MPs) agrees to combine with one or other of the minor parties to form a Government. A compromise must be made over policies. Inevitably disagreements arise and dissentient members may resign from the coalition government. This weakens the administration and eventually the Government resigns and an appeal is made to the electorate. Another general election is then held. In peacetime coalition governments tend to be weak in policy and may fall apart, ending in resignation or dissolution. Vacillating policies and numerous changes of Government produce uncertainty, cynicism and disillusionment in the people (see pp. 123, 131). 'England does not love coalitions' (Disraeli, 1852).

In times of emergency, however, coalition governments may be successful. During the Second World War (1939–45) a National Coalition Government made up of members of all parties (Conservative, Liberal, and Labour) held the keys of power. Parties and party members sank their political differences in the national interest and presented a united front against the common enemy. It had one aim—the prosecution of war in defence of the realm. The existence of the State and its people was at stake and the national interest overrode all others. This is common sense and was the best thing to do.

It is a necessary part of the working of the party system in this country for the parties to know when to suspend party controversy. (Viscount Samuel (1870–1963), *Our Parliament* by Strathearn Gordon.)

Coalitions are commonplace in some countries. Thus, for example, in 1974 France, West Germany, Italy, Holland, Finland, and Canada had coalition governments. Denmark, Norway, and Sweden each had a **minority** government, that is a government which has the most seats of any party, but fewer than the combined seats of two or more other parties.

In March 1974 the Labour Party was able to form a minority government. In that situation the Government party has to act circumspectly, dropping those proposals which would be opposed by the other parties acting in unison. In the election of October 1974, the Labour Party gained a small overall majority (of three) but the Prime Minister was still obliged to tread carefully. Indeed, during 1977–78 there was an agreement or 'pact' with the Liberals whereby the latter gave the Labour Government support in Parliament in exchange for modifications in the Government's policies (e.g. the withdrawal of a proposed increase in petrol tax).

If a National Coalition Government comprising the most able men in the State can wage a mighty war and protect the lives and rights of its people why may not this form of government be equally successful in time of peace? The proposition is simple and attractive. It is difficult to justify its opposite. Why not a Government of the best men or women in the State elected by all the people to govern our lives, free of party squabbles and ties, and free to devote themselves to producing the 'good' life for all in justice, equity, and peace?

However, such a 'Council of State' style or form of Government presupposes facts which do not accord with the harsh realities of life. There is no agreement as to who are, or what is meant by, 'the best'. All have faults and weaknesses. Moreover history shows that even when such elite groups are formed there is no certainty that the best people will agree among themselves. Without parties we could have 650 MPs with varied backgrounds and interests and widely different policies. Dissensions and disagreements arise among the best of men and women; such differences may be deep and irreconcilable.

It is impossible to assemble 55 million together to vote. The electors have diverse interests, opinions, and views both as to their representatives and the policies they should follow. Let us now suppose a group of the 'best' do succeed to power. Might they not merely become another party and would they give up power having gained office? Political power has always had a fatal attraction for ambitious men. 'Power tends to corrupt, and absolute power corrupts absolutely,' said Lord Acton (1887).

History provides astonishing examples, and England has had its share of despotic monarchs and its taste of a dictator in Cromwell (1599–1658). The country remembers its experience.

Criticisms of the Two-Party System

No system of government is perfect. The experience of Parliamentary government in this country has been one of continuous adaptation to the challenges, changes, and crises which are the lot of man and of nations.

We may applaud the virtues of a two-party system while acknowledging certain weaknesses:

(i) The expression of minority views which are not a part of any one of the major parties is limited. Party discipline in the House, party loyalty, and the self-discipline of party members prevent individual MPs who are members of one of the major parties from supporting minority views.

(ii) Independent MPs (who disclaim allegiance to any party) are handicapped. An independent may not afford now to become an MP if he depends on his Parliamentary salary alone, and he cannot rely on promotion to ministerial rank. He also lacks the help of a party 'Whip' and the consequential party assistance, e.g. in being kept informed by literature, research and notices. An independent has to frame his own Private Member's Bill (if he has one). For all their value in Parliament itself (we remind ourselves of the late Sir Alan Herbert, W. J. Brown, and others), the independent MP has been virtually squeezed out by the monolithic major parties. This is a loss: a lone voice may be a wise one.

(iii) If a voter casts his vote for a party and not for the individual candidate on his merit and personal qualities there can be danger in ignoring the personal element in politics. Essentially a Member represents constituents; there is a personal and human relationship, an identification with the people of an area.

(iv) The *raison d'être* of the small minority party (e.g. Liberals) is similar to that of the independent MP. Each has a value. A minority party should be kept in being: its policy may be right and good and may yet appeal to the best in men to give it the necessary support to grow. A minority party is an insurance against having no Government at all (e.g. if both parties fall apart, disagree, and disintegrate). Men, like bees, may regroup.

(v) The adversary or 'yah-boo' approach to politics of Government *v.* Opposition may slow progress and undermine business and foreign confidence.

Advantages of the Two-Party System

For some two hundred years there has been virtually a two-party system: (i) Whigs and Tories, (ii) Liberals and Conservatives; and (iii) Labour and Conservatives. We may justify the system on the following grounds:

(i) *Natural Division*. The two-party system follows the basic division existing between men: (*a*) **radicals**, i.e. those who wish to reform thoroughly and immediately; and (*b*) **conservatives**, i.e. those who prefer gradual change within existing institutions which may be adapted to change.

(ii) *It Works*. The two-party system is now one of the main features of the constitution. It has been tried and found **successful**, it has developed empirically—by experience.

(iii) *The Will of the People*. The electorate chooses a Government and also, in effect, lays down the broad lines of policy which the electorate expects a Government to follow, e.g. as expressed in a party's manifesto. The system is democratic, and the elector himself can compare the actions of a Government with its party programme announced before election.

(iv) *Provides Strong Government*. The two-party system ensures stable and strong government during its term of office—usually four to five years. During this period the Government has virtually unlimited powers to legislate as it will.

(v) *Ensures Strong Parties*. Each major party has an efficient party political organisation (see below) and each has a declared policy. The Opposition Party has its Shadow Cabinet ready to accept office immediately on failure of the Government. This system therefore allows for continuous and strong Government. Weak parties with few MPs, or a party which is divided by disagreement and dissension cannot form an Administration though it may join in a coalition which may be unstable in peace-time.

(vi) *For and Against*. Voters have a simple choice between two rivals— 'For' or 'Against'. If there are many parties and policies confusion may arise in the electorate. Thus the two-party system focuses *responsibility*.

(vii) *Floating Voters*. These voters who can be instrumental in changing a Government do not generally like voting for a party unable to form a Government. These are regarded as 'wasted' votes.

(viii) *Right and Left Wings*. Each major party has a right and a left wing. Each party can, therefore, absorb factions and persons holding widely different views and coming from different areas of society. There are Trade Unionists in the Conservative Party; professional men and industrialists in the Labour Party. Each party has its cross-section of social and religious groups: they are 'broad churches'. A third political party finds difficulty in framing a distinct policy of its own different from the other two parties.

(ix) *The Debating Chamber and the Houses of Parliament*. People are affected by the buildings or institutions in which they live and work. 'We shape our buildings, and afterwards our buildings shape us,' said Winston Churchill in 1943 (October) in the Debate on the rebuilding of the House of Commons. The seating arrangements of the House of Commons (see p. 63) and the lobby arrangements (separating 'Ayes' and 'Noes') support or preserve a two-party system of Government and Opposition. The **structural form encourages good debate**. A Government can be criticised openly, and its weaknesses or strengths can be exposed or appraised in full view of all members, the Press, and the public. It has been proved by actual experience; it is satisfactory and it works well. Moreover, the atmosphere of the House can tame the wildest spirits and induce respect for constitutional method.

These are some of the points which justify a two-party system of Government. There are others.

The two-party system is the natural concomitant of a political tradition in which Government as such is the first consideration and in which the views and preferences of voters and of members of Parliament are continuously limited to the simple alternative of 'for' and 'against'. (L. S. Amery: *Thoughts on the Constitution*.)

Party Organisation Today

All three major parties are organised to maintain their existence, fight elections, win voters to their cause, and return members to Parliament. We shall deal with (i) the Conservative Party, (ii) Labour Party, and (iii) the party organisation in Parliament.

The Conservative Party Organisation

(i) *The Constituency Association*. The constituency is the unit of the party organisation. Each is divided into wards or polling districts.

The objects of a Constituency Association are:

(*a*) to recruit members;
(*b*) to fight elections;
(*c*) to select or adopt prospective candidates (usually with the approval of an Advisory Committee of the National Union);
(*d*) to raise election funds (by subscriptions, donations, bazaars, etc.).

The Constituency Association appoints its own executive committee and Chairman, and has various sub-committees (Trades Union Committee, Young Conservatives' Committee, Women's Advisory Committee, Education Committee). It is responsible for appointing a certificated agent (see below) to carry on the full-time work of the constituency. He is assisted by a woman organiser and office staff.

(ii) *The Area Councils*. There are twelve Area Councils in England and Wales. Each Area comprises several constituencies, and these are linked together on a provincial basis by the Area Council which co-ordinates the resources of the Area to advise the Central Office in London.

(iii) *The Central Council of the National Union*. The Central Council is composed of (*a*) the Leader, (*b*) the Officers of the Party, (*c*) the Parliamentary Party, (*d*) all adopted candidates, and (*e*) four representatives from each constituency association. This group amounts to nearly 6,000. Only about 3,500 attend the Central Council. Theoretically, the Central Council is the governing body at national level, but in practice it is too large to carry out executive functions, and it merely acts as a two-way link between MPs and the rank and file in the country. It also serves as a centre for Conservative interests. It does not control the Central Office of the Parliamentary Party. One standing committee of the Central Council vets prospective Parliamentary candidates.

(iv) *The Executive Committee of the National Union*. This comprises 150 members mainly from the provincial Areas. The body includes the Leader and other principal officers of the Party. It deals with the affairs of the Central Council. There are important sub-committees, e.g. Local Government, Trade Union Advisory Committee, Young Conservatives' Committee, Central Women's Advisory Committee, and the Conservative Political Centre Committee.

(v) *The Leader*. The Leader of the Party is elected by the Parliamentary Party, adopted prospective Parliamentary candidates and the Executive Committee of the National Union. She/He selects the Chairman of the Conservative Party who heads the Central Office. The Leader determines the Party programme and policy on the issues of the day. She/He must always consult with the other leading members of the party and must also have regard to the views of backbenchers in the '1922 Committee'.

(vi) *The Central Office*. Founded in 1870 by Disraeli, this office is under the control of the Leader. Located in Smith Square, London with some 300 staff it is the permanent Headquarters of the Party. It co-ordinates preparations, workers and the resources for an election campaign. It supplies information, arranges speakers for the Party for local Constituency Associations. It carries out studies of public issues. It has charge of the Party's finances, and makes grants to constituencies, if needed. It also vets prospective candidates. It is responsible for recruiting and training the paid agents and organisers in the constituencies.

(vii) *Conservative Research Department.* This body undertakes long term research to assist in party policy. It also provides official secretaries for Parliamentary Committees and prepares briefs on issues coming before Parliament. It provides party members with information and guidance, and assists all departments of the Central Office. The Research Department comes within the framework of the Party Headquarters.

(viii) *The Election Agent.* These are the full-time officials employed by each constituency. They are trained by Central Office, which conducts examinations for them and issues them with certificates of proficiency.

The main duties of an agent are:

(*a*) To act as link between the MP and his constituency.

(*b*) To account for money spent at an election.

(*c*) To inform the MP of local matters requiring his attention.

(*d*) To arrange the MP's speaking engagements.

(*e*) To arrange for the MP to meet electors who wish to see him.

(*f*) To inspire local voluntary workers and co-ordinate the ward and the constituency activities.

(*g*) To provide an efficient administrative office.

(*h*) To get his Parliamentary candidate returned at the next general election (i.e. *to win*).

Fig. 6. Conservative Party Organisation

(ix) *The Annual Party Conference.* About 4,000 persons attend the Annual Party Conference. The conference comprises all the members of the Central Conference of the National Union, election agents, and an additional three representatives from each constituency association. Delegates representing various groups put forward motions which are debated by the conference and replied to by the leaders of the Conservative Party i.e. the frontbenchers or principal Parliamentary spokesmen and women. Although resolutions may influence the Leaders in forming their policy, they are not instructions and are not binding. The Conference is virtually a 'sounding board' of opinion and a Party rally. Conference gives a sense of unity and renews the enthusiasm of party members (currently about 1½ million compared to 3 million in 1952).

The Labour Party Organisation

(i) *The Constituency Organisation.* Each local Constituency Labour Party (CLP) is in fact a federation of a number of organisations, including the Young Socialists, local trade unions, representative socialist societies, and local branches of the co-operative societies. Representatives of all affiliated groups serve on a General Management Committee which elects the officers, viz. Chairman, Secretary. The objects of the constituency organisation are similar to those of the Conservative Association listed above.

The constituency appoints its Secretary, and where the constituency employs an agent he usually occupies both posts.

(ii) *Regional Councils.* There are eleven Regional Councils with full-time staff controlled by Party Head Office.

(iii) *National Executive Committee (NEC).* The Annual Conference elects the NEC, which comprises the Party Treasurer, 12 members elected by various groups of Trade Unions, 7 by CLPs and regional federations, 1 by socialist and co-operative societies, 1 by the Young Socialists and 5 women are appointed to represent the women's sections of the party. The Leader and Deputy Leader of the Party are ex-officio members. The NEC meets regularly to: (*a*) interpret and implement Conference decisions, (*b*) manage party finances, (*c*) maintain liaison with the Parliamentary Party, (*d*) supervise local CLPs, and (*e*) enforce discipline.

(iv) *The Leader.* He was elected by the Parliamentary Labour Party for a year at a time and customarily re-elected (but see p. 47). He exercises considerable influence, but is not so dominant as the Conservative leader. He does not control the officials of the Party Head Office.

(v) *Annual Party Conference.* Over 1,100 delegates from the affiliated organisations, including 37 Trade Unions attend the Annual Party Conference. Delegates vote according to the number of 'due-paying' members in the group they represent. The Trade Unions dominate the 'card vote' (with their six million affiliated members as compared to about one third of a million ordinary party members). Members of Parliament, prospective candidates, members of the NEC, and local agents are ex officio members of the conference. A programme is drawn up by the NEC; motions are debated, and the conference determines the Party's general policy in that those resolutions which get passed by a majority of two-thirds or more become official party policy.

(vi) *The Head Office.* This is the counterpart of the Central Office of the Conservative Party. It is headed by the General Secretary, who is appointed by the NEC. The Head Office is the national Headquarters of the Party and deals with the same matters as those carried out by its Conservative counterpart. The Head Office, with some 140 staff, also provides organisers for the Regional Councils. It is located in Walworth Road, London.

Recent changes. Disappointed at losing the 1979 election, the Labour Party 'lurched to the Left' by adopting more socialist policies (nuclear disarmament, nationalisation, withdrawal from the EEC) and by significantly amending its own constitution. Thus Labour MPs are now obliged to undergo re-selection procedures (where candidates are 'adopted') in their constituencies (CLPs) before each general election (this has meant 'deselection' for some—see p. 97). And the election of the Leader (and Deputy) is now undertaken by an electoral college comprising the PLP, Trade Unions and CLPs (with voting shares of 30, 40 and 30 per cent respectively).

These developments alarmed many Labour 'moderates' including prominent members such as Roy Jenkins, Shirley Williams, David Owen and William Rogers—the 'Gang of Four'. In 1981 they and 22 other Labour MPs (plus 35 Labour peers) broke away from the Labour Party and formed the Social Democratic Party (see p. 39). This would represent a watershed in Britain's party and Parliamentary system if the SDP, perhaps in Alliance with the Liberals, were to gain many votes and MPs in the general election, especially if it were to result in a 'hung' (or balanced) Parliament.

Party Finances

Party politics is expensive. Thus, in the 1983 general election for example, the Conservatives spent an estimated £3.8 million, while Labour spent £2.2 million. £20 million is the estimate for 1987. Generally, the parties rely upon membership subscriptions and voluntary fund-raising (jumble sales, coffee mornings, etc.). Thus it is said that we get our politics 'on the cheap'. Another criticism is the heavy dependence of the Labour Party on Trade Union funds (75 per cent) and the Conservatives' reliance on donations from private businesses. Consequently it is often suggested that parties should receive State aid. Yet this too might bring undue influence and also diminish the parties' links with the community. However, since 1975 Opposition parties have been able to receive State grants (currently on the basis of £1,500 for each MP plus £3 for every 200 votes received in the election, up to a maximum of £450,000). In 1986 Labour received £440,355, Liberals £88.641, Social Democrats £62,562 and Ulster Unionists £20,397.

Party Organisation in Parliament

Each political party in the House of Commons has what is called a Parliamentary Party, made up of MPs of the same political persuasion. Thus we have the Parliamentary Labour Party (PLP), the Conservative Private Members' (or '1922') Committee, the Liberal Parliamentary Party and the Social Democratic Parliamentary Party.

These groups of MPs meet (separately) once or twice weekly during a session to discuss the business of the House and in particular important matters of the moment, some of which may be controversial.

First, we recall that the two major political parties will form the Government and the Opposition. The Government will have its Cabinet (twenty or more members), the Opposition will have its 'Shadow Cabinet' (see pp. 40, 80). All MPs who are not members of the Cabinet or Shadow Cabinet are known as 'backbenchers' (Government backbenchers or Opposition backbenchers).

Here we shall discuss a Government Party and its Parliamentary Party (the same general principles apply to the Opposition Party in its relation with its Parliamentary Party). A Government Minister may be invited to attend a Parliamentary Party meeting and will meet and hear the views of backbenchers. The Government policy on an issue may have been or be about to be decided in the Cabinet, and the Minister will explain this to the party group and expect and encourage support. Party members may not, of course, always agree with Cabinet policy. In this situation the Minister must handle the issue skilfully and carefully. The Cabinet must have behind it the strong support of its party members (i.e. the backbenchers) if it is going to push its policies through Parliament. It cannot afford a defeat on a division of the House. Backbenchers, for their part, seek to know what is the policy of the Cabinet and to be kept 'in the picture'. Communication between a Minister (and his colleagues in the Cabinet) and the backbenchers is vital. This is a two-way matter and involves the 'Whips' (see p. 72). Both sides must try to co-operate, and there must be give and take or compromise on occasions.

A Parliamentary Party group may not instruct or control a Cabinet. The basic constitutional doctrine is that the Cabinet is responsible to the House of Commons as a whole. A Government's (i.e. a Cabinet's) essential duty is to govern, but it can only do this if it has the solid support of its party members. Hence the need to obtain harmony with its backbenchers and to present a united team in the event of a Division (i.e. vote) of the House. If an individual MP feels strongly about an issue he can abstain from voting or vote against the policy of his own party, though this is attended by certain risks (see p. 72).

In addition to the full meetings of Parliamentary Parties there are numerous committees or meetings to discuss particular matters, e.g. trade, economic affairs, industrial relations, agriculture, education, and so on. These party subject committees are sometimes attended by a Minister (or Shadow Minister in the case of the Opposition party) or a representative of a Minister. In addition, the Whips (see p. 72) will also attend to get to know the feelings, views and interests of party members on the various committees.

The term Opposition Party suggests continual obstruction, contest, and contention; this is not the case. Many matters are dealt with in agreement with the Opposition—'behind the Speaker's chair' or 'through the usual channels' i.e. the Chief Whips—and the House does not divide. Moreover, on occasions a 'free vote' may be taken when MPs of all parties may vote according to their own consciences free from the party line, as in the vote in Parliament in 1975 on Britain's continued membership of the EEC. (This vote preceded the Referendum (see p. 373).) A further example of party collaboration is the system of all-party committees in Parliament (see p. 76) and the Select Committees (see pp. 77–83).

Exercises

1. Give a short historical account of the development of the franchise.

2. What are the main provisions of the *Representation of the People Act, 1969*?

3. What criticisms may be made of the electoral system?

4. What do you understand by: (i) The second ballot; (ii) The alternative vote; (iii) proportional representation?

5. How did Burke define a political party?

6. What, in your opinion, has contributed to the decrease in the number of Liberal MPs to the House of Commons?

7. Account for the growth of the Labour Party since its inception.

8. Coalitions seem to work in war but not in peace. Why is this?

9. What are the advantages of the two-party system in the British Constitution?

10. Describe the organisation of (i) the Conservative and (ii) the Labour Party.

11. Can a one-party State be democratic?

12. Comment on the fact that the Labour Pary has 70 full-time agents while the Conservatives have 300 (1982 figures).

13. Members of affiliated trade unions pay a political levy as a part of their union subscription though there is a procedure which enables them to 'contract out' of this. In total this levy raises about £2.5m p.a. for the Labour Party. Comment on this arrangement.

3
The Legislature

The British Parliament comprises (i) HM The Queen, (ii) The House of Lords, and (iii) The House of Commons. It is sometimes technically described as The Queen in Parliament. The Legislature is **bi-cameral**, i.e. it consists of two chambers: the House of Lords and the House of Commons.

Unlike most legislatures, the British Parliament does not have a set 'life' or term of office. The law (i.e. the *Parliament Act, 1911*, merely lays down a legal maximum term of 5 years. In practice General Elections are held at any time within that 5-year period (see p. xiv) as the Prime Minister decides (see p. 124). As this flexibility may give the Government of the day an unfair advantage, there have been calls for fixed term Parliaments. (This may cause problems when no party has an overall majority in Parliament; but it may induce parties themselves to become more flexible and form coalitions.)

The House of Lords

This is the older of two Houses. Originally the Anglo-Saxon Kings were advised and assisted by the Witan; and the Norman Kings by the Great Council (the *Magnum Concilium*). This latter body was an assembly of feudal barons, nobles, and vassals, together with the bishops whose appointments were in the gift of the Monarch. All were powerful magnates summoned by the King and consulted by him on matters of importance.

Another Norman institution—the *Curia Regis* (the Court of the King) comprised a smaller group of advisers who carried on day-to-day government and thus ensured continuity. The *Curia Regis* had two main functions which tended to separate: one was **judicial** which, in the time of Henry II (1154–89), gave rise to the Courts of Law (see p. 215); the other was **administrative and advisory** to give continuous governmental advice to the King. The House of Lords is the successor of the old *Curia Regis*, a feudal body.

The Norman Kings summoned not only the barons on matters of great importance, but after 1265 another group which included the knights from the shires and the burgesses from the cities and boroughs as representatives of the communities or 'Commons'. These two groups met separately from each other in private assemblies—the Lords in one group and the Commons in another. Each body was constituted on entirely different principles.

The period between the seventeenth and nineteenth centuries witnessed the rising power of the wealthy commercial class who became the middle class. Members of this group of people pressed for reform of the Commons to ensure fairer representation in Parliament. Eventually, after a period of great political agitation, the *Reform Bill* of 1830–2 was passed. It was strongly opposed by the House of Lords mainly because of the threat to their own political power and influence. The Lords rejected the Bill twice. When, however, Lord Grey's Government induced the King to agree to create enough peers in favour of reform to swamp the Lords, the Upper House at last gave way and the Reform Bill was finally passed. This was a strong indication that the power of the Lords, great as it may have been in the past, would have to give way in face of the rising power of the Commons.

The Period 1832–1911

The *Reform Act, 1832*, introduced a wider voting franchise, and the House of Commons became more representative of the people. The *Reform Acts of 1867 and 1884* introduced an even wider franchise which resulted in an increased representative and democratic House of Commons. Some politicians in the nineteenth century pressed for the reform or abolition of the House of Lords which was described as an undemocratic anomaly.

Changes were, however, slow. Prime Ministers were still largely peers. Their presence and that of other leading Ministers of the Government in the House of Lords lent authority to the proceedings in that chamber. But, towards the end of the nineteenth century the number of peers (as distinct from commoners) in the Government became fewer. The last peer to be Prime Minister was the Marquess of Salisbury who resigned in 1902.

The Commons continued to grow in status and power, and the debates and struggles in the Lower House determined the course of political life and growth. The Lords' power was still in theory equal with that of the Lower House except that, by convention, the Lords did not interfere with financial questions. Meanwhile many old Whig peers joined the Tories in the House of Lords and this increased the Conservative strength of that chamber. In the Commons the party division between Liberals and Conservatives became more bitter. Social change was needed and many industrial problems arose. This state of affairs precipitated another crisis which resulted in the *Parliament Act, 1911*, by which the power of the House of Lords was much curtailed.

The Parliament Acts of 1911 and 1949

Theoretically, the Lords' power of veto over measures proposed by the Commons used to be unlimited. In 1909 **David Lloyd George**, Chancellor of the Exchequer under **Mr H. H. Asquith**, Prime Minister, tried to push forward a programme of democratic legislation. The Finance Bill which contained the financial proposals was passed by the Commons, but was rejected by the Lords. This rejection infringed the convention that the Lords ought not to oppose a **Money Bill** sent up by the Commons. The Bill was introduced again, dissension followed, and eventually the Prime Minister threatened that unless the Bill were passed by the House of Lords he would arrange for the King to create a sufficient number of Liberal peers to ensure its passage. In the circumstances the Bill was finally passed by the Lords and became law.

The Government felt that it ought not to be baulked in this way and thereupon introduced a Bill to curtail the powers of the House of Lords itself. This Bill was passed by the House of Lords under the same threat as before of 'flooding' the Upper House with sufficient Government peers to ensure its passage. The *Parliament Act, 1911*, is the result of the struggle and provides that:

> If a Money Bill, having been passed by the House of Commons and sent up to the House of Lords at least one month before the end of the session, is not passed by the House of Lords without amendment within one month after it is so sent up to that House, the Bill shall, unless the House of Commons direct to the contrary, be presented to His Majesty and become an Act of Parliament notwithstanding that the House of Lords have not consented to the Bill.

This in practical terms meant that the House of Lords no longer had any power to interfere with the policy of the Government so far as finance was concerned. If, therefore, the House of Lords does not pass a Money Bill as it stands within one month, the Bill may receive the Royal Assent without the concurrence of the House of Lords.

A 'Money Bill' is defined as:

> A Public Bill, which, in the opinion of the Speaker of the House of Commons, contains only provisions dealing with the imposition, repeal, remission, alteration or regulation of taxation . . . or subordinate matters incidental to those subjects or any of them.

Every Money Bill must be endorsed by the Speaker to the effect that it is a Money Bill. The Speaker's decision is made after consultation with two members of the Chairman's Panel.

To fall within the provisions of the Act, Money Bills certified by the Speaker must be sent to the Lords at least one month before the end of the session.

Other Bills. The *Parliament Act, 1911*, made certain provisions regarding Bills other than Money Bills. The Act laid down:

> If any Public Bill (not a Money Bill) is passed by the House of Commons in three successive sessions and is sent up to the House of Lords in each of those sessions, that Bill on rejection by the House of Lords a third time be presented to His Majesty and become an Act of Parliament provided that two years have elapsed between the date of the Second Reading in the first of these sessions of the Bill in the House of Commons and the date on which it passes the House of Commons in the third of these sessions.

The effect of this was that the Commons could get their own way and that the House of Lords could only delay, not prevent, legislation.

After 1911

The House of Lords accepted their minor role in the legislature, and there was less disagreement between the political views of the Government and the majority of the Lords. The decline in the importance of the Upper House was reflected in fewer peers holding Government office. Moreover the **convention** now emerged that the Prime Minister must be a member of the House of Commons. **Lord Curzon** was passed over for Prime Minister in 1922 and **Stanley Baldwin** was chosen in compliance with the convention.

Another struggle, however, lay ahead. In 1947 a Labour Government was obstructed by a mainly Conservative Upper House over the proposals to nationalise steel. Accordingly another Parliament Bill was introduced which provided that a Bill rejected or amended by the Lords can go for the **Royal Assent** provided it has been passed by the Commons in two successive sessions (not three as provided in the Act of 1911). As two successive sessions may be held in one year, the *Parliament Act, 1949*, reduced the delaying period of the Lords from two years to one. This power was used in 1977 to pass the Aircraft and Shipbuilding Bill of 1976.

Composition

The House of Lords consists of two classes: **the Lords Spiritual** and the **Lords Temporal**. For our purposes there are, however, four main groups:

(i) *The Lords Spiritual*. There are twenty-six Spiritual Lords who hold office by virtue of being bishops of the established Church of England. They comprise:

(*a*) The Archbishops of Canterbury and York and the Bishops of London, Durham and Winchester who are each entitled to a seat.

(*b*) Twenty-one diocesan bishops being the senior bishops of the Church. When one of this number dies or resigns his seat he is succeeded by the next most senior diocesan bishop of the Church.

(ii) *Hereditary Peers*. These number about 800 and are peers of the United Kingdom or of Scotland. Under the *Act of Union, 1707*, the Scottish peers elected sixteen of their number to represent them in the Lords. Now, however, by s. 4 of the *Peerage Act, 1963*, all Scottish peers are entitled to a seat.

Peerages are occasionally granted immediately to ladies of distinction or the widows of distinguished men. Peeresses in their own right (as they are called) frequently acquire their title by lineal inheritance which means that females succeed to the title in default of males. The rank of peeress in her own right is inherited by her eldest son (or perhaps daughter). There are some 19 peeresses in this rank.

(iii) *Lords of Appeal in Ordinary*. These are sometimes referred to as the Law Lords. They hold the rank of baron and are appointed for life (*Appellate Jurisdiction Act, 1876*, as amended). They perform the judicial work of the House of Lords when sitting as the final Court of Appeal, hearing some 50–70 cases a year. Although there are currently some 20 of them, they only sit as 3 or 5 when hearing a case.

(iv) *Life Peers*. These are men and women appointed to the rank of baron or baroness under the *Life Peerage Act, 1958*. There are about 320 at the present time (including 43 peeresses).

Creation and Renunciation of Hereditary Peerages

The creation of peerages is one of the Monarch's prerogatives. Originally the method adopted was to issue a writ of summons to an individual to the House of Lords followed by his taking a seat. This conferred a hereditary peerage, i.e. the right to attend descended to the Lord's heir at law. Since the fifteenth century the creation of hereditary peerages has been by **Letters Patent** which enabled descent to be directed into a certain line of heir different from those ascertained by reference to feudal customary law. Today all hereditary and life peerages are conferred by the Sovereign on the advice of the Prime Minister.

The Scottish peers are those who held titles which existed before the *Act of Union, 1707*. Since that time there has been no power to create Scottish peers as such though they may be created peers of the United Kingdom.

There is a common belief that most of the peerages date from feudal times. In fact only about sixty can be traced to a date before the eighteenth century; the rest have been created within the last two hundred years. As no hereditary peers were created during the period 1964–79 (i.e. when Wilson, Heath and Callaghan were Prime Ministers) it began to appear that the institution was being phased out, that a new convention was emerging. However, in 1983, Mrs Thatcher created three such peers (Whitelaw, Tonypandy and Stockton).

Fig. 7. Peers of the Realm (1986)

The *Peerage Act, 1963*. Before 1963 a hereditary peerage could not be surrendered or disclaimed. The Act now permits this, so that a person who succeeds to a peerage may disclaim that peerage for his or her lifetime and thereby becomes a commoner. Any person who disclaims his peerage loses his right to sit in the House of Lords, but he is able to vote at Parliamentary elections and is now eligible for election to the House of Commons.

The Act was passed as a result of the case of Anthony Wedgwood Benn who, in 1960, was MP for the constituency of Bristol South-East. His father, Viscount Stansgate, died in 1960. Mr Wedgwood Benn, an able politician, became a peer immediately and was automatically disqualified from membership of the House of Commons. His seat was accordingly declared vacant, and a by-election was held. The new Viscount Stansgate stood as a candidate (quite legally as there are few restrictions on being a candidate as such). He was re-elected by a large majority and presented himself as a member of the House of Commons. He was refused entry to the House and his opponent (who had in fact lost the election) was declared the member for the constituency. As a consequence of the publicity attending the case the Government introduced the *Peerage Act, 1963*, which provided (as we have noted above) for disclaimer and renunciation of a peerage. The Act enabled Viscount Stansgate to resume his former status and to become again Anthony Wedgwood Benn. The existing member gallantly resigned his seat and a further by-election was held. Mr Wedgwood Benn won the seat and took his place once more as the duly elected member for Bristol South-East (as Tony Benn).

Sir Alec Douglas-Home (formerly Lord Home) and Quintin Hogg (formerly Lord Hailsham), both prominent politicians also took advantage of the Act and became members of the House of Commons. Quintin Hogg (a distinguished lawyer and politician) was in 1970 made Lord Chancellor and once again resumed his former title of Lord Hailsham—as a life peer under the 1958 Act (as subsequently did Lord Home). To date 15 peers have disclaimed their peerage.

The *Peerage Act, 1963*, does not extinguish a peerage when a disclaimer is made. The next heir upon the death of his father can either elect to assume the peerage or to disclaim.

Disqualification. There are certain categories of person who are disqualified from membership of the House of Lords. These are:

(i) Persons who are aliens, bankrupts, or infants.

(ii) Persons convicted of treason or felony (serious crime) may not sit or vote until the sentence has been completed or pardoned.

(iii) Civil servants who are peers may sit in the House of Lords, but they may not speak or vote on issues. This rule is contained in a Treasury Minute. On resignation from the Civil Service he may resume the full rights of his peerage.

Officers of the Lords

Both Houses of Parliament have some members concerned with the management of business. The most important of these in the House of Lords are:

(i) *The Lord Chancellor*. Presides over the House in his capacity as

Speaker of the House and takes his place on the **Woolsack**, the traditional name given to a broad red-covered seat in front of the Throne.

The Lord Chancellor is recommended for appointment by the Prime Minister who is not required to consult the House. The Lord Chancellor is a member of the Government and usually a member of the Cabinet. As a member of the Executive, the Legislature, and the Judiciary he forms an exception to the doctrine of the separation of powers to which we referred previously (see p. 11).

As Speaker, the Lord Chancellor has fewer and less important powers than his counterpart in the Commons. The House of Lords is master of its own procedure, and matters of order are decided by the House itself.

As an important member of the Government the Lord Chancellor frequently takes an active part in debates. He may speak and vote as a member of his party, and on these occasions he rises from the Woolsack and moves a few feet so that he may be technically 'in' the House.

The Lord Chancellor is reponsible for the control of services and accommodation in that part of the Palace of Westminster and precincts occupied by or on behalf of the House of Lords. In the absence of the Lord Chancellor a Deputy Speaker presides. The Crown appoints several peers, in order of precedence, to the office of **Deputy Speaker**.

(ii) *The Chairman of Committees.* The first of the Deputy Speakers is the **Lord Chairman of Committees** who is appointed by the House at the beginning of each session. His duties include the following:

    (*a*) He takes the chair in all Committees of the House.
    (*b*) He is ex officio chairman of all other Committees of the House.
    (*c*) He acts as Speaker in the absence of the Lord Chancellor. He does not usually take part in the debates on ordinary topics.

(iii) *The Clerk of Parliaments.* He is appointed by the Crown and is removable only on an address of the House. His duties include keeping the records of proceedings and judgements and administering the judicial business of the House. He also pronounces the words by which the Royal Assent to Bills is signified (see p. 105).

The Clerk Assistant and the Reading Clerk record the daily attendances and read the Commission for Royal Assent.

(iv) *The Gentleman Usher of the Black Rod.* He is a member of the Royal Household. He enforces the orders of the House.

(v) *The Serjeant-at-Arms.* He attends the Lord Chancellor and carries the Mace.

Organisation of the House of Lords

Attendance. Although actual membership is over 1,000 (1,162 in 1986), average daily attendance is about 300, but in the course of a year some 700 take part. More attend when some matter of special interest is under discussion. In recent years the workload has increased and the Lords has become less leisurely and more workmanlike, with the length of sittings averaging some six hours. During the session the House of Lords meets on most Mondays, and on Tuesdays and Wednesdays at 2.30 p.m., on Thursdays at 3 p.m. and on Fridays at 11 a.m.

To ensure that only those peers who are interested in the general work of Parliament attend, holders of hereditary peerages are asked at the beginning of each session whether they will attend the sittings of the House as often as they reasonably can, or whether they wish to be relieved of the obligation to attend. If they so desire they are requested to apply for *leave of absence* either for the duration of a particular Parliament or for a single session (in 1986, 140 peers did so.). During that time they are expected not to attend the sittings of the House. A peer who wishes to terminate his leave of absence may do so on giving a month's notice.

Peers in constant attendance at the House of Lords are generally elder statesmen and others who have spent their lives in public service.

Peers receive no salary for their parliamentary work. They are, however, entitled to (i) travelling expenses from their homes to the Palace of Westminster (provided they attend at least one-third of the number of sittings); and (ii) expenses incurred for the purpose of attendance within a maximum of £52 (a figure which would cover overnight expenses).

The minimum number of members required to form a duly constituted House is three, but a vote cannot be taken unless there are thirty peers present.

Political Parties in the Lords. Like the Commons, the House of Lords has a Government bench and an Opposition bench. There are, however, a number of peers who have no party affiliations who sit on the **'cross-benches'**. There are, too, the Law Lords and the Lords Spiritual whose special position excludes party politics. (Such neutral positions do not exist in the Commons, apart from the Speaker and the three deputy Speakers; non-government party MPs must sit with the Opposition.) Thus in 1985–6, the party composition was:

Conservative peers	418
Labour	136
Liberals	41
SDP	41
Crossbenchers	219

On the Government side there must be by law at least three Ministers of the Crown as members of the House of Lords in addition to the Lord Chancellor. One of the three will be the Leader of the Government party in the House, and one will be the **Chief Whip** who is in charge of the party organisation in the Lords. The Government Ministers in the Lords deal with all questions or debates on behalf of the Government, and inevitably they will have to cover a wide parliamentary field, not necessarily those subjects falling within the sphere of their own department.

The Opposition Party in the Lords follows the usual party organisation found in the Commons, with a Leader, Chief Whip, and party spokesmen i.e. there is a 'front bench' team of about twenty peers and peeresses.

Superficially there are certain resemblances to the Commons, but we must remember that the power of the Upper House has been much eroded (*Parliament Acts, 1911 and 1949*). Moreover, peers do not have the risk of elections and loss of their seat or status. As to the conduct of business we have already noted that this falls to the Lord Chancellor who is **Chairman** of the House. He differs from the Speaker in the Commons in that he (the Lord Chancellor) is not impartial for he is a member of the Government, and may take part in debates. He may vote, but has no casting vote. He has little power over members (unlike the Speaker) and procedure in the Lords is much more flexible.

The Present Functions of the Lords

The main duties of the House of Lords, bearing in mind the limitations imposed by the *Parliament Acts, 1911 and 1949*, are summarised as follows:

(i) *Initiation of Legislation.* As we have noted the House of Commons is the chamber which initiates almost all the important Bills. The only Bills introduced first in the House of Lords are (*a*) those of a legal character, (e.g. the *Courts Act, 1971*), (*b*) Bills of a non-financial or non-controversial character, and (*c*) those of a minor character. The House of Lords contains many distinguished lawyers, including the Law Lords, in addition to experienced politicians well acquainted with the legislative process of Parliament, and they are therefore well qualified to deal with all of the above types of Bills. Moreover this duty saves the time of the Commons.

As to the procedure, we should note that the same legislative process applies in the Lords as in the Commons: Bills are read three times, and there is a **Committee stage** and a **Report stage**. Where Bills are received from the Commons, the Lords now usually content themselves with making minor changes only, such as verbal alterations (see p. 104).

(ii) *Revision of Legislation.* Formerly, where the House of Lords held fundamentally different views about a particular Bill the ensuing disagreement could precipitate a constitutional crisis, as we have already noted (see p. 52). Today this does not present a serious problem. The main Bills are introduced first in the Commons and constitute part of the political programme or mandate of the Government. The Upper House must therefore content itself with making only those amendments designed to improve the proposals.

Where fundamental disagreement does occur over a Bill, it can be submitted (under the 1949 Act) for the Royal Assent without the concurrence of the House of Lords. If, however, the Lords decide to merely amend the Bill it must be returned to the Lower House where it originated for consideration of those amendments. If the Commons reject the amendments made by the Lords, a committee is set up to show the reasons for the disagreement, and a message is sent to the Lords. The amendment may then be dropped, or alternative ones adopted. Negotiation proceeds until agreement is reached. Only if it is impossible to reconcile the different points of view would the Commons invoke the powers of the *Parliament Acts, 1911 and 1949*, to present the Bill for Royal Assent after one year (with the exception of Money Bills, see p. 52); this procedure was used in 1977 (see p. 53). Notwithstanding these technical procedures to achieve agreement, we must not forget that the House of Lords *is* the second stage in the legislative process and that this allows time for reflection, eliciting new points of view and for detecting errors not discovered in the Commons. This applies particularly in the case of delegated legislation (see p. 286).

(iii) *Examination of Government business.* It is the duty of Parliament as a whole to keep an eye on the work of the Government. This is done by the House of Lords in several ways. Firstly, as we have seen the Government's legislation is scrutinised and perhaps amended by the Lords. Secondly, the Lords' debates (see (iv) below) frequently focus on Goverment policy (or lack of it). Thirdly, the Lords have a regular daily period of Question Time (for about 20 minutes). Sometimes a question may lead to a short debate. In either case Government Ministers are obliged to reply. Finally, the Lords may set up Select Committees to investigate general subjects or problems, some of which may naturally involve Government activity. Thus in recent years, the Lords have had a Committee on Science and Technology and a Committee on Unemployment. The committees can call witnesses (civil servants, business managers etc.) and subsequently produce a report containing recommendations for action.

(iv) *Discussion on Current Affairs.* Most persons would say that the Commons has too much to do and too little time in which to do it. Because of this it follows that the Commons cannot give many hours to discussing current affairs. The Upper House is not pressed in this way. Many peers have wide experience and knowledge, and some are specialists. The debates in the Upper House are usually informed with good sense, of high quality and (because peers do not fight elections) they are disinterested. The contribution of Life Peers has added to the standard, and a reading of *The Times*, *The Daily Telegraph*, *The Independent*, *The Guardian* or of *Hansard* will reveal the general level attained and the detachment which the Upper House achieves.

(v) *Examination of European proposals.* Since joining the Common Market in 1972, we have become subject to the laws of the European Economic Community (EEC). When the EEC proposes new laws which will affect Britain, they are investigated by a Select Committee in each House of Parliament. The Lords' Committee has 7 sub-committees (which specialise in particular subjects like agriculture, environment etc.) and the reports of the Committee can give rise to Parliamentary debates which may influence the attitude of the British representative in Europe (a Minister) to the proposed laws and this may help to shape the laws themselves.

Reform of the House of Lords

All institutions have their critics, and the House of Lords is not exempt. These allege long-windedness, a lack of urgency and sense of reality. Critics point also to the high average age of the members and conclude that this relects a lack of modernity in thought, approach, and attitude.

The reform of the Upper House has agitated the minds of thoughtful persons for many years. In 1649 the House was abolished on the grounds that it was 'useless and dangerous to the people'. It was restored in 1660.

Since then it has been commonly attacked on the ground that the hereditary principle (of feudal origin) is incompatible with representative democracy. A Conference on the Reform of the Second Chamber was held in 1918, presided over by Lord Bryce. He stated:

The need of two chambers has been an axiom of political science based on the belief of the innate tendency of an assembly to become lazy, tyrannical and corrupt, a tendency which can only be checked by the co-existence of another house of equal authority.

Even if all these points were true it is extremely doubtful whether the House of Lords would be the corrective to re-establish industry and efficiency, benevolence and propriety, particularly having regard to the present diminished powers of the Upper House. We have already noted (p. 52) that the *Parliament Acts, 1911 and 1949*, have considerably reduced the effectiveness of the House of Lords as part of the supreme legislative assembly.

The main criticisms may be listed thus:

(i) *The House of Lords is unrepresentative.* Most members claim noble birth or are there by reason of past political service, church office or as Law Lords. The majority are drawn from a special section of the people.

(ii) *Conservative bias.* Members tend to belong to a property-owning class and are conservative (see p. 57). Labour peers are generally but a small proportion of total membership. They are, therefore, ineffective in voting power.

(iii) *Unsuitable Membership.* Some peers have not the interest or capacity for politics. Most are hereditary peers, and this is not a satisfactory qualification for deliberative or legislative duties. Some hereditary peers must earn a living, and may be prevented from attending the House for that reason.

(iv) *Attendance.* Many of the peers do not attend regularly and their attendance is sparse.

The result of these and similar criticisms is that there has been a decline in the public esteem of the Upper House as a second chamber.

Is the Lords as a Second Chamber Necessary? There is no general agreement on this point for the following reasons. It is generally held that a second chamber should not:

(*a*) Be a duplication of the other chamber and should differ in qualifications for membership.

(*b*) Represent a single or a few classes or interests.

(*c*) Predominantly favour any of the parties which alternately govern the country.

It is frequently held that a second chamber should:

(*a*) Have a fixed term of life i.e. have renewable membership.

(*b*) Be independent, without fear of punishment for the expression of opinion.

(*c*) Represent all bodies of opinion, even those who do not accept the whole programme of any party.

(*d*) Provide opportunity for 'second thoughts', reconsideration and deliberation.

The question of reform was debated in the House of Lords itself in 1946. Some twelve years later the *Life Peerages Act, 1958*, was passed, which overcomes, to some extent, the criticism of the hereditary character of the House. The Crown may now confer peerages on men and women who have proved themselves worthy of the honour in public service and in many walks of life including industry, commerce, the professions, and the Commonwealth. A life peerage, as its name implies, terminates on the death of the recipient of the honour.

Paradoxically, the Lords is in some respects more representative of the population than the Commons is. Thus, the Lords have four non-white members, has one Communist and proportionately more women members. It has also been responsible, in the 1980s, for imposing substantial and widespread amendments to Government legislation (e.g. on local government, education, immigration, dockyards and financial services).

The *Government White Paper (Cmnd 3799) of 1968*. This document, issued in November 1968, represented the agreed conclusions of a joint party conference established in November 1967. The Government stated four propositions on which reform should be based:

(*a*) The second chamber has an essential role to play, **complementary** to, but not rivalling, that of the Commons.

(*b*) The present composition and powers of the House of Lords prevent it from performing that role as effectively as it should.

(*c*) The reform should therefore be directed towards promoting the more efficient working of Parliament as a whole.

(*d*) Once the reform has been completed the work of the two Houses should become more closely co-ordinated and integrated, and the functions of the House of Lords should be reviewed.

The White Paper further stated that reform should ensure that:

(*a*) The hereditary basis of membership should be eliminated.

(*b*) No one party should possess a permanent majority.

(*c*) In normal circumstances the Government of the day should be able to secure a reasonable working majority.

(*d*) The powers of the House of Lords to delay public legislation should be restricted.

(*e*) The Lords' absolute power to withhold consent to subordinate legislation against the will of the Commons should be abolished.

The Labour Government introduced the *Parliament (No. 2) Bill, 1969*, to give effect to the proposals in the White Paper, but it was withdrawn following opposition from backbenchers of both main parties who saw the reforms as either too radical or too moderate. Neither the Government nor the Opposition regarded the Bill as of much importance, and it was realised that legislation might create additional problems.

Conclusion. There is no special sanctity in a second Chamber. New Zealand manages her affairs successfully without one. Sweden abolished its second Chamber in 1971. However, most national systems of government contain two chambers (bi-cameral), especially those with a federal constitution such as the USA, West Germany, Canada and Australia. In a debate on the subject in 1970 Lord Shinwell said: 'Let us face the problem frankly. Either we create an elected senate sharing authority with the Commons or leave the subject alone. As a debating chamber the House of Lords can do no harm and may even do some good.'

It has long been held that the House of Lords will continue so long as it 'behaves itself' in its relationship with the Commons. However, the future of the Lords is now once again in question: this follows the Labour Party's Annual Conference of 1978 when, by an overwhelming majority, the abolition of the House of Lords became official party policy. Nevertheless, there was a distinct lack of enthusiasm by the Party's leadership, and indeed no action was taken during the Labour Government's period of office which ended in 1979 (inaction largely attributed to the Prime Minister, James Callaghan).

The House of Commons

We have already traced the history of the House of Commons from the time of Simon de Montfort in 1295 and the so-called Model Parliament, and have noted the great constitutional struggles of the seventeenth century which culminated in the *Bill of Rights, 1689*, and the *Act of Settlement, 1701*. These two documents finally assured the supremacy of Parliament over the Monarch and all other institutions, and settled the succession to the English throne.

Democracy, as we understand the word, was not attained overnight. Our institutions and procedures have grown step by step for some 250 years following the Bill of Rights.

In this chapter we shall examine the existing House of Commons to which Members of Parliament are elected and where the will of the people finds its highest democratic expression.

Composition

The House of Commons is a representative assembly of men and women who are Members of Parliament (MPs). There are at present 650 seats in the House of Commons (since 1983) and these are distributed as follows: England, 523; Wales, 38; Scotland, 72; Northern Ireland, 17.

Constituencies. The United Kingdom is divided into 650 constituencies each of which returns one member to the House of Commons.

Parliament itself determines where those constituencies are located. Under the *House of Commons (Redistribution of Seats) Acts, 1949 and 1958*, there were set up four permanent **Boundary Commissions** for England, Scotland, Wales, and Northern Ireland. The Chairman of each Commission is the Speaker of the House of Commons. The Vice-Chairman is a judge.

The duty of the Commissions is to keep constituencies constantly under review, to submit periodic reports at intervals of not less than ten years nor more than fifteen years and to recommend changes in the boundaries of any constituency. Broadly, each constituency should be for an area containing 60,000 to 70,000 voters (e.g. the target figure or quota for England is 65,750). Roughly half of the 650 members represent urban boroughs, and half the rural counties. A city (or borough) with a population of half a million inhabitants may return to Parliament seven or eight members.

The reason for the constant review of constituency boundaries is the changes of population arising from the local industrial growth or decline, building of new towns, new housing estates, and similar factors (e.g. in 1982 eleven constituencies had over 100,000 people and fourteen less than 40,000). The reports of the Boundary Commissions are made to the Home Secretary and require Parliamentary confirmation. The 1982 review introduced considerable changes and the addition of 15 seats to the previous

Fig. 8. House of Commons Seating Plan

635 MPs. The Labour Party, predicted to lose 20 seats, challenged the validity of the report's proposals on the grounds that it allowed excessive disparities between constituencies from the given quota of 65,750 (e.g. it allowed Isle of Wight 88,500 cf. Surbiton 46,500). The challenge was rejected by the High Court (December 1982).

Qualifications for Membership of the House of Commons

Any British subject (or Irish citizen) may be a member of the House of Commons, except the following: (i) Aliens. (ii) Infants, i.e. persons under 21. (iii) Mental patients. (iv) Members of the House of Lords. (v) Clergymen of the Churches of England, Scotland, and Ireland, and the Roman Catholic Church. (vi) Bankrupts (for a period of five years from their discharge). (vii) Persons convicted of treason provided they have not been pardoned. (viii) Persons convicted of corrupt or illegal practices at Parliamentary elections. (ix) Persons disqualified by the *House of Commons Disqualification Act, 1957*. The principal persons in this category are:

(*a*) Judges and stipendiary magistrates.
(*b*) Civil servants.
(*c*) Members of the regular Army, Navy and Air Force.
(*d*) Police Officers (except Special Constables).
(*e*) Members of Public Corporations.

Under the *Representation of the People Act, 1981* prisoners serving a sentence of one year or more are disqualified from standing for election and membership of the House of Commons. (This followed the case of the IRA hunger-striker Bobby Sands who stood for Parliament, and was legally elected—though he could not take his seat.)

Any dispute as to qualification for membership is decided by the House of Commons, not a court of law. Thus, the **Committee of Privileges** (which exercises the jurisdiction) held that when Lord Stansgate (formerly Anthony Wedgwood Benn) wished to claim his seat in the Commons in 1961 it was decided that he was disqualified by reason of his peerage (see p. 53).

Generally, practically anyone is entitled to *stand* for election as an MP. In practice, there are many factors which affect candidature. Primarily, a candidate must possess certain important personal attributes, an interest in people, politics, and a capacity for hard work. But, apart from these factors, there is usually the need for financial backing and the support of a political party. Some (Labour) MPs are 'sponsored', i.e. they are nominated by a trade union which then provides election finance and/or funds to the constituency Labour Party (CLP). Over half of the present (1987) MPs are sponsored.

Attendance

The House of Commons meets in Westminster from Mondays to Fridays throughout the year. There are 160 sitting days per year, and these are divided roughly into four periods:

(*a*) From November to Christmas   30–40
(*b*) From January to Easter   40–50
(*c*) From Easter to Whitsun   30
(*d*) From Whitsun to end of July   40

When Parliament is not sitting it is said to be **in recess**.

Hours. On Mondays, Tuesdays, Wednesdays and Thursdays the official hours of sitting are from 2.30 p.m. to 10.30 p.m. There are certain classes of Parliamentary business which are always exempt from normal closing time. Moreover, if the House so desires and chooses any other business may necessitate going on longer than 10.30 p.m. If the business of the House is urgent or important (as is frequently the case) the sittings continue much later. All-night sittings sometimes occur.

Fridays are exceptional in that the House assembles at 9.30 a.m. and usually rises at 3 p.m. (since 1979). This enables Members to return to their constituencies, some of which are far distant from Westminster. On Saturday mornings, most members engage in political activities, attend to complaints of constituents (at their 'surgeries') or attend other local functions.

Only in exceptional circumstances does Parliament sit on Saturdays or weekday mornings of Monday to Thursday.

Members of Parliament are not expected to be in constant attendance in the debating chamber. Some are members of the numerous committees of the House, and all have many and varied duties to perform. When, however, specially important business is to be dealt with such as a vote on important legislation, special steps (through the Whip system, see pp. 72–6) are taken to ensure that members are present. Apart from these times the House of Commons chamber may be relatively full or empty, dependent on the speakers and the subject-matter of the debate. The majority of members remain within the precincts of the House so that they may be available to reach the voting lobby within a few minutes of being called. Some members may leave the House of Commons altogether for a few hours.

Formerly, if members desired to be away from the House for some days at a time during the session they had to apply formally for leave of absence. This is not now considered necessary. But, if an official delegation of members of the House of Commons is visiting a foreign country, for example, formal permission to be absent is granted.

Ministers in the Commons

All Ministers of the Crown must sit in one or other of the Houses of Parliament. The *Ministers of the Crown Act, 1965*, and the *House of Commons Disqualification Act, 1957*, governs the number of Ministers who may sit in the Commons. At the present time ninety-one holders of Ministerial office are entitled to sit and vote in the House of Commons at any one time.

Resignation of Members

A member elected to the House of Commons may, for some reason, e.g. ill health or incapacity, wish to resign during a Parliament. One might suppose that a letter sent direct to Mr Speaker and the Chairman of his constituency party might dispose of this matter, but this is not so.

Technically speaking, a Member of Parliament cannot resign his seat. The reason is historical. At one time the Crown wanted to ensure that members of the House would not escape their important responsibilities to vote money (i.e. to impose taxation on the public) for carrying on the government of the country simply by resigning from the House. Taxes had to be imposed, and the **Royal power** was applied in earlier times to ensure that the reluctant member did not evade his duty.

Today a member resigns by an indirect method of applying for 'an office of profit under the Crown'. The holding of such an office (except Ministerial office) has been a disqualification for membership of the House of Commons since the *Act of Settlement, 1701*. The application is automatically granted and the member vacates his seat.

The two appointments to 'an office of profit' are: (i) Steward of the Chiltern Hundreds, or (ii) Bailiff of the Manor of Northstead. Both are ancient offices, though neither exists in fact today. Both are nominally in the gift of the Chancellor of the Exchequer who may grant them in quick succession where more than one member wishes to vacate his seat at the same time. No remuneration attaches to the two posts, and, in practice, a request is never refused. The former MP thereupon resumes his status as an ordinary citizen and a by-election is held in his constituency.

Officers of the Commons

The Speaker

The office of Speaker dates back to Simon de Montfort and the Model Parliament of 1295, and we know from the Parliamentary Rolls that the office has been held continuously from 1377.

From the earliest times the Speaker was the spokesman of the Commons to the King. But his exact relationship *vis-à-vis* the Crown was anomalous and precarious, for the Speaker was at one and the same time the spokesman (hence the name Speaker) *to* the House of Commons on behalf of the Crown. We know that in the sixteenth century he was appointed by and paid by the Crown and was, therefore, looked upon as the agent of the King. The Tudor and Stuart sovereigns ensured that all Speakers should be of their choosing. They were, therefore, compliant to the Royal wish, managing Royal business in the Commons and reporting on the attitude of members. This was not satisfactory to the Commons.

In 1629 Mr Speaker Finch was held down in his chair by the Commons while resolutions were passed condemning the Crown's taxation of 'tunnage and poundage', whereupon (we are told) the Speaker stated: 'I am none the less the King's servant for being yours'.

In 1642, however, the attitude of the Commons stiffened. When Charles I came into the House to arrest five members of the Commons he demanded of the Speaker where the members were. The Speaker replied bravely: 'I have neither eyes to see nor tongue to speak in this place, but as the House doth direct me whose servant I am.'

The constitutional struggles of the seventeenth century finally resulted in the *Bill of Rights, 1689*, and the supremacy of Parliament over the King. Thenceforward the Speaker was undoubtedly the servant of the Commons. From that time forward his modern duties as spokesman of the Commons to the Crown and as chairman have evolved.

Such in broad outline is the history, and it is small wonder that the office and 'Mr Speaker' himself are accorded traditionally great respect by the public and by all members of the House. Thus, when during proceedings the Speaker rises to his feet all other members in the Chamber must sit down; when he speaks in the proceedings all other members remain silent. If a member disobeys the Speaker he will first be given a warning. If the member persists he may be ordered to leave the House. This is effected traditionally by stating the name of the offender instead of referring to him by the customary manner of 'The Honourable Member for . . .' (the constituency for which the member stands). At this point the Government Minister in charge of the business being debated will move a resolution that the offending member be expelled. The resolution is carried usually unanimously and the offender must leave the House for a certain period (usually five days for a first offender.)

In 1968 Dame Irene Ward, Conservative Member for Tynemouth, who first entered the House in 1931, made a protest during a debate on the Finance Bill. During the division she took a stand before the mace at the foot of the clerks' table, obstructed the tellers when they returned to announce the voting figures and failed to obey the Speaker's request, several times repeated, to resume her seat. The Speaker eventually 'named' Dame Irene, and the Leader of the House moved her suspension. This motion was carried, and as Dame Irene persisted in trying to voice her protest from where she stood the Speaker directed the Serjeant-at-Arms to escort her from the Chamber. She went quietly, and was debarred from entering the Chamber for a week. The Revd. Ian Paisley was so named in 1982.

Present Functions of the Speaker. The Speaker is the chief officer of the House of Commons, and his main duties are as follows:

(i) He is the mouthpiece of the House of Commons in its relation with (*a*) the Crown, (*b*) the House of Lords, and (*c*) other representative bodies and organisations.

(ii) He presides over the House in its debates, and enforces the rules for preserving order in its proceedings.

In addition, the Speaker has a number of administrative and statutory duties in relation to the function of the Commons. Among these are the following:

(*a*) He certifies whether a Bill is a **Money Bill** for the purposes of the *Parliament Acts, 1911 and 1949.*

(*b*) He executes the orders of the House.

(*c*) He signs warrants for the issue of writs for by-elections.

(*d*) He issues warrants for committal for contempt of the House, and warrants for witnesses to attend the House to give evidence.

(*e*) He issues reprimands to members or 'strangers' (i.e. members of the public) for contempt of the House or breach of privilege.

(*f*) He supervises and controls all the departments of the House of Commons.

Election of the Speaker. The Speaker is elected by the House from among MPs. Usually the Prime Minister and the Leader of the Opposition consult together and agree to propose a member who has taken no recent part in party controversy and who is acceptable to all sections of the House. Qualities of good temper, common sense and scrupulous fairness are looked for.

When elected, the Speaker must, in his chairmanship of the most important and powerful body in the country, be impartial. He does not, therefore, take part in debates (i.e. he does not speak on party political matters). This practice has been observed by all previous Speakers over the last hundred years. He has a casting vote, but, in the event of a tie, he uses that vote to keep the issue open.

When the House of Commons sits, for certain purposes, 'in committee' the chair is occupied by the Chairman of Ways and Means, the Deputy Chairman of Ways and Means, or a temporary chairman. The debates and business done by the House 'in committee' are more informal.

Residence. The Speaker may be called upon to chair a meeting of the House at any time of the day or night, and should as servant of the House be available to perform his important duties. He is given an official residence within the precincts of the Palace of Westminster.

Salary. The Speaker receives a salary of £46,650 per annum, payable out of the Consolidated Fund (see p. 111). On retirement the Speaker is offered a peerage and is awarded a pension.

The Chairman of Ways and Means

This officer is elected by the House from among its members at the beginning of each Parliament. He presides over the House when it is in Committee and maintains order in its business. He must be impartial in the chair. He acts as Deputy Speaker of the House as do the three Deputy Chairmen of Ways and Means.

The Chairman of Ways and Means and the Deputy Chairmen are party appointments and the holders receive salaries for their work in the House.

The Clerk of the House

This office dates from 1388. The Clerk is appointed by the Crown and is removable on an Address from the House. The Clerk keeps the records, prepares the journals, endorses Bills sent or returned to the Lords.

He is assisted by two Clerk Assistants who are similarly attired in wig and gown and sit at the Table of the House and formally record the proceedings.

The Clerk of the House controls a staff of about thirty officers whom he appoints. The Clerk's experience, knowledge of procedure and advice are available to the House, its committees and members.

The Serjeant-at-Arms

He is the officer who ceremonially attends the Speaker with the Mace (the symbol of the Speaker's authority). He executes the Speaker's warrants for commitment to prison (if need by), maintains order in the galleries, controls the messengers and porters, and arranges the policing of the House.

The Serjeant-at-Arms is appointed by the Crown and he is provided with an official residence in the House.

The Speaker's Counsel

This is a lawyer whose duty is to assist the Chairman of Ways and Means in the examination of Private Bills (see p. 100).

The Librarians

Their duties include the provision of literature, journals, books of reference and similar material for the use of members.

Parliamentary Privilege

The House of Commons and the House of Lords enjoy certain rights and privileges. These privileges are part of the common law (see p. 215 and are enforceable as such.

Broadly the privileges of Parliament govern the relation of each House with (i) each other, (ii) the Crown, (iii) the Courts, and (iv) the public.

The rights (or privileges) have been won largely as the result of the former struggles of Parliament with the Crown over the question of the 'supremacy' of Parliament and with the Courts over the question of jurisdiction. The main object of Parliamentary Privilege is to protect the rights of the House of Commons and its members inside Parliament to enable them to do their duty. Parliamentary Privilege ensures the efficiency of Parliament. In a sense it forms a special law which is interpreted and administered in each House and not in the ordinary courts of law. It is nevertheless part of the law of the land and is recognised constitutionally by the Courts of Law.

Privileges of the House of Commons

At the opening of Parliament the Speaker lays claim to the privileges in the name of the Commons thus:

their ancient and undoubted rights and privileges; particularly that their persons may be free from arrests and all molestations; that they may enjoy liberty of speech in all their debates; may have access to Her Majesty's Royal person whenever occasion shall require; and that all their proceedings may receive from Her Majesty the most favourable construction.

To this request the Lord Chancellor, acting for Her Majesty, replies:

Her Majesty most readily confirms all the rights and privileges which have ever been granted to or conferred upon the Commons, by Her Majesty or any of her royal predecessors.

The main privileges may, therefore, be listed thus:

   (i) Freedom from arrest.
   (ii) Freedom of speech and debate.
  (iii) Right of access to the Queen.
  (iv) Right to regulate its own proceedings.
   (v) Right to regulate its own composition.
  (vi) Right to have the most favourable construction placed on the deliberations of the Commons.
 (vii) The power to punish for breach of privilege or for contempt.

   (i) *Freedom from Arrest.* This has lost much of its former importance. MPs are not exempt from the criminal law and, if they commit arrestable criminal offences they may be arrested if need be at any time. The privilege relates to civil arrest, i.e. arrest for civil cause. A member may not be arrested on a civil matter during a session and forty days before and forty days after a session. The privilege is practically obsolete. It was formerly invoked when a member was arrested for civil debt (*Ferrer's Case, 1543*), but since the *Debtor's Act, 1869*, which precludes arrest for civil debt, the privilege is not now of importance, and a Select Committee on Parliamentary Privilege in 1967 recommended its abolition.

Where a member is convicted of crime the judge notifies the Speaker, and the House may, if the crime be of a serious nature, pass a motion expelling the member concerned.

(ii) *Freedom of Speech.* This is one of the main freedoms which is jealously guarded. The *Bill of Rights, 1689 (Article 9)* declares:

That the freedom of speech and debates on proceedings in Parliament ought not to be impeached or questioned in any court or place out of Parliament.

No legal proceedings have since then been taken by the Crown or a private person against any member for words spoken in the House. So a member may not be prosecuted for sedition nor may he be sued for libel or slander in respect of anything said by such member during proceedings in the House or published on its order paper. Members are also exempt from the provisions of the *Official Secrets Acts, 1911–1939*, in respect of anything said by them which would in other circumstances be a criminal offence.

The privilege of freedom of speech is not a personal right of any individual MP but a necessary protection and guarantee that a member should be able to defend to the full the interests of the electors, and is, therefore, an indirect constitutional privilege of every citizen.

Allied to the right of freedom of speech is the right of the Commons to debate (*a*) in private, and (*b*) in secret session. The Commons may at any time exercise the right to exclude strangers (i.e. the public) from the public galleries. The right may be exercised by the Speaker on his own initiative or on a motion by a member that strangers be ordered to withdraw. A vote is then taken and the Speaker may thereupon order members of the public to withdraw from the Chamber.

A secret session is one in which vital matters of national importance are discussed, e.g. shipping losses in time of war, the revelation of which would be helpful to an enemy. The House may resolve that its proceedings or debates be held in secret and that the public (including the Press) be excluded.

(iii) The *Right of Access to HM The Queen*. In the thirteenth and fourteenth centuries the Commons were sometimes admitted to the Royal presence to give answers to the demands or requests put before them. The privilege is formally requested today by the Speaker. It is a collective right and is exercised through the elected representative of the House, namely the Speaker.

(iv) The *Right to Regulate its own Proceedings*. The House of Commons has the right to determine its own constitution, e.g.:

(*a*) To settle disputed elections where irregular practices are alleged.
(*b*) To suspend or expel a member.
(*c*) To decide what it will discuss and the order of so doing.
(*d*) To settle its own procedure in the chamber and in the House as a whole.

Bradlaugh, an atheist MP for Northampton, refused to take the oath on his admission to the House of Commons and claimed the right to make an affirmation instead under the *Evidence Acts, 1869 and 1870*. The House refused to permit this and Bradlaugh challenged the ruling in the Courts of Law. He also sought an order to restrain the Serjeant-at-Arms (Gossett) from preventing him from entering the House and a declaration that the resolution of the House was void. The Court held that: 'For the purpose of determining on a right to be exercised within the House itself, and in particular the right of sitting and voting, the House and the House alone could interpret the Statute'. Bradlaugh was subsequently allowed to affirm in 1886 and took his seat. *Bradlaugh* v. *Gossett* (1884).

(v) *The Right to Regulate its own Composition.* This privilege is closely allied to the previous one. The right is best exemplified by the right:

(*a*) To fill a casual vacancy by the Speaker issuing a warrant instructing a writ to be issued authorising an election (i.e. a by-election) to be held in a constituency when a casual vacancy occurs.
(*b*) To decide disputed elections. This is done by an order of the House to HM judges who are directed to hear the petition. The House invariably accepts the determination of the judges.
(*c*) To determine whether a person claiming to be lawfully elected is or is not legally disqualified. See the case of Anthony Wedgwood Benn (p. 55).
(*d*) To expel a member or suspend a member.

(vi) *The Right to have the Most Favourable Construction placed on its Deliberations.* This is a reminder of former times when the business of the House was reported to the Monarch by the Speaker in his own words. This was sometimes a very tricky duty demanding the utmost tact and discretion. The privilege is now of no great practical importance.

(vii) *The Power to Punish for Breach of Privilege or Contempt.* The privileges are those listed above. Contempt means 'any act which offends the dignity of the House or which obstructs or impedes any member or officer of the House in the discharge of his duty or which tends to produce such a result', e.g. disorderly conduct in the House, abuse of the Speaker, throwing a tomato at him.

Enforcement. The House may punish offenders by imprisonment, fine, reprimand, admonition, or, in the case of a member, expulsion or suspension. Imprisonment may be for a specified time or until the end of the session when the committal automatically lapses. The prison itself is located in the Clock Tower. Warrants for the arrest of a member or non-member are drawn up by the Speaker and executed by the Serjeant-at-Arms with the aid of the civil police.

Complaints of breach of privilege or contempt are investigated by the **Committee of Privileges** which has power to summon witnesses and hear evidence. The House itself decides what amounts to breach of privilege. Nevertheless the Courts of Law have laid it down that it is for the Courts, as a matter of law, to determine the existence and the limits of a privilege claimed by a litigant. The Courts will not consider mere resolutions of either House as sufficient justification for a privilege, for a resolution as such is not law. The following case is relevant to the privilege of freedom of speech and debate (No. (ii) above):

The House of Commons ordered the publication by its printer (Hansard) of certain matters which were defamatory of Stockdale (plaintiff). Copies of Hansard were sold outside Parliament and Stockdale sued Hansard in defamation. Hansard's defence was that an order of the Commons granted privilege from action in the Courts of Law and that a resolution of the Commons and a declaration of its privilege excluded the Courts of Law from jurisdiction. *Held:* That the mere resolution or order of the House will not justify an act otherwise illegal, and that the House had no privilege to authorise publication of libel outside the House. *Stockdale* v. *Hansard* (1839).

The *Parliamentary Papers Act, 1840*. As a result of the decision in *Stockdale* v. *Hansard* (1839) the *Parliamentary Papers Act, 1840*, was passed which extended absolute privilege to any publication made by authority of either House of Parliament. Accordingly an action for defamation in any such publication (or broadcast) will be stayed on production of a certificate from an officer of the relevant House.

Privileges of the House of Lords

The House of Lords is the descendant of the medieval Council. The Lords were in those early days the tenants in chief of the Crown. One of the incidents of feudal tenure was that a tenant had a right or duty to attend his lord's (i.e. the King's) court, known as suit of court. The Lords attended court and gave advice to the Crown personally, if need be.

The privileges of the Lords are practically the same as those enjoyed by the Commons, namely:

  (i) Freedom from arrest.
 (ii) Freedom of speech and debate.
(iii) Right of access to the Crown. This is a personal right since each peer is a Counsellor of the Sovereign.
 (iv) The right to regulate its own proceedings and composition.
  (v) The right to enter a protest in the journals against a resolution of the House.

The Whips

The name 'Whip' derives from the hunting field. Many MPs of former days were country gentry and rode to hounds. The 'whipper in' kept the hounds in a pack or in line. The 'Whip' is a well-known parliamentary term and has two meanings. It refers to:

  (i) An important party official (Government and Opposition):
 (ii) A written notice or direction to an MP to attend the House to vote.

Party Official

After a General Election each major party appoints a Chief Whip and assistant Whips. The Government Chief Whip usually holds the office of Parliamentary Secretary to the Treasury, a salaried post. The holder has few departmental duties. The Chief Whip lives in 12 Downing Street. Other Whips (about 12) are also appointed to lesser Government posts as Junior Lords of the Treasury. These also are salaried, and some are sinecures (i.e.

with few departmental or ministerial duties). The freedom from departmental duties enables the Whips to manage their party politically within Parliament.

The main duties of the Government Whips are *managerial*. They include the following, namely to:

(*a*) Arrange the business of the House and its time-table.
(*b*) Advise MPs how to vote and of the relative importance of a motion or debate to the Government.
(*c*) Inform the leaders of the feelings and views of backbenchers on party policy.
(*d*) Discipline MPs if need be.
(*e*) Arrange 'pairing' of MPs (see p. 74).
(*f*) Act as 'Patronage Secretary' (Government Chief Whip).

The Whips are the agents through whom the party machinery is used for the conduct of the business of the House. They are the eyes and ears of the party chief. It is their business to try and discern the direction in which sections of opinion are moving, to hear any mutterings of discontent, and to suggest methods for mitigating them. (Sir Courtenay Ilbert.)

The Opposition leader also appoints Whips for each House, though in the case of the Labour Party, when it is in opposition, it elects its Whips. In the Commons, the Opposition Chief Whip and two assistant Whips are salaried appointments. Their duties correspond with those of their counterparts on the Government side. They are salaried appointments.

(*a*) *Arranging business*. The Government Chief Whip consults with (i) the Prime Minister and the Leader of the House (a senior politician) as to the time-table of the business, and (ii) the Opposition Chief Whip who also confers with the Leader of the Opposition. When done and agreed the Government Chief Whip confers with the Speaker for his approval of the time-table of business.

This is not always easy. Sometimes a Government party wishes to get an important Bill through Parliament quickly, e.g. an Industrial Relations Bill. The Opposition may require to debate the Bill to which it is fundamentally opposed. A compromise has to be reached to enable the Opposition to debate and object while also enabling the Government to pass the Bill with its majority.

(*b*) *Advising MPs*. The Whips usually attend the Parliamentary Party meetings each week, and there outline the business of the following week indicating the relative importance of pending matters. The Chief Whip sends formal notices (also called 'Whips') to all members of the Parliamentary Party detailing the matters to be dealt with in the House.

The notices are underlined in three ways: one-line; two-line; and three-line, in ascending order of urgency or importance, thus:

One-line whip = least vital.

Two-line whip = a division is expected. MPs must attend (unless firmly paired—see p. 74).

Three-line whip = attendance vital. Only seriously ill MPs will be excused.

(c) *Informing the Leader*. MPs of a particular party will be expected to follow the main policies of the party, in or out of office. The Cabinet or the Shadow Cabinet each gives a lead, but neither of these groups may expect automatic obedience from its MPs in the Parliamentary Party. The leaders require to know how the rank and file feel about a particular matter, and the Chief Whips must inform them of the views of MPs. The aim is to achieve agreeement and unity.

Nevertheless it is true that a Government and an Opposition may each act unwisely. Neither claims final wisdom. Where a substantial group within a party disagrees with its leaders a dangerous situation arises. A house divided against itself will fall; and so will a Government or Opposition Party.

Where an individual MP disagrees with his party he may say so. The Whip will try to alter his view by discussion, persuasion, or advice with a view to compromise or agreement. In the final resort an MP may on conscientious grounds refrain from voting or vote against his own party.

(d) *Discipline*. The basic principle of the party system is that each party accepts certain defined policies, and that MPs of the party act in concert to present a united front, voting 'Aye' or 'Nay' in accordance with the agreed policy. Nevertheless, each MP has, in the final resort, after pondering the issues at stake, a freedom to act as his conscience dictates even if this amounts to a vote against his own political party.

If no compromise can be reached with a dissentient MP the question arises as to how far and how long a party may carry a rebel within its ranks. If an MP consistently votes contrary to the direction of the Whip he will first be tactfully warned against continual opposition. If the MP persists the ultimate sanction is expulsion from the party and the withdrawal of the Whip and the benefits from adherence to a politically powerful party group. The MP then virtually becomes independent. How long that lasts depends on many factors. Sometimes an expelled member is readmitted later. Certain MPs have even after expulsion achieved great prominence and Cabinet rank.

(e) *Pairing*. If an MP has an engagement away from Parliament a system of 'pairing' is applied, i.e. the Whips of both Government and Opposition agree that e.g. Mr. *A*, MP (Con.) who is away, shall be paired with Mr. *B*, MP (Lab.) also away; or that Mr *C*, MP (Con.) is paired with Mr *D*, MP (Lab.) who are both members of a Parliamentary delegation or ill, etc. If each party thus loses an equal number of members the majority in a division of the House will not be affected. Pairing is a long-term, not a one-off arrangement.

(f) *Patronage Secretary*. The Government Chief Whip is known as the Patronage Secretary. As we have seen, the appointment is an important one (his official office is at 12 Downing Street, London) and the holder exercises considerable influence in the award of honours. Moreover, since the Government Chief Whip is the 'eyes and ears' of the Prime Minister he may recommend to the leader any MP with the necessary ability and character for advancement to Ministerial office.

Moreover, where a MP is competent in a particular subject and wishes to speak in debate as a backbencher the Government Whip will make arrangements for him to be given the opportunity—sometimes called

SECRET

On MONDAY, 15th November, 1982, the House will meet at 2.30 p.m.

Transport Bill: 2nd Reading and related Money Resolution.
(Money Resolution EXEMPTED BUSINESS for 45 minutes)

Important divisions will take place, and your attendance at 9.30 p.m. for 10.00 p.m. and until the Money Resolution is obtained is essential.

Motions on the Customs Duties (ECSC) (Quota and Other Reliefs) (Amendment) Order, and on the Customs Duties (ECSC) (Quota and Other Reliefs) (Amendment No. 2) Order.
(EXEMPTED BUSINESS for 1½ hours)

Motion on the Summer Time Order.

(EXEMPTED BUSINESS for 1½ hours)

Divisions may take place, and your continued attendance until the business is concluded is particularly requested unless you have registered a pair.

On TUESDAY, 16th November, the House will meet at 2.30 p.m.

Water Bill: 2nd Reading and related Money Resolution.
(Money Resolution EXEMPTED BUSINESS for 45 minutes)

Water Bill: Ways and Means Resolution.
Opposition Prayer relating to the Devon Trial Area Order.
(EXEMPTED BUSINESS until 11.30 p.m.)

Important divisions will take place, and your attendance at 9.30 p.m. for 10.00 p.m. and until the business is concluded is essential.

> *NOTE*: A Motion to suspend the ten o'clock rule for the Ways and Means Resolution will be moved at 10.00 p.m.

On WEDNESDAY, 17th November, the House will meet at 2.30 p.m.

British Shipbuilders Bill: 2nd Reading.

Important divisions will take place, and your attendance at 9.30 p.m. for 10.00 p.m. is essential.

Motion on the Supplementary Benefit (Housing Benefits) (Requirements) Consequential Amendment Regulations.
(EXEMPTED BUSINESS for 1½ hours)

Motion on the Employment Subsidies Scheme.
(EXEMPTED BUSINESS for 1½ hours)

Divisions may take place, and your continued attendance until the business is concluded is particularly requested unless you have registered a pair.

On THURSDAY, 18th November, the House will meet at 2.30 p.m.

Agricultural Marketing Bill: 2nd Reading.
Motion on the Wages Council (Northern Ireland) Order.
(EXEMPTED BUSINESS for 1½ hours)

Divisions may take place, and your attendance from 7.00 p.m. until the business is concluded is particularly requested unless you have registered a pair.

On FRIDAY, 19th November, the House will meet at 9.30 a.m.

Debate on the First Report from the Select Committee on Agriculture in Session 1980–81 on Animal Welfare in Poultry, Pig and Veal Calf Production (HC 406) and the relevant Government Observations, on a Motion for the Adjournment.

Your attendance is requested.

11.11.82
MICHAEL JOPLING

Fig. 9. Example of a 'Whip'

'catching the Speaker's eye' if circumstances of the business of the House permit.

Committees

Both Houses of Parliament have an organised system of committees. This is inevitable. Parliament does what any other institution does when faced with a formidable amount of work: it distributes its work to smaller bodies which report back to the main body—the House of Commons or the House of Lords.

Parliamentary Committees serve two distinct purposes:

  (i) To represent the whole House in the detailed scrutiny of legislation:

  (ii) To inquire into matters which may only be satisfactorily investigated by a small number of persons.

Another important feature which we may mention here is that committees are constituted to enable Parliament to consider matters in a less formal atmosphere than that which obtains during an ordinary sitting of the House.

The Committee system of the House of Commons is made up of:

(1) Committees of the Whole House.

(2) Standing Committees.

(3) Select Committees.

(4) Joint Committees (i.e. committees of (*a*) the Commons and (*b*) the Lords).

(5) Committees on Private Bills.

In addition to the above we should note the existence of Parliamentary Party Committees (referred to on pp. 48, 80), the Scottish Standing and Grand Committees, and the Welsh Grand Committee (see p. 77).

There are also about 100 (unofficial) all-party groups or committees of MPs and Peers. They are concerned with a wide variety of matters—human rights, smoking, the Channel tunnel, youth affairs, a wide range of industries etc. They fluctuate according to members' interests and topical issues. Basically they allow members to follow particular interests, but they may also inform and influence government policy.

(*1*) *Committees of the Whole House*

A Committee of the Whole House is the technical name given to the whole House presided over by the Chairman of Ways and Means (or a Deputy) instead of the Speaker. It constitutes itself in this form by resolution to enable the House as a whole to consider important Bills in detail, clause by clause, after their second reading.

The procedure generally in a Committee of the Whole House is the same as that when the House sits formally, except that the Committee operates under more flexible rules. Thus a member may speak more than once on the same motion. The mace is placed by the Serjeant-at-Arms under the Speaker's table, signifying the proceedings are of less formal character.

Committees of the Whole House are appointed for a specific purpose (e.g. the consideration of a particular Bill) and with limited powers. When the matter to be dealt with is completed and the deliberations ended a report is made to the House formally (the Speaker then resuming his chair and the mace being replaced). The report to the House is made by the Chairman of the Committee.

(2) Standing Committees

Public Bills which, after a second reading, are *not* committed to Committees of the Whole House, to Select Committees, to Joint Committees or to the Scottish and Welsh Grand Committees (see below) are sent to Standing Committees.

A Standing Committee considers and amends Public Bills. Standing Order 38 requires that all public Bills, except:

(a) Bills for imposing taxation and Consolidated Fund and Appropriation Bills, and

(b) Bills confirming Provisional Orders,

shall be committed to a Standing Committee unless the House otherwise directs. Bills of first class constitutional importance would be dealt with by a Committee of the Whole House, as would those which are required to be passed quickly into law.

Today the House of Commons appoints six Standing Committees designated Standing Committee *A*, *B*, *C* to *F*. Any number of Standing Committees may be appointed by the House, but it is rare for more than five such committees to sit simultaneously.

Constitution. An ordinary Standing Committee consists of a Chairman and not fewer than twenty nor more than fifty members nominated in respect of each Bill the committee is to consider. Members are appointed by the Committee of Selection, regard being had to the interest and experience of members and to the composition of the House, i.e. party strengths.

Scottish Standing Committee. This consists of thirty members nominated from Scottish constituencies with up to twenty other nominated members. In its plenary (i.e. full) form the committee is known as the Scottish Grand Committee and comprises *all* the members for the Scottish constituencies and not less than ten nor more than fifteen others. These committees consider Scottish estimates and other matters relating exclusively to Scotland as well as Scottish Bills. In December 1982, this Committee sat in Scotland—the first time it had met outside Parliament since 1707.

Welsh Grand Committee. Consists of thirty-six members for constituencies in Wales and Monmouthshire, with up to five other nominated members. This committee considers Welsh estimates, and matters relating exclusively to Wales in addition to Welsh Bills.

Procedure in Standing Committees. This is similar to that followed by a Committee of the Whole House. Since 1980 Special Standing Committees have been set up from time to time. These incorporate some of the features of Select Committees in that they can hold preliminary discussions on the legislation and have witnesses to present evidence (see p. 81).

(3) Select Committees

These are committees which are *not* (1) Committees of the Whole House or (2) Standing Committees. They are generally quite small with about twelve members and they are set up to take evidence on some particular matter and to report their opinion to the House. Select Committees may be grouped under three heads: (i) Committees supervising Government Administration; (ii) *Ad hoc* committees; (iii) Domestic committees.

(i) *Committees Supervising Government Administration.* Examples of these include the following:

(*a*) Public Accounts Committee (see p. 113).
(*b*) The Statutory Instruments' Joint Committee (see p. 289).
(*c*) The Committee for the Parliamentary Commissioner (see p. 305).

Since the 1950s, a number of other Select Committees were developed, each focusing on a separate area (such as Science and Technology, the Nationalised Industries or Immigration). In 1977 the Committee on Expenditure was established: it not only reviewed Government expenditure generally, but also investigated particular areas of Government activity (education, defence, employment, etc.) by means of its six functional subcommittees. However, following a report of the Committee on Procedure in 1978 these committees were rationalised and most of them were replaced by a battery of fourteen new Select Committees each one of which is geared to a particular Government Department (see pp. 80–83).

(ii) *Ad hoc Committees.* These are set up on a short-term basis to investigate a particular matter (i.e. *ad hoc*). An example in 1971 was the Committee on the Civil List (see p. 120). This Committee was appointed to investigate the expenses of the Royal Family. The Chairman was Lord Boyle and the Committee reported in December 1971, as a result of which the House approved the revised allowances shown on page 121.

Another example was the Select Committee set up in February 1969, to investigate certain claims made by Sir Gerald Nabarro, MP, that he had 'irrefutable evidence' of the Chancellor's intention to increase the price of Road Fund Licences for motor-cars in the impending Budget of 1969. The matter was investigated and the claims were rejected as unfounded.

After an *ad hoc* committee has investigated and reported upon the particular subject matter within its terms of reference it ceases to exist.

(iii) *Domestic Committees.* These are constituted to enable the House to manage and run its own affairs more efficiently. One finds in a college usually a Library Committee or Restaurant Committee and so on; such committees being 'domestic' to the particular institution. It is in this sense that we use the word domestic committee in relation to the House of Commons. Examples of these committees include:

(*a*) The Committee of Selection. (This names the members of the Standing Committees and other committees mentioned above.)
(*b*) The Committee of Privileges (see p. 71).
(*c*) The Select Committee on Procedure. (This makes recommendations in the rules and orders giving the procedure of the House to ensure more efficient administration.)

(*d*) The Select Committee on Debates and Reports. (Arranges publication of official matters for the members, the House and the public.)

(*e*) The Kitchen and Refreshment Rooms Committee. (Makes provision for and supervises running of kitchens, etc.)

(*f*) The Standing Orders Committee.

(*g*) The Select Committee on Members' Interests (Declaration) (p. 99).

Powers of Select Committees

The Commons' Select Committees have important powers. They may: (i) Order production of documents such as official reports made to Government Ministers. (ii) Summon witnesses to give evidence to the committee (e.g. civil servants of any department, expert witnesses such as scientists or technologists).

In the Lords these powers are not given automatically. Witnesses may be requested to attend there or to produce documents to its Select Committees. If need be an Order of the House of Lords may be made to ensure compliance.

Attendance of Public. Members of the public may be allowed to be present while evidence is being given before a committee. During the deliberating stages, e.g. when members discuss the truth or worth of the evidence, or the contents of their report and its recommendations the public may be excluded. MPs (not members of the committee) may be present during the deliberative stages, though they usually withdraw as a mark of courtesy. When a committee reports to the House the document is made public and is usually reported in the Press as part of the Parliamentary proceedings.

(4) Joint Committees

These are committees composed of (i) members of the House of Commons and (ii) members of the House of Lords, usually in equal numbers. Such committees may be appointed to deal with (*a*) a particular subject, (*b*) a particular Bill, or (*c*) Bills of a particular kind. A joint committee to consider a particular subject may be appointed at the instance of either House. A proposal that a particular Bill should be committed to a joint committee must come from the House in which the Bill originated. Members of a joint committee are chosen by each House in equal numbers. The Chairman is elected by the joint committee. Decisions are taken by vote in the normal way. A joint committee has only that authority which is given to it by both Houses. The time and place of meetings are fixed by agreement between the two Houses. An example is the SI Committee (see p. 289).

The report of a joint committee is presented to both Houses by the Chairman to the House of which he is a member, and by a member selected by the Committee for the purpose to the other House.

(5) Committees on Private Bills

Private Bills are those which are usually of a local character and are most commonly presented by a local authority, a Port Authority, or similar body requiring an extension of its powers (see p. 100). Private Bills may be opposed or unopposed. An *opposed* Bill is one which is opposed, e.g. by a group of persons, another local authority, or a private company whose rights may be adversely affected were the Bill to become law. Opponents thereupon present a petition to the House against the Bill. (Even where no such petition has been presented the Chairman of Ways and Means for the Commons and the Lord Chairman of Committees for the Lords may report that any particular Bill should be treated as opposed.)

The committee on an opposed Bill before the Lower House consists of four MPs (who are appointed by the Committee of Selection). The members must have no local or personal interest in the Bill since their function in relation to the Bill is quasi-judicial. In the case of an *unopposed* Bill the committee comprises the Chairman of Ways and Means, the Deputy Chairman and three other members chosen by the Chairman from a panel appointed by the Committee of Selection at the beginning of each session.

In the House of Lords committees on opposed Bills consist of five members; unopposed Bills are referred to the Lord Chairman of Committees.

Parliamentary Party Committees

In addition to the above committees, we must also note that both the Government and the Opposition have their own **Parliamentary Party Committees**. These backbench committees cover such areas as defence, transport, foreign affairs and trade, etc. Each Committee has its Chairman, Vice-Chairman and secretaries chosen from party MPs. The Shadow Cabinet stands at the apex of the Opposition committee structure. In the Labour Party the **Shadow Cabinet** is actually called the 'Parliamentary Committee': its members are elected by the PLP, though the leader may add others and is responsible for allocating shadow posts. In the Conservative Party, the leader chooses and appoints members of the Shadow Cabinet.

The Shadow Cabinet has a designated room in the precincts of Parliament where it meets regularly.

Committees: Recent Changes and Comment

One of the problems facing the House today is its weakness to control the Government. The growth of powerful party loyalties has meant that Parliament has virtually lost its capacity to defeat or even influence a Government. We say the Government must govern; but we also say the House should control the Government, or at least the Government should be responsible (i.e. answerable and responsive) to Parliament. How to restore Parliament's power, particularly to allow discussion of policy before decisions are taken and the stamp of party approval has been applied?

One suggestion was the creation of small, specialist Select Committees. Such committees were in fact set up in the 1960s, and were of two kinds: (i) 'subject' committees to consider a range of related subjects (such as Race Relations or Science and Technology) and (ii) 'Departmental' committees, to consider the work and activities of particular Government Departments (such as the Ministry of Overseas Development).

Policy and finance are closely interwoven, and thus the investigatory powers of Parliament were considerably increased by the creation in 1971 of the Public Expenditure Committee (and its sub-committees—see p. 108). However, it was increasingly felt that the assortment of Select Committees was too piecemeal and unsystematic in form, and consequently certain areas were being overlooked. Furthermore, the existing committee arrangements were held to be deficient on the grounds that membership was too shifting and unstable; support services were underprovided; and committee powers were inadequate (e.g. in 1976 the Prime Minister, Harold Wilson, refused to allow a Minister, Harold Lever, to appear before the committee investigating State aid to Chrysler). Thus, in general, it was felt that the committees' inquiries were not as effective or comprehensive as they might be.

Consequently, following the Report of the Committee on Procedure (1978), fourteen new **Departmental Select Committees** (plus a Liaison Committee) were established and began work in February 1980. They cover the subject areas of the main Government Departments—viz. Agriculture, Defence, Education, Employment, Environment, Foreign Affairs, Home Affairs, Industry and Trade, Social Services, Transport, Treasury and Civil Service, Scotland and Wales. They are charged with *examining the expenditure, administration and policy of their respective Departments and associated public bodies*, for which purpose some are empowered to appoint one sub-committee and possibly more than one. These Select Committees have similar but rather greater powers than their predecessors. They are able to summon and question Ministers (though by convention, not the Prime Minister), Civil Servants and other interested bodies and individuals, and they can send for 'papers and records'. Their servicing support and ability to engage advisers is also strengthened. In thus monitoring the work of Government Departments they can check how policies are developed and how they operate, and they can oversee the process of Government expenditure. The Report envisaged that ultimately these Departmentally-related committees may 'become the "eyes and ears" of the House in relation to government departments, drawing the attention of members to matters which require further political consideration and providing members with advice and informed comment which can nourish the work of the House in scrutinising and criticising the activities and proposals of the executive.' Through their hearings and published reports, they increase the accountability of Ministers to the House especially now that the new committees can examine the whole area over which a Departmental Minister has direct authority. They thus bring before Parliament and the public generally a body of fact and informed opinion on many important issues. Membership of these committees broadens an MP's experience and awareness; MPs are thus able to ask more pertinent questions on the floor of the House and suggest possible remedies which a Government ought to apply. They may even have a direct and immediate impact on policy (e.g. the abolition of the 'sus' law in 1981).

Members (about 11 on each committee) are drawn from backbenchers on both sides of the House, reflecting the balance of the parties there. For example, the present Treasury and Civil Service Committee has the following composition: 6 Conservatives, 4 Labour, 1 Liberal. (The chairman is a Conservative.) In the pursuit of their responsibilities, committee members put aside their party affiliations and aim to work as a united team. This bi-partisan approach is seen as an advantage, even perhaps as the key element in the success of these Select Committees. But some people are sceptical: they fear that the crucial sting will be taken out of the party conflict as committees produce anodyne compromise or watered down reports in their quest for unanimity. Furthermore, do the committees have enough expertise amongst their members to ask the right questions and develop a systematic strategy for questioning rather than a piecemeal, round-the-table approach?

There are other **dangers and problems**. Will the Party Whips manipulate the Committee membership? With so many Members engaged in committee work, will the floor of the House become emasculated and devalued? Will a two-tier system develop by the creation of a privileged band of MPs with access to more information than their colleagues? Is there a danger that in getting into close contact with the executive, members will be won over and develop too cosy a relationship with their 'adversaries'? Will so many Committee reports get read or used? Will the Government allow time for their debate? And will the debates be influential? For example, of the 275 Select Committee reports issued 1979–85, only four have been the principal subject of Debates.

Ultimately, decisions rest with the Cabinet and individual Ministers (see p. 128). These are the executive Ministers in the Departments who are supplied with up-to-date information in their bid to grapple with the nation's problems. In the last resort, the Government's policy will prevail by reason of its Parliamentary (party) majority upon which it can rely. But how far it will be chastened and influenced by Parliament's committees is uncertain especially where committees are themselves divided (as occurred in the reports of those Committees examining such contentious issues as the reinstatement of miners sacked during the pit strike of 1984–5, the sinking of the Argentine ship 'Belgrano' during the Falklands war and the role of the Special Branch police in Britain). Equally, the impact of the Committees is undermined to the extent that they are denied evidence or witnesses. The latter has occurred on a number of occasions e.g. in relation to the Defence, Public Accounts and Treasury Committees, but most notably in the 1985–86 investigations into the Westlands (helicopters) Affair. Here the Prime Minister refused to allow certain key civil servants to appear before the Defence Committee: the Head of the civil service, Sir Robert Armstrong, attended instead. (In its Report, July 1986, the Committee severely criticised the Secretary of State for Trade and Industry, Leon Brittan, and five senior civil servants for the parts they played in the affair. But the Government, in October 1986, flatly rejected the criticisms.) Meanwhile, in the same Parliamentary session, the Trade and Industry Committee had been refused documentary evidence by the Bank of England concerning its role in the crisis in the tin industry 1985–6. In such cases the Committee can only report the fact to the House; but it is doubtful whether parties will break ranks to take effective action in these circumstances to deal with a determined Government. Indeed, in November 1986, the Government publicly threatened to instruct civil servants appearing before Select Committees not to answer questions about their own or their colleagues' conduct. But in a subsequent report (*Accountability of Minister and Civil Servants*, February 1987) the Government declared that in future civil servants may answer questions before Select Committees concerning their **actions**: but where their **conduct** is concerned (especially involving any criticism or blame) then the Minister should be consulted.

A recent study of the Select Committee system has concluded that: 'It cannot be doubted that increased accountability of government has been the outcome of the Select Committees' (G. Drewry, *The New Select Committees*, CUP, 1985). But Frank Field, MP, declares that 'they do little to strengthen the position of the Commons over the Executive. Under a two party system, with each side getting regular turns in government, and with almost half of the winning side expecting government office ... the chances of the Commons being able to wrestle power back from the Executive are limited' (*Listener*, 5 September 1985). His hopes for any significant change lay in the re-emergence of a multi-party system.

The Commons at Work

Cabinet Ministers hold the keys of executive power at the head of the State, making decisions which affect the lives of millions. Parliament has an essential role to play: in considering legislation; voting State finance; questioning Ministers; and debating issues of public importance. All these matters are dealt with in detail later. In this section we consider the House of Commons at work generally.

The Year's Work

A Parliamentary session lasts for one year approximately, i.e. from November to November. Each session is usually broken up by adjournments to allow for vacations. When Parliament is not sitting it is said to be in recess.

During each session there are approximately 160 'sitting days'. This amounts to thirty-three weeks of the year during which MPs carry on their work at Westminster. At the beginning of the present century Parliament was in full session for some twenty-six weeks only. In 1939 the number of weeks increased to twenty-nine. Parliamentary work increases year by year, it becomes more complex and exacting and consequently more time is needed.

Parliament is summoned by the Queen in November and it is prorogued or dissolved by the Queen. The modern practice is that the same Royal proclamation dismisses a Parliament and summons a new one.

Each Parliamentary session is officially opened by the Queen. In the **speech** from the Throne the achievements of the Government during the past year (if it has been in office during the year) are briefly reviewed. Then follows the future intentions of the Government and its legislative programme. The speech is usually delivered by Her Majesty in person; otherwise it is read by the Lord Chancellor or by a Royal Commission. The speech is delivered in the House of Lords where the Commons are summoned to hear it.

Then follows what is described as the 'grand inquest of the nation', i.e. a general debate and discussion on the political situation, domestic and foreign, takes place. But, before an address is moved in answer to the Speech, a formal first reading of an obsolete Bill is performed in both Houses. In the Commons this is known as a 'Bill to prevent Clandestine

Outlawries'. This quaint formula or document acknowledges the rule of 'redress of grievances before supply'. In other words, before the Commons is prepared to vote the money necessary to carry on government the Crown must attend to the grievances of subjects. Once that formality is over a full-scale 'inquest' or inquiry into the state of affairs of the nation takes place when backbenchers on the Government side move the address in reply to the Speech.

The work of the House is roughly divided into three parts: legislative, control of finance, and the checking of the work of the Government by questioning of Ministers (administration). The time devoted to each of these subjects is as follows:

(i) Legislation	50 per cent
(ii) Finance	30 per cent
(iii) Administration	20 per cent

This is a broad analysis of the time. We shall deal with each of the headings in more detail later, in particular considering the steps in the enactment of legislation, the raising of finance by taxation, and the appor- tionment or distribution of the monies so raised to Departments of Government. The checking by the House of the administration of Govern- ment is the last of the three duties, and this involves questions raised in the House or a full-scale debate and, if need be, a vote of censure on the Government. The object of this is to ensure that the Government Ministers and their departments or agencies are working efficiently, are subject to the control of Parliament, and ultimately to the people of the country.

Question Time

At about 2.45 p.m. Question Time begins. For 45 minutes members may ask questions of Ministers who reply 'on the floor of the House'.

Question Time is a useful Parliamentary device to enable any member to:

(*a*) Obtain information.
(*b*) Publicise a grievance.
(*c*) Stimulate, challenge or embarrass a Minister.
(*d*) Show that the member asking the question is active in the House.

All MPs receive complaints and information from constituents. Some disclose injustices or maladministration and may be genuinely critical of Government. A member may, after verifying the facts, direct a question to the appropriate Minister and ask for an explanation in Parliament. A member may have certain information gained from his own resources which warrants a question in the House. He need not wait to be moved by a constituent.

Parliamentary questions are of four types:

1. 'Oral', requiring an oral answer in the House; known as 'starred' questions.
2. 'Non-oral' or 'written' requiring a written reply.
3. 'Private Notice'—in effect oral questions of an urgent nature which

by special permission from the Speaker receive a reply at the end of Question hour, even on the day when first raised.

4. 'Supplementary', which follow replies to 'oral' questions. The supplementary questions are presumed to arise impromptu in the mind of the questioner, though in fact they are often prepared for previously by the member.

Most proceedings in Parliament are governed by rules. Question Time has evolved its rules. Thus a question must be written on paper and handed to the Clerks of the House who may rephrase it in parliamentary language. A question must relate to the department of the Minister questioned, and a minimum of forty-eight hours' notice to a Minister is required. A questioner must verify his facts and figures, if any, which he quotes. Hearsay and rumour should be avoided. A question must be interrogative in form, not a statement or a speech. It must not be argumentative or merely rhetorical and must not refer to a debate in the current session or be critical of a decision of the House; nor must it contravene constitutional usage or etiquette.

As noted above, the supplementary question is the chief counter to an unsatisfactory, vague, or evasive reply. Although a Minister will be briefed by his Department, the supplementary question may be an accurately aimed blow which the Minister must parry as deftly as he can or reply to as best he can with the information available. Sometimes a supplementary question may result in a minor debate particularly if other members join in the fray. However, we must note that a Minister is not bound to reply to a question, and (rarely) he may refuse to do so on occasion, e.g. on security grounds.

Question Time is limited to three-quarters of an hour. Consequently time is short, and if long answers are required this necessarily means that fewer questions can be answered. Where questions on the list are not answered on a particular day they receive a written reply. There may be 50 or even 70 starred questions, but up to half may not be reached and answered.

If a member is not satisfied with an answer given by a Minister he may 'raise the matter on the adjournment'; that is, in the half-hour debates which take place at 10 p.m. each evening. This can only be done if the questioner secures a place by ballot to raise the matter.

During Question Time a member may move the immediate adjournment of the House under Standing Order No. 10 (a procedural rule of the House for emergency debates) to 'discuss a specific and important matter that should have urgent consideration'. This depends on whether the Speaker allows the motion. If he does the motion is moved and a speech is made involving the point of the question to which a reply is made by a Government Minister on behalf of the Government. If the matter is of sufficient importance the Prime Minister or Leader of the House may reply.

By the nature of things Opposition front- and back-benchers ask more questions than members on the Government side. No Government back-bench member would wish to embarrass his side if he can, by discreetly securing a written reply, obtain the required action or information (though some oral questions are 'planted' with its MPs by the government (see below)).

There is never a division during Question Time. Consequently there is no motion which is likely to bring down a Government. Nevertheless questions do ensure that a Government is kept on its toes; that faults are brought to light; inefficiencies exposed and malpractices prevented. The right of any subject to petition the Crown or a Government is beyond doubt; the right of a member to question the Government is another freedom which should be jealously guarded.

Answers. On receiving a question the Minister passes it to civil servants of the Department to obtain details and facts for a reply. The Minister is then 'briefed' with information to enable him to answer clearly and accurately the point raised. Civil servants also provide background information in case supplementary questions are asked. The Minister is politically responsible for his Department and the civil servants for their part try to ensure that their chief makes a good showing when on his feet facing a critical House.

Ministers appear in the House and answer questions on a rota system. Normally two Ministers appear each day and take all the questions relating to both Departments. The Prime Minister answers questions on two days a week, at 3.15 p.m. on Tuesdays and Thursdays.

Generally the questioners are Opposition front- and back-benchers and, to a lesser extent, Government back-benchers. It sometimes happens, however, that the Government may itself arrange for a question to be asked to enable a Prime Minister or other Minister to disclose certain information of importance which the House and the public ought to know.

All Oral Answers are reported in *Hansard* (the official Report of the House of Commons) and sometimes in *The Times* and other newspapers. A study of *Hansard* is necessary to reveal the kind of question to which Government Ministers are exposed (see p. 88).

The Debate on the Adjournment

In addition to Question Time (2.45–3.30 p.m.) a member may raise a matter on the motion 'that the House do adjourn' which is moved at the end of the day's business at 10 p.m. The last half-hour before the House rises at 10.30 p.m. will then be devoted to debating any important topic a member seeks to introduce.

The normal rule since 1945 is that the main business of the House is finished at 10 p.m. unless it is 'exempted business': see p. 64). Any debate which is then allowed takes place between that hour and 10.30 p.m.

Where an 'all-night' sitting occurs the ten o'clock rule is thereupon suspended, in which case no one may take advantage of a debate on a motion which he seeks to move.

Many members have matters which they seek to raise. Consequently a ballot is held or the Speaker makes a decision as to the member who will be allowed to move a motion.

The Ten-Minute Rule

This is another method of raising a subject in Parliament. A member may introduce a Bill under what is called the 'Ten-Minute Rule' which is the time allotted at certain specified times during a session to enable a member to introduce a Bill with a ten-minute speech. A ten-minute speech may be allowed in reply, and the House may vote or accept the Bill unopposed. Even if the Bill is not accepted the member has the satisfaction of bringing public attention to his cause as contained in the Bill.

Procedure

All institutions in which groups of people reach decisions and take action on those decisions have rules of procedure for the conduct of business. The rules of the House of Commons are contained in:

  (i) Acts of Parliament (e.g. *Parliament Acts, 1911* and *1949*).
  (ii) Standing Orders of the House.
  (iii) Precedents in the Journals of the House and in text books.

  (i) *Statutes.* We have already referred to the rules relating to Money Bills and the particular rules which apply to these as laid down in the *Parliament Acts, 1911 and 1949* (see p. 52). Another statute containing procedural rules is the *Parliamentary Papers Act, 1849*.

  (ii) *Standing Orders.* These number over a hundred and have been hammered out over the years to ensure efficient dispatch of the business of the House. Only three orders date back to before 1832. The orders lay down the time-table for each day (see p. 91), the manner in which motions may be moved, the form of debate, the rules for adjournment, the rules for the closure of a debate (see p. 90).

The Speaker or the Chairman of the House for the time being or of a Committee of the House enforces the rules. Thus a Speaker may 'name' a member who refuses to desist from interrupting the proceedings or for disobedience of the rules. 'Naming', i.e. calling the member by his name rather than the 'Honourable Member for . . .' entails automatic suspension from the House (see p. 67). This particular rule was first formed in 1641 by Mr Speaker Lenthall and has been followed since as the accepted procedure for suspension of a member.

The standard work on Parliamentary Procedure was written by **Thomas Erskine May** (a former clerk of the House of Commons) in 1844 and was entitled *A Treatise upon the Law, Privileges, Proceedings and Usages of Parliament*. This work which is shortly referred to as 'May' is still the standard authority and is periodically revised.

The justification of these procedural rules is that they:

  (*a*) Ensure fairness in the conduct of the proceedings.
  (*b*) Protect the rights of the Opposition and minorities.
  (*c*) Promote efficient and orderly dispatch of business.

Just as the common law has evolved over the years to form the basis of an efficient legal system so too have the Parliamentary Rules of Procedure emerged. They are flexible and allow for growth and modification to enable

House of Commons

Thursday 15 July 1982

The House met at half-past Two o'clock

PRAYERS

[MR. SPEAKER *in the Chair*]

PRIVATE BUSINESS

DERWENT VALLEY RAILWAY BILL *[Lords]*
Read a Second time and committed.

BRITISH RAILWAYS (LIVERPOOL STREET STATION) BILL
(By Order)
Order for Third Reading read.
To be read the Third time upon Tuesday 20 July.

Oral Answers to Questions

NATIONAL FINANCE

Inflation

1. **Mr. Greenway** asked the Chancellor of the Exchequer if he will give the average annual rate of inflation for 1979 to 1982 compared with 1974 to 1977.

The Chief Secretary to the Treasury (Mr. Leon Brittan): The average annual rate of inflation between May 1979 and May 1982 was 14·2 per cent. From February 1974 to February 1977 the averge annual rate of inflation was 19·6 per cent.

Mr. Greenway: Does my right hon. and learned Friend agree that those figures speak volumes for the value of a Conservative Government as against a Socialist Government? What effects will that have on Britain's future and its position in the world?

Mr. Brittan: The continued fall in inflation is the biggest single contribution that we can make towards sustained recovery. It will improve our competitiveness and the prospect of lower interest rates.

Mr. Eggar: I welcome my right hon. and learned Friend's reply, but will he confirm that if we are to sustain the fall not only in inflation but in interest rates, it is essential that the Government should do everything in their power to limit increases in public sector wages?

Mr. Brittan: I readily confirm that.

Mr. Flannery: In his last answer the Chief Secretary mentioned the continued fall in inflation, but he neglected to mention the catastrophic rise in unemployment. Will he tell us something about that?

Mr. Brittan: When I am asked I will——

Mr. Flannery: I am asking.

Mr. Brittan: There is no shortage of questions on unemployment on the Order Paper. This question is about inflation.

595

Recession (Economic Indications)

2. **Mr. Deakins** asked the Chancellor of the Exchequer what indicators now lead him to believe that the recession is ending.

The Chancellor of the Exchequer (Sir Geoffrey Howe): Industrial production in the three months to May was about 3 per cent. higher than in the spring of last year. The prospect is for further gradual recovery. This is supported, for example, by the central statistical office's index of leading cyclical indicators, and most recent independent forecasts.

Mr. Deakins: Are there any signs of increased job opportunities in British industry to combat the present disastrous levels of unemployment?

Sir Geoffrey Howe: There are two foundations upon which the prospects of improved employment are to be built. One is the continued success against inflation, and the second is the improvement in output that is likely to follow that. All our policies are directed to that end.

Mr. Richard Wainwright: Is the Chancellor aware that his own central statistical office states that the figures to May are incomplete until we have the June figures, partly because of this year's exceptional incidence of the spring bank holiday and, secondly, because of the frenzied industrial activity due to the Falklands crisis?

With regard to the ending of the recession, what is the Chancellor's reaction to the recent surge in imports due to the sabotage of the home industrial sector?

Sir Geoffrey Howe: I agree that the surge in imports is to be regretted. That is a consequence of the continued lack of competitiveness of Britain's economy, which has nevertheless made substantial improvements in recent months. It is also aggravated by continued examples of industrial unrest.

It is because the figures for one month are not representative that I founded my answer on industrial production in the three months to May, which was 3 per cent. higher than it was in the spring of last year.

Mr. Rippon: Does my right hon. and learned Friend believe that the record number of bankruptcies in the first six months of this year, mostly among small businesses and largely due to high interest rates, suggests that the recession is ending?

Sir Geoffrey Howe: I understand my right hon. and learned Friend's anxiety about the record level of bankruptcies, which is not confined to this country. He rightly draws attention to the importance of lower interest rates in improving prospects for small businesses as well as others. As a result of the Government's economic policies interest rates are now 4 per cent. lower than at the end of last year.

Mr. Straw: On 30 July 1981 the Chancellor of the Exchequer told an incredulous House that the recession was at an end. Is the right hon. and learned Gentleman aware that in the past 12 months—not three months—manufacturing production slumped still further and has only recently returned to the level of last July? With the right hon. and learned Gentleman's track record of predictions the House and the country would do far better to take notice of people such as the chairman of the Yorkshire and Humberside CBI, who last Saturday said that the economy was as dead as a dodo?

Fig. 10. A page from *Hansard*

the House to meet the demands of modern Parliamentary life. Yet at the same time they produce certainty, and represent 'the distilled common sense of centuries'.

Sir Reginald Palgrave ('The House of Commons') said:

> The House conducts both its business and its manners according to chance remarks, or casual rules, recorded in journals of about three centuries ago; which rules were, in their turn, founded upon custom and usage of immemorial antiquity.

Under this heading we may include 'Sessional Orders' which, as their name implies, are special orders applicable during the session for which they are laid down and are therefore temporary.

Ceremony still continues to play its part in national and Parliamentary life. The ceremonial procedures of the House—e.g. (1) the summons of Black Rod to attend the House of Lords to hear the Queen formally opening Parliament; (2) the Speaker's Procession to the Lords; (3) The Royal Assent to Bills which is given in Norman-French—all conduce to dignity and tradition. Those procedures (quaint though they may appear to other eyes) are a constant reminder of the history and the continuity in English Parliamentary democracy. A modern form of Royal Assent by Commission is now used (see p. 105).

(iii) *Precedents* in the Journals of the House are kept by the Clerks of the House of Commons and are the 'case law' of the operative rules of the present.

Motions

The business of the House of Commons is conducted by means of motions. A motion is merely a proposal which a member wishes to submit to the House. If the motion is agreed it may result in (1) an Order by which the House gives an instruction to some person or official; or (2) a Resolution by which the House expresses its corporate opinion.

Motions may be moved by the Government or the Opposition or a member. Most frequently in important debates the two major parties are involved. In some debates only one motion is moved, e.g. a motion of censure, and the battle ensues on the single proposal and is resolved by a division almost always in the Government's favour. Amendments are merely alterations to a motion. Amendments may be moved by an opponent.

The procedure of a debate follows well-defined rules as applied in debat-

GOVERNMENT PARTY   AYE   NO   OPPOSITION PARTY

Cabinet   Chief Government Whip   Party Members Government   Party Members Opposition   Opposition Whip   "Shadow" Cabinet

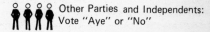

Other Parties and Independents: Vote "Aye" or "No"

Fig. 11. Division of the House

ing societies. The Government side puts its case through speakers selected for their particular position as Cabinet Minister, Departmental Minister, or by reason of special experience and interest. The motion will be opposed by the Opposition whose speakers will be selected practically on the same principles as the Government speakers.

Backbenchers in the House who wish to speak in the debate try to catch the Speaker's eye so that they too can contribute their knowledge, insight, and relevant comments for or against the motion. If the Government moves a motion and the Opposition has replied with its speakers the Government spokesman proposing the motion is entitled to wind up the debate by replying to the points made against the motion and recapitulating the reasons for the motion.

After a debate the House may divide i.e. vote; those members for the motion go into the Government lobby (the 'Ayes'); those against go into the Opposition lobby (the 'Noes'). The number of members voting is counted and the result is recorded in the journals of the House together with the names of voting members. To ensure accuracy 'tellers', i.e. pairs of members (one Government and one Opposition) are posted at each of the lobby doors and count members as they pass through.

The result of a debate on most issues and in all major matters is a foregone conclusion, if the Government has a majority and uses it to ensure that its will prevails. Parliamentary debates on important issues are reported in the Press, on the radio and television, and the electorate is kept well informed of the issues and the outcome. All the speeches are recorded in *Hansard*, the official report of the proceedings, and this is on sale to the general public.

Terminating Debates

In the eighteenth and nineteenth centuries any member who wished to speak on an issue could do so. Nowadays it is well known that a Government is committed to the passage of a number of Bills as outlined in the Queen's speech, and that Parliamentary time is limited.

In the nineteenth century the Irish Nationalists adopted 'filibustering' tactics, i.e. speaking for long periods with the object of preventing the enactment of legislation. In 1881 in a Parliamentary session of 154 days fourteen Irish members delivered 3,828 speeches, and asked numerous questions. Although within the rules of the House at that time, these tactics threatened to wreck the entire business of the House.

Accordingly, means have been evolved to prevent such obstruction by the Opposition. There are three devices to overcome delaying tactics. By these means Bills can be given speedy passage through the House. They are:

1. The Ordinary Closure.
2. The Kangaroo.
3. The Guillotine (or Closure by Compartment).

The Ordinary Closure. The origin of this is traceable to 1881 and to a resolution emanating from W. E. Gladstone (Prime Minister) and approved by the House. It has now been incorporated in Standing Orders (No. 29). At any stage in the debate any MP may move 'that the question be now put'. If the Speaker (or Chairman of the House if it is in Committee) permits, the motion is put to the House. If the motion that the debate shall end is carried, the debate is brought to an end. The mover of the motion in the full House must have the support of 100 members. The rule of the Ordinary Closure also applies to Standing Committees though in those assemblies only twenty members are needed to support the motion.

The Kangaroo. This form of closure applies to the Committee Stage and Report Stage of the consideration of Bills. The Speaker (on the Report Stage) and the Chairman (in the Committee of the Whole House or a Standing Committee) may select a certain number of clauses of a Bill which he considers important. Only those clauses are discussed, the remainder are not debated. This procedural rule evolved from 1919 and is now incorporated in Standing Order No. 31. This was repealed in 1986 and the Chair given the general power to select amendments.

The Guillotine. This form of closure is adopted if the House by resolution so ordains. It is usually invoked when a comprehensive or a long Bill is debated. Such a Bill may be divided into compartments, and any debate on the Bill or a part of the Bill may be 'cut off' ('guillotined') at a predetermined time. The 'guillotine' is used by all Governments in modern times e.g. for Acts covering Transport (1968), Industrial Relations (1971), Devolution (1978), Local Government Finance (1987) and Finance (frequently).

The objection to the closure devices named above are that they restrict consideration of a Bill and, therefore, prevent Parliament fulfilling its essential role. The Opposition naturally find the devices unpopular. Moreover, legislation hurried through Parliament may be defective in clarity and meaning and difficult to enforce. On the other hand a Government must in an emergency ensure that legislation is passed without delay (e.g. the *Emergency Powers Act, 1939*). Moreover a Government is pledged by its mandate to pass legislation and may claim that it is acting efficiently if it goes ahead and enacts speedily those Bills which it promised to introduce. The use of its political majority in the House is a constitutional means to that end.

Governments do not, or cannot, always close down debates. E.g. in December 1986, the House of Commons held its longest sitting this century with a debate on the Teachers' Remuneration Bill which lasted 23 hours, interrupted only by divisions (votes). However, the longest recorded debate was that of 1881 when the sitting lasted a continuous $41\frac{1}{2}$ hours.

The Daily Time-Table of the House of Commons

The time-table of the House of Commons is regulated by Standing Orders. The following is the usual order of events:

Time:	Business.
2.30 p.m.	House meets.
	Prayers.
	Mr Speaker in the Chair.
2.35 p.m.	**Preliminary Business.**
	Motions for new writs, e.g. to fill vacant seats in constituencies.
	Unopposed Private Business (Bills).
	Presentation of public petitions to House.

Time:	Business.
2.45 p.m.	**Questions to Ministers. Oral answers given by Ministers.**
3.30 p.m.	'Private Notice Questions' (i.e. Questions allowed to be asked on grounds of urgency).
	Requests to move the Adjournment of House under Standing Order 10 (i.e. to debate a specific and important matter which should have **urgent** consideration).
	Ceremonial speeches, statements by Ministers in personal explanation, or ex-Ministers giving reasons for resignation.
	Public Business.
	Presentation of Public Bills.
	Government Business Motions (e.g. on Public Expenditure).
	Public Business: 'Orders of the Day'.
	Motions for Leave to introduce Bills.
10.00 p.m.	**Public Business ends.**
	Minor business.
	Motion for the Adjournment of the House.
10.30 p.m.	**House Adjourns.**

Note: The above applies generally from Mondays to Thursdays. On Fridays the House meets at 9.30 a.m. and adjourns at 3 p.m. The Prime Minister answers questions at 3.15 p.m. on Tuesdays and Thursdays.

Criticism of Procedure

Since the beginning of the present century Government activities have increased greatly. The jurisdiction of the Government has extended into more areas of society, and at the same time most of them have become more technical. All Government Departments have advisory committees feeding Ministers with information and data. The total number of these committees alone is 900 (see p. 144).

Since 1964 several prominent politicians (Mr R. S. Crossman was one) have advocated a closer examination of the Commons' procedure in managing its work. The fact remains that the Commons has too much to do and too little time in which to do it. The following, however, are some of the recent suggestions and changes which have been made to ensure a better use of Parliamentary time:

(i) *Improved Voting Methods.* This was examined by the Select Committee on Procedure during 1966/7. Press-button voting (as occurs in the UN) was not accepted. The saving in time was held to be small. Moreover, the physical gathering in the lobbies may help to lower tensions.

(ii) *An Increase in the Number of Days Parliament Sits.* This was also rejected by the same committee. Ministers would be overworked, and MPs must have time for constituency duties and for rest. They need rest as do all other individuals.

(iii) *Morning Sittings.* These were introduced in 1967 when the House met on Mondays and Wednesdays to deal with unopposed Bills, Ministerial Statements and adjournment debates. It was soon abandoned, however, partly because MPs normally used the mornings for correspondence, attending committees, etc., and Ministers were busy at their Departments.

(iv) *Question Time.* The aim is to increase the number of questions asked. Only a certain number can possibly be asked. The MP who asks long questions may get long answers. The moral is for a brisker approach by both MPs and Ministers. A further recommendation, now implemented, is that questions should be answered more quickly. The maximum limit is now twenty-one days from notification of the Question.

(v) *Improving Public Bill Procedure.* Since 1967 the Second Reading stage of Public Bills of a non-controversial character has been dealt with by a Second Reading Committee, i.e. 'upstairs' (subject to the proviso that if twenty MPs object, the Bill will be dealt with in the normal way). During the 1979–80 session, there began the experiment of limiting some Second Reading speeches to ten minutes. In 1984 and 1986, this was extended, experimentally, to other, especially crowded, debates.

The Select Committee on Procedure recommended that there should be a carry-over of bills from one session to the next. (At present Bills not passed in one session must be reintroduced in the following and pass through all stages again.) This has not been implemented. Another recommendation was that more preliminary discussion take place before a Bill is introduced, through White Papers, Specialist Committees, etc. This would ensure that Bills would be better drafted to take account of the feeling and views of the House. This will occur to some extent under the new Select Committee system. But more significant is the experiment (since 1980) to allow Standing Committees to operate for up to three meetings on a Select Committee basis. The recommendation that the Report Stage of *minor* Bills should be taken in Committee was implemented in 1968, but the recommendation that the Third Reading stage should be taken without amendment or debate was not adopted.

(vi) *Improving Financial Procedure.* In order both to increase flexibility and to simplify financial procedure, the (Whole House) Committees of Supply and Ways and Means were abolished in 1967. It was also recommended that the Committee Stage of the Finance Bill (i.e. the Budget) should go to a Standing Committee. This happened in 1968. But since then the Finance Bill has been split, with the more technical elements going to the Finance (Standing) Committee and the more general aspects staying 'on the floor' in a Committee of the Whole House. In 1971, the Committee on Expenditure was created (to replace the Estimates Committee) but this lapsed in 1980 with the creation of the new Select Committees (see p. 80).

(vii) *Increasing Opportunities for Private Members.* Standing Order No. 10 (see p. 85) should be interpreted more liberally. This has been put into effect.

The suggestion was made that sittings on Fridays be lengthened. This has not been accepted. Members return to their constituencies usually at weekends and must have time to do so.

The Member of Parliament

There are 650 MPs in the Commons. This group is made up of men and women from all walks of life: laywers, doctors, ex-service personnel, teachers, lecturers, financiers, businessmen, farmers, trade union leaders, and so on (see p. 203). It is interesting to note that a majority of MPs are middle class and have had a university education. Roughly 1 in 6 MPs will be a journalist, teacher, or university lecturer. Men outnumber women by 20 to 7 though in 1987 the number of women MPs rose from 27 to 41 (i.e. 6 per cent). Four black MPs were elected in 1987. The party composition is outlined on p. vi.

Part-time or Full-time MPs

Should MPs be full-time or should they be part-time representatives, i.e. able to carry on other work outside Parliament? One view is that part-time occupation while an MP increases the MP's usefulness in the House. He is more 'in touch' with life, more keenly aware of the pressures and problems of industry, for example, if he is a Trade Unionist or a company director; more conscious of the problems of education if he is a teacher or lecturer, and so on. In effect he broadens his outlook by practical experience in life generally over which he exercises political control or leadership. Another possible merit is that it enables the MP to be more independent of political party constraint. The other view is that the work of an MP is itself so exacting and the responsibilities so heavy and complex that he cannot, by the very nature of political life today, discharge those essential duties unless he gives himself wholly to his work as MP.

The salary of an MP is £22,548 a year (in 1985), plus £21,000 for secretarial and research expenses. The salary is small by comparison with that received by professional men whether company directors, administrators, trade unionists, and so on. Some MPs may feel compelled and justified in earning extra money to maintain a standard of living compatible with a member's duties and position. Some write for the Press, take part in radio and television discussions. MPs may, as a concession, claim income tax relief for expenses actually incurred. The general view, however, is that British MPs are not well paid in comparison with those in other countries (though many gain from consultancy roles).

To avoid public disquiet when MPs vote increases in their salaries it was agreed in 1983 to start linking their pay with an appropriate Civil Service grade (Grade 6: Senior Principal), thus enabling automatic increase.

The MP's Duties

The duties of an MP are so varied that it is convenient to classify them:

(a) The MP and the Nation

The first duty of an MP is to do what, in his faithful and disinterested judgement, he believes is right and necessary for the honour and safety of the country. His second duty is towards his constitutents, of whom he is the representative and not the delegate. Only in the third place does his duty lie to the party organisation or programme. (W. S. Churchill in an address to his constituents 1955.)

Every one knows that, by our Constitution, after a gentleman is chosen, he is the representative, or, if you please, the attorney of the people of England, and as such is at full freedom to act as he thinks best for the people of England in general. He may receive, he may ask, he may even follow the advice of his particular constituents;

but he is not obliged, nor ought he, to follow their advice if he thinks it inconsistent with the general interest of his country. (A speech by Sir William Yonge, MP, in 1745.)

It follows, therefore, that the over-riding duty of an MP is to play his part in safeguarding the security and prosperity of the United Kingdom and its peoples. That security includes making the Constitution work, observing the rules of Parliament, and using his judgement in the best interests of the nation. If an MP is a Minister he will have much to do in an executive capacity; if he is a backbencher he should learn as much as possible of national and international affairs, the pros and cons of the cases and problems on which he must decide and vote. 'The prerequisites of the successful politician are: common instincts combined with uncommon ability.' (W. Bagehot) (Note: Four MPs—as well as three peers—have a 'dual mandate', having been elected to serve in the European Assembly i.e. MEPs: they might find their loyalty stretching beyond the UK.)

(b) The MP and his Constituency

Once elected to Parliament an MP becomes the representative of some 50,000 to 70,000 electors within his constituency. All persons, whether they voted for him or not, may look to him. It is his duty to serve them. Accordingly most MPs hold their 'clinics' or 'surgeries' (usually on Saturdays) where constituents may bring their complaints, problems, difficulties, or alleged injustices. Some may seem trivial, some are important. *A* may have received no Old Age Pension to which she is entitled; *B* may have been refused redundancy payment; *C* may be unable to find accommodation for her family, or is destitute; *D* may seek the member's support in a national wage claim about which the Minister has done nothing or has delayed setting up the necessary machinery for settlement; *E* may wish to become a naturalised British subject and does not know how to proceed.

The consultations may be dealt with by personal advice; by referring the constituent to a local authority official; by writing a letter to a Minister. If no other method is suitable and the matter is important enough an MP may raise a question in the House of Commons or the point may be made on the ten o'clock adjournment of the House. Ordinary people like to be able to meet their MP face to face, to get to know him, to feel that he is interested in them. An MP increases his standing if he gets things done for his constituency. In addition MPs receive an average of 33 letters per day, mainly concerned with housing, social security or education.

They must concern themselves with local industry. If an important local industry collapses or fails (e.g. steel-making, textiles) numbers of persons may be unemployed. The local MP must press for Government help, if necessary, draw attention to the circumstances, call for help for the unemployed, in finding new jobs, retraining, rehabilitation, etc.

An MP must attend local civic and social functions. A Royal visit may be planned, a new Mayor may be installed, a new school opened, a new factory is built, receptions, dinners, bazaars are held, and to most of these the Member of Parliament will be invited.

The constitutional position of an MP in relation to his constituency and the electorate was well expressed by Edmund Burke, the distinguished Irishman, in his address to the electors at Bristol in 1774:

Speeches : In Parliament
Party Conferences
Local Constituency, local debates
Radio, T.V.

Meetings : In Parliament
Party Meetings
Constituency
Special Interests

Consultation : In Parliament
Constituency "clinics"
Groups (Chambers of Commerce,
pressure groups etc.)

Correspondence : With Constituents
Pressure Groups
Government Departments
Ombudsman

Fig. 12. Responsibilities of an MP

Certainly, gentlemen, it ought to be the happiness and glory of a representative to live in the strictest union, the closest correspondence, and the most unreserved communication with his constituents. Their wishes ought to have great weight with him; their opinion high respect; their business unremitted attention. It is his duty to sacrifice his repose, his pleasures, his satisfactions, to theirs; and above all, ever, and in all cases, to prefer their interest to his own. But, his unbiased opinion, his mature judgment, his enlightened conscience, he ought not to sacrifice to you, to any man, or to any set of men living. . . . *Your representative owes you, not his industry only, but his judgment; and he betrays, instead of serving you, if he sacrifices it to your opinion.*

To deliver an opinion is the right of all men; that of his constituents is a weighty and respectable opinion, which a respresentative ought always to rejoice to hear and which he ought always seriously to consider. *But authoritative instructions, mandates issued, which the member is bound blindly and implicitly to obey, to vote and to argue for, though contrary to the clearest conviction of his judgment and conscience—these are things utterly unknown to the laws of this land, and which arise from a fundamental mistake of the whole order and tenor of our constitution. . . . You choose a member indeed; but when you have chosen him, he is not a member for Bristol, but he is a Member of Parliament.*

So, a Parliamentary constituency elects an MP to Parliament as a representative, **not a delegate** (i.e. one subject to instructions from his constituency). Actually, an MP must consider the views of his constituents as a matter of prudence. All agree that he is **not absolutely bound** by their instructions.

The tension between an MP and his constituents is always present. Thus when Nigel Nicholson, MP for Bournemouth East, did not support the Government in the Suez crisis of 1956 his decision incensed the local constituency party representatives. In the 1959 election he was not re-adopted by the local constituency party. In 1972 Dick Taverne, QC, MP, Labour member for Lincoln, disagreed with his party and local constituency leaders over Britain's entry to the EEC. In October 1974 he campaigned as a social democrat and was defeated by the Labour candidate.

Over the past ten years a number of Labour MPs have been in trouble with their constituency party caucuses (e.g. Bob Mellish, Roy Mason, Reg Freeson, Norman Atkinson, Robert Kilroy-Silk). Some resigned; others failed to get re-adopted i.e. were 'de-selected'. Should they 'toe the line' as *delegates* or risk political suicide as more independent minded *representatives*? Burke's view is constantly being questioned and challenged (especially in the Labour Party: see p. 47).

No one should minimise the difficulties surrounding the judgements which an MP has to make in his voting and decisions. There are occasions in all our lives when on a point of principle and rightness a stand must be made. This takes courage; men are not gifted with foresight. The judgement as to what best to do in the complexities of modern life is the common problem of all politicians.

(c) The MP and his Party

An MP is in Parliament because he is a member of a party. Today the Independent MP who owes allegiance to no party is rare indeed. Usually a prospective candidate chooses the party which reflects most closely his own political philosophy, Conservative, Labour, or Liberal. If adopted as a candidate at a political election the prospective MP will get the support of the party machine (see p. 43). He is thereupon expected to support the party view, its political manifesto, and, if successful at the election, he will take his place as a member of the House of Commons pledged to support the party in the Government or Opposition as the case may be. Accordingly he votes in the Divisions of the house in compliance with the instructions of the party whip (see p. 70).

Where a 'free' vote in the House is decided upon an MP may vote as his conscience dictates. Where an MP disagrees with his own party he may vote against it, but this course is attended with the risk of an admonition or warning from the Whips. No party can afford recalcitrant members in important issues when a division occurs, particularly where a Government has a small majority only. Party unity is vital, and it takes courage to ignore the Whips. An MP must also bear in mind the reaction his adverse vote may have on his local Constituency Party group (cf. Nigel Nicholson's experience, see p. 97). Usually, therefore, an MP must compromise, and seek other means to bring his views to notice, e.g. in the Parliamentary Party meetings, at Party Conferences and among other unofficial groups of MPs with similar views in Parliament.

MPs are not 'rubber stamps', automatons, members of a regiment, acting in accordance with instructions on all conceivable occasions. Democracy recognises the existence of minorities, and political parties do likewise. Each has groups, e.g. Left and Right wing of a party, and a centre group. All parties have meetings, conferences, or groups where policy can be thrashed out, and it is here than an MP may find opportunity to get his particular viewpoint accepted by the leaders. Additionally, an MP may be a member of the specialised party committees, e.g. on trade unions, foreign affairs, economic policy, where he may seek to air his views in an attempt to change the accepted party policy.

(d) The MP and his Interests

In addition to (i) the national interest (which has overriding claim on his vote), (ii) party interests, and (iii) constituency interests, an MP may have special personal interests. Thus he may be interested in reform of abortion laws, liquor licensing reform, the abolition of blood sports, crime prevention, protection against pollution, consumer protection, and so on. He may represent a particular section of workers, e.g. consultant or adviser to the Police Federation, a particular professional body or trade union, from which he receives a fee in return for any assistance he may give in the conduct of their affairs or in achieving particular objects. Thus he may make speeches in debates in the House, make representations to a Government Minister for the particular group whose special interests he protects or furthers. He may produce a Private Member's Bill and endeavour to get that through the House. He may, or may not, be successful but he will certainly draw public attention to the subject matter in which he is personally interested. Examples of Private Members' Bills which have become law are cited on page 100.

Where a Government is committed to a heavy legislative programme there is scant opportunity for the debate of sectional or minority interests or the enactment of Private Members' Bills which may be important to an individual MP but relatively unimportant nationally. Government is the art of the possible, and what is possible is conditional on the capacity of Parliament, time and finance, and other factors.

Declaration of MP's Interests. Where an MP speaks in the Commons he is expected, by convention, to declare any financial interest or pecuniary relationship he has in the matter under debate. The convention has been shown to be too narrow in scope particularly having regard to the growth in public relations and consultancy work undertaken by some MPs.

A compulsory Register of Members' Interests published by HMSO began in November 1975 and is available for public inspection. The convention is transformed to a Rule of the House. The registrable interests are:

1. Directorships.
2. Employment of office.
3. Trades or Professions.
4. Clients.
5. Financial sponsorships.
6. Overseas visits.
7. Payments, etc., from abroad.
8. Land and property.
9. Declarable shareholdings.

The Register follows the lines of the Select Committee's Report which was agreed to by the House on 12 June 1975. The Registrar is an officer of the House of Commons. On one hand the public have a right to know the 'interests' of an MP and on the other he has a right to privacy. It was a question difficult of satisfactory solution. Some felt it should be left to an MP's own judgement. For the social background of MPs see p. 203.

Legislation

We have already noted that the Legislature comprises the Queen, the House of Lords, and the House of Commons, and that one of the chief duties of Parliament is the enactment of legislation.

Legislation first finds expression in the form of a Bill, which is in effect draft legislation. A Bill is divided into clauses and sometimes sub-clauses. During the process of passing through Parliament a Bill undergoes scrutiny and debate, and changes, called amendments, are often made to a Bill. When a Bill passes into law it becomes a statute and the clauses become sections (sub-clauses become sub-sections). A specimen first page of a Bill appears on page 381. A copy of the first page of a statute appears on page 382. You will observe from the statute that underneath the official reference and the short description of the object of the statute there follows the *enacting clause* which normally reads thus:

Be it enacted by the Queen's Most Excellent Majesty, by and with the advice and consent of the Lords Spiritual and Temporal, and Commons in this present Parliament assembled, and by the authority of the same, as follows:

Kinds of Bills

There are four types of Parliamentary Bills, viz.:

  (i) Public Bills.
 (ii) Private Members' Bills.
(iii) Private Bills.
(iv) Hybrid Bills.

In addition to the above classification we have also noted that there are
(*a*) Money Bills (see p. 52), and (*b*) Non-Money Bills, not requiring the
expenditure of money.

(i) *Public Bills.* These alter the general law of the land and are normally
introduced by the Government. We recall that when a Government is
returned with a mandate to pass certain legislation the electorate will expect
the promise to be kept. Examples of Public Bills include the *National Health
Service Act, 1946*, the *Race Relations Act, 1965*, the *Sex Discrimination
Act, 1975*, the *Data Protection Act, 1984*.

(ii) *Private Member's Bill.* This type of Bill differs from a Public Bill
(above (i)) only in being introduced by a member of either House who is
not a member of the Government. A ballot is held for the opportunity to
introduce such Bills. The first twenty members are successful, and certain
Fridays in each session are allocated to enable members successful in the
ballot to introduce their Bills. It must be remembered, however, that
Government Bills (i.e. Public Bills) are most important and since Parliamentary time is limited there is little time left for Private Members' Bills.

Apart from the ballot method a private member may seek leave to introduce a Bill under the 'ten-minute' rule (see p. 87) which permits the proposer
enough time to make a brief speech outlining the case for his Bill. An
objector member is permitted a few minutes to oppose the Bill saying why
the Bill should not go forward. Following this the question is put to the
House that leave be given to bring in the Bill.

The increasing pressure on Parliamentary time precludes many Private
Members' Bills from being debated, and even some that are debated do
not reach the stage of Second Reading. A few Bills do become law, and we
may mention far-reaching measures such as the *Murder (Abolition of Death
Penalty) Act, 1965*, introduced by Mr S. Silverman, the *Abortion Law
Reform Act, 1967*, by David Steel, the *Video Recordings Act, 1983*, by
Graham Bright and the *Chronically Sick and Disabled Persons Act, 1970*,
by Alfred Morris the *Disabled Persons Act, 1986*, by Tom Clarke.

It may be considered that too little time is allowed for Private Members'
Bills, some of which are of greater importance than the time spent on them
might suggest, and they do provide the ordinary MP with the opportunity
to introduce legislation which is not necessarily of importance to the
Government of the day. Governments may however support Private
Members' Bills because they lack time in their own legislative programme.

(iii) *Private Bills.* Private Bills are (*a*) **Local**, and (*b*) **Personal**.

(*a*) **Local Bills** deal with (i) the construction or alteration of works, e.g.
bridges, canals, docks, ports, roads, railways, tramways and waterworks,
and (ii) others—e.g. extending the powers of local authorities, and of gas,
electricity and other public utility undertakings; altering the powers of

charters of public corporations, and dealing with Crown and Church property.

(*b*) **Personal Bills** are now rare and must be started in the House of Lords. They relate to estates, names, naturalisation, divorce, peerage, and other matters not classified as 'local'.

As to (*a*) Local Bills we should note that during the eighteenth and nineteenth centuries this was the only means by which local authorities were able to acquire legal powers to initiate new schemes. Parliament was forced to develop some procedure to protect private interests against the excessive powers which local authorities and other *ad hoc* bodies acquired.

Today a local authority (or other public body) may wish to acquire additional powers not available under the general law. To do this it may promote a private Bill. The procedure is complicated, lengthy, and expensive. The Standing Orders of both Houses must be complied with as well as certain Acts. Procedure requires that notice of the intention to present a Bill should be given to the public, and in some cases to individuals affected by the Bill. If opponents of the Bill wish to challenge it in Parliament they may do so before the Private Bill Committee. The proceedings here are judicial in character; the contest is between the promoters (represented by lawyers) and the opponents who may also be legally represented. Witnesses for and against the Bill may be examined or cross-examined as in a court of law. The committee then decides for or against the Bill on the evidence adduced. The main interest of the Committee is to resolve or reconcile the clash between the private and the public interest. The Committee has powers of alteration or amendment of a Bill, and finally the Bill is reported to the House.

(iv) *Hybrid Bills*. These partake of the characteristics of both (*a*) Public and (*b*) Private Bills, i.e. they alter the general law, but have particular effect upon certain bodies or individuals, e.g. the *Parliament Square Improvement Act, 1949*, the *British Museum Act, 1964*, the *Severn Bridge Tolls Act, 1965*. Hybrid Bills are referred to a Select Committee for examination, but at a later stage in the legislative process they proceed as Public Bills. An important point to note in these Bills is that persons affected by a Bill may lodge a petition against it, as in the case of a Private Bill. The Committee Stage is taken as for a Private Bill, i.e. a quasi-judicial procedure is followed with an opportunity to make petitions of objection by private persons affected.

The Origin of Bills

Legislation springs from many and varied sources: a declared policy of a political party which seeks power; a declared Government policy (i.e. once it is in power); a departmental policy; a Royal Commission; a committee appointed *ad hoc* by the Government (to consider one particular matter and to make recommendations); a research group, a public outcry.

Whatever the source of a Bill, there will certainly be discussions, negotiations, consultations (sometimes taking months), and meetings before the Bill is drafted. Groups and interests affected will be approached and their views ascertained. Thus legislation on health matters would involve medical organisations representing the medical profession, nursing societies, local authorities; law reform would be preceded by discussion with the Law Society, the General Council of the Bar; road traffic law would involve motoring organisations, AA, RAC, local authorities, police, highway surveyors, motor manufacturers, and so on. This time given to discussion with affected groups and interests is the period of gestation of the Bill.

Once a Minister adopts an idea, or policy, or scheme for a Bill he must obtain Cabinet approval that it is a suitable measure. The proposed Bill is drafted and perused by a committee of the Cabinet at which the draftsman and the Government Chief Whip are normally present.

Out of the 160 days in a parliamentary session only sixty are available for public legislation. It follows, therefore, that only a certain number of Bills can find room in the legislative programme. The most that Parliament can manage during one year is between sixty and seventy Public Bills. Some of these are large comprehensive measures (e.g. the *National Health Service Act, 1946*, the *Sex Discrimination Act, 1975*, the *Health and Safety at Work Act, 1974*); others merely amend, or consolidate previous Acts, or merely deal with small (though important) matters.

Drafting. This is a skilful and sometimes a long process if the proposed Bill is complicated. The task is undertaken by lawyers (known as Parliamentary Counsel) attached to the Parliamentary Counsel's Office at the Treasury. Amendments and redrafts are made and, when completed, the draft Bill is considered by the Cabinet who scrutinise it to ensure it accords with intentions and purpose. A memorandum is attached to the draft Bill to explain its objects.

Stages in Legislation for Public Bills

A Bill passes through the following stages to enable Parliament to consider and reconsider its provisions as thoroughly as possible.

   (i) First Reading.
  (ii) Second Reading.
 (iii) Committee Stage.
 (iv) Report Stage.
  (v) Third Reading.
 (vi) Amendments in the Upper House.

(i) *First Reading.* This is a formality. The Clerk of the House reads out the short title of the Bill and the Minister names a day for Second Reading. This is formal acknowledgement that the Government intends to bring in a Bill. The Bill is then printed and published. The Opposition may then study it with a view to criticism and amendment if need be.

(ii) *Second Reading.* This is the effective stage at which there is the first opportunity for debate on the Bill and its principles. The Minister or member in charge of the Bill explains its purpose and the main issues of policy involved, and he moves that the Bill be read a second time. The debate is limited to the purpose of the Bill and the means proposed for giving effect to it. Detailed discussion, which includes criticisms which could be met by amendment, is reserved for the Committee Stage or Report Stage.

If the Opposition decide to vote against the Bill an amendment is moved by one of their number to prevent the Bill being read a second time. If the amendment is defeated the Speaker declares the Bill to be read a second time.

In the Commons a **non-controversial Bill** may be referred to a **'Second Reading Committee'** to recommend whether or not it should be taken as read a second time. This procedure saves the time of the House as a whole.

(iii) *Committee Stage*. The next stage in the legislative process is the reference of the Bill to a Committee, normally to a Standing Committee but sometimes to a Committee of the whole House or even a Select Committee (see p. 77). Each clause in the Bill is considered and voted on. The Committee Stage may take several days if the Bill is lengthy or controversial.

Fig. 13. The House of Commons in session

We consider the part played by committees generally in the House on page 76. All we need to remark here is that the House of Commons has six Standing Committees, *A* to *F*. The committees are made up of between twenty-five and forty-five members and the members are appointed by another committee called the Committee of Selection (an all-party committee run by the Whips). The Standing Committees are not permanent committees (or 'standing' for a considerable time) but are constituted afresh for each Bill as it arises. The membership of the Standing Committee is in **proportion to the respective political parties** and where a member has special interest or experience in the subject of a Bill he will usually be appointed to a committee. Thus let us suppose that a House of Commons is made up of:

Conservative	400
Labour	200
Alliance	50
Total members	650

A Standing Committee might be made up thus:

Conservative	18
Labour	9
Liberal	2
	29

The Government (Conservative) would have a majority in the Committee and would thereby ensure its will prevails.

The purpose of the Committee Stage is to consider the **details** of a Bill, clause by clause and word by word. The Chairmen of the Standing Committees are appointed from a panel of twelve members. Debates in Committee are freer, a member may speak on a point more than once, but business is conducted expeditiously and, if need be, the debate may be closed by resolution. The Standing Committees meet in the morning usually twice a week.

(iv) *Report Stage.* Having passed the Committee Stage the Bill is formally reported to the House by the Chairman of the Committee. The House then considers the Bill as amended, and it may then make any additional amendments needed. The Report Stage is similar, in practice, to the Committee Stage, except that, in the House of Commons, the amendments are discussed rather than the clauses of the Bill.

(v) *Third Reading.* This is a purely formal stage, where the Bill is reviewed in its final form after the amendments have been made at earlier stages. There is normally no debate, though verbal amendments may be made.

(vi) *Amendments in the Upper House.* A Bill may originate in either House. Normally legislation starts in the Commons and is then sent to the Lords. A Bill which deals with taxation or expenditure (i.e. a Money Bill) **must** be introduced in the Commons.

Legislation of an intricate, but not of controversial character, may be introduced in the House of Lords where it may be fully discussed before being sent to the Commons, e.g. the *Crown Proceedings Act, 1947* (see p. 171) and the *Courts Act, 1971* were dealt with in this way. The Lower House may then deal with the Bill more quickly.

After a Bill has passed the third reading in the House of Commons it is ready for sending to the House of Lords where it passes through a similar series of stages (though the Committee stage in the Lords is usually a Committee of the Whole House). If the Bill originated in the House of Lords it goes to the Commons after its third reading. If there is no disagreement between the two Houses the Bill is submitted for the Royal Assent (see below). If, however, the second House amends the Bill it must be returned to the House where it originated for consideration of the amendments. If the first House rejects the amendments made by the second House, a committee is set up to show the reasons for the disagreement. A message embodying the reasons is sent to the second House. The amendments disputed may then be dropped, or alternative ones adopted. This process continues until agreement is reached. If agreement proves impossible, the Commons may make use of their powers under the *Parliament Acts, 1911* and *1949* (see p. 51) to present the Bill for Royal Assent after one year without the concurrence of the Lords.

The Royal Assent

The Royal Assent is given (*a*) by the Sovereign in Letters Patent and is declared to both Houses by their Speakers, or (*b*) periodically by Royal Commission. The Royal Commission is composed of three Lords Commissioners who sit before the throne in the House of Lords. The Speaker and Commons are summoned by Black Rod to the bar of the House of Lords, the title of the Act is read out and the Royal Assent is signified by the Clerk of Parliaments in Norman–French thus:

1. Public Bills (except Money Bills)   'La reyne le veult.'
2. Money Bills   'La reyne remercie ses bons sujets, accepte leur bénévolence, et ainsi le veult.'

Formerly a Monarch could veto a Bill, but this power has not been exercised since Queen Anne (1702–14) and has fallen into disuse. By convention the Royal Assent is never withheld.

If a Bill is urgent it will be presented for Royal Assent forthwith after passage through the Commons and the Lords. Otherwise Bills are presented in batches before a long adjournment or at the end of a session.

The stages through which a Bill is passed occupy a long process. Nevertheless, in an emergency such as an outbreak of war, emergency legislation may be passed through all stages in a few hours, as occurred with the *Defence of the Realm Act, 1914* and the *Emergency Powers Act, 1939*.

Broadcasting Parliament

The broadcasting of Parliamentary proceedings has been debated since 1960. On 24 February, 1975, the Commons decided to permit a four-week experimental *radio* broadcast of their proceedings. (This occurred in June 1975.) The House rejected (275 to 263) a three-week experimental televising of their proceedings. Both were free votes. Since then the proceedings of Parliament (including committees) have been sound recorded and selections broadcast. In addition, after a period of the live radio transmission of Question Time, there are occasional live broadcasts of special Parliamentary events—such as the Budget speech or emergency debates (e.g. the Falklands crisis (April 1982), disarmament (December 1982) Westland helicopters (1985), State Security and the BBC (1987)).

The main reason for broadcasting proceedings was that the British people were missing history every day because the workings of Parliament were relatively shrouded and kept from the public view. Today democratic parliaments need broadcasting just as much as broadcasting needs Parliament. This would lead to more open government.

The reasons advanced against the experiment were that the presence of television cameras might change the nature of parliamentary proceedings; that in editing recordings for transmission the broadcasters might attach too much importance to the frivolous and eccentric; and editors would select portions of speeches which were dramatic, entertaining and sensational. A fair and balanced summary posed difficult problems.

However, in 1985–6 and again in 1986–7 the House of Lords agreed to some live and regular recorded television broadcasting of its proceedings without apparent deleterious consequences and often with impressively high viewing figures.

Finance

All Governments need money to carry on their essential functions. The very existence of Parliament is due primarily to the need of the early Norman and later Monarchs to obtain money from their subjects. Kings taxed the people to pay for wars or to provide for the King's courts and their amenities.

Today money is needed to carry on the essential functions of Governments, e.g. maintenance of order, and defence against external enemies. These are in themselves costly but, in addition, all modern Governments expand their control over the economy to maintain a high level of employment, to raise the standard of living of all inhabitants, year by year. A Government may seek to organise a prices and incomes policy; it must assist local authorities to provide essential services such as housing and education, for which they are responsible in partnership with the central Government; and, above all, these economic activities must be fitted within the international scene by trying to ensure the country's balance of payments stands at a proper level.

In 1900 taxation took ten per cent of the nation's income. Today taxation takes over forty per cent of the nation's income, which indicates the growing cost of all the activities of Government in controlling the affairs of the nation as a whole.

The Main Principles of Parliament's Control

We have already mentioned the long struggle between the Crown and Parliament from the Middle ages to the seventeenth century when Parliament gradually established the principle that taxation could not be imposed by the Crown (by prerogative) at its will. Parliament grudgingly voted or granted the money, but always insisted that its grievances be met or answered before any grant was made. To justify its demands to Parliament for money the Crown had to specify in detail the reasons for the expenditure it proposed to make. We see therefore that today we have the principle that the estimates of expenditure of the Crown (i.e. the Government departments) must be presented to Parliament before Parliament will vote the income (in the form of taxation) to meet the proposed expenditure.

By the seventeenth century after the *Bill of Rights, 1689*, Parliament firmly established the principle that taxation could not in future be imposed by the Crown or Monarch but must be approved by Parliament. Moreover, a Minister is no longer responsible to the Monarch, as was formerly the case, but he is responsible to Parliament as the supreme authority in the State. We have already mentioned that the House of Commons achieved supremacy in Parliament, so that the next principle to note is that only a Minister (as a member of the House of Commons) could propose the spending of money by the Government.

The House of Commons is today the chamber which controls national finance both as to (*a*) raising money, and (*b*) spending it. The House of Lords has practically no powers now in this regard (see p. 50), in that the House of Lords is powerless to reduce or veto a Money Bill.

During the course of time Parliament has evolved three important financial or accounting principles to control the expenditure of monies by the Crown:

(i) Any sum granted is a **maximum** and may not be exceeded.

(ii) Money authorised to be spent for **one purpose** may not be spent on another purpose.

(iii) Money granted for any purpose may be used only during the **financial year** for which it is voted. Surpluses may not be carried forward but must be paid over to the Exchequer (i.e. the Treasury).

It should also be noted that the nation's *financial* year begins on 1 April and ends on 31 March of the following year. A Parliamentary session runs from November to November and thus straddles two financial years. The *tax* year runs from 6 April each year to 5 April of the following year. These two dates determine the schedule of time to which Government Departments and Parliament work.

Expenditure: the Procedure

Broad indications and plans for public (State) expenditure are outlined each November in the Chancellor of the Exchequer's 'Autumn Statement' to Parliament. More details and 3-year forward plans are provided in the Public Expenditure White Paper, published early each year: these provide the basics for supply estimates for the coming year.

There are, broadly, two kinds of State expenditure: (i) Consolidated Fund Services, which run continuously and only need Parliamentary approval when they need to be altered, e.g. to take account of inflation (see p. 112); (ii) Supply Services, which need the annual approval of Parliament before spending can take place. In this section we are concerned with **Supply Services**.

Every year, during October and November, the Government Departments prepare their **estimates** of expenditure. These estimates show what individual Departments require during the following financial year. The estimates are sent to the Treasury where they are checked during December. By about January all the Departmental estimates will be ready for discussion by the Cabinet. The estimates are then published in February. During February and March the House of Commons begins to consider the published estimates before it grants supplies of money to the Government. In the estimates, the Chancellor of the Exchequer will have information on which he will be able to base his Budget (to raise finance) which he will present to the House early in April. This is one of the important events in the Parliamentary session, and is equally important to the public.

The place of the Treasury (the finance Department) in the scheme of financial control is crucial. Firstly, it co-ordinates the estimates after scrutinising them to prevent waste or excess by consulting each Department's top civil servant (the Permanent Secretary) or his Accounting Officer. With inflation and the advance of modern technology, costing presents very great difficulty. After collating the estimates the next duty of the Treasury and the Chancellor is to consider means by which the sums required will be met, i.e. by taxation, the main source, or borrowing money.

How the Chancellor will meet the requirements will depend on a number of factors. In particular he will pay regard to whether the nation is in an inflationary situation or its opposite, deflationary. There is inflation when prices and incomes are rising. In that case the Chancellor must budget for more income to cover this situation. He may increase taxation to meet the proportionate increase in the expenditure of the Government Departments. If he increases taxation he will thus take from the public their spending power, for the public will have less money to spend.

The Chancellor possesses the facts and figures from the Central Statistical Office, from the Departments of Trade and Industry and from his own Ministry. The Chancellor analyses the nation's position and forms his policy. He discusses with the Prime Minister his recommendations for raising the extra money required. The Chancellor may recommend: (i) raising the income tax; (ii) corporation tax; (iii) road fund (car) tax; (iv) VAT, and so on. Most of us will be familiar with the problem and dilemma. If he taxes necessities the Government will be unpopular; if he taxes cigarettes, tobacco, wines, spirits, and luxuries he will also be unpopular. No tax is popular with the payer. Someone will be disappointed, inevitably. The Prime Minister may suggest amendments to the Chancellor's proposals.

Supply Debates

Once the estimates for the ensuing financial year have been finally agreed between the Chancellor and the Cabinet they are published at about the beginning of February. This leaves six weeks before the Chancellor presents his Budget proposals to the House of Commons.

The estimates—known as 'Votes'—are presented in tabulated form to the Commons under three main heads: (i) the Defence Departments; (ii) the Revenue Departments; and (iii) the Civil Estimates. The whole of the estimates covers 450 pages. Hence it is highly technical.

The House of Commons comprises 650 members. This is much too large a body to examine in detail the provisions of the estimates. Moreover, only a few days are allowed for their consideration between the publication of the estimates and some time in August by which the Appropriation Bill must be passed. The House also lacks the necessary expert and technical knowledge to criticise properly the estimates. Accordingly the House sets up a committee to do its work. This task was formerly allotted to the Estimates Committee comprising MPs drawn from all parties. But in 1969 the **Select Committee on Procedure** recommended that the **Estimates Committee** should become a **Select Committee on Expenditure**. This operated from 1971 to 1979.

Broadly, this Committee was charged with the duty of examining closely all areas of Government expenditure to consider whether the sums asked for were indeed necessary. Do we, for example, need nuclear submarines? If so, are they built to the best specification, and are they built economically without waste? What equipment is needed today by the Army and Air

Force and Navy for their tasks? Is that equipment the best available and is it costing too much? How many people must be employed? Crime is increasing, more prisons are required as well as better security. What type of prison is the best, how many do we need, and are they built economically? How many prison officers are required? The financial implications of all such questions are considered and immediately policy is involved. The task, therefore, of considering estimates is highly important. Such questions will now fall to the **Departmental Select Committees** (see p. 81).

Up to 1981, 29 days were devoted to general discussions on matters of policy, the topics being chosen by the Opposition. These were known as 'Supply Days'. But as 'supply' or finance was (by convention) barely touched, they were more realistically re-named 'Opposition Days'. Of the 20 days provided each year, 17 go to the Opposition and three are used by the second largest opposition party. (For example in 1986 Labour used one of its days to debate 'insider dealing' in the City, while the Alliance used one for a debate on the State Security Services.) In addition there are now three more days, known as 'Estimates Days' when, on the recommendation of the Liaison Committee (see p. 75), certain estimates are debated. By about July, all the remaining items are voted through the House without discussion and are approved by the annual Appropriation Act.

The Interim Period

If the Appropriation Act (which finally approves Supply Services) is not passed until early August how are the Government Departments financed between 1 April (the beginning of the financial year) and August? We must remember that no expenditure (Supply Services) may be made without the approval of the Commons. The answer is that the House passes a Vote on Account with a *Consolidated Fund Bill* immediately after the Budget. This will enable the Government Departments and the Defence Forces to draw enough money on account until the Appropriation Act is passed in August.

We have mentioned that the estimates are very detailed. The need for this is justified by the fact that money authorised for one purpose may only be spent on that specific purpose. Moreover, strict control is maintained by the Comptroller and Auditor-General. And he may only do this if he knows specifically for what purpose money is being used. **Virement** is a technical term and in practice means merely that it is permissible to transfer a sum of money voted for one branch of the Armed Forces to another. Virement has been extended to a limited extent in Departments other than the Defence Services. In all cases, however, Treasury approval must first be obtained.

Income: the Budget

In all matters of finance the lead must be taken by the Government. The Government proposes how it intends to spend money and the Government proposes how it will raise money. A Government may, of course, borrow money, e.g. for capital expenditure and for loans to local authorities or to the nationalised industries. But the main source of supply is taxation.

Fig. 14. Taxing and spending

The Chancellor of the Exchequer prepares his Budget, the details of which are disclosed only to the Cabinet a few days before presentation to the House of Commons. Strict secrecy is maintained as to the details right up to the moment the Chancellor makes his speech to the House of Commons (usually in early April). Any leakage may cause the resignation of the Chancellor himself, as was the case with Dr Hugh Dalton who made a chance remark on his way into the Commons itself to a lobby correspondent in 1947.

The manner of presentation is usually a report on the financial year just ended. He then compares the result with the forecast. There follows a review of the general economic situation anticipated during the year just beginning. The Chancellor then sets out his proposals for alterations in taxation. See, however, p. 118.

Until 1967 all work in the Commons relating to new or altered taxation was dealt with by a committee of the whole House (called the Committee of Ways and Means). A new procedure was adopted in 1968; the Budget speech and Budget debate now take place in the House of Commons as such. The House considers the Budget statement over a number of days and must vote upon proposals for new or altered taxation, including income tax, which has to be approved each year. (Customs and excise taxes, estate duty, etc., continue automatically from year to year unless altered by Parliament.) At the Committee stage many of the detailed and more technical aspects of the Budget are considered in the Finance (Standing) Committee.

The House of Commons, after debate, finally approves the Chancellor's proposals and, subject to any minor amendments, the results are enacted in the Finance Act which then becomes law.

Some time elapses between the announcement of the Budget proposals and the enactment of the Finance Act. To enable the Board of Inland Revenue to collect taxes between 6 April and the date of the passing into law of the Finance Act, we should note there is the *Provisional Collection of Taxes Act, 1913*. This Act authorises the Board of Inland Revenue to collect the proposed new taxes from the date of their announcement in the Budget to the date of passing of the Finance Act.

The Consolidated Fund

Instead of having separate funding arrangements for each Department, there is a Consolidated Fund for all Departments. Thus all Government receipts (e.g. taxes and certain other revenues) are paid into this account at the Bank of England. Payments on behalf of the Government are made out of the Consolidated Fund.

Certain Officers of State are paid directly out of the Consolidated Fund, e.g. High Court Judges, the Speaker, the Leader of the Opposition, the Comptroller and Auditor General and the Ombudsman. The Fund also pays the Queen's 'Civil List' (see p. 120). Certain regularly recurring payments such as interest on the National Debt are also made out of the Fund. All these form part of the Consolidated Fund Services (see p. 107).

The purpose of making such payments is to protect the political independence of the recipients i.e. their payment runs continuously from year to year, without the need for Parliamentary debate and approval. However, the effects of inflation in recent years is such that these payments are coming before Parliament with greater regularity e.g. the Civil List is now revised virtually each year instead of merely once in a monarch's reign.

Expenditure Committees

We have noted that the House of Commons is much too large to examine estimates in detail. Since 1912 it has appointed annually an **Estimates Committee** (except during the War years). In 1960 this was made a Select Committee set up each session under Standing Orders. The Committee's functions were to examine the estimates, to report how, if at all, the policy implied in the estimates could be carried out more economically, and to consider the principal variations between the estimates of the current year and those of the previous year and the form in which the estimates should be presented. Usually, the committee selected each year a few Votes to review.

A new and larger committee, the Select Committee on **Public Expenditure**, was appointed in 1971 to replace the Estimates Committee. It had similar functions (see above) but was given the additional power to consider not just the annual estimates but any papers on public expenditure presented to the House—in particular the five-year forward projections, as set out in the annual White Paper. Its terms of reference also allowed it to examine the methods by which the Government planned and controlled State expenditure (e.g. the basis upon which the Government draws up its expenditure projections). Otherwise it had the usual powers of a Select Committee, namely: to send for persons and papers, to sit during any adjournment of the House, to appoint people with technical knowledge to help it with its work and to form sub-committees. It immediately took advantage of this last power and divided into six functional sub-committees covering the following general areas of administration: (i) Public Expenditure (General); (ii) Trade and Industry; (iii) Employment and Social Services; (iv) Defence and External Affairs; (v) Education and Arts; (vi) Environment and Home Office.

The Public Expenditure (General) Sub-committee concerned itself mainly with studying the central area of Government financial control at the Treasury and the Cabinet levels and within the Civil Service Department.

The general purpose of the Committee was to give much more detailed consideration to the estimates than can the entire House of Commons. This responsibility (since 1980) now rests with the **Departmental Select Committees** (see p. 81) who are enjoined, in addition to their more general functions, to pay special attention to the expenditure of the relevant Government Departments. The Select Committee on the Treasury and the Civil Service has broadly assumed the role of the former Public Expenditure (General) Sub-committee.

Additional Parliamentary time was set aside for the consideration of the reports of the Public Expenditure Committee. This should continue and perhaps even increase under the new committee system. In practice, however, the estimates for the *current* year are unlikely to be affected; but the committees may influence *future* plans (see p. 115) and will seek to ensure that the money voted by the House is properly used. In this respect their work is facilitated by the existence of:

(i) the Comptroller and Auditor-General, and
(ii) the Public Accounts Committee.

The Comptroller and Auditor-General (C&AG)

This post was created first by Gladstone in 1866. The C&AG is neither an MP nor a civil servant; he is an Officer of Parliament. His salary is charged on the Consolidated Fund which gives him a certain independence of Parliament. With a staff of 830, his functions are:

1. As Comptroller he controls receipts and issues of public money to and from the Consolidated Fund and the National Loans Fund. (The latter is concerned solely with the Government's loans and borrowings.)
2. As Auditor-General he audits departmental accounts and submits his report (or 'certificate') on the Appropriation Accounts and other accounts (some 500 in all), as required by statute, to Parliament.

His statutory function is to ensure that all expenditure is properly incurred (e.g. that no payments are made which go beyond any relevant statutory authority) and that Treasury sanction has been obtained whenever necessary. In addition, however, he has been encouraged by successive Public Accounts Committees (see below) to examine Departmental expenditure with a view to drawing attention to any case of apparent waste or extravagance. And more recently (since the *National Audit Act, 1983*, which converted his former department into the National Audit Office, his work has extended to 'value-for-money' inquiries i.e. providing information, advice and assurance to Parliament about 'economy, efficiency and effectiveness' in the use of resources by Government departments and related bodies, though not local authorities or nationalised industries. In fact, because the remit of the C&AG only covers some 40 per cent of State expenditure, there are moves to extend his authority and scrutinise State industries and other public bodies.

The Public Accounts Committee (PAC)

This is a Select Committee of the House of Commons. It was first set up under Mr Gladstone in 1861 to ensure that expenditure was properly incurred in accordance with the purpose for which the expenditure was voted and with any relevant statutes.

We note that the accounts of each Government Department are examined by the Comptroller and Auditor-General who reports on them. The Public Accounts Committee have the duty to examine the accounts also. This duty is widely interpreted by the PAC to ensure that full value has been obtained for the sums spent by the Government Departments. The PAC have examined cases where the administration has been faulty or negligent. The PAC is, therefore, another 'watchdog' to expose waste and inefficiency.

The PAC sits weekly throughout the Parliamentary session, and prepares reports which are then presented to the House of Commons. The Committee has power to call for persons (e.g. civil servants) or papers (the actual accounts if need be). Questions may be put to the individual concerned and any papers examined. The PAC, invariably chaired by a leading opposition MP, is advised by the Comptroller and Auditor-General and his professional staff to assist in the analysis and investigation of the public accounts.

The PAC operates 'after the event' as it were. Its main function is to be critical of expenditure already made. Its work, therefore, lacks the interest of current events. Any recommendations made by the PAC are considered by the Treasury which may accept them and put them into effect to avoid the pitfall the following year e.g. a report in 1986 drew attention to the saving of some £75 million a year by improved stores purchasing methods in the NHS. In 1962 the Report of the Comptroller and Auditor-General drew attention to the excessive profit made by Ferranti Ltd on a Government contract for constructing Bloodhound missiles. The matter was investigated by the PAC; created a public stir and the company finally agreed to repay £4,500,000. Thus the PAC's 'inquisitions' and subsequent reports can have a salutory effect on spending officials. But like other Committees, the PAC may be denied access to information (see p. 82); thus, in February 1982 it was reported that the Comptroller was refused access to certain persons and papers of British Leyland. In December 1986, the C&AG drew attention to his being denied access to the accounts of the BBC concerning overseas broadcasting services.

Supplementary Estimates

These are necessary when during a financial year a Department finds it has underestimated the cost of a particular service, or it has not made provision for something which arises unexpectedly or which could not reasonably be foreseen. Thus a crisis in the Middle East (cf. Suez crisis of 1956) or further afield (such as the Falklands War of 1982) could well involve a Supplementary Estimate for the Defence Services. Where a demand is thus made by a Department it is passed to the Treasury, and the Chancellor may (if he approves) then place before the House of Commons a Supplementary Estimate. This would pass through the same Parliamentary process as that for the annual estimates. Supplementary Estimates arise usually in the latter part of the financial year, but could occur earlier, e.g. as a result of a national epidemic of foot-and-mouth disease among cattle, or freak weather conditions.

Excess Votes

These are necessary when a Department has underestimated an item of expenditure and the mistake is discovered after contract has been made. Money must, therefore, be voted to avoid breach of contract by the Government. An Excess Vote must be obtained from the House of Commons. In practice, of course, the money is invariably found. The occasion for the vote does, however, provide a chance for the Opposition to criticise the Government for its failure in budgeting or for its maladministration. Excess Votes are usually for comparatively small sums. They differ from Supplementary Estimates in that Excess Votes arise from over-spending which has already occurred, the fact being revealed when accounts are presented at the end of the financial year. Supplementary Estimates provide for foreseen additional expenditure.

The Paymaster-General

The Paymaster-General is a political post, not normally of Cabinet rank. The holder is responsible for signing documents permitting a Government Department to receive money from the Consolidated Fund after the Treasury has given authority for payment.

The office has few responsibilities attached to it (other than the above). This enables a Prime Minister to appoint some person to this junior post who is allocated some additional responsibility in the Government. In 1981 the post was held by Cecil Parkinson, who combined the position with that of Chairman of the Conservative Party, and as such he attended Cabinet meetings. In April 1982 he was given the additional role of Chancellor of the Duchy of Lancaster. In 1986, Kenneth Clarke combined the post with that of Minister for Employment.

Forward Planning

In the past a Government was concerned solely with the estimates for the ensuing financial year. The estimates were, and still are, difficult to analyse and control. Parliament has an opportunity to consider the Annual Estimates for the next financial year and the Opposition may propose a motion criticising the Government on its inadequacy and mishandling. Naturally the Government, Opposition and individual MPs are interested in what is happening now.

But Government should be concerned with the future: indeed, forward planning is now essential. On assuming office, a Government may look forward to holding the keys of power for five years. It will have a broad plan of what it hopes to accomplish during each Parliamentary session. But it can put through its policies only if there are sufficient resources to meet them: hence the need for long-term financial and economic plans.

Since 1961, following the Plowden Report, Governments have operated a system of forward planning (over a five-year period) for public expenditure. All Government Departments are called upon to forecast proposals and expenditure both for the next year and up to five years ahead. The Department of Education and Science will indent for new schools and colleges to replace old ones and provide for increasing numbers of students. A new Government faced with rising crime may promise to 'strengthen the forces of law and order'. The Home Office will have to state its requirements for more police, vehicles, training establishments, radios and other equipment. The prison service will be considered: more prisons may be required and better arrangements for after-care of offenders and so on. The Lord Chancellor may require new courts and staff to man them. The

Defence Minister must look ahead and plan for new defence equipment to match the needs of modern defence, e.g. to replace Polaris. The Secretary of State for the Environment has to forecast the need for new motorways and roads which will be required in five years' time. Britain's contributions to the Common Market must be allowed for.

On the basis of the figures supplied by Departments the Treasury is able to assess the probable future demands for finance and the likely tax changes or borrowing which will be necessary. Such decisions are of vital importance to the economy generally and to the Public Sector Borrowing Requirement (PSBR) and the money supply in particular.

Such tasks have involved the creation of the **Public Expenditure Survey Committee** (PESC), an inter-departmental committee of civil servants from various Departments and chaired by a Treasury official. Its general purpose is to co-ordinate the financial planning work of the individual Departments. More specifically, PESC, beginning in about February each year,

Table 3. Income and Expenditure for the Public Sector 1986–7

Receipts	£m	%	Expenditure	£m	%
Income tax	39,120	24	Defence	17,930	11
Corporation tax	11,410	7	Foreign and		
Capital taxes	3,260	2	Commonwealth Office	1.630	1
Value added tax	21,190	13	Agriculture, Fisheries		
Local authority rates	16,300	10	and Food	1,630	1
Duties on petrol, alcoholic			Trade and Industry	1,630	1
drinks and tobacco	16,300	10	Employment	3,260	2
Other expenditure taxes	9,780	6	Transport	4,890	3
Petroleum revenue tax and			Environment—housing	3,260	2
oil royalties	3,260	2	Environment—other		
National Insurance and			environmental services	3,260	2
other contributions	26,080	16	Home Office	4,890	3
Interest and dividends	6,520	4	Education and Science	14,670	9
Gross trading surpluses			Health and Social		
and rent	3,260	2	Security—health and		
Other items and			personal social services	17,930	11
adjustments	1,630	1	Health and Social		
Public sector borrowing			Security—social security	42,380	26
requirement	6,520	4	Scotland	8,150	5
			Wales	3,260	2
			Northern Ireland	4,890	3
			Chancellor's departments	1,630	1
			Other departments	3,260	2
			Reserve	4,890	3
			Gross debt interest	17,930	11
			Adjustments (net of		
			privatisation proceeds)	1,630	1
Total	163,000	100	**Total**	163,000	100

Sources: *Financial Statement and Budget Report 1986–87* and *The Government's Expenditure Plans 1986–97 to 1988–89.*
Note: Difference between total receipts and the sum of component parts is due to rounding.

examines the existing state of the expenditure plans, scrutinises any Departmental proposals for changing them (and their reasons for so doing, such as population changes) and inquires where reductions could best be made in existing plans if this proved necessary.

Meanwhile, the Departments have become involved in policy review exercises known as **Programme Analysis and Review** (PAR). These began in 1971 and sought to ask questions about certain existing programmes of expenditure (different ones were selected each year): are the policies adopted in the past still relevant today? If so, are the objectives being achieved in the most effective way? Could they be achieved as effectively but more efficiently or economically? Examples of such policy stocktaking occurred in education (resulting in 1972, in a Green Paper, *Education: a Framework for Expansion*), and in housing (resulting in the Green Paper *Housing Policy*, plus four technical volumes, 1977, though most PARs have not been published). Other efficiency and waste-cutting procedures have been developed, such as MINIS (management information for ministers) and, since 1982, FMI financial management information. **FMI**

In 1979, Sir Derek Rayner was appointed part-time from business to advise the Prime Minister on the elimination of waste in Departments. This responsibility now rests with a senior civil servant who heads a special unit in the cabinet office.

This responsibility now rests with a senior civil servant. Meanwhile departments are developing efficiency and waste-cutting procedures known as MINIS (management information for ministers).

Generally, therefore, the expenditure survey system seeks to examine current and future spending plans with a view to determining priorities both among Departmental programmes and within those programmes.

Normally the PESC exercise is completed by June and results are then submitted to the Cabinet Ministers. They discuss the plans and, taking account of the overall economic prospects, reach collective decisions both on the total volume of expenditure in each of the next four years and on the allocation to (and within) the various expenditure programmes (some 17 of them). Where there remains a disagreement over any programme, it or they are referred to a committee of senior Ministers, known as the 'Star Chamber' (currently chaired by Lord Whitelaw) whose aim is to conciliate and reach agreement, ready for the Chancellor's Autumn Statement (see p. 107). Unresolved issues may go to the Prime Minister or a full cabinet. The Treasury Ministers play a leading role in this. This part of the process is normally complete by about November of each year.

Since 1969, these final decisions on the Government's expenditure plans have been published as White Papers, usually at the turn of the year, and presented to Parliament (see Table 3). This publication provides important background material for the annual current estimates. Consequently, it usually forms the basis of a debate in which MPs may hope to influence plans for two or three years ahead. Such debates have often been guided by the inquiries conducted by the Public Expenditure Committee or, more recently, the Select Committee on the Treasury and the Civil Service, whose proceedings have sometimes been broadcast.

Recent developments

Important changes have been introduced in response to the report of the Select Committee on Procedure (Finance) (1981) and the promptings of the Select Committee on the Treasury. First, Supply Days (p. 109) as such have been abolished: instead 20 days are set aside for Opposition-chosen debates, and 3 days are to be devoted exclusively to consideration of the Estimates (as selected by the liaison committee—see p. 81). Second, the Government now provides more and earlier information on its spending and borrowing plans, and on the budget options available to the Chancellor. Thirdly, the value-for-money scrutinies by the C&AG are revealing greater opportunities for Parliament to examine various schemes and procedures of government. These are modest steps: some reformers wish to see select committees empowered to adjust estimates and also seek to bring government borrowing under Parliamentary scrutiny; others want a more comprehensive provisional (or Green-Paper type) budget. But they are significant steps in settling the balance of power between Parliament and Government.

Exercises

1. Describe the composition of the House of Lords.
2. Should the House of Lords be reformed or abolished?
3. Name and explain the Lords' reform Acts dated 1911, 1949 and 1963.
4. What are the disqualifications for membership of the House of Commons?
5. Describe the election and functions of the Speaker.
6. What is the role of the Whips?
7. List the main types of committee in the House of Commons.
8. Explain (a) Oral, (b) Written, (c) Private Notice, (d) Supplementary Rule?
9. What is (a) the Debate on the Adjournment, (b) the Ten-Minute Rule?
10. What is (a) PESC, (b) PAR, (c) MINIS, (d) FMI?
11. Describe (a) the Ordinary Closure, (b) the Kangaroo, (c) the Guillotine.
12. What do you understand by (a) the PLP and (b) the 1922 Committee?
13. What are the four types of Parliamentary Bill? Give examples.
14. Describe the stages through which a Bill must pass to become law.
15. What is the purpose of Departmental Select Committees?
16. How far does, and how far should, Parliament control the Government?

4
The Executive

The Monarchy

The United Kingdom is a monarchical State, sometimes described as a **limited hereditary Monarchy**. The origin and history we have already noted on page 18.

The Crown

When we use the phrase 'the Crown' we must distinguish two meanings:

(i) The Crown may mean the Monarch or Sovereign, who personally holds office, or

(ii) The Executive, i.e. the Prime Minister, Cabinet and Ministers with the Civil Service who exercise governmental powers in the name or on behalf of the State.

The Crown is the visible symbol of supreme executive power which is vested in the Queen but exercised by her Ministers who, as we have noted, are responsible to Parliament and ultimately the electorate for their actions. It is, therefore, a 'constitutional' Monarchy: 'The Queen reigns, but does not rule.' The Queen may be said to be the personification of the State.

Tenure

The Queen occupies the throne by virtue of statute, viz. the *Act of Settlement, 1701*, whereby in default of issue of Princess Anne of Denmark and of William III, the Princess Sophia Electress, grand-daughter of James I, and the heirs of her body being Protestant succeeded to the throne.

Title

The Royal Title is now: 'Elizabeth II, by the Grace of God of Great Britain, Ireland and the British Dominions Beyond the Seas, Queen, Defender of the Faith' (*Royal Titles Act, 1953*). The Coronation took place on 2 June 1953, at Westminster Abbey, London.

Regency

By the *Regency Acts, 1937–1953*, provision is made for certain con-

tingencies. (e.g. illness, incapacity of mind or body). Thus, if on accession
to the Crown the Sovereign is under the age of 18 years, or is incapacitated
through illness of performing the Royal functions, a Regent may be appointed to exercise the powers of the Sovereign. The first potential Regent
should be the Prince Philip, Duke of Edinburgh.

The *Regency Act, 1943*, amended the 1937 Act by providing that Counsellors of State may be appointed to whom the Royal functions may be
delegated if the Sovereign is ill or absent from the United Kingdom (e.g.
on a prolonged visit to a Commonwealth country). The Counsellors shall
be the wife or husband of the Sovereign, and the four persons next in line
of succession to the Crown, or, if those persons are less than four, then all
such persons.

The heir apparent or presumptive to the throne if not under 18 shall not
be disqualified from being a Counsellor of State. The *Regency Act, 1953*,
provided for the Duke of Edinburgh to act as Regent in the event of the
Heir Apparent acceding to the throne before he reached the age of 18
years.

The Civil List

In medieval times a Monarch paid all expenses of government (i.e. court
expenses, army, navy, and government officers) out of feudal dues payable
by the tenants of land to the Lord Paramount (the King). Taxes were then
(and are always) burdensome, and the Royal claim to impose taxes by
right of his prerogative was one of the main causes which precipitated the
struggle between the Crown and Parliament in the seventeenth century.
Finally, this struggle resulted in the House of Commons claiming the exclusive right to tax, and then the right to complete control of how the
revenue raised should be spent.

If royalty was to be maintained, the King had to have some money to
keep him in existence. Charles II was granted the proceeds of the duties on
spirits, cider, and beer, and these dues became part of the Royal income.
In the reign of William III this grant of money by the Commons became
known as the 'Civil List'. The grant is still in being and now includes the
money allocated by Parliament and charged on the Consolidated Fund
(see p. 111).

Today the Civil List covers the personal income of the Sovereign, together with expenses of the Royal Household and any allowance which
Parliament may make for other members of the Royal Family. The Civil
List is embodied in a statute (*Civil List Act, 1952*) and in that year was
fixed at £475,000 per annum. In December 1971 the Commons Select
Committee on the Civil List made recommendations increasing the figure
to £980,000. To meet rising costs, the Committee suggested a system in
which the Treasury could bring forward Orders in Parliament to make any
necessary adjustments. The Committee found that the Royal Household
was run very economically and that increases were justified. Today the
Civil List covers the Queen's expenses for running the machinery of
monarchy, and includes allowances to other members of the Royal Family
as follows (1986–7 figures):

HM the Queen Elizabeth II	£4,136,000
Queen Elizabeth the Queen Mother	359,000
The Duke of Edinburgh	200,000
Princess Anne Princess Royal	124,800
Princess Margaret	121,000
Prince Andrew	20,000
Prince Edward	20,000

Most of the Civil List is spent on wages and salaries for the 350 staff employed in the Royal Household (secretaries, cleaners, etc.). (There were 530 in 1952). The Queen is exempt from taxes, except for rates on the estates of Balmoral and Sandringham which are part of the Queen's private property rather than Crown land (i.e. former Royal property which has reverted to the State). Civil List annuities to other members of the Royal Family are only taxable in so far as they are not used to meet official expenses incurred in carrying out public duties. In addition, about 75 per cent of the cost of the monarchy's official duties (upkeep of palaces, travel at home and abroad, the Royal Yacht and Royal Flight, etc.) is met by annual Parliamentary Departmental Votes. Members of the Royal Family also have some private sources of income (and occasionally the Queen uses part of this to meet deficits in the Civil List expenditures).

The Civil List no longer includes a personal allowance for the Queen whose principal source of income, some £1.5 million p.a., is derived from the lands of the Duchy of Lancaster.

Duties of the Sovereign

Our State may be described as a representative Parliamentary democracy in a monarchical framework. The real rulers are 'Her Majesty's Ministers' i.e. the Cabinet and Ministers in whom are vested the executive powers of government which were once claimed by the Kings of Britain. Today the Queen by convention always acts on the advice of Her Ministers, and never vetoes a statute enacted by Parliament. As we have observed 'the Queen reigns but does not rule'. In 1867, Walter Bagehot said that the King had three rights: 'the right to be consulted, the right to encourage, and the right to warn'. 'And,' he adds, 'a King of great sense and sagacity would want no others.'

In brief, the main functions of the Queen today may be listed thus:

(i) To open and close Parliament.
(ii) To dissolve and summon Parliament.
(iii) To appoint a Prime Minister.
(iv) To be the Fountain of Justice.
(v) To be the Fountain of Honour.
(vi) To be the Head of the Commonwealth.
(vii) To exercise the right of advice to Her Ministers.
(viii) To take part in the formal and ceremonial events observed by the Constitution.

(i) *Opening and Closing of Parliament*. The dates on which Parliament is opened (summoned) and closed (prorogued), i.e. the beginning and end of a Parliamentary session, are fixed by Parliament itself. The Queen attends the formal opening of Parliament which is characterised by traditional pomp and pageantry. The Queen drives in State from Buckingham Palace to Westminster accompanied by the Household Cavalry. The event is an important event constitutionally and is notable for its traditional ceremony and dignity.

Her Majesty sits on the Throne in the House of Lords which is crowded for the event. The Commons are summoned to the bar of the upper chamber to hear the Queen's Speech. The Speech is prepared by the Prime Minister and Cabinet and, as we have noted (see p. 83), is usually a review of the past with proposals for new legislation in the ensuing Parliamentary session.

(ii) *Dissolution and Summoning of Parliament.* Parliament is dissolved at the end of a five-year period (*Parliament Acts, 1911 and 1949*). If, however, a Government is defeated on a major issue in the House of Commons during the five-year period the Prime Minister must, by convention, resign or test his or her credibility in a general election.

A Prime Minister may at any such time during the five-year life of a Parliament request a dissolution. The Sovereign may not constitutionally refuse the request. Normally, however, where a Government has a workable majority in the House of Commons a Prime Minister will not wish to dissolve Parliament. But, where this is not so and a Government has only a small majority a Prime Minister may feel that an appeal should be made to the electorate to enable strong and effective government to be carried on. Accordingly a request is made to which the Monarch accedes.

Sir Alan Lascelles (Private Secretary to King George VI) considered that a Sovereign *could* refuse dissolution where three conditions were fulfilled:

(*a*) The existing Parliament was still vital, viable and capable of doing its job.

(*b*) A general election would be detrimental to the national economy.

(*c*) The Sovereign could rely on finding another Prime Minister who could carry on his Government, for a reasonable period, with a working majority in the House of Commons.

It is very seldom that the above three conditions will co-exist.

The problem of a request for dissolution sometimes arises where a Government has a small majority. A Prime Minister in this situation may request dissolution if the Government is not strong enough to carry on or carry out its policies. If a request by a Prime Minister for dissolution is refused by the Sovereign the Prime Minister may, of course, resign. His successor, nominated by the Sovereign, would in the circumstances face the same problem as before, and, if he also requests a dissolution this would place the Sovereign in a difficult situation and, in the event, the Sovereign would have to accede to the dissolution.

(iii) *Appointment of the Prime Minister.* The Prime Minister is chosen and appointed by the Queen by right of her prerogative. The choice is frequently automatic, and her appointment is bound by convention. Thus:

(*a*) Where a party has a majority in the House of Commons and a recognised leader in the House that person will be appointed to the office of Prime Minister.

(*b*) If the Government is defeated in the Commons and the Prime Minister resigns, the Monarch must send for the leader of the Opposition who will be asked to form a Government. If, by reason of a lack of a majority in the Commons, he or she is unable to form a Government a general election will be held, following which the recognised leader of the majority party in the Commons will be appointed.

If a Prime Minister dies in office and there is no recognised leader of the party to succeed him, the Monarch must make a personal choice. Normally this is the person recommended to the Monarch by the Prime Minister before his death. Winston Churchill, for example, recommended two successors (1) Anthony Eden; and (2) Sir John Anderson. If both Churchill and Eden died, Sir John Anderson was to succeed.

If a Prime Minister wishes to resign (e.g. if he is too ill to perform his office) the Monarch may ask his advice as to his successor. This situation arose on the resignation of Sir Anthony Eden in 1957. There were two contenders for the position: Mr R. A. Butler and Harold Macmillan. As a result of her own inquiries, and after consultations with Sir Winston Churchill and Lord Salisbury, Mr Macmillan was appointed.

Where the political situation is confused the Sovereign may intervene. Thus in 1931 no one party had a clear majority. At the time the Liberal Party had a stronger membership in the Commons. The Labour Party Prime Minister, Ramsay MacDonald, could not secure agreement within the Labour Party on the means to combat the economic crisis of the time and he tendered his resignation, but recommended to King George V that the King should consult with the leaders of the other two parties, namely Stanley Baldwin (Conservative) and Sir Herbert Samuel (Liberal). As a result of the King's intervention a conference of the three party leaders was held and a National Government under Ramsay MacDonald was formed. The coalition so formed was, however, weak due to basic differences in political philosophies.

Where the Sovereign has, in the particular circumstances of the times, to make a personal decision he may consult whom he pleases. Normally, as we have noted, the practice is to consult the Prime Minister who resigns or seeks to resign. But there is no rule to this effect, and sometimes the Sovereign may consult Privy Counsellors (see p. 127) or the Monarch's Private Secretary. Thus, we are told, it was as a result of meetings between the Private Secretary to George V, Mr L. S. Amery and Mr Bridgman that Stanley Baldwin was chosen in 1923 to accept the premiership in place of Lord Curzon.

Appointment of Ministers. Originally the Ministers of the Crown were appointed by and dismissed by the Sovereign to whom they were personally responsible for carrying out the Royal commands. Since 1832 the appointment of Ministers has been the responsibility of the Prime Minister who selects his team of Ministers some of whom will be of Cabinet rank and some not.

The list of Ministers is by convention submitted to the Sovereign for approval. Queen Victoria made her opinions known, but today the appointments are little more than a formality. We know, however, that a Sovereign may still make his or her opinion known. George VI, we are told, preferred Ernest Bevin as Foreign Secretary to Dr Hugh Dalton, and that recommendation took effect. Ultimately, however, the responsibility is the Prime Minister's, not the Sovereign's.

Dismissal of a Government. Formerly it was within the prerogative of a Sovereign to dismiss a Government. The last time this was done was in 1783 when George III dismissed Mr C. J. Fox and Lord North who were replaced by Pitt.

Since the *Reform Act, 1832*, the effective political power reposes with the Prime Minister and the Cabinet responsible to Parliament. By convention the Monarch is now above party politics.

In theory, a Sovereign could still invoke the prerogative to dismiss a Government, which was acting unconstitutionally. But this presupposes a great deal, since all Governments today are democratically elected and therefore responsive (albeit crudely) to the will of the people. If a Government acts constitutionally there would be no need for intervention by the Sovereign. In this respect Sir Ivor Jennings comments:

> It (the Constitution) functions in a normal manner so long as the electors are asked to decide between two competing parties at intervals of reasonable length. She (the Queen) would be justified in refusing assent to a policy which subverted the democratic basis of the Constitution, by unnecessary or indefinite prolongations of the life of Parliament, by gerrymandering of the constituencies in the interests of one party, or by fundamental modification of the electoral system to the same end. (*Cabinet Government.*)

This leaves open many questions, and a dismissal of a Government would in fact be a last resort, as, for example if a Government after a vote of censure in the House of Commons on a vital matter refused to resign, or resolved to continue in power indefinitely.

Generally (as Bagehot states), the Monarch is entitled to be informed and consulted, and in practice the Prime Minister has audience with Her Majesty frequently. The Queen on her part develops considerable experience of Constitutional matters. Elizabeth II, since ascending the throne in 1952, has had eight different Prime Ministers, has visited all the Commonwealth countries and has therefore a store of useful wisdom and advice which she may impart to her Ministers which may be heeded in the national interest.

(iv) *Fountain of Justice.* The Queen is the 'fountain of justice'. The Courts of Law are the Royal Courts, and Justice is administered by Her Majesty's Judges, appointed by the Crown. Senior counsel who are senior members of the Bar are known as 'Queen's Counsel' (QC).

The Queen can, by prerogative, remit all or part of any sentence or penalty inflicted on a person convicted of crime. Formerly persons sentenced to death for murder could be reprieved. In all such cases where a sentence is remitted or a pardon granted Her Majesty acts on the advice of one of her Ministers—the Home Secretary—who makes his own inquiries, reads the files and advises Her Majesty accordingly.

(v) *Fountain of Honour.* In exercise of her prerogative, Her Majesty confers peerages, baronetcies, knighthoods, and other honours. Most honours are, however, conferred by the Sovereign on the advice of the Prime Minister. Under this heading we include all important state offices to which the Sovereign makes appointments, for example, judges, officers in the Armed Forces, Governors of Commonwealth countries or colonies, diplomats, and the leading positions of the established Church of England. We have noted already the Queen's consent and approval of the appointment of Cabinet and other Ministers.

Notwithstanding the above list, there are a few honours which are the personal gift of the Sovereign. These are the Order of Merit, the Royal Victorian Order, the Most Noble Order of the Garter, and the Most Noble and Most Ancient Order of the Thistle.

(vi) *Head of the Commonwealth*. The Queen is Head of the Commonwealth (see the Royal Title on page 119). The Commonwealth has been described as a free association composed of some thirty independent nations which owe allegiance to the Queen as the symbol of their free association. The Queen is Head of State in twelve countries.

The seat of the Monarchy is the United Kingdom. In the nations of the Commonwealth the Queen is represented by a Governor-General, Lieutenant-General or Governor; in the Channel Islands and the Isle of Man, by a Lieutenant-Governor. In the other member nations of the Commonwealth the Queen is represented by a Governor-General who is appointed by the Crown on the advice of the Ministers of the country concerned and is wholly independent of the UK Government.

In dependencies the Queen is represented by Governors appointed by the Crown. These have varying legislative and executive functions, but are responsible to the UK Government for the good government of the countries concerned.

It was in her capacity as Head of the Commonwealth that, in 1986, it was alleged that differences arose between The Queen and Mrs Thatcher as it was felt that the latter's resistance to Britain's imposing sanctions on South Africa would jeopardise this country's relations with the rest of the Commonwealth and put a strain on the whole institution.

(vii) *To Exercise the Right of Advice to Her Ministers*. As Walter Bagehot has stated, the Sovereign has three rights: 'the right to be consulted, the right to encourage, the right to warn. And a King of great sense and sagacity would want no others.' The broad rule is that by convention the Monarch always acts on the advice of her Ministers, but this ignores certain important aspects and practices.

First, the Prime Minister has an audience with the Queen once a week (when Parliament is in session) usually at 6 p.m. on a Tuesday evening (for about an hour) before a Cabinet meeting. Here the Prime Minister may explain why and when he desires the exercise of the prerogative powers of the Queen, e.g. in the summoning, prorogation, or dissolution of Parliament, the conferment of peerages, titles, and honours. This is essentially an important constitutional event. The Queen may make her own observations on proposals.

The Queen today has much work to do. She must read a great deal. Thus, Sir Michael Adeane, Private Secretary, stated:

There is reading of all sorts—not only familiarising herself with the Government papers which are produced in this country, which she does with great regularity, but keeping fairly well in touch, though perhaps not in so much detail, with what is going on in a great many other countries. This is mainly done by reports from governors, governors-general, ambassadors and so forth . . .

The Queen is fortunately a quick and accurate reader and the many people who have audiences with her during the year find that she is remarkably well informed on all these important matters. If she is not, I can guarantee that it is because I have not given her the right papers. . . . But she can be relied upon to read the papers and to remember them.

This goes on 365 days in the year and it is something which cannot be skipped, and is not skipped, and something she does very well. But it is something which has increased and goes on increasing.

(Report from the Select Committee on the Civil List 1971) (*The Times*, 3 December 1971.)

Governments and Prime Ministers come and go. The Monarch is the continuing element. Queen Elizabeth has had eight Prime Ministers, and it is clear that her knowledge and experience in the affairs of state are invaluable. Moreover she has visited all parts of the Commonwealth, knows personally the leading figures there and in many foreign countries. Again that experience is unique. The Queen is above party politics, yet at the same time (as Sir Ivor Jennings put it) the Monarch is 'the nearest approach to the ordinary man provided by the British constitutional machine' (*Cabinet Government*). Any advice the Queen may give in a particular situation is disinterested and not partisan. How far a Prime Minister accepts or bows to that advice is a matter for him or her in the final event. Mr Asquith's memorandum to George V runs as follows:

In the last resort the occupant of the Throne accepts and acts on the advice of his Ministers. . . . He is entitled and bound to give his Ministers all relevant information which comes to him; to point out objections which seem to him valid against the course which they advise; to suggest (if he thinks fit) an alternative policy. Such intimations are received by Ministers with the utmost respect and more deference than if they proceeded from any other quarter. But, in the end, the Sovereign always acts upon the advice which Ministers, after (if need be) reconsideration, feel it their duty to offer. They give that advice well knowing that they can, and probably will, be called upon to account for it by Parliament.

(viii) *Pageantry, Pomp, and Circumstance.* Any brief sketch of the Sovereign's function is incomplete without reference to the role which the Monarchs in the last two hundred years have played in the British Constitution. All have set an example of service to the nation and, at the same time, taken a leading part in the pageantry and the traditional ceremonies which are part of the British scene.

British subjects support the Monarchy with respect and affection. They delight in the ancient forms with which Parliamentary government, national, and state affairs are preserved and carried on. The Monarch symbolises the unity of the State and imparts dignity to its proceedings. The pageantry is merely the visible splendour of the important occasions in national life. Behind the outward splendour lies the difficult, strenuous, and exacting work of ensuring that the rights and duties inherent in democracy are upheld and preserved.

Notwithstanding the fact that the Crown has lost its original great powers it can be said, certainly of the present century, that as those powers passed and the Monarchy became strictly constitutional, the Monarch has become increasingly popular in the hearts and minds of the British people. (Lord Morrison: *Government and Parliament*.)

The visits made by the Sovereign to Commonwealth countries are always notable for the friendly way in which Her Majesty is received. These overseas activities help in uniting the independent members of the Commonwealth and their peoples and serve to reinforce friendships and loyalties to the common ideals which underlie the free association of member States.

The Cabinet

The Privy Council was at one time the formal source of executive power in the State. In medieval times there were the *Magnum Concilium* (the Great Council), a smaller body, the *Curia Regis*, and in addition a body known as the Privy (Private) Council of the King made up of those people on whose advice the Monarch depended and on whom he relied to carry out his decisions and commands.

In the seventeenth century the Monarch held conferences or meetings with his leading Ministers apart from the Privy Council. These meetings were confidential and took place in the King's 'cabinet' (derived from the French '*cabinet*' meaning a private room set apart for interviews).

Charles II and William and Mary did not attend some of the meetings, and, although George I, of Hanover, attended cabinet meetings at the beginning of his reign he could not speak English, did not understand English institutions or our way of life and was not interested in political affairs. By the end of his reign he attended only rarely, and ceased to attend after 1717.

The following factors influenced the growth of cabinet power: (i) the withdrawal of the Sovereign from active politics; (ii) the development of organised political parties; and (iii) the extension of the franchise following the *Reform Act, 1832*.

As the Cabinet grew in importance the Privy Council declined. Many of the former powers of the Privy Council were transferred to the Cabinet, and many of the executive duties of the Privy Council were transferred to newly formed Government Departments.

The link between the Privy Council and the Cabinet is today preserved, however, in that all Cabinet Ministers (past and present) and other Senior Ministers are **Privy Councillors**—of whom there are currently some 400—are formally appointed by the sovereign, and may be removed at will but rarely are. On being nominated they take the oath of office, binding themselves among other things to 'keep the Queen's council secret'. Membership is a coveted distinction and Privy Councillors are entitled to be addressed as 'Right Honourable'. They also have precedence in Parliamentary debate.

The Privy Council still plays an important part in the Constitution. Apart from many functions vested in it by statute, it is the body on whose advice the Queen in Council exercises certain prerogative powers and a large number of powers vested in Her Majesty by statute.

The centre of the political power of the State at the present time is the Cabinet which is presided over by the Prime Minister and meets usually at No. 10 Downing Street, London.

Composition

The Cabinet is a group of party representatives which depends for its continued existence in power upon the ability to command the support of a majority of Members of Parliament in an elected legislature, the House of Commons. That support is derived from members of the same political party or a group of parties, e.g. in the event of a coalition of parties.

Most members of the Cabinet are appointed to head Government Departments. The number of members forming a cabinet varies. In 1886 there were fourteen members; in 1971 seventeen; in 1987 twenty-two. These form the 'inner core' of the ruling political party.

The Cabinet has the following main characteristics. The Cabinet:

   (i) Exists purely on convention; it has no statutory basis.
   (ii) Operates on the principle of secrecy about its deliberations.
  (iii) Consists of MPs (and Peers) of the same political views.
  (iv) Is chosen from the Party with a majority in the House of Commons.
   (v) Carries out a concerted or commonly agreed policy.
  (vi) Has to resign collectively in the event of Parliamentary censure on a vital issue.
 (vii) Is selected by the Prime Minister, whom members acknowledge as leader and chairman.

Walter Bagehot emphasised the importance of the Cabinet thus:

> The efficient secret of the English Constitution may be described as the close union and nearly complete fusion of the executive and legislative powers . . . The Cabinet is a combining committee—a hyphen which joins, a buckle which fastens the legislative part of the State to the executive part of the State. In its origin it belongs to one, in its function it belongs to the other. (*The English Constitution*, 1867.)

Functions of the Cabinet

Policy Forming. The main task of the Cabinet is to form the policy of HM Government with regard to home and foreign affairs. This task faces all governments, but it is essential here to bring it into focus.

The broad outlines of a Government's policy will have been laid before the electorate in its political manifesto before a general election. A programme of legislation will, therefore, be drawn up and followed so far as possible. Industrial relations, unemployment, housing, the reform of local government, the question of joining or leaving the European Common Market, immigration, and race relations are a few of the matters to be decided.

Relations with foreign states, international co-operation with such bodies as the United Nations Organisation, are continuous. All governments are concerned with protecting vital national interests, maintaining the peace and at the same time meeting the challenge of the inevitable changes and events which occur in the world scene.

The Cabinet governs the country as a whole in the interests of the entire nation. The leaders must be wary of too doctrinaire an attitude against which the electorate may react unfavourably, thus leading to defeat at the next general election.

Filling in Details of Policy. Where a broad policy only is decided upon before an election, the Cabinet is faced with the task of filling in the details.

Fig. 15. Government: Cabinet: Parliament: Electorate

For example the reform of Industrial Law relating to trade unions is a policy matter, but the form of the changes in the law is a matter for the Cabinet, with the assistance of its advisers. The Cabinet therefore draws up the annual Parliamentary legislative programme. Frequently lack of time and finance dictate necessary limitations on what the Cabinet can determine. Government, it has been said, is 'the art of the possible'.

Co-ordination of Policy. Effective and convenient government requires that all Government Departments concerned with the same problems work together. For example, raising the school-leaving age in 1973 involved:

   (i) The Secretary of State for Education and Science.
  (ii) The Secretary of State for Social Services.
 (iii) The Secretary of State for the Home Department.
  (iv) The Chancellor of the Exchequer.
   (v) The Secretary of State for Trade and Industry, and President of the Board of Trade.

The broad dovetailing of policy and oversight of its execution is achieved at Cabinet level while the lower executive authorities in the provinces, e.g. the local authorities, act in concert with the policy laid down.

Major Unforeseen Problems. Granted that a Government proposes certain reforms which it hopes to carry through during its five-year period of office, some, perhaps all, will be achieved, but it is certain there will also be many emergencies or contingencies which cannot be foreseen. Thus there may be a revolution in the Middle East, a break in East–West relations or the reverse, a capture of an ambassador by terrorists, unrest or violence in Ulster. All such matters fall within the purview of the Cabinet, and evoke response and, if need be, immediate action, as in the oil crisis of 1974 or the Falkland crisis, 1982.

The world seethes with problems: over-population and disease; pollution of earth, seas and atmosphere; the threat of war with its vital and complicated defence implications; international trade disputes; poverty and inequality (see the Brandt Report, 1980). The Cabinet lays down its short- and long-term policies. But it must do even more by giving to the country as a whole an energetic lead, motivating the Executive (civil service and local government) and demonstrating that it can govern. 'The cabinet pushes a stream of tendency through affairs' (per Professor H. J. Laski). Once the dynamic is lacking, government stagnates. Thus the Cabinet is both a political and an administrative body.

Principles of Cabinet Government

There are certain well-established principles on which the Cabinet works.

Cabinet and Parliamentary majority. The exercise of the important functions of the Cabinet, for example, its supreme control of the national executive, is vitally affected by the fact that the Cabinet is a group of party representatives depending for its existence upon the support of a majority of members in the House of Commons. As we have noted, it is an important convention that a cabinet which loses that support must resign or face a General Election. This is rare, though it did in fact occur in April 1979 (when James Callaghan's Labour Government was defeated in a vote of Confidence by one vote).

The value of this convention is that the Cabinet, through its control of the Commons, can frame policies and pass them into law, or raise any funds necessary for governmental purposes.

Some critics describe this system as 'Cabinet tyranny' or 'elective dictatorship'. The charge of 'dictatorship' suggests uncontrolled or absolute powers, leading to tyrannical government. The view ignores the checks which operate in the British Constitution in fact. Thus, we have noted that the Cabinet is dependent upon its majority in the House of Commons which can only be maintained by keeping the support of MPs, and, through MPs, the general public (the electorate) who have entrusted them with power. Moreover, a cabinet which heads a Government must know that its power will end at the expiration of five years in any event (*Parliament Acts, 1911 and 1949*).

A dictator on the other hand relies on armed force, a state-controlled police, repressive laws, an absence of a rival political party or group and an absence of free elections. The dictator may, of course, go to the lengths of destroying 'unhealthy' factions and liberties. Dictators are above the law by definition.

The power of the British Cabinet rests ultimately on the will of the people and the support of MPs of the same political beliefs. All Cabinet Ministers are subject to the law of the land (see the Rule of Law) in the same way as ordinary citizens. They have no power to imprison arbitrarily or destroy the opposition, and may indeed be prosecuted for crime or sued for their wrongs even in purported execution of their lawful powers.

Party Composition. All Cabinet members must be members of the same political party, or at least agreed upon a common policy. Unless there is membership of a party or fundamental agreement upon a common policy a Government cannot command a majority in Parliament to pursue a consistent policy.

In time of war, coalition Governments have been formed from the leaders of the different parties. This form of Government has worked mainly because all MPs have sunk their differences in pursuit of the overriding united purpose of winning the war.

In peace, however, coalitions have not worked well. For example, in the financial crisis of 1931, at a time of trade recession and mass unemployment there was a national emergency. The coalition Government formed at the time was an uneasy combination and was not successful. One half of the Government thought that expansion of financial credit was essential while the other thought restriction of credit was the cure for the prevailing crisis (see also pp. 40, 123).

It appears, therefore, that only in war is a coalition Government likely to work. In peace a coalition cabinet is ineffectual if it lacks a common policy and aim and is composed of members of fundamentally divergent philosophies.

'*Collective Responsibility*' became accepted as a doctrine by the middle of the nineteenth century. It means that the Cabinet is bound to offer unanimous advice to the Sovereign even when its members do not hold identical views on a given subject. It implies, therefore, that the policy of Departmental Ministers must be consistent with the policy of the Government as a whole. In principle it means that once the Government's policy on a particular matter is decided each Minister is expected to support it and share responsibility for it. If he cannot agree with his colleagues on a matter of general policy or on a single major issue he should resign. In February 1938 Anthony Eden (the late Lord Avon) resigned as Foreign Secretary because he disagreed with the appeasement policy of the Prime Minister Neville Chamberlain. In October Duff Cooper (later Lord Norwich) resigned from his office of First Lord of the Admiralty because of his disagreement with Chamberlain's Munich Agreement with Nazi Germany, and the dismemberment of the democracy of Czechoslovakia. Similarly, Aneurin Bevan resigned in 1951 from his office of Minister of Labour over disagreement with the Labour Government's policies of rearmament and with its proposals to impose charges for medical prescriptions under the hitherto 'free' National Health Service. Sir Edward Boyle resigned from his appointment as Economic Secretary to the Treasury because of his disagreement with the invasion of Egypt during Suez crisis of 1956. George Brown resigned unexpectedly in 1968 from the Labour Government. In May 1981, Keith Speed (the Navy Minister) was dismissed for his outspoken criticism of Government reductions in our naval forces. In the same year, Norman St John-Stevas was forced to resign because of his lack of support for the Government's economic (monetarist) policy. In 1986 Michael Heseltine resigned over the Cabinet's policy in the Westland affair and the Prime Minister's apparent refusal to have it discussed in cabinet.

'*Ministerial Responsibility*' means that as political head of a Department, a Minister is responsible or answerable for all its acts or omissions. He must also bear the consequences of any defect of administration, any injustice to an individual or any aspect of policy which may be criticised in Parliament, whether or not he is *personally* responsible. There is some doubt as to the validity of this doctrine today, as occasionally Ministers have failed to observe the consequences of such responsibility. But the principle was dramatically illustrated in April 1982 when the Foreign Secretary, Lord Carrington (together with two of his Ministers), resigned over their much criticised handling of the Falkland Islands crisis (occasioned by Argentina's sudden invasion and occupation of the islands). In January 1986, the Home Secretary, Leon Brittan, resigned because of the role he and his Department played in the Westland affair (especially the leaking of a confidential letter).

Most Ministers are members of the House of Commons. They are there able to answer questions and to defend themselves against criticism in person. Departmental Ministers who are in the Lords answer questions in that chamber, but must also be represented in the Commons by someone qualified to speak on their behalf for the Department, usually by their Parliamentary Secretaries (who are, of course, MPs).

The work of the various Government Departments is examined in more detail later (see pp. 143–57). Normally Departmental Ministers decide all matters within their responsibility. For example, the Home Secretary deals with all matters relating to police and prisons and their administration. On important matters, however, e.g. a proposal to 'nationalise' the police or the CID, a Minister will usually wish to consult his colleagues collectively through the Cabinet or a Cabinet committee. Any decision by a Departmental Minister binds the Government as a whole.

The responsibility of Ministers for their departments is one effective way of bringing the Government under public control. The knowledge that any departmental action may be reported to and examined in Parliament discourages the taking of arbitrary, ill-considered, or irresponsible decisions and high-handed action.

Cabinet Secretariat. All committees must have secretarial staff to record the business transacted. It is surprising, therefore, to notice that there was no true secretariat of the British Cabinet until 1916 when Lloyd George, as Prime Minister, created one. He transferred the then Secretary of the Committee of Imperial Defence (Colonel M. Hankey) to become the first secretary to the Cabinet. The secretary's main duties were to take charge of all cabinet papers, prepare agendas for meetings, prepare summaries of evidence, provide information of previous decisions of the Cabinet, to record decisions, and to notify Government Departments concerned. All such work was and still is highly confidential.

During the course of the past sixty years Cabinet responsibilities have grown increasingly complex. The work of the Cabinet has been divided and allocated to specialist committees. All such committees require the best and most accurate information available on which to reach decisions. Accordingly the Cabinet office staff has increased (from 407 in 1965 to 789 in 1985) and now includes scientific and specialist advisers. The Central Statistical Office (CSO) is one of the most important of the offices used by the Cabinet and its sub-committees for the supply of statistics and data on which the best decisions can be reached.

The Secretariat staff today includes one Secretary of the Cabinet, three

Deputy Secretaries and four Under Secretaries, plus ten Assistant Secretaries. All assist by being present at and servicing Cabinet meetings or the numerous committees of the Cabinet.

Today the Cabinet Office is an extremely important body. It is at the very centre of Government, recording decisions and precedents and co-ordinating the work of the various Cabinet committees. The Secretariat provides an element of permanence and continuity to the Cabinet (which must itself change at least once in every five years), and provides also considerable knowledge and experience which inevitably carry great weight. For these reasons the official Secretary to the Cabinet (formerly Sir Robert Armstrong now Robin Butler) is now the most important appointment in the Civil Service.

Cabinet Office Advisers. As part of the reorganisation made by the Prime Minister in October 1970, there was created a **Central Policy Review Staff** (also known as the CPRS, 'think-tank' or 'capability unit'). The team of some twelve advisers were drawn from many specialised fields. Their function was to question and objectively challenge policies put to the Cabinet by individual Departments in order that Ministers (especially Cabinet Ministers) should make better policy decisions. In the words of the White Paper *Reorganisation of Government 1970*, this unit seeks to enable Ministers:

to take better policy decisions by assisting them to work out the implications of their basic strategy in terms of policies in specific areas; to establish the relative priorities to be given to them; . . . and to ensure that the underlying implications of alternative courses of action are fully analysed and considered.

The CPRS has produced many reports (on energy, the computer industry, counter-inflation, race relations, regional policy *et al*). However, it was abolished in July 1983 on the grounds that it was superfluous, since other bodies had developed similar roles (viz. policy units in Departments, a policy unit in Downing Street, the Secretariat itself preparing issues for Cabinet discussions).

In addition, the Cabinet may engage individual experts to advise it on economic or scientific matters. Some such advisers may also be brought into Government Departments. In recent years, we may note the employment of the following advisers to the Cabinet: Sir Derek Rayner, Terry Burns and Sir Leo Pliatsky, advising on Government waste and over-manning, economic policy and Government agencies respectively.

Cabinet Committees. The Cabinet is composed of the principal officers of State. All Cabinets include the Lord Chancellor, the Foreign Secretary, the Home Secretary, the Chancellor of the Exchequer, the Minister of Defence. There is no fixed composition. It rests with the Prime Minister to decide who has a seat in the Cabinet. Most members are placed in charge of important Ministries, but sometimes holders of minor offices and Ministries without Portfolio (i.e. having no Departmental responsibilities) are appointed members of the Cabinet. Much depends on the personality and capacity of the individual, the availability of Government offices at the time and, of course, the handling of a particular problem or project of the times. Thus, in 1970 the Rt. Hon. Geoffrey Rippon, QC, MP, was appointed Chancellor of the Duchy of Lancaster (a Cabinet appointment with few duties) to handle negotiations for Britain's entry into the European Economic Community.

Cabinet meetings are held once or twice a week and usually last for two hours. Everything depends on the state of affairs at home and abroad. The agenda, prepared by the Secretariat, is discussed, the decisions recorded and notified to the Government Departments concerned or affected by the decisions. Each member of the Cabinet is free to express his views on topics introduced by the Prime Minister or other Ministers. All cabinet business follows that general pattern.

Government problems become increasingly complex. The machinery and institutions of government must change to cope with the problems and opportunities which constantly arise. The Cabinet has resorted to the use of committees. These smaller bodies relieve the burden on the main Cabinet. They also provide opportunity for more detailed discussion not suitable for the full Cabinet. Moreover, Cabinet Committees enable non-cabinet Ministers to be associated with policy decisions on matters affecting their own Departments; this also provides useful Cabinet experience.

The work of Cabinet Committees (like that of the parent body) is secret. Their existence, scope, and composition are not normally revealed during the life of a particular Government. However, there are certain well-known ones. Thus the Defence Committee exists and its importance in the provision of men and equipment for the defence of the nation needs no stressing here. The Committee is composed of the principal members of the Cabinet, the Service Ministers, and the Chairman of the Chiefs of Staff Committee who is the military head of the Forces. All defence matters are dealt with by this Committee and only major matters are reported to the full Cabinet with recommendations for approval. The Legislation Committee considers draft Bills and watches their progress through Parliament. The Leader of the House of Commons, and the Departmental Minister specially concerned with the subject-matter of a Bill attend the Committee. The Future Legislation Committee considers policy on **future** proposals and Bills to be considered by Parliament. The Lord President's Committee is a General Purposes Committee, i.e. one dealing with matters not specially assigned to a special committee. There is also an Economic Committee (chaired by the Prime Minister) and a Home and Social Affairs Committee (chaired by the Home Secretary). Special and sub-committees may be appointed to consider some particular matter as need arises, e.g. terrorism or an international event. (In 1976 it was estimated that as many as 118 various Cabinet Committees existed, *The Economist*, 6 February 1982, details 43 of them. See also P. Hennessy, *Cabinet*, in which he estimates some 160, including a number of informal advisory groups which the PM has created.) These may take decisions without reference to the full Cabinet, but normally all important matters are decided by the full Cabinet to whom the Committees report. The PM keeps in contact with all Committees, a fact which reinforces the leader's position since he or she may well be the only member who is in touch with all.

The Committee system has been adopted on the grounds of efficiency; the complexity and pace of modern government demands a division of responsibility and specialisation. Committees also give valuable experience to Junior Ministers. However, the Committee system has also tended to change the conduct of Cabinet proceedings. Formerly all Cabinet Ministers attended all Cabinet meetings and contributed their store of common sense and judgement to the solution of the current problems. Now Cabinet meetings may become rather formal, even ceremonial affairs as many important decisions are taken by Committees and thus by-pass the full Cabinet. (Over the years some of these Committees have virtually constituted a Prime Minister's 'inner Cabinet' and there have been allegations of 'Cabinet disintegration'.)

Co-ordination. The chief co-ordinator in the Cabinet is, of course, the Prime Minister whose task is to adjust and harmonise the work of the various constituent committees and individual members of the Cabinet. Senior members of the Cabinet also co-ordinate the work of the various committees of which they are appointed Chairmen. The Chancellor of the Exchequer must co-ordinate the work and decisions of all committees involving finance. The Secretary of State for Defence also co-ordinates defence matters and the work of the service Ministers who are not members of the Cabinet.

Another means to achieve co-ordination is to group related Departments or Ministries in one Department. The Secretary of State for the Environment is now responsible for: (i) Local Government (ii) Environmental Services and (iii) Housing and Construction, each in charge of a Minister. The Foreign Secretary is responsible for: (i) Foreign and (ii) Commonwealth and Colonial affairs and (iii) Overseas Development (since 1979).

In 1951 Sir Winston Churchill appointed three Ministers (known as 'Overlords') to supervisory positions in the Cabinet: (i) Lord Woolton (Lord President of the Council) to supervise Agriculture and Food; (ii) Lord Leathers (Secretary of State for the Co-ordination of Transport, Fuel and Power) to supervise Transport, Fuel and Power; (iii) Lord Cherwell (Paymaster-General) to supervise Research and Scientific policy. This followed the pattern set during the Second World War when Churchill appointed Ministers without departmental duties, e.g. Lord Privy Seal, the Chancellor of the Duchy of Lancaster, the Paymaster-General and a Minister without Portfolio, whose main task was to act as Chairmen of two or three closely connected Cabinet committees and the co-ordination of a group of related services. In 1953, however, the practice of appointing peers (hence the name 'Overlords') was criticised by Labour spokesmen mainly because the holders of such powerful positions were not responsible to the Commons. Moreover there was a blurring and confusion of political responsibility. Was the Minister responsible (see p. 131) or was the co-ordinator (the 'Overlord')? Accordingly, the arrangement was withdrawn in 1953.

Co-ordination involves (i) a clear objective to be achieved; (ii) a plan and time-table; (iii) efficient administrative machinery (committees, sub-committees, and administrative staff); and (iv) effective leadership in the persons of the Prime Minister and leading Ministers who can issue directives to members, reconcile differences in the achievement of the overall policies and master the art of getting things done.

The Government: 1987

The Cabinet

1. Prime Minister and First Lord of the Treasury and Minister for the Civil Service.
2. Secretary of State for the Home Department.
3. Secretary of State for Foreign and Commonwealth Affairs and Overseas Development.
4. Lord Chancellor.
5. Chancellor of the Exchequer.
6. Lord President of the Council.
7. Secretary of State of Defence.
8. Secretary of State for Social Services.
9. Chancellor of the Duchy of Lancaster.
10. Secretary of State for Employment.
11. Secretary of State for Education and Science.
12. Secretary of State for Scotland.
13. Lord Privy Seal.
14. Secretary of State for the Environment.
15. Secretary of State for Wales.
16. Minister of Agriculture, Fisheries, and Food.
17. Secretary of State for Trade and Industry.
18. Secretary of State for Northern Ireland.
19. Secretary of State for Energy.
20. Paymaster General and Minister for Employment.
21. Chief Secretary to the Treasury.
22. Secretary of State for Transport.

(Each member is currently paid a salary of £51,000, which includes £17,000 for MPs. Peers thus receive less, except the Lord Chancellor who receives £79,400. The PM declines to take her full entitlement of £62,700.)

Ministers Not in the Cabinet

Minister of State for Foreign and Commonwealth Affairs (4).
Financial Secretary, Treasury.
Economic Secretary, Treasury.
Minister of State, Treasury.
Minister for Housing, Urban Affairs and Construction.
Minister for Local Government.
Minister for Environment and Planning.
Minister of State, Department of Energy.
Minister of State, Department of Education and Science.
Minister for the Arts.
Minister of State, for Armed Forces.
Minister of State, for Defence Procurement.
Minister of State, Home Office (3).
Minister for Trade.
Minister for Information Technology.
Minister for Industry.
Minister for Health.
Minister for Social Security.
Minister of State, Transport.

Minister of State, Scottish Office.
Minister of State, Northern Ireland Office.
Minister of State, Ministry of Agriculture, Fisheries and Food (2).

(Each is currently paid £40,000 p.a. except for a Minister of State in the Foreign Office, the DOE, the Scottish Office and the MAFF, who receive £47,000 p.a., and the Parliamentary Secretary to the Treasury who receives £44,000 p.a.)

Law Officers

Attorney General.
Lord Advocate.
Solicitor General.
Solicitor General for Scotland.

In addition there are fifty-four other members of the Government, including Parliamentary Secretaries, Under-Secretaries and Whips. Collectively known as 'Junior Ministers'.

The Prime Minister

History

When political parties began to form in the eighteenth century certain dominant personalities emerged as leaders. Sir Robert Walpole who headed the Government from 1721 to 1742 is generally regarded as the first Prime Minister. There was, however, no clearly defined office as such nor was the Cabinet constituted as it is today. English institutions have grown from experience and need. The former executive powers of the Sovereign in the early Privy Council were transferred to a Prime Minister and a Cabinet. This body (the Cabinet) is now the effective apex of the political power in the State.

This transfer of power was more a gradual evolution. Thus in Walpole's administration the King selected the Ministers, not Walpole. Nevertheless, Walpole unified the group of Whigs, and dissentient members unable to support his policies were dismissed or compelled to resign. This foreshadowed the later principle of 'collective responsibility' (see p. 131). When Walpole resigned in 1742 his Ministers did not, however, resign with him. The only resemblanace between Walpole and a Prime Minister today is that the latter still holds the office of First Lord of the Treasury and resides at 10 Downing Street, London, W1.

William Pitt, the Younger, who was in office between 1783–1801 and 1804–6, was a strong Prime Minister, and further consolidated the work of Walpole. In 1834 Sir Robert Peel became Prime Minister and formed a Cabinet of fourteen members. He was able to oversee all the government business of the day whether home or overseas affairs.

The *Reform Act 1832*, and the extension of the franchise had a great effect on the general political scene, and the modern Cabinet began to take shape.

During the nineteenth century Mr W. E. Gladstone (Liberal) and Benjamin Disraeli (Conservative), were the important Prime Ministers who both further developed the office. Disraeli signed the *Treaty of Berlin* in 1878 as 'Prime Minister of England' the first time the office was officially named. In 1905 the Prime Minister was granted by Royal Warrant precedence next after the Archbishop of York.

The Prime Minister is now normally the acknowledged head of the party commanding a majority in the House of Commons. We have noted (see p. 123) that it is only on occasions when no party commands an absolute majority in the House, or when the majority party has no acknowledged head that the Royal discretion as to choice of a Prime Minister may be exercised.

Offices held

There is no salary assigned to the office of 'Prime Minister'. S/He draws the salary of whatever **other** office s/he holds. The Lord Treasurer was regarded at the end of the seventeenth century as the most important Government official, and the leading Minister (i.e. the Prime Minister) has normally held the office of First Commissioner (or First Lord) of the Treasury since that time. By virtue of this post the Prime Minister may draw a salary of £62,700 per annum (under the *Ministers of the Crown Act, 1937*, as amended) though in practice Mrs Thatcher takes only £51,000 (1988).

The Earl of Chatham (PM in 1766) was also Lord Privy Seal; the Marquess of Salisbury (PM in 1895) was also successively Foreign Secretary and Lord Privy Seal. Winston Churchill, during the Second World War, was both Prime Minister and Minister of Defence. Edward Heath acted as First Lord of the Treasury and Minister for the Civil Service. Harold Wilson followed suit in 1974, as did James Callaghan (1976) and Margaret Thatcher (1979).

Residence

The official residence of Prime Ministers is 10 Downing Street, London. They also have the use of *Chequers*, a country mansion in Buckinghamshire.

The PM as an MP

In the eighteenth century Cabinets consisted almost solely of peers, though the Leading Minister (the Prime Minister) was frequently recruited from the Commons. In the nineteenth century, however, MPs formed the bulk of the Cabinet though, curiously enough, the Prime Minister was frequently a peer.

With the expansion of the franchise and the reduction of the powers of the Lords (by the *Parliament Act, 1911*) it became difficult for a peer to exercise the premiership from the House of Lords. The last peer to be Prime Minister was Lord Salisbury who resigned in 1902. In 1923 Lord Curzon (a contender for the post) was passed over in favour of Stanley Baldwin. This showed decisively the need for a Prime Minister to be a member of the Commons and thus answerable to that Chamber. In 1963

Lord Home was appointed Prime Minister. He thereupon immediately disclaimed his peerage, and was subsequently elected to the House of Commons as Sir Alec Douglas-Home, MP.

The Power of the Prime Minister

In considering the power of Prime Ministers, we look first at their main functions. Thus a Prime Minister:

  (i) Is leader of the majority party in Parliament.
 (ii) Is Head of the Government (i.e. the Administration).
(iii) Selects Cabinet Ministers.
 (iv) Appoints other members of the Government (i.e. non-Cabinet Ministers) numbering about 100.
  (v) May move Ministers from one post to another (a 'reshuffle').
 (vi) May dismiss Cabinet (or other) Ministers, or call upon a Minister to resign from the Government.
(vii) Is Chairman of the Cabinet and several Cabinet Committees.
(viii) Co-ordinates policy and supervises Departments' activities.
 (ix) Is the nation's chief spokesman in international and domestic affairs.
  (x) Is ultimately responsible for party discipline. He appoints the Chief Whips who maintain close contact with him.
 (xi) Exercises patronage (i.e. he appoints to more than 180 offices, including judicial and ecclesiastical), dispenses titles, peerages.
(xii) Is political head of the Civil Service, and collaborates with the Head of the Home Civil Service over senior Civil Service appointments and promotions.
(xiii) Communicates the Government's decisions to HM The Queen, and advises when Parliament may be dissolved.

This is a considerable list of functions and powers vested in the Prime Minister under the Constitution. Indeed, Richard Crossman has declared that, 'The post-war epoch has seen the final transformation of Cabinet Government into Prime Ministerial Government.' When one adds to these the fact the Prime Minister is frequently in the public eye, on television and radio and in the Press, his impact on the public can be very great, particularly if he has a 'good public image'. There is a tendency nowadays to personalise organisations and ideas, e.g. 'the Wilson era', 'the Heath Government', 'Thatcherism' and the leader's performance as Prime Minister can influence the people's voting decisions. In these various roles, the Prime Minister has to decide whether to act as a leader and initiator or rather as a conciliator, waiting for events to happen.

Mrs Thatcher has been portrayed as a very autocratic (or Boadicean) Prime Minister. She has declared herself to be a 'conviction politician', and on different occasions has stated that this 'lady's not for turning' and, 'as Prime Minister I could not waste time having any internal arguments'. It is widely believed that she dominates (even browbeats) her Cabinet, and that she by-passes or manipulates it on occasion by use of Cabinet committees or other smaller consultative groupings (see P. Hennessy, *Cabinet*). One ex-Minister, John Biffen, even described her Cabinet style as 'Stalinist'! (1986).

The Limits of Power of the Prime Minister

Providing Prime Ministers have the support of their Cabinet colleagues and command a majority in the Commons they may expect to serve out their five-year term of office. But if a Government is defeated on a major issue in the Commons then, by convention, the Prime Minister must request a dissolution of Parliament, whereupon a general election will be held (as happened with Mr Callaghan's Government in 1979, it resulted from the Government's loss of support by the Scottish Nationalist MPs who were upset at the Government's plans to abandon devolution).

A Prime Minister may be forced to resign from his office by his own party. In 1916 Mr Asquith was forced to resign as Prime Minister following dissatisfaction within the Cabinet over his conduct of the war of 1914–18. Similarly Neville Chamberlain was forced to resign in 1940 by dissentient members in the Cabinet and Parliament, again over his leadership in war. There was discontent over Eden's policy in 1956, and Mr Macmillan's in 1963.

If a Prime Minister becomes ill he may of course resign. But if he does not do so, pressure may be brought to bear on him to resign.

Although a Prime Minister is legally free to select whomsoever he will to be a member of the Cabinet there are practical and political limits to this power. One is the availability of talent within his own party. For example, if a party has been in opposition for some time there will be few MPs with previous Cabinet experience (cf. Attlee's Labour Government of 1945).

Another limitation on Cabinet composition is the standing of certain members in the party. Some may have a large following and cannot be omitted for fear of alienating sympathisers within the party. Some MPs are outstanding personalities and have obvious political abilities. If such are omitted they may cause splits or splinter groups to form within the party. A Prime Minister must be careful to avoid giving important ministerial posts to minor figures. Friendship is important in all walks of life. Hence to be friends with a Prime Minister is an asset, but that alone is insufficient and there is little evidence that well qualified politicians (unfriendly to a Prime Minister) have been deliberately excluded from office on that account alone. Some MPs, particularly if they have had successful Cabinet experience already, are able by their importance to nominate their own departments in which they would be prepared to serve.

Dismissals

Clearly, a Prime Minister may dismiss a weak and ineffectual Minister. It has been said that a Prime Minister must be a 'good butcher'. Macmillan, in 1962, for example, dismissed one-third of his Cabinet, i.e. seven Cabinet Ministers, and the loyalty of the Conservative Party endured that strain. Margaret Thatcher has dismissed, in a period of five years, over a dozen of her Ministers. But a Prime Minister cannot go too far for fear that the dismissals may recoil on his own head by spreading discontent among backbenchers and insecurity among the remaining Cabinet Ministers. Prime Ministers must, in the last resort, **earn** the support and confidence of their party members. They cannot compel it.

Policy Determination

A Prime Minister cannot alone determine policy. Each Minister, e.g. the Chancellor of the Exchequer, Foreign Secretary or Home Secretary, will have a strong brief for certain action or policy. Moreover, policy information occurs within the party, research bodies, Cabinet Committees, and many decisions are formed before reaching the Cabinet when it is too late for the PM to alter them. A PM will, therefore, be unwise to drive through a policy which is disagreeable. A Minister whose particular view or policy is already made public can, of course, resign, thus weakening the Cabinet. We must not forget that Ministers' political careers and party unity are at stake if a PM over-rides an accepted or formulated policy.

A Prime Minister cannot, in the complex situation and flux of modern life, keep in touch with all aspects of administration. Peel, in 1840, was able to know all that was going on in Government. It is different today.

The power of a Prime Minister to take decisions alone or after consulting an individual Minister is limited. Important decisions (i.e. those likely to affect the nation as a whole) must go through the whole Cabinet. Similarly where there is no unanimous agreement in a Cabinet Committee the matter must be decided by the full Cabinet. However, some important decisions are known to have been taken in small, inner groupings and the Cabinet has been virtually by-passed (e.g. the decision to make the A-bomb, by Attlee in 1951; the Suez invasion, by Eden in 1956; the adoption of the Chevaline missile, by Callaghan in 1978 and the ban on trade unions at GCHQ by Mrs Thatcher in 1984).

Generally we may say that the power of a PM varies with the times (e.g. in war or peace), with the style and aptitude of the Prime Minister, and the ability, experience and determination of his colleagues in the Cabinet.

Mrs Thatcher has proved to be a 'strong' PM who has determined the direction of a number of government policies—notably in the economic field (though cuts in public expenditure have been somewhat resisted by some spending Ministers). She has appointed a policy unit containing a number of advisers (on economic policy, foreign policy, etc.) to strengthen her hand: thus something of a Prime Minister's Department appears to be emerging.

Qualities of Leadership

A Prime Minister is the leader of his political party which wins an election. What, we may ask, are the specifications for the ideal PM? No clear answer can be given to this question. History shows that each occupant of the office has different capacities and skills. Moreover the times and circumstances may call for different personalities: a good war-time leader, e.g. Lloyd George or Churchill, may not be equally effective in peace time.

The demands of office, both physical and mental, are extraordinarily heavy. It follows that a Prime Minister must be physically strong and have a good constitution. S/He must be able to work twenty hours a day on occasion, and be able to eat and drink at all hours of the day. S/He must be able to snatch sleep whenever possible, relaxing completely.

Educationally it is not necessary that s/he hold a first-class honours degree or have high academic qualifications. Ramsay MacDonald, Lloyd George, Winston Churchill and James Callaghan had no university education. Nevertheless any Prime Minister today must have the capacity to assimilate much knowledge and possess an orderly vigorous mind.

S/He must be industrious and able to work under pressure. S/He must possess initiative, be able to organise others and get his policies accepted and pushed through Parliament. In short an ability to get things done.

S/He must possess judgement in public affairs, knowing when and where to intervene in a political situation. S/He must on occasions be patient. When political storms and crises arise (e.g. a threat of war) he must show courage. S/He must also possess the strength of mind not to worry, and a sense of humour capable of riding out the daily rebuffs and criticism which are the lot of all politicians in a free democratic society. S/He must have the strength to dismiss Cabinet colleagues (even friends) if need so dictates.

Finally we may mention the ability to use television and radio effectively. When a Prime Minister speaks on the television s/he is watched by millions at home and possibly overseas. A good 'public image' is a useful asset.

Cabinet Ministers, no less than a Prime Minister, must show leadership and possess the qualities mentioned above. A Prime Minister cannot make all decisions; certain important ones are left to a Departmental Minister. For example, the Home Secretary formerly had the awesome responsibility of deciding life or death when a convicted murderer appealed to the Monarch for reprieve.

Government intervenes more and more in public and social affairs, and the actions and decisions of Government Ministers vitally affect the lives of millions. The pace and stress of life are reflected in Government, making more and greater demands on those persons in whom political power has been lawfully vested to act in the best interests of the nation. A study of the newspapers will reveal current topical issues at home and abroad to which Government must react and in respect of which vital decisions must be made.

Government Departments

Government Departments are the main instruments for putting into effect Government policy after Parliament has passed the necessary legislation. Departments (i.e. Ministers and civil servants) are required to ensure that services already in existence are carried on efficiently and smoothly until such time as the Cabinet or Minister thinks fit to change them by legislation.

Departments are formed mainly on the basis of the *service* they provide (such as education or defence). The alternative is to establish Departments on the *clientele* principle (such as Departments for children or the unemployed). The service principle was favoured by the Haldane Report (*Committee on the Machinery of Government*, 1918) but it has not been slavishly followed, for example, some Departments are geographically based (Scottish Office, Welsh Office).

A change of government does not necessarily affect the number or general functions of Government Departments, though a change in policy

may be accompanied by organisational change. The scope of Government activity has, however, in the last fifty years led to the formation of many new Departments. In 1970, for example, Mr Heath created two new posts, both of Cabinet rank: (i) Secretary of State for Trade and Industry and President of the Board of Trade, and (ii) Secretary of State for the Environment (their functions and responsibilities are described below). A few Departments such as the Home Office, the Foreign Office and the Treasury have existed for over two hundred years. Some Departments are very recent creations—the result of new problems (e.g. energy). But sometimes they are created to give a public impression of Governmental activity; or they may even result from the whim of a prominent politician.

The work of some Departments, e.g. the Board of Customs and Excise, covers the United Kingdom as a whole. Other Departments such as the Departments of Trade or Industry cover Great Britain (England, Wales, and Scotland, but not Northern Ireland) and the Department of Housing and Local Government (which now falls under the general control of the Department of the Environment) covers England only. There are separate Departments (or Offices) for Scotland, Wales and Northern Ireland.

Departments are usually headed by Ministers, mainly known as Secretaries of State with salaries of some £51,000 (1988 figure). There are, however, certain Departments in which questions of policy do not normally arise and which are headed by a permanent official, a Minister with other duties being responsible for them to Parliament. Thus, Treasury Ministers are responsible for a number of Departments, e.g. Her Majesty's Stationery Office, the Central Office of Information, the Treasury Solicitor's Department, the Department of the Government Actuary, the Royal Mint, the National Debt Office, the Public Works Loan Board, and the National Savings Committee. The staff of the Departments are all members of a body of Crown servants known as the Civil Service (see p. 157).

Internal Organisation of Government Departments

Departments of Government vary in size and in the volume, type and complexity of their work. Each Department makes its own arrangements for discharging its duties and there are variations in internal organisation. However, most Departments have certain features in common.

The Minister is, of course, at the head of his Department and is politically responsible to Parliament. Under the Minister there is usually a **Permanent Secretary**. In those departments where the Minister is a 'Secretary of State', the chief civil servant in the Ministry is known as Permanent Under-Secretary of State. Below this office there will be one or more Deputy Secretaries; below these a number of Under-Secretaries and Assistant Secretaries.

Major Departments (e.g. the Home Office) have a Principal Finance Officer and Organisation Officer. A number of Establishment Divisions within a Ministry have their own Organisation and Methods Branch (O and M Branch), the members of which act in an advisory capacity to the Permanent Under-Secretary. Many Government Departments also have their own legal advisers or solicitors, and their own Information Divisions.

Some Government Departments maintain a regional organisation, and some have direct contact with the public throughout the country by maintaining local offices, e.g. the Department of Employment which, through the Manpower Services Commission, maintains Job Centres for employers seeking labour, for workers who are unemployed or who wish to change jobs, and also for the validation of unemployment benefits.

Advisory Bodies

One device to ensure that a Minister is adequately informed on matters falling within his Department is the Advisory Council or Committee (or 'Quango'). Most Departments are assisted by such bodies of which there are now hundreds (see p. 377). This in itself gives an indication of the complexity of public administration. The object of these bodies is to enable the Minister to be the better informed so that any executive action or proposed legislation is taken on the best available information or professional opinion.

Sometimes a statute lays down that a Minister is *required* to consult a Standing Committee; on other occasions he *may* seek their advice. In either case the final decision is the Minister's, not the Committee's. Examples of these advisory bodies are: (i) Central Advisory Councils for Education (*Education Act, 1944*); (ii) Police Council (*Police Act, 1914*); (iii) Central Advisory Council for Science and Technology; (iv) Social Security Advisory Committee (*Social Security Act, 1980*).

Membership of the advisory committees varies. Some contain experts including scientists, medical practitioners, pathologists, agriculturalists and veterinary surgeons and the like, while others include civil servants (who serve to act as a link with a particular Government Department) and representatives of various interests, e.g. industrialists, trade unionists, educationists, lawyers, local government councillors and local government officers.

In addition to these committees a Minister may set in motion a **Royal Commission** with a chairman of some standing and a membership representing informed opinion from various walks of life. A commission examines written and oral evidence from Government Departments and other interested organisations—official and unofficial—and individuals. A commission (or committee) will then submit a report with recommendations. It is for the Government to accept the report in whole or in part, or to take (or defer) action as a matter of policy. A recent example is the Redcliffe–Maud Commission on Local Government Reform (see p. 327) or the Royal Commission on the NHS, 1979.

In addition to the above a Minister may at any time cause an inquiry to be undertaken within his own Department by a 'Departmental Committee', e.g. the Maud Report, 1967 (see p. 363), the Widdicombe Report on the Conduct of Local Government, 1986, or the Peacock Report on Advertising in the BBC, 1986.

Today there is a proliferation of reports and an abundance of advice, all emanating from reputable sources. The problem of the Government (or Minister) is the arrangement of priorities.

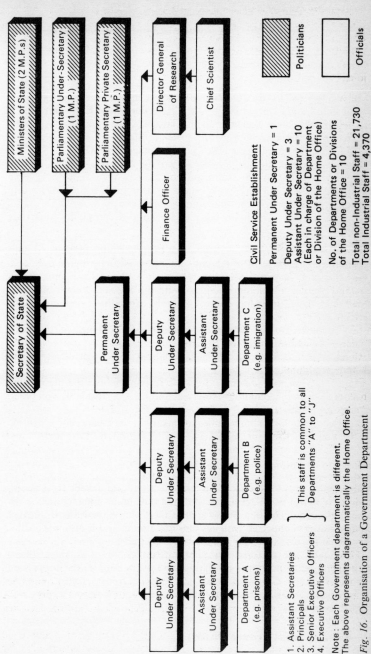

Fig. 16. Organisation of a Government Department

Politicians

Officials

Civil Service Establishment

Permanent Under Secretary = 1

Deputy Under Secretary = 3
Assistant Under Secretary = 10
(Each in charge of Department
or Division of the Home Office)

No. of Departments or Divisions
of the Home Office = 10

Total non-Industrial Staff = 21,730
Total Industrial Staff = 4,370

1. Assistant Secretaries
2. Principals
3. Senior Executive Officers
4. Executive Officers

} This staff is common to all
Departments "A" to "J".

Note: Each Government department is different.
The above represents diagrammatically the Home Office.

Ministers of State (2 M.P.s)

Parliamentary Under-Secretary
(1 M.P.)

Parliamentary Private Secretary
(1 M.P.)

Director General
of Research

Chief Scientist

Secretary of State

Permanent
Under Secretary

Finance Officer

Deputy
Under Secretary

Assistant
Under Secretary

Department C
(e.g. imigration)

Deputy
Under Secretary

Assistant
Under Secretary

Department B
(e.g. police)

Deputy
Under Secretary

Assistant
Under Secretary

Department A
(e.g. prisons)

The Treasury (14,000 staff)

The nominal heads of the Treasury are the Lords Commissioners, viz.:

The First Lord of the Treasury (now always the Prime Minister).
The Chancellor of the Exchequer.
Five Junior Lords.

In practice the Lords Commissioners never meet as a board, and their responsibilities are carried out by the **Chancellor of the Exchequer** who is assisted by the Chief Secretary to the Treasury, the Financial Secretary, the Economic Secretary and two Ministers of State.

All the above are political posts, i.e. the holders are MPs.

There is also a Parliamentary Secretary to the Treasury, who is the Chief Government Whip in the House of Commons whose duties have been outlined on page 72. The Treasury, as its name implies, is the Government Department primarily responsible for the development of Britain's overall economic strategy. The main body of its work is carried by four large groups or Sectors, viz.:

(i) *Public Services Sector* is responsible for controlling aggregate public expenditure and for most of the individual expenditure programmes.

(ii) *Domestic Economy Sector* is concerned with fiscal (i.e. tax), monetary and counter-inflation policies, and with the Treasury's contribution to industrial policies, including control of public expenditure on industry and agriculture.

(iii) *Overseas Finance Sector* is responsible for balance of payments policies, the management of Britain's foreign currency reserves, international monetary questions, financial relations with other countries and the aid programme.

(iv) *Chief Economic Adviser's Sector* is responsible for the preparation of short-term and medium-term forecasts and for specialist advice on broad economic policies.

In discharging his responsibilities for taxation, the Chancellor is assisted by the Board of Customs and Excise, and by the Inland Revenue.

The Board of Customs and Excise (25,000)

The primary duty of the Board is to collect and administer the customs and excise duties and VAT as laid down in the annual Finance Acts or by other legislation. The Board also advises the Chancellor of the Exchequer on any matters connected with customs and excise, and is also responsible for preventing and detecting the evasion of the revenue laws.

The Board also performs miscellaneous duties for other Departments such as the enforcement of prohibitions and restrictions on the import and export of certain classes of goods, exchange currency control, and the compilation of UK overseas trade statistics from customs export and import documents.

The Board of Inland Revenue (70,000)

The Board administers the laws relating to (i) income tax; (ii) corporation tax; (iii) capital gains tax; (iv) stamp duty; (v) estate duty, and certain other direct taxes. It also advises the Chancellor of the Exchequer on any matters connected with the taxes. The Board of Inland Revenue is also responsible for the valuation of real property (i.e. land and buildings for such purposes as compensation for compulsory purchase), local rates in England and Wales and for estate duty. It also collects tithe redemption annuities. Up to 1968, the Treasury was also responsible for Civil Service matters. In that year, following the Fulton Report (see p. 159) a separate Ministry—the **Civil Service Department**—was created. It was placed under the control of the Prime Minister with responsibility for its day-to-day work delegated to a senior Minister. The new Department became responsible for all matters pertaining to the Civil Service—recruitment, training, grading, pay, management services, etc.

From the beginning doubts had been expressed about the wisdom of such a move, many feeling that the Treasury was the natural locus of establishment (personnel) matters. Following an official review in January 1981, the Government rejected suggestions for a restoration of Treasury responsibility for the Civil Service. However, in November 1981 a partial re-integration took place when the Civil Service Department was abolished. Consequently, the Treasury now has responsibility for Civil Service manpower, pay, pensions, and the central computer and telecommunications agency. The other aspects of the Civil Service, i.e. organisation, management, recruitment policy, training and personnel management, are now the responsibility of a new **Management and Personnel Office (MPO)**, responsible on a day-to-day basis to the Chancellor of the Duchy of Lancaster, but ultimately to the Prime Minister. This functions within the **Cabinet Office** (which also contains the Cabinet Secretariat and the Central Statistical Office, see p. 132) whose Permanent Secretary (formerly Sir Robert Armstrong now Robin Butler) is the Head of the Civil Service.

It should be noted that the *Civil Service Commission*, formerly part of the Civil Service Department, now forms part of the new Management and Personnel Office. The Civil Service Commission was first constituted by Order in Council in 1855. It is responsible for the examination and selection of permanent civil servants, and in the discharge of this function specific and formal arrangements have been made to ensure its independence and impartiality (see p. 158). In this respect it is assisted by the Civil Service Selection Board ('Cisbee').

Parliamentary Counsel to the Treasury. The Office of the Parliamentary Counsel is responsible for the drafting of all Government Bills (legislative), except those Bills or provisions of Bills exclusively affecting Scotland, which are dealt with by the Lord Advocate's Department. The Office drafts all financial and other Parliamentary motions and amendments moved by the Government during the passage of Bills. It also advises Departments on questions of Parliamentary procedure, and its officials (lawyers) attend sittings and committees in both Houses. The Office also drafts subordinate legislation (see p. 286), and advises the Government on legal, parliamentary, and constitutional questions falling within its special experience.

The Ministry of Agriculture, Fisheries and Food (12,000)

This Department is responsible in England and Wales for administering government policy for the agriculture, horticulture, and fishing industries.

It is directed by the Minister of Agriculture, Fisheries, and Food, assisted by two Ministers of State and a Parliamentary Secretary.

Today the Department is concerned with the administration, in co-operation with the Intervention Board for Agriculture Produce, of the agricultural support system arising from the Common Agricultural Policy of the enlarged EEC. The Ministry also administers schemes such as the control and eradication of animal and plant diseases and for the improvement and drainage of agricultural land; and it has responsibilities for applied research and development.

As to food, the Ministry is concerned with the safety and quality of food and with food hygiene, including standards of composition, labelling and advertising, food additives and contaminants; and has some responsibilities for public health standards in the production and handling of basic foods in cargoes, stores and slaughterhouses. The Ministry also has overall responsibility for questions of food supply, food, and drink industries and also acts as agent of the Department of Prices and Consumer Protection for the detailed administration of subsidies on food.

As to Wales, the Secretary of State for Wales has joint responsibility with the Minister for a number of functions. The Minister has also operational control of certain diseases of animals in Scotland.

The Ministry maintains relations with Commonwealth and foreign countries and takes part in the activities of a number of international organisations, e.g. the Food and Agriculture Organisation of the UN and the Organisation for Economic Co-operation and Development (OECD).

Under the *European Communities Act, 1972*, the Intervention Board for Agricultural Produce was set up. It is responsible for implementing market support arrangements in the UK and certain other aspects of the European Community's Common Agricultural Policy provided for under the guarantee section of the European Guidance and Guarantee Fund.

The Ministry of Defence (MOD) (200,000)

This Government Department is responsible for (i) defence policy, and (ii) the control and administration of the three fighting Services—the Navy, Army, and Air Force.

The Secretary of State for Defence has a seat in the Cabinet and is in charge of the Department. He is assisted by a Minister of State for Defence who is responsible for personnel and logistics (moving men and supplying them with equipment, etc.), research, development and production. There are also three Parliamentary Under-Secretaries with responsibilities for the respective Services.

The Department of Education and Science (DES) (2,400)

This falls under the control of the Secretary of State for Education and Science (a Cabinet post). The Department is organised into various branches: (i) schools; (ii) further education (including vocational, recreational, and adult education and the youth service); (iii) teachers, and kindred subjects in England and Wales; (iv) universities; (v) civil science; and (vi) support for the arts throughout Great Britain. The Department is also responsible for National Libraries policy and all general policy matters relating to libraries. There are specialist branches within the Department which advise on health, building, planning (e.g. educational research and statistics), law. The Department also has an information service.

The Department's responsibilities for the development of Primary, Secondary, and Further Education include dealing with the supply, training, and superannuation of teachers, the building of new schools and other institutions, the school health service, the special educational treatment of handicapped children, and the provision of school meals.

The Department works in co-operation with local education authorities who are required to secure adequate facilities for all forms of education in their areas. The Department's relations with the universities are conducted through the University Grants Committee. Its activities in the field of civil science are discharged through five research councils: the Medical Research Council, the Agricultural Research Council, the Natural Environment Research Council, the Economic and Social Research Council, and the Science Research Council. The Council for Scientific Policy advises the Secretary of State. A Minister of State and two Parliamentary Under-Secretaries assist the Secretary of State in the discharge of the duties of the Department.

The Department of Employment (30,000)

This Department has general responsibility for manpower policies and the formulation of labour legislation. It is also responsible for monitoring and producing statistics on labour market trends, pay and prices. More specifically it deals with the payment of unemployment benefit and tax refunds to the unemployed; the issue of work permits to workers from overseas; the Race Relations and Employment Advisory services; and Britain's relations with the International Labour Office and other such international bodies.

The Secretary of State for Employment is assisted by a Minister of State and two Parliamentary Under-Secretaries of State.

Members of the Advisory, Conciliation, and Arbitration Service or ACAS (6,500 staff who deal with industrial disputes), the Manpower Services Commission (22,000 staff responsible for running the Jobcentres and training schemes) and the Health and Safety Commission (3,500 staff responsible for the formulation at national level of policy and accident prevention under the *Health and Safety at Work Act, 1974*) are appointed by the Secretary of State for Employment. (These bodies are further examples of quangos—see p. 377.)

The Foreign and Commonwealth Office (FCO) (10,000)

The Secretary of State for Foreign and Commonwealth Affairs is one of the most important officials and is a member of the Cabinet. The Department acts as a channel of communication between the British Government and the governments of foreign and overseas Commonwealth countries for the discussion and negotiation of all matters (including economic issues) falling within the sphere of international and Commonwealth relations.

One of its functions is the drawing up of international treaties and agreements.

The Department provides the means by which the British Government is represented in the United Nations Organisation and other bodies and by which it is kept informed about developments in countries overseas; by which British subjects and interests abroad are protected and trade promoted; and by which British policy is explained to governments and peoples overseas. It also discharges the British Government's responsibilities in the Associated States (e.g. Antigua, Dominica, Grenada, St Kitts-Nevis, Anguilla and St Lucia) and the Dependent Territories of the Commonwealth. In the cases of the Associated States the British Government's responsibilities relate mainly to defence and external affairs. In the Dependent Territories, each of which has its own internal administration, the British Government is finally responsible for good government and for the relations between these territories and other countries.

The Secretary of State (Foreign Secretary) is assisted by four Ministers of State (one of whom has special responsibility for Overseas Development) and a Parliamentary Under-Secretary. He is the UK representative in the Council of Ministers of the European Community.

The Department of Health and Social Security (DHSS) (94,000)

This Department is under the charge of the Secretary of State for Social Services (a Cabinet post). The Department is responsible (in England) for the administration of the National Health Service, the social services provided by local authorities for the elderly and handicapped, socially deprived families and aspects of public health, including hygiene. Throughout Great Britain the Department is responsible for (i) the payment of benefits (e.g. sickness benefits), (ii) the collection of contributions under the national insurance and industrial injuries' schemes, and (iii) the payment of family benefits. The Department also makes reciprocal social security arrangements with other countries, and represents the United Kingdom on the World Health Organisation (WHO) of the United Nations.

The Department is responsible (i) for determining awards of non-contributory benefits (e.g. for the destitute); (ii) for reception centres (e.g. for vagrants or those having no home to go to); and (iii) for assessing the means whereby people can apply for legal aid (see p. 239). In addition, the Department has responsibilities in connection with pensions and welfare services (including in some cases medical and surgical treatment) for war pensioners in the United Kingdom, the Channel Islands, the Isle of Man, and the Republic of Ireland, and for UK war pensioners living in Northern Ireland or in countries overseas.

The Secretary of State is assisted by two Ministers of State (one each for Health and Social Security) and two Parliamentary Under-Secretaries.

The Home Office (36,000)

The Ministerial head of the Home Office is the Secretary of State for the Home Department (the Home Secretary) who is always accorded Cabinet rank by virtue of the importance of his responsibilities. First we should observe that all matters of national administration not specially assigned to other Ministers are entrusted to the Home Secretary. For this reason he is sometimes described as the 'residuary legatee'. His duties are now practically restricted to the domestic affairs of England and Wales, the Channel Islands, and the Isle of Man.

The Home Secretary's duties may be classified thus:

(i) He is the recognised channel of communication between the Crown and the subject in all cases where no other special procedure is laid down.

(ii) He is responsible for the maintenance of internal law and order.

(iii) He administers much statute law, particularly in regard to the welfare of the community, though some of this work has been redistributed to other Departments: the Department of Health and Social Security; the Department of Employment.

The chief matters falling within the scope of the Home Office are:

(i) *Police*. The Home Secretary is directly in control of the Metropolitan Police and assumes indirect control of provincial forces.

(ii) *Administration of Justice*. The Home Secretary has control over the organisation of magistrates' courts, the appointment of Metropolitan magistrates and stipendiary magistrates; the introduction of legislation on criminal justice; the criminal injuries' compensation scheme.

(iii) *Extradition*. The Home Secretary exercises control over the extradition of criminals.

(iv) *Prerogatives of Pardon and Mercy*. The Home Secretary advises the Monarch on these matters.

(v) *Immigration and Aliens*. The Home Secretary is responsible for immigration and for the admission, supervision and deportation of aliens. He also grants certificates of naturalisation to aliens desirous of becoming British subjects.

(vi) *Prisons, Probation, After-care of Prisoners*. The Home Secretary is responsible for these services.

(vii) *Fire Service*. The Home Secretary maintains central control of the Fire Service.

(viii) *Parliamentary and Local Government Elections*. The Home Secretary is responsible for the administration of the law relating to these matters.

(ix) *By-laws of Local Authorities*. The Home Secretary is responsible for sanctioning by-laws made by local authorities in so far as they relate to 'law and order' and 'good governance'.

(x) *Petitions and Addresses to the Sovereign*. The Home Secretary is responsible for receiving and submitting addresses and petitions to the Sovereign and preparing presentations to Parliament.

(xi) *Miscellaneous*. These matters include preparing patents of nobility for peers and formal proceedings for the bestowal of honours; granting licences for scientific experiments on animals; ordering the exhumation and removal of bodies; supervising the control of explosives, firearms and dangerous drugs; deciding general policies on the law of liquor licensing and of shops; the general policy on the law relating to music and dancing;

community relations problems; the regulation of employment of children and young persons; co-ordinating government action in relation to the voluntary social services; equal opportunities for women.

Finally, the Home Secretary controls the relations with Northern Ireland, the Channel Islands, and Isle of Man, and is the medium of communication between the Established Church and the Crown.

In the discharge of his duties the Home Secretary is assisted by two Ministers of State (not of Cabinet rank) and one Parliamentary Under-Secretary.

The Central Office of Information (COI)

This is a common-service Department which produces information and publicity material, and supplies publicity services required by other Government Departments. In the United Kingdom it conducts Government press, television and poster advertising, produces booklets, leaflets, films, television material, exhibitions, photographs and other visual material, and distributes Departmental press notices.

For the Foreign and Commonwealth Office it supplies British information posts overseas and similar publicity material, and manages schemes for promoting the overseas sale of British books, periodicals, and newspapers.

It is responsible for British pavilions at world exhibitions (e.g. Expo' 70) and for exhibition services on behalf of the Board of Trade at overseas trade fairs and British Weeks. It also organises tours for visitors officially invited to Britain. Nine regional information offices are maintained in England, which provide services for the Home Departments and assist the overseas services by providing material.

The Central Office of Information is administratively responsible to Treasury Ministers, but the Ministers whose Departments it serves are responsible for the policy expressed in its work.

The Department of the Environment (DOE) (35,000)

This Department is responsible in England for a wide range of functions relating to the physical environment in which people live and work. It is under the control of a Secretary of State and is concerned primarily with the strategic issues of policy and priorities, including public expenditure, which determine the operations of the department as a whole. The Secretary of State is assisted by two senior ministers:

(i) The Minister for Local Government and Environment Services, who is responsible for statutory and regional planning; development control; land policy; commercial property; new towns; local government, structure and finance; water and sewerage; minerals; and conservation.

(ii) The Minister for Housing and Construction is responsible for the policy and finance of the housing programme; the construction industries; and the Property Services Agency (which provides nearly all Government common services relating to land, property, buildings and furnishings).

Of the four Parliamentary Under-Secretaries, one acts as Minister for Sport; another has, since February 1982, special responsibility for race relations.

Department of Transport (DOT) (14,000)

This Department, headed by a Secretary of State assisted by two Under-Secretaries, is responsible in England for the main inland transport industries (including railways, buses, freight and ports). It is also responsible for the planning and construction of motorways and trunk roads (though matters arising from public inquiries are shared with the Department of the Environment). This Department also has responsibility for local transport, road and vehicle safety, and for vehicle and driving licensing.

The Department of Trade and Industry (DTI) (15,000)

This Department has two broad areas of responsibility. First, it is responsible for general industrial policy, both national and regional. Particular functions include sponsorship of private industries; provision of technical services to industry as a whole; and oversight of industrial development and finance. The Department exercises government policy in relation to aerospace and industrial research and development (including supervision of industrial research establishments). It acts as the 'sponsoring' department and is responsible to Parliament for British Aerospace, British Shipbuilders, British Steel and the Post Office Corporation (see ch. 5). Second it is responsible for commercial policy and Britain's trade relations with other countries. It promotes Britain's commercial interests overseas, negotiates trade and commercial matters and administers Britain's protective tariffs. It sponsors the work of the British Overseas Trade Board in export services and Government support for overseas trade fairs and provides an information service to industry. The Department is also responsible for **consumer affairs** and business competition policy. It also supervises companies legislation, the insurance industry, and the insolvency service together with patent work, trade-mark and copyright matters. Other responsibilities include civil aviation, marine and shipping policy, tourism, hotel and travel industries, the newspapers, printing, publishing and film industries and the distributive and service trades.

The Department's regional offices also serve the Department of Energy. The Secretary of State is assisted by three Ministers and three Parliamentary Secretaries.

The Department of Energy (1,000)

This Department is concerned with the development of government policies for the supply and use of all forms of energy. It discharges functions connected with the nationalised coal, gas, and electricity industries; it is responsible for the Atomic Energy Authority; and is the sponsoring department for the nuclear power and oil industries. It is also responsible for the development of off-shore oil and gas resources in the British sector of the continental shelf, and deals with the international aspects of energy problems including relations and co-operation with oil-producing countries. It is the co-ordinating and sponsoring body for energy conservation policy, in addition to implementing measures not falling directly to any other department. The department also encourages the development of new sources of energy, being assisted by the Energy Technology Support Unit at Harwell, Oxfordshire.

The Secretary of State for Energy is supported by a Minister of State and two Parliamentary Under-Secretaries of State, one of whom is concerned with the development of oil and gas from the North Sea.

The Paymaster-General's Office (800)

This office acts as a banker for Government Departments (except the Boards of Inland Revenue and Customs and Excise for which separate arrangements exist). Money granted by Parliament is transferred, in such sums as may be required from day to day, from the Exchequer account to the account of the Paymaster-General at the Bank of England. Most payments of Government Departments are made by means of payable orders drawn on the Paymaster-General's Office. The orders are similar to cheques and the recipients (i.e. payees) obtain payments through the commercial banks, whose accounts at the Bank of England are in turn reimbursed by the Paymaster-General's Office.

The Paymaster-General's Office is also responsible for the regular payment of many public service pensions, including those of civil servants, teachers, and members of the National Health Service, as well as the retired pay and pensions of officers of the Armed Forces, their widows and dependants.

The Stationery Office (3,500)

Her Majesty's Stationery Office (HMSO) is responsible to the Chancellor of the Exchequer. The office is the central Department for providing Government printing, binding, and publishing, and for providing Government Departments with office machinery, equipment, and supplies, together with desk stationery.

The Controller of HMSO is the Queen's Printer of Acts of Parliament. The Stationery Office maintains thirteen printing and binding works where about one-third of all official printing is done, the remainder being carried out under contract with private printers. The Stationery Office maintains eight Government bookshops for the sales of official publications.

The Welsh Office (2,000)

The Secretary of State for Wales (a Cabinet minister) has for some time had full responsibility for government functions relating to child care, health, housing, local government, primary and secondary education, town and country planning, new towns, water and sewerage, roads, forestry, tourism, national parks and historic buildings, and shared responsibility for the administration of urban grants to areas of acute social deprivation and (with the Minister of Agriculture, Fisheries, and Food) for agriculture in Wales.

The Minister has direct responsibility in Wales for selective financial assistance to industry, and exercises a general responsibility for Welsh economic development. This part of the Secretary of State's work is strengthened by the establishment of a Welsh Development Agency, responsible to him, with important industrial and environmental functions. The Secretary of State has certain responsibilities for the National Library and National Museum in Wales.

The Welsh Office works closely with government departments concerned with economic and social planning through the Welsh Planning Board and Welsh Council.

The Secretary of State is assisted by two Parliamentary Under-Secretaries of State. There is a small ministerial office in London, but the Welsh Office is situated in Cardiff.

The Scottish Office (13,000)

The Secretary of State for Scotland is responsible for a number of functions which, in England and Wales, are distributed among a number of Government Departments. The Secretary of State is assisted by a Minister of State and three Parliamentary Under-Secretaries of State. The Scottish Law Officers are: (i) The Lord Advocate, and (ii) the Solicitor-General for Scotland.

The Secretary of State's duties are discharged by five Departments (each of equal status) collectively known as the Scottish Office:

(i) The Department of Agriculture and Fisheries for Scotland.
(ii) The Scottish Development Department.
(iii) The Scottish Education Department.
(iv) The Scottish Home and Health Department.
(v) The Scottish Economic Planning Department.

The Secretary of State is responsible for preparing and implementing economic plans for Scotland, applying regional policies of the EEC, and development of North Sea oil. He is advised as to this by the Scottish Economic Planning Council and the Scottish Economic Planning Board, together with officials of Government Departments concerned.

Day-to-day administration is carried on in Edinburgh, but each Department has representatives in London (where the Scottish Office is also located) for liaison and Parliamentary duties.

The Northern Ireland Office (200)

The Secretary of State for Northern Ireland (Ulster) has direct responsibility for constitutional developments, law, order and security and electoral matters. He also directs the work of six departments:

(i) The Department of Agriculture.
(ii) The Department of Economic Development.
(iii) The Department of Education.

(iv) The Department of the Environment.
 (v) The Department of Finance and Personnel.
(vi) The Department of Health and Social Services.

The Secretary of State is assisted by one Minister of State and four Under-Secretaries. (Northern Ireland has its own Civil Service and Civil Service Commission modelled on the counterpart in Britain.)

The Lord Chancellor's Department (10,000)

The Lord High Chancellor of Great Britain, more usually known as the Lord Chancellor, ranks eighth in order of precedence in England after the Queen, a status which reflects his importance as a Minister of the Crown chiefly responsible for the administration of justice.

The Lord Chancellor is appointed by the Crown on the advice of the Prime Minister. His position combines duties which are legislative, executive, and judicial. It is, therefore (somewhat controversially), an exception to the constitutional doctrine of the 'separation of powers'.

In his *legislative* capacity the Lord Chancellor presides over the House of Lords. He may take part in its debates and can vote in all of its divisions.

As an *executive* or administrative officer he is a member of the Cabinet, its chief legal and constitutional adviser and one of its representatives in the House of Lords. He is the Ministerial head of the Land Registry, the Public Record Office and the Public Trustee, and he provides assistance in cases of difficulty in the administration of these departments. He is also responsible for the custody and use of the Great Seal which authenticates important legal documents such as Letters Patent.

In his *judicial* capacity the Lord Chancellor is head of the judiciary, President of the House of Lords (in its appellate capacity) and President of the Supreme Court. He is the most important member of the Judicial Committee of the Privy Council, and is head of the Chancery Division of the High Court. However, he rarely sits as a judge other than in the House of Lords and the Judicial Committee of the Privy Council. He appoints, in the name of the Crown, the following judicial officers: puisne judges of the High Court, Crown Court, and Circuit Judges, and magistrates. The appointments of legally qualified chairmen of certain administrative tribunals are subject to his approval.

The Lord Chancellor is served by a staff of professional assistants and his office in the House of Lords.

The Law Officer's Department (20,000)

The Attorney-General and the Solicitor-General are together known as Law Officers. They are political appointments (see p. 194), and the holders are precluded from private practice.

(*a*) *The Attorney-General* is usually a member of the House of Commons. His duties comprise the following:

(i) He represents the Crown in the courts in civil matters, and may prosecute in important and difficult cases in the criminal courts.

(ii) He advises Government Departments on important legal matters and may take part in many judicial and quasi-judicial proceedings affecting the public interest, e.g. the administration of charities and patent laws.

(iii) Certain criminal offences must be reported to the Attorney-General (e.g. by the police) and his consent is necessary before criminal proceedings may be taken in certain cases, e.g. bribery, incest, corrupt practices, and offences against the *Official Secrets Acts, 1911 and 1939*, the *Dangerous Drugs Act, 1951*, the *Public Order Act, 1936*, the *Prevention of Violence (Temporary Provisions) Act, 1939*, and various other Acts.

The Attorney-General superintends the work of the Director of Public Prosecutions. He is head of the English Bar, and points of professional etiquette may be referred to him.

(*b*) *The Solicitor-General* is deputy to the Attorney-General and his duties are similar. He is a barrister-at-law and is usually a member of the House of Commons. By the *Law Officers Act, 1944*, any functions authorised or required to be discharged by the Attorney-General may, unless expressly excluded, be discharged by the Solicitor-General if the office of Attorney-General is vacant, if the Attorney-General is absent or ill, or if the Attorney-General authorises his deputy to act in any particular case.

The Civil Service

History

Kings, Presidents, dictators, and Governments of all kinds require officials to enforce the orders or laws made by the rulers. In early times the civil servants (clerks and administrators) were employed directly by the King or by his Ministers. Appointment was by patronage, in the gift of the King (or his Ministers) and depended on personal relationship, or friendship or knowing the 'right people'.

Some posts were often given as a reward for political services and were regarded as part of the 'spoils' of office. Many posts were sinecures, the appointee receiving a salary but performing no real work. Sometimes the holders of Government posts were empowered to charge fees for their services to the public.

Such was the broad picture until the end of the eighteenth century, when there was a movement for reform. Royal patronage was reduced, sinecures became fewer and the charging of fees was abolished. The *Reform Act, 1832* left the Civil Service untouched; but attacks were made on its inefficiency and corruption by J. S. Bentham (1748–1832) and J. S. Mill (1806–73). Important reformers, e.g. Benjamin Jowett, Macaulay, Trevelyan and Northcote, became interested in the reform of the Civil Service, particularly following the changes in recruitment by competitive examination to the Indian Civil Service and the reform of the examination system at Oxford and Cambridge Universities.

Parliament appointed a Select Committee to inquire into the cost of the civil administration, and as a result of evidence given to the committee Trevelyan and Northcote were asked to prepare a report on the reorganisation of the Permanent Civil Service to ensure its efficiency in administration. This report (the Northcote–Trevelyan Report) of 1854 made 4 main recommendations which laid the foundation of the present Civil Service:

  (i) Recruitment should be by competitive examination.
 (ii) Promotion should be by merit and not seniority.
(iii) The separation of the 'intellectual' from the 'mechanical' side of administration.
(iv) The unification of the Civil Service; the unification of recruitment and inter-departmental promotion.

During the next seventy years these recommendations were all adopted. In 1855 the *Civil Service Commission* was set up by Order in Council as an independent body controlling the recruitment of civil servants. It established rules regarding age, ability, knowledge, health, and character of entrants. Originally the Commission tested by examination only those nominated by Departmental heads, but after 1870 open competition became the only method of entry to the Civil Service, except for the Foreign Office and Home Office. The Commission is today made up of six Commissioners (with a staff of roughly 1,000) and continues its main function in the appointment of Civil Servants. Formerly the Treasury answered in Parliament for the Commission; but was replaced in 1968 by the Civil Service Department when it took over certain Treasury functions. Since November 1982 Civil Service responsibilities have been divided between the Treasury and the Management Personnel Office (see p. 147). The Civil Service Commission comes under the latter.

Description Today

Definition. 'A civil servant of the Crown (not being the holder of a political or judicial office), who is paid wholly and directly out of money voted by Parliament and works in a civil capacity in a department of government.'

  Numbers. Including part-time staff (two part-time officers being reckoned as equivalent to one full-time) there are about 594,000 civil servants in 1986 (compared with 732,000 in 1979 and nearly half of this number are women).

  Roughly 300,000 are engaged in the provision of public services: paying sickness benefits and pensions, collecting taxes and contributions, running employment services, staffing prisons, and providing services to industry and agriculture. About 250,000 are employed in the Ministry of Defence, including the Royal Ordnance factories and Royal Dockyards. Of these there are about 150,000 industrial staff; they are mainly manual workers in government industrial establishments, whose pay and conditions of service are largely separately administered, and differ, quite substantially, from those of non-industrial grades. The remainder are about equally divided between: central administrative and policy duties; support services, such as accommodation, printing and information; and services which are largely self-supporting financially, e.g. those provided by the Department for National Savings and the Royal Mint.

  In addition there are some 5,000 staff employed in the **Diplomatic Ser-**

vice. They work for the Foreign and Commonwealth Office, and at UK embassies and consulates abroad.

About 75 per cent of civil servants work outside the London area, and plans in 1973 (the Hardman Report) for further dispersal from the capital have been partially implemented.

The Development of the Modern Civil Service

The great expansion in State activity in the first half of the twentieth century involved the recruitment of many scientific and professional classes in addition to those employed in administering the many new services provided by the State itself. These latter are by far the most common groups of civil servants who formulate policy and advise Ministers or apply established procedures in the lower ranks of the service. The Civil Service Commission controls recruitment which has been adapted to a developing educational system. Moreover, co-ordination between the various Departments of Government has been improved.

Between 1920 and 1968 there were three 'Treasury Classes' of civil servants which were linked with the educational system, viz.

Class	Education	Age
Administrative	Degree	22
Executive	'A' Levels (GCE)	18+
Clerical	'O' Levels (GCE)	15/16+

Following the report of the **Fulton Committee**, 1968, which made a detailed scrutiny of the structure and management of the Civil Service, changes were made to re-shape and modernise the Civil Service to make it more effective in carrying out its changing tasks. The pace of this change has now diminished.

Present Structure

The Civil Service is now being redesigned to provide a more flexible deployment of staff so that talent can be used to the best advantage, and the highest levels of the Civil Service are seen to be open to the people of outstanding ability, whatever the specialist background of the candidate or the original method of entry to the service.

These structural changes involve the abolition of classes (i.e. the former Treasury Classes, which were rigid and tended to preclude entry to the highest ranks unless one were educationally qualified on entry). The changes now being made are allied with personnel management policies designed to ensure that, although work requiring *specialist* skill (about 25 per cent of the Civil Service) is always done by appropriately qualified persons—e.g. chemists or lawyers or explosives experts—people with the necessary aptitudes are given suitably wide experience to fit them for higher posts. Consequently at the top levels of the Civil Service, where staff are predominantly concerned with higher management and policy, there is now an *open and unified structure* covering, since 1984, some 10,000 staff from the former grades of Permanent Secretary, Deputy Secretary, Under Secretary, Assistant Secretary, Senior Principal and Principal. (They are simply numbered Grade 1, 2 . . . to 7.) In theory these posts are filled by people most suitable for them without regard to their academic background or to whether they were previously in a specialist or generalist stream.

At other levels the structure of the Civil Service is based on a system of *categories*. These are pay and grading structures and occupational groups—groups of staff within each category whose members have common personnel management and recruitment needs. Twelve categories have been created, covering 75 per cent of staff, including:

(i) **General Category.** The Administration Group contains some 270,000 staff. Their functions range from co-ordination and improvement of government machinery and the formulation of advice to ministers on matters of policy to the performance of normal clerical duties connected with the running of departmental business at lower levels.

The Economist Group contains some 300 staff. They provide economic advice and undertake economic analysis.

The Statistician Group (some 450 staff) undertakes the collection and analysis of statistics required for government policies.

The Information Officer Group (some 1,350 staff) carries out a variety of specialised press, publicity, public relations and information work.

(ii) **Science Category.** Contains the Science Group (18,000 staff), which is responsible for conducting research and testing in government laboratories and testing establishments, and for providing advice on scientific policy. Its members also participate in the planning and management of advanced technology procurement projects.

(iii) **Professional and Technical Category.** This contains some 40,000 staff and includes a range of professionals—architects, quantity surveyors and electrical and mechanical engineers—and supporting staff whose main function is to plan and oversee a wide range of government construction and procurement activities, and to carry out certain inspection and regulatory activities.

The Illustrator Group contains about 500 staff responsible for the preparation of all forms of artwork to the wide range of requirements within the Government service.

(iv) **Training Category.** Within this Category the Instructional Officer Group comprises some 4,000 staff employed on instruction in a trade, craft, or subject, or ancillary or supervisory duties connected with instruction.

Other Categories. The four categories outlined above account for some 60 per cent of the non-industrial civil service. Another 15 per cent fall into the following categories: Legal, Police, Secretarial, Data Processing, Research, Social Security, and Museums categories.

Typists. The Civil Service employs about 24,000 shorthand typists, audio typists and copy typists, who work mainly in small groups, and about 4,500 personal secretaries who work mainly for senior civil servants.

Other Support Staff. There are about 29,000 other support staff, including paper keepers, office cleaners and messengers. As far as possible, posts of messengers are reserved for ex-servicemen, although other men and women over the age of 30 may be recruited.

Recruitment Today

The Administration Group. We have mentioned that recruits to the permanent staff enter by means of open competition. Before 1970 university graduates with 1st- or 2nd-class honours degrees were recruited by two methods:

Method I: Candidates took a qualifying written examination, an interview before an Interview Board under a Civil Service Commissioner, and a written examination in optional academic subjects at honours degree level.

Method II: Candidates took (*a*) a written qualifying examination, followed by (*b*) two days of tests and interviews by the Civil Service Selection Board ('Cisbee'). The tests and exercises were intended to provide evidence of intellectual ability, practical ability, and judgement. The candidate was awarded marks. The last hurdle (*c*) the candidate appeared before the Final Selection Board for final interview. The Board made its evaluation of the candidate's personal qualities and determined the successful ones.

Before 1970 over eighty per cent of the successful candidates were selected in this way. From 1970 Method II was the only mode of qualification, and the requirement of a 1st- or 2nd-class honours' degree for eligibility was abolished. Method II had previously been used for the selection of mature candidates from outside the service (e.g. from industry, local government, etc.) and is continued for this class of entrant in view of its superiority over the alternative Method I. Members of the Scientific Officer Category who wish to transfer to the Administration Group may apply, and these entrants also take Method II. Of the 250 or so administrative trainees admitted each year about 80 per cent are direct entrants; the other 20 per cent come from internal recruitment.

The Executive Officer Grade. Recruitment is by the following methods:

(i) Open competition for persons between $17\frac{1}{2}$ and 28 years who have two 'A' levels or a degree (those with a degree make up ten per cent of the total recruited in this way).

(ii) A qualifying written examination followed by interview for candidates serving in HM Forces and former members of Overseas Civil Service.

(iii) An annual limited competition by written examination and interview open to permanent officers in the Clerical Class aged 19–24.

(iv) Promotion by Departmental board of clerical officers.

The Clerical Grade. These are recruited by educational attainments of five 'O' levels for candidates of 16 years, and by written examination for older candidates including clerical assistants. who are recruited similarly, the educational standards being lower.

Professional and Technical Categories. These are recruited from candidates with specialist or professional qualifications, followed by an interview. Many are recruited on a temporary basis and are then offered permanent appointment later. For the higher posts in these classes a degree or diploma in technology is required; for the lower posts two 'A' levels and four 'O' level passes are required.

Salary and Conditions of Service

The machinery for negotiation on conditions of service affecting the Civil Service as a whole is provided by the **National Whitley Council**, first set up in 1921. The Council is composed of two sides: (i) the Official Side, and (ii) the Staff Side. The Official Side acts in co-operation with the Treasury and is made up of senior Treasury officials and the Establishment Officers from the main Departments. The Staff Side is made up of the various staff associations which civil servants are encouraged to join (e.g. Civil and Public Services Associations, the Society of Civil Servants, the Institution of Professional Civil Servants, and the Association of First Division Civil Servants). The Official Side and the Staff negotiate through the Whitley Council machinery. Where there is disagreement between the two sides on matters of pay, hours of service, and leave, provision is made for arbitration.

Salary. The salary which a civil servant receives is based on a fair comparison with that paid for similar work outside the service. Annual increments are usually paid until the civil servant reaches the maximum for the grade to which he belongs. Civil servants hold office 'at the pleasure of the Crown', subject to the *Trade Union and Labour Relations Act, 1974*. In practice, one of the attractions of civil service life is that of security of tenure of employment. Provided he is capable and efficient a civil servant may reasonably expect a full career in the public service and a pension on retirement. In 1982, the Megaw Report on civil servants' pay recommended that market forces (i.e. the demand for and supply of civil servants) should be given more weight in determining civil service salary levels. This would suit the present Government's general approach.

As in most other employments a specified number of hours is laid down as the working week. Certain grades are paid overtime, but members of the higher grades are paid salaries on the assumption that, if need be, they will work long hours without additional pay. The standard working week is 40 hours. All civil servants receive annual leave. The Secretary to the Cabinet, who is head of the Civil Service has a salary of £77,400. Other Permanent Secretaries receive some £65,000. Grade 7 civil servants (formerly known as 'Principals') had a salary range of £16,000–£20,000 (1986/7 figures).

Characteristics of the Civil Service

The State is today the largest employer of labour, and Government touches almost every activity or aspect of life. Generalisations as to features and characteristics of the Civil Service may be misleading particularly where changes in the structure and operation of the service are continuously being made to enable the administrative machine to adapt to modern conditions.

E. N. Gladden states:

The requirements of the Civil Service are that it shall be impartially selected, administratively competent, politically neutral and imbued with the spirit of service to the community.

(i) *Impartial Selection.* Civil Servants are appointed by open competition (see pp. 158, 161) and there is no patronage.

(ii) *Permanence*. The Civil Service is permanent; its members continue in office notwithstanding changes of Government or Ministers. This permanence ensures continuity in Government administration. Ministers may come and go; civil servants continue, carrying on services vital to the community. Civil servants have a security of tenure of office and may look forward to a full and worthwhile career with reasonable pay and prospects.

(iii) *Neutrality*. Civil servants are non-political, i.e. they serve different Governments in power impartially and disinterestedly. Lord Attlee, Sir Winston Churchill, and Sir Harold Wilson have all testified to the vigour of the Civil Service in applying policies under their administrations. Thus in 1949 Labour proposed that the Iron and Steel Industry be nationalised. In 1951 the Conservatives proposed denationalisation. Both policies were carried through by virtually the same officials.

In their relations with the public also civil servants must be impartial. This implies no discrimination, except so far as special circumstances justify this, between one member of the public and another. If Mrs *A*. of Newcastle on Tyne is entitled to a pension, Mrs *B*, from Norwich, is entitled also, if the circumstances are similar.

(iv) *Anonymity*. This means that the Civil Service must work behind the scenes, without praise or blame. We have mentioned that a Minister is primarily concerned with policy. He runs his Department, and is politically responsible for its activities. He will, of course, consult his Permanent Under-Secretary on major policy decisions. (Collectively these top civil servants are known unofficially as 'mandarins'.) The latter may suggest two or three alternative courses, pointing out the difficulties of each or the advantages and disadvantages. Finally the Minister must decide which course to follow. He alone will be answerable in Parliament for the results, good or bad, not the civil servant. Recently this tradition has been broken. Some civil servants have been named and revealed quite publicly, not only as a result of Select Committee inquiries, but as a result of political incidents (e.g. the Westland affair, 1985–6; the MI5/Wright trial in Australia, 1986).

When a Minister knows that he cannot put the blame on his civil servants he is stimulated to judge their advice independently and carefully, and to insist that they shall do their best. That he is answerable to Parliament causes him to insist that others shall be answerable to him. Further, the efficiency of representative government depends upon the use of the expert knowledge of the officials. (Finer: *Theory and Practice of Modern Government*.)

All civil servants within a Department are loyal to their political head and wish to avoid placing the Minister in an embarrassing position in Parliament or in public. They do this by carrying out the Minister's policy faithfully, by applying the appropriate administrative procedures as honestly and fairly as possible and by working efficiently. A good leader inspires confidence in the subordinate staff in the Department: there is mutual trust.

Mistakes and maladministration, however, occur from time to time. Where these happen and a civil servant is at fault he may be removed from the Department or his promotion prospects may be impaired.

The question of Ministerial responsibility for the work of officials within a Department was highlighted by the **Crichel Down case of 1954**. The facts of this case in brief were that farmland owned by Lt-Com. Marten was compulsorily purchased by the Ministry of Agriculture in 1937. The land was used during World War II and, subsequently, as a bombing range. By 1952 Lt-Com. Marten applied to buy back his former farmland which he proposed to use again as agricultural land. Meanwhile officials at the Ministry wanted to acquire the land for a model farm. Many difficulties were placed in the way of Lt-Com. Marten's repurchase of the land. The former owner persisted in his endeavours and eventually (as a result of pressure in Parliament) the Minister (Sir Thomas Dugdale) agreed to a public inquiry, conducted by Sir Andrew Clark, QC. His report criticised the work of the officials of which the Minister had no knowledge and some of which had been performed before the Minister had taken office. A debate was subsequently held in the House of Commons, Sir Thomas Dugdale assumed moral responsibility and as a result of pressure from his own political backbenchers he resigned his office. (It should be noted that he had not forfeited the Prime Minister's confidence. This was the case too with Lord Carrington in 1982 see p. 132.)

Sir David Maxwell Fyfe (later Lord Kilmuir), the Home Secretary in 1954, made the following statement during the debate:

Where action has been taken by a civil servant of which the Minister disapproves and has no prior knowledge, and the conduct of the official is reprehensible, then there is no obligation on the part of the Minister to endorse what he believes to be wrong, or to defend what are clearly shown to be the errors of his officers. The Minister is not bound to approve an action of which he did not know, or of which he disapproves. But of course he remains constitutionally responsible to Parliament for the fact that something has gone wrong, and he alone can tell Parliament what has occurred and render an account of his stewardship.

Owing to the complex nature of government work today a Minister cannot know all that goes on in his own Department, much less take all the decisions done in his name. The Crichel Down case alerted public attention to the difficulty of an individual in getting his case aired in public, and calling the decision-making civil servants to account for their actions where maladministration is alleged or prejudice occurs. This and similar cases showed the need for some machinery to enable grievances to be brought to light and the inadequacies or inefficiencies of public administration to be exposed. The *Parliamentary Commissioner Act, 1967*, was eventually passed into law and the office of **Parliamentary Commissioner for Administration** was created (see p. 305).

Criticism of Civil Servants

Bearing in mind that recruitment to the Civil Service is now by open competition; that candidates for the top positions must be highly qualified intellectually; show qualities of leadership; possess personal qualities of service and a capacity to work with others; what criticisms may be made of the service? The main standard of judgement is **efficiency**. The difficulty of measuring efficiency in public administration is great, mainly because the tasks of Government are so complex.

The general criticisms which are popularly made of the Civil Service are:

(i) Lack of vitality, imagination, drive, and initiative.
(ii) Addiction to 'red-tape' and precedent, leading to inflexibility.
(iii) Bureaucracy.
(iv) Secrecy (see pp. 262, 374).
(v) The Administrative Class tends to be made up of persons of middle class, and are therefore drawn from a narrow social background.
(vi) Tendency to departmentalism, i.e. strong support for own Department, to the detriment of public administration as a whole.
(vii) Excessive caution and an unwillingness to admit mistakes.
(viii) Higher civil servants assume excessive self-importance, yet are protected by the anonymity of the Civil Service from criticism for errors.

Some of these criticisms may be true. Doubtless there are some members of the Administrative Class who lack vitality; some may have been worn out by the administrative machine. The same point may be made of those working in the lower clerical classes who can see no way to improve their lot by promotion. A civil servant who is expected to conform to tradition and the rules of the Service or his Departmental head is hardly likely to show initiative or drive if by so doing he will antagonise his superiors. Precedent and 'red tape' are inherent in governments of all kind. Formal procedures must be laid down in all offices and these must be followed if chaos is to be avoided. Order is better than disorder. A file in writing is prepared and all applications from the public are dealt with in the same way. The simplest example is the income tax return. Documents have to be prepared, facts stated by the member of the public are recorded in the proper column, the formula of assessment is applied to each, and the amount due is notified. In unusual cases a civil servant will look for a precedent from past files to indicate how he is to deal with a problem. Precedents are useful guides. What was approved in the past should be applied in the future, unless there are contrary reasons. In law and public administration precedents are valuable in achieving certainty.

Bureaucracy is allied to the problem of precedent. Civil servants are trained in the methodical treatment of claims, petitions, applications, and complaints. This leads to officialism which in turn is criticised as inhumanity or indifference to individual and personal merits of the claimant. The Civil Service has its own Organisation and Methods Branches (O and M) which reviews continuously the methods and procedures used in all departments.

In 1982, the Treasury and Civil Service Committee was very critical of civil service efficiency. The Government has responded (in a White Paper *Efficiency and Effectiveness in the Civil Service*) by pressing departments to more clearly define their objectives and more closely assess related achievements.

The criticism that the Administrative grades largely emanate from the middle classes is no longer so true. Changes in the educational system and particularly the more open entries to Oxford and Cambridge Universities have meant that candidates for the higher posts are drawn from a wider range of classes. Since 1964 there had been (according to the Fulton Report of 1968) 'a distinct and progressive change towards greater representation of people from less privileged backgrounds'. And, in its assessment of Method II procedures (see p. 161), the report stated: 'The principles on which it operates are sound and its duration is appropriate in the light of those principles; it provides equality of opportunity; it maintains a proper balance between the personal and intellectual qualities which are needed in the Administrative Class. It confers no advantage on those who merely have a small veneer of social graces, but it does give due weight to effectiveness in personal relations. Nevertheless, a report of the House of Commons' Expenditure Committee in 1977 remained highly critical of recruitment bias, with over 60 per cent of administrative entrants coming from Public School and/or Oxbridge.

Departmentalism is inevitable in all organisations. It is known in colleges and schools, in industry and Government. It engenders pride in one's own Ministry, loyalty between members, and a common ideal. It may stimulate competition between departments in service to the public. The difficulties may be overcome by proper and effective co-ordination, particularly by Ministers and senior Civil Servants.

As to excessive caution in public affairs one has to bear in mind that any individual who is unjustly treated by a public official (civil servant, local government official, or the police) may complain to his MP. The result may be a Parliamentary Question which exposes the Minister responsible to public attack, or, if the matter is serious enough, a public inquiry (see the Crichel Down case). All civil servants are aware of the risk and tend to exercise that care which will avoid exposing the Minister (and indeed himself) to criticism. Moreover, the Press is always alert to maladministration and vigorously attacks injustices arising from carelessness of public officials.

It is doubtful whether the higher civil servants are excessively self-important. Certainly they have ability and exercise influence at the centre of government power, and are therefore important by right. It is their job to point out the snags of a Minister's policy, to act as a brake at times rather than a spur; to understand how the Minister thinks; to set aside their own vision on policy, and to be disinterested. The absolute 'non-entity' of the British administrator is said to be his chief merit. In practice the main characteristic of the British Civil Service is that it is non-political, and successive Prime Ministers (Attlee, Churchill, and Wilson) have all paid tribute to the capacity of the Civil Service to serve Governments (Conservative and Labour) with equal vigour.

However, a number of observers remain sceptical. Some Labour politicians believe that the Civil Service is actively biased against socialist policies (though in 1979 some Conservative Ministers were protesting at what they perceived as *socialist* bias in the civil service). Others, on a wider front, suggest that *any* radical policy measures will be opposed by the Civil Service and, indeed, it has been suggested that the scheduled reform of the Civil Service itself has (since 1968) been quietly but firmly diluted, delayed or devitalised by the civil servants (see *The Civil Servants*, P. Kellner and N. Crowther-Hunt).

Training

Most civil servants on entry into the profession are untrained in the techniques of administration. Some entrants to the Professional and Technical classes must be professionally qualified before appointment, e.g. doctors, lawyers, and certain scientists and engineers.

Before 1943 civil servants who were appointed to administrative posts (at the top or bottom) 'learned by doing', performing the simpler tasks first and gradually moving on to the more complex and responsible. The method (or absence of method) was wasteful and uneconomical overall. Before 1943 the Civil Service gave little encouragement to those already established to prepare for degrees or diplomas in suitable subjects, e.g. public administration or political or government subjects. In 1943 a Committee on the Training of Civil Servants was set up under the chairmanship of Sir Ralph Assheton (a former Civil Servant). Its reports criticised the lack of system and recommended a three-month course for new entrants to the Service on the general aspect of administration, periodic refresher courses, and up to twelve months' leave for members of the Administrative Class on reaching 30 years of age to carry out approved research. Financial restrictions in the 1950s prevented the full implementation of the Report.

The Fulton Report of 1968, however, gave added impetus to training and the position today is that full-time Training Officers and instructors are appointed to all the major Departments of Government. Their task is to state the training needs of the staff and to organise courses, general and technical, to provide for the varying requirements.

Civil servants under 18 are granted Day Release to attend local Colleges of Further Education. Adult staff are assisted financially and by the giving of 'time off' to undertake private study to enable them to pursue studies leading to recognised educational or professional qualifications. Certain civil servants may be granted sabbatical leave to undertake research in areas of interest to themselves and their departments.

The co-ordination of training is carried out by the Management and Personnel Office (see p. 147) which has central responsibility for personnel management, including training and career management, as well as organisation and recruitment and the development and dissemination of administrative and managerial techniques.

The main training centre is the Civil Service College at Sunningdale Park, Berks. There is also a London Centre for training. Courses and seminars are run on a variety of subjects: management, economics, statistics, industrial growth, social administration, operational research, computers and information systems. Some civil servants attend external management courses at Business Schools, the Administrative Staff College and elsewhere.

Apart from formal educational instruction, there is also 'on the job' training. In addition, civil servants are regularly moved among different branches of the Government Department to which they are attached; sometimes they move among Departments to give wider experience of Civil Service work; and some will interchange with outside employments.

Generally, therefore, we may say that there has been a considerable expansion of training within the Service with particular emphasis placed upon management skills. The aim is to enable personnel to keep abreast of the changes in society and to meet the demands for an efficient public service.

Political and Private Activities of Civil Servants

All Civil Servants enjoy the electoral franchise in common with all other adult citizens; they may vote in Parliamentary and local elections, but there are necessarily some restrictions on their activities.

The Masterman Committee on the Political Activities of Civil Servants in its report (Cmnd. 7718 of 1949) stated:

(i) In a democratic society it is desirable for all citizens to have a voice in the affairs of the State and for as many as possible to play an active part in public life.

(ii) The public interest demands the maintenance of political impartiality in the Civil Service and of confidence in that impartiality as an essential part of the structure of Government in this country.

The broad position is that industrial staff and the minor grades of the clerical class (numbering about 60 per cent of the service) are not restricted at all politically. They are 'politically free'; they may stand for Parliament and represent a political party. Any such candidate must resign his appointment before nomination day on the understanding that if not elected he will be reinstated in his previous capacity within a week of the declaration of the election result. This group was categorised as 'below the line'.

The 'politically restricted' group comprises Higher Executive Officers, Administrative Trainees, Principals (who are now superseded as Grade 7) and above grades: they are not allowed to participate in national politics at all. They must abstain from party office, speeches, canvassing, and public manifestations of views that might associate them with a political organisation or political controversy (though they may, with permission, take part in local political activity). The third, intermediate, group may seek permission to take part in general political activities.

Generally, where required, permission is granted to the extent consistent with the reputation of the Civil Service for political impartiality and the avoidance of conflict with official duties, and subject to a code of discretion requiring moderation and avoidance of embarrassment of Ministers. We have already noted that one of the leading characteristics of the British Civil Service is that it is 'non political', and it was noted by the Masterman Committee that 'any weakening of the existing tradition of political impartiality would be the first step in the creation of a "political" Civil Service . . . Such a system would be contrary to the public interest and, in the long run, the Civil Service itself.'

In 1978, the **Armitage Committee** on the Political Activities of Civil Servants proposed a modification in the system which they saw as unnecessarily restrictive. Instead of debarring whole categories of civil servants on the basis of their *grades*, the Committee suggested that the criterion should be the *type of work* the civil servant is engaged in. Apart therefore from senior servants (Principal grades and above, whose work tends to be sensitive or near the 'political-official interface'), individual decisions should be based on reasoned assessments of the nature of the applicants' official duties. The effect of this proposal (yet to be adopted) would be to reduce the 'restricted' category from 196,000 (26 per cent) to 23,000 (3 per cent). (In 1952 the figure was 100,000, or 14 per cent.)

Civil servants in all classes are subject to the very wide provisions of the *Official Secrets Acts, 1911–39* which make it an offence 'to make, obtain or communicate to any person, any sketch, plan, model or other document or information which might be useful to an enemy for any purpose prejudicial to the safety of the State' (*1911 Act s.1*). Furthermore, 'If any person having in his possession or control . . . any information . . . which has been entrusted in confidence to him by any person holding office under Her Majesty . . . communicates the . . . information to any person other than a person (authorised) . . . shall be guilty of a misdemeanour' (*s.2*).

Thus, broadly, Section 1 of the Act deals with espionage, while Section 2 is much wider (and consequently controversial—see pp. 262, 374) and covers unauthorised disclosure of official information of all kinds.

There have been a number of illustrative cases in recent years. Thus, under Section 1 there were prosecutions against Geoffrey Prime (1982), Professor H. Hambledon (1982), Michael Bettaney (1984) (the latter himself an MI5 officer!). Under Section 2, a policeman was prosecuted for supplying information to a criminal (1970); John Berry was sentenced for passing on details of his work in signals intelligence (1978); Miss Rhona Ritchie was found guilty of divulging details of the work of her department (the Foreign Office) (1982). More recently (1984) was the case of a clerical officer Sarah Tisdall, who was imprisoned for 6 months after pleading guilty to sending confidential documents about the arrival in Britain of the cruise missiles to *The Guardian* (on the grounds that the Minister, Mr Heseltine, was exercising undue delay in informing Parliament). And in 1985, Clive Ponting, a civil servant in the Ministry of Defence, admitted sending confidential documents about the Falklands war to an MP; but he pleaded not guilty to the charge of breaking the *Official Secrets Act*. He did this on the grounds that an MP was a proper person to whom information could properly be disclosed*, and that, as a result, his loyalty to the Crown (and his own conscience) was not diminished. The trial judge, however, declared that the interests of the state was synonomous with the interests of the government of the day.

Much to many people's surprise, the jury acquitted Ponting. As a result, the Head of the Civil Service issued guidelines to civil servants which said that they 'are under an obligation to keep . . . (official) confidences. There must be a general duty upon every civil servant . . . not to disclose . . . any document or information . . . which has come his way . . . in the course of his duty . . .'. (When confidential information was 'leaked' by a civil servant about the Westland affair, there was no prosecution on the grounds that the action has been authorised by the Minister—see p. 132.)

The *Prevention of Corruption Act, 1906*, also contains wide provisions which are designed to protect the State against corruption by its officials, e.g. *A*, a civil servant, receives £1,000 from *B*, a public contractor, on condition that *B* is awarded a contract to build a Government office, bridge, etc.

A civil servant must not use his experience or official position to further his private interests and is subject to certain restrictions in commerce and business. Thus, he may not hold private interests in public contracts, and he may not use official information in writing, broadcasting, or lecturing

---

* In 1987, the Government successfully applied for an injunction which prevented MPs viewing a BBC film about Britain's security satellite 'Zircon'.

without the approval of his Department. Concern has been expressed that senior officials, who are offered business appointments following their retirement from public service, may deviate from giving impartial advice while still in their posts. Normally (since 1975) they have to obtain clearance from an advisory committee which reports to the Prime Minister.

Security. The general rule is that the private political views of civil servants are not official concern. But, there are some Civil Service duties (e.g. defence or foreign relations) in which secrecy is vital to State security. Civil servants employed on these matters must be reliable. Any civil servant who is known to be a member of, or actively associated with Communist or Fascist organisations, or is known to be a 'security risk', will not, therefore, be employed on secret work. A 'screening' process known as the Positive Vetting System is operated to check the credentials of individuals before a civil servant undertakes secret work. Where a civil servant is found to have Communist or Fascist sympathies he may be dismissed or transferred to other work. This occurred several times in recent years (see p. 169).

Each Government Department is responsible for its own internal security. The Security Service operates independently under a Director-General, responsible to the Home Secretary. In addition to the above arrangements there is a Security Commission which may investigate and report on breaches of security in the public service. Such investigation may only be carried out if requested by the Prime Minister in consultation with the leader of the Opposition.

Crown Proceedings

The expression 'the Crown' may be used to describe (i) the Sovereign in her personal capacity, and (ii) the Sovereign as Head of State, in her corporate capacity. The Crown, in its corporate capacity, includes Her Majesty's Ministers, the Government Departments, and the Civil Service.

Two ancient maxims of the common law determined the relationship of the Crown to a subject: 'No action can be brought against the King personally, for he cannot be sued in his Courts'; and 'The King can do no wrong'. The Sovereign could not be sued personally for any alleged wrongs he may have committed in person. As a corporate body, the Crown was similarly immune from legal liability. The doctrine of vicarious liability (whereby at common law a master is liable for the wrongs of a servant committed in the course of his employment) did not apply to the Crown.

Petition of Right

The apparently harsh principle whereby the Crown escaped liability in contract and tort (a civil wrong) was mitigated, however, by an action known as the Petition of Right. This lay for the recovery of: (*a*) Property in the possession of the Crown (the subject claiming restitution or compensation). (*b*) Money due under contract made with the Crown by its servants. (*c*) Unascertained damages for breach of contract. (*d*) Sums payable to the petitioner under a grant from the Crown.

The *Petition of Right Act, 1860*, regulated the procedure to be followed by the applicant seeking redress in claims of a contractual nature mentioned above. However, it was first necessary to obtain the *fiat* (order) of the Attorney-General before proceedings could be commenced. There was no appeal against his refusal of the *fiat*, and the Act itself did not apply to claims in tort against the Crown.

Although the Crown itself was immune from legal action in respect of torts committed by a servant in the course of his duties, nevertheless it was possible to sue the Crown servant personally. For example, where a Ministry's van driver negligently knocked down a pedestrian, action could be taken against the 'tortfeasor' personally. In such cases the Government Department stood behind the civil servant and paid damages awarded against him. This protection was a matter of grace, and the claimant had no legal right to *enforce* payment from the Crown.

This action was abolished when it became subject to the *Trade Union and Labour Relations Act, 1974*.

The Crown as Employer

The Crown is now one of the largest employers in society. The legal relationship of master and servant in private life is governed by both the common law and statute. Each party has rights and duties in respect of the other, such rights and duties being enforceable in a court of law. In regard to Crown service, however, the position is somewhat different in that a civil servant holds office 'at the pleasure of the Crown'. The phrase 'Crown employment' does not include employment in the police, the NHS or the local government service.

Generally British civil servants enjoy greater security of employment than most people. In fact, the Crown endeavours to act as a model employer, and internal Treasury regulations ensure just treatment of employees both during employment and on retirement. What it does mean is that the civil servant cannot sue the Crown at law to enforce 'rights' which apply in the normal relationship of master and servant. In recent years civil servants have become noticeably more militant (and thus more 'political') over pay, conditions and redundancies, industrial action is no longer unthinkable.

The Crown Proceedings Act, 1947

This act was passed as a result of the unsatisfactory state of the law regarding legal proceedings against the Crown. The main object was to place the Crown in the same position, as far as possible, as a private person or employer; i.e. able to sue and be sued for breaches of contracts or for torts committed by servants. The Act does not affect the Queen's personal immunity from legal proceedings.

Liability in Contract. The Act provides that actions for breach of contract may now be brought as of right against the Crown.

Liability in Tort. Section 2(1) of the Act provides that 'the Crown shall be subject to all those liabilities in tort to which, if it were a person of full age and capacity, it would be subject:

(*a*) In respect of torts committed by its servants or agents.

(*b*) In respect of any breach of those duties which a person owes to his servants or agents at common law by reason of being their employer.

(*c*) In respect of any breach of the duties attaching at common law to the ownership, occupation, possession or control of property'.

As an example of (*b*): A master is under a common law duty to provide reasonably safe plant and machinery for his employees. If, therefore, the Crown provides a faulty vehicle for use by its servant *B*, as a result of which *C* is injured, an action will lie against the Crown under s. 2(1).

As an example of (*c*): A private person visits the local office of the Inspector of Taxes to discuss his income tax assessment. A defective electric light fitting falls from the ceiling and lacerates the caller's head. An action will lie for the tort at the instance of the injured person.

Procedure. Action is brought against the appropriate Government Department. The Treasury publishes a list of the Departments and names the solicitor to accept service of process on behalf of each Department. Where the Department is not named, or uncertainty exists as to the Department's identity, the Attorney-General may be made defendant.

The legal action then follows the usual procedure of a High Court or county court action. The Act provides, however, that:

(*a*) Judgement against the Department cannot be enforced by the ordinary methods of levying execution or attachment. The Department is required to pay the amount certified due as damages.

(*b*) An injunction and a decree of specific performance are inappropriate to the Crown. Instead, the court makes an order declaratory of the rights of the parties.

(*c*) No order for restitution of property will be made against the Crown. Instead, the court may declare the plaintiff entitled as against the Crown.

Under the *National Health Service (Amendment) Act, 1986*, health authorities (see p. 181) lost their immunity and became subject to the laws on food provision and health and safety. Thus, hospitals now risk prosecution for the dirty kitchens which were often alleged to exist (especially following outbreaks of food poisoning).

The Armed Forces. Special provision is made in the Act with regard to the Armed Forces of the Crown. Nothing done or omitted by a member of the Armed Forces of the Crown while on duty shall subject him or the Crown to liability for inflicting death or personal injury on another member of the Armed Forces if (i) the latter is on duty or is on any land, premises, ship, aircraft, or vehicle used for the purposes of the Armed Forces, and if (ii) the Minister of Social Security certifies that the victim will receive an award.

Adams v. *War Office* (1955). *A* was killed on duty by a shell fired by other members of the Armed Forces on duty. The Minister certified that *A*'s death was attributable to service for the purpose of entitlement to an award, but it was also held that *A*'s father did not satisfy the conditions of the Royal Warrant under which parents might claim a pension in respect of the loss of a son.

The Government is, however, currently considering changing this rule, so that, say, a soldier injured in training may in future be able to claim damages.

Crown Servant. Section 2(6) of the Act defines the term 'officer' (in respect of whose actions the Crown now assumes liability in tort) as follows: the 'officer' shall (i) be appointed directly or indirectly by the Crown; and (ii) be paid in respect of his duties as an officer of the Crown at the material time *wholly* out of the Consolidated Fund, moneys provided by Parliament, the Road Fund, or a fund certified by the Treasury.

The police are not *wholly* paid out of such funds, hence the Crown is not subject to liability for torts committed by them.

Exercises

1. 'The King', said Bagehot, 'has three rights: the right to be consulted; the right to encourage; and the right to warn. And a King of great sense and sagacity would want no others.' Discuss.

2. The Queen is said to be the 'fountain of justice' and the 'fountain of honour'. Explain.

3. 'Royal pageantry and pomp are significant features of the British way of life.' Discuss.

4. Name the main functions of a Prime Minister.

5. The power of a Prime Minister is not without limits. What are they?

6. Enumerate the qualities you consider most desirable in a Prime Minister.

7. Trace the history of the Cabinet.

8. What are the main functions of the Cabinet?

9. What is meant by the phrase 'Ministerial Responsibility'?

10. Describe the Cabinet Committees.

11. Describe briefly the organisation of a Government Department.

12. What part is played by Advisory Committees in assisting a Minister to run his Department? Discuss the composition of some.

13. Consider the suggestion that the government creates a Minister for the Nationalised Industries.

14. Who are Parliamentary Counsel to the Treasury?

15. What duties fall to be discharged by the Home Secretary?

16. Discuss the duties of the Minister of the Environment?

17. 'Road and Rail Transport are now so important to all of us that a Minister should be placed in sole charge answerable only to the Cabinet and Parliament.' Do you agree?

18. Outline the duties of (a) the Paymaster-General and (b) the Lord Chancellor.

19. What duties are carried out by the Law Officers of the Crown?

20. Outline the history of the Civil Service.

21. How do candidates now qualify to enter the Administrative Class of the Civil Service?

22. Describe the characteristics of the Civil Service.

23. 'It is absurd that a Minister should have to resign over a dispute about a piece of farm land' (Crichel Down). Comment, and outline Sir

David Maxwell Fyfe's views on the question of responsibility for administrative error.

24. 'The Civil Service is eaten out with red-tape, precedent, bureaucracy and dilatoriness.' Do you agree?

25. *A*, who is a clerical assistant in the Civil Service, wants to stand for Parliament as an anarchist. Advise him.

26. What provisions exist to maintain security within the section of the Civil Service handling specially secret matters?

27. Comment on the description of top civil servants as 'permanent politicians'.

28. In October 1982, Sir John Hoskyns (a former policy adviser to the PM for 3 years) controversially declared that exhausted Ministers were advised by pessimistic civil servants who did not believe Britain could avoid continued decline. He suggested that the civil service needed an infusion of new blood and ideas, and said this could be done either by having Ministers bring in more outside advisers, or simply by dismissing all top civil servants over the age of 50. Comment on these ideas.

5
Public Corporations

Introduction

The basic functions of the State are (i) the maintenance of internal order and (ii) defence against external aggression. These duties remain today, but we have already noted that the State has increased the range of its functions, e.g. by creating social services of many kinds, so that we have today what is termed a Welfare State.

The main philosophy until the end of the nineteenth century was *laissez-faire* which implied that any goods or services required were best supplied by private enterprise. The Government ensured peace and good order, in which atmosphere private initiative and enterprise could flourish. This lasted until the Great War (1914–18) by which time the Government responsibilities were mainly limited to:

  (i) Administration of Justice.
 (ii) Defence (by maintaining Armed Forces).
(iii) Education (elementary).
 (iv) Conducting foreign relations.
  (v) Regulating conditions under which private enterprise could flourish, e.g. by administering Factory Acts, Weights and Measures Acts, and similar statutes.

These matters were dealt with by various Government Departments, the main ones being the Home Office, the War Office, the Admiralty, the Board of Education, the Foreign Office, the Board of Trade, and the Treasury.

The State itself did not initially carry on an industry; that was not its function. But, of course, there is no reason why a State should not do so. We may note the Communist States profess this to be one of their basic beliefs. We concede that a public service or an industry may be administered (i) by the State itself acting directly through a Government Department or indirectly through local government, or (ii) by private enterprise, acting through a public or private company, the main interest of which is profitability. In the first case the State owns and directs the service or industry and is accountable to Parliament, while in the second case private enterprise is not accountable to Parliament and must make a profit or go bankrupt.

In this chapter we are concerned with a third form or method, namely the public corporation, which is neither a Government Department nor a public or private company, but a semi-independent body which purports to combine the benefits or advantages of both forms.

The idea of the semi-independent body is not new. In Tudor times Parliament appointed **Commissioners of Sewers** to supervise the disposal of sewage (a basic health measure of great importance). In the eighteenth century **Turnpike Trusts** were set up to supervise the provision and maintenance of roads locally in the towns and counties. Commissions for local lighting and paving in towns, and Commissions to provide and supervise canals were also set up. The Commissioners were appointed to perform limited functions, each group of men being responsible for a particular job. It was the age of *ad hoc* authorities, for local government authorities did not exist to do the necessary work or provide the services.

The practice of appointing *ad hoc* authorities continued. School Boards were created by the *Elementary Education Act, 1870*. In 1834 **Poor Law Commissioners** were appointed to provide a public service to enforce the poor law throughout the country. Many of these powers were taken over by the local authorities created in the nineteenth century. The *Municipal Corporations Act, 1835*, gave corporate status to the towns; the *Local Government Act, 1888*, set up **County Councils** and **County Borough Councils**; in 1894 the **Urban District Councils** were created. All these authorities absorbed a number of the public services formerly carried on by the *ad hoc* Commissions and Boards (e.g. roads, sewers, canals, paving, lighting, and education).

Other notable examples of semi-independent bodies performing public services were the Mersey Docks and Harbour Board (1857) and the Port of London Authority (1908) which administered the docks at Liverpool and London respectively; the Metropolitan Water Board (1902), and the London Passenger Transport Board (1933). Each of these authorities was created to bring order into the use and facilities of the ports or to create a unified system of passenger transport in London. These particular matters were important nationally and were considered to be outside the scope and function of local government, and the Boards continued their existence independently.

We note that the special bodies mentioned did not come directly under Government control, though some of the public corporations (as they became to be called), included representatives of a Government Department on their executive bodies (i.e. the Boards) in whom powers of management were vested.

Similar bodies were created and constituted, notably the Forestry Commission (1919), the Central Electricity Board (1926), the British Broadcasting Corporation (1927), and the British Overseas Airways Corporation (1939), all following the same sort of pattern of previous bodies mentioned, i.e. the members of the corporations were appointed by the Government, but the bodies themselves had a degree of independence of the Government by which they were individually and collectively appointed.

Nationalised Industries and Services

Since its creation in 1900 the Labour Party has been committed to the policy of the nationalisation or common ownership of the basic industries of the nation. When, therefore, the Labour Government came to power in

1945 under Mr C. Attlee, it already had a definite programme of nationalisation to carry through. The Port of London Authority, the London Passenger Transport Board and the other authorities already in existence were models on which the nationalisation programme of the basic industries were built. Coal (1946), electricity (1947), transport (1947), gas (1948) and steel (1949) industries were nationalised by means of statutes, and public corporations were created. These have been described as 'managerial–economic' bodies and are highly important in the nation's economy. Most are members of the Confederation of British Industry (CBI).

The former owners and shareholders were divested of their ownership and were compensated by the Government for their properties which were then vested in the **Corporations** or **Boards** set up by the various statutes to manage and supervise the industries as efficiently as possible in the interest of the public. How far this has been achieved is always open to controversy.

The Conservatives have traditionally opposed nationalisation as ultimately leading to the totalitarian state and viewed the inroads of Government control of industry with suspicion. The outcome of the clash between the main parties has been the creation of the **public corporations**. (The alternative has been for the State to acquire partial or major shareholdings in private companies, e.g. BP.)

Apart from the industrial corporations (sometimes called 'managerial–economic corporations') such as those created for coal, gas, electricity, transport, etc., there are also non-industrial corporations (sometimes called 'managerial-social corporations') which were created after the Second World War to provide various social services. Thus, the *National Health Service Act, 1946* imposed on the Minister of Health a duty to create a comprehensive health service through Regional Hospital Boards (now Regional Health Authorities). The *New Towns Act, 1946* (now consolidated in Acts of 1965 and 1968) empowers a Minister to order the site of a new town to contain the overspill of city populations where these have become too crowded. Thirty-two new towns have been established in Britain, and their origin is due to the creation of a public ('development') corporation to initiate the acquisition of land and to develop the site for the new inhabitants. The **Development Corporations** produce a master plan, the capital cost is advanced from public funds, officials are appointed, houses, schools, etc., are built, and on completion the town becomes a local authority with powers similar to those possessed by all similar bodies. The **Arts Council** was set up in 1946 and given funds to encourage cultural life in Britain.

Current Policy

The present Conservative Government, since 1979, has sought to **'privatise'** or de-nationalise certain areas of State activity. This may take the form of selling off the assets in whole or in part to private owners (e.g. this is happening with British Airways, British Aerospace, British Rail Properties, British National Oil Corporation (BNOC), National Freight, British Gas, etc. Altogether it will affect up to half of the State industries). Secondly, the Government is breaking into the monopoly position of some corporations by allowing private firms to set up in competition (e.g. in the case of telecommunications a private firm called 'Mercury' was allowed to compete with British Telecom before it was privatised; and competition in passenger transport has been introduced following de-regulation of the buses under the *Transport Act, 1985*). Thirdly, by seeking to improve the management and efficiency of the industries which remain in the hands of the State, especially by means of clearer objectives, performance targets and tighter financial discipline (especially by limiting external financing limits: these so-called EFLs comprise the total of Government grant, borrowing (State or private), leasing and any share capital arrangements).

Another aspect of this policy is to privatise the management of public services, as with naval dockyards under the *Dockyard Services Acts, 1986*. (In so far as foreign companies win such contracts, this raises the question of the security of our nuclear and other weapons systems.)

The Government aims both to increase efficiency in these industries and raise funds in order to reduce State borrowing (PSBR). De-nationalisation and de-municipalisation (e.g. through private refuse collections) are also regarded as elements in traditional Conservative ideology. On the other hand the Labour Party has threatened re-nationalisation (perhaps without compensation) and the additional State takeover of banking and insurance enterprises.

Government Department Form of Organisation

Where a Government Department carries on a service or an industry, a Minister is appointed to be in charge of it and is politically responsible for its administration. His policy will be criticised in Parliamentary debates, for example, and he will be accountable to Parliament for the decisions of civil servants in the Department in the normal way (see p. 131). Estimates will have to be submitted and approved by Parliament. The Department will be subject to close control by the related Select Committee (see p. 81), the Public Accounts Committee (see p. 113) and the Treasury.

It is argued that Parliament is not the place for debates on details of business or commercial administration. Its main function is the discussion of major political issues. MPs and Ministers lack the experience, technical knowledge, and skill to exercise proper control and management of an industry. Civil servants who are appointed to run or manage an industry frequently lack enterprise and initiative and the desire to make a profit— qualities which are the life-blood of successful commercial undertakings. Moreover, if they are subject to attack or criticism in or out of Parliament they will tend to play for safety, avoiding the risks which bold and imaginative policies entail. A cautious, middle-of-the-road approach ensures a more peaceful existence. Civil servants tend also to follow precedent, the usual procedures, and these tend to make for inefficiency and unprofitability. Each item of expenditure may be questioned and each item of service is provided at the lowest possible cost. **State-owned industries** are usually monopolies. This lack of competition is traditionally held to be wasteful. Hence the current policy (see pp. 177, 186).

On the other hand efficient **private enterprise** is usually characterised by (i) the need for profit, (ii) speedy production of goods or services at the lowest cost and sale at the best price, (iii) all financial risk being taken by the owner, e.g. he invests his capital, in buildings, plant, or goods, provided the ultimate end is a potentially higher overall profit, (iv) competition, which ensures greater efficiency, since the owner who produces the best goods at the lowest price will command a market.

General Characteristics of Public Corporations

The following are the main features common to all public corporations:

(i) *Creation*. They are corporations created by statute.

(ii) *Ownership*. The corporations are publicly owned.

(iii) *Legal Capacity*. They can sue and be sued in their corporate names.

(iv) *Employees*. They are not civil servants. Each corporation recruits its own staff and lays down its own conditions of service.

(v) *Profit*. The corporations are not solely profit-making, but each corporation must balance its accounts taking one year with another.

(vi) *Accountability*. The corporations are exempt from Parliamentary control of their day-to-day management but not policy.

(vii) *Finance*. Revenue is obtained from the goods and services they provide. They may borrow money from the Government (the Treasury) for long-term capital development; they may also borrow privately. In addition they may receive grants or subsidies, and some raise a proportion of their capital from share issues. They do not submit estimates to Parliament.

Altogether, they currently account for some 7 per cent of national production and they employ over one million people. (In 1979, the figures were 10 per cent and 2 million.)

Examples of Public Corporations

Public corporations are amongst the largest employers in the country, and they are responsible for huge expenditures. Collectively they form part of the area of the constitution known as 'intermediate Government'; individually they are sometimes known as 'quangos' (see p. 377). The number of corporations is too great for detailed account here. The following notes will help to show the main features of some of the public corporations prominent in national life today.

National Coal Board

This body was created by the *Coal Industry (Nationalisation) Act, 1946*. The Board comprises a Chairman and eight to eleven members. The Board is appointed by the Energy Minister. Members must be paid and are selected from qualified persons. The Minister may give directions of a general character on matters appearing to affect the national interest, after consultation. The main function of the Board is to work and get coal, to secure the efficient development of coal-mining industry, and to make supplies of coal available. The Industrial Coal Users and Domestic Users Consumers' Councils exist to allow of official representation to the Board by the users. The NCB received heavy financial support (£47 million) under the *Coal Industry Act, 1967*, to relieve hardship caused by the diminution of the coal industry.

Electricity

The Central Electricity Generating Board was set up under the *Electricity Act, 1957*. It comprises a Chairman and seven to nine members, one of whom is Deputy Chairman. The Board members are appointed by the Energy Minister and must be chosen from qualified persons. The principal function of the Board is that it may give directions to the Area Boards (see below) and must co-ordinate the distribution of electricity. It may generate and acquire supplies of electricity.

The Electricity Council was constituted by the *Electricity Acts, 1947 and 1957*. The Council comprises a Chairman, two Deputy Chairmen, and three members, together with three members of the CEGB, and the Chairmen of the Area Boards. The Energy Minister appoints only the Chairman and the Deputy Chairman, and he may give such directions of a general nature as seem to be in the national interest. The principal function of the Electricity Council is to advise the Minister and to promote and assist maintenance and development by Area Boards of 'an efficient, co-ordinated and economical system of electricity supply'.

The Area Boards. There are twelve Area Boards. All owe their existence to the Electricity Acts mentioned above. Each Area Board consists of a Chairman and five to seven members. One may be Deputy Chairman. The Energy Minister appoints from qualified persons, and may give similar directions as those to the Electricity Council. The Area Boards' function is to acquire bulk electricity, and carry out efficient and economical distribution in their Area. There is a Consumer Council attached to each Area Board. (*Note*: there are plans to sell the industry off by 1990.)

Gas

Up to 1986 when it was sold off to private shareholders the British Gas Corporation comprised a Chairman, Deputy, and the Chairmen of the Area Gas Boards (see below). The Energy Minister appointed the members who were paid. The Chairman and the Deputy Chairman had to be qualified persons. The Minister could give directions of a general character after consultation. The function and duty of the corporation was to advise the Minister, to promote and assist the efficient exercise and performance by the Area Boards of their functions.

The Area Boards. There were twelve Area Boards, each made up of a Chairman, Deputy, and four to six members, plus the Chairman of the Area Consultative Council. The members were paid, and the Chairman and Deputy Chairman had to have had experience and shown capacity in gas supply. The Minister could give directions of a general character after consultation with the Gas Council and the Board. The duty of each Area Gas Board was to develop and maintain an efficient co-ordinated and economical system of gas supply for their area. There was a Gas Consultative Council attached to each Area Board through whom the public could make representations or complain.

Health

The *National Health Service Act, 1946*, imposed on the Minister of Health
a duty to create a comprehensive health service. Hospital and specialist
services are administered on behalf of the Minister. The *National Health
Service (Reorganisation) Act, 1973*, created a three-tier structure in England:

   (i) Regional Health Authority (14);
  (ii) Area Health Authority (90);
 (iii) District Management teams (DMTs).

In 1982, the Area Health Authorities were replaced by 192 District
Health Authorities, which incorporated the DMTs.

The chain of responsibility moves upwards from district to region, and
finally to the Department of Health.

The Act specifies a number of bodies—e.g. local authorities, trade unions,
and professional organisations—which the Secretary of State must consult
before making appointments to the regional authorities. Local authorities
nominate members to District Health Authorities, and the regional
authorities must consult the appropriate bodies before making their nom-
inations.

The aim of the reorganisation was to create a more unified health service,
and, after 1982, a more streamlined and responsive service. After the
Griffiths inquiry (1983) the emphasis turned to effectiveness and efficiency:
general managers have been appointed to all levels of the service, and
more managerial attitudes are being introduced with a view to giving better
value for money.

In Wales, Scotland, and Northern Ireland there are no regional authorities; each district authority is directly responsible to the relevant Minister
and central department. In Northern Ireland both health and personal
social services are the responsibility of one authority in each area.

The British Broadcasting Corporation

The BBC was incorporated under Royal Charter (see p. 193) as successor
to the British Broadcasting Company, Ltd., whose licence expired in 1926.
Then followed the grant of a Charter which expired in 1964. The present
Charter, renewed in 1981, expires 1996. The BBC forms an exception to
the general rule in that it owes its corporate status to the Charter and not
statute.

The BBC was created as a corporation to avoid the possibility of political interference in so important a matter as broadcasting—radio or TV.

The Chairman, Vice-Chairman, are other Governors (ten), drawn from
a range of interests, and appointed by the Crown. They appoint the Director-General (i.e. chief executive) and can dismiss him (as occurred to Mr
Alisdair Milne in 1987). The part-time Governors receive £8,300 per annum
apart from the Chairman who receives £32,700.

The BBC is financed by revenue from receiving licences for the Home
Services and by a Grant in Aid from Parliament for External Services. The
total number of television licences in force (1987) was 18,887,211 (4,887,663

monochrome and 13,779,548 colour). Radio-only licences were abolished on 1 February 1971.

The Independent Broadcasting Authority (IBA)

Under the *Television Act, 1954*, the IBA was created to provide television and (since 1972) local radio with information, education and entertainment services. The Chairman and members of the Authority are appointed by the Home Secretary. The programmes transmitted from the Authority's forty-five stations are provided by fifteen independent programme contractors whose revenue derives from the sale, subject to controls exercised by the Authority, of advertising time. The contractors pay a rent to the Authority to meet the IBA's own requirements and a levy based on net advertising revenue to the Exchequer.

There is a Chairman, a Deputy Chairman and nine Governors, and like the BBC it has its Director-General with supporting staff. Its general role is that it acts as a competitor with the BBC but like the BBC is a public corporation and adopts similar standards of public responsibility.

Both the BBC and the IBA have a considerable degree of freedom in the programmes they produce, but where matters are raised in Parliament, the responsible Minister is the Home Secretary.

Management

One problem facing the nationalised industries is the engagement of outstanding individuals to fill the management posts at the head of the important industries entrusted to their direction. As to salary, the nationalised industries stand half-way between private industry and the Civil Service. It is clear that unless attractive salaries are paid the best men will not accept the posts available. In 1980, in order to appoint Ian MacGregor as chairman of the British Steel Corporation, the Government agreed to pay a 'transfer fee' of £1.825 m. to secure his release from an American merchant bank where he was currently engaged. Chairmen's salaries are currently (1987) about £90,000 p.a. They have formed themselves into the Nationalised Industries Chairmen's Group, which meets regularly with Ministers.

Some of the members of the corporations are part-time and others full-time. The constitution of each of the Boards varies widely. There are former senior civil servants, industrialists, professional men (lawyers, accountants, etc.), university professors, engineers, scientists, and senior personnel of the Armed Forces. Sometimes senior trade union leaders have been appointed to management posts. Engagements are offered for five years, on occasions, but at any time the Minister may dismiss a member or call upon a particular individual to resign. Full-time members must devote their whole time to the corporation; part-time members may continue other employment.

The selection of the best personnel is one of the current problems. The leadership of an industry is vital to its success; the increasing complexity of the technical aspects demands that the managers must know more of the detail of the industry and they must possess the personal qualities which command respect of the lower ranks of the industry and the public—the consumers or customers at large. The tendency today is to appoint to the management career administrators or scientists already employed within the particular industry.

Personnel Policy

The efficiency of an industry depends on good management guiding the industry and efficient execution at all levels, from the top administrator or scientist to the newest recruit in the office or on the factory floor. Each corporation is responsible for salary policy and must compete for available men and women by offering a satisfactory and worthwhile career within its own industry. All public corporations must, therefore, adopt high standards in relation to employment policy: thus they must provide good conditions of service, pension schemes, adequate holiday arrangements, sickness pay, and provide training schemes for staff.

Arrangements are made for workers' consultation with the management through consultative committees. Trade Unions negotiate at national, regional, or local level to ensure satisfactory wages and conditions of employment, including safety precautions, health measures, and amenities for staff. Despite the *Trade Union and Labour Relations Act* strikes continue in the nationalised industries, the most notable illustration of which was the coal miners' strike of 1984–5.

The Problem of Control

If we assume the public corporation is a semi-independent body, 'publicly owned', producing goods and services for the public generally, the questions arise as to who exercises control over it and as to how that control is exercised. The Electricity and the Gas Boards are obvious cases in point, though other corporations may be cited where the problem of political and managerial control and responsibility arises.

There are two opposite viewpoints: (i) a public service or industry may be managed and operated as a Government Department. The GPO provided a service and until 1968 all the staff were civil servants with a Ministerial head, the Postmaster-General. From 1968 it became a public corporation; (ii) A public service may be managed in the same way as an efficient private enterprise, i.e. a private or public company.

If the corporations spend, or are financed by, public money and, if they administer services on behalf of the public, they ought in theory to be subject to public (i.e. Parliamentary) control through a Minister. The need for such control is undeniable. If all competition is eliminated (as it normally is) by the creation of a State-owned monopoly, periodic inquiries by the elected representatives of the people (i.e. Parliament) are necessary. The public are taxpayers and, in essence, replace the original shareholders (e.g. of the former gas companies existing before 1946) and they are entitled to know how their affairs are being run. The advocates of nationalisation say that the nationalised industries are too important to be left in the hands of private individuals.

If, on the other hand, an industry or trading service is to operate on commercial or semi-commercial lines, it follows that good business management cannot be maintained by the appointment of elected members to run them. Elected members are not *ipso facto* good managers. Moreover, good management which is noted for its drive, initiative, inventiveness and similar qualities cannot thrive or survive if it is subject to detailed control by Parliament or by a Minister.

The art of government is the art of compromise. The result has been an attempt to combine the virtues of both forms, leading to the creation of the public corporations of today.

Ministerial Control

Most public corporations act today in association with or under the general surveillance of a Minister (e.g. see p. 153). The extent of a Minister's control can be ascertained only from the statute creating the corporation. Generally, Ministerial control is exercised in the following ways:

(i) *Appointment of Members*. The Minister appoints members of the corporation and may remove members if he is not satisfied with their work.

(ii) *Directions*. The statute usually authorises a Minister to give **general directions** where the national interest is involved, e.g. such as price restraint policy.

(iii) *Specific Controls*. A Minister may appoint auditors and approve programmes of reorganisation or development involving capital expenditure and use of surplus revenues. The Minister controls borrowing powers e.g. how much can be borrowed, from what source (private or State), etc.

Where a corporation requires public money to meet losses or finance its investment or expand its building or machinery it is right that a Minister keeps a close watch on why the particular industry needs the money. How far a corporation should be aided is a matter of political controversy. Where public money is invested and a Minister begins to interfere in the management this may lead to inefficient operation. The closure of an uneconomic railway line may be justified on grounds of economy, but it may be attacked by those members of the public immediately affected by the loss of rail service and inconvenience.

Parliamentary Control

A Minister is now required to answer in Parliament only generally concerning the aims, activities, and problems of a particular corporation. Parliamentary controls operate in the following ways:

(i) *Annual Report*. Each public corporation is required by statute to submit an annual report. This is sent to the Minister who must lay it before Parliament, together with any report made by him.

(ii) *Annual Accounts*. A copy of the annual accounts is required to be submitted to the Minister. A copy is also laid before Parliament.

(iii) *Debates.* The annual report and the accounts may be the subject of debate. The House may debate the conduct of the public corporations on special motions and on Opposition (formerly Supply Days (see p. 118). The debates are limited to general issues of policy and have little value in practice.

(iv) *Finance.* The Financial Committees of the House of Commons have little influence over the public corporations. Each corporation is expected to pay its way, taking one year with another. But, sometimes a failure results, or money is asked for from Parliamentary funds. Parliament may then debate the motion for financial aid.

(v) *Parliamentary Questions.* Because the Minister is not wholly responsible for the work of the corporation he cannot be called to account for the administration of the industry. Parliamentary questions on the corporations may only be asked on matters for which the Minister is responsible, i.e. general directions, and matters of public importance.

We have noted the reasons for this already. Good management is hindered and harassed if it is subjected to scrutiny, controversy, and interference by Parliament. The opponents of this view stress that the object of creating the nationalised industries (usually a monopoly) was to make them subject to popular (i.e. Parliamentary) criticism and that real grievances of the public should be expressed in Parliament and that the corporations should not be protected from Parliamentary criticism. The Parliamentary Commissioner for Administration does not handle complaints against public corporations.

(vi) *Select Committee on Nationalised Industries.* Set up in 1956, this Committee was required 'to examine the report and accounts of the nationalised industries' and 'to obtain further information about their current policy and practices'. The Committee has made visits, heard evidence, and produced reports. These reports have kept other MPs informed of what is happening and many of their recommendations have been accepted by Ministers. Though limited to examining one industry a year (through lack of time) it has been one of the most effective Parliamentary controls. Its primary duty has been to call the attention of MPs to all matters affecting the efficiency of the nationalised industries. In this way Parliament can protect the public interest while not making the industries themselves accountable to the House for their day-to-day administration. These responsibilities now, for each industry, fall within the scope of the relevant departmental Select Committee (see pp. 80–2) e.g. the coal industry would be of special interest to the Energy Select Committee, though matters affecting more than one industry may be considered by a joint sub-committee of these committees.

Funding by Treasury loans or by guarantees or external borrowing is important. So is pricing. To keep pace with requirements the nationalised industries must be properly managed. Strong managers are appointed; they see what needs to be done but may then be prevented by Government. Clashes occur and resignations or dismissals often result. Sir Richard Marsh (British Rail), Sir Monty Finneston (British Steel), and Sir Arthur Hawkins (CEGB) in 1976 joined the other leaders who 'fell on the field of battle', as did Lord Robens, Sir Brian (now Lord) Robertson, and others.

Parliamentary control over the public corporations is not very effective. Having regard to the underlying dilemma of management (already discussed) this seems inevitable. But current reform plans may alter this if State industries come within the purview of the C&AG (see p. 108).

Consumer Protection and the Nationalised Industries

Consumers' Councils have been set up in relation to certain industries. Thus two Consumers' Councils exist in regard to the coal industry, namely, (i) the Industrial Consumers' Council, representing merchants and industrial users, to whom coal is supplied in bulk; and (ii) Domestic Coal Consumers' Council, which represents groups concerned with the domestic use of coal. These bodies report to the Minister. Another example is the Post Office User's National Council (POUNC).

Consultative Councils have also been appointed, and can be found, for example, in the gas (formerly) and electricity industries. Each area of the country has its Consultative Council (twenty to thirty members) mainly nominated by local authority associations and by bodies representing industry, commerce, trade, and similar activities and associations. The duties of the Consultative Councils are to hear complaints from the public and to raise general matters affecting the rights of consumers. The object of the Councils was to act as bodies to which users could turn for defence and protection and to which management could turn for views of persons using the services, i.e. consumers. In practice their existence is little known to the public and they are generally felt to lack 'teeth', but they are not without value to the community. Nevertheless, there is a danger of their developing a 'cosy relationship' with the industry and too great a readiness to accept uncritically the views of their industry's management rather than pursue the interests of consumers.

Recent Developments and Current Issues

The principle underlying the Public Corporation is that of semi-independence: of an 'arm's length' relationship between the State industry and the Government to allow the former's freedom to operate appropriately in a business context. But it is a vague concept, lacking a clear definition of just how long the 'arm' should be. Consequently Ministers interfere as they see fit or as conditions require or allow—though the intervention is usually unofficial or covert: 'nods and winks' and 'lunchtable directives' e.g. to buy British materials, fly uneconomic routes, keep particular (uneconomic) pits or rail lines open.

The present Conservative Government has sought to exercise control over the industrial Corporations by control of their borrowing. It was argued that their borrowing 'crowded out' private sector access to funds, and also increased the State's total borrowing (the PSBR, which according to the *monetarist* view influences inflation by affecting the money supply). But the Government is also committed to a policy of **privatisation** of State industries. Some have been sold outright to private ownership (e.g. National

Freight); others are having a substantial private shareholding introduced into them (e.g. British Telecom; Aerospace; Cable and Wireless). Alongside this, some State monopolies are beginning to face competition as private enterprises are allowed and encouraged to trade in their field. And the State industries are to be subject to greater scrutiny of their efficiency by the Monopolies and Mergers Commission e.g. one such scrutiny in 1984 resulted in a doubling or more in the rate of return on the assets of an Electricity Board's appliance retailers.

Privatisation is also being applied to certain non-Corporation State activities such as Ordnance Survey and the Royal Ordnance Factories; and at local level, services such as refuse collection, catering, laundering and vehicle testing, which are being sold off or contracted out to private business. And another form of privatisation has been the introduction of private management into State-owned establishments (e.g. the management of the dockyards, under the *Dockyards Act, 1986*).

Some of these moves have met strong resistance from employees, unions and some chairmen, and some have successfully resisted certain plans (e.g. sale of gas showrooms in 1982). But some industries welcome the policy as it frees them from 'the dead hand of the Treasury'.

From the Government's point of view, the policy brings in revenue and lowers the PSBR, and it makes for the more efficient allocation of the nation's resources by subjecting them to market forces rather than central State direction. But time will tell. And there is always the possibility of re-nationalisation (although the Labour Party is committed to a policy involving greater variety in the forms of State or 'Social Ownership', including partial ownership, worker participation on boards or worker co-operatives).

Exercises

1. Compare the 19th century boards with today's public corporations.
2. Evaluate the concept of the public corporation.
3. Explain Parliament's relationship to the public corporations.
4. Discuss the operation of consumer protection in the public enterprise sector.
5. Describe the distinction between the BBC and the IBA.

6
Public Opinion, Pressure Groups, and the Mass Media

Public Opinion and the Government

Public opinion is a vague concept. All we may note is that it is the attitude of mind of most people. There are certain matters about which most people are commonly agreed. Most people in this country support the Monarchy; most people support Parliament and its institutions; most people support the judiciary and its traditional independence; most people support the police in their task to preserve public order. But, by the very nature of things, there is a division of opinion concerning politics, i.e. policies, leaders, and MPs.

Some of the problems facing Government today are highly controversial. For example: (i) the future of the House of Lords; (ii) Britain's membership of the European Economic Community; (iii) British action towards nuclear disarmament; (iv) British intervention in Northern Ireland and the cure of the civil disturbances there, (v) the cure of unemployment involving $3\frac{1}{4}$ million; and (vi) the legal control of Trade Unions.

Most people do have views. Some think deeply about a problem; others accept what is printed in the Press or broadcast on radio or television. There are people, too, who do not bother to go beyond the headlines and have no opinion worthy of the name.

If a Government controls (i) the Press, and (ii) radio and television, it may control public opinion to a large extent. Totalitarian or authoritarian states like the USSR do this. As everyone knows, the first requirement of a valid opinion is (i) the ascertainment of the true facts, (ii) the application of rational thought, to which may be added (iii) experience of life and judgement of the practicalities of the situation which enable a forecast of probabilities or possibilities. Mankind is, however, not gifted with foresight, and sometimes reaches conclusions by using false data and imperfect reasoning.

In wartime a democratic State through its Government is justified in suppressing information or controlling it, first because the release of vital information may be useful to the enemy, and secondly because a Government does not want to spread alarm or despondency or to disseminate false news or rumour which can be damaging to the war effort. The *Defence Regulations, 1939*, operated certain controls.

In peace-time no such controls operate. The Press is free **within the law**, the BBC and IBA are independent institutions and are not controlled by the Government as to what is transmitted by these powerful organs. Each body is controlled by Governors who, although appointed by a government

Minister (the Home Secretary), have practically autonomous powers to administer the service. Both the BBC and IBA have resisted Government interference and notable figures, e.g. Lord Reith, a former Director-General, have withstood pressures from outside so that independence is assured but see pp. 193–4.

Public Opinion Polls

Formerly, public opinion was considered to be too vague to predict or to form a useful guide in politics. Politicians formed their own idea of public opinion (some still do). They had hunches and moved among the people to find out how they felt about policies and events.

Today public opinion or public reaction can be more accurately ascertained by **sample** and **research** techniques. Broadly speaking, this involves making a sample survey of, say, one person in a 1,000, all over the country. Questions are asked, and answers are recorded. By this means a fairly accurate guide can be obtained of public reaction to a particular issue. For example, the popularity-rating of a Prime Minister, or Leader of the Opposition, can be assessed and charted on a graph which shows how people think over a period of months as a result of policies proposed or applied, or stemming from his personal impact on TV or radio. It has also been possible to forecast the result of an election with considerable accuracy.

This system of sampling and research was first introduced in America by **Dr Gallup** in 1941. The techniques achieved a certain fame, and were introduced into this country later. The **National Opinion Poll** is another organisation (privately financed) which also conducts surveys on similar lines. Similar methods are used by industry to forecast possible demands for certain goods. Politically, therefore, the surveys or polls are an important part of the present political scene. The main 'public opinion' companies operating in the UK in 1983 are (i) Gallup, (ii) National Opinion Poll (NOP), (iii) Marplan, (iv) Harris, (v) Opinion Research Centre, (vi) Research Services Ltd. and (vii) Market and Opinion Research International (MORI). They are all independent of the Government. NOP, for example, is owned by Associated Newspapers, Ltd. But the forecasting or sampling of political views held by the public is merely one aspect of the research sampling undertaken by these groups.

Parliamentary By-Elections

Where a by-election is held for a Parliamentary seat, much attention will be paid by the Government and the Opposition to the result. Let us examine the following example for the 'Oxbridge' Constituency:

Table 4.

Party	1983 General Election	Party	1986 By-Election
Cons.	20,000	Lab.	22,000
Lab.	15,000	Cons.	14,000
Lib.	5,000	Lib.	4,000
	40,000		40,000

If we assume the same number of people turned out for both elections (say eighty per cent), then we may conclude that there is evidence which indicates a large swing away from Conservative which lost 6,000 votes (20,000–14,000). Labour, on the other hand, increased its vote by 7,000 (from 15,000 to 22,000). The Liberal candidate lost 1,000 (5,000–4,000) votes. The change in representation may be due to various factors: (i) the unpopularity of present Government measures; (ii) increased activity of the local Labour organisation in getting voters out to the election booths; (iii) a change of candidate; (iv) local unemployment; or (v) a basic desire on the part of the voters to give the other fellow a chance to prove what he can do. There are many factors to consider. But, all parties will regard the by-election as significant, though by no means conclusive, that the same sort of result would be recorded all over the country if a general election were to be held in the next year.

Local Government Elections

Local government seats are contested each year. The local authorities are usually composed of (i) Conservatives, (ii) Labour, (iii) Alliance and (iv) Independent candidates. Although only thirty to forty per cent of the electorate turn out for these elections, they do serve as a guide—but only a guide—as to what people in the constituencies feel and think about politics.

The above factors, namely Public Opinion polls, Parliamentary by-elections, and local government elections, are important indications of public feeling to which politicians of all parties pay heed.

The following list indicates some of the other sources available to Government and Opposition parties to gauge public opinion:

    (i) Letters to Government Departments and Ministers.
   (ii) Letters to MPs.
  (iii) Letters in the Press.
  (iv) Press comments.
   (v) **BBC** and **IBA** broadcasts, showing how the 'man in the street' feels and thinks about persons and policies, or even politics in general.
  (vi) Films such as 'Cathy Come Home' depicting the experiences of a family evicted from their home and the processes followed by local authorities, social services, the police, court officials and others.
 (vii) Pressure Groups, e.g. CBI, TUC, Local government representative organisations, and the other bodies referred to on p. 191.

By tapping all these sources it is possible to build up a picture of public opinion on which, in the long run, a Government wins or loses.

As we have seen, a Government influences public opinion by means of policies, personalities, and events, and the people (the governed) in their turn influence their representatives. It is a case of action and reaction.

We may say, therefore, that today Prime Ministers will pay heed to all the above sources in fixing the date of the general election when they put themselves and their parties to the test of public approval or rejection via the ballot box.

Pressure Groups

Pressure groups are groups of people who seek to change or influence the policy of a Government by persuasion, but without themselves assuming or usurping the power of Government.

The phrase 'pressure group' is not a precise term and may be misleading. All persons or groups have an inherent right in a civilised democratic society to approach or to try to influence an MP or a Government Minister. It is inevitable, therefore, that democratic legislatures must be subjected to 'lobbying'. The larger the number in a particular group the greater will be its persuasive force or pressure. There is strength in numbers. Generally, we may say also that the wealth of a group or its social or economic power increases its importance and the strength of its pressure.

Any persuasion or pressure applied must be lawful. Thus threats of personal violence to a MP or Minister constitute a crime; threats to Parliament as an institution could amount to sedition (the use of any form of physical force in any public matter connected with the State) and would be a breach of the privilege of either House. The forms of pressure usually include the following: (i) approach to MP or Minister personally or by letter; (ii) contacts with Government officials (e.g. via consultative and advisory committees—see p. 144); (iii) deputations to Parliament; (iv) mass meetings; (v) Press propaganda, TV and radio interviews; (vi) demonstrations and marching with banners through the streets.

Types of Pressure Group

In a complex society there are many interests and minority groups. In the past some have had worthy and beneficial ideals, e.g. the Anti-Slavery League or the Suffragette Movement. Their activities have resulted in enlightened public attitudes and progressive changes in the law. The various kinds of groups existing today may be broadly classified as:

(i) *Promotional* (or *Sectional*), where they seek to promote or protect the interests of members. Trade Unions provide an example. The Trades Union Congress (TUC) has a total membership of over 9 million members and maintains systematic relations with the Government and its Departments. The Transport and General Workers' Union has over $1\frac{1}{2}$ million members. Other unions include the NUT (teachers), NGA (printers), MU (musicians), NUM (miners), NUR (railmen). The Confederation of British Industry (CBI) represents the management side of industry and advises the Government on all aspects of state policy affecting business interests. Membership consists of 11,500 companies and over 200 trade associations and employers' bodies. The National Farmers Union represents 90 per cent of British farmers. Similarly, the British Medical Association protects the interests of doctors, while the legal profession is represented by the Law Society (solicitors) and the Bar Council (barristers).

(ii) *Cause groups* seek to influence official policy on behalf of others or the whole of society e.g. the Lord's Day Observance Society, the Howard League for Penal Reform, the Campaign for Nuclear Disarmament (CND), the National Council for Civil Liberties (NCCL), and Age Concern. They are described as 'groups for' (cf. 'groups of', above).

This classification is not perfect for some groups may fall into both categories (e.g. as when the TUC presses for better state pensions). And for many organisations, acting politically is only incidental to their main activities (e.g. Trade Unions, Women's Institutes, motoring or sports clubs).

The Case For

(i) People form groups through identity of interest, so pressure groups are natural and necessary in a democratic society.

(ii) Groups educate (*a*) the public, and (*b*) their own members by clarifying the issues or moderating the extreme views of some members.

(iii) Minority views may be more effectively expressed through group pressure, and social justice more quickly and easily achieved. Old Age Pensioners unable to cope with the rise in the cost of living are examples of this.

(iv) Pressure groups may act as watchdogs in keeping track of issues that the general public might overlook.

(v) The Government is entitled to the best information available and habitually consults affected interests before proposed legislation. Thus the Minister of Transport Industries proposes to raise to 17 the age at which a person may ride a motor-cycle. He will consult the AA, the RAC, the police, vehicle manufacturers, RoSPA (Royal Society for the Prevention of Accidents), the medical profession, Road Research Laboratories and others. There are 7,500 deaths and 400,000 persons injured on the roads each year and the Minister's responsibility is to try to reduce this appalling number of deaths and injuries.

The Case Against

(i) Some groups are too powerful, e.g. the Confederation of British Industry (CBI), the Trade Unions, and the NFU.

(ii) The interests of consumers (i.e. the public) are not adequately protected, despite the existence of Consumer Associations. Producers organise themselves in their own economic interest.

(iii) Persons unable to organise themselves through illiteracy, lack of education, or ability are at a disadvantage in competition with those who can.

(iv) Poverty or the dispersal of a group frequently results in its ineffectiveness (contrast the CBI and the TUC and the Trade Unions which are financially powerful).

(v) Groups can sabotage or blackmail a Government. Thus if all doctors agreed to opt out of the National Health Service the service would be brought to a standstill; if all dockers refused to unload ships, or the police refused to enforce the law, or teachers refused to teach, or if all Trade Unions refused to co-operate in the administration of an Industrial Relations Act, the country could be brought to a standstill, and much damage could be done.

Resolving the Difficulties

In the final analysis, the elected Government must govern. It follows that a Government must reach decisions, impose legislation or issue its instructions. But only after it has weighed (i) the interest of the nation, and (ii) the interest of the minority group or factions which exert pressure. The over-riding duty of a Government is to safeguard the security and prosperity of the United Kingdom and its peoples, and to achieve that a Government must make decisions now for long-term as well as short-term benefits. But Parliament has similar responsibilities, and it may take a different view of what is right. Since ultimately Parliament is sovereign, it can impose its will on the Government of the day—as happened in 1986 when the legislation to allow Sunday trading was defeated, due in large measure to the efforts of the Lord's Day Observance Society and its campaign to 'Keep Sunday Special'.

The Mass Media

We have already discussed the Press (see p. 188) and the BBC and IBA (see p. 181) and their place in the Constitution.

The law relating to the Press has also already been noted in broad outline (see also pp. 260ff.). Under the terms of its Charter the BBC is a Broadcasting Service as 'a means of information, education and entertainment'.

Radio and Television

The Government appoints a Board of (part-time) Governors, under a Chairman. Their role is to allocate resources, ensure balance in programmes and ensure respect for public taste and decency (though the day-to-day management responsibilities are delegated to the Director-General and senior managers).

The BBC is required to broadcast any announcement when so requested by a Minister of Her Majesty's Government (Clause 13(3) of the BBC's licence). In practice, important Government announcements find their place in the regular news bulletins, but the Government may also from time to time require the BBC to make Special 'News Flash' announcements of items of pressing importance such as police messages or outbreaks of war or violence.

The BBC is also required to broadcast an impartial account day by day, prepared by professional reporters, of the proceedings in both Houses of Parliament (Clause 13(2)).

As has been noted, the Governors of the BBC have been granted practically autonomous powers of running the service. Nevertheless under Clause 13(4) the Home Secretary may from time to time by notice in writing require the Corporation to refrain at any specified time or at all times from sending any matter or matters of any class specified in such notice. Ministers have respected this independence and the power to direct the withdrawal of a programme has never been used in peacetime. But in 1985 the Home Secretary *requested* the BBC not to transmit a programme (which included an interview with a leading member of Provisional Sinn Fein). Despite the views of the board of management, the Governors acquiesced in the request—provoking an unprecedented strike by broadcasters, and casting doubt on the impartiality or independence of the broadcasting authorities. This was reinforced early in 1987 when, at Government request (on grounds of national security) the BBC withheld the showing of a film involving plans for a secret defence satellite ('Zircon'), though this was followed by a (Special Branch) police raid on the Scottish BBC to obtain the film material for scrutiny, and the removal (using a warrant under the *Official Secrets Act*) of film material for scrutiny. Such an intrusion was unprecedented and understandably gave rise to considerable public concern. (The search warrants, issued under the *Official Secrets Act*, were initiated by the Advocate General—the Scottish equivalent of the Attorney General—and subsequently there were suggestions that those offices should no longer be political i.e. MPs.)

Under clause 13(4) the Minister requires the Corporation to refrain from expressing in broadcasts its own opinion on current affairs or on matters of public policy. The BBC's policy in controversial matters must be one of **impartiality.** However, in April 1981 a group of academics, MPs and trade unionists accused the broadcasting authorities of lacking such impartiality. And in 1986, the Chairman of the Conservative Party (Norman Tebbit) severely criticised the BBC for its anti-Government bias, and provided an analysis of its news coverage (on the bombing of Libya by the USA from bases in Britain) to illustrate the point. The allegation was rebutted, though the BBC did admit one significant error. However, the BBC has also had to deal with complaints of unfair treatment from the other parties too—and as a result, has claimed that it must have the balance about right!

There is an independent **Broadcasting Complaints Commission** (established 1971) to consider complaints from the public of unfair treatment in radio and television programmes. Its three members are appointed for three year periods. The Commission has no sanctions other than publicity (which itself is not insignificant). In 1986, it upheld 12 such complaints.

Mass communication through radio, television, and the Press (which term includes newspapers, books, periodicals, magazines, comics, etc.) must influence the minds of recipients and, therefore, behaviour. The exact effect—whether for good or ill—is the subject of fierce debate. Strong views are often held by individual citizens, no less than by powerful group interests, as to what should or should not be printed in the Press or be broadcast in the way of 'information, education, and entertainment'. It is the duty of the BBC to keep in touch with public opinion and to weigh such representations as may be made to them. It maintains its own Audience Research and notes carefully what is said in Parliament, the Press, or elsewhere. The Press, too, maintains a close watch on public opinion, but unlike the BBC the Press is not a public corporation providing a public service. The Press exists to make a profit and need not be impartial—and clearly is not (see p. 197).

The evidence suggests (see I. Crewe et al, *Political Communication*, CUP, 1986) that most people today get their knowledge of politics from television. (Such is this importance recognised by the parties that they undertake training in the techniques of television interviewing and discussion.) The consequence of this, bearing in mind the required political neutrality of the broadcasting services, is that people are no longer exposed to a particular political point of view, as in the past, when much of their political 'socialisation' tended to be one-sided i.e. family, neighbourhood or a (biased) newspaper, Hence voters have become more fluid and volatile (see pp. 204ff.).

Party Political Broadcasts (PPBs)

These are provided throughout the year by the various political parties. The broadcasting authorities (BBC and IBA) make available to them (without charge) facilities for 3 hours of broadcasting a year (worth some £9m.) and more in the year of a General Election (when they are known as Party Election Broadcasts). The allocation of time is determined for 12 months at a time by the Committee on Party Political Broadcasting, a non-statutory body comprising representatives of the parties and the broadcasting authorities (with a secretary who is a civil servant from the Whips Office in 12 Downing Street). The working principle appears to have been established that parties are allowed 10 minutes broadcasting time for every 2 million votes received. The broadcasting authorities decide broadly what is acceptable and the parties themselves determine the editorial content of the broadcasts. In addition to ordinary PPBs, Governments are given suitable opportunities to explain matters of national importance (including new legislation), and this is always balanced by equal opportunities for the Opposition to reply or respond. And during a General Election, the major parties are given equal exposure in general news items.

For 1983, the Conservative and Labour parties (who always get the same amount of time) had 60 minutes each of television time (and 45 minutes of radio time) and the Liberals got 20 minutes. On a different ratio for their electoral support, the SNP got 30 minutes on the Scottish network and the Welsh Nationalists (Plaid Cwmru) got 10 minutes. The SDP had no General Election vote to indicate their support (having only 2 MPs elected on the SDP 'label' from by-elections in 1982). But they were offered 5 minutes to broadcast under the label 'SDP-Liberal Alliance'.

In 1984–5, Conservative and Labour parties were allocated 6 television and 8 radio broadcasts; the Liberal and Social Democratic parties were given (separately) 2 television and 1 radio broadcast, while as the Alliance they had 1 television and 3 radio broadcasts.

One innovation agreed in January 1980 was the splitting of permitted TV broadcasting time into five-minute slots. Also broadcasts need no longer go out simultaneously on all channels.

How far, it may be asked, do pre-election party political broadcasts affect voting behaviour? The Television Research Unit at Leeds University, sponsored by Granada TV, carried out a survey covering a three-week period only during an electioneering programme. The study revealed that whilst viewers are not influenced significantly to change their attitudes, previously held views, opinions, or attitudes are reinforced (see p. 212). Mass media are more likely to create opinion where the individual has no preconceived viewpoint or clear viewpoint. This particular survey may have been too short for conclusions to be drawn as to the overall effects of mass media. Exposure to political broadcasts over a long period of time may produce different results. It appears that more research is needed into the whole question of the effects of mass media (particularly TV) on the population.

Since 1965 various Select Committees considered the question of broadcasting the proceedings of Parliament, and selective broadcasting. This began in 1975 (see p. 105).

Statistics

Over ninety per cent of the people living in Great Britain have TV and of those with both BBC and ITV channels the average person watches ITV more than BBC.

Time spent per day. One-third of the viewers watch TV for one hour per day, one-third for two hours, and one-third for three to five hours.

During the year October 1968 to September 1969, the amount of time devoted to viewing BBC television amounted to 7.4 hours per week per head of population. By 1980 the average viewing time was 17.5 hours per person per week. The overall average is now 25 hours per week.

To sum up, the BBC and ITV are extending their programmes nationally and locally. Their effect cannot yet be gauged with accuracy. Lord Hill of Luton (Chairman of the Governors of the BBC) referring to the duty of **impartiality** said:

The BBC has no editorial opinion, and its reputation for impartiality is jealously guarded not only within the BBC but by people outside. That is why any critic with a suspicion that the Corporation is showing bias is liable to express shocked resentment—and the outcry is all the sharper when the matter of dispute arouses bitter personal feelings. One of the hardest tests in the history of the BBC came in 1969 when we were broadcasting to the people of Northern Ireland at a time when argument had burst into the violence of stones, petrol bombs and firearms. At such times, those who are most hotly partisan do not want impartiality; they want the news and views that support their own fiercely held opinions. In this difficult period the BBC was assailed by both sides, creating at least a presumption that it had held the middle ground. Tempers were roused, too, though not from such deep emotions, over the Nigerian Civil War and over the attempts to break up the sporting fixtures of South African visitors to Britain. Those who were angered by what they heard, or saw, in our broadcasts found it hard to believe that the BBC was not espousing the cause they detested. But the BBC espouses no cause; it tries to hold the ring in argument. The job of getting the facts right and holding the balance of opinion fairly is a difficult one, and it requires constant vigilance. We may err from time to time but impartiality remains our duty and our objective. (BBC 1970 Handbook.)

Finally it must be noted that the BBC and IBA are subject to the law (see p. 15) and may be prosecuted or sued in their corporate names (e.g. for defamation). Films, radio, and television broadcasts which are defamatory are treated as libel (*Defamation Act, 1952*).

The Press

The Press is a general term which includes daily and weekly newspapers, as well as magazines and specialised papers which appear on the news-stands and in the book shops of all towns in the United Kingdom. There are in fact 124 daily newspapers and Sunday newspapers, and over 1,000 weekly newspapers published in Britain (though they are owned in effect by four company groups). Annual circulation has fallen from 37 million in 1970 to 33.5 million in 1980 and 33.7 million in 1985.

So far as the British Constitution is concerned there is no special press law. The State does not control the Press and does not impose censorship. The Press is, of course, subject to the law. The editor or proprietor of a newspaper or magazine or book may print or publish anything providing such publication does not offend the law.

The main newspapers with their circulations are listed in Table 5. Most are Conservative or Labour but some are independent in outlook or reporting slant. The effect of this is that although in general tone a paper may be politically biased this does not prevent the paper from criticising the Government of the day whatever its political colour. A vigorous and free press is, therefore, essential to a free society, speaking out clearly and strongly when a policy is improper or when corruption is located in public affairs. On the other hand, a newspaper may approve and congratulate Government leaders or private citizens at will, providing the event, incident, or the individual is newsworthy and interesting. The newspaper or magazine is a commercial enterprise. It exists to make a profit, and if it fails to do so it risks bankruptcy or liquidation. Nevertheless editors may still be quite independent from proprietors.

The Press and the Law. In Britain the Press has the same freedom as the individual. In other words it may print or say what it likes so long as it does not transgress the law. The Press (and broadcasting) also has 'qualified privilege' i.e. it can report items from Parliament which would otherwise be libellous or actionable (see p. 261)

There are certain statutes which require the registration of newspapers for postal purposes, but there are no specific press laws. There are, how-

Table 5. The main newspapers and their circulations (1987)

Title	Ownership/control	Political tendency	Average circulation = 34 m
Dailies			
The Times (1785)	News International	Ind./Cons.	503,000
The Daily Telegraph (1855)	Telegraph Newspaper Trust	Cons.	1,140,000
The Independent (1986)	Newspaper Publishing	Ind.	310,000
Daily Express (1900)	United Newspapers	Cons.	1,810,000
Daily Mail (1896)	Associated Newspapers	Cons.	1,830,000
The Sun (1969)	News International	Cons.	4,000,000
Morning Star (1966)	People's Press	Comm.	28,000
Daily Mirror (1903)	Pergamon Press	Ind./Lab.	3,060,000
Financial Times (1888)	Pearson Longman	Ind.	258,000
Today (1985)	Lonrho Group (up to 1987)	Ind/All.	300,000
Daily Star (1978)	United Newspapers	Cons.	1,400,000
The Guardian (1821)	Guardian & Manchester Evening News	Ind./All.	538,000
London Evening			
The Standard (1827/1980)	Associated Newspapers	Ind./Cons.	517,000
Evening News (1881/1987)	Associated Newspapers	Ind./Cons.	100,000
Sundays			
The Observer (1791)	Lonrho Group	Ind./All.	782,000
The Sunday Times (1822)	News International	Ind./Cons.	1,120,000
The Sunday Telegraph (1961)	Telegraph Newspaper Trust	Cons.	675,000
News of the World (1843)	News International	Ind./Cons.	4,800,000
The Sunday People (1881)	Pergamon Press	Ind./Lab.	2,980,000
Sunday Express (1918)	United Newspapers	Cons.	2,310,000
Sunday Mirror (1963)	Pergamon Press	Ind./Lab.	2,990,000
Mail on Sunday (1982)	Associated Newspapers	Cons.	1,630,000

ever, clauses or sections in statutes which apply in particular to the Press. Thus, the extent of newspaper ownership in television companies is limited and there are restrictions on newspaper reporting of preliminary hearings of indictable offences (in England, Wales, and Northern Ireland). The object of this is to preclude prejudice on the accused at his trial before a judge. The Press has the right to attend meetings of local authorities and their committees though they can be required to withdraw from parts of their proceedings.

There are certain restrictions on the publication of: (i) divorce and domestic proceedings in law courts; (ii) advertisement and investment circulars (certain Acts deal with the publication of false or misleading descriptions of goods and services and with fraud); (iii) advertisements of remedies for certain diseases which are covered by public health legislation; (iv) certain types of prize competitions; (v) copyrights.

Of particular importance to the Press are the laws relating to defamation (see p. 261) or contempt of court. A newspaper may not publish comments on the conduct of judicial proceedings which are likely to prejudice their reputation for fairness before or during the legal proceedings. The Press may not, for example, publish before or during a trial anything which might tend to influence the result. The publication of seditious libel, incitement to disaffection, or of official secrets (see p. 262) is unlawful. Libel actions (mostly brought by individuals) render the editor, proprietor, publisher, printer, and distributor liable. The author of any particular article which transgresses the law will, of course, also be held responsible. The courts (via injunction) may ban certain publications e.g. the *Sunday Times* revelations re. MI5 (1987) or Thalidomide drug (1972)

There is also a system of voluntary self-censorship. This operates under the **'D-Notice' system** whereby proposals to withhold the publication of information on defence (hence 'D') and intelligence subjects go before the Defence, Press and Broadcasting Committee for approval. Established in 1912, this Committee comprises civil servants and representatives of the media, the latter having a veto power. On approval a notice is issued urging editors to refrain from publishing certain information (e.g. defence and civil defence plans).

The Press Council. In April 1947 a Royal Commission was appointed to inquire into the control, management, and ownership of the Press and news agencies, and to make recommendations thereon. The Commission, which reported in June 1949, recommended that a Press Council be formed. This was established on 1 July 1953. This constitution was amended in 1963 by the introduction of an independent chairman and up to twenty per cent lay membership. The objects of the Council are:

(i) To preserve the established freedom of the British Press.

(ii) To maintain the character of the British Press in accordance with the highest professional and commercial standards.

(iii) To consider complaints about the conduct of the Press or the conduct of persons and organisations towards the Press; to deal with these complaints in whatever manner might seem practical and appropriate and record resultant action.

(iv) To keep under review developments likely to restrict the supply of information of public interest and importance.

(v) To report publicly on developments that may tend towards greater concentration or monopoly in the Press (including changes in ownership, control and growth of Press undertakings) and to publish statistical information relating thereto.

(vi) To make representations on appropriate occasions to the Government, organs of the United Nations and Press organisations abroad.

(vii) To publish periodical reports recording the Council's work and to review, from time to time, developments in the Press and the factors affecting them.

The Press Council has an independent Chairman, eighteen professional members of the press (representatives of Newspaper Publishers Associations and the National Union of Journalists and the Institute of Journalists), and eighteen lay members representing the public. Reports are published annually.

The Press Council is frequently attacked as being too slow or ineffectual. The National Union of Journalists often claim it too readily takes the management side. Many MPs feel the press should be under statutory control.

The number of complaints against the press has doubled in the past decade. In 1986, the Council received 1,136 complaints, though most were settled or withdrawn before final judgement. Of the 118 cases which were concluded (of which 70 involved national newspapers) 57 were upheld and 61 rejected. When a judgement goes against a paper (as did six involving the *Daily Express* in that year) it is required to publish Council's finding in full. Some feel there should be stiffer sanctions, such as a fine.

Social Class

All societies broadly conform to the pattern of a pyramid with (1) a king, dictator or leader at the apex (surrounded by government staff and aides), (2) a middle group of persons of lesser standing, and (3) a lower group at the base. The pyramid pattern perpetuates itself, and you will see this structure in a modern State, Government Department, factory and office.

In medieval times there were nobles and peasants; Lords, Knights of the Shires, freemen and serfs or villeins. We may note also the 'Three Estates of the Realm': the Monarch, the Lords Spiritual and Temporal, and the Commons. The Lords and Commons continue today, as we have seen. The modern classification is: (1) upper class, (2) middle class, and (3) lower class. That is a broad classification only and we shall note other groups at p. 200.

Objective and Subjective Assessments

Objective assessment of class membership is made by other members of a group or society of another individual member. It is made by using certain characteristics, e.g.

Wealth	Kinship	Occupation
Education	Customs	Leisure
Speech	Manners	Culture
Clothing	Physical movement	Ethnic group

Subjective assessment is made by one person of himself. Mr A puts himself in, say, the middle class because he earns £x per annum and is an accountant. He uses two criteria of measurement: wealth and occupation.

Where kinship is important in a particular society, blood relationship might count more than occupation. So a person of mediocre professional accomplishment who has eminent ancestors might rank higher in the social class than a wealthy and more successful person without eminent ancestors. A bastard son of a king may be instantly ennobled on birth, while a bastard son of a peasant girl was regarded as 'illegitimate' and prejudiced through life.

'The essence of social class is the way a man is treated by his fellows (and, reciprocally, how he treats them), not the qualities or the possessions which cause the treatment. Social class unites into groups people who differ from one another by overriding the differences between them.' (T. H. Marshall, *Citizenship and Social Class*, Cambridge University Press, 1950.)

In developed industrial societies of the modern world the groups or grades or classes are complex and less distinct. In Western liberal democracies, including the US, greater mobility between one group and the other exists. A person can move up or move down. Despite the mobility, classes or social groups continue to exist. People with common interests—religion, education, culture or other factors—combine themselves into groups and classes. 'Birds of a feather flock together,' and persist in so doing.

In the UK, classes in society continue, although they are becoming more blurred. The Registrar-General in the UK, in presenting census data, groups classes by applying criteria to the 'head of the household'. He adopts five classes.

Table 6. Population of Great Britain classified by Social Class (Census 1971)

Social class	Occupation of head of household	Percentage of total population
I	Owners, Managers, Professional	3.6
II	Lower and Intermediate non-manual	17.8
III	Skilled manual and routine non-manual	49.5
IV	Semi-skilled	20.9
V	Unskilled	8.2
	Total	100

The above classification may be broken down further, as shown in the classification opposite also used by the Registrar-General.

This practice raises another factor: once we categorise or classify the 'head of the household'—let us say the male—as belonging to a certain class, his wife and children may partake of a similar status. Others defer to him and he defers to those above him in the class structure. Wives or children reflect the same status and enjoy or suffer (if one moves up or down) the enhanced or diminished status.

Communism and Class

Communism refers to a type of society where all resources belong to the community as a whole and the fruits of the productive process (i.e. goods and services) are distributed according to individual and group needs. No such society yet exists though some claim to be moving in that direction.

Such societies and the whole modern communist movement are based on the theory of Karl Marx (1818–83) as developed by Lenin and others who have sought to apply Marx's analysis to the changed conditions of the twentieth century. (There is continuous argument about how far the basic principles of Marxism–Leninism should be adopted—or revised—to changing circumstances to avoid errors of dogmatism.)

Table 7. Population of England and Wales classified by Socio-Economic Groups Census 1971 (and 1961)

Socio-economic group	Occupation of head of household	Percentage of population	
1	Employers and managers—large establishments	3.4	(3.6)
2	Employers and managers—small establishments	7.9	(5.9)
3	Professional workers—self-employed	0.8	(0.8)
4	Professional workers—employees	3.8	(2.8)
5	Intermediate non-manual workers	5.3	(3.8)
6	Junior non-manual workers	11.9	(12.5)
7	Personal service	1.0	(0.9)
8	Foremen and supervisors—manual	3.5	(3.3)
9	Skilled manual workers	29.0	(30.4)
10	Semi-skilled manual workers	12.6	(14.7)
11	Unskilled manual workers	7.8	(8.6)
12	Own account workers—non-professional	4.2	(3.6)
13	Farmers—employers and managers	0.8	(1.0)
14	Farmers—own account	0.8	(1.0)
15	Agricultural workers	1.6	(2.3)
16	Members of armed forces	1.4	(1.9)
17	Unclassified	4.0	(2.9)
	Total	100.0	

Generally, communists believe that their ultimate task is the establishment of socialism under which all property belongs to the community and social life is based on the principle 'from each according to his *ability*, to each according to his *needs*'. Initially, the envisaged revolution would involve the overthrow of the capitalist system and the establishment of 'the dictatorship of the proletariat' in which the state is regulated on the basis of the principle of 'from each according to his *ability*, to each according to his *work*'. The state would belong to the people, whose energies would be directed to shaping it for the common good. The ownership of property, apart from personal needs, would cease. The aim is thus to establish a classless society in which the exploitation of any section of the community no longer exists and the over-riding precept is that of social equality.

For our purposes we should note that Marx identified two well-known classes:

(i) The bourgeois class (sometimes called '*bourgeoisie*'), made up of property-owning people or the middle class;

(ii) the proletariat class, made up of wage-earners or labouring classes.

The class struggle would ultimately result in the domination of the proletariat after the overthrow of the *bourgeoisie*.

Today the USSR claims to have abolished 'classes'. It has not. Persons in responsible positions in the USSR, e.g. party officials, bureaucrats, top artists, sportsmen and sportswomen, etc., have access to restricted goods and services, privileged medical treatment, special shops and subsidies on houses. The élite thus receive enormous 'fringe benefits'. The ratio of top salaries to the national average is very similar in both the UK and USSR. The pursuit of egalitarianism has no more acceptance in the USSR than in any other developed country. Indeed, there is much evidence to show that the opposite is true, e.g. where a child in the USSR shows signs of exceptional talent or skill more resources are devoted to him or her than is the case in the UK. Little is done in the UK either to identify the gifted child or provide the opportunity to the child to develop the gifts and talents he or she has. The consequent loss to the child or young person and indeed to the nation as a whole is considerable.

Summary

1. Some form of class structure emerges in every society.

2. The form the structure takes depends on the type of society: communist or capitalist, industrial or pre-industrial, or (in the third world) urban or rural classes.

3. Divisiveness and tensions occur once classes form.

4. To reduce dangerous divisiveness and tensions there should be equality of opportunity and mobility in society.

5. Class affects voting behaviour at elections (see later).

6. Universal franchise (one man, one vote) gives the people an opportunity to decide what kind of society it wants.

7. Some politicians emphasise the existence of the 'class struggle' (extreme Left); others seek to promote tolerance, privacy, individuality, freedom from Governmental bureaucracy—or so much of these as our crowded modern life in a crowded island permits.

Social Class and MPs

On p. 94 we referred to the occupations of MPs. For most, this refers to their former occupation (i.e. prior to election; but some MPs continue to combine the job of an MP with another occupation (this is discussed on p. 94).

Occupation is one of the most important features or determinants of social class. The following gives some details of the occupations of MPs at the 1983 General Election. For purposes of comparison, the figures are broken down by party, the overall figures for which are Conservatives 397/Labour 209/Alliance 23. (The 1970 figure is also provided.)

(i) *Professions*

Barrister 56/9/4; solicitor 26/8/1; doctor/dentist 2/2/1; architect/surveyor 6/0/1; civil engineer 7/1/1; chartered secretary/accountant 19/3/1; civil servant/local government 16/10/1; armed services 18/0/1; teaching (university, adult, school) 20/52/3; other consultants 4/0/0; scientific research 3/2/0.
Total in group (i) = *278 of which C 177, L 87, A 14 (1970 figure = 291).*

(ii) *Business*

Company director 33/0/0; company executive 67/5/0; commerce/insurance 31/4/0; managerial/clerical 4/8/1; general business 7/2/0.
Total in group (ii) = *162 of which C 142, L 19, A 1 (1970 figure = 129).*

(iii) *White collar and miscellaneous*

Publisher/journalist 31/9/5; farmer 19/1/1; politician/organiser 12/7/1; miscellaneous white collar 6/14/1; local administrations 0/2/0; Housewife 6/0/0.
Total in group (iii) = *115 of which C 74, L 33, A 8 (1970 figure = 125).*

(iv) *Manual workers*

Miner 0/20/0; skilled worker 4/35/0; semi/unskilled worker 0/15/0.
Total in group (iv) = *74 of which C 4, L 70, A 0 (1970 figure = 74).*

The significant features of the composition of the House of Commons are that (*a*) professional occupations dominate, and within the professions Labour is best represented by teachers; (*b*) busines is overwhelmingly represented in one party, the Conservatives; (*c*) manual workers form a small proportion of MPs, and are virtually only found in Labour.

Clearly every General Election will yield people from different backgrounds. But broadly, nearly half of all MPs are from professions, one fifth from business, one fifth are 'miscellaneous white collar' and one eighth are from a working class background.

Another indicator of class is education. The following data reveals significant variations among MPs elected in 1983:

Education institution	Conservatives	Labour	Alliance
University	282	111	15
Oxford/Cambridge	190	31	7
Public school	278	30	12
Secondary only	29	34	4

Thus 70 per cent of Conservative MPs went to university, compared to 66 per cent of Alliance and about 50 per cent of Labour MPs; and 70 per cent of Conservatives had a Public School background while for Labour the figure was 30 per cent, and for the Alliance, 50 per cent. About 20 per cent of Labour and Alliance MPs left full-time education at the secondary school stage.

Left, Right and Changing Class

The two major parties have moved noticeably apart since the mid-1970s. Prof. Dahrendorf (*On Britain*) suggests this is due to the replacement of the traditional upper class dominance of the Conservatives by the new forces of a radical, thrusting, individualist middle class; whilst in the Labour Party, the traditional trade union, working class dominance is being displaced by the more radical, egalitarian and intellectual middle class activists. (see p. vi)

Voting Behaviour

Human nature is infinitely varied and puzzling. 'Man know thyself,' said Seneca, the Roman philosopher. And we still do not know. Fallen angel or risen ape? Much can be said either way.

In this chapter we study voting behaviour—the behaviour of electors at elections of MPs and local councillors. Why does Mr A vote Labour, while Mr B votes Conservative, Mr C votes Liberal, and Mr D abstains from voting? Voting behaviour in modern times has been carefully studied, but the subject is not an exact science. We have mentioned National Opinion Polls (p. 189), which attempt to forecast results of elections based on data obtained from surveys and interviews of random groups and people. Frequently the polls are right, but they are fallible, e.g. four (Marplan, Gallup, NOP and Harris) forecast a Labour win at the General Election on 18 June 1970. In fact the result was a decisive victory for Conservatives, who obtained 46.4 per cent of the votes cast as against Labour's 42.9 per cent.

Definitions and Terminology

The experts in this field of voting behaviour use words and phrases about which we should be clear. Here are some:

Floating voter. At each election there are some voters who change their party allegiance for one reason or another, some abstain from voting, and some, who become 18 and are 'qualified' by registration, vote at an election for the first time. These and others are able to affect decisively an election result.

In one election there may be only two candidates, e.g. Labour and Conservative. In a later election in the same constituency there may be three or more candidates, e.g. Labour, Conservative, Liberal, and Independent. So a Liberal supporter who would normally support a Liberal candidate, might have to choose between, say, the Labour or Conservative candidate. He may vote for one or the other, or he may abstain from voting. This kind of person is a distinct type of 'floating voter'.

A floating voter is, therefore, one who is not committed continuously to one political party but votes at any particular election according to his own political judgement of (1) self-interest, (2) party political programme, (3) candidate's personal qualifications, or (4) some other reason. Although the definition of a floating voter is not exact, nevertheless this type of voter affects the outcome of an election in marginal constituencies.

Deferential and Secular Voters. R. McKenzie and A. Silver (*Angels in Marble: Working-Class Conservatives in Urban England*, Heinemann, 1968) distinguished two classes of voters thus:

Deferential Voter. A deferential voter is that kind of voter who tends to invest the Conservative Party with an inborn superiority of talent and responsibility and who believes the Conservative Party to be a 'national institution'. Such a voter sees the policies which benefit the working class as stemming from the success of élitist leaders, manufacturers and others.

Secular Voter. These voters base their support of the Conservative Party on a pragmatic assessment of the Conservative policies and performance in office; in other words, they base their judgement on historical experience of sound policies and successful management of the economy. The assessment is based on merit, and the secular voters prefer those who achieved office or results by their own merits.

The working-class Conservative is moving away from being a deferential voter to secular voter. Other findings by McKenzie and Silver show that in general more women than men are deferential voters, due

Table 8.

Party	Percentage of vote in 1974 (Oct)	Percentage of vote in 1979
Labour	40.2	37.8
Conservative	36.7	44.9
Liberal	23.1	17.3
	100.0	100.0
Conservative majority over Labour	-3.5	7.1

Swing to Conservatives 7.1 + 3.5 = 10.6 divided by 2
                               = 5.3 (the biggest swing since 1945)
In 1983 the swing to Conservatives was 3.9.
In 1987 it was 2.5 to labour (GB not UK).

perhaps to women reacting more slowly than men to political and social perspectives.

Swing

Where one election follows another and a different result occurs in the second election, political analysts refer to a 'swing to Conservative' or a 'swing to Labour'. It indicates the extent to which people change sides.

The swing is a technical expression. It is calculated by taking the **averages** of the differences in the Labour and the Conservative share of the **total** votes cast, comparing the current (or present or second) election with the previous election. (See table 8, p. 205.)

Why do People Vote as They do?

The present law on voting franchise is contained in the *Representation of the People Acts*, which broadly means that all British subjects resident in the UK and registered as prescribed and over the age of 18 years may vote at General Elections and at Local Government Elections (see p. 30). The graduate vote and the vote in respect of business premises' qualification is abolished (*Representation of the People Act, 1948*).

Here we examine the question: Why do people vote as they do? Until the nineteenth century it was generally thought by many that people being reasonable creatures voted by using their reason in the choice of party and candidate. Disraeli, realising the great voting power vested in the lower class and poor class, sought to unite the 'two nations', the rich and the poor, into one, and relied on the traditionalism of the lower classes. He thought that a socially responsible upper class could retain the loyalty at the polls of the poorer members of society.

Karl Marx asserted that politics was primarily a struggle between classes, and rejected the purely rational analysis that ordinary people applied reason to guide their behaviour.

Sociologists and psychologists suggested that **values** play some part. Some voters support political actions which they consider *right*, and disregard their own personal advantage and probability of winning. This view detracted from the widely held supposition that the majority of the electorate voted out of **self-interest**, or in modern terms, 'I vote for the party which promotes and protects my prosperity'—prosperity being looked upon in terms of material wealth.

Voting behaviour could be looked upon as purely a rational matter, or a desire to do the right thing (values playing a part), or in terms of self-interest or personal advantage.

Experience in Germany, the US, Israel, Australia, and Sweden showed that the less privileged in a society tended to vote for leftist parties, while the well-to-do voted for the more conservative parties which defend some form of equality and oppose redistribution by the state. But the examination of voting behaviour also showed that this was affected by (*a*) age, (*b*) sex, (*c*) economic characteristics, (*d*) social class, (*e*) workplace, (*f*) neighbourhood, (*g*) trade union membership, (*h*) family, and (*i*) religion.

Voting Turnout and Social Factors

You will note that at some elections there is a large turnout whilst at others there may be a small turnout. At Parliamentary General Elections there is usually participation or turnout of just over 70 per cent of the total electorate; while at Local Government elections the turnout is roughly 37 to 40 per cent.

The social characteristics related to turnout may be seen from the following table:

Higher Turnout	*Lower Turnout*
High income	Low income
High education	Low education
Men	Women
Middle-aged (35–55)	Young people (under 35)
Old residents	Newcomers in community
Businessmen	Unskilled workers
White-collar employees	Servants
Government employees	Service workers
Married people	Single
Crisis situation	Normal situation

Groups of potential voters will have a higher turnout if

  (i) their interests are strongly affected by Government policies (e.g. school-teachers where schools may be closed down);
 (ii) they have information about the relevance of political decisions to the group's interests;
(iii) the group is subject to social pressures demanding voting;
(iv) the group is not pressed in different directions, e.g. by conflicting information, interests, or group pressures.

(*Source:* abstracted from *Political Man: the Social Bases of Politics* by Seymour Martin Lipset, Doubleday & Co., Inc.)

Social Class and Voting

H. Durant, in Rose's *Studies in British Politics* (Macmillan, 1967), shows that there is a definite and persistent relationship between social class, as objectively determined, and voting behaviour. The studies mentioned found that the middle class gives great support to the Conservatives and the working-class voters favour the Labour Party.

These are broad generalisations and are common knowledge. However, within the middle class there are also groups, especially State employees, which support the Labour Party, and conversely there are numbers in the working class who support Conservative policies, such as sale of council houses or immigration control (see also p. 213). Indeed, since the 1970s, there has been considerable support for the view that a 'de-alignment' has occurred between party support and class e.g. in the 1974 General Elections, over 30 per cent of the managerial and professional occupational groups (the so-called A/B groups) did not vote Conservative; and in 1983, more of the skilled working class (the C2 group) voted Conservative than Labour (40 per cent as opposed to 32 per cent). (See B. Sarlvik and I.

208   *British Constitution Made Simple*

Crewe, *Decade of Dealignment*.) Table 9 gives some detail for the 1983 (and 1979) election. *Note*: see p. vii for 1987 figures

Table 9. Class and Sex voting in the 1983 (and 1979) election

	Middle Class (A, B, C1) (%)	Skilled working class (C2) (%)	Unskilled working class (D, E) (%)	Men	Women
Conservative	55(59)	40(40)	33(35)	42(45)	46(45)
Labour	16(22)	32(42)	41(50)	30(40)	26(36)
Others	29(19)	28(18)	26(15)	27(15)	29(19)
	100	100	100	100	100

(Based on MORI poll. (See D. Butler and D. Kavanagh, *The British General Election 1983* and *1979*, Macmillan.)

However, a new study suggests that class allegiances have not eroded to the extent claimed. The new analysis re-classified women according to their own occupations and not, as previously, on the basis of their husbands' jobs. Social class categories were also more carefully defined, with the following result:

Table 10. Voting and class in 1983, another interpretation.

	Conservative (%)	Labour (%)	Alliance (%)
Petty bourgeoisie (self-employed)	71	12	17
Salariat (managers, professionals)	54	14	31
Foremen/technicians (supervisors)	48	26	25
Routine non-manual (clerks)	46	25	27
Working class (supervised at work)	30	49	20

Source: A. Heath et al, How Britain Votes, Pergamon, 1985

Sex Differences and Voting

Men, it is said, show a consistent bias in favour of the Labour Party, while women favour the Conservative Party. According to Seymour Lipset these differences are also found in a number of Western countries. The conclusion is, however, that the effect of gender on voting is *marginal* and has little accuracy as an indication or prediction of a person's vote.

Age Differences and Voting

Durant (above) claims that persons aged between 21 and 29 show a preference for the Labour Party; those between 30 and 49 were evenly divided, and those aged between 50 and 64 consistently favoured the Conservatives. Class remains an important influence, but is weakening (see *The Economist*, 11.3.78).

Durant analyses the relation between class, sex, age and voting and states that it is misleading to explain voting behaviour in terms of a single *social* characteristic. He also states that a *third* of the British electorate does not vote in agreement with its objective social class.

Religion and Voting

Religion in some countries, particularly where there are identifiable religious parties, e.g. Christian Democrat, plays a part in voting behaviour. In Britain there has been a general decline in religious observance if not practice during the present century, with consequent smaller influence exerted on voting behaviour.

In Northern Ireland, with its strong Catholic and Protestant groupings and antipathy, voting behaviour is correspondingly influenced. In Wales there is a noticeable Nonconformist tradition. In England there are local variations, e.g. in Liverpool there are many Roman Catholics, but generally and overall there is a tendency for Catholics and Nonconformists to support Labour, and members of the Church of England to support Conservative. The latter tendency may be explained on the grounds that there is a higher proportion of middle-class supporters in the Church of England, while a high proportion of Catholics are working class. Summing up, Professor Blondel notes: 'the precise impact of religion on voting is difficult to determine'.

Family Influence

In the normal family of a man, a wife and two or three children where there is a loving and caring relationship, the children on reaching the age of discretion take on the attitudes and political viewpoint of parents. This is particularly the case where both parents support the same political party. The family influence is generally strong and durable.

A child is very likely indeed to share his parents' party preference. Partisanship over the individual's lifetime has some of the qualities of a photographic reproduction that deteriorates with time: it is a fairly sharp copy of the parents' original at the beginning of political awareness, but over the years it becomes somewhat blurred, although remaining easily recognisable. (D. Butler and D. Stokes, *Political Change in Britain*, p. 47.)

Again this is a general truth. One finds frequently that 17–21-year-olds espouse a revolutionary cause (sometimes extreme left) in defiance of conservative parental influence, and seek to put the world to rights. After blowing off steam for two or three years the large majority then revert to the more middle-of-the-road stance of parents and home and acquire a political maturity from their own experience, particularly so if they find that the words of the political theorists have to be applied practically to the hard realities of the modern world—the confused babel of voices and the economic market-place.

Neighbourhood, Workplace, and Trade Union

The neighbourhood where one lives can be influential in voting behaviour. Thus a working-class person residing in a middle-class area is less likely to vote Labour than a working-class person living in a working-class area. The apparent rule is that 'the more the middle class predominates in a district, the more working-class people identify themselves with it' (M. Young and P. Willmott, *Family and Class in a London Suburb*).

Where a person has his workplace in his neighbourhood there is an added pressure. Thus manual workers employed in small family businesses are more likely to vote Conservative than manual workers employed in large factories (Stacey, *Tradition and Change in Banbury*). This may be due to such workers identifying their own with their employer's interests—in other words, it may be self-interest.

The trade unions (see p. 191) traditionally support the Labour Party. Membership of a TU as usually understood *prima facie* indicates membership and support of the Labour Party. However, in a British Institute of Public Opinion survey in 1964 some 41 per cent were trade unionists, and of this 41 per cent there were some 53 per cent who were *regular* Labour voters, and some 22 per cent were Conservative supporters. In 1979, of TU voters, 50 per cent voted Labour and 35 per cent voted Conservative (and vice versa for non-members). For 1983 and 1987 TU Labour voters were 39 and 42 per cent.

The phrase 'trade union' has a technical and general meaning. In those industries where trade unionism is stronger there is nevertheless a sizable minority of Conservative supporters which is considerably larger than the minority of Labour voters among professional and managerial employees (see T. Brennan, *Politics and Government in Britain*).

Where neighbourhood, workplace, and trade union influences combine—for example, where miners live on housing estates, work nearby, are members of a trade union, and have a family tradition of mining—there are many pressures which operate on the individual person to influence his voting behaviour.

Party Image

The majority of voters interviewed during surveys or by those conducting opinion polls indicate from replies given that they have only *general views* of what particular parties stand for—in other words, their policies. This general view of assessment is summed up by the phrase 'Party image'.

The Labour Party is, for example, seen as a party 'standing for the working class'; the Conservative party 'standing for the middle class'. Another generalisation appears that the Labour Party is 'for more Government control and nationalisation of industry'; the Conservative Party is 'for freedom from Government control and less bureaucracy'.

Party image, i.e. the general impression made on the average person (if there be such) of the political party as a whole, is still important. That image is the result of history, general political stance and values implanted on the minds of the masses. Thus the support for a party given by numerous people is often based on continuing emotional loyalty rather than on a cool rational analysis, an evaluation of policies, political representatives and leaders, and their integrity in honouring pledges given.

In 1908 Graham Wallas, in *Human Nature in Politics*, noted the enduring allegiance of some voters to a political party. He wrote:

'Something is required simpler and more permanent . . . which can be recognised at successive elections as being the same thing that was loved and trusted before; and a party is such a thing.'

Leaders in all political parties know there is a dedicated loyal group upon whom they can rely. Whatever the tensions and stresses there may be within a political party, the Right pulling against the Left over a particular issue, when the time for voting comes the emotional tie asserts itself.

Party Leaders and Party Candidates

Leaders. Party leaders are chosen (by election) by members of their parties (see pp. 44–7, 123).

Apart from the qualities of leadership referred to, one quality which a modern leader requires is the ability to make an impact on the electorate on radio and television. Only a few thousands could hear Gladstone, Disraeli, or Lloyd George at their open-air meetings. When mass communication became possible through popular newspapers and particularly radio and television, the chance to reach a wider audience was quickly taken. The US Presidential election campaign in 1980 between Ronald Reagan and Jimmy Carter was watched by millions in the US, in Europe and throughout the world over many weeks.

Granted that the press, radio and television provide the media to reach an increasingly wide public, we may ask how far a leader's performance and image at election time affects the vote. On the available evidence the conclusion is that only *some* voters' attitudes towards the party leaders do in fact involve shifts in votes between parties (Butler and Stokes, *Political Change in Britain*, Chapter 17).

However that may be, the history of mankind shows that at various periods a few beings emerge as leaders with an appeal and charisma which can affect millions. What the future holds we do not know, but the lack of positive evidence of the ability to change voters' attitudes *strongly* may be due to one or more of many factors, e.g. the mediocrity of present leaders and/or the fact that no powerful political leader has yet emerged, or that there is scepticism about the extravagant promises made to the electorate by those seeking power at all costs.

Candidates

When a prospective candidate seeks adoption by the local constituency party committee, the selection committee try to pick the best man who has the requisite qualifications and who will win. What sort of appeal will he make to the average voter in the constituency? Can he speak well in public, is he persuasive, and what of his personality?

One investigation (R. Milne and H. C. McKenzie in 1951 and 1955) showed that only 1 per cent of the electorate felt that the local candidate influenced their decision. Similarly, in a national sample (NOP) in 1966, only 3 per cent mentioned the qualities of the candidate.

There are exceptions to this: where a well-known and popular personality

on radio or television decides to enter politics he has a decided advantage
e.g. Clement Freud and Andrew Faulds—who both became MPs.

Another factor which must be taken into account is the organisation
and vigour with which a local candidate campaigns. The effect of the personality of the candidate must be distinguished from the part played by
the campaign organisation—which may be arranged by a committee or the
candidate himself, who may 'barnstorm' the constituency.

The evidence so far collated since the war indicates that the number of
'personal' votes, i.e. votes for the candidate personally, are few. The truth
appears to be that parliamentary elections are contests between *parties* and
not personalities.

Electioneering

What influence does electioneering have on voting behaviour? In each constituency there is a hard core of workers who get together at election time
to canvass houses, produce and distribute literature, and generally seek to
get all likely supporters of the party to turn out and vote.

British elections take on the appearance of an exciting sporting event;
each party uses its political colour, badges, and rosettes; there is door-to-
door canvassing; and loudspeakers introduce candidates to all districts or
villages. What effect does all this have on voting behaviour? Here are some
points to be borne in mind:

1. **Information.** Voters are informed and made aware that there is an
   election, which ensures a high turnout.
2. **Morale** must be sustained. An election campaign fought with enthusiasm helps people to maintain good hope and spirits.
3. **Marginal seats.** Where these occur, electioneering is specially important. One or two votes can decide an election in marginal seats, so
   electioneering here is *essential*.
4. **Knowledge of politics.** Elections help people to get to know what politics is about. Apathy and ignorance (there are said to be 2 million
   illiterates and innumerates in the UK) and cynicism have to be
   combated.

There are many lonely people in the UK. A visit from a canvasser shows
that he or she living alone is important. The truth is that each individual in
a democracy is important. Man is not a cog in a machine or an automaton
who clocks in and out of a massive factory or office. In the political constitution he or she is endowed with rights and privileges and is subject to
duties, one of which is the duty and right to vote to ensure that the values
underlying our society are preserved for those who follow us. However, in
narrowly electoral terms, research suggests that contrary to popular belief,
the efforts of constituency party organisations have little effect on voters'
behaviour (see Rose, *The Problem of Party Government*, Pelican, 1976).

Interest, Apathy and Ignorance: A Case for Political Education?

There are vital problems facing the country: the relationship between
Government and business; between Government and the TUC and indivi-

dual unions, such as the NUM, NALGO, NUPE, the Police Federation and others. Why is British productivity so low? What do we do about long-term unemployment; race relations; the decay of many of our towns; the education of children and young persons for the twentieth century; energy, and the time when coal and oil run out; and what, if nuclear power is one answer, do we do about nuclear waste?

All such problems are political. Yet, in a survey conducted by Mark Abrams (*Social Trends and Electoral Behaviour*) only 15 per cent of those interviewed described themselves as 'very interested' in politics. Some 85 per cent were thus 'not very interested', 37 per cent were 'interested', 33 per cent 'not really interested', and 15 per cent 'not at all interested'.

The future is uncertain, and the struggle appears to be between those who believe in the collectivist approach where the state and government are supreme and inviolate, and those who believe that every human being is unique and must play his part in working out his own salvation. The great figures of Wycliffe, Cranmer, Adam Smith and Gladstone all believed in this principle. It formed the mainspring of many Victorians who wished to change British society. 'All good things which exist are the fruits of originality,' said Adam Smith, and originality belongs to individuals, not to collectives. Each person has to choose whether he wants the right to decide his own life or to have others decide for him. If he wants to choose between spending and saving, between sending his child to one school instead of another, between joining or not joining a union, he is a disciple of freedom. If he wishes to adopt a wholly different philosophy which finds its future and salvation in the collectivist theory he will decide differently. What is at issue is a man's place in society, and whether he will be able to make the choice to enable him, according to his lights and understanding, to lead the good life.

That is why voting at democratic elections in a liberal democracy is vital and why it is significant and depressing that some 85 per cent of the persons interviewed (see above) were 'not very interested' in politics. The situation seems unlikely to improve judging from the results of a recent survey conducted for the Hansard Society (*The Political Awareness of the School Leaver*, 1977). This showed a considerable degree of apathy and cynicism about politics. It also revealed a great deal of ignorance in that 50 per cent could not name the Foreign Secretary or their own MP; nor could they name a pressure group; only 20 per cent could name their own constituency; 6 per cent could not even name the Prime Minister. On political issues about 20 per cent believed it was Conservative policy to nationalise industries and Labour policy to provide for private health and education; and some 44 per cent thought that the IRA was a Protestant organisation. But perhaps of greater potential significance was the MORI poll finding that nearly half of the young unemployed believe that violence to bring about political change can be justified (see *Sunday Times*, 6.9.81).

However, the idea of political studies in schools and colleges creates anxiety in many people owing to their fear of political bias and indoctrination by teachers and local education authorities. The present Government has cast grave doubts on the validity of Peace Studies in schools, and despite the efforts of the Politics Association and even school HMIs to encourage political education, no significant progress has occurred.

Exercises

1. What are Public Opinion Polls?
2. How important are they to (i) a Prime Minister; and (ii) a back-bencher?
3. What factors or agencies would you as an MP take into account in estimating public opinion in Britain?
4. Distinguish between (i) a political party, and (ii) a pressure group.
5. State (i) the case for, and (ii) the case against pressure groups.
6. What are the duties of the BBC under its charter?
7. What are party political broadcasts? What arrangements exist for these in the United Kingdom?
8. What controls operate on (i) the BBC and IBA; and (ii) the Press?
9. State the composition and functions of the Press Council.
10. Voting behaviour at a General Election is largely determined by two factors: (i) social class and (ii) workplace. How far is this true?
11. What is meant by (i) a secular voter, (ii) a deferential voter and (iii) 'swing' in an election.
12. In the 1950s and 1960s it was believed that increased affluence (or 'embourgeoisment') was causing more workers to vote Conservative. Equally in the 1960s and 1970s it was believed that dependence on State employment was inducing more middle class (the 'salariat') to support Labour to protect their jobs. Comment on these ideas.

7
The Law and the Courts

The Nature of Law

The term 'law' is used in many senses: we may speak of the laws of physics, mathematics, science, or the laws of football or health. When we speak of the law of a State we use the term 'law' in a special and strict sense, and in that sense law may be defined as *a rule of human conduct, imposed upon and enforced among, the members of a given state.*

If a group or society is to continue, some form of social order is necessary. Rules or laws are, therefore, drawn up to ensure that members of the society may live and work together in an orderly and peaceable manner. The larger the community (or group or state), the more complex and numerous will be the rules.

If the rules or laws are broken, compulsion is used to enforce obedience. We may say, then, that two ideas underlie the concept of law:

  (i) **Order,** in the sense of method or system.
 (ii) **Compulsion,** i.e. the enforcement of obedience to the rules or laws laid down.

The English Legal System

We have three main streams; (i) the Common Law; (ii) Equity; and (iii) Statute Law.

  (i) *The Common Law* is that part of the law which was formed by the royal judges out of the varied customs of the realm from the twelfth century onwards. It is largely judge-made law. The judicial decisions and principles were treated with respect and followed by succeeding judges. Judicial precedent gave certainty to the Common Law which is still with us and constantly adapting itself to the changed conditions of today. (See pages 9, 255, 258 for some Common Law cases.)

 (ii) *Equity* is a system of justice which supplements the Common Law. It is based on principles formulated by the early Chancellors who acted as Keepers of the King's Conscience. Where the Common Law was defective or injustice resulted from too strict adherence to precedent, Equity intervened as a corrective. Today Equity is applied in all civil courts and takes precedence in the event of conflict with the Common Law.

(iii) *Statute Law* is the main source of English law today (see pages 8 and 99).

Sub-Divisions of the Law

It is impossible to give more than an outline of the subjects which are today covered by the law. Law may, however, be classified in various ways. The main division is into:

(i) Criminal Law
(ii) Civil Law

(i) *Criminal Law*

That part of the law which characterises certain kinds of wrongdoings as offences *against the State*, not necessarily violating any private right, and punishable *by* the State. Crime is defined as an act of disobedience of the law forbidden under pain of punishment. The punishment for crime ranges from death or imprisonment to a money penalty (fine) or absolute discharge.

The police are the public servants primarily concerned with the enforcement of the criminal law and in keeping the peace (see p. 272). However, the police service has no monopoly and a private person may bring a prosecution though this is rare in practice.

(ii) *Civil Law*

That part of the law which is primarily concerned with the rights and duties of *individuals towards each other*. It includes the following:

(*a*) Law of Contract
(*b*) Law of Tort
(*c*) Law of Property
(*d*) Law of Succession
(*e*) Family Law
(*f*) Admiralty Law

This list is not exhaustive—for example, there is the growing volume of international law: the Law of the Air, the Law of the Sea, and so on to outer space, where man is now prone to go and hurl or leave certain sophisticated hardware in orbit.

Civil Courts Today

The House of Lords stands at the apex of the judicial system, and is the final court of appeal in civil and criminal matters.

As a court of appeal, it is composed of the Lord Chancellor, the Lords of Appeal in Ordinary, and other peers who have held high judicial office. A quorum of three is necessary to constitute the court. Each judge may deliver a separate judgement, the verdict being by majority.

Jurisdiction. In civil matters the court hears appeals from the Court of Session of Scotland, the Court of Appeal in Northern Ireland, and the Court of Appeal (Civil Division) in England. There is no general right of appeal: leave of the Court of Appeal or the House of Lords must first be obtained to appeal to the House of Lords.

The *Administration of Justice Act, 1969*, provides a new form of appeal in *civil* actions from the High Court (or Divisional Court) direct to the House of Lords, 'leap-frogging' the Court of Appeal. An appeal will lie only subject to the following conditions: (i) that, on application of any of the parties, the trial judge grants a certificate of appeal; (ii) that the certificate will only be granted if the judge's decision involves a point of law of *general public importance*; (iii) that this point of law either relates to the construction of an enactment or statutory instrument, *or* is one in respect of which the judge is bound by the Court of Appeal or the Lords.

In criminal matters the court hears appeals from the Court of Appeal (Criminal Division) and the Divisional Court of Queen's Bench. Both parties (appellant and respondent, or prosecutor and defendant) may appeal, but leave of the Court of Appeal or the House of Lords must first be obtained on the ground that the case involves a point of law of general public importance (*Administration of Justice Act, 1960*). In all, some 5 per cent of appeals go to the Lords.

Before 1948 peers accused of serious criminal offences were entitled to be tried by the House of Lords, but this right was abolished by the *Criminal Justice Act* of that year.

Most proposals for the reform of the House of Lords retain the 15 or so Lords of Appeal in Ordinary as members, which indicates their worth in the Upper House when acting as a legislative body. There are usually three or four ex-Lords Chancellor who are able to bring wide experience to bear on the proceedings, as well as act as judges in the cases which come before the Lords when acting as an appellate court.

Moreover, if Britain were to devise a Bill of Rights, or to go further and

Fig. 17. The present structure of the Civil Courts

draw up a written constitution, there would need to be a supreme court (as in the USA) to act as guardians and interpreters of the constitution (see p. 379). These matters are speculative, but we have to face the fact that so far in our recent history we have managed to avoid a *political* judiciary. The absolute independence of the judiciary is vital (see pages 11–14) to our democratic way of life. That fact was apparent to those who framed the written American Constitution, and it will be foremost in the minds of those who will have the task of drafting the British Constitution, even if it be drawn in broad terms.

Judicial Committee of the Privy Council. The Privy Council originated as the *Curia Regis* of the Norman kings, to which reference has been made earlier (see p. 127). The Council retains certain advisory and formal functions, but it also exercises judicial authority through a committee known as the Judicial Committee of the Privy Council.

Composition. The 'court' is made up of all Privy Councillors who hold, or have held, high judicial office in the United Kingdom (including Lords of Appeal in Ordinary), the Lord Chancellor, former Lord Chancellors, and Commonwealth judges who are Privy Councillors. The quorum of the Committee is three, but in important cases five members are usually present.

Jurisdiction. The Committee hears appeals from those Commonwealth countries which have retained the right of appeal (some such countries on acquiring independence abolished the right) and from colonial territories. More specifically the Committee hears appeals from:

(i) Prize courts. Jurisdiction extends over claims to captured ships during time of war.

(ii) Ecclesiastical courts.

(iii) Courts of the Isle of Man, the Channel Islands, British Colonies, British Protectorates and Trust Territories, and from Commonwealth countries retaining the right of appeal. Australia opted out after a controversial action by the Governor-General (the Queen's representative) in 1984.

(iv) Tribunals of the medical, dental, and opticians' professions.

Procedure. The Committee sits as an advisory board and its procedure is informal. Judges, for example, are not robed. No judgement is given as in a Court of Law. The Committee tenders advice to the Monarch upon which an Order in Council is made to dispose of the issue in question. No dissentient opinions are given.

The decisions of the Judicial Committee are not binding on itself or on the lower Courts of Law of the United Kingdom, but a decision on appeal from a colony is binding on the colonial courts of that territory. Generally and in practice the judicial strength of the Committee is such that its decisions are treated with great respect.

Court of Appeal (Civil Division). This court is composed of ex officio judges and other judges. Ex officio judges include the Lord Chancellor, the Lord Chief Justice, the President of the Family Division, the Lords of Appeal in Ordinary and the Master of the Rolls. In practice the Master of the Rolls is President of the court and he is assisted by a permanent staff of eight to eleven Lords Justices of Appeal. However, any High Court judge may be requested by the Lord Chancellor to sit. The quorum of the court is three and the court may sit in four Divisions at the same time.

The court may uphold, amend, or reverse the decision of a lower court, or order a new trial.

Jurisdiction. The court hears civil appeals from all Divisions of the High Court, from county courts and certain special courts.

The High Court of Justice. This court consists of:

(i) The Queen's Bench Division (QBD).
(ii) The Chancery Division (Ch. Div.).
(iii) The Family Division (F. Div.).

The three Divisions are of equal competence, so each is empowered to try any action, but for administrative purposes and convenience specific matters are allocated to each Division as described below.

The Presidents of each of the respective Divisions are (i) QBD: The Lord Chief Justice; (ii) Ch. Div.: The Lord Chancellor (in practice the Vice-Chancellor presides); (iii) F. Div.: The President, Family Division. These are assisted by approximately 70 puisne (lesser) judges who are allocated to each Division. The Lord Chancellor may require any judge to sit in any Division.

(i) The **Queen's Bench Division** is composed of the Lord Chief Justice and approximately thirty puisne judges. It exercises three kinds of jurisdiction: (*a*) **original** (i.e. at first instance); (*b*) **appellate**; (*c*) **supervisory**.

(*a*) *Original Jurisdiction* is of three kinds. As a result of the *Administration of Justice Act, 1970*, the jurisdiction of the Admiralty Court has now been added to the Queen's Bench Division and a new Commercial Court has been added to deal with court cases involving traders and merchants. The characteristic of this court is that cases entered on the 'Commercial List' are tried in a simpler and quicker way than ordinary cases.

The effect of this is that the QBD jurisdiction comprises (i) all civil cases not specifically assigned to other Divisions of the High Court, such cases including tort cases, breaches of contract and actions for the recovery of land; (ii) Commercial Court cases as described above; and (iii) Admiralty cases, such as claims and actions involving ships with regard to collisions,

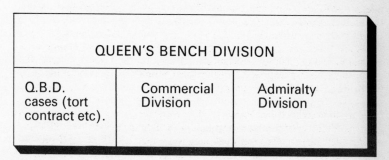

QUEEN'S BENCH DIVISION		
Q.B.D. cases (tort contract etc).	Commercial Division	Admiralty Division

Fig. 18.

salvage, towage, and prize jurisdiction. A diagrammatic representation of the functions of the QBD is shown on p. 219.

When hearing cases, the judges sit singly, but in exceptional cases (for example, defamation) a jury may be empanelled to assist the court. Jury verdicts may now be majority verdicts. There is no limit to the amount which may be claimed in the QBD. Some cases involve hundreds of thousands of pounds.

(b) *Appellate Jurisdiction* is exercised by two or three judges sitting as a 'Divisional Court' to hear appeals from magistrates' courts and some Crown Courts by means of a process known as 'case stated'. These appeals are on points of law, the subordinate court setting out the facts of, and reasons for, the decision for solution by the Divisional Court.

(c) *Supervisory Jurisdiction* is exercised over inferior courts, tribunals, and administrative authorities 'acting judicially', by means of the writ of *habeas corpus* and the prerogative order of *certiorari, prohibition*, and *mandamus* (see p. 296).

(ii) The **Chancery Division** deals generally with matters which before 1873 fell within the jurisdiction of the old Court of Chancery. Certain other matters have, however, been added by statute, for example bankruptcy, claims, and company matters.

Composition. The court is composed of the Lord Chancellor, a Vice-Chancellor and seven puisne judges. The Lord Chancellor has, however, so many duties to perform as head of the judiciary, President of the House of Lords and member of the Cabinet, that he does not in practice take part in the work of the court, such duties falling to the Vice-Chancellor.

Jurisdiction of the division includes: (i) the administration of estates of deceased persons; (ii) the dissolution of partnerships and taking of partnership accounts; (iii) mortgages and charges on land; (iv) trusts, both private and public (or charitable); (v) the sale of property subject to a lien or charge; (vi) wardship of infants and care of infants' estates; (vii) company matters, e.g. dissolution and winding up; (viii) revenue matters, e.g. taxation; (ix) partition and sale of real estates; (x) rectification and setting aside of deeds or other written instruments of cancellation; (xi) bankruptcy matters; and (xii) specific performance of contracts.

(iii) The **Family Division** of the High Court deals mainly with the following matters: (a) divorce; (b) marriage of minors; (c) appeals from magistrates' courts on matrimonial matters, such as separation orders, maintenance, etc.; and (d) non-contentious probate business (probate means proving a will).

County Courts. These were first established by the *County Courts Act, 1846*, to provide cheap, speedy, and local justice—so obviating the need for bringing actions at Westminster or before the courts at *nisi prius*. The county courts proved efficient and their jurisdiction has been enlarged from time to time. The *County Courts Act, 1959* (a consolidating Act) now governs the composition and jurisdiction of these useful courts.

There are at present over four hundred such courts in England and Wales; and there are about ninety-eight county court judges, some of whom have charge of two or more courts. The number of cases dealt with annually amounts to over $1\frac{1}{2}$ million. Most actions are, however, disposed of or settled out of court before hearing.

Composition. The court is composed of one judge, known as a Circuit Judge (see p. 224), who sits singly. Circuit judges are appointed by the Lord Chancellor. They must be barristers of at least seven years' standing. In rare cases a jury of eight persons may be empanelled to assist the court.

The **registrar** of the court keeps the records of the court and performs the administrative work attached to it. He must be a solicitor of at least seven years' standing, and is appointed by the Lord Chancellor. A registrar may hear and adjudicate on certain small claims in place of the judge.

Jurisdiction. As a general rule the plaintiff must bring his claim or action in the court of the district where the defendant (or one of several defendants) dwells or carries on business. Actions relating to land must be brought in the court of the district wherein the land is situated.

Matters falling within the jurisdiction of the county courts include: (i) actions founded on contract or tort up to £5,000; (ii) equity matters (trusts, mortgages, etc.) up to £30,000; (iii) actions for the recovery of land, and questions of titles to land, where the net annual rateable value does not exceed £1,000; (iv) bankruptcies; (v) probate proceedings where the value of the deceased's estate is less than £30,000; (vi) winding up of companies with a paid-up capital of less than £120,000; (vii) supervision of the adoption of infants; (viii) Admiralty matters (in some courts only); and (ix) actions in relation to rent-restriction, hire-purchase, landlord-and-tenant, and similar matters as laid down by statute.

To relieve the burden of work falling on the Family Division of the High Court in regard to divorce petitions, and with a view to reducing legal costs, the county courts were given a limited divorce jurisdiction. The Lord Chancellor may designate any county court as a 'Divorce County Court' with power to hear and determine any *undefended* matrimonial cause.

Appeal from a county court lies to the Court of Appeal.

Since 1974 small claims—e.g. for debts, whether for goods sold, work done, or money lent, or for damages for negligence—where the amount in dispute does not exceed £500, may be dealt with **informally** before an arbitrator, who is usually the Registrar. The object is to enable persons to bring or defend actions without a solicitor, and perhaps running up costs and long delays. This court is in an experimental stage, but it meets a genuine need where people have been unjustly treated over small matters and they require quick settlement.

Criminal Courts Today

The courts in which criminal cases are tried are:

  (i) The House of Lords.
 (ii) The Court of Appeal (Criminal Division).
(iii) Crown Courts.
(iv) Magistrates' Courts.

In addition, the following court acts as an Appeal Court:

 (v) Divisional Court of Queen's Bench.

The House of Lords. This court hears appeals from the Court of Appeal (Criminal Division) and from the Divisional Court of Queen's Bench. Either prosecutor of defendant may appeal, but an important requirement is that leave of the Court of Appeal (Criminal Division) or the House of Lords must be obtained on the grounds that the case involves *a point of law of general public importance*. This is to prevent frivolous or minor cases going to this final court.

Composition. As already explained (p. 217), this court is composed of the Lord Chancellor, the Lords of Appeal in Ordinary, and other peers who have held high judicial office. The quorum is three, and each judge delivers a separate judgement, the verdict being by a majority.

Court of Appeal (Criminal Division). The *Criminal Appeal Act, 1966,* provides that the Court of Appeal shall consist of two divisions: one exercising civil jurisdiction and one criminal.

Composition. The court is composed of the Lord Chief Justice and the Lord Justices of Appeal. The Lord Chief Justice, or, in his absence, the Master of the Rolls, may require any judge of the Queen's Bench Division to sit. A quorum of three is necessary, and only one judgement is delivered except where the presiding judge permits separate verdicts to be pronounced on a question of law.

Appeals shown thus: ⟶
Committals for trial: — — ⟶ — — —

Fig. 19. The Criminal Courts

Jurisdiction. The court may dismiss the appeal or allow the appeal, and may order that any conviction recorded in a lower court shall be quashed. The court may order a new trial (*Administration of Justice Act, 1964*). The court may not increase the sentence against which appeal is being made. (Formerly a convicted person who wanted to appeal against what he considered too long a sentence ran the risk of having his sentence increased by the Court of Appeal, but this risk is now eliminated; the number of appeals on this ground has grown accordingly.)

To hear these appeals two courts sit full-time, while a third sits as and when required by the number of appeals listed.

Crown Courts. From medieval times the Royal judges went on circuit from Westminster administering justice in the provinces. They sat as **Courts of Assize** ('assize' means a 'sitting' or 'session') and had both a civil and criminal jurisdiction, although in modern times the criminal jurisdiction was the more important. The judges sat with juries and a Court of Assize could try, at first instance, any case in the criminal calendar, from treason and murder to simple theft. In practice, an Assize Court tried the serious crimes committed locally. If, therefore, *A* was brought before a magistrates' court charged with murder or some other serious offence, the magistrates would make a preliminary investigation and if the court decided that the prosecution had made out a *prima facie* case against *A*, the accused person would be committed to an Assize Court to stand trial.

Quarter Sessions Courts were also of medieval origins. These survived also until 1971. There were two kinds, namely a **County Quarter Sessions** and a **Borough Quarter Sessions Court**. The former was presided over by a chairman (who might be legally qualified or who might not, i.e. not a barrister or solicitor). The Chairman was assisted by magistrates drawn from the county. Most County Quarter Sessions in modern times had legally qualified chairmen. The Borough Quarter Sessions Court was presided over by a Recorder (usually a practising barrister who acted as a judge for the Borough). Their jurisdiction included less serious criminal cases than those reserved for the Courts of Assize. In addition, the Quarter Sessions court had an **appellate jurisdiction**. Thus if *A* were convicted of theft at a magistrates' court he could appeal to a Quarter Sessions Court against (*a*) his conviction, or (*b*) his sentence if it was too severe for the offence he had committed. Where *A* was prosecuted for an offence before a magistrates' court he had the option, if he was liable to three months' imprisonment or more, of (*a*) being dealt with by magistrates there and then, or (*b*) trial before a jury either at Assizes (if the offence was serious) or Quarter Sessions in other cases.

It is not possible here to outline in full the jurisdiction of each of these courts, or their efficiency. Certainly they had served their purpose well and were trusted. Nevertheless, no judicial system can stand still. A Royal Commission on Assizes and Quarter Sessions was appointed under the Chairmanship of Lord Beeching and the Commission reported in 1969 (*Cmnd. 4153* of 1969). It proposed sweeping reforms and both the Government and Opposition regarded the report as radical and spectacular.

The old circuit system was out of date. Many of the assize towns were situated in the country and the Assizes and Quarter Sessions Courts did not serve the interests and convenience of people in the large conurbations. There was inefficient use of judges, the administration of the judicial work needed rationalising, so that the most serious cases were directed to those best qualified to handle them, and there was a growing back-log of appeals together with delay in handling the numerous cases due to the increase in crime.

The *Courts Act, 1971*, gave effect to most of the proposals. Only the main points are noted here:

(i) Assize Courts and Quarter Sessions Courts were abolished.

(ii) Crown Courts were established. (In general terms the Crown Court takes over all **first instance** business above magistrates' court level and all appeal business of Quarter Sessions, previously mentioned.)

The structure of the criminal courts from 1972 is as follows:

(i) House of Lords.
(ii) Court of Appeal (Criminal Division).
(iii) Crown Court.
(iv) Magistrates' Court.

Crown Court Jurisdiction. The Crown Court is a superior court, and it exercises original criminal jurisdiction. All proceedings on indictment must be brought in the Crown Court. (An indictment is merely a document which sets out the crime(s) with which a person is charged. Any offence punishable with three months' imprisonment or more is 'indictable', i.e. the accused may claim trial by jury—which will be in the Crown Court.)

The jurisdiction of a Crown Court will depend on how the Court is manned. The broad principle is that the higher the status of the judge the more serious will be the cases he will try. So we must look at the judges of the Crown Court. They are:

(i) A judge of the High Court.
(ii) A circuit judge.
(iii) A Recorder.

(i) A **High Court judge** is a *puisne* (lesser) judge of the Queen's Bench Division. His position is similar to that of his predecessor (Assize Court Judge).

(ii) A **circuit judge** is a judge appointed by the Crown to serve in both (*a*) Crown Courts, and (*b*) County Courts. He must be a barrister of ten years' standing, or a person who has held the office of a Recorder (see p. 223) for five years. He must retire at 72 years of age, but may be allowed to extend his period of office until he is 75. All former county court judges (see p. 220), the Recorders of Liverpool and Manchester, a number of full-time Chairmen and Deputy Chairmen of Quarter Sessions, and certain other holders of judicial office can become circuit judges.

(iii) A **Recorder** is a **part-time** judge of the Crown Court. He is appointed for a fixed term. Appointments are made from men of high professional standing, who are prepared to commit themselves to **not less than one month's work** on the bench each year.

The new Recorders must not be confused with those referred to on page 223 (Recorders of Boroughs whose office now lapses under the Act). The new Recorders are not associated with particular Boroughs.

The new system will give the authorities (e.g. the Lord Chancellor) the chance to assess the Recorders, as to their suitability for appointment to the High Court Bench, or to circuit judgeships.

The Division of Offences. Offences triable in Crown Courts are divided into four classes:

Class 1. Triable by High Court judge only.

(i) All offences punishable by death; (ii) misprision of treason and treason felony; (iii) murder; (iv) genocide; (v) offences under section 1 of the *Official Secrets Act, 1911*; (vi) incitement, attempt or conspiracy to commit any of the above offences.

Class 2. Triable by High Court judge only unless a particular case is released to be tried by a circuit judge, or Recorder.

(i) Manslaughter; (ii) infanticide; (iii) child murder; (iv) unlawful abortion; (v) rape; (vi) sexual intercourse with a girl under 13; (vii) incest with a girl under 13; (viii) sedition; (ix) mutiny; (x) piracy; (xi) offences under section 1 of the *Geneva Conventions Act, 1957*; (xii) incitement, attempt or conspiracy to commit any of the above offences.

Class 3. All indictable offences (i.e. triable before a jury) other than those in classes 1, 2 and 4).

Such offences may be tried (i) by a High Court judge, or (ii) a circuit judge or Recorder.

Class 4. Triable by a circuit judge or Recorder. (Sometimes by a High Court judge—see below.)

(i) Indictable offences which may be tried summarily (i.e. before magistrates' court) or on indictment. For example, theft in a supermarket is indictable and may be tried (*a*) before magistrates' court, or (*b*) before the Crown Court. (ii) Causing death by reckless or dangerous driving; (iii) wounding or causing grievous bodily harm; (iv) burglary; (v) robbery, or assault with intent to rob; (vi) forgery; (vii) incitement, attempt or conspiracy to commit any of the above offences.

Considerable discretion is given to the presiding High Court judge responsible for a particular circuit, to allocate particular cases. For example, even if a substantive offence is not grave or serious in itself the circumstances or the points of law likely to arise may justify trial by a High Court judge rather than by a Recorder, who is a part-time judge and consequently has less experience.

Crown Courts and Justices of the Peace. The *Courts Act, 1971*, provides that the Crown Court shall consist of (*a*) a High Court judge, or (*b*) a circuit judge, or (*c*) a Recorder, sitting with not less than two nor more than four Justices of the Peace:

(i) At the hearing of an appeal.

(ii) In cases where a defendant has been committed for sentence (for example, when a magistrates' court finds a man guilty, and that he should be sentenced by a Crown Court).

Furthermore, any jurisdiction (i.e. any case triable at a Crown Court)

CROWN COURT

1.	High Court Judge, Circuit Judge or Recorder	11.	Court Usher
2.	Justices of the Peace (not more than 4)	12.	Witnesses who have given evidence
3.	Clerk of the Crown Court	13.	Jury
4.	Defending Barrister (standing)	14.	Press reporters
5.	Prosecuting Barrister (seated)	15.	Public
6.	Solicitor or solicitor's clerk in attendance (Defence)	16.	Witnesses for Prosecution outside court waiting to give evidence
7.	Solicitor or solicitor's clerk in attendance (Prosecution)	17.	Witnesses for Defence outside court waiting to give evidence
8.	Probation Officer	18.	Witness
9.	Accused	19.	Shorthand writer
10.	Warder from prison		

Fig. 20. The Crown Court

may be exercised by a court consisting of a professional judge and not more than four Justices. When they are members of a Crown Court, the Justices have one vote each and a decision is carried by a majority vote. The principle is that 'team effort' shall be fostered in the administration of justice.

Crown Courts and Solicitors. Solicitors of ten years' standing are eligible for appointment as **Recorders**. Moreover, if a solicitor holds the appointment of Recorder for five years, he is eligible for appointment as a **Circuit Judge**. This is the first breach in the monopoly exercised by the Bar.

Under the Act a provision has been made whereby solicitors can appear in court, and address the court in some proceedings in the Crown Courts. Hitherto the right to appear in the superior courts has been limited exclusively to barristers.

Appeal by Way of Case Stated. This form of appeal may be used in a magistrates' court and in a Crown Court, when the Crown Court re-hears a case on appeal from a magistrates' court. The court to which appeal is made is the Divisional Court of Queen's Bench, which is constituted by not less than two judges of that Division (the usual number sitting is three).

Where either party (prosecutor or defendant) is dissatisfied on a point of law with the decision of, for example, a Crown Court, that party may require the Crown Court to 'state a case' for the opinion of the Divisional Court of Queen's Bench. The Crown Court states the case in writing, giving the facts and the reasons for the decision. The Divisional Court then adjudicates on the written evidence submitted and gives its ruling.

There are two points to be noted: (i) the appeal must be on a point of law, not fact; (ii) both prosecutor and defendant may appeal. This is contrary to the general rule that where a charge is dismissed or the defendant

Fig. 21. Appeal by way of 'Case Stated'

Points to note:
    Applies to magistrates' courts *and* Crown Courts.
    Defence *and* prosecution can appeal.
    Must be on *a point of law*.

is acquitted, the prosecution has no general right of appeal to a higher court. We should further observe that this form of appeal applies to a magistrates' court as well as to a Crown Court when the latter sits in its appellate capacity (hearing a case from a magistrates' court).

Magistrates' Courts. The first Justices were appointed in 1327 as 'conservators of the peace'. For more than six hundred years their successors, now known as Justices of the Peace or magistrates, have performed the duties of enforcing the common law and statute law and of preserving locally the public peace and good order.

During the past fifty years Parliament has burdened magistrates' courts with enforcing increasing quantities of legislation, much of it highly complex. Magistrates' courts (or courts of petty sessions) today exercise wider jurisdiction and deal with more cases than any other court in the English legal system. For example, over ninety-eight per cent of all criminal prosecutions in England and Wales are dealt with by magistrates. Magistrates also deal with a wide variety of civil cases and perform certain administrative duties, particularly in licensing matters.

There are two kinds of Justices of the Peace: (i) County Justices and (ii) Stipendiary Magistrates.

(i) **County Justices** are appointed by the Lord Chancellor on the recommendation of the Lord Lieutenant of the county assisted by an advisory committee. They have jurisdiction throughout the county.

The important features of the local county magistrates are that they are unpaid (though they may receive out-of-pocket expenses when adjudicating) and they are laymen.

Because of the importance of the work falling to magistrates, it is now ordained that all magistrates appointed after 1 January 1966, must undergo basic training in the duties of their office. They must understand the meaning of 'acting judicially', elementary legal procedure and sentencing policy, so as to preserve the highest standards of efficient judicial administration. The total number of lay magistrates in England and Wales is approximately 23,000.

(ii) **Stipendiary magistrates** or **'stipes'** are full-time paid magistrates. They are appointed by the Lord Chancellor and must be barristers or solicitors of at least seven years' standing. Stipendiary magistrates (eleven) are found in the larger cities, application for such appointments being made by the municipal corporations. A stipendiary magistrate can do alone any act which requires two or more lay Justices sitting in petty sessions.

Metropolitan magistrates are stipendiary magistrates appointed for the Metropolitan Area, which includes the City of London and the County of London, the latter being divided into court areas; there are 39 in all.

The Clerk to the Justices is the official attached to each magistrates' court who advises the Justices on points of law and procedure, makes a record of evidence and prepares depositions (i.e. statements sworn on oath in the presence of an accused person) made by witnesses in those cases sent forward for trial at a Crown Court. He also performs the administrative work of the court such as preparing informations, summonses and warrants granted by the magistrates, and collecting fines.

The *Justices of the Peace Act, 1949*, provides that a clerk must be a

1. Chairman of Justices
2. Justices of the Peace
3. Clerk of Magistrates
4. Prosecuting Lawyer (seated)
5. Defending Lawyer (standing)
6. Probation Officers
7. Defendant
8. Police Officer
9. Witness
10. Other witnesses
11. Press
12. Public

Fig. 22. The Magistrates' Court

barrister or solicitor of at least five years' standing. The Act also provides for the setting up in the counties of committees to supervise the administrative work of the magistrates' courts.

A clerk to the Justices must not retire with the Justices to consider their verdict, such matters being solely for the magistrates.

Jurisdiction of Magistrates' Courts. The jurisdiction of these courts falls under three main headings: (*a*) as a court of trial; (*b*) as a court of preliminary investigation; (*c*) miscellaneous.

(*a*) *Court of Trial.* The jurisdiction is exercised by from two to seven justices, and the maximum punishment that may be imposed for any one offence is six months' imprisonment or a fine of £1,000. A single Justice in petty sessions may try trivial cases such as simple drunkenness.

Criminal offences can be divided into three classes:

(i) Indictable offences, i.e. those triable on indictment at a Crown Court. All offences punishable with three months' imprisonment or more are indictable. The magistrates must ask any person accused of such an offence whether he wishes to be tried on indictment or to be tried summarily (see below). An indictment is simply the document used in jury trials which names the offence(s).

(ii) Offences triable summarily, i.e. there and then in a magistrates' court. Offences which can only be tried summarily include riding a pedal cycle at night without lights, begging in a public place, and being found drunk and incapable on the highway.

(iii) Indictable offences triable summarily in the magistrates' court if the accused so elects. Let us take by way of example a case where the accused is alleged to have stolen a penknife. Since theft is an indictable offence (it is punishable by seven years' imprisonment), the accused may claim trial before a jury. However, the magistrates will offer him the choice of either trial at a Crown Court or trial by the magistrates. If he chooses the latter, the magistrates will try the case there and then, i.e. summarily. If he chooses to be tried at a Crown Court, the magistrates will sit as a court of preliminary investigation.

The agenda of a typical magistrates' court reveals a wide variety of offences: petty theft, wilful damage, common assault, drunkenness, driving a motor-car without a driving licence, driving without insurance, failing to obey traffic signs, parking offences, driving without due care and attention, and similar road-traffic offences. Some offenders will be dealt with then and there (even though they qualify for trial by a Crown Court), while defendants who elect for trial by jury will be committed for trial if the prosecution makes out a *prima facie* case in respect of each. (A *prima facie* case is one which appears 'at first sight' or 'from the first impression' to be an offence.)

The *Criminal Justice Bill, 1987*, proposes to reduce the opportunities for trial by jury for a number of minor offences. Thus driving while disqualified, taking and driving away, common assault and criminal damage valued below £2,000 become trialable only by magistrates.

(*b*) *Court of Preliminary Investigation.* In this capacity the magistrates' court is called upon to determine whether an accused person, who is brought before it by means of a summons or by arrest, shall be committed to stand trial at a Crown Court.

The prosecution calls its witnesses and produces exhibits (e.g. a gun or knife). The evidence of the prosecution witnesses is taken down in writing in the presence of the accused, and the document (called a deposition) is signed by the witness (called a deponent) and by the Justice present at the hearing. After all the evidence for the prosecution is heard, the accused is charged with the alleged offence. He may plead 'guilty' or 'not guilty'; he may give evidence himself and call witnesses in his support, or he may reserve his defence until the actual trial. Usually an accused reserves his defence.

After hearing the evidence the magistrates decide whether the prosecution has made out a *prima facie* case. If it has, the accused and the witnesses are bound over to attend the trial at a Crown Court. These proceedings are known as **committal proceedings**, and although they may be taken before one Justice, in practice two or more lay magistrates usually preside over this important step in the judicial process.

If the prosecution has not made out a *prima facie* case against the accused, the magistrates must release him. When an accused is committed for trial he may be either remanded in custody (i.e. to a prison to await trial) or remanded on bail (i.e. liberated from the magistrates' court on condition that he turns up at the trial at a later date when his case will be heard).

The *Criminal Justice Act, 1967*, provides that, in certain circumstances, an accused person may be committed for trial on **written** evidence alone instead of oral evidence taken down in the form of depositions.

The Act also restricts the publication of reports of committal proceedings to purely formal matters, i.e. the identity of the court and magistrates, the names of the parties, and the nature of the charges. The object is to avoid prejudicing the accused by pre-trial publicity.

(*c*) *Miscellaneous Jurisdiction.* In addition to the foregoing duties, the magistrates perform administrative functions in regard to liquor licensing (approving applicants and premises), betting licensing, theatre and cinematograph licensing, and have a limited jurisdiction in regard to civil debts (e.g. unpaid income tax where the amount due is less than £30).

Other important duties include: (i) making matrimonial orders for separation and maintenance of spouses; (ii) affiliation orders; (iii) consent to marriage; (iv) guardianship of infants; (v) adoption of children; (vi) orders under the *Mental Health Act, 1959* and (vii) orders in regard to children and young persons in need of care, protection or control.

Juvenile Courts. Certain magistrates attached to a petty-sessional division form a special panel to deal with offences committed by children (i.e. persons under 14) and young persons (i.e. over 14 and under 17). The juvenile court is formed by three lay Justices, one of whom must be a woman. All such Justices retire at 65 years of age. A stipendiary magistrate may sit in this court.

The juvenile court sits separately from the adult court: if it cannot sit in a different room it must sit on a different day. Proceedings in juvenile courts are shielded from publicity. The Press must not disclose the identity of the child or young person unless the court, in exceptional cases, permits.

Where a child or young person is charged jointly with an adult the case is dealt with in an adult court, i.e. the usual magistrates' court.

Appeals from magistrates' courts are organised as follows:

(*a*) Where the defendant wishes to appeal against (i) conviction and/or (ii) sentence, appeal lies to the Crown Court.

(*b*) Where the defendant wishes to appeal against conviction or sentence on a point of law, appeal lies to the Divisional Court of Queen's Bench by way of 'case stated'.

(*c*) Appeals concerning separation and maintenance orders, affiliation, adoption, and consent to marry lie to the Family Division of the High Court.

Special Courts

Central Criminal Court. This famous court, commonly known as the Old Bailey, was set up by the *Central Criminal Court Act, 1834*. It exercises the criminal jurisdiction of a Crown Court and hears cases on indictment committed from the City of London and the Greater London area. In addition, the Central Criminal Court may try any crime committed at sea.

Proceedings may be removed into the Central Criminal Court from a provincial court if there is a risk that strong local feelings might otherwise prejudice the accused's case.

The court is held at least twelve times a year and is, in practice, very busy and is in almost continuous session.

Composition. The judges of the court are the Lord Chancellor; the judges of the Queen's Bench Division; the Lord Mayor, Aldermen, Recorder, and Common Serjeant of the City of London; and the judge of the City of London Court. In practice, the judges are those of the Queen's Bench Division and judges appointed by commission.

The court is constituted by a single judge who sits with a jury.

Restrictive Practices Court. This court was set up by the *Restrictive Trade Practices Act, 1956*, and is a new superior court of record. Its purpose is to consider and adjudicate on agreements entered into between firms, suppliers, or buyers, in which restrictions are imposed on the price, quantity, quality, or method of distribution of goods.

Restrictive agreements must be registered with the Director-General of Fair Trading, whose duty it is to refer to the court any agreement deemed to offend against the public interest.

Composition. The court is equal in standing to the High Court, and consists of three judges of the High Court, a judge of the Court of Session of Scotland, and a judge of the Supreme Court of Northern Ireland. In addition there are ten lay members experienced in industry, commerce or public affairs, two of whom with one presiding judge form a quorum. The court may sit in two or more Divisions. Appeal lies to the Court of Appeal.

Coroners' Courts. The office of coroner and the coroner's inquest (or inquiry) are of ancient origin. The first coroners were appointed in the reign of Richard I in 1194. Originally they had wide powers concerning local administration and the criminal law, but these have now been shed and the coroner of today carries out those duties laid down in the *Coroners Acts, 1887 and 1954*, and rules made thereunder. (Local authorities retain administrative responsibility for them however.)

The main duties of the coroner are to investigate the death of any person which has been (i) sudden, (ii) violent, or (iii) unnatural (i.e. against the course of nature), (iv) deaths of prisoners, and (v) deaths of persons in mental institutions where there is no satisfactory medical evidence as to the cause of death. The coroner may, however, hold an inquest into *any* case of death.

A coroner *must* summon a jury when there is reason to suspect that death is due to murder, manslaughter, infanticide, a road accident, poisoning, or notifiable disease. An inquest may be held in any place (e.g. a court or a private house). Proceedings are carried out in a formal manner. The public are admitted to the court except when this would be prejudicial to national security.

The purpose of the inquest is to enable the coroner, with the aid of a jury when so required, to ascertain the identity of the deceased person and the place and cause of death. If the jury find that the cause of death is murder, manslaughter, or infanticide they may name the person responsible, and the coroner must then issue a warrant of arrest. However, if some person has already been arrested and charged with the murder, manslaughter, or infanticide of the subject of the inquest, the coroner must adjourn his inquiry until the criminal proceedings are ended.

Money, coin, gold, silver, plate, or bullion found hidden in the earth or a private place, the owner of which is unknown, is called **treasure trove** and belongs to the Crown. When such articles are uncovered, the coroner holds an inquest to establish whether they are in fact treasure trove. If so, the finder and the owner of the land on which they were found are customarily recompensed by the Treasury.

A coroner must be a barrister, solicitor, or medical practitioner of at least five years' standing. He is appointed by a county council or a borough council having a separate commission of the peace. The Lord Chancellor may dismiss a coroner for inability or misbehaviour amounting to misconduct.

Law Reform

The law is open to the criticism that in general it is conservative. Many statutes are ancient, appertaining to a bygone age and feudal system; some common law offences are inappropriate today. For example, the offences of challenging to fight, eavesdropping, being a common barrator, a common scold or common night walker were abolished only in 1967 by the Criminal Justice Act of that year. Furthermore, it is argued that legal procedures are unduly formal and slow, and that the system of courts needs overhaul and remodelling.

Another criticism is the variation in sentencing for similar offences by different judges or magistrates e.g. in two different rape cases in 1987, two offenders got 3 and 5 years, while another two got fourteen and sixteen year jail sentences. Guidelines on sentencing (laid down by the Lord Chief Justice) do exist. But recent cases have brought into question their adequacy and clarity. Plans to codify and publish these on a statutory basis were dropped in 1986. Instead, under the *Criminal Justice Bill, 1987*, it is proposed that cases of apparently over-lenient sentencing may be referred by the Attorney General to the Court of Appeal which would then provide guidelines or principles for future similar cases.

Some of these criticisms may seem fair and reasonable; but it is clear that reform of the law and the machinery of the courts are matters which cannot be approached carelessly, irresponsibly, or hurriedly. Nevertheless, law is a living thing and reform is continual. The agencies through which reform is effected include the following:

(*a*) Law Reform Committee.
(*b*) Criminal Law Revision Committee.
(*c*) Law Commission.
(*d*) Royal Commissions.
(*e*) Government Legislation (Public Bills).
(*f*) Private Members' Bills.

(*a*) *The Law Reform Committee* began in 1952 and took over the work of the Law Revision Committee set up in 1934. It is made up of judges and

Fig. 23. A Royal Commission

practising and academic lawyers, and deals with civil-law matters referred to it by the Lord Chancellor. Members of the committee, and the general public also, may raise matters and suggest subjects for consideration. The following statutes reformed parts of the civil law and were passed as a result of the recommendations of the committee:

The *Limitation Act, 1939.*
The *Law Reform* (*Contributory Negligence*) *Act, 1945.*
The *Occupiers' Liability Act, 1957.*
The *Law Reform* (*Husband and Wife*) *Act, 1962.*

(*b*) *The Criminal Law Revision Committee.* While the Lord Chancellor is concerned with the Law Reform Committee and the reform of the civil law, the Home Secretary is primarily concerned with the administration of the criminal law. The Criminal Law Revision Committee (a Standing Committee) was set up in 1959 to examine aspects of the criminal law, to consider whether the law requires revision, and to make recommendations.

The Committee has issued several reports; the seventh (Felonies and Misdemeanours) and eighth (Theft and Related Offences) have resulted in the *Criminal Law Act, 1967*, and the *Theft Act, 1968*, respectively.

(*c*) *The Law Commission.* The *Law Commissions Act, 1965*, set up a full-time Commission whose duty is to keep under review the English law as a whole with a view to its systematic development and reform, including, in particular, its codification, the elimination of anomalies, the repeal of obsolete and unnecessary enactments, the reduction of the number of separate enactments, and, generally, the simplification and modernisation of the law. Pursuant to programmes approved by the Lord Chancellor, the Commission undertakes the examination of particular branches of the law and the formulation, by means of draft Bills, of proposals for reform. It is responsible for the consolidation and revision of statute law.

The five commissioners and a legal staff are appointed by the Lord Chancellor. The Commission issues an annual report which is laid before Parliament.

(*d*) *Royal Commissions* are appointed by the Crown on the advice of a Minister who names a Chairman. The membership of each Royal Commission varies, but it usually reflects expert, professional, and lay opinion. The duty of a Royal Commission is to investigate some matter of public importance, to take evidence and to make recommendations. On receipt of its report, the Government may give legislative effect to the recommendations. Recent Commissions have dealt with the press, the NHS, pollution and pornography. The *Royal Commission on the Constitution (1969–73)*, under the chairmanship of Lord Kilbrandon, considered and made recommendations on devolution in the UK (see p. 372 below).

The Royal Commission on Local Government Reform (1966–9) resulted in the *Local Government Act, 1972.* (See p. 334.)

(*e*) *Government Legislation.* A Government's legislative programme varies with the political party in power. Some Bills may inaugurate entirely new services, e.g. the National Health Service legislation of 1946, but some legislation may aim at tidying up, consolidating, or reforming the law in a particular respect. The *Road Traffic Act, 1972*, and the *Town and Country Planning Act, 1971*, consolidated and reformed existing law in these two matters. Moreover, delegated legislation may be passed into law by Ministers to whom Parliament has entrusted its power. Thus many statutory instruments amend, reform, or consolidate existing rules.

(*f*) *Private Members' Bills* (see p. 100) may reform existing law in important respects. Examples include the *Defamation Act, 1952*, and the *Chronically Sick and Disabled Persons Act, 1970.* Parliamentary time is, however, limited, and Government Bills must come first. Hence the Private Members' Bill is not the most important medium of reform.

Juries

(*a*) *The Criminal Jury* comprises twelve persons of either sex and is found in the Central Criminal Court and the Crown Courts. Juries are not used in magistrates' courts, juvenile courts, the Court of Appeal or the House of Lords. The sworn duty of the jury is 'to well and truly try the case and give a true verdict according to the evidence'.

The defence and the prosecution have a right of challenge to the array of jurors or to individual jurors. Those jurors objected to will be asked to stand down and others will be empanelled to take their places.

Formerly the verdict of a jury had to be unanimous. Now, the *Juries Act, 1974*, provides that a majority verdict may be allowed. The court cannot, however, accept a majority verdict unless the jury has been deliberating for not less than two hours, when the verdict need not then be unanimous if (i) in a case where there are not less than eleven jurors, ten of them agree; or (ii) in a case where there are ten jurors, nine of them agree.

Where a juror dies or is ill, provided that both sides agree and the number of jurors is not reduced below ten, the case may continue and a verdict may be given.

(*b*) *The Civil Jury* is not used as frequently as its criminal counterpart. Certain civil actions are unsuitable for trial by juries, e.g. taxation cases and company matters involving detailed examination of accounts. The general rule following the *Administration of Justice (Miscellaneous Provision) Act, 1933*, is that the civil court has a discretion in its use of a jury. A jury may, however, be ordered on the application of either party in cases of defamation, malicious prosecution, false imprisonment and fraud, unless the court considers that, for example, the trial will involve prolonged examination of documents or accounts.

In actions in the Chancery Division juries are used only rarely. In defended divorce cases or contested probate actions a jury may be applied for.

In High Court cases the jury comprises twelve persons. A majority verdict is now accepted. In county court actions the jury numbers eight. In coroners' courts the jury comprises from seven to eleven persons; the coroner may accept a majority verdict, provided that the number of dissentients does not exceed two.

When a judge sits without a jury, he determines questions of law and fact. (The most controversial use of such a system occurs in Northern Ireland, under the *Northern Ireland (Emergency Provision) Act, 1983*, for trials concerning terrorism, see p. 284.)

Qualifications of Jurymen

The *Criminal Justice Act, 1972*, abolished the former property qualification for jury service in England and Wales. The basic qualification is that of **citizenship** as evidenced by inclusion in the Electoral Register. Anyone between the ages of 18 and 65 (70 under the *Criminal Justice Bill*, 1987) registered as an elector who has lived here for five years or more since the age of 13 becomes liable for jury service.

Payments in respect of jury service for travelling, subsistence, and financial loss are made to jurors.

Ex-prisoners are disqualified from serving on a jury. Mentally ill persons are ineligible. Sick, blind, and deaf persons may be excused on compassionate grounds.

Peers, judges, MPs, clergymen, barristers, solicitors, medical practitioners, members of HM Forces and police officers are among the more notable persons exempt from jury service. The *Juries Act, 1974*, consolidates the law.

The **advantages** of trial by jury are:

(*a*) Jurors are independent of the parties to a trial.

(*b*) Juries represent the verdict of ordinary people of common sense, and this fact can act as a corrective to the harshness of the law.

(*c*) There is public confidence in jury trials.

(*d*) In jury trials the judge explains the facts to be proved and the law to be applied, which tends to clarify the issues verbally. The public thus sees that justice is done.

(*e*) The English jury trial has been copied by other countries (e.g. the United States) and is found satisfactory.

The **disadvantages** of trial by jury are:

(*a*) Complicated financial frauds may be incomprehensible to ordinary folk. (The Government is currently proposing to remove complex fraud cases from jury hearings.)

(*b*) Jurors have no physical or educational test for their task.

(*c*) Jurors may be too easily impressed and swayed by advocacy of experienced counsel.

(*d*) Juries are too prone to leniency to an accused or defendant in criminal trials. Too many cases are committed for trial; many could be dealt with summarily.

(*e*) Local prejudice may exist, and this may be reflected in local jurors.

(*f*) Jurors are susceptible to corrupt influences, threats, and intimidation from outside parties.

(*g*) Some trials are long and, as a consequence, cause inconvenience to jurors; self-employed jurors may suffer financially. Hence the jury system is expensive.

(*h*) Persons at 18 may be considered too inexperienced.

The issue of **jury vetting** has been prominent in recent years. The procedure involved rests on two foundations:

(i) The long-standing right of counsel for the prosecution (and indeed for the defence) to object to particular jury members. Under the *Criminal Justice Bill, 1987*, this right (known as 'peremptory challenge') is to be abolished owing to its over-use and abuse by the defence in a number of trials

(ii) The screening of jury members by the prosecution to ascertain their eligibility to serve (e.g. to exclude illiterates where a case deals with fraud and may involve the examination of documents).

It is sometimes felt that the screening or 'standby' process itself can go too far and lead to abuse by the authorities. The Attorney General has declared that the police should check criminal records of jurors only in exceptional cases. Indeed, many people, including Lord Denning, have expressed the view that such scrutiny is not only unnecessary but also dangerous and unconstitutional. However, others say that if jury formation is left to chance (i.e. random choice) then impartiality may on occasion be threatened. The issue remains unresolved except that in December 1979 the Attorney General said that there would be no further jury vetting without his direct approval.

Legal Aid and Advice

Free legal assistance to persons of limited means has existed at least in a few courts since the thirteenth century. Such schemes were run by unofficial voluntary organisations known as the Poor Man's Lawyers. Apart from such schemes, the general situation before 1949 was that legal aid and advice were available only to those who had the money to pay for them.

The *Legal Aid and Advice Act, 1949*, revised existing schemes and expanded them into a service covering the full range of needs and providing (i) free, or assisted, representation for all who require it; and (ii) virtually free legal advice on matters unconnected with court proceedings (known as non-litigious matters). The *Legal Aid Act, 1974*, consolidates the law on this matter.

Legal Aid in Civil Proceedings

Legal aid is available for proceedings in the House of Lords, Court of Appeal, High Court, county courts, and certain tribunals, and to civil proceedings in magistrates' courts. Proceedings wholly or partly in respect of defamation, decree proceedings for undefended divorce and separation and proceedings by way of Judgement Summons in a county court are excepted from the scheme. All other civil proceedings, including matrimonial causes, qualify for legal aid.

Eligibility for legal aid in civil proceedings depends on an applicant's 'disposable income' and 'disposable capital'.

In practice a 'means test' is operated thus:

(*a*) *Free* legal aid is available to those with a disposable income not exceeding £2,325 p.a. and whose disposable capital is £3,000 or less.

(*b*) *Contributory* legal aid is available to those with a disposable income which does not exceed £5,585 p.a. and whose disposable capital is less than £4,850 or such larger figure as may be prescribed (1987 figures).

Aid is now available for persons of average income. The 'disposable income' and 'disposable capital' are assessed by the Department of Health and Social Security in accordance with regulations, taking into account any maintenance expense of dependants, interests on loans, income tax, rent, etc., as well as the value of an applicant's house, furniture, and household effects. *Note*: Some may be repayable where a recipient wins a case involving finance.

The Legal Aid Scheme is run by the Law Society under the general guidance of the Lord Chancellor. There are twelve area committees and a network of local committees composed of barristers and solicitors (who may be paid a fee) with a salaried staff. The cost of operating the scheme is met by (i) contributions from assisted persons; (ii) costs recovered from opposite parties in litigation; and (iii) grants from the Exchequer.

Procedure. An applicant for legal aid must approach the local committee and show that he has reasonable grounds for his claim. If successful he is entitled to select from a panel a solicitor, who, if necessary, will instruct a barrister. The case then proceeds in the normal way, payments being made into and out of the Legal Aid Fund. The costs of an action which an assisted litigant loses to an unassisted opponent may also, if the court so orders, be met out of the Legal Aid Fund (*Legal Aid Act, 1974*). For example, let us suppose that *A*, an assisted person, sued *B*, an unassisted person, in negligence. *A* loses his case against *B* who is now faced with paying his solicitor's fee and other incidental expenses arising from his successful defence. The court may, at its discretion, order that *B*'s costs be paid out of the Legal Aid Fund.

Legal Advice. Anyone over 16 may obtain legal advice under the 'Green Form Scheme', which enables a solicitor to provide advice and letter-writing (but *not* representation in court) up to value of £50 (£90 for divorce cases) without the need for approval of the Legal Aid Committee. Poor persons (i.e. disposable income not more than £56 per week, 1987 figures) may thus get free advice and help; otherwise a 'means test' operates.

Legal Aid in Criminal Proceedings

A criminal court, e.g. magistrates' court, or Crown Court, has power to order legal aid to be granted where it appears desirable to do so in the interests of justice. Trivial cases, e.g. simple drunkenness, do not qualify. The court *must* make an order in cases where a person of limited means is committed for trial on a charge of murder.

The court will not make an order for legal aid unless it is satisfied that the person's means are such that he requires assistance in meeting the cost of the proceedings. Legal Aid is free if disposable income is no more than £48 per week and capital is under £3,000. Above these figures, contributions are required.

Application for legal aid should be made to the appropriate court where proceedings are to take place. An applicant may be required to make a contribution towards the costs of the action. To ascertain the amount of this contribution he will be required to produce written evidence of means. An assessment of means will be carried out by the DHSS, which reports to the court. No contribution is required from a person who has insufficient means. Any doubt which exists as to the means of the defendant is resolved in his favour. The court has power to amend or revoke a legal-aid order.

As a general rule, legal aid in criminal cases includes representation by counsel and solicitor. In magistrates' courts, however, representation will be by solicitor alone unless the offence is serious. Legal aid may also be granted in connection with appellate proceedings, e.g. on appeal to the Court of Appeal (Criminal Division), and, if need be, to the House of Lords.

Dock Briefs

Where a person is committed for trial from a magistrates' court he will, should his means be insufficient, be granted facilities for legal aid in the form of advice and representation of his case in court during the committal proceedings. A barrister then represents him at a Crown Court.

If, however, a prisoner has no barrister to represent him at a Crown Court, he may (irrespective of his means) choose any counsel, robed and in court, to defend him. By tradition the barrister selected will never refuse to take his 'dock brief', and will defend the prisoner to the best of his ability for a very small fee. This customary aid has fallen into disuse because of the statutory provisions, i.e. *Legal Aid Act, 1974.*

Problems

Concern has been expressed recently at (i) the growing cost of legal aid (for criminal cases it rose from £0.5 million in 1961 to £133 million in

1985; for civil cases it was £139 millions); (ii) the great variations which occur over the country in the local granting of legal aid; and (iii) the non-availability of legal aid in childcare and mental review proceedings.

Law and Laymen

The making of law, the administration of law, and the administration of justice in the courts and tribunals are matters of supreme importance to civilised men everywhere.

Laymen in Anglo-Saxon and Norman times participated closely in making and administering the law. They were, as we have noted, responsible for keeping the King's Peace. If crimes were committed they had forthwith to raise the 'hue and cry' and to surrender the criminal (if known) to the Courts of Law; for failing to do so they were collectively held responsible and fined. The laymen or their representatives attended the Anglo-Saxon dooms; they attended the hundred court, the shire court, the manorial court, and the Royal court. They adjudged, as jurymen, in disputes as to ownership and possession of land and cattle and goods, and they pronounced on innocence or guilt—giving the verdict of the country. They petitioned successive Monarchs to change the laws and to grant remedies or relief when the laws pressed heavily upon themselves. Ultimately they achieved a great constitutional reform of Parliament in 1689, which ensured that the will of the people (laymen) should prevail against the supreme might and power of a despotic King. Such, in broad outline, were some of the reforms by laymen who played their part—sometimes at great personal risk—in the creation of the English legal system we now enjoy.

Today in a free society the will of the people finds its highest democratic expression in a Parliament composed of representatives of all classes, elected by popular vote of laymen who hold universal franchise.

As to making the law, we may note that a layman can offer himself as a Parliamentary candidate; he can, as of right, make representations to change the law to his MP, to a Minister of a Government Department, to the Prime Minister, if need be. He can offer advice and evidence to Royal Commissions set up to inquire into a matter of immediate public importance, and he can suggest reform or improvement of the law itself, e.g. to the Law Commission (see p. 234).

As to administration of the law today, we may note particularly the part played by laymen (*a*) as Justices of the Peace, (*b*) as jurors, and (*c*) as lay assessors who assist a professional judge or lawyer acting judicially in the special courts and administrative tribunals already described.

(*a*) *Justices of the Peace*. A description of the composition and jurisdiction of the magistrates' courts has already been given. All we need to note here is that there are some 21,500 lay Justices regularly adjudicating on a wide variety of matters and performing numerous administrative duties. These Justices deal with more than ninety-eight per cent of the criminal cases in Britain, and they may now sit in the Crown Courts.

Lay Justices appointed after 1 January 1966, are required to undergo training in the basic duties of their office. This does not render them professional lawyers, but assists them in understanding the meaning of 'acting judicially' so that they may more efficiently administer justice to the local people, from whose numbers they are drawn and whose public interests they serve.

(*b*) *Juries*. A detailed description of the different kinds of juries is given on p. 235. We should bear in mind that juries are composed of laymen on whose shoulders rests the final determination of verdicts in civil and criminal cases in a wide variety of courts.

(*c*) *Lay Assessors in Special Courts*. Examples of this form of participation are found in:

(i) *The Admiralty Court*. This is presided over by a High Court judge with jurisdiction to decide cases involving ships, shipping disputes, collisions at sea, etc. There is no jury, but in suitable cases (e.g. negligent navigation) the judge may call on the assistance of two nautical assessors (Elder Brethren of Trinity House) who are competent to advise on technical maritime matters.

(ii) *The Restrictive Practices Court*. The jurisdiction of this court has been dealt with on p. 232. It is a superior Court of Record and is composed of professional judges and men experienced in commerce and business. Each court sits with a High Court judge and two laymen.

(iii) *Administrative Tribunals*. These have an increasingly important part to play in the lives of all people, and mention may be made of Rent Tribunals, National Insurance Tribunals, National Insurance Industrial Injuries Tribunals, Pensions Tribunals, National Health Service Tribunals, Transport Tribunals, and those of the Area Traffic Commissioners.

Although the constitution of each may vary in detail, the common factor is the presence of laymen, usually representing interests or bodies such as local authorities, employers' organisations, and employees' organisations. Usually the Chairmen are legally qualified persons (*Tribunals and Inquiries Act, 1971*), but the presence of the laymen ensures that tribunals display the characteristics of 'openness, fairness, and impartiality' and helps to achieve a just and proper balance of opinion on the tribunal bench (see p. 290).

Administrative Personnel

The distinction between laymen and professional lawyers is not always clear. The Welfare State has enormously increased the number of local and central Government servants and has introduced a whole range of enforcement officers who must specialise in and enforce certain parts of the law. Pre-eminently, the police must know the criminal law and the powers of arrest and procedure very well indeed if they are to enforce its detailed and complicated provisions. They receive special training throughout their careers to equip them to discharge their duties efficiently. Many legal battles in the criminal courts revolve around whether the particular police officer has, or has not, acted in accordance with the law (common law or statute law), all of whose precepts he is presumed to know.

Other officials include probation officers, inspectors of factories, local authority social workers, and standards control officers. Like the police, these officials who execute or administer the law may lay information for summonses, may prosecute cases before the magistrates' courts, and in some cases may detain persons. They are therefore in a special class and do not strictly fall under the headings of laymen or professional lawyers.

For some nine hundred years laymen have played their part in the creation of the legal system and the constitution which we inherit. The word 'justice' appeals to the idealism in men the world over. Laymen have seen to it that it is much too important a matter to be left to professionals or to be dispensed in secret. 'Every court of justice is open to every subject of the King,' said Lord Halsbury in *Scott* v. *Scott* (1913). The public, or laymen collectively, recognise the truth of the following utterance in a court of law: 'Justice is not a cloistered virtue; she must be allowed to suffer the scrutiny and respectful, even though outspoken, comments of ordinary men' (*Ambard* v. *Attorney-General of Trinidad and Tobago*, 1936).

All laymen, whether officiating as magistrates, assessors, jurors, witnesses, or merely spectators in the public gallery, ought to ensure that full and positive meaning is given to the words of Lord Chief Justice Hewart: 'It is not only necessary that justice should be done, but also that it should manifestly be seen to be done.'

The Royal Commission on Legal Services, 1976–79 (Cmnd. 7648)

After producing a lengthy report and costing £1¼ m. this Royal Commission concluded that lawyers were generally competent and (contrary to much popular opinion) not overpaid for the work they do. The Commission also concluded that the basic structure and role of the legal profession should be preserved (see next chapter).

However, it made a number of detailed suggestions for change (over 350 in all) among which we note the following: (i) extensions to the legal aid and advice scheme by increasing income limits (see p. 238); (ii) better support from the Central Government for local law centres; (iii) the encouragement of competition among solicitors by allowing some (limited) advertising; (iv) the review and simplification of procedures in tribunals (see p. 290) and the facilitation of representation therein (including legal aid if necessary); (v) the need to reduce excessive delay in the litigation process.

Some of the recommendations are easier said than done, and, in particular, a number would involve unfashionable increases in public expenditure. However, while the *Legal Aid Act, 1982* seeks to extend the right of access to legal aid, it also increases the financial contributory element: thus, of the 451,000 who received criminal legal aid in 1981, 32,000 made some contribution: this is now expected to double to 67,000 (15 per cent). Meanwhile, the *Mental Health* (*Amendment*) *Act 1982*, now extends legal aid to those engaging legal representation in mental health tribunals.

Exercises

1. What is the composition and jurisdiction of the House of Lords when sitting as a Court of Appeal?

2. Outline the composition and jurisdiction of the Judicial Committee of the Privy Council.

3. The Queen's Bench Division of the High Court exercises (i) an original jurisdiction, and (ii) an appellate jurisdiction. Describe its jurisdiction carefully.

4. What is the composition and jurisdiction of the Court of Appeal, Criminal Division?

5. Describe the composition of the Crown Courts, and give an outline of their jurisdiction.

6. Distinguish between (*a*) a High Court judge; (*b*) a circuit judge; and (*c*) a Recorder.

7. What is meant by 'an appeal by way of Case Stated'?

8. Distinguish between a stipendiary magistrate and a county magistrate.

9. Outline the jurisdiction of a magistrates' court.

10. What is a court of preliminary investigation?

11. Indicate the main agencies responsible for Law Reform.

12. What qualifications have jury members? Outline the arguments (*a*) for, and (*b*) against the jury system.

13. What are the main provisions of the *Legal Aid Act, 1974*?

14. What part do laymen play in the administration of English law?

8
Judicial Officers, Law Officers, and the Legal Profession

The Lord Chancellor

The Lord High Chancellor of Great Britain, more usually known as the Lord Chancellor, ranks eighth in order of precedence in England after the Queen: a status which reflects his importance as a Minister of the Crown chiefly responsible for the administration of justice.

The Lord Chancellor is appointed by the Crown on the advice of the Prime Minister. His position combines duties which are legislative, executive, and judicial: it is therefore an exception to the constitutional doctrine of the 'separation of powers'.

In his *legislative* capacity the Lord Chancellor presides over the House of Lords. He may take part in its debates and can vote in all of its divisions.

As an *executive* or administrative officer he is a member of the Cabinet, its chief legal and constitutional adviser and one of its representatives in the House of Lords. He is the Ministerial head of the Land Registry, the Public Record Office and the Public Trustee, and provides advice and assistance in cases of difficulty in the administration of these departments. He is also responsible for the custody and use of the Great Seal, which authenticates important legal documents such as Letters Patent.

In his *judicial* capacity the Lord Chancellor is head of the Judiciary, President of the House of Lords (in its appellate capacity) and President of the Supreme Court. He is the most important member of the Judicial Committee of the Privy Council, and is head of the Chancery Division of the High Court. However, he rarely sits as a judge other than in the House of Lords and the Judicial Committee of the Privy Council. He appoints, in the name of the Crown, the following judicial officers: puisne judges of the High Court; Recorders; Circuit judges, and magistrates. The appointments of legally qualified chairmen of certain administrative tribunals are subject to his approval. He thus holds a key, and somewhat ambiguous position in the scheme of things, for which he is entitled to a salary exceeding that of the Prime Minister.

The Lord Chancellor is served by a staff of professional assistants and his office is in the House of Lords.

Judges

(i) *The Lord Chief Justice* (LCJ) is appointed by the Crown on the advice of the Prime Minister. He is head of the Court of Appeal (Criminal Division) and of the Queen's Bench Division. He is also a member of the House of Lords.

(ii) *The Master of the Rolls* (MR) is appointed by the Crown on the advice of the Prime Minister. He is deputy to the Lord Chancellor and is head of the Court of Appeal (Civil Division). He supervises the admission of solicitors to the Rolls of the Supreme Court.

(iii) *The President of the Family Division* is appointed by the Crown on the advice of the Prime Minister, and is responsible for the work of this Division of the High Court.

(iv) *The Vice-Chancellor of the Chancery Division.* This post was re-created in 1971 after one hundred years. The Vice-Chancellor is head of the Chancery Division under the Lord Chancellor (the official President).

(v) *The Lords of Appeal in Ordinary* are known as **Law Lords** and are appointed by the Crown on the advice of the Prime Minister from among existing judges or barristers of at least fifteen years' standing. They are life peers and can adjudicate in appeal cases heard in the House of Lords. They are also *ex officio* members of the Judicial Committee of the Privy Council. There are ten Law Lords (current salary is £71,400 p.a.).

(vi) *Lords Justices of Appeal* are appointed by the Crown on the advice of the Prime Minister from among existing judges or barristers of at least fifteen years' standing. They are judges of the Court of Appeal. They are twelve in number.

(vii) *Judges of the High Court* are known as puisne judges and are appointed by the Crown on the recommendation of the Lord Chancellor from among barristers of at least ten years' standing. Nine judges are assigned to the Chancery Division, forty-four to the Queen's Bench Division and seventeen to the Family Division of the High Court.

Each of the above judges receives a substantial salary which ensures independence and reflects the importance of judges in society.

All the judges referred to above hold office 'during good behaviour' and may be removed by the Crown on an address presented by both Houses of Parliament. Their salaries are fixed by statute and form a charge on the Consolidated Fund. The effect of these two important provisions is to ensure judicial independence: a vital feature in the administration of law and justice within the State.

Judges of the High Court retire at the age of 75, and are eligible for pensions granted by statute. Today judges hold exercises and conferences in penology and sentencing policy to ensure uniformity in judicial administration.

(viii) *Circuit judges* are judges appointed by the Crown on the advice of the Lord Chancellor to serve in both (i) Crown Courts, and (ii) county courts. A circuit judge must be a barrister of 10 years' standing or a person who has held the office of a recorder for five years. The retiring age is 72, with the possibility of extension to 75. All existing county court judges can become circuit judges, as can the Recorders of Liverpool and Manchester, a number of whole-time Chairmen and Deputy Chairmen of

Quarter Sessions and certain other holders of judicial offices. (*Courts Act, 1971.*)

(ix) *Recorders.* Under the *Courts Act, 1971* (see p. 224) these are part-time judges of the Crown Court. Appointments are made to men of high professional standing who are prepared to commit themselves to not less than one month's work on the bench each year. Solicitors of 10 years' standing (as well as barristers) are eligible for appointment to this office. If a solicitor holds the appointment of Recorder for five years he may then be appointed a circuit judge (see above).

Criticisms

There has been mounting criticism of judges in recent years, in particular of the way in which they are appointed. Not only is the process felt to be un-necessarily secretive, but it results in a distorted composition, with only 17 per cent women, one in three being over the normal retirement age, and the vast majority drawn from a highly privileged section of society (e.g. of the 10 current Law Lords, nine went to Public School and eight to Oxbridge). This may be considered unfair. But it may also be dangerous since senior politicians tend to come from the same background, so that there may be a tendency to share values and views (often called the 'establishment view') e.g. it is alleged that the judiciary accepted too readily the Government claim about the national interest when they accepted the ban on trade unions at Government Communications Headquarters (GCHQ) in 1984.

There is also some concern that judges are appointed (by the Queen or the Prime Minister) on the advice of the Lord Chancellor—a senior politician in the Government of the day. The alternative might be an apparently more impartial Judicial Appointments Board.

Attorney-General and Solicitor-General

Together these are known as Law Officers. Both are appointed by the Crown on the advice of the Prime Minister. They are political appointments, and the holders are precluded from private practice.

(*a*) *The Attorney-General* is usually a member of the House of Commons. His duties comprise the following:

(i) He represents the Crown in the courts in civil matters, and may prosecute in important and difficult cases in the criminal courts.

(ii) He advises Government departments on important legal matters and may take part in many judicial and quasi-judicial proceedings affecting the public interest, e.g. the administration of charities and patent law.

(iii) Certain criminal offences must be reported to the Attorney-General, and his consent is necessary before criminal proceedings may be taken in certain cases, e.g. bribery, incest, corrupt practices, and offences against the *Official Secrets Acts, 1911 and 1939*, the *Dangerous Drugs Act, 1951*, the *Public Order Act, 1936 and 1986*, the *Prevention of Violence* (*Temporary Provisions*) *Act 1939*, and various other Acts.

The Attorney-General superintends the work of the Director of Public Prosecutions. He is head of the English Bar, and points of professional etiquette may be referred to him. The equivalent in Scotland is the Lord Advocate.

(*b*) *The Solicitor-General* is deputy to the Attorney-General and his duties are similar. He is a barrister and is usually a member of the House of Commons. By the *Law Officers Act, 1944*, any functions authorised or required to be discharged by the Attorney-General may, unless expressly excluded, be discharged by the Solicitor-General if the Office of Attorney-General is vacant, if the Attorney-General is absent or ill, or if the Attorney-General authorises his deputy to act in any particular case.

Director of Public Prosecutions (DPP)

The office of Director of Public Prosecutions was created by the *Prosecution of Offences Act, 1879*. The Director must be a barrister or solicitor of at least 10 years' standing. He is a civil servant who has had wide experience of the criminal law in the courts. He acts under the superintendence of the Attorney-General, and is assisted in his work by a staff of professional barristers.

The Director and his staff advise the police, clerks to magistrates, and other persons enforcing the criminal law on prosecutions in serious or difficult cases. He must prosecute in offences punishable by death (e.g. treason), and in cases of murder and manslaughter. He may also prosecute in any case referred to him by a Government Department or in any case which, because of its importance or difficulty, requires his intervention. Chief officers of police must report to him all offences formerly punishable by death, offences under the *Incitement of Disaffection Act, 1934*, the *Official Secrets Acts, 1911 to 1939*, the *Forgery Act, 1913, Punishment of Incest Act, 1908*, and other enactments. The Director appears for the Crown in every appeal to the Court of Appeal (Criminal Division).

The Legal Profession

There are two branches of the legal profession in Britain: viz. barristers and solicitors of the Supreme Court. Their roles are rather like that of the specialist and the General Practitioner in medicine. In most other countries, including some parts of the Commonwealth, there is no such division.

Solicitors

The modern solicitor is the successor of three former ancient professions known as attorney (or representative), solicitor, and proctor. These assisted judges in the King's Bench in the early stages of litigation or carried out the less skilled work in the ecclesiastical and Admiralty courts. By a succession of *Solicitors Acts* (*1839–1974*), the profession has been unified and regulated.

The regulations of the Law Society provide for:

(i) The scales of remuneration and fees of solicitors.
(ii) The terms and conditions of articles of clerkship for new entrants.

(iii) Courses for the education and training of students.
(iv) The conduct of examinations.
 (v) The discipline of all solicitors.

A person who has served articles (from $2\frac{1}{2}$ to 5 years) to a solicitor, and who passes the examinations of the Law Society, may be admitted a solicitor by having his name enrolled. He thereby becomes an officer of the Supreme Court, and receives his Certificate to Practise which is renewable annually. There are some 26,000 solicitors in England and Wales.

Solicitors have a professional body known as the **Law Society**, which controls entry to the profession and regulates legal education and training. The Law Society is responsible for conduct and discipline, which in the last resort may include the power to withdraw the right to practice, in the cases of professional misconduct.

The *Administration of Justice Act, 1985*, established the **Solicitors' Complaints Bureau**. This body has the power to deal with lesser complaints of shoddy work, such as undue delay, incompetence in drafting a conveyance, incorrect instructions or explanations to clients.

Duties of a Solicitor. Most solicitors are employed in private practice, either alone or in a partnership firm. Others are employed in the public service, industry, and commerce.

Practising solicitors are consulted by, and receive instructions from, lay clients on a wide variety of matters both civil and criminal, e.g. the making of wills, administration of estates, family matters, the formation of companies, drawing up of documents, conveyancing, and criminal offences of all kinds. In cases of unusual difficulty or where a trial is to take place in the superior courts, the solicitor takes his instructions from the client, prepares briefs and approaches a barrister (counsel) who thereupon gives an 'opinion' or represents the client at the trial.

Solicitors have a right of audience only in certain courts, e.g. Magistrates' Courts, County Courts, and Crown Courts (if the solicitor defended the accused in the Magistrates Court).

The relationship between solicitor and client is based on professional confidence, and a solicitor cannot be compelled to disclose in court communications made in a professional relationship. Nor is a solicitor liable for defamation in respect of statements made in court during the course of a trial. A solicitor is, however, liable to be sued for damages for negligence in the conduct of his profession: e.g. where he has carelessly lost documents entrusted to him.

Solicitors may now be appointed as Recorders in Crown Courts (see p. 224), and many have opted to join the recently established Crown Prosecution Service as Crown Prosecutors.

Crown Prosecutors

A new role for qualified lawyers appeared in 1986 with the introduction of the Crown Prosecution Service. Its introduction under the *Prosecution of Offenders Act, 1985* represents the biggest change in the criminal justice system this century as it involves the police relinquishing responsibility for prosecutions to a new salaried service of public prosecutors; thus prosecuting crime is now separated from its investigation. Anxiety about police procedures in their dual role led to the *Royal Commission of Criminal Procedure* (1977–81) which recommended a new statutory framework for police investigation of offences (which took form in the *Police and Criminal Evidence Act*, 1984: see pp. 270–2, 276). The Commission also recommended a new prosecution system, which was to be both fairer and more efficient (as about half of the cases going to the Crown Court resulted in acquittals, often on grounds of insufficient evidence). Hence, one of the functions of the new service is to sift out the weaker cases and stop them going forward.

At a time when the police have been given additional powers (see p. 266–8, 270ff.) the new independent system provides an additional safeguard for the rights of the individual within the criminal justice system, though initially, there have been difficulties recruiting the necessary 1,600 prosecutors (solicitors) in England and Wales.

Barristers

Anyone wishing to become a barrister must join one of the four Inns of Court: Gray's Inn, Lincoln's Inn, Inner Temple, and Middle Temple. These four Inns of Court are unincorporated bodies of medieval origin, owned and controlled by their senior members called the Masters of the Bench. There are currently some 15,000 barristers.

In 1966 a Senate of the Inns of Court was created to take over the functions previously exercised by each of the four Inns. The Senate deals generally with conditions for the admission of students, legal education and welfare; a Disciplinary Committee has been established.

Each intending barrister must make a certain number of attendances (known as 'keeping terms') at his Inn, and to qualify for Call to the Bar he must pass the examinations conducted by the Council of Legal Education. After passing the examinations a barrister intending to practise must undertake one year's pupillage in chambers, following which he has the right of audience in any court of law in England and Wales. As noted above, he may take instructions only from a solicitor, not from a lay client direct. Unlike the solicitor, he may not sue for his fees and is not liable in negligence in the conduct of a case.

Duties of a Barrister. Many barristers take positions in industry, commerce, the universities, and the public service. A barrister intending to practise must choose in which part of the law he intends to specialise. A barrister is essentially an advocate whose task is to present his client's case effectively in court. To be successful he must possess certain personal and intellectual qualities and, above all, a capacity for hard work. A portion of his work includes the drafting of opinions on difficult points of law, the settling of pleadings and advice on evidence and procedural matters.

The difference between the two branches of the profession may be summarised as follows:

(*a*) Solicitors have a right of audience in inferior and Crown Courts; barristers may appear in all courts.

(*b*) Solicitors are liable for negligence in the conduct of a case; barristers are not so liable (*Rondel* v. *Worsley*, 1967).

(c) Solicitors are agents for their clients and can bind them by what they say; barristers cannot so bind their clients.

(d) Solicitors may make binding contracts with clients; barristers cannot make such contracts with clients.

(e) Solicitors deal with clients direct; barristers deal with clients only through the medium of a solicitor, as a matter of professional etiquette.

(f) Solicitors are in close touch with the community and are to some extent businessmen; barristers are less so, and need a specialised knowledge of law and skill in forensic advocacy, i.e. in presenting a case in court.

(g) Solicitors are controlled by statute (*Solicitors Acts, 1839–1974*); barristers are controlled by their Inns of Court and the recently established Senate, non-statutory bodies.

When a barrister has acquired practical experience, skill, and distinction in his profession, he may apply to the Lord Chancellor to 'take silk', i.e. become a Queen's Counsel. If the applicant's request is granted, Letters Patent are issued and he will then be called by his Inn of Court 'within the bar' thus relinquishing his former status of 'outer' or 'utter' barrister.

By his new status the successful applicant will expect to attract more difficult cases and to command higher fees. He will no longer draft pleadings, conveyances, or similar documents. Thenceforward he will have the assistance of junior counsel who will be briefed with him and who will receive a proportion of his fee. A Queen's Counsel is distinguished by the letters QC after his name, and is referred to as a 'Leader'.

A Minister of Justice

The question whether there should be a Minister of Justice in the Government has agitated the minds of some people for years past. Jeremy Bentham urged this over a century ago. France, West Germany, Switzerland and Italy each has a Minister of Justice who holds one of the most important posts in the respective Governments.

In the United Kingdom the functions performed by such a Minister are distributed among:

  (i) The Lord Chancellor.
  (ii) The Home Secretary.
  (iii) The Attorney-General.

In 1918 Lord Haldane, Chairman of 'The Machinery of Government Committee' recommended to Parliament that the Home Secretary should be 'Minister of Justice' under the Lord Chancellor. Nothing has been done since, though the functions and powers of each of the three officers of State have widened considerably during the years since 1918.

The Arguments For

The following are some of the points which may be advanced in favour of such an appointment:

  (i) The administration of justice is one of the most important of the social services. A senior Minister should be appointed to the post and should be a member of the House of Commons responsible to that Chamber. The Lord Chancellor sits in the Lords and cannot answer in the Commons.

(ii) A Minister of Justice should be responsible for:

(*a*) The appointment of all judges.

(*b*) The legal profession (barristers and solicitors).

(*c*) The administrative arrangements by Circuit Administrators, Clerks of Courts (County Courts and Magistrates' Courts) and recording judgements.

(*d*) The police and criminal law enforcement.

(*e*) The prisons, detention centres, borstals, and similar institutions, and the after-care of prisoners.

(iii) Reform of the Law has traditionally been slow. The reform of the legal system, particularly the courts has also been slow. A Minister with political drive would ensure that the administration of justice would keep pace with the needs of the times. These are constantly changing and will continue to change at an increasing rate, hence the need for constant review by one person specially charged with responsibility.

(iv) The growth of Administrative Tribunals (see p. 290) and Industrial Courts itself imposes an increasing responsibility. These tribunals proliferate with no single Minister in charge of them. The tribunals represent almost another legal system dispensing 'administrative justice', and their numbers will increase as the State intervenes in the private lives of subjects more and more.

(v) A Minister or Justice should recommend appointments to the office of Parliamentary Commissioner for Administration. More commissioners are now created, e.g. for complaints against local government authorities (see p. 367) and the Health Service and hospitals (see p. 310). A Minister could co-ordinate in this field.

(vi) The post is a logical one. If such Ministers are found satisfactory and compatible with liberal democracy in the main European countries there is no reason why a similar post may not be created in the United Kingdom. The responsibilities and powers are essentially the same.

The Arguments Against

The following are some of the arguments against such an appointment:

(i) The appointment of a Minister of Justice would violate the doctrine of the separation of powers (see p. 11), in that he would purport to combine (i) executive and (ii) judicial duties in one office. His roles must inevitably conflict.

(ii) English law is different from the European systems and the United Kingdom has one of the finest legal systems in the world. The main characteristics are (i) its age and continuity; (ii) an independent judiciary; and (iii) an independent legal profession.

(iii) A Minister of Justice may not be a trained lawyer who is familiar with the problems inherent in law and the administration of justice. If a

Minister is not himself a lawyer he would be 'in the hands of' the higher civil servants.

(iv) The police are traditionally independent, and it would be wrong in principle if a Minister were directly responsible for police and police action. In the hands of the Executive the police service is a powerful weapon.

(v) The judges in the past have stood against the Executive and guarded individual private rights, and declared as wrongful and illegal 'Acts of State' (see p. 255) and Ministerial orders (e.g. Regulation 18B, Defence Regulations, 1939 (*Liversedge* v. *Anderson* (1942))).

(vi) The 'administration of justice' itself is too vast a subject for one Minister effectively to control. It is better that the responsibilities be shared so that each of the present officers of State can act as a check on the other(s).

(vii) The division of responsibility: the Lord Chancellor, responsible for the administration of the civil law, with the Home Secretary, responsible for the administration of the criminal law, is a partnership which works well. Each has Law Reform or Law Revision Committees (see p. 233) under his surveillance, and the Law Commission is effectively working through the law with a view to its eventual codification. Law Reform does keep pace; see the *Courts Act, 1971*, the *Administration of Justice Act, 1970*, which have inaugurated changes in the criminal courts (see p. 224) and the High Court (see p. 219).

(viii) There is public faith in the present office holders and, although change inevitably takes place, the law and its administration is one subject where changes and modifications ought to be made slowly. It is better that law be certain even if there are occasional injustices. A reformist zeal is inappropriate in a Court of Law. The wheels of the law grind slowly—and not without purpose.

Conclusion

There is no absolute conclusion here. There are views for and views against, and there are many other implications which would have to be weighed in the balance.

The prime duty of any Government is the preservation of law and order. That is the basic duty which must be discharged. Only an independent and disinterested stranger can properly evaluate the freedoms which we enjoy within the law. Although there are inevitably strains on the forces of law and order and the administration of justice, ordinary citizens may live out their lives in reasonable safety and peace. Any disturbance of the delicate 'checks and balances' which operate on the constitution must be measured with care. It is no justification to say that if other countries have Ministers of Justice we must follow suit. It may well be that British people like British justice as it is, which is justification enough for Parliament to be satisfied with the present arrangements and its present officers.

Exercises

1. Describe the office and functions of the Lord Chancellor.

2. What is meant by the phrase 'The Law Officers of the Crown'? What are their duties?

3. Describe the office held by the Director of Public Prosecutions and indicate his duties.

4. Describe the duties of a solicitor, and indicate the functions of the Law Society.

5. Describe the profession of barrister, and distinguish it from that of a solicitor.

6. Who are Queen's Counsel?

7. There is no Minister of Justice in Britain. How are the functions performed by such a Minister in other countries distributed in Britain?

8. What are the main arguments for and against the creation of the post of Minister of Justice?

9. Comment on the following figures (1987):

Circuit judges: 373 men, 16 women

High Court judges: 76 men, 3 women

Recorders: 512 men, 22 women

10. Comment on the suggestion that a judicial board be appointed to advise the Lord Chancellor on the dismissal and appointment of judges.

9
Liberties of the Subject

Personal liberty, freedom of thought and freedom of speech are familiar to British people. We accept them as part of the British way of life, the British tradition, yet it is unwise to take them for granted. Their safeguard today lies in representative government, in the power of the body of citizens to express their will through their Government, in the use they make of that power, and in an independent judiciary.

Freedom is dear to the hearts of most people; men have given their lives for it and will doubtless do so again. Yet freedom is by no means a simple conception. It may take many forms: national, political, religious, economic, and personal.

There is no formal guarantee under the British constitution that all subjects shall be free. Magna Carta, 1215, (Art. 39), which is still the law of the land, lays down:

No free man shall be taken or imprisoned or dispossessed or outlawed or in any way destroyed . . . unless by the lawful judgment of his peers (equals) or the law of the land.

Outlawry is no longer permitted, and a man may no longer be 'destroyed' (killed). The main point of this provision is the declaration that there shall not be arbitrary or illegal arrests, in other words it was an early manifestation of the 'Rule of Law'. There are, however, declarations of rights in the Bill of Rights, 1689, and the Act of Settlement, 1701, but there is no written statement by Parliament or the law that you or I have a legal right to our freedom. Under the American Constitution (a written constitution) we see:

Congress shall make no law respecting an establishment of religion, or prohibiting the free exercise thereof; or of abridging the freedom of speech or of the Press; or the right of the people peaceably to assemble, and to petition the Government for a redress of grievances.

These rights, and others, have been incorporated as fundamental rights, but they have necessarily been curtailed or qualified by law, making the fundamental rights not absolute but relative.

What English law says is not 'You can do this' but 'You cannot do this.' I am free within the limits of the law; I can do what I please so long as I do nothing prohibited by law i.e. what is not prohibited is permitted. For example, if I trespass on your land the law gives you a legal remedy against me for my wrong to your rights of possession. If I drive a car dangerously down the road a police prosecution may follow whereupon a court of law may punish me for my offence.

Freedom of the Person

Briefly, therefore, we may say that *A* can do anything or go wheresoever he wishes in this country so long as he does not offend the law. If therefore *A* does not trespass on another's property or commit nuisance, and behaves as a rational civilised being he will not be interfered with by the Government or its agents (the police) responsible for maintaining the law.

Under the Rule of Law (discussed on p. 15) we mentioned that no one, not even a Secretary of State acting in the name of the Crown, may interfere with my personal freedom by arresting me unless he has legal power so to do. Governments have in the past, in moments of crisis and emergency, tried to arrest those of whom they were suspicious or did not like. Secretaries of State have tried to act under the authority of 'Act of State' and have issued general warrants which purport to authorise the arrest of *unnamed persons* and search *unnamed premises*. Such documents virtually authorise officials (e.g. police) to search any house or building or arrest any person.

By a series of cases in the eighteenth century these warrants were declared illegal by the courts. Thus in *Leach* v. *Money* (1765) a general warrant to arrest unnamed printers and publishers of the 'North Briton' (a journal), which the Government sought to suppress, was declared illegal. In *Entick* v. *Carrington* (1765), it was held that there was no inherent power in a Secretary of State (i.e. the Home Secretary) to order arrest except in cases of treason.

Where it is necessary for the police to obtain a warrant of arrest or search they will (on sworn information in writing) obtain a warrant from a JP (or a judge). The person to be arrested is named (or identified) in the warrant and the premises to be searched are described. Search warrants are necessary for a number of offences, e.g. stolen property, possessing explosives, dangerous drugs, firearms, and the law authorises their issue to enable search to be made. Any stolen articles, drugs, firearms, etc., discovered will be seized in accordance with the warrant and brought before a court of law, together with the alleged culprit.

An interesting case arose in 1968:

Chic Fashions (West Wales) Ltd. v. *Jones* (1968). The police, under a search warrant which referred to clothing stolen from a particular manufacturer, searched the Chic Fashion shop. During the search the police seized other items of clothing which they believed to have been stolen, although made by another manufacturer. None of the clothing was, in fact, stolen. The company sued the police. *Held*: (by the Court of Appeal) that the police have power under a search warrant to seize *any* goods which they believe to have been stolen.

Lawful Imprisonment

A person may be lawfully arrested either under the common law or under powers granted by statute. For example at common law a police officer or a private person may arrest any person found committing treason, murder, theft, or dangerous wounding, or a breach of the peace. There are numerous statutes which give legal power of arrest to (*a*) a private person, and (*b*) a police officer. These will be referred to later. A police officer has wider powers of arrest than a private citizen.

The following are the occasions when **lawful** imprisonment is permitted:

(i) By arrest pending trial (e.g. for murder, arson, burglary, theft, breach of the peace, and many other offences).

(ii) By sentence of imprisonment or detention after trial by a court, e.g. a judge or magistrate may issue a warrant of commitment to a prison.

(iii) By detention of a mentally sick patient or lunatic. (*Mental Health Act, 1959.*)

(iv) By detention of a child (i.e. a person under 14), or a young person (14–17 years) where such person is found by a court as being in need of care, protection, or control. (*Children and Young Persons Acts, 1933 and 1969.*)

(v) By parental authority, as where a parent detains his child in a room (technically an imprisonment).

We have mentioned that a person may lawfully be arrested by (*a*) a police officer, and (*b*) a private person, and that there are two types of arrest: (i) by a warrant, and (ii) without a warrant. Moreover, a person may be arrested under **common law powers** and by **statute**.

Warrant. First, what is a warrant? It is, of course, a legal document authorising some act to be done, and has been defined thus:

A warrant is a written authority signed by a Justice (or a judge) directing the person or persons to whom it is addressed to (*a*) arrest an offender to be dealt with according to law, (*b*) to take a person to prison, (*c*) to search premises, or (*d*) to levy distress for the non-payment of a legal penalty.

Where a constable sees *A* committing a serious offence (e.g. murder or theft) the constable may arrest *A* immediately. He does not need a warrant at all. But suppose *A* commits a theft and absconds from the district. A constable will make inquiries and ascertain that *A* is the probable culprit. The constable may then lay his information before a magistrate, giving details of the alleged offence and the name or identification of the alleged culprit, upon which information the magistrate may then issue a warrant which authorises the arrest of *A*.

In 1987 there was considerable public disquiet over the warrant issued to allow the (Special Branch) police to enter the BBC in Glasgow and remove film and other material. The warrant was felt to be too general or unspecific. (There was similar concern in 1979 when the police entered the business premises of Rossminster in their search for evidence of tax evasion.)

We have mentioned that there are several statutes which give powers to police and private persons to arrest another. The common law and the statutory powers of arrest before 1967 were confusing mainly because of the medieval distinction between felonies (serious offences such as murder, manslaughter, and theft), and misdemeanours (i.e. all other offences, except treason which was in a special category of offences altogether). The misdemeanours included certain offences such as fraud which could be very serious indeed but in respect of which the power of arrest was circumscribed. There were some anomalies in this part of the law and as a result the *Criminal Justice Act, 1967*, was passed which clarified the position and created what is called an **arrestable offence**. This phrase, arrestable offence, means:

(i) an offence for which the sentence is fixed by law (i.e. where the magistrates or judges have no discretion as to the penalty on a finding of guilt); and

(ii) an offence for which a person may be sentenced to five years' imprisonment on *first* conviction.

There are very few offences under the heading (i) above. Murder was formerly punishable by death, the judge having no discretion once a person was found guilty of that offence. But now, of course, the death penalty for murder has been abolished. As regards (ii), the following are the main arrestable offences:

Assault causing bodily harm.	Possessing firearms with intent to endanger life.
Assault with intent to rob.	Using firearms to resist arrest.
Indecent assault on a girl under 13.	Assisting prisoners to escape.
Armed assault.	Criminal damage.
Burglary.	Living off immoral earnings.
Conspiracy to murder.	Manslaughter.
Causing death by dangerous or reckless driving.	Murder.
Drug offences.	Piracy.
Using explosives with intent to cause grievous bodily harm, or causing injury by using explosives.	Rape.
	Theft.
	Treason.
Obtaining property by deception.	Wounding causing bodily harm.
Possessing firearms while committing another offence.	Wounding with intent to murder or maim.

All the above are punishable with imprisonment for five years. Some, e.g. murder, manslaughter, piracy, and rape are punishable with life imprisonment.

The *Police and Criminal Evidence Act, 1984*, (which largely replaced the *Criminal Justice Act, 1967* in this respect) lays down the following:

Arrest by any Person

(i) Any person may arrest without warrant anyone who is or whom he, with reasonable cause, suspects to be in the act of committing an arrestable offence. (s. 23.)

(ii) Where an arrestable offence has been committed any person may arrest without warrant anyone who is, or whom he, with reasonable cause, suspects to be guilty of the offence.

Arrest by a Constable

(i) Where a constable, with reasonable cause, suspects that an arrestable offence has been committed, he may arrest without warrant anyone whom he, with reasonable cause, suspects to be guilty of the offence.

(ii) A constable may arrest without warrant any person who is, or whom he, with reasonable cause, suspects to be, about to commit an arrestable offence.

To arrest any such person, under the powers noted above, a police officer may **enter** (if need be, by force) and **search any place** where that person is or where the constable, with reasonable cause, suspects him to be. (On this and the subject of arrest, see also p. 270).

A word of warning is necessary in regard to the use by a private citizen of the powers of arrest. Although there may be, for example, legal power to arrest another for 'breach of the peace' (which can be a fight or the use of insulting words or behaviour) a private citizen is ill advised to use it, since if he interferes unlawfully, he may be sued or prosecuted for assault or false imprisonment by the supposed culprit.

Remedies for Infringement of Personal Freedom

We have seen that any interference with the personal freedom of another, whether by assault, removal from premises, or arrest is unjustified unless there is some lawful authority for that interference.

The person interfered with is not without remedy, and he may look for protection in the following:

  (i) Self-defence.
 (ii) Prosecution or civil action for assault.
(iii) An action for wrongful arrest (false imprisonment).
(iv) Right of bail, if arrested.
 (v) Habeas Corpus.

(i) **Self-defence.** If a man is attacked by an assailant in such a manner as to cause him reasonable fear of danger to himself, his wife or child, he is justified in adopting **proportionate** means to ward it off; and if, having retreated as far as he can, until he has no means left of escaping from the attack, he turns upon his assailant and kills him in order to avoid his own death, he will not be guilty of murder. For example, if A, B, and C come towards D at the top of a cliff intent on killing D, the latter may have no means of escape, and is entitled to kill A, B, and C.

What the law permits is a reasonable or proportionate degree of force, and it is not reasonable if it is either (i) unnecessary (i.e. greater than is requisite for the purpose); or (ii) disproportionate to the evil to be prevented. Thus if A throws a tennis ball at B (technically an assault and battery), B cannot turn round and shoot A.

The use of self-defence against the police is a dangerous expedient. It is an offence to assault or resist or wilfully obstruct a constable in the execution of his duty, or to assault, resist, or wilfully obstruct a person assisting a constable in the execution of his duty:

Donnelly v. *Jackson* (1970). A constable approached Donnelly as he was walking along a road to enquire about an offence which he suspected Donnelly to have committed. Donnelly ignored requests to stop, and the police officer touched him on the shoulder intending to stop him and speak to him, but not to arrest him. Donnelly then struck the constable. Donnelly was convicted of assault, but he appealed to the Court of Appeal: *Held*: a constable is acting in the execution of his duty when, if he wishes to speak to someone, he touches them on the shoulder to attract attention. Accordingly Donnelly's appeal was dismissed.

(ii) **Action for Assault.** An assault is some act accompanied by such circumstances as indicate an intention of using actual violence against the person of another, providing the attacker has the means of carrying out his intention. A battery is the actual application of unlawful force to another. Any hostile touching, however slight, is a battery. Every battery, therefore, includes an assault.

Where, therefore, an assault or battery is committed an aggrieved party may take civil action in a county court or a prosecution in a magistrates' court for redress of the wrong done. If the attack is a serious one the police will undertake the prosecution, otherwise the matter will be left to the injured party to pursue in his own way.

(iii) **Action for False Imprisonment.** False imprisonment is any unjustified act of arresting, imprisoning, or otherwise preventing a person from exercising his right of leaving the place in which he is. To constitute imprisonment actual force is unnecessary; threats procuring submission are sufficient. Actual imprisonment in a room or cell is unnecessary, but the deprivation of liberty must be complete, as e.g. by putting handcuffs on another or merely holding his arm so that he cannot leave. No imprisonment arises by preventing a man's going in some direction while leaving him free to go in others, as by blocking a path or roadway against him. (*Bird* v. *Jones* (1845).)

Because the police must arrest persons they are particularly exposed to the risk of legal actions for false imprisonment. A constable who, let us say, arrests *A* must inform *A* of the true grounds for the arrest in accordance with rules laid down in *Christie* v. *Leachinsky* (1947).

(iv) **Right of Bail.** Where *A* is arrested without warrant by the police, the officer in charge of the police station to which *A* is taken *may* grant bail to *A*. If no bail is granted (*A* being placed in police cells), then *A* must be brought before a magistrates' court within twenty-four hours of the arrest.

When before the court *A* may apply for bail to the magistrate who will hear what the police say and will then make up his mind, having regard to all the circumstances, and grant or refuse bail. If bail is refused the magistrate must inform *A* that he (*A*) may apply to a judge of the High Court or Crown Court for bail.

The police may have very good reason for refusing or opposing bail by the court, e.g. the seriousness of the offence, fear that the prisoner on release will interfere with witnesses, or will abscond overseas, etc. On the other hand it is clearly wrong to imprison a man for a long time awaiting trial. Good justice is speedy justice; but, on occasion, the police cannot complete their inquiries to proceed with the prosecution and must, consequently, ask for further remands in custody.

Where bail is granted, the *Bill of Rights, 1689*, states that excessive sums cannot be imposed, as, for example, where *A* is released from custody and bailed in the sum of £250,000. If *A* does not turn up at court on the day named for trial the rule is that the sum named is forfeited to the Crown unless the court otherwise directs.

(v) **Habeas Corpus.** This is the name given to a writ of the Queen's Bench Division addressed to the person who holds another in custody, directing him to produce the body (corpus) of the prisoner and show cause for his detention. The writ first appeared in the reign of Edward I (1272–1307), and was issued under the common law. Habeas corpus is now governed mainly by two Acts, the *Habeas Corpus Act, 1679* (which applies to criminal matters) and the *Habeas Corpus Act, 1816* (which applies to detainees under the civil law, e.g. an inmate of a Mental Hospital).

The procedure for grant of the writ is as follows: an application is made by **affidavit** (sworn statement) to the Divisional Court of the Queen's Bench Division, (if in vacation, to a judge in chambers) by the prisoner, his lawyer or friend, setting out the reason why the detention is unlawful. The court may then grant the application immediately if urgent, but may, of course, hear the other side (e.g. the Governor of the prison who may have very good reason for the detention). Where the Divisional Court makes an order, either party (i.e. the prisoner and the person or body imprisoning) may appeal to the House of Lords with leave of either Court.

Where a writ is granted the prisoner must be released forthwith; otherwise the refusal so to do would amount to contempt of court, a punishable offence.

Privacy

An Englishman's home is his castle. And we have seen how there are limits placed on the powers of the police to detain, arrest or search people, or enter and search premises (pp. 255ff. and 270). Yet their powers are substantial and therefore controversial. Moreover, there are over 180 different statutory provisions vesting numerous officials with the power of entry for purposes of inspection, testing survey, taking possession or demolition.

Of equal concern is the question of the interception of post and tele-communications ('tapping'). This is dealt with on p. 283.

Freedom of Speech

As with personal freedom, there is no constitutional or positive right to say or write whatsoever one wills. The right is residual. In effect, *A* may say or write anything so long as he does not offend the law. Although we shall consider the legal limitations on the freedom of speech, in practice we know that this liberty is one of the most precious in the land. Indeed, were it otherwise there would be an end of democracy itself. Small wonder, therefore, that there are few prosecutions, say, for sedition, if enforcing that law entails the sacrifice of democracy.

The main restrictions on freedom of speech are found in the law relating to: (i) defamation, (ii) sedition, (iii) blasphemy, (iv) obscenity; (v) *Official Secrets Acts, (1911–1939)*, (vi) *Incitement to Disaffection Act, 1934*, (vii) *Public Order Act, 1936 and 1986*.

We shall deal with these in order, although space will not permit a full account of these detailed subjects.

(i) **Defamation.** Defamation is 'the publication of a statement which tends to lower a person in the estimation of right-thinking members of society generally; or which tends to make them shun or avoid that person' (per Professor Winfield)

There are two forms of defamation: (i) **libel**; and (ii) **slander**. Libel is defamation in some **permanent** (usually written) form, while slander is defamation in some **transitory** form, such as speech. What the law does here is to provide the machinery to enable a person to protect his good name. If, therefore, *A* writes to *B*'s employer falsely describing *B* as a rogue who has been guilty of theft, great harm and mischief can be done. This is clearly a defamatory statement, and since *A* has published the statement to the employer the law allows *B* to sue *A* in defamation (libel) to recover damages.

We have all seen caricatures of politicians and statesmen. Some of these are defamatory from a legal standpoint, but the politician may do nothing about it, letting the 'dirty water' splash off his shoulders. That is all part of politics. If, of course, the cartoon or the statement goes too far, then a politician may have recourse to the law and sue the artist or author and publisher. The usual remedies available are (i) damages, and (ii) an injunction against repetition of the libel or slander.

Some statements are protected by what is known as **Absolute Privilege**. Thus, it is not possible to sue in respect of statements, however defamatory they may be, in the following cases:

(i) Statements made in the course of judicial proceedings.

(ii) Statements made in either House by a member of either House. (Parliamentary Privilege.)

(iii) Statements made in Parliamentary papers and published by the order of either House of Parliament. (*Parliamentary Papers Act, 1840.*)

(iv) Statements made by one officer of State to another in the course of their official duty.

Qualified Privilege is something different again. The main examples of this are statements made in pursuance of a legal, moral or social duty to a person who has an interest in receiving them. For example, *A*, an employee of *B* applies for a post with *C*. *C* writes to enquire of *B* as to *A*'s character. *B* may give an honest reply or he may write a dishonest assessment of *A* (to prevent *A* leaving his employment or merely out of spite). In the latter case, if *A* knows of the defamatory statement he may sue *B* and the Qualified Privilege is withdrawn with the possibility of damages being awarded to *A*. Qualified Privilege extends to all such statements, but they will be protected only where there is no malice, ill-will, fraud or other motive of which the law disapproves. The Press have such privilege when reporting Parliamentary speeches. Local authorities also have qualified privilege in relation to their own debates.

(ii) **Sedition.** This usually takes the form of a seditious libel which is the publication of something with intent to excite disaffection against the Sovereign, the Government or the administration of justice, or to incite crime or disaffection. Thus advocating rebellions, insurrections, assassinations, outrages, or physical force or violence of any kind may be held seditious (*R.* v. *Aldred* (1909)). In practice, very few prosecutions of this nature occur, and the consent of the DPP (see p. 247 must first be obtained.

(iii) **Blasphemy.** This is committed *where a person denies and ridicules the Christian religion in a scandalous or scurrilous manner* (Blackstone). Prosecutions are rarely undertaken. In practice, there is freedom of religion and anyone may practise any form of religion (or no religion) as he pleases.

(iv) **Obscenity.** This, in the context of freedom of speech, means the publication of matter which has a tendency to deprave and corrupt those into whose hands it might fall. As we all know, greater freedom in literature and the Press is now permitted, yet the law must still be upheld. A trial in 1982 concerned the play *The Romans in Britain* containing rape scenes: it illustrated the difficulty of drawing the line between liberty and licence.

(v) **Official Secrets.** The *Official Secrets Acts, 1911–1939*, are the main statutes dealing with spying and other practices prejudicial to the safety and interests of the State. The statute is widely drawn and makes it an offence, 'to make, obtain or communicate to any other person, any sketch, plan, model, or other document or information which might be useful to an enemy for any purpose prejudicial to the safety of the State' (1911 Act. s. 1). And, 'If any person having in his possession or control . . . any information . . . which has been entrusted in confidence to him by any person holding office under Her Majesty . . . communicates the . . . information to any person other than a person (authorised) . . . shall be guilty of a misdemeanour' (s. 2).

Thus, for example, it is an offence for an officer of the Inland Revenue to disclose information on an income tax return form to an unauthorised person. We have seen other examples on p. 169. It should be noted that Ministers, civil servants, members of the armed forces, and the police are all restricted by the Acts in the giving of confidential information to unauthorised persons.

Recently there has been some concern about the way in which the statutes were drafted. The safeguard against over-zealous enforcement of this part of the law is that the consent of the Attorney-General is required to any prosecution under the Acts, and all offences must be reported by the police to the Director of Public Prosecutions. Clearly, spies must be brought to trial, and the purpose of this legislation is the prosecution of such persons, together with those ('moles') who divulge confidential information and thereby damage the nation's interests or inhibit the policy-formation process. Nevertheless many people feel that the safeguards are inadequate, and that all-embracing Section 2 should be more strictly drawn, or even replaced with a Freedom of Information Act: see p. 374.

(vi) **Incitement to Disaffection.** The *Incitement to Disaffection Act, 1934*, makes it an offence to seduce any member of HM Forces from his duty or allegiance to Her Majesty, and for a person to have in his possession or under his control any document of such a nature that the dissemination of copies thereof among members of HM Forces constitutes an offence. Similarly it is an offence to cause disaffection among members of the police (*Police Act, 1964*, s. 53).

(vii) **Public Order Act, 1986.** This Act substantially modifies and extends the Act of 1936 and introduced a new offence of **disorderly conduct** i.e. such behaviour, including abusive language, that threatens others. Under the Act, a person is guilty of an offence if he:

(*a*) uses towards another person threatening, abusive or insulting words or behaviour, or (*b*) distributes or displays to another person any writing, sign or other visible representation which is threatening, abusive or insulting, with intent to cause that person to believe that immediate unlawful violence will be used against him or another by any person, or to provoke the immediate use of unlawful violence by that person or another, or whereby that person is likely to believe that such violence will be used or it is likely that such violence will be provoked (s. 4).

and if he

(*a*) uses threatening, abusive or insulting words or behaviour, or disorderly behaviour, or (*b*) displays any writing, sign or other visible representation which is threatening, abusive or insulting, within the hearing or sight of a person likely to be caused harassment, alarm or distress thereby (s. 5).

The Act also reinforces existing provisions to outlaw acts intended or likely to stir up racial hatred, including the use of words, behaviour or broadcasts, and the display of written material and recordings.

In *Jordan* v. *Burgoyne* (1963): *J* (a teacher) addressed a meeting in Trafalgar Square, London, of 5,000 people. *J* said: 'Hitler was right. Our real enemies—the people we should have fought—were not the National Socialists of Germany, but World Jewry and its associates.' *J* was convicted at a magistrates' court and appealed to Quarter Sessions which allowed the appeal. The prosecution then appealed (by way of case stated) to the Divisional Court of the QBD. *Held*: *J* should be convicted: It was said: 'a speaker must take his audience as he finds it. If those words to that audience are likely to provoke a breach of the peace the speaker is guilty of an offence. The right of free speech is not in question: he may express his views as strongly as he likes, but he must not threaten, abuse or insult that audience.'

General. In addition to the above restrictions, we may note also the *Race Relations Act, 1968*, which makes it an offence to publish and distribute any written matter, or to use insulting or abusive words at any public meeting, which is likely to stir up hatred against a section of the community on grounds of colour, race, ethnic or national origins. s. 6.

We may note also that it is a tort to publish an **injurious falsehood**, i.e. an oral or written statement which is maliciously published and calculated to injure some interest of the plaintiff other than his reputation.

Censorship

The *Theatres Act, 1968*, repeals the *Theatres Act, 1843*, and abolishes the Lord Chamberlain's powers of censorship in regard to films, plays and similar productions intended for public performance. The new Act of 1968 makes it an offence 'publicly to perform plays which tend to deprave and corrupt the audience, or are intended or likely to incite racial hatred, or are intended or likely to cause a breach of the peace'. It is a defence to a charge of 'depravity and corruption' that performance is for the public good as being in the interests of art or learning (see p. 262). No prosecutions may take place without the consent of the Attorney-General.

The State takes no part in the censorship of films. The British Board of Film Censors (set up in 1912) grades films into four categories:

'U' suitable to be seen by any person not less than 5 years.
'PG' (Parental Guidance) for persons of 5 or over, but containing material that some parents might prefer their children not to see.
'15' for persons of not less than 15 years.
'X' for persons of not less than 18 years.

The local authority has powers under the *Cinematograph Acts, 1909–1952*, to license the showing of films and may prevent the showing of any particular film. Generally, however, the local authorities rely on the gradings of the Board of Film Censors referred to above.

Freedom of Association and Assembly

Association

The right to associate is the freedom of two or more to combine or meet together providing such combination or meeting does not infringe the common law or statute. The right is clearly supremely important, for only by securing the support of others in a common purpose can political objects normally be achieved or meet with success.

The right of association and the right of assembly or meeting are closely allied. A meeting or an assembly may amount to a conspiracy.

Conspiracy. The crime of conspiracy is defined as the 'agreement of two or more persons to do some *unlawful* act or to do some lawful act in an *unlawful* manner'. Everything said, written or done by any one of the conspirators in furtherance of their common purpose will be evidence against the other conspirators. Thus it is a conspiracy for '*A*' and '*B*' to agree to steal another's property, to injure another by blackmail or to corrupt public morals.

But, in addition to the **crime** of conspiracy, there is also the **tort** of conspiracy which is committed where there is a combination of two or more persons to effect an unlawful purpose resulting in damage to a plaintiff.

In the early days of their history, trade unions were looked upon as criminal conspiracies, and we recall the Tolpuddle martyrs. Since 1871 various Trade Unions Acts have legalised their activities. The *Trade Union and Labour Relations Act, 1974*, inaugurated a new era with regard to employer–employee relations. The act recognises the legality of trade unions and requires that all such bodies be registered. Industrial disputes will be resolved in the QBD and by tribunals set up under this very important Act. Today the legal control of trade unions is a sensitive political issue.

Picketing, which means setting or posting persons round a place, is a form of activity commonly used to draw public attention to a grievance and to persuade fellow-workers or the public to adopt a course of action in industrial disputes. Peaceful picketing is lawful, but where it is accompanied by violence or intimidation, the law gives protection to the person whose freedom of action is violated. There are many provisions to ensure that no undue pressure is placed upon a worker (e.g. under the *Employment Act, 1980* pickets are limited to six at any one works' entrance), and a criminal prosecution may follow if the law is broken. The police are usually present at strikes to ensure the rule of law prevails and that public peace is preserved.

Assembly

The law recognises no **legal** right of public meeting. But this does not mean of course, that public meetings are never held. They occur everywhere—in the smallest parish or hamlet, at the Royal Albert Hall, Trafalgar Square or Central Hall, London or at the Pier Head, Liverpool, where hundreds of people may foregather at one time. As with other forms of freedom, a public meeting may be held in any place and at any time so long as it does not offend the law.

For example, there is no right of public meeting on a highway. Any interference with the right of passengers to pass and re-pass on the highway is an obstruction. That is an offence against the criminal law and those holding such a meeting may be prosecuted: (*R.* v. *Cunninghame, Graham and Burns* (1888).) The holding of a meeting on occasions in a place of public resort (e.g. a public park) without protest does not confer a right to do so in the future. In other words one cannot acquire a *legal* right to hold meetings by *long usage* or **prescription** under the *Prescription Act, 1832*.

Where a meeting is held on *private* premises, the law as to trespass and nuisance applies, as well as the general law affecting property.

The law as to public meetings has until recently (see p. 266) been dealt with under headings:

(i) Unlawful assembly.
(ii) Rout.
(iii) Riot.

Unlawful Assembly. An assembly of persons is unlawful when it is composed of three or more persons who have met together to carry into effect some illegal purpose or who have met in such numbers or under such circumstances at to endanger the public peace or cause alarm and apprehension to Her Majesty's subjects.

A lawful assembly is not rendered unlawful merely because those taking part are aware that *other* persons, hostile to the assembly, will probably cause a breach of the peace. The following case illustrates the point:

Beatty v. *Gilbanks* (1882). The Salvation Army assembled at Weston-super-Mare and marched through the town. Opponents (called the Skeleton Army) interfered with them violently on several occasions. The police, to maintain the peace, reported the Salvationists for unlawful assembly. The Justices thereupon bound the Salvationists over to keep the peace and took sureties from them. The Salvationists appealed by 'case stated' to the QBD on the ground that as they had not committed any offence they could not lawfully be 'bound over' to keep the peace. *Held*: the disturbances were caused by the opponents. The Salvationists had not committed acts of violence and therefore could not be convicted of unlawful assembly or be bound over to keep the peace.

If a meeting is constituted in such numbers or under such circumstances so as to endanger the public peace it is an offence. If, therefore, a constable (or indeed any other person) of reasonable firmness and courage fears a breach of the peace, the meeting *prima facie* becomes unlawful and is an unlawful assembly.

Wise v. *Dunning* (1902). A protestant crusader held meetings in a public place in Liverpool and, when addressing the assembly used words and gestures highly insulting to Roman Catholics of whom a number were present. *Held*: the meeting was unlawful and the speaker could be bound over to keep the peace.

All persons who join an unlawful assembly and all who give support to it are liable to prosecution. If the circumstances are likely to endanger the public peace it is immaterial that the purpose of the meeting is lawful.

It is the duty of the police to disperse an unlawful assembly and to prosecute those responsible for holding the meeting and those who offer resistance by obstruction of the police.

Duncan v. *Jones* (1936). Mrs D. held a meeting near the entrance to a training centre for unemployed. No obstruction of the highway was alleged, the purpose of the meeting was lawful and its conduct orderly and peaceable. Mrs D. was ordered by a police officer to stop the meeting, but she continued it. She was arrested and convicted of obstructing the police in the execution of their duty. The police stated that disturbances had occurred at a previous meeting held by Mrs D. at the same place, and the police feared a breach of the peace if a further meeting were held. *Held*: The police had a duty to stop the meeting.

A public meeting may be held on private premises. The question of police power to enter such premises was dealt with in the following case:

Thomas v. *Sawkins* (1935). A meeting was held in a Welsh town to protest against a Parliamentary Bill and to demand the dismissal of the Chief Constable of Glamorgan. Admission to the meeting was open to the public free of charge. Police attended and were requested to leave. Proceedings were taken before the magistrates' court where it was found that the police had reasonable grounds for believing that seditious speeches would be made and that incitement to violence and breaches of the peace would occur. Appeal was made (by case stated) to QBD. *Held*: Police had power to enter and remain on the private premises when they had reasonable grounds for believing that the commission of an offence was imminent even though not accompanied by a breach of the peace.

The effect of this case is therefore that police may **enter private premises** when they have reasonable suspicion that seditious speeches will be made or a breach of the peace may occur. The police have no right to enter private premises (e.g. a garage) in connection with a summary offence (e.g. parking a car on a highway) not involving a breach of the peace (*Davis* v. *Lisle* (1936)). Where a police officer enters on private premises, e.g. to make an enquiry, and is then requested to leave by the occupier, the police officer should leave. He becomes a trespasser if he remains (*Bailey* v. *Wilson* (1968)).

Under the *Public Order Act, 1986*, the common law offence of unlawful assembly has been abolished. So too have the old offences of riot, rout and affray. These have been replaced with the following offences:

Violent disorder. This is where 3 or more persons who are present together use or threaten unlawful violence and the conduct of them (taken together) is such as would cause a person of reasonable firmness present at the scene to fear for his personal safety.

Affray. This is where one or more persons uses or threatens unlawful violence towards another, and the conduct is such as would cause a person of reasonable firmness present to fear for his personal safety.

Riot. This is where 12 or more persons who are present together use or threaten unlawful violence for a common purpose and the conduct of them (taken together) is such as would cause a person of reasonable firmness present at the scene to fear for his personal safety.

Under the *Riot (Damages) Act, 1886*, as amended by the *Police Act, 1964*, where a house, shop or building, in any police district, or the property therein, has been injured, destroyed or stolen owing to a riot, compensation to the person(s) aggrieved is to be paid out of the police fund.

Munday v. *Metropolitan Police District Receiver* (1949). A large crowd invaded the plaintiff's premises in order to see a football match on an adjoining ground after the gates to the ground were closed. Plaintiff's daughter and gardener were assaulted during the invasion, and damage was done to plaintiff's premises. *Held*: Plaintiff could recover from the police rate for damage done by the crowd.

The *Riot Act, 1714*, which empowered a magistrate (or sheriff, or a mayor) to read the Riot Act, calling upon a riotous assembly to disperse and peaceably to 'depart to their habitations or to their lawful business' has now been repealed. The police are the responsible authority to suppress a riot, and may use force if need be. Moreover, a police officer is empowered to call upon all other subjects of the Queen to assist him, and it is the duty of every citizen (whether called upon or not) to assist in suppressing a riot. If a person refuses to assist a constable in the execution of his duty when called upon to do so, and such person is capable of doing so and has no lawful excuse, he commits an offence.

Disturbances at Public Meetings

The *Public Meetings Act, 1908*, as amended by the *Public Order Act, 1936 and 1986*, makes it an offence, punishable summarily (i.e. before a magistrates' court) or on indictment (i.e. before a Crown Court) for any person at a lawful public meeting to act in a disorderly manner for the purpose of preventing the transaction of the business for which the meeting was called.

The *Representation of the People Act, 1949*, makes it an offence to incite disorder at a Parliamentary or a local government election meeting.

The Public Order Act, 1936 and 1986 are the main Act under which most prosecutions are taken today. The Act of 1936 contains important powers in regard to political uniforms, quasi-military organisations and processions. Thus the following acts are prohibited:

(i) *Wearing Uniforms*. The wearing in a public place of a uniform signifying association with a political organisation or with the promotion of any political object. (1936 Act, s. 1.)

(ii) *Quasi-Military Organisations*. Taking part in the control or management, organising, or training of any association (*a*) for the purpose of enabling the members to be employed in usurping the functions of the police or Armed Forces of the Crown; or (*b*) organised to use or display force in promoting any political object. (1936 Act, s. 2)

(iii) *Offensive Weapons*. It is an offence for any person while present at any public meeting or procession to be in possession of any offensive weapon, otherwise than by lawful authority (e.g. rifle club, cadet corps, and similar bodies). (1936 Act, s. 4.)

Processions and assemblies. Under the *Public Order Act, 1986*, the police must be informed in advance of public processions. And where they reasonably believe that the procession or any public assembly (*a*) may result in serious public disorder, serious damage to property or serious disruption to the life of the community, or (*b*) that the purpose of the gathering is the intimidation of others they may impose conditions as to location, duration, maximum number of participants (e.g. pickets), or route. Processions may even be *disallowed* where it is felt that the imposition of conditions may not be sufficient to prevent serious public disorder.

These restrictions are not entirely new. But they do represent an extension of powers. Although the changes were mooted as long ago as 1979, and again in the Scarman Report, 1981 (see p. 277), they were given a new urgency by the violent events which occurred in the miners' strike 1984–5 and at the picketing of the News International premises at Wapping in 1986 and 1987 and marches by the National Front in the 1970s.

We have already mentioned the frequently used provision under s. 5 which makes it an offence for any person in a **public place** or **meeting** to use threatening, abusive or insulting words or behaviour with intent to provoke a breach of the peace, or whereby a breach of the peace is likely to be occasioned.

The general effect of all these provisions in practical terms is that although there is no constitutional right to hold meetings or take part in processions, meetings do, of course, take place both on private premises and in public places. Moreover, everyone is aware that processions are today part of the common scene. The law does not generally prevent meetings or processions, but it does ensure that both are held peaceably and in good order. So one sees a police officer accompanying a group to Westminster to petition MPs. The procession is orderly, the peace is kept and the petition reaches its destination, i.e. Parliament. That is the civilised form of protest. Where the forces of law and order break down, the foundations of democracy crumble.

Freedom of Religion

Many times in the course of history, Kings, rulers, and dictators have tried to impose particular religious beliefs on their subjects. Rulers have repeatedly gone to the extremes of war against infidels (e.g. The Crusades) and neighbouring states with the avowed object of converting others to their particular beliefs. In medieval times the Church, through its bishops and clergy, maintained a strict discipline over the religious beliefs of the people, and punished members of the flock for heresy or unorthodox beliefs.

For centuries there was no freedom of religion in Britain. The main division was between the Roman Catholics and the Protestants. Henry VIII (1509–47) broke from Rome and declared himself to be Head of the Church of England. Those who were Royalists adhered to the newly established Church. The *Test Act, 1673*, was passed which prevented Catholic and Protestant-Non-Conformists from holding State or municipal office. Life for the Catholics and Protestant dissenters, who did not support the Established Church, was very difficult. Eventually, in 1828, the *Test Act* and the *Corporation Act* (which also prevented those not of the Established Church from election to the municipal authorities) were repealed, and in 1829 the *Catholic Emancipation Act* removed the disabilities imposed on Roman Catholic believers. The only real survival today is the prohibition excluding a Roman Catholic from accession to the Throne of the Kingdom. (*Act of Settlement, 1701*.)

The Queen is Head of the English Church, and the Archbishops and certain bishops have seats in the House of Lords. There has, however, been a decline in Christian belief and in Church membership in modern times.

The position today, therefore, is that any person may practise any religion he pleases providing that in so doing he does not infringe the general law of the land. Blasphemy, which is the offence of vilifying the Christian religion or bringing its beliefs into contempt, is still a common law offence, though in practice few prosecutions are brought mainly because of the tolerance and restraint observed by most members of society.

In the United States *Bill of Rights* we note in Article I:

Congress shall make no law respecting an establishment of religion, or prohibiting the free exercise thereof; of abridging speech, or of the Press or the right of the people to assemble, and to petition the Government for a redress of grievances.

There is under the British Constitution no guarantee of freedom of religion since we have no written constitution. Here we may say there is freedom of religion—within the law. Though nominally Christian, the country contains adherents of practically every world religion who are free to practise their particular beliefs in a tolerant and free society.

Detention by the Police

We have seen (p. 257) how the law applies to arrest. The Rule of Law applies to the police just as it does to other officials purporting to exercise legal powers. A constable who trespasses on the lands or goods of another or arrests another person must, if sued, be prepared to justify his action in a Court of Law.

Mr Justice Devlin (now Lord Devlin) stated:

You sometimes read in novels and detective stories, perhaps written by people not familiar with police procedure, that persons are sometimes taken into custody for questioning. There is no such power in this country. A man cannot be detained unless he is arrested.

This does not mean that the police cannot arrest on suspicion—but that they have no power to detain a person *merely* for questioning. If, for example, PC X has reasonable grounds for suspecting that Y has committed or is about to commit an arrestable offence he may arrest Y. If PC X later discovers that Y is innocent Y must be released forthwith. If Y thereupon decides to sue PC X he may do so (he may also sue the Chief Constable of the force—see p. 278). If the case proceeds to trial it will be for the judge (not the jury) to say whether PC X had reasonable suspicion that Y had committed the offence mentioned. *McArdle* v. *Egan* (1933).

Much depends on the words 'reasonable suspicion'. Clearly, if A is discovered at midnight emerging furtively through the front window of a house, he should not be surprised if he is arrested by a constable who sees him. There is reasonable suspicion. It is one of the risks which everyone is exposed to. The only true safeguard lies in trusting that the police will be adequately trained to know their wide powers and to use them with discretion and tact. This they do, and the public considers the police to be efficient and fair and carry out their duties honestly. The relations between the police and the public are generally good. Where, however, a police officer oversteps the bounds of his authority and makes a wrongful arrest (there being no 'reasonable suspicion') or where he has no statutory authority so to do a civil action in tort may be brought against him and his chief officer for assault, battery (if he is manhandled) and false imprisonment. (*Police Act, 1964*.) Complaints against the police are referred to on p. 311.

Apart from increasing the definition of 'arrestable offence' and extending the powers of the police to investigate such offences, the *Police and Criminal Evidence Act, 1984*, introduced a new general power of arrest for minor offences viz. where it would be inappropriate to serve a summons because of doubts over the offender's proffered name or address, or where it was believed to be necessary in order to prevent injury, damage to property, obstruction of the highway or offence against public decency.

Police Interrogation and the Code of Practice ('Judges' Rules')

The primary duty of the police is the prevention and detection of crime. The police are also responsible for the maintenance of peace and good order within our society. One of the main tasks of any Home Secretary is to ensure that the police are efficient in the discharge of their important duties which increase in range and scope year by year.

When a crime is reported to the police, an inquiry is made (*a*) to ascertain the facts, and (*b*) to detect the author of the crime from the available evidence. Once the preliminary inquiries are completed, a police officer will have to decide whether he has sufficient evidence to justify proceedings against the suspect. If so, the police officer may interview the suspect and report him for summons, or he may arrest the suspect. In either case the suspect will be interviewed and a statement may be obtained in accordance with the rules mentioned below.

Sometimes the police will have insufficient evidence to justify arrest or summons, but the evidence may suggest that A could be the culprit. A may be interviewed by the police. If he satisfies the police that he is innocent he will hear no more about it. A may know (if he is guilty) that the police have insufficient evidence to charge him with the offence. He may lie to the police and may decline to make any statement to them.

The cardinal rule of English law is that a confession made to a person in authority such as a police officer will only be admitted in evidence at the trial when such confession has been made freely and voluntarily, i.e. without constraint, force, or as a result of inducement held out by the officer (*Ibrahim* v. *R.* (1914)). A valid confession is itself sufficient to enable a Court of Law to convict an accused person, without corroborative evidence (*R.* v. *White* (1823)).

Confessions obtained by threats of physical punishment, or promises of favour, e.g. 'If you tell me where the goods are I will be favourable to you' (*R.* v. *Cass* (*1784*)) have been held inadmissible. Similarly, in *Regina* v. *Richards* (1967) when a police officer was questioning a suspect (Richards) concerning a housebreaking the police officer said: 'I think it might be better if you made a statement', it was held that the officer's remark was clearly capable of constituting an inducement, and the statement was held inadmissible.

What are sometimes called 'third degree' methods are clearly wrong and unlawful. Any officer using threats or violence against a suspected person or a prisoner is liable (*a*) to disciplinary proceedings under the Police Discipline Regulations, and (*b*) to civil or criminal actions at the instance of the person injured. However, the use of such methods is often alleged.

The origin of the Judges' Rules (see below) is traceable to an approach made by the police themselves to the Lord Chief Justice in 1906, requesting guidance in the correct police procedure in the interrogation of suspects and the obtaining of statements of confessions of guilt. Certain rules were formulated in 1912 and these were approved by the judges of the King's Bench Division. Further rules were added in 1918 and in 1964. The present Judges' Rules (which, under the *Police and Criminal Evidence Act, 1984* have been re-stated and incorporated into the law as Codes of Practice) are as follows:

1. When a police officer is trying to discover whether, or by whom, an offence has been committed he is entitled to question any person, whether suspected or not, from whom he thinks that useful information may be obtained. This is so whether or not the person in question has been taken into custody so long as he has not been charged with the offence or informed that he may be prosecuted for it.

2. As soon as a police officer has evidence which would afford reasonable grounds for suspecting that a person has committed an offence, he shall caution that person or cause him to be cautioned before putting to him any questions, or further questions relating to that offence.

The caution shall be in the following terms: 'You are not obliged to say anything unless you wish to do so but what you say may be put into writing and given in evidence.'

When after being cautioned a person is being questioned, or elects to make a statement, a record shall be kept of the time and place at which any such questioning or statement began and ended and of the persons present.

3. Where a person is charged with or informed that he may be prosecuted for an offence he shall be cautioned in the following terms: 'Do you wish to say anything? You are not obliged to say anything unless you wish to do so but whatever you say will be taken down in writing and may be given in evidence.'

There are three additional rules. Thus, where two or more persons are charged with the same offence and statements are taken separately from the persons charged each person should be furnished with a copy of such statements. If the person charged desires to make a statement in reply the usual caution should be administered.

Any statement made in accordance with the above rules should, whenever possible, be taken down *in writing and signed by the person making it* after it has been read to him and he has been invited to make any corrections he may wish.

A record should be kept by the police officer of the times at which the taking of the statement started and finished, and of any intervals and refreshments. It is for the judge at the court of trial to say whether a statement obtained by the police shall be admitted in evidence.

The (1984) Code of Practice (on Detention Treatment and Questioning) introduced the right of access to a legal adviser, whereby detainees must now be told of their right to consult a solicitor at any time, including before making a statement—though the police may, on narrowly prescribed grounds, refuse the request for up to 36 hours (48 in terrorism cases). Interrogation may now be tape recorded too. The *Police and Criminal Evidence Act, 1984*, allows a general right of search of arrested persons on grounds that they might have evidence relating to the offence, may have anything which might aid their escape or may present danger to themselves or others. Again, as with arrest, the officer must have reasonable grounds for the search. Only removal of outer clothing can normally be required, except for intimate searches (which require higher authorisation and normally a medical practitioner's participation).

The Code requires that a careful Custody Record is kept to register the events of the suspect's detention, including reasons for detention, any delay in the right to have someone informed or of access to legal advice; a list of all personal belongings at the time of detention; and the extent of any searches etc.

In general, the purpose of the Code is to balance the extension of police powers elsewhere under the *Police and Criminal Evidence Act 1984* (see pp. 257, 270), and a breach is grounds for complaint and may lead to disciplinary proceedings against the offending officer.

The Police Service

The first duty of any government is to maintain peace and promote good order within the State. The preservation of the peace is supremely important to ourselves as citizens, to Parliament and, indeed, all branches of the Executive. We cannot go about our work or perform our functions as citizens unless we have a reasonable assurance that we shall not be molested in what we do, and that our property will be reasonably secure.

The agents appointed to ensure the peace is preserved and that crimes are prevented and detected are the police. The advent of the Welfare State has not, alas, resulted in a reduction in crime. On the contrary, crime has increased since the Second World War. This has meant increasing burdens on the forces of law and order, in particular the police.

Organisation

The police service of Great Britain is organised in a number of large forces (i) linked with local government, and (ii) subject to the influence and final control of the Home Secretary in England and Wales. In Scotland the final responsible authority is the Secretary of State for Scotland. In Northern Ireland there is one police force only (the Royal Ulster Constabulary) the final responsibility resting in normal times (before 1972) with the Minister of Home Affairs at Stormont.

The number of regular police forces is (1987) fifty-two, comprising forty-three in England and Wales, eight in Scotland and one in Ulster (the RUC).

In England and Wales the forces are defined according to the area of responsibility: following the reorganisation of local government the areas correspond to counties or (in Scotland) regions.

Combined forces are forces whose area of responsibility extends over two or more counties or country boroughs. In addition to the above there is the Metropolitan Police Force which is responsible for an area within a radius of approximately fifteen miles from Charing Cross. Within this area (separate from the Metropolitan Police Force) is the City of London Force which operates within the one square mile of the City of London.

The strength of the regular police force in the United Kingdom is over 130,000, of which nearly 10,000 are women. The size of each force depends on the population and size of the police area. The Metropolitan Police Force has a strength of 22,600 and outside this force most establishments range within 1,000 to 2,500.

Note that the police service is not a 'national' service directly controlled by and responsible to a Secretary of State. Each force is headed by a Chief Constable who is appointed by and dismissible by a police authority (see next paragraph). This arrangement disperses police power amongst a number of local bodies (Police Authorities or Committees) who supervise the administration of each separate police force.

Police Authorities

Each police force is maintained by a police authority. In the counties of England and Wales the authority is the Police Committee. Committees of the local council consist of (*a*) councillors, and (*b*) magistrates, in the proportion of two to one. Combined police authorities (which arise as the result of the amalgamation of small forces into large police forces) consist of councillors and magistrates from each constituent area covered by the amalgamation scheme. In Scotland the police authority is the regional council. Here too we find combined police authorities in the same way as in England and Wales.

The police authority for the London Metropolitan Police Force is the **Home Secretary**. (In the City of London the Court of Common Council is the police authority.)

Duties of the Police Authority

The duties of the police authority are:

(*a*) To maintain an adequate and efficient force for the area.

(*b*) To appoint the Chief Constable, and any deputy or assistant chief constable (in each case subject to the approval of the Home Secretary).

(*c*) To determine the establishment of the force.

(*d*) To provide premises and equipment.

(*e*) To require the officers referred to at (*b*) to retire in the interests of efficiency (again subject to the approval of the Home Secretary).

(*f*) To appoint a member of the police authority to answer questions on the discharge of the functions of the police authority put to him by the county or county borough councils.

(*g*) Reports. The chief constable is required to submit an annual report in writing. The police authority can require a Chief Constable to submit a report on policing of the area. The Chief Constable may, if the matter required by the police authority to be reported on is against the public interest, refuse until permission is granted by the Secretary of State.

The duties of the Chief Constable are to see that the force under his control is used efficiently. The Home Secretary is responsible for ensuring that the police authority and the Chief Constable are enabled to exercise their powers and do so. This redefinition of function of the police authority means that the Home Secretary is answerable in Parliament for the efficient policing of the country as a whole rather than for the defaults of a particular force. In the first half of the nineteenth century when police forces were originally founded, their control was deliberately vested in the local authorities so as to ensure that there would be no authoritarian use of police forces by the central Government which could, were a Government so minded, be dangerous. There is a tendency now against the diffusion of power to the smaller authorities; the forces are becoming larger (as combined forces) and there is a lobby for the whole of the police forces to be 'nationalised' or regionalised on the grounds of efficiency, e.g. in the CID, where some benefits might accrue. On the other hand, there is the view that powerful forces of law and order need to be democratically controlled in the interests of civil liberty. Police authorities often complain that they lack the powers to make their Chief Constable truly accountable, and the Greater London Council decries its lack of a proper Police Committee (as the Metropolitan Police are run from the Home Office). Chief Constables are jealous of their operational independence, and fear the intrusion of party politics into police matters (as might occur in Ulster, for instance, because of the Catholic suspicions of the Royal Ulster Constabulary).

Central Control of Police Forces

Co-ordination in the administration of the police forces is ensured through powers granted by Parliament to (i) the Home Secretary in respect of England and Wales, and (ii) the Secretary of State for Scotland in respect of the Scottish forces. Each Minister has power under the *Police Act, 1964*, to:

(*a*) Make regulations as to the government, administration and conditions of service throughout the police service.

(*b*) Approve voluntary or initiate compulsory schemes for the amalgamation of police forces.

(*c*) Recommend the appointment of inspectors to inspect and inquire into the efficiency of the police forces outside the Metropolitan Police Area.

(*d*) Withhold the whole or part of the police grant.

(*e*) Approve appointment of Chief Constables, Deputies and Assistants.

(*f*) Adjudicate on appeals in disciplinary matters.

(*g*) Require co-operation between forces (e.g. lend manpower).

(*h*) Order a local inquiry into a police matter.

(*i*) Obtain any report he wants from the Chief Constable.

(*j*) Retire a Chief Constable in the interests of efficiency.

The police *regulations* cover such matters as ranks; qualifications for appointment; promotion and retirement; discipline; hours of duty, leave, pay, and allowances, and uniform and equipment. Some of these (e.g. pay, allowances, and leave) are first negotiable with the **Police Council for Great Britain** which is the negotiating body for the police. It is constituted on **Whitley Council** lines with representatives from the Home Office, Scottish Office, local authorities, and all ranks of the police service. Other matters are discussed by the Home Secretary (or his representative) with representative advisory bodies. Thus before making regulations under certain sections of the *Police Act, 1964*, the Minister sends a draft to the Police Advisory Board.

The Home Secretary is advised on all matters concerning police efficiency by Her Majesty's Chief Inspector of Constabulary and nine Inspectors of Constabulary. Two of the latter are concerned with crime and traffic respectively; one is concerned with Police Planning Organisation and six are individually responsible for the inspection of a number of forces. They also deal with individual forces and their Chief Constables when particular problems arise. The inspectors report annually to the Home Secretary on the state of efficiency of all forces except the Metropolitan Police Force. Similar administrative arrangements are made for the inspection of Scottish forces, reports being made to the Secretary of State for Scotland.

All police authorities receive a grant of one-half of their net expenditure. (The Common Council for the City of London Force receives one-third.) Both the Home Secretary and the Secretary of State are empowered to withhold the grant, in whole or in part, permanently or for such time as they may determine, if they are not satisfied that a police area is efficiently policed, that a police force is not maintained and administered, or that the rates of pay or allowances are as prescribed or approved by them.

Police Officers

Entry to the regular police force is open to both men and women. The usual recruitment ages are between 19 and 30 years (men) and 19 and 35 (women), subject to extension in special circumstances. The examination for entry is of modest standard, but in recent years there has been a drive to recruit graduates, and there are now over several hundred serving in the police forces in the United Kingdom. Moreover, certain candidates are selected to pursue courses at universities to read for degrees.

The ranks of the police forces are: Chief Constable, Superintendent, Inspector, Sergeant, and Constable. Most forces now have intermediate ranks (e.g. Chief Superintendent and Chief Inspector). In the Metropolitan Police the chief officer is known as the Commissioner of Police of the Metropolis who is assisted by a Deputy Commissioner and four Assistant Commissioners. Below these are Commanders responsible for a specific area of the Metropolis. The City of London has its own Commissioner of Police.

Police officers may not belong to a trade union. It is a basic principle of the police service that there shall be no political bias in the discharge of their duties. The various ranks have their representative organisations, the most important being the **Police Federation**. This body has a central committee which is able to negotiate with the Home Secretary and the police authorities. It has been the practice to engage as a consultant an MP to represent the police service point of view in Parliament. James Callaghan and Eldon Griffiths were formerly consultants and advisers to the Police Federation.

In addition to the main body of police there are Police Cadets. These are young persons aged between 16 and 18 who are given training in preparation for entry to the force on reaching the minimum age. There is also a considerable civilian staff performing much of the clerical work.

All police forces have Special Constables (about 15,000 in all) who assist the regular police. They act as auxiliaries and perform their duties part-time and without pay. They have similar powers, however, to the regular police.

Traffic wardens are also employed to deal with traffic duties and offences, and they may serve fixed penalty notices for minor traffic offences. The traffic wardens remain under the control of the Chief Constable of the force to which they are attached, whatever duties they perform.

Police Duties

The main duties are to: (*a*) preserve the peace (*b*) prevent crime, (*c*) protect life and property (*d*) maintain public order.

For these purposes the police have powers of arrest, as we have seen (pp. 257 and 270). They also have considerable powers (made wider by the *Police and Criminal Evidence Act, 1984*) to 'stop and search' for stolen or prohibited articles (e.g. skeleton car-keys which could be used to steal vehicles, or a steel comb which could be used as an offensive weapon). As with the power of arrest, the constable must have reasonable grounds for his or her suspicion, and must follow certain procedures (e.g. identify him or herself, state reason for search, undertake the search quickly and without force, except as a last resort, and make a written record of the incident as soon as practicable).

In addition, the police have general powers to enter and search premises for evidence and seize items, or to arrest, or save life or property usually with consent, or if necessary on a magistrate's warrant (see p. 256). Again the constable must have reasonable grounds for the intrusion—so-called 'fishing expeditions' are no longer permissible. The Code of Practice (see p. 270) provides further safeguards viz. the search must be at a reasonable hour, must have regard for property and privacy; permission must be given in writing; officers must identify themselves; only reasonable force may be used, where necessary.

But there are many other duties. For example, the police are the main service to organise emergency aid schemes in case of local disasters such as train crashes. They also attend road accidents, give first-aid to the injured, and have the duty to enforce many regulations governing road vehicles, licensed houses, and many other matters.

In 1981, the **Scarman Report** on the Brixton riot sought general improvements in urban social conditions and particular changes in police methods, including (i) more community policing and greater police-community consultation (now compulsory under the *Police and Criminal Evidence Act, 1984*), (ii) a more independent police complaints procedure (also introduced under the 1984 Act, see p. 311); (iii) better training for the police in handling public disorder situations (this constitutes part of the *Public Order Act, 1986*: see pp. 263, 266, 268).

Status

The office of constable has been in existence since the eleventh century. Between the eleventh and fourteenth centuries a constable was the executive agent and representative of the village or township, the local keeper of the peace, exercising his powers under the common law as 'a person paid to perform, as a matter of duty, acts which if he were so minded he might have done voluntarily'. Thus he kept the peace, arrested felons (i.e. criminals suspected of murder, housebreaking, theft, or other crimes), and brought them to justice before the magistrates of his area. As with other services of medieval origin, the industrial revolution and the changes in society generally imposed too heavy a burden on the old system, and a reorganisation took place in the early nineteenth century, inaugurated by Sir Robert Peel. It was Peel who in 1829 introduced the modern police in London at first as an experiment. This was successful and eventually civilian police forces were established in all areas during the middle of the nineteenth century.

In modern times their duties have become increasingly complex and responsible, demanding physical fitness, courage, discretion, and tact, as well as initiative of a high order.

The exact legal and constitutional status of a police officer is unique, and one must look to both the common law and numerous statutes to ascertain his powers. A constable is not a Crown servant, and the Crown is not liable for his acts or omissions during his employment. The *Crown Proceedings Act, 1947*, does not apply to a police officer. Nevertheless a constable is a person who 'holds office under Her Majesty' for the purpose of the *Official Secrets Acts, 1911–1939*, and may be prosecuted if he commits any offence under these statutes. On joining the police, a constable makes a solemn attestation, declaring that he will 'well and truly serve Our Sovereign Lady the Queen in the office of constable, without favour or affection, malice or ill will', and that he will to the best of his power cause the peace to be kept and preserved and prevent all offences against the persons and properties of Her Majesty's subjects. (*Police Act, 1964*, s. 18.)

A constable is not a 'local government servant'. In *Fisher* v. *Oldham Corporation* (*1930*) it was held that a police constable is not the servant of the borough. He is a servant of the State, a ministerial officer of the central power, though subject, in some respects, to local supervision and local regulation. In another case, *Att.-General for New South Wales* v. *Perpetual Trustee Co.* (1955) Viscount Simond said:

His authority is original, not delegated, and is exercised at his own discretion by virtue of his office: he is a ministerial officer exercising statutory rights independently of contract. . . . His relationship to the Government is not in common parlance described as that of servant and master.

Under the *Police Act, 1964*, a chief officer of police has vicarious liability for any wrongful act a constable may commit in the performance of his functions as a constable. A constable is himself also liable and may be sued in respect of his wrongful act. This creates by statute the same sort of relationship as applies in the general law of master and servant. A constable has a certain independence in enforcing the law. Thus he, and he alone, must make up his mind whether to arrest for a suspected offence. Although a constable must obey the **lawful** orders of a Chief Constable and is liable for disciplinary proceedings if he does not, a constable is not bound even if ordered by a Chief Constable to make an arrest which is manifestly illegal. (*Keighley* v. *Bell* (1866)). (For complaints against the police see p. 311.)

The main departments in all police forces are: (i) Uniform department; (ii) CID; (iii) Road Traffic Department. Specialised departments include the River Police (e.g. in London for the River Thames), the Mounted Branch, the Training Branch, and certain others with particular functions such as the use of police dogs and special patrol groups.

The work of **Special Branch** (with some 1,200 officers) is concerned with threats of terrorism, subversion, espionage and public order. As with the work of MI5 (see p. 283) this is a controversial area of police work since it may represent a threat to civil liberties. Thus, in 1985, a report on Special Branch by the Parliamentary Select Committee on Home Affairs revealed some concern about possible harassment and interference (e.g.) through telephone tapping: see p. 283) in the lawful activities of pressure and protest groups (trade unions, peace groups, etc.). The activities of Special Branch were well illustrated in their searches of the offices of the BBC in Scotland and of the *New Statesman* journal, following the latter's revelations about a secret intelligence-gathering satellite (code-named 'Zircon') in January 1987. (This affair also raised questions about the breadth of the terms of the search warrants: see p. 256.)

The use of scientific aids in the prevention and detection of crime has grown increasingly in recent years: £12 million is spent annually on police equipment, including £2 million on radio-communications. A national computer is used for the keeping of records and dissemination of information (see p. 313).

The Home Office has introduced a **Police Planning Organisation**, staffed by senior police officers, scientists, and accountancy and management experts. Its duty is to study police methods and the development of new equipment and new techniques throughout Great Britain, so that the police service generally will be able to match the increasing demands made upon them by the increase in crime and by the use of more sophisticated methods on the part of the criminals.

New Scotland Yard, the Headquarters of the Metropolitan Police, performs special duties on behalf of all police forces, such as the publication of the *Police Gazette* (for wanted criminals, etc.), the investigation of company frauds (by the Fraud Squad), the execution of extradition orders made by the courts, and it also maintains relations with the **International Criminal Police Commission** (Interpol) on behalf of all forces in Great Britain.

Nationality and Domicile

By a person's nationality we mean his status as a citizen or member of a particular state to which he owes allegiance. Everyone is the subject of some state to which he owes political allegiance and loyalty, for which he may be called upon to fight, pay taxes, and from which he may expect protection. These are broad general statements only. For instance, although we say that all persons must be national subjects of some state or other, we know that due to upheavals of war there are some unfortunate 'stateless' persons who have been disowned by, or expelled from, their country of birth and origin.

Nationality is of great importance in the field of public law. Thus, British subjects enjoy universal franchise, i.e. the right to vote in elections. Aliens in Great Britain have no such right. Some aliens disapprove of all that is fundamental to the British way of life, and it would be highly irregular for them to be accorded the rights which have been won by hard struggles in the past to create this way of life. Aliens, therefore, are subject to certain restrictions concerning entry into the United Kingdom and employment after entry; furthermore they must register certain particulars with the police.

Apart from these requirements, English law treats aliens in much the same way as ordinary British subjects: for example, they are subject to the same rules of criminal law and the same laws of tort and contract. Some special disabilities or restrictions apply. Thus an alien may not own or part-own a British ship registered at a British port and sailing under the British flag.

The following pages deal with the acquisition of British nationality and the allied question of domicile, which is becoming increasingly important as travel makes it easier for people to move from one country to another.

British Nationality

The *British Nationality Act, 1948*, as amended, divided 'British subjects' into two classes:

(*a*) Citizens of the independent nations of the British Commonwealth. Into this class fall citizens of Canada, Australia, New Zealand, India, Pakistan, Sri Lanka, Ghana, Nigeria and the other twenty independent Commonwealth countries. These persons were known as 'Commonwealth citizens'.

(*b*) Citizens of the United Kingdom and Colonies. This type of citizenship could be acquired by way of birth or descent, naturalisation, registration, marriage or by incorporation of territory.

However, the *British Nationality Act, 1981*, introduced a number of fundamental changes in the law of citizenship (as from 1983). Consequently, there are now *three* types of citizenship:

(*a*) *British Citizenship* i.e. those who are citizens of the UK and Colonies who have the right of abode in the UK.

(*b*) *Citizenship of the British Dependent Territories* i.e. those citizens of the UK and Colonies by birth, naturalisation or registration in a Dependent Territory (these include Hong Kong, Gibraltar, the Falkland Islands, St Christopher and Nevis and St Helena).

(*c*) British Overseas Citizenship i.e. those UK and Colonies Citizens who, on 1 January 1983, did not fall into (*a*) or (*b*) above.

Each status brings with it a different set of rights and entitlements, especially concerning entry to the UK.

Acquisition of British Citizenship

British citizenship is acquired automatically by those born in the UK who have a parent who is a British citizen or a parent who is settled in the UK. (Certain other categories of children born in the UK may qualify too e.g. foundlings or adoptees.)

A person born outside the UK may acquire British Citizenship as follows:

(*a*) If one of his or her parents is a British Citizen otherwise than by descent (e.g. the parent was born in UK).

(*b*) If one of his or her parents is a British Citizen serving the Crown overseas.

(*c*) If the Minister consents to his or her registration while he or she is a minor.

(*d*) If, as a Citizen under (*b*) or (*c*) above, or as a British Protected Person (see below), he or she has been lawfully resident in UK for 5 years.

(*e*) If he or she is naturalised. This applies only to adults, and the conditions of approval (which is at the discretion of the Home Secretary) include five years' residence, good character and a sufficient knowledge of the English language. (The requirements are somewhat less for an applicant who is married to a British Citizen.)

Note: Legislation provides for many citizens of the Republic of Ireland (Eire) to claim British citizenship.

Loss of Nationality

British citizenship may be lost by:

(i) *Renunciation.* This is effected by a person making a declaration of renunciation, which must be registered with the Home Secretary.

(ii) *Deprivation.* This applies *only* to citizens who acquired citizenship by naturalisation or by registration, and may be ordered by the Home Secretary for serious misconduct, e.g. criminal acts.

Where a female citizen of the United Kingdom and Colonies marries an alien under whose national law she acquires her husband's nationality, she does not automatically lose her citizenship of the United Kingdom and Colonies. In all such cases her British citizenship is retained unless she expressly renounces it.

British Protected Persons

So far we have been dealing with British subjects and aliens. A third group of persons, known as British Protected Persons, must be mentioned. These are members of those territories described as Protectorates, Protected States or Mandated or Trust Territories and declared as such by an Order in Council.

Aliens

All persons other than British subjects and British Protected Persons are aliens. The following general restrictions apply to an alien:

(i) He may not vote at local or Parliamentary elections.

(ii) He may not become a Member of Parliament.

(iii) He may not work in the United Kingdom unless specially permitted.

(iv) He must register with the police and notify changes of address.

(v) He is liable to deportation if he engages in crime.

Domicile

Most persons make their homes permanently within the state of which they are subjects. Danes live in Denmark, Dutchmen in the Netherlands, and so on, each national being subject to his own country's laws. Some members, however, uproot themselves and make their permanent homes outside their own country. For example, an Italian may decide to live permanently in England, a Frenchman may decide to live permanently in Italy. In such cases, under English law, the Italian and the Frenchman are held to have acquired domiciles in the countries where they intend permanently to reside.

The concept of domicile, under English law, involves two elements: (i) actual residence; and (ii) *animus manendi*, i.e. the intention to remain in that place or country. Where these two elements co-exist a person is said to have a domicile in that country.

Whereas nationality implies a political relation existing between a person and the state to which he owes allegiance, domicile determines important civil rights and obligations which will be discussed later. First we must note that under English law it is an inflexible rule that (i) every person must possess a domicile, and (ii) no person can have more than one domicile.

There are three classes of domicile:

(*a*) *Domicile of Origin*. This domicile attaches at birth. A legitimate child takes the domicile of the father; an illegitimate child that of its mother. A foundling (deserted infant without known parents) acquires the domicile of the place where found. A domicile of origin cannot be entirely lost or extinguished. If a person with a 'domicile of choice' (see later) abandons his present domicile, the domicile of origin revives and attaches to him until he acquires a new domicile.

(*b*) *Domicile of Choice*. Where a person sixteen or over establishes his home permanently in a country with the intention of remaining there permanently (such country being different from his last domicile), he is regarded as acquiring a domicile of choice.

(*c*) *Domicile of Dependent Persons*. (i) A minor takes the domicile of his parent as at (*a*) above. Where the spouses are separated and the child makes his home with his mother he may take his mother's domicile. (*ii*) Since 1974 a married woman is capable of acquiring a domicile independent of her husband. The *Domicile and Matrimonial Proceedings Act, 1973*, states that a person is capable of acquiring an independent domicile when he reaches sixteen.

The above represent the main rules regarding the concept of domicile in English law. This law of domicile is important in regard to:

(*a*) *Jurisdiction in Divorce*. For example, Atkins, a British subject domiciled in Nevada, USA, is granted a divorce by the Divorce Court of Nevada on the grounds of 'incompatibility of temperament'. The divorce is recognised in English law even though the grounds are much less than those required to sustain a divorce in England.

(*b*) *Validity of Wills of Movable Property and the distribution of such property on an intestacy*. For example, Brown, a British subject domiciled in Ruritania, makes a will attested by one witness. English law requires two witnesses to a will, whereas the law of Ruritania requires one witness only. Brown's will is regarded as valid in English law because it complies with the law of the domicile.

(*c*) *Legitimation*. The law which gives legal status to children born before marriage of their parents.

(*d*) *The Essential Validity of Marriage*. The 'essential validity' includes the form of celebration, age of parties, etc. It is possible for an English court to decide that a marriage contracted without the form required in England is valid because it complies with the law of the domicile.

English law takes the view that a person who establishes a domicile in a country attracts to himself the rights, duties, and obligations of that country; he therefore assumes the law of the domicile.

Proof of Domicile. Although long residence in a country affords strong proof that a person has acquired a domicile in that country, we must note that residence and domicile are not the same thing. The English court decides the question of domicile by applying English law, taking account of the *intention* of the party. Evidence of intention may include correspondence, oral or written declarations, the purchase of a house, or even a grave. Inquiry by the English court may range over the whole of a person's life to enable the court to establish where a domicile has been acquired.

State Security

Every state needs to protect itself from those, at home and abroad, who would wish to see it harmed, undermined or transformed politically (e.g. by foreign takeover). For such purposes we have established military and police forces, and law courts.

But operating much more under cover we have the **Security Services**. These were established formally in 1909 (as Military Intelligence). They comprise MI5, (the Security Intelligence Service, or 'molehunters') responsible for counter-espionage in the UK and Commonwealth, and MI6 (the Secret Intelligence Service) which is responsible for intelligence gathering outside Britain. Each is headed by a Director General who is responsible for day-to-day operations and accountable to the Home Secretary (MI5) or the Foreign Secretary (MI6).

With any sort of policing, there is always the risk of abuse of authority or that innocent people will be harmed or harrassed. There is the problem of balance: how much public accountability and control is compatible with the necessary secrecy of operations. It is an ancient problem: *Quis Custodiet Ipsos Custodes?*

There have been a number of recent allegations of illegal and politically biased activities by the Security Services, e.g. by Kathy Massiter in 1985 and, more startlingly, by a retired senior MI5 officer, Peter Wright, in 1986 in his book *Spycatcher*. The latter not only alleged infiltration into MI5 by Soviet sympathisers—including perhaps a former head of MI5— but also that MI5 had, among other things, planned to destroy the 1974 Labour government by undermining its chances in the October election (e.g. by illegally 'bugging' the Prime Minister's telephone, and by fabricating bank account documents in order to discredit the then deputy leader of the party and according to one of the Intelligence Officers responsible, Colin Wallace, by a whole 'tide of smears, leaks and fabrications' otherwise known as black propaganda and disinformation schemers).

In a Parliamentary debate in December 1986, a number of MPs called for a special commission (comprising peers and MPs) to supervise the work of the Security Services. The Home Secretary (Douglas Hurd) rejected this and claimed that a review of the Service, following the Bettaney case (see p. 169) had already resulted in reformed and better management and improved vetting of personnel.

Many people remain sceptical and dissatisfied, particularly with regard to **telephone tapping.** The eavesdropping on private telephone calls and the opening of mail by the Security Services, the police and by customs officials may take place legally, on the authority of a warrant issued by the Home Secretary or other designated Minister, with the aim of detecting or forestalling crime, sedition or terrorism. Thus, for example, in 1979 467 (excluding Ulster) such warrants were issued (compared with 150 in 1958), though it is alleged that in practice many thousands of 'taps' occur unofficially. MPs have expressed disquiet and sought statutory controls. In response, the Home Secretary in 1980 appointed a senior judge to act as an independent watchdog to monitor these surveillance procedures. Lord Diplock's Report (March 1981) declared satisfaction with the system. But MPs condemned the Report as inadequate and a 'whitewash'.

Consequently, the *Interception of Communications Act, 1985*, was passed to provide a statutory framework which now governs the interception of telephone and postal services. The legislation sets out the grounds on which the Secretary of State is empowered to give such authorisation.

These include:

(*a*) The prevention or detection of serious crime.
(*b*) Securing national security.
(*c*) Safeguarding the nation's economic wellbeing.

Interception outside of these areas is a criminal offence. A Commissioner (Lord Justice Lloyd) has been appointed to report on the working of the Act. His report for 1986 showed that some 317 warrants were in operation in December 1986 to allow telephone tapping and mail interception.

Ulster

Extra-special state powers exist in, and in relation to, Northern Ireland, under the *Northern Ireland (Emergency Provisions) Act, 1978* (first introduced in 1973). Under this law, the police and army have special powers to question and arrest people, and to search persons and premises; a person arrested as a suspected terrorist may be detained for up to 72 hours; those arrested for serious offences may be tried by a judge alone (i.e. without a jury, in a 'Diplock' court); and the Secretary of State had the power (up to July 1980) to detain suspected terrorists without trial (i.e. internment). Furthermore, under this Act, a number of organisations are proscribed, including the IRA and the UVF: thus it is an offence to belong to them or to make any financial contribution to them.

Applicable to the whole of the UK is the *Prevention of Terrorism (Temporary Provisions) Act, 1984* (first introduced in 1974). This Act allows the Minister to make exclusion orders to bar entry to, or remove from, mainland Britain and/or Ulster any persons connected with terrorist activities related to Northern Ireland affairs. He is also empowered to ban organisations which appear to be concerned with terrorism. The Act also gives the police the power to arrest and question suspects, and detain them for up to seven days without charge or appearance before a court.

Terrorism Acts

Clearly such significant powers give rise to concern and misgivings. They have been described as a drastic response to drastic events i.e. the sporadic terrorist bombings in mainland Britain and the more regular killings in Ulster itself (numbering some 100 a year). And the powers are used. Thus for example, in 1980–81, 49 people were denied entry to Britain, 515 were detained and 30 charged with offences under the Prevention of Terrorism Acts.

However, there are safeguards in that both Acts have to be reviewed regularly by Parliament, the former every 6 months, and the latter annually. And there have been successful appeals over the treatment of individuals under these powers to the European Court of Human Rights (see pp. 25 and 380).

Exercises

1. When may a person be lawfully imprisoned?
2. What is meant by Bail? Who may grant it and when?
3. Explain the main rules of law relating to public meeting in Britain.
4. Describe the main rules relating to detention by police.
5. How does the Government control the police?
6. How far can a democratic society go to protect itself from anti-democratic movements without itself becoming undemocratic?

10
Administrative Law and Justice

Delegated Legislation

Parliament can grant to some other person or body the power to make orders, regulations, or rules which have the force of law. In strict legal theory, Parliament ought to retain in its own hands the power and duty to enact all the laws and rules affecting the State and its peoples. In practice, Parliament cannot discharge this duty mainly because it has so much to do and so little time in which to do it. To overcome this difficulty it resorts to **delegated legislation**, sometimes called subordinate legislation or indirect legislation.

Statutes nowadays tend to lay down general principles or policy and to leave the working out of the administrative details to subordinate authorities who are responsible for carrying the statutes into effect. For example, the *Road Traffic Act, 1972*, empowers the Minister for Transport to make regulations in respect of road traffic matters by means of statutory instruments; the Home Secretary may make orders and regulations under the *Police Act, 1964*, in relation to the government, administration, and conditions of service of police; and the Secretary of State for Education and Science may make orders under the *Education Act, 1944*.

Forms of Delegated Legislation

Delegated legislation is comprised of:

(*a*) **Orders in Council** are Orders made by the Queen in Council and have been described as the most dignified form of subordinate legislation. In practice, the Minister of a Government Department usually drafts and makes the Order in the name of the Queen, whose approval 'in Council' is a formality. They may be issued (i) under statute, or (ii) under power of the Royal Prerogative.

(*b*) **Statutory Instruments, Rules and Orders** are normally made by Ministers in charge of Government Departments, but such rules must be submitted to Parliament either before or after they come into force.

(*c*) **Bye-Laws** are made by local authorities, railways, water boards, and similar bodies and, like statutory instruments, derive their authority from Acts of Parliament. Bye-laws require the approval of the appropriate Minister before they have legislative force.

All the forms of subordinate legislation noted above are enforced equally with statutes. For example, infringements of bye-laws, such as misconduct of some kind on a railway platform or damage to trees or seats in a public park, are enforced equally with offences such as simple theft, in the magistrates' courts. Appeal lies to higher courts against conviction or sentence imposed by the lower court.

The Government of a country of fifty-five million people is a highly complex matter. The most that Parliament can get through in the legislative field in one session (one year) is between sixty and seventy Acts of Parliament. On the other hand more than two thousand statutory instruments are issued each year and, in addition, bye-laws increase annually.

Growth of Delegated Legislation

The following reasons are advanced for the growth of delegated legislation:

(*a*) **Lack of Parliamentary time.** The Legislature has insufficient time to deal with and debate all the measures necessary for efficient government.

(*b*) **Urgency.** Parliament is not always in session, and its legislative procedures are slow. Emergencies and urgent problems arise, and delegated legislation is the best means of meeting the situation.

(*c*) **Flexibility.** A statute requires elaborate and cumbersome procedures for its enactment and can be revoked or amended only by another statute. A Ministerial order or statutory instrument can be made speedily and if it proves unworkable or impracticable, it can be quickly revoked.

(*d*) **Technicality of subject-matter.** Modern legislation tends to be technical and detailed, e.g. road traffic matters which may deal with 'special type' vehicles; building regulations; dangerous drugs regulations. Such legislation is best dealt with by Ministers, advised by experts familiar with the technical or scientific problem, rather than MPs who may be unfamiliar with the technicalities involved and who do not have access to experts.

(*e*) **Future needs.** Parliament cannot foresee the difficulties which may arise when new major schemes like the National Health Service or National Insurance are launched. Unforeseen difficulties are better dealt with by delegated legislation rather than statutes.

Criticisms of Delegated Legislation

The processes of Government and, in particular, the making of statutes are continuously subject to critical examination and analysis. Among the criticisms frequently levelled at delegated or subordinate legislation are:

(*a*) **Matters of Principle.** These are the primary concern of Parliament and Ministers ought not to be empowered or entitled to legislate by means of orders in respect of matters of principle.

(*b*) **Delegation of Taxing Power.** Parliament fought for years for the sole and exclusive right to impose taxes. History shows that the right can be abused and should not be yielded to subordinate authorities or Ministers. The *Import Duties Act, 1932*, gave the Treasury the power to legislate on taxation by fixing import duties and altering the 'free list', which usurped the sole right of the House of Commons to levy taxes.

(*c*) **Sub-delegation.** The *Emergency Powers (Defence) Act, 1939,* provides a clear example of five-tier legislation as it embraces: (i) the parent statute (made by Parliament); (ii) regulations made under the statute; (iii) orders made under the regulations; (iv) directions made under the orders; and (v) licences issued under the directions.

In its Report of 1946, the Select Committee on Statutory Instruments condemned the practice of delegation at four removes from Parliament of the power to make subordinate legislation.

(*d*) **Exclusion of the Jurisdiction of Courts.** The power of the courts to declare the regulations void on the ground of *ultra vires* ought not to be excluded either in the parent Act or the delegated legislation.

(*e*) **Authority to Modify an Act of Parliament.** This power, known as 'the Henry VIII clause', enables a Minister to modify the Act itself and thus usurp the essential function and duty of Parliament.

(*f*) **Inadequate Publicity.** The Press usually reports the purpose and effect of new statutes, but there is frequently inadequate publicity given to the numerous statutory instruments (over 2,000 annually) made by Ministers. A citizen reported for an offence against a statutory instrument of whose existence he was unaware, cannot plead in court that he did not know of it: ignorance of the law is no excuse (*ignorantia juris non excusat*).

Control of Delegated Legislation

The main forms of control over the power of a Minister to make delegated legislation are: (*a*) Consultation of interests. (*b*) Control by the courts. (*c*) Control by Parliament. (*d*) Publication.

(*a*) **Consultation of Interests.** In practice Ministers consult experts both within their own Departments and outside, and take the advice of various interests and bodies likely to be affected by proposed legislation. Thus road traffic legislation would involve consultation with local authorities, the police, the AA, the RAC, motor manufacturers, and others likely to be intimately affected. Sometimes a Minister must, as set down in a statute, consult an advisory body or submit a draft of any statutory instrument to it for approval. For example, under the *National Insurance Act, 1946,* regulations proposed by the Secretary of State for Social Services must be submitted in draft to the National Insurance Advisory Committee. When a Minister proposes to make rules of procedure for tribunals set up within his own Department, he must consult the Council on Tribunals (*Tribunals and Inquiries Act, 1971*).

(*b*) **Control by the Courts.** Rules and regulations made by Ministers and other administrative bodies under statutory authority are liable to be subject to challenge in the courts on two grounds: (i) *ultra vires* and (ii) unreasonableness. While a court cannot invalidate an Act of Parliament, it may declare that statutory instruments, rules or bye-laws are void on the ground that they are *ultra vires*, i.e. beyond the powers conferred by the Act under which they were made. In practice, Ministerial rules and orders are only rarely challenged on this ground because great care is taken by the legal advisers of the Minister on such procedural matters.

By-laws may be challenged on the grounds of **unreasonableness,** i.e. they are partial and unequal in operation as between different people. If rules are manifestly unjust, if they disclose bad faith, or they involve 'such oppressive or gratuitous interference with the rights of those subject to them as can find no justification in the minds of reasonable men, the court might well say Parliament never intended to give authority to make such rules; they are unreasonable and *ultra vires*' (Lord Russell in *Kruse* v. *Johnson*, 1898).

(*c*) **Control by Parliament.** (i) Parliament may revoke or vary the delegated power. (ii) Certain Acts require that regulations made under them shall be laid before Parliament. This is to enable MPs to know what has been done by a Minister, or what he proposes to do. (iii) A Select Committee on Statutory Instruments was set up in 1944 to consider every statutory instrument, rule or order laid before the Commons. A Special Orders Committee exists in the Lords to do similar work. In 1974, to avoid duplication in the two Houses, a Joint Statutory Instruments Committee (SIC) was created, comprising members of a Select Committee from the Commons and members of the corresponding committee in the Lords. The SIC, which replaces the two former committees in their consideration of SIs, reports to the House on any order or regulation deserving special attention on the following grounds:

(i) That it imposes a charge on the public revenue, or imposes or prescribes charges for any licence or consent or for any services from a public authority.

(ii) That it is made under an Act which precludes challenge in the courts.

(iii) That it appears to make some unusual or unexpected use of the powers conferred by the statute under which it is made.

(iv) That there appears to have been unjustifiable delay in publication or laying before Parliament.

(v) That for any special reason its form or purpose calls for elucidation.

(vi) That the drafting is defective.

(vii) That it purports to have retrospective effect.

The SIC may require a Department to submit a memorandum or explanatory note on any SI, and may request a representative of the Department to appear and explain a document personally. Before the Committee reports that the special attention of the House should be drawn to an instrument, it gives the Department concerned the opportunity to furnish an explanation.

In addition to this *technical* consideration the *merits* of SIs can be considered by each House, and in the Commons (since 1973) they can be considered (though not decided) in Standing Committee if the Government so decides. But SIs are 'take-it-or-leave-it': they cannot be amended. Secondly many are subject to a time limit (40 days) which can expire before debate takes place.

(*d*) **Publication.** HM Stationery Office publishes lists showing dates of issue of statutory instruments, and the *Statutory Instruments Act, 1946*, provides that 'it shall be a defence to prove that the instrument had not been issued by HMSO at the date of the alleged contravention, unless it is proved that at that date reasonable steps had been taken for the purpose of bringing the purport of the instrument to the notice of the public or of persons likely to be affected by it, or of the person charged.'

Administrative Tribunals

From early times special courts of local or limited jurisdiction have been set up apart from the main Courts of Law forming the English judicial system (see p. 215). The Tolzey Court of Bristol, the Piepowder courts (from *pieds poudrés* Fr. = dusty feet) set up to administer mercantile and commercial law for merchants attending local fairs in the Middle Ages, and the early Church Courts which dealt with disciplinary offences by the clergy and offences by the laity, such as blasphemy, heresy, and similar matters were some examples of the early tribunals.

For the past fifty years, successive Governments have been concerned with regulating the social life of the people and social legislation to improve the general well-being of the country has included the *National Health Service Act; National Insurance Act; Education Act; Housing Acts; Town and Country Planning Acts; Rent Restriction Acts;* and other Statutes. Although the collective good and the welfare of the community are admirable aims, the effect of much of the legislation is that, while promoting the public interest, it also circumscribes the rights of private individuals.

For example, Adams owns a field which the local education authority proposes to purchase compulsorily as a site for a technical college. Adams wishes to retain his valuable field for grazing and to contest the right of the education authority to acquire it. If the field is compulsorily acquired, Adams may further dispute the amount payable to compensate him for the loss of his land. Tribunals decide (i) whether the field may be acquired, and (ii) the amount of compensation if the field is taken by the authority.

Similarly, Black receives an injury at work which disables him from continuing his employment. He claims a pension under the National Insurance Industrial Injuries Acts, but his claim is repudiated by the National Insurance Officer on the ground that the injury is not within the Act: it was sustained after working hours or not 'during the course of employment'.

Many such disputes occur between a private individual seeking to protect his own private rights and a Minister, Government Department, local authority or other body, or person to whom authority has been given by law to administer a particular Act. In 1970 it was estimated that more than 150,000 people in Britain had their lives affected by Government-sponsored tribunals of one kind and another.

There are now some forty-five different types of tribunals dealing with a variety of cases ranging from mental health review boards (e.g. where *A* wishes to obtain his release from a mental institution) to air transport licensing boards. Each tribunal has its own jurisdiction and rules, and in many cases they either overlap or are confusingly different. One of the latest set of tribunals are the appeal committees established under the *Education Act, 1980* and allow parents to question LEA allocation of pupils to schools.

It may be argued that disputes of the kind mentioned ought to be decided in the impartial atmosphere of a Court of Law which follows a known procedure and applies a known system of law—common law or statute. In practice the disputes are frequently decided by special tribunals, not on the basis of law, but on grounds of policy and discretion. The difficulty faced by the tribunals lies in trying to reconcile the rights of the individual with those of the general public in whose interest the particular legislation may have been passed.

The position occupied by administrative tribunals in the Constitution and the type of law applied therein, known as **administrative law**, is a matter of great importance. Administrative law is defined as *that body of legal principles which concerns the right and duties arising from the impact upon the individual of the actual functioning of the executive instruments of Government.* (C. K. Allen, *Law and Order.*)

Types of Tribunals

There are three main types of administrative tribunals dealing with three different areas of jurisdiction:

(i) Deals with disputes in which a Government Department or a public authority is involved. These tribunals hear, and usually decide, appeals from the decisions or proposed decisions of Government Departments. The decision may be made either by a tribunal (e.g. a local valuation court on rating) or by the relevant Minister after an inquiry.

(ii) Deals with disputes between individual and individual. These are concerned with disputes between private persons and interests which result from attempts by the Government to regulate a particular aspect of the economy (e.g. rents and roads) or the functioning of a particular service (e.g. the National Health Service).

(iii) Deals with the enforcement of professional discipline such as the General Medical Council for doctors, the Law Society for solicitors. The constitution and procedure to be followed by these tribunals are determined by the respective professional body. They have no jurisdiction over the general public.

At this stage we may conveniently examine some of the reasons advanced for the creation of tribunals and the advantages and disadvantages which administrative tribunals display.

The reasons usually given for the establishment of administrative tribunals are:

(*a*) Ordinary courts are already overburdened with work, and additional jurisdiction would cause a breakdown.

(*b*) The costs of judicial proceedings in ordinary courts would be heavy.

(*c*) The Courts of Law are slow and the procedure is too elaborate.

(*d*) Matters involving a public service are best administered by specialists in that service.

(*e*) Policy decisions are best settled by an administrative authority, e.g. a Minister.

The *advantages* of administrative tribunals are:

(i) Decisions are quick and delays are avoided.

(ii) The procedure is cheap; no fees are payable usually.

(iii) The informal atmosphere and less rigid procedure suit the litigant.

(iv) They have wide discretionary power. This avoids the rigidity which the doctrine of judicial precedent imposes on Courts of Law.

(v) Tribunals are often staffed by experts: e.g. doctors on Pensions or Injuries Tribunals determine disability or extent of injury.

(vi) Tribunals aim for efficient administration of social or economic policies found in statutes; while Courts of Law sift facts and decide on the basis of established rules of law different in character from social policy.

The *disadvantages* are:

(i) Administrative tribunals are sometimes held in private and lack publicity. Suspicion may therefore be aroused as to 'administrative justice'.

(ii) The parties are sometimes prohibited from being represented by lawyers. The inarticulate person is therefore at a disadvantage in explaining his case. Legal aid is not generally available.

(iii) Reasons for decisions are not always published.

(iv) Technical experts and administrators are not always capable of acting impartially or of sifting the facts accurately. The lawyer-chairman is more suitable and qualified in this field.

(v) Tribunals sometimes include a civil servant of the Ministry directly involved in a dispute. He is, therefore, not sufficiently independent or impartial to give a just decision.

(vi) Rights of appeal are limited in some cases, and they differ as between tribunals.

(vii) Discretion of a tribunal is sometimes so wide as to make decisions inconsistent and unpredictable.

Examples of Tribunals

National Insurance. Claims for benefits under the *National Insurance Act, 1965*, are dealt with locally by an insurance officer. If disagreement arises the applicant for benefit has a right of appeal to a local tribunal composed of a Chairman, who is a lawyer, and two lay members, one representing employers' organisations and one representing employees' organisations. From the tribunal's decision appeal lies to the National Insurance Commissioner, a senior barrister appointed by the Crown.

There is no right of appeal either on a point of law or on a matter of fact from the Commissioner's finding. Some technical questions are reserved for decision by the Minister who may refer the matter to a judge of the High Court. From the Minister's decision on such question, there is a right of appeal to the High Court whose decision is final.

Industrial Injuries. There is a similar system of adjudication in respect of industrial-injuries claims under the *National Insurance (Industrial Injuries) Act, 1965* (as amended). The insured person must establish that his injury arose during the course of his employment. If the insurance officer disallows the claim the applicant may appeal to the tribunal applicable to National Insurance (see above).

If the applicant establishes that his injury did arise in the course of his employment, the next question to consider is the extent of the disablement.

This claim is decided first by a medical board of two doctors. Further appeal lies to a medical appeal tribunal made up of two doctors with a lawyer as Chairman. From the medical appeal tribunal appeal lies to the National Insurance Commissioner.

Decisions of the Commissioner in national insurance and industrial injuries cases are published officially, and such decisions bind insurance officers and local tribunals.

Industrial Tribunals: Redundancy Payments. The *Redundancy Payments Act, 1965*, created an obligation on employers to make payments to employees who have been dismissed, laid off or kept on short time, by reason of redundancy. The Act established a Redundancy Fund, to which employers must contribute, and from which payments are made to redundant employees according to their lengths of continuous employment.

Where an employee disputes the redundancy payment (e.g. as to amount) he has the right to appeal to an industrial tribunal. This consists of a Chairman (legally qualified) and two lay members representing (*a*) employers' organisations and (*b*) employees' organisations, respectively. The tribunal sits in various parts of the country as required.

The appellant may be legally represented or may be represented by a trade union official; send written representations setting out the facts and arguments; require the production of documents, and request the tribunal to order the attendance of any person to give evidence or to produce documents.

The decision of the tribunal is given in writing with reasons. The decision is final, subject to a right of appeal to the High Court on a point of law.

Rent Tribunals. Under the *Rent Act, 1965*, restrictions are placed on the rent payable for 'regulated' tenancies, i.e. lettings of unfurnished dwellings with a rateable value on 23 March 1965, not exceeding £400 in Greater London, and £200 elsewhere in England and Wales.

Disputes may arise between landlord and tenant over the assessment of a fair rent. If the assessment of the rent officer (an official appointed for an area) is disputed, a party may appeal to a rent tribunal (or rent assessment committee).

Members of the panel of adjudicators are appointed by the Secretary of State for the Environment and the Lord Chancellor, and are comprised of one-third lawyers; one-third valuers or surveyors; and one-third lay people. Rent Assessment Committees are appointed from the panel and have three members and the Chairman is usually a lawyer. Each Committee is served by a clerk who is a civil servant.

Legal representation is allowed, hearings are open to the public and the Press, and evidence is never taken on oath. If requested, reasons for the decisions of the Rent Assessment Committee may be given in writing or orally. Appeal, on a point of law only, lies to the High Court.

Domestic Tribunals. Domestic tribunals exist to determine questions, decide disputes and maintain discipline among members of a particular trade or profession. Thus a trade union or a professional body may lay down its set of rules governing membership and conduct. If the rules are infringed a tribunal may be set up to deal with the incident, and it may punish or expel an offender.

Three important examples of domestic tribunals are:

(*a*) **Trade Unions.** The disciplinary tribunals of trade unions are created by members themselves. A governing committee frames the rules of membership, the rules constituting a tribunal, rules of procedure and the forms of punishment. Members who violate the rules may be expelled or fined. Expulsion from a union could mean that an individual member is prevented from following his former trade. Such powers are, however, controlled by the Courts of Law and a member may claim the protection of the law if the union acts unlawfully. In *Bonsor* v. *Musicians Union* (1955) it was held that a musician who had been wrongly expelled by his union could obtain damages to compensate him for his financial loss resulting from the expulsion.

The *Trade Union and Labour Relations Act, 1974*, altered the law relating to trade unions, and protects employees against unfair dismissal. Its provisions are too detailed for consideration here (see p. 264).

(*b*) **Solicitors.** The *Solicitors Act, 1972*, provides for the setting up of a committee to exercise disciplinary powers over solicitors. The disciplinary committee sits as a board with a minimum of three members, and follows the usual legal procedure of a Court of Law. The Board may strike a solicitor off the roll, suspend him from practice, impose a fine of up to £500, or order the payment of costs. Appeal from the committee lies to the High Court.

(*c*) **Doctors.** The General Medical Council has power under the *Medical Act, 1956*, to strike a doctor off the Medical Register for infamous conduct in his profession, and he can be barred from further practice. Appeal against the decision of the General Medical Council lies to the Judicial Committee of the Privy Council.

The General Dental Council has similar powers under the *Dentists Act, 1957*, concerning dentists, and the Central Midwives Board has similar authority over midwives. There are, however, many more tribunals (forty-five different types) but lack of space prevents their description here.

Judicial Control of Administrative Tribunals

A tribunal is another name for a court, but to avoid confusion the term is applied here to those bodies possessing judicial power which operate outside the traditional Courts of Law described on page 215.

The essential purpose of a tribunal is adjudication in a particular type of dispute; to follow proper procedures; to act fairly and impartially, and finally to reach a decision. Many of the tribunals today have very wide powers indeed, therefore, their judgements and decisions must be subject to the supervisory control of the Courts of Law. Such control is exercised mainly by the Queen's Bench Division which continues the ancient jurisdiction of the original Royal court of King's Bench, in seeing that justice is done by a tribunal, local authority or other body acting judicially.

As a rule Parliament leaves the professional organisations to form their own rules and procedures and to discipline their membership. Only in exceptional cases will the Courts of Law interfere with these. But, where the administration of a statute, the exercise of powers under it, and the setting up of tribunals to decide disputes are entrusted to a Minister, Parliament generally requires that certain rules be framed to ensure fairness in the administration of the statute and of any tribunals set up, (cf. the

National Insurance Tribunals on p. 292). Nevertheless injustice does sometimes occur and the purpose of this section is to examine the grounds on which the Courts of Law exercise their supervisory jurisdiction, and the procedures that are followed.

Where a tribunal acts **judicially** it must follow certain unwritten rules of common law known as **natural justice**. Natural justice embraces two main rules:

(*a*) The rule against bias ('no man may be a judge in his own cause').

(*b*) *Audi alteram partem* ('hear the other side').

(*a*) **The Rule against Bias.** A true judicial decision can be reached only if the judge himself is impartial. This is an obvious requirement in a Court of Law or a tribunal. It was held in *R*. v. *Rand* (1866) that a judge is disqualified where (i) he has a direct pecuniary interest, however small, in the subject matter in dispute; or (ii) there is a real likelihood that the judge would have a bias in favour of one of the parties.

For example, if a judge is related to, or is a friend of, one of the parties to a dispute there would be a real likelihood of bias. It is immaterial whether a judicial decision was **in fact** biased, for as was said by Lord Chief Justice Hewart in *R*. v. *Sussex Justices, ex parte McCarthy* (1924): 'Justice should not only be done, but should manifestly and undoubtedly be seen to be done.'

As an example of pecuniary bias we may note:

Dimes v. *Grand Junction Canal* (1852). Lord Chancellor Cottenham made judicial decrees in a Chancery suit in favour of a canal company. Lord Cottenham held several shares in the company. *Held* (by the House of Lords): that the decrees be set aside on the ground of pecuniary interest. No bias was proved in fact, nor could it be shown that Lord Cottenham was in any way influenced by his own shareholding.

(*b*) **Audi Alteram Partem.** The second rule of natural justice is that a man has the right to be heard in his own defence. 'It is contrary to the spirit of our laws that anyone should be convicted without having an opportunity of being heard in his own defence,' said one judge in 1795, and that principle still holds good.

The rule embraces the propositions that a party sued or prosecuted should have the opportunity to:

(i) Know the case against him.

(ii) State his case (orally or in writing).

(iii) Make submissions on relevant rules of law.

(iv) Comment on all material considered by the judge.

Ridge v. *Baldwin* (1964). The Chief Constable of Brighton was dismissed from his post by the local Watch Committee for certain acts of misconduct (alleged). The Chief Constable was not present at the meeting of the Watch Committee, nor given the grounds of the proposal to dismiss him nor any particulars of the facts alleged. The Chief Constable appealed to the Courts of Law and eventually in the House of Lords it was held: that the rules of natural justice required that a hearing should have been given to the Chief Constable before the Watch Committee exercised its power of dismissal. Failure to give a hearing invalidated the dismissal.

The above basic rules of natural justice, together with the further rule that neither side may communicate with the judge behind the other's back, are in truth elementary and procedural. The courts follow strict procedural rules which have been hammered out over the centuries to ensure fairness. Administrative tribunals, however, are not bound to follow exactly the same rules which are applied by the courts, but they must apply the general basic principles of justice as noted above.

Supervision by the Queen's Bench Division

The Monarch is 'the fountain of justice' and the Queen's Bench Division of the High Court, acting for the Crown, supervises the administration of justice by inferior courts (e.g. magistrates' courts, administrative tribunals and subordinate tribunals) throughout the Kingdom. Moreover the QBD exercises supervisory control over Ministers of the Crown, civil servants, local authorities, or other authorities purporting to exercise statutory powers. If such authorities act *ultra vires* (i.e. beyond the powers conferred on them by law) the QBD may declare such excess of power to be void.

Control is exercised by the QBD by means of prerogative orders of (*a*) **mandamus**, (*b*) **prohibition**; (*c*) **certiorari**; and (*d*) **declaratory judgement**.

(*a*) **Mandamus** is an order issuing out of the QBD commanding (*mandamus*: we command) a person or body to perform a duty imposed by common law or statute. The order is available to enforce administrative duties, e.g. to compel a local authority to produce its accounts for inspection by a ratepayer; to enforce judicial duties, e.g. to compel a housing tribunal to hear and determine an appeal, or magistrates to decide a case in petty sessions.

(*b*) **Prohibition** is an order issuing out of the QBD to prohibit an inferior court or tribunals from continuing to exceed, or threatening to exceed, its jurisdiction. The order may be directed to magistrates, coroners, and all statutory tribunals.

(*c*) **Certiorari** is an order removing the decision of an inferior judicial body into the QBD to have its legality enquired into. The word *certiorari* means 'to be informed'; in effect the QBD reviews the decision. The order may be used (i) to secure an impartial trial; (ii) to review an excess of jurisdiction; (iii) to challenge an *ultra vires* act; (iv) to quash a judicial decision made contrary to natural justice (see above); and (v) to correct errors of law on the face of the record of the lower court or tribunal.

An order of *certiorari* will lie 'whenever any body of persons having legal authority to determine questions affecting the rights of subjects, and having the duty to act judicially, act in excess of their legal authority'. Again the order can be issued to magistrates' courts, administrative tribunals, disciplinary tribunals of, e.g. the police and fire service, and to arbitrators.

(*d*) **Declaratory Judgements.** These are simply judgements which declare what the law is on a particular point and are not accompanied by any sanction or means of enforcement. The Rules of the Supreme Court, Order 25, r. 5 provides:

No action or proceeding shall be open to objection on the ground that a merely declaratory judgment or order is sought thereby, and the Court may make binding declarations of right whether any consequential relief is or could be claimed, or not.

The remedy is particularly useful where a local authority or public body (or a private person) proposes to spend a large sum of money and is unsure of the law. To forestall subsequent proceedings which may invalidate the project (and cost the local authority much to defend), the local authority may apply to the High Court for a Declaration as to what the law is.

The Court will not adjudicate on hypothetical issues. A concrete case must have arisen.

The Law Commission has proposed (Working Paper No. 40) that there should be a single remedy for judicial review of administrative action and orders, and should be called 'the application for review'.

Tribunals and Inquiries Act, 1971

The wide powers granted to tribunals and the varied procedures which each followed in determining the private rights of individuals caused considerable disquiet in the period following the Second World War. This came to a head in the Crichel Down case in 1954, concerning the acquisition by a Government Department of privately owned land, which eventually resulted in a special inquiry by the Government. This inquiry revealed inefficient administrative procedures by the Civil Service and apparent injustices to the person whose land was taken and who wanted it back. As a result, a committee was set up in 1955 by the Government under Sir Oliver Franks (now Lord Franks). Its terms of reference were to examine and make recommendations on (i) the constitution and working of tribunals set up by statute; and (ii) the working of administrative procedures, e.g. the holding of an official inquiry or the hearing of appeals by a Minister as the result of objections, particularly in relation to the compulsory purchase of land.

The difference between a tribunal and an inquiry is that a tribunal is, in general, constituted under statutory authority; it has a regular or permanent existence; a defined jurisdiction to hear and determine disputes; and resembles a judicial body such as a court in reaching a decision or finding. An inquiry, on the other hand, is set up at the instance of Parliament, the Government, or a Minister, to hear and receive evidence concerning a matter and to report the facts to some other body, e.g. Parliament, a Minister, or some other body, or to make recommendations. Important inquiries are those like the Aberfan Disaster Inquiry of 1966, and the Inquiry regarding the Third London Airport. An inquiry is most frequently employed in disputes over the compulsory purchase of land by a Government Department or a local authority and in appeals against refusal of planning permission by a planning authority. The Minister appoints an inspector to hold an inquiry the purpose of which is to ascertain the facts and details from the parties, the local authority, the public. The inspector submits his report to the Minister who comes to a decision.

The Franks Committee reported in 1957 and some of its main recommendations passed into law in the *Tribunals and Inquiries Act, 1958*.

The general provisions of the *Tribunals and Inquiries Act, 1971* (a consolidating statute), include:

(*a*) **A Council on Tribunals** shall be formed of ten to fifteen members appointed by the Lord Chancellor. (A Scottish committee is appointed to deal with Scottish matters, the members being appointed by the Secretary of State for Scotland.)

(*b*) **Duties of the Council** are to keep under review the constitution and working of the tribunals listed in a schedule to the *Act of 1958*. The Council acts in an advisory capacity and does not itself hear appeals.

(*c*) **Reports** of the Council are made annually to Parliament.

(*d*) **Chairmen** of the various tribunals to which the Act applies are selected by the appropriate Ministers from a panel of names suggested by the Lord Chancellor. This ensures that nominees have the qualifications, legal or otherwise, for appointment.

(*e*) **Membership** of tribunals can be terminated only with the consent of the Lord Chancellor.

(*f*) **Reasons for decisions** made by tribunals must be given in writing or orally, if the tribunal is requested by a party, even before the decision itself has been announced.

(*g*) **Appeal** on a point of law to the High Court is given in the case of a number of tribunals (e.g. rent, schools, and employment tribunals) where the right had not existed before the Act.

(*h*) **Prerogative Orders**; judicial control by resort to *certiorari, mandamus,* and prohibition is safeguarded.

Tribunals of Inquiry (Evidence) Act (1921)

Under this Act both Houses of Parliament may resolve that it is expedient that a tribunal be appointed to inquire into 'a matter of urgent public importance'. Since 1921 there have been seventeen such tribunals dealing with various matters: allegations of bribery of Ministers and public servants over the issue of licences; disclosure of Budget secrets; the loss of a submarine during diving trials; corruption in municipal offices; complaints against police; a spy (Vassall) at the Admiralty; Aberfan disaster (144 children and adults killed) in 1966; civil disturbance in Ulster (13 deaths) in 1972—the Widgery Tribunal.

The instrument appointing the tribunal may confer on it all the powers of the High Court to examine witnesses, order production of documents, etc. Usually a High Court judge is appointed to preside, and he is assisted by two independent members who may or may not be lawyers. There is no accused person. The case is presented by a Law Officer of the Crown or counsel who may call witnesses. Legal representation is allowed to witnesses whose interests might need to be protected.

The purpose of the inquiry is to ascertain the truth of a particular matter. At the end of the inquiry the President of the court submits his report to the Home Secretary.

A Royal Commission on Tribunals reported in November, 1966, that 'there is need for standing legislation to permit the setting up whenever necessary of an inquisitorial tribunal and for this purpose the *Tribunals of Inquiry (Evidence) Act (1921)* subject to certain amendments and safeguards should be retained'.

Statutory Inquiries

Efficient decision-making involves, as a first step (1) an inquiry to ascertain the facts of a situation; (2) reasonable thought and judgement; and (3) the actual decision. This is prudent whenever an important action is proposed both in private or public life. Administrative authorities are expected to act responsibly in public affairs and it follows that many inquiries must be made in a wide variety of matters, before a final decision is arrived at.

These inquiries range from the preliminary investigation of an executive of a local authority—e.g. a sanitary inspector or public health inspector, or a police officer before a summons is issued or an arrest is made—to the full-scale inquiry presided over by a judge and (say) two independent members forming a tribunal.

Ministerial Statutory Inquiries

In some cases a statute imposes a *duty* on the Minister to hold an inquiry. This form of inquiry has been defined by section 14(1) of the *Tribunals and Inquiries Act, 1958*, thus: 'an inquiry or hearing held or to be held in pursuance of a duty imposed by any statutory provision . . .'. Examples of statutes requiring such an inquiry are: the *Town and Country Planning Act, 1971*; and the *Housing Act, 1957*.

In other cases a statute gives a *power* to a Minister to hold an inquiry. Thus under the *Police Act (1964)*, s. 32(1), we find 'The Secretary of State *may* cause a local inquiry to be held by a person appointed by him into any matter connected with the policing of any area'. For the rules as to the procedure to be followed at the inquiry one must look to the statute itself.

In addition to inquiries initiated under a power given or a duty imposed by statute, a Minister may order an inquiry on his own volition. Such an inquiry may be called an extra-legal inquiry—e.g. the Crichel Down Inquiry of 1954, the Mountbatten inquiry into Prison Administration following the escape of Blake (a spy) in 1967 the Cleveland child abuses 1987.

Generally, therefore, although inquiries may be held for any purpose whatsoever, the term 'statutory inquiry' is used to refer to the obligatory inquiry to enable objections to be made to some scheme, for example, the siting of a New Town, the compulsory purchase of land, before a final decision is made by the Minister. It is a useful administrative device to that end. A recent example is the 1983 public inquiry into the Sizewell nuclear power station (the Layfield inquiry).

Compulsory Acquisition of Land

Government Departments and local authorities may purchase or acquire land by agreement. The normal rules of contract generally apply to these. Authorities may also purchase land *compulsorily*—for, e.g. airfields, fire-stations, cemeteries, children's homes, drainage schemes, police-stations, markets, swimming-baths, and so on. The local authority may wish to clear an area of bad housing (slum clearance) or to pull down a single house as unfit for human habitation.

Statutory authority for such schemes is found in various acts: the *Housing*

Act (1957), which prescribes the procedure to be followed in the Inquiry. The *Acquisition of Land (Authorisation Procedure) Act, 1946*, is a general act which may be applied whenever land is to be compulsorily acquired, and lays down the procedure to be followed.

Thus, the steps to be followed in the compulsory acquisition of, say, a portion of land known as Blackacre are:

1. Resolution of the local authority to purchase Blackacre.
2. Compulsory purchase order made by the local authority.
3. Advertisement of the order in local Press.
4. Notices served on every owner, lessee, and occupier of Blackacre.
5. Objections to the proposal may be made by any person within time permitted (must be not less than twenty-one days from notice).
6. If an objection is made the Ministry may:
   (*a*) hold an Inquiry; or
   (*b*) give objector right to be heard in private.
7. Inquiry is held. (If objector pursues his rights).
8. Assuming objections are over-ruled, the Minister may make a confirmation order.
9. Minister publicises the making of the compulsory purchase order.
10. Within six weeks of confirmation order an objector may apply to the High Court for the order to be quashed on two grounds:
    (1) that the order is *ultra vires*; or
    (2) that the interests of applicant were substantially prejudiced by failure to òbserve proper procedure.
11. If no proceedings under '10' are taken within the six-week period the order 'may not be questioned in any legal proceedings whatsoever'.

No. 10 is described as 'the standard form of challenge' and applies in other statutes where compulsory powers of acquisition are given to administrative authorities. In practice the land or house is usually acquired by agreement before the complete procedure is gone through.

Town and Country Planning

Under the *Town and Country Planning Act (1971)*, the 'responsible authorities' are (1) the Minister for the Environment; and (2) County Councils and District Councils who are designated 'local planning authorities'.

The main duties of the local planning authority are to (1) submit planning proposals for the area to the Minister; and (2) control local 'development' by owners, occupiers, etc. Under (1) the local authority must submit to the Minister a 'development' plan allocating areas for residential, agricultural, or industrial purposes. Notice of the submission of the plan to the Minister must be published in the *London Gazette* and local Press. Objections may be sent to the Minister within a specified period. The Minister must consider all objections either at (1) a public local inquiry; or (2) private hearing. The procedure follows that outlined in previous paragraph. The Minister may approve the plan with or without modifications. The 'standard form of challenge' within six weeks applies in this case.

Where a person wishes to 'develop' his land he must obtain planning permission from the local planning authority. 'Development' means:

the carrying out of building, engineering, mining, or other operations in, on, over or under land, or the making of any material change in the use of any buildings or other land.

If the planning authority refuses permission or permission is granted subject to conditions the applicant may appeal to the Minister who may (i) dismiss the appeal; (ii) allow the appeal; (iii) reverse or vary any part of the authority's decision.

Before determining the appeal the Minister must, at the request of either the applicant or the planning authority hold an inquiry. Both the applicant and the authority will have an opportunity to be heard. The inquiry is held by an inspector appointed by the Minister, and the report of the inquiry is sent forward for decision by the Minister. Subject again to the standard form of challenge, the Minister's decision 'shall not be questioned in any legal proceedings whatsoever'.

The holding of a 'local inquiry' or 'statutory inquiry' is required under various acts—e.g.:

1. *New Towns Act, 1946.* A site is chosen to build a new town—e.g. Stevenage; a 'development corporation' is constituted, and the plan is publicised. Objections may be made at the statutory inquiry; a confirmation order is made with the standard form of challenge.

2. *Pipe Lines Act, 1962.* This act empowers the Ministry of Power to control the construction of cross-country pipe-lines (e.g. for oil, gas). Again objections are heard at the statutory inquiry and the standard form of challenge applies also in this case.

3. *Local Government Act, 1972.* Two local government commissions (one for England, and one for Wales) were set up to review the organisation of local government, and to make proposals for the alteration, amalgamation, and extinction of certain existing local authority areas. A statutory inquiry may be held in some cases to consider objections. Otherwise a local conference will be held.

Accident Inquiries

Where a serious railway accident occurs or where, for example, there has been serious loss of life at sea, the Minister for Transport is responsible for ascertaining the cause and circumstances. To do this an inquiry is set up, evidence is taken and a report is made to him officially. We may note the following inquiries.

1. **Shipping Casualties.** The Minister of Transport Industries is empowered under the *Merchant Shipping Act* (*1894*) to hold an inquiry into the loss, stranding or abandoning of a ship and other shipping casualties, whether or not there is loss of life. Where a formal investigation is made a court of inquiry is set up presided over by a Wreck Commissioner, who is assisted by two expert assessors. Such a court has all the powers of a court of summary jurisdiction. The findings are announced in public, they may recommend or stipulate the suspension or revocation of the certificate of the ship's officers. They may also recommend the substitution of a certificate of lesser competence as—e.g. a mate's certificate for a master's. Copies

of the findings of the court are printed by HM Stationery Office and made available to the public e.g. the Channel Ferry disaster 1987.

2. **Railway Accidents.** The Minister has statutory powers to order inquiries into train accidents and other accidents involving railway personnel. Train accident inquiries are investigated by the Inspecting Officers of Railways.

The object of the inquiry is to ascertain the cause of the accident and to make recommendations to prevent recurrence. The rules of evidence are relaxed, and the inspecting officer may in his discretion take any part of the evidence in private, an expedient which is adopted where there is a possibility of criminal proceedings—e.g. manslaughter involving a train-driver or signalman. Trade union representatives and railway officers may put questions to witnesses on points relevant to the purpose of the inquiry. On completion the inspector's report is sent to the Minister indicating the circumstances of the accident, its cause, and any observations arising out of the investigation. The report is printed by HM Stationery Office and made available to the public. In some cases where proceedings are pending against a person (e.g. a train-driver) the report is withheld until the judicial proceedings are concluded.

3. **Air Accidents.** The Civil Aviation (Investigation of Accidents) Regulations (1951) direct that when an accident occurs to a civil aircraft involving death or serious injury to any person, or serious damage to an aircraft, particulars should be notified to the Minister of the Department of Trade and Industry.

An inspector of accidents will be required to investigate the accident and a special court will be appointed to hold a public inquiry, the findings of which will be reported to the Minister.

Extra-legal Inquiries

Non-statutory or extra-legal inquiries may be held at the initiative of the Minister and are therefore discretionary. The Crichel Down case of 1954 is an example (see p. 163).

Comment

Tribunals decide; inquiries, at most, recommend. A statutory inquiry is not an engine of bureaucracy designed to over-ride private interests in any event. It is an administrative process. The judicial procedure is ordered by Parliament to deal with objections, to assuage the mind of the objector, to enable him 'to blow off steam' in the hope of rallying public support to his view, but primarily to enable the facts to be brought to the mind of the Minister. He is responsible to Parliament, must carry out the policy of the Government—e.g. to create the new town, clear slums, eliminate bad housing, build schools, prisons, a new airport and the like, and must have first regard for the public interest and welfare generally. The evidence produced by one objector is part only of the facts, pressures and responsibilities to which he must pay attention. Administrative justice is difficult to attain and there is no ideal solution. Lawyers have not always understood the problem clearly and the distinction between an 'administrative decision' and a 'judicial decision' is not helpful.

As a result of these and other criticisms two committees were set up: (1) The Committee on Ministers' Powers in 1932, which made a report, but little action was taken; and (2) the Franks' Committee (chairman Sir Oliver Franks, now Lord Franks) in 1955 (following the Crichel Down case of 1954) which made its report in 1957. The *Tribunals and Inquiries Act* (*1958*) followed upon the Report (see p. 297).

Redress of Grievances

Introduction

In all civilised states injustices occur from time to time. The Cabinet Ministers, the Civil Service, local authorities, police, public corporations, and other bodies have enormous powers to regulate the lives of us all. Despite the fact that the authorities purport to act 'in the best interests of the community' or for the common good, somewhere there will be a person who has been unjustly treated.

The Crichel Down affair, which arose out of the acquisition of land in Dorset in 1937, and finally resulted in an independent inquiry and a Report to Parliament in 1954 (*Cmnd. 9176, 1954*) brought into focus some of the problems facing administration today, including ministerial responsibility and the techniques of administration in the Civil Service. The report disclosed an apparent injustice to a citizen who persisted in securing his private rights to property he formerly owned and of which he was dispossessed (see p. 163).

Following the report the Government appointed the Franks Committee in 1955 to consider the working of statutory tribunals and the administrative procedures followed in holding an inquiry on an appeal or as a result of objections or representations. Where a citizen's rights are prejudiced there may, in some cases, be formal procedures laid down by statute to be followed whereby the decisions questioned can be pursued or appealed against. The Courts of Law may also control the actions of administrative authorities (see p. 294), but there are limitations to those controls. The Franks Committee observed:

> Over most of the field of public administration no formal procedure is provided for objecting or deciding on questions. For example, when foreign currency or a scarce commodity such as petrol or coal is rationed or allocated, there is no other body to which an individual applicant can appeal if the responsible administrative authority decides to allow him less than he has requested. Of course the aggrieved individual can always complain to the appropriate administrative authority, to his Member of Parliament, to a representative organisation or to the Press. But there is no formal procedure on which he can insist.

Channels of Complaint

These are some of the channels through which a citizen may complain:

(i) A statutory inquiry (e.g. compulsory acquisition of land).
(ii) Statutory tribunals (e.g. National Insurance Tribunal).

  (iii) Parliamentary Inquiry (*ad hoc*, e.g. Crichel Down Inquiry).
  (iv) Courts of Law.
  (v) Consumer Council (e.g. gas, electricity, etc.)
  (vi) Representative Organisations (e.g. TUC, NALGO, to act as a pressure group or for remedy).
  (vii) The Press.

In 1960 the British section of the International Commission of Jurists ('Justice' for short) initiated an inquiry into the problem of the redress of grievances against administrative authorities such as the Civil Service and others, and produced a report in 1961 called *The Citizen and the Administration: the Redress of Grievances*. It became known as the Whyatt Report, Sir John Whyatt being the Chairman of the committee initiating the inquiry. The report mentioned two types of complaint: (i) those alleging that a decision affecting the individual was wrong; and (ii) those alleging maladministration.

Examples of complaints. The following are some of the many instances in which there was no effective machinery for securing redress to the person aggrieved:

(*a*) **Education.** The selection of a child for a particular school following an '11-plus' examination. The local education authority (LEA) decides, and the parent has no right of appeal. A parent may wish his child to attend school *X* near his home, but the LEA may direct that the child attend school *Y* at a distance from the home. (Under the *Education Act, 1980*, some choice is allowed and such appeals are now possible—see p. 290.)

(*b*) **Health Service.** 'Marginal benefits', e.g. a mechanically propelled invalid chair is granted or withheld at the discretion of civil servants in the Ministry, or a hospital authority. There is no formal machinery for review of a disappointed applicant's case; nor for similar local social services.

(*c*) **Telephones.** The allocation or refusal of a telephone to a would-be subscriber is a matter for a local Telephone Manager. An applicant who is refused may appeal only to a higher official in the Post Office (i.e. before it became the private company British Telecom).

(*d*) **Farmers' Subsidy.** The amount of agricultural subsidy to be paid to individual farmers is decided by officials. No statutory right of appeal exists but a farmer may complain to an agricultural executive committee, a body independent of the Ministry. In practice the decisions of the committee are almost always accepted by the Minister.

In these types of cases the Whyatt Report suggested that 'the guiding principle should be that the individual is entitled to have an impartial adjudication of his dispute with authority'. It was acknowledged that in some cases the Minister should, in the public interest, retain responsibility for the final decision.

The Report suggested that a **general tribunal** should be set up to deal with miscellaneous appeals from discretionary decisions made by authorities. It was also recommended that the Council on Tribunals should be empowered to keep this aspect of public administration under review, and to make proposals for new tribunals.

After reviewing the remedies and procedures available and the channels through which an aggrieved citizen might pursue his complaint the Report noted:

a continuous flow of relatively minor complaints, not sufficient in themselves to attract public interest, but nevertheless of great importance to the individuals concerned, which give rise to feelings of frustration and resentment because of the inadequacy of the existing means of seeking redress.

The Parliamentary Commissioner for Administration (PCA)

The 'Justice' Report then examined the office and function of the **Ombudsman** which has existed in Sweden for 150 years, and in more recent years is found in Denmark, Norway, Finland, and New Zealand.

The function and powers of each Ombudsman vary, but the common characteristics are that the Ombudsman (*a*) is an impartial person (*b*) is independent of the Government, although appointed by and acting on behalf of the Parliament of his country (*c*) has the duty to investigate complaints of **maladministration** made to him by members of the public against any person acting in the service of the State.

In October 1965 the Government produced a White Paper *The Parliamentary Commissioner for Administration* (Cmnd. 2767). In 1967 the *Parliamentary Commissioner Act* was passed which created the post of **Ombudsman** and Sir Edmund Compton was duly appointed to discharge the duties laid down.

Appointment

The Commissioner is appointed by Letters Patent. He may be removed from office by an Address from both Houses of Parliament and shall vacate this office on reaching 65 years of age. The Commissioner shall not be a member of the House of Commons. He shall be an *ex officio* member of the Council on Tribunals and of the Scottish Committee of that Council (see p. 298).

The Commissioner's salary is some £62,000 a year, the appointment carries a pension and the salary and pension are paid out of the Consolidated Fund.

In Britain it is emphasised that he is a **Parliamentary Commissioner**: he reports to Parliament, is backed up and overseen by a Select Committee, and he only normally acts on cases referred to him by MPs, i.e. MPs are 'filters'. It should be noted that his investigations form, in any one year, a small fraction of the investigations by Departments in direct communication with MPs.

Departments and Authorities Subject to Investigation

A schedule to the Act lists the Departments and authorities subject to investigation. Broadly these include all the Government Departments (see pp. 146–57) and the other 'authorities' include, the Public Trustee, the Public Records Office, Registry of Friendly Societies, the Royal Mint, bodies ancillary to or under the supervision of a Government Department or Minister. The Departments and bodies must exercise functions 'on behalf of the Crown'.

How may a Complaint be made?

A has a complaint of maladministration in respect of some act or omission by the Ministry of Social Security. *A* now wishes to complain to the Parliamentary Commissioner for Administration.

(*a*) *A* makes a **written** complaint to an MP.
(*b*) The complaint must amount to **maladministration**.
(*c*) *A* **consents** to the reference to the Commissioner.
(*d*) The MP **refers complaint** to the Commissioner for investigation.

Matters not Subject to Investigation

The Commission will not investigate any matter where *A*, the aggrieved person, has a right of appeal or review before a statutory tribunal (e.g. National Insurance Tribunal), or where *A* has a remedy in a court, unless in the latter case *A* has a reasonable excuse for not taking proceedings.

The following matters are specifically excluded:

(*a*) **Foreign relations.** Dealings between Governments or international organisations.

(*b*) **Ambassadors, Consuls.** Action by, outside the UK. In 1979 this was amended to allow investigation of actions relating to UK citizens who have the right of abode in this country.

(*c*) **HM Dominions.** Action by Dominion Governments outside the UK.

(*d*) **Extradition and Fugitive Offenders.** Action taken to retrieve offenders who escape from the United Kingdom to other countries.

(*e*) **Criminal Investigation.** Action taken by the Home Secretary for the security of the state, and respecting passports.

(*f*) **Legal Proceedings.** Commencement or conduct of civil or criminal proceedings before the courts or the Navy, Army, or Air Force tribunals (Military Tribunals).

(*g*) **Prerogative of Mercy.** Action taken by the Home Secretary respecting the prerogative of mercy.

(*h*) **Contracts and Commercial Transactions.** Action taken in contracts, etc., made in the United Kingdom or elsewhere by a Government Department or authority to which the act applies. The following, however, are **within the jurisdiction of** the Commissioner: (i) transactions for or relating to the acquisition of land compulsorily or in circumstances in which it could be acquired compulsorily; (ii) the disposal of surplus land acquired compulsorily or in such circumstances as described at (i) above.

(*i*) **Personnel Matters re Armed Forces, Crown Servants.** Action taken in respect of appointments, removals, pay, discipline, superannuation or other personnel matters in relation to (*a*) Armed Forces and their auxiliary forces; (*b*) civil servants.

(*j*) **Honours.** The grant of honours, awards, or privileges within the gift of the Crown, including the grant of Royal Charters.

Who May Complain?

The broad rule is that any individual, including a body corporate, such as a company, may complain through the proper channels to the Commissioner.

Who may not Complain?

Local authorities, nationalised corporations, and any other authority or body, whose members are appointed by Her Majesty or any Minister of the Crown or Government Department, or whose revenues consist wholly or mainly of money provided by Parliament, may not complain.

Where *A* an aggrieved person, had a complaint but dies, provision is made for the complaint to be made by *A*'s personal representatives (i.e. the executor of his will, or the administrators of his estate if he left no will), or a member of *A*'s family.

Time Limit for Complaints

The broad rule is that a complaint must be sent to an MP within one year of the time when the aggrieved party had notice of the matters alleged in the complaint. Where special circumstances apply the Commissioner may extend the period.

A complaint shall not be entertained unless the aggrieved person is resident in the United Kingdom or the complaint relates to action taken in relation to him while he was present in the United Kingdom.

Procedure in respect of Investigations

The main points to be observed in regard to procedure are the following:

(*a*) **Audi Alteram partem** ('Hear the other side'). The Commissioner will hear views expressed by the Government Department against whom complaint is made.

(*b*) **Privacy.** Proceedings may be conducted in private. The Commissioner has a discretion to order otherwise.

(*c*) **Legal Representation.** The Commissioner decides whether any person may be represented by a lawyer.

(*d*) **Information.** The Commissioner may obtain information from such persons, in such manner and may make such inquiries as he thinks fit.

(*e*) **Expenses.** The Commissioner may pay reasonable expenses to persons who attend or furnish information for investigation, and may make compensation for loss of time.

(*f*) **Evidence.** The Commissioner may require any Minister, officer, or member of the Department or authority concerned, or any person who is able to furnish information or produce documents relevant to the investigation to furnish any such information or produce such documents.

(*g*) **Attendance of Witnesses.** Witnesses may be compelled to attend and/or to produce documents. The Commissioner has virtually the same powers as a Court of Law in this respect.

(*h*) **Secrecy or Claim of Privilege.** In effect this means that a witness (e.g. a member of a Government Department) may not claim that his information is secret. Nor may such person claim 'privilege' and refuse to disclose information. The broad rule here is that the same procedure applies as that followed in a Court of Law.

(*i*) **Cabinet Proceedings.** Information concerning Cabinet matters are secret and may not be disclosed.

(*j*) **Obstruction and Contempt.** Obstruction of the Commissioner or a member of his staff in the execution of their duties amounts to contempt. Where the Commissioner certifies that an offence has been committed the matter is referred to a Court of Law which will deal with the matter.

Reports

The first duty is to notify the MP who forwarded the complaint whether the PCA has decided to investigate the complaint or not. Many complaints are received which do not warrant any action at all. If the PCA conducts an inquiry he notifies the result to the MP sending the complaint: where he makes no inquiry the PCA states his reasons for not proceeding.

Annual Report. The Commissioner shall annually lay before the House of Commons a general report on the performance of his functions under the Act.

Special Reports. The Commissioner may lay a special report before the House of Commons where the Commissioner believes that an injustice has not been, or will not be, remedied.

The reports are specially protected from action for defamation, and they are protected by the rule of absolute privilege. Special provision is made in regard to the disclosure by a Minister of documents which would be prejudicial to the safety of the State or contrary to the public interest. In these cases the Commissioner is not authorised to communicate to any person the contents of the document or the information referred to.

Limitations

There are certain important fields of public service which are immune from investigation. The most important of these are: (i) the Police, (ii) nationalised industries, (iii) local government, (iv) the NHS (but see p. 310).

In regard to the local authorities, **local government commissioners** are appointed each working independently in a particular part of the country. Complaints are routed through councillors (see p. 367). As for the police, this is a very sensitive area. By the nature of their work they are in a very exposed position (see p. 270). The procedure is outlined on p. 311.

The nationalised industries are in a somewhat different position since they are in fact hybrid bodies. Nevertheless there ought, in principle, to be some method whereby maladministration can be complained about and injustices prevented or rectified (see p. 186).

Maladministration

The term 'maladministration' is not defined in the 1967 Act, though in introducing the legislation the Minister (Richard Crossman) suggested that it included 'bias, neglect, inattention, delay, incompetence, ineptitude, perversity, turpitude and arbitrariness'. In addition the Select Committee has urged the PCA to find maladministration in decisions which appear to him to be 'thoroughly bad in quality' or 'clearly wrong'.

The following are *examples*: official error which led to accumulated tax arrears for which interest was demanded; similar Government properties being sold to tenants at arbitrarily different prices; error in handling application for war pension (which led to the payment of twenty years' arrears); failure to warn an individual of the procedure in the event of a driving licence being revoked on grounds of health; inadequate publicity for rights of compensation for depreciation in the value of homes affected by road works; delay in payment of child benefit for eleven months; a Jobcentre mistakenly told an ex-serviceman he was eligible for financial aid under the Employment Transfer Scheme; lack of proper care in advising someone on registration for VAT; undue delay in purchasing property for road construction purposes; undue delay in taking action against gypsies whose unauthorised occupation of Government land had adverse effects on a local neighbourhood; failure to apply the correct criteria in determining eligibility for house insulation against noise.

Apart from these routine cases, the PCA also draws Parliament's attention to particular issues by producing special reports. For example, in May 1968 he issued a Special Report on the *Sachsenhausen Case*. Certain British ex-prisoners of war (Servicemen) claimed compensation from the Foreign Office for exclusion from the Anglo-German relief fund set up for victims of the Nazis. The Foreign Secretary ruled that the claim was made too late and that no further money was available for the claimants. They complained through an MP who passed the application to the Commissioner for investigation. The Commissioner found there had been maladministration and submitted that funds should be provided to compensate the complainants. The Special Report was debated in the House of Commons and the Foreign Secretary said that although he did not accept the findings of

Table 11. Cases referred to the Parliamentary Commissioner for selected years

Year	Cases referred	Cases outside jurisdiction	Cases fully investigated	Maladministration* (no. and %)
1967	1,069	561	188	19 (10%)
1968	1,120	727	374	38 (10%)
1969	761	445	302	48 (16%)
1970	645	362	259	59 (23%)
1977	901	528	318	171 (57%)
1978	1,259	962	343	189 (55%)
1979	758	563	238	124 (56%)
1980	1,031	702	225	144 (63%)
1982	838	574	202	131 (65%)
1983	751	605	198	155 (78%)
1985	759	606	177	155 (87%)
1986	719	549	168	153 (91%)

* Including cases in which complaint not upheld but departmental action criticised.

the Commissioner as regards maladministration by the Foreign Office, he would act on the Commissioner's Report and make financial awards to the claimants.

Over the years of its operation, the distribution of complaints and declared maladministration has remained quite constant: the Inland Revenue and the Department of Health and Social Security receive by far the greatest number of valid complaints (about fifty each per annum in recent years). This is not surprising in view of their widespread and frequent dealings with the public and the complexity of their transactions. The Departments of Employment, Transport, Home Affairs, Environment and the Board of Customs and Excise manifest around five to ten cases of maladministration a year. (It should be noted that the PCA receives direct from the public a number of complaints equal to those referred by MPs. These are of course not acceptable.)

Appraisal

The first three PCAs were all ex-civil servants. Since then two have been from the legal profession, including the current incumbent, A. R. Barrowclough, who was appointed in 1984.

The general evaluation since the 1967 Act is that the PCA has an important office in the Constitution and he has performed his duties efficiently. On balance, his inquiries have not revealed widespread maladministration among Government Departments, and Ministers and the Civil Service have vindicated the belief that they are generally efficient and fair in the discharge of their duties. But his office might be more effective if there was more publicity, if it was made directly accessible and faced fewer excluded areas. (In 1981 the Government rejected the Select Committee's request that State personnel matters and Government contracts be de-classified. The Committee feared, for example, use of contracts as political weapons.) However, in a White Paper, Cmnd 9563, July 1985, the Government announced its intention (confirmed July 1987) of amending the 1967 Act to bring some 50 quangos (Government agencies) into the jurisdiction of the PCA. This had been urged by the Select Committee in 1984.

The Second Report of the Select Committee on the PCA (in 1986) again complained about restrictions on his jurisdiction which compelled him to turn away 80 per cent of the complaints made to him, many of which the Committee felt may well involve some injustice. But the Committee was more specifically concerned with the long delays by the Ombudsman in reporting, with the average time taken to report on a complaint being just over 12 months. It was felt to be unacceptable and was putting the credibility of the office at risk. (For critical review of PCA see *New Society*, 13 January 1983.)

The Health Service Commissioners

The *National Health Service* (*Reorganisation*) *Act, 1973*, makes provision for the appointment of Health Service Commissioners for (1) England, and (2) Wales, and (3) Scotland (a separate Act applies to Scotland). The three offices are held by the Parliamentary Commissioner.

The Health Service Commissioner is responsible for investigating complaints against the National Health Service authorities that are not dealt with by those authorities to the satisfaction of the complainant.

Complainants have **direct access** to the commissioner, but he will not investigate a complaint until he is satisfied that the Health authority concerned has had a reasonable opportunity to investigate it and to make a reply. If the complainant is still dissatisfied the Ombudsman will take up the case. When the patient is unable to act for himself in pursuit of his rights, another person can lay the complaint for him. However, the Ombudsman will *not* investigate complaints (i) that in his opinion relate to the exercise of **clinical judgement** by doctors and other staff, (ii) for which statutory procedures already exist, e.g. those about family doctors, dentists, pharmacists and opticians, which will continue to be dealt with under the family practitioner service procedure, (iii) which he thinks could reasonably be pursued through the courts or before a tribunal. (In his 1980 Report, the Commissioner called for the power to start investigations on his own initiative.)

In 1985–6, the Health Service Commissioner received a record 926 complaints, and on average complaints took 47 weeks to complete. Examples of grievances include a case of next of kin not being informed of the death and burial of a patient; extracting children's teeth without proper parental consent; non-availability of ambulances; inadequate consultation with local residents over the siting of a community home for discharged mentally handicapped adults.

Complaints against the Police

Complaints against a police officer by a member of the public may allege (*a*) a crime, or (*b*) irregularity of procedure or (*c*) incivility or other impropriety which may be an offence against the Police Discipline Code. The *Police Acts, 1964* and *1976* apply and the *Police and Criminal Evidence Act, 1984*.

In 1981, there were some 32,400 complaints against the police (in England and Wales). They may come via MPs, Citizen's Advice Bureaux and other bodies, or direct from the public (or perhaps even from the police themselves). Complaints must be recorded and (unless withdrawn) investigated.

The long-standing criticism of the procedure on complaints is that the police are themselves involved in the pursuance of the investigations and may therefore not be impartial or diligent. The *Police and Criminal Evidence Act, 1984* seeks to overcome this by introducing an independent element into the investigation of complaints in the form of the Police Complaints Authority (or PCA). This body, of some 14 lay people, appointed by the Home Secretary for a three year period, has the power to supervise police investigations (unlike the Police Complaints Board which the PCA replaced). The new scheme also introduced an informal conciliation procedure.

There are basically three categories or avenues of procedure in dealing with such complaints:

(*a*) Informal conciliation (for less serious cases).

(*b*) Full investigation (involving the PCA for serious and some inter-mediate cases).

(*c*) Full investigation leading to referral to the Director of Public Pro-secutions or DPP (for serious cases involving criminal charges).

Conciliation may occur where the Chief Constable (CC) considers the complaint to be minor in character e.g. discourtesy or inconsiderate be-haviour. Here he may seek an informal resolution such as an apology or an explanation.

More serious cases may be (i) investigated by the CC without reference to the PCA, (ii) referred by the CC to the PCA or (iii) not originally referred but subsequently called in by the PCA. Where the complaint is very serious (e.g. involving death or serious injury) it *must* be referred to the PCA. Where the PCA is involved, it will appoint the (independent) investigation officer and perhaps give instructions.

Following the inquiry, a report is sent to the PCA, to the officer com-plained of and the Chief Constable or his police authority. And, where a criminal offence is involved, a copy is sent to the DPP who will then decide whether criminal proceedings are to be brought before the courts in the normal way (e.g. as in the case of the mistaken shooting of Mrs Cherry Groce in 1986, the child John Shorthouse in 1985 or Stephen Waldorf in 1983. In all these cases the police officers were acquitted and did not have to face disciplinary charges).

On receipt of the report, the CC may decide (*a*) a criminal offence has been committed but no charge should be made or (*b*) no criminal offence has occurred. In either case, he must inform the PCA and state whether or not disciplinary charges are to be made. (The PCA can insist that they are made if it wishes.)

Where the investigation does not involve supervision by the PCA, the CC must send a copy of the investigation report to the PCA, which will then decide whether to refer the case to the DPP, and/or, if it wishes, insist on disciplinary charges being brought.

Disciplinary proceedings are held at a tribunal or at a hearing before the CC, and penalties may include dismissal; reduced pay or rank, fine, re-primand or caution. Of the 32,400 cases referred to above, 48 per cent were withdrawn and 47 per cent were unsubstantiated, leaving five per cent substantiated. There were 212 cases of disciplinary proceedings (not all arising from complaints by the public) and criminal proceedings in 39 cases (mostly motoring offences).

Traditionally the British police have been held in high esteem as an unarmed civilian force. However, they are in an exposed position in society and subject to the pressures and stresses all around them. There is a decline in the respect for authority generally; there is great instability in the modern family creating very complicated relationships for children; crime appears to be increasing and is certainly becoming more sophisti-cated.

In response the police have developed sophisticated methods for the detection and prevention of crime. We have mentioned telephone tapping (p. 283), which raises the issue of the balance between the security of the state and the liberties of the individual. The same question arises from the existence of the **police computer** which contains the names (over one million) and information on criminals, other offenders and, allegedly, many innocent people who are included through official error. It is sometimes suggested that people should have the statutory right to inspect and if necessary challenge these and other (e.g. medical, social security, social casework or creditworthiness) records by means of a Privacy or Databank Control Act. Some protection is afforded by the *Data Protection Act, 1984*, under which every computer system which processes personal, name-linked data (*except* those concerned with national security or crime investigation) has to register and comply with a code of practice, and citizens have right of access to the records held on them. (Another large area which is excluded is *manual* records e.g. medical, educational and social work. But the Access to Personal Files Act, 1987 (a private members Bill) allows more access now.

It is felt by many that recent events (e.g. the miners' strike 1984–5) have led to a greater centralisation of the police and their activities. Developments in technology (such as the police national computer) has contributed to this.

Another area of concern arises from the Government's proposals (in the Ministry of Defence Police Bill, February 1987) to extend the powers of the (5,000) Ministry of Defence police. Instead of their jurisdiction being confined, as previously, to an area of 15 miles around military establishments, it is planned to extend their powers throughout the country. Like the Metropolitan police, the MoD police are accountable only to a single Minister (the Secretary of State for Defence).

Of more immediate concern has been the number of deaths of people in police custody in recent years. In the period 1970–79 there were 274 such deaths. Of the twenty-six cases sent to the Director of Public Prosecutions, none was sent forward for prosecution. The public disquiet which this has caused prompted an investigation by the House of Commons' Select Committee on Home Affairs. Its report, in July 1980, concluded that there was no evidence to support a generalised accusation of police brutality towards people in custody. Although the police are subject to a stringent code of discipline, the Committee was unhappy at the amount of secrecy surrounding the investigation of complaints, including the way in which the DPP reaches his decision whether to prosecute. (The Police Complaints Authority is currently supervising a number of investigations following complaints against the Metropolitan police arising from the trouble outside the News International publishing plant at Wapping, East London, in January 1987 and the London abattoir robbery killings July 1987.)

Exercises

1. What reasons are advanced for the growth of delegated legislation?
2. What criticisms may be aimed at delegated legislation and what controls exist?
3. What are Administrative Tribunals and why do they exist?

314 British Constitution Made Simple

4. By what means may a Court of Law control Administrative Tribunals?

5. What are the Prerogative Orders issued by the QBD of the High Court?

6. What are Declaratory Judgements? Why are they useful?

7. State what you know of the *Tribunals and Inquiries Acts, 1958–71*.

8. Discuss the procedure of the PCA ('ombudsman') in the investigation of complaints.

9. Outline the procedure for dealing with complaints against the police.

10. Consider the suggestion that (i) the Police Complaints Authority should undertake police complaints inquiries rather than supervise such investigations as at present (ii) there should be local police complaints bodies.

11
Local Government

Introduction

Most civilised states have some form of local government, although theoretically it is possible for a central Government to administer all public services in the regions and in the local areas. In the United Kingdom there are local authorities (Councils) which are not part of the Civil Service but are local bodies which work in partnership with the central Government.

The structure of local government broadly is the same for England, Wales, and Scotland, the minor differences in regard to Scotland being due to historical reasons.

History of Local Government in England and Wales

It is important to know something of the history of local government in order to understand the present composition and the functions it performs in the British Constitution. There are four main periods of development of local government in the United Kingdom: local government before 1830; local government from 1830 to 1880; local government from 1880 to 1945; and local government from 1945 to the present.

Local Government before 1830

Before 1066 there were regional Kings, such as Alfred the Great (849–99), King of Wessex. In Anglo-Saxon times the country was divided into shires which were ruled or presided over by the sheriff who was the King's outpost officer or agent.

William I (1027–87) invaded the country in 1066, defeated the English, proclaimed himself King at Westminster and set up a strong central Government and unified the Kingdom. William I retained the office of sheriff which was useful in curbing the rebellious English feudal barons. The sheriff was appointed by the King and presided over the shire court, which was primarily an administrative body, maintaining local control, collecting the Royal revenues and paying these taxes over to the Monarch. The sheriff was also a judicial officer who decided civil and criminal disputes in the shire court where he was assisted by the bishop and the ealdormen. The sheriff was also responsible for military organisation; for keeping the King's peace and arresting those persons accused of crime; justice being administered according to the customary law of the English people. The sheriff in Norman times was a powerful figure, deriving authority from the Monarch himself.

The shires were divided into **hundreds** (an area of land) each under the control of the medieval hundredman. Below the hundred was the manor, the vill or small township.

The Boroughs. There were in Anglo-Saxon and Norman times certain Roman cities still inhabited; York, Chester, Winchester, and London, to name a few, and some new towns which sprang up as a defence against the Danes. Until the beginning of the twelfth century there was no separate form of government for these. The Monarch then began the practice of granting charters to the boroughs (townships), giving some of them corporate status which enabled them to organise some form of local government. The rights in the charters varied from borough to borough. Some boroughs were governed by guilds or companies of merchants (a comparison exists in the City of London today) and some were granted a special 'court' composed of favoured persons of the King, the privilege of attending court passing lineally from father to son. Sometimes a borough was honoured by having its own sheriff. Elsewhere in the shires the sheriff was the important figure.

The Decline of the Sheriff. In many areas the sheriffs were oppressive, which caused disquiet and unrest, and in 1327 Edward II created **Conservators of the Peace** (Justices of the Peace) from among the knights of the shires. Their duties were to preserve the peace and to administer a primitive police system by the appointment of a Constable or Head Constable to act as the executive officer of the Justices, arresting those people accused of a crime, and executing the Justices' warrants and orders.

The Justices of the Peace, as they came to be called, grew in importance and power as the local controllers and judicial officers primarily responsible for maintaining peace and good order. They were leaders in the localities, were efficient and as their power and prestige grew that of the sheriffs declined. The office of sheriff still exists today, but the holders of this ancient office now carry out only formal and nominal duties.

The Justices of the Peace. The feudal system began to decay in the thirteenth and fourteenth centuries and the changes in the social structure caused labour troubles and much poverty. The magistrates were empowered by law to regulate wages. Where the highways fell into disrepair the magistrates were empowered to maintain them and the *Statute of Bridges, 1530*, authorised JPs to compel landowners or corporations to repair them. At the same time, the *Highways Act* empowered the JPs to appoint surveyors to each parish to ensure that the inhabitants repaired the roads and bridges.

In 1563 the first Poor Law made contributions for the relief of the poor compulsory. In 1601, the *Poor Law Act* made each parish responsible for providing work for the unemployed and for giving poor relief. The officials responsible for seeing that the law was carried out were the churchwardens and the **Overseers of the Poor**, who were given the power to tax all the inhabitants of the parishes for the relief of the poor. These officials acted under the control of the JPs, who were authorised by statute to levy a 'poor rate' (tax). The Parish Vestry was the meeting place of the local leaders responsible for the elementary and basic duties of local government.

In the boroughs control was vested in the corporations. JPs were nominated to their posts by the corporations, but the appointments were made by the Crown. Their responsibilities were the same as those of the county JPs, i.e. local order, highways, and relief of the poor.

The Industrial Revolution. From 1750 the Industrial Revolution changed the country from an agricultural to an industrial society. Large urban areas grew apace as people left the land and their agricultural work for industry and the industrial towns of the midlands and the north. The existing local government in the towns, operated by the JPs and the corporations, was quite inadequate to cope with the bad social conditions which industrialisation brought in its train: the factories were insanitary; there was poor housing, unemployment, and poverty.

Some boroughs obtained local Acts to ensure the towns were paved, lit, and policed, sometimes a local Act empowered a corporation to build a hospital; but, generally, the local services were quite inadequate to cope with the problems of ill health, poverty, and the high death rate among young people which resulted from the industrial changes taking place. In the early nineteenth century there were no local services for public health; no arrangement for the care and needs of special groups such as children, the sick and the elderly, no adequate police to cope with the prevalent crime and there were no fire-brigades.

Local Government: 1830–1880

The Change in Thinking. Robert Owen (1771–1858) and Thomas Paine (1737–1809) preached against the existing conditions in society. Later Thomas Carlyle (the writer); Benjamin Disraeli (the politician); John and Charles Wesley (the religious leaders) and members of the Established Church agitated with Lord Shaftesbury for legislation to reduce the misery of the Industrial Revolution.

Jeremy Bentham (1748–1832) also advocated changes in the law and the Government and preached the doctrine of **Utilitarianism**, i.e. that the test of good law was whether that law promoted the greatest happiness of the greatest number of people. If laws or government (central or local) failed in that test they were not good. Edwin Chadwick (1800–90) became a follower of Bentham and adopted utilitarianism as a philosophy. Chadwick held important Government posts and tried to improve conditions, particularly by changing the Poor Law. A Poor Law Commission was set up by the Government in 1831 which included Chadwick. The Report of the Commission resulted in the *Poor Law Act, 1834*. This Act provided:

(i) The Poor Law was to be administered by Local Boards of Guardians, elected by the local people. This was an important step forward in that local people (householders) elected local representatives.

(ii) The area of the Board was a 'union' of parishes, i.e. a convenient and efficient local area (several parishes joined or united) to serve the needs of people within that area.

(iii) The Board employed paid officials to do the work, who were controlled by the Guardians.

(iv) Poor Law Commissioners were appointed to ensure central control (i.e. from the central Government).

The Poor Law Commissioners could make orders, appoint paid officials, and inspect local administration. In effect, therefore, the Commission was the forerunner of the Ministries of the present century, responsible for the vast services administered by local government. The Commission was followed by (i) the Poor Law Board which in time became; (ii) the Local Government Board which subsequently became; (iii) the Ministry of Health which was succeeded by; (iv) the Ministry of Housing and Local Government and now; (v) the Department of the Environment.

At the same time that the Poor Law Commission was set up in 1831, the great *Reform Act of 1832* was passed, which greatly altered the political representation in Parliament (see p. 27).

The *Municipal Corporations Act, 1835*. This Act, the result of another Commission, introduced certain important changes in the boroughs, which were now agitating for reform:

(i) A municipal corporation was defined as a 'legal personification of the local community, represented by an elected council, and acting for, and responsible to, the inhabitants of the district'.

(ii) The vote was given to all rate-payers who resided within the area of the corporation for three years.

(iii) Council meetings were to be open to the public.

(iv) The council was empowered to appoint paid officials.

(v) Provision was made for levying a rate.

(vi) An annual audit of accounts was provided for.

(vii) Three-quarters of the council were elected by the householders and one quarter were nominated and elected by the councillors and were called **aldermen.**

The 1835 Act deprived the municipal council of the power to nominate the Justices: from that time the JPs of the boroughs were solely concerned with judicial work; while the councillors and aldermen performed the administrative work of local government. In 1888 the county justices were similarly deprived of their administrative functions in the local government of the counties and from then onwards they devoted themselves to judicial work in the county magistrates' courts and Quarter Sessions.

The defects of the *Municipal Corporations Act, 1835*, were that it did not apply to all urban areas; London was too large to be subject to the Act, and there was still left in the country 'a chaos of areas and a chaos of authorities'. If a borough wanted to extend its powers it had to promote a private Bill in Parliament. Central control was also defective and inadequate, except in the auditing of accounts.

In 1872 the corporations became Public Health Authorities, and in 1882 they were given powers to regulate roads and streets; drainage and sewage; public health; gas and water supply. In addition, some of the larger boroughs (such as Liverpool and Manchester), secured the passing of special statutes to enable them to deal with sanitation and unfit housing.

The Development of the Public Health Movement. In 1850 half the population of the country lived in towns, but by 1880 this number had increased to two-thirds. The early pioneering work of Edwin Chadwick, who was secretary of the Poor Law Commissioners, showed up the many defects in urban living and the inadequacies of local administration and the local authorities. He advocated enlarging the areas and authorities and granting increased powers to the local bodies. The *Public Health Act, 1848*, set up the General Health Board and local health boards in areas with high death rates. Some 670 of these local boards were established and designated as urban and rural sanitary authorities.

In 1868 the Royal Sanitary Commission was set up. This body reported in 1871, and recommended:

(i) That the numerous existing laws on public health matters should be consolidated in one or more Public Health Acts.

(ii) That the administration of the law be made uniform throughout the country, instead of depending on local initiative. The operation of the main powers should be compulsory, so that all areas should reach minimum standards in street cleansing, water supply and similar matters.

(iii) All local health powers should be the responsibility of one authority in each area, instead of being spread over several sets of authorities. The local authorities should be supervised by a central Government Department, on the lines of the Poor Law Board.

This Report was followed by the *Local Government Act of 1871*, which set up the central authority, the Local Government Board, and took over the powers of the other Government agencies. In 1872 the *Public Health Act* of that year set up local sanitary authorities for the whole country. The law was consolidated by the *Public Health Act, 1875*, which dealt with public health generally and also highways.

Under this revised system England and Wales were divided into sanitary districts: urban sanitary districts for the boroughs and rural sanitary districts for the Poor Law Unions. The authority, responsible for the administration of these local bodies, was the elected representatives in the urban districts, and the Poor Law Guardians in the rural districts. In the urban areas the sanitary authority was also responsible for highways.

Education was another service which needed attention. The Government took the view that education of the masses was not their responsibility. There were voluntary and religious bodies which ran schools and to which the Government made grants, but only a small number of children received any form of education, and it was not till the *Education Act, 1870*, that a move was made. The Act provided for the setting up of School Boards to provide education. The Boards were under the control of the Privy Council and were required to provide education of an elementary kind.

Local Government, 1880–1945

Between 1835 and 1888 there was a confusing number of authorities, each with their own separate power and function. It is true that in urban districts the health authority was also the highway authority and that the guardians of the poor were also responsible for public health in rural districts. Generally, however, the pattern was 'one service, one authority', and local government powers were distributed among various authorities: the Justices of the Peace, borough councils, sanitary authorities, poor law guardians, improvement commissioners, vestries and similar bodies. The areas for which each body was responsible varied and the consequence was a confusion in which order had to be restored. The first important change was brought about by the *Local Government Act, 1888.*

The *Local Government Act, 1888.* This important Act set up the county councils as elected bodies, applying the same kind of local self government as that found in the boroughs. The principal features of the Act were:

(i) **Transfer of Powers.** The powers of the JPs in Quarter Sessions were transferred to county councils, which were directly elected by the people.

(ii) **Areas.** The county councils were responsible for county areas which were retained.

(iii) **London.** A new London County was created from three geographical counties adjoining the Metropolis.

(iv) **Boroughs.** The largest boroughs, with populations of 150,000 and over, were excluded from the county council structure. These boroughs were called 'county boroughs' and became (like the county councils) multi-purpose authorities exercising all the local government functions for their areas, independent of the county. Some older boroughs with smaller populations than 150,000 agitated against the loss of borough status and against their being incorporated within the county councils. These boroughs were allowed to become 'county boroughs'. Altogether there were fifty-seven, four of which had populations of less than 50,000.

The *Local Government Act, 1894.* This Act completed the programme of local government reform by renaming the urban and rural sanitary districts, within the counties, **urban districts** and **rural districts**, and by putting them under the control of elected councils. There are no aldermen found in these elected councils. The district councils were given the powers of the former sanitary authorities (urban and district). The newly created urban and district councils took over the function of the highway boards which were then abolished.

The position of the parishes in the structure of local government declined after the loss of their poor law functions in 1834. The new 1894 Act created within the rural districts (i) **parish councils**, and (ii) parish meetings, both with limited powers.

With the passing of the 1894 Act, the pattern of local government was complete and the system lasted till 1972. The reformed system was based on elected councils, to which the responsibility of administering public services was entrusted. It was, however, impossible to remove all the *ad hoc* authorities at one sweep and some remain today. However, the functions of most of them were gradually taken over by the local councils. The last important one to disappear was the Poor Law Guardians, a body which was finally abolished by the *Local Government Act, 1929*, which transferred the duties to the county councils or county borough councils.

From 1894, therefore, there was a general enlargement of local services and responsibility transferred to the general-purpose or all-purpose authorities, e.g. the county councils, the county borough councils. The *Education Act, 1902*, enlarged the scope of the system of education in the United Kingdom and transferred responsibility from the School Boards, which were then abolished, to the county councils and county borough councils. Certain large urban districts within counties were, however, enabled to be an educational authority separate from the county.

The *Housing Act, 1919*, imposed on county district and county borough councils a duty to provide new houses for the working classes and, at the same time, the Act gave generous financial assistance for this purpose. Subsequent Housing Acts continued this principle, although the Government grants (subsidies) were restricted.

The *Housing and Town Planning Act, 1909*, gave urban local authorities an optional power to control town planning. From 1919 town planning became compulsory and today this aspect of local government work is very important indeed.

The *Rating and Valuation Act, 1925*. Rating, which was formerly dealt with by the Overseers, as a heritage of the Poor Law, was taken over by the borough, urban and rural district councils under the *Rating and Valuation Act, 1925*. The various rates, which had been levied, were consolidated in one general rate and this simplified financial procedure.

The *Local Government Act, 1933*. This Act was passed to consolidate the law relating to local government and was the first Act to contain all the provisions regarding the structure and constitution of local authorities outside London. Previous legislation passed in the 1880s was repealed.

Other important Acts passed around the same time were the *Housing Act, 1936*, the *Public Health Act, 1936*, and the *Food and Drugs Act, 1938*.

The new structure, as noted in the diagram (on page 324) exists, in broad outline, now, but the complex and confusing system of *ad hoc* authorities gave way to the general-purpose or multi-purpose authorities of today.

During the Second World War the United Kingdom was divided into regions for civil defence purposes, each under a Civil Defence Regional Commissioner responsible for co-ordination of the civil defence arrangements organised by individual local authorities. The fire service was nationalised during the war, but afterwards the counties and county boroughs were made responsible for the administration of the fire service.

Local Government, 1945–58

In 1944 the *Education Act* was passed which made provision for wider educational facilities ranging from nursery schools to colleges of further education and colleges of advanced technology.

In 1945 the Labour Government came to power and the nationalisation measures then enacted removed from local authority control the utilities, for example, gas and electricity.

The main aspects to be considered are: (1) the transfer of certain functions from the smaller local authorities to the larger; and (2) the transfer of functions away from local government to central Government Departments or new *ad hoc* bodies, and the preference for larger units for the new functions.

(1) Transfer of Functions to Major Authorities

The *Education Act of 1944* made the county councils and the county borough councils the educational authorities for the country. County districts lost their duties in relation to education, except that some were made **agents** of the county council. The reason for this transfer of duty was the knowledge that the provision of a wide range of schools, from nursery schools to Colleges of advanced technology, could only be undertaken by the larger authorities. A major service ought to be administered by major authorities. Moreover it was administratively more convenient to deal with only 140 education authorities rather than the many hundreds which existed independently before the 1944 Act.

The *National Health Service Act, 1946*, introduced a new set of local health services: home helps, vaccination and immunisation, health centres, and ambulances. Some of these services had previously been run in another form by the district councils, while others were new. The county councils and the county borough councils were made responsible for the services.

The National Fire Service was disbanded after the war, and, by the *Fire Services Act of 1947*, services were returned to the county councils' or county borough councils' control.

Similarly the *Police Act, 1946*, abolished some separate small police forces and absorbed them into the larger forces: examples of this were Penzance (Cornwall) and Tiverton (Devon), small towns with their own forces, which were incorporated into the forces of Cornwall and Devon respectively.

The *Town and Country Planning Act, 1947*, made county borough councils and county councils the planning authorities, but enabled the county councils to delegate power to county district councils, if they so wished.

The *Children Act, 1948*, placed on the county councils and the county boroughs responsibilities under this Act and, at the same time, deprived the county district authorities of their powers.

Similarly the *National Assistance Act, 1948*, more or less abolished the old Poor Law, leaving the few remaining local assistance (welfare) services with the county and county borough councils.

(2) Transfer of Functions from Local Government

After the Second World War it was felt that county councils and county boroughs were too small to administer certain services. Consequently the Government reverted to *ad hoc* authorities and transferred responsibility for certain services away from local government control.

(i) **Hospitals.** The hospital service was, under the *National Health Service Act, 1946*, transferred to Regional Hospital Boards, below which were the local Hospital Management Committees, both bodies being appointed by the Minister. A few services (e.g. the ambulance service) were left with local government.

(ii) **National Assistance.** The *National Assistance Act, 1948*, placed responsibility for public assistance on the National Assistance Board (below which were regional offices and local offices), which was controlled by the Minister. The Act took away from the local authorities the responsibilities for poor relief.

(iii) **Trading Undertakings.** Certain local authorities operated gas and electricity services for their areas. The *Electricity Act, 1947*, and the *Gas*

Act, 1948, nationalised both industries and created public corporations with responsibility allocated to Area Boards (see Public Corporations, p. 175).

(iv) **New Towns.** Most towns in the past grew up spontaneously for geographical or industrial reasons. The *New Towns Act, 1946*, provided for the establishment of new towns to relieve the congestion in certain over-populated urban areas. The Minister appoints members of a Development Corporation to start the work and when the town is built and completed it is transferred to local authority control.

(v) **Valuation for Rating.** The valuation of property for rating purposes has since 1601 been undertaken by the local authorities. The *Local Government Act, 1949*, transferred from local authorities to the Inland Revenue Department the duty of valuation of property and premises.

Therefore, after 1945 there was a conscious reduction in the functions traditionally performed by the local authorities by transferring certain of those duties to *ad hoc* authorities, by appropriating them to Government Departments, or Boards acting as agents of Government Departments.

At the same time, however, the local authorities enlarged certain of their services, particularly social services and the expansion of those services retained by local authorities involved closer central control by Ministers, operated mainly through:

(i) **Inspection.** For example, the educational service is a wide and important one. HM Inspectors are appointed at the Ministry whose task is to ensure uniformity of standards and efficiency in the expanded educational services.

(ii) **Appeals.** When decisions made by local authorities adversely affect the rights of citizens, provision is made for statutory appeals to be made to the Minister, for example, planning appeals. Similarly if a local authority wishes to clear slum dwellings or make new roads, a scheme is prepared, published locally and an appeal against this may be made to the Minister, who makes the final decision.

(iii) **Finance.** If local authorities wish to engage in capital projects, e.g. buildings, houses, and schools they must if they have insufficient finance, apply for loans or grants of money from the central Government. There is a great deal of dependence therefore, by local authorities on the central Government for grant aid for new projects, improvement of existing projects, buildings, services, etc. This dependence on central Government aid means that a closer watch, in the interests of national economy, must be kept on the local authorities to ensure that national policy, national planning and national standards are maintained. Ministry supervision by this budgetary control extends into the field of policy and administration. Inevitably, conflict arises between local authorities, who wish to initiate new schemes and the central Government, which must take account of its national, or regional, plan and the economy of the country as a whole. Tensions between the local authorities at the periphery and the central Government are endemic in all Governments.

Reversion. Whereas in the early nineteenth century this country had a range of *ad hoc* authorities dealing with specific services, by the end of the century there were a series of local authorities which took over practically all the *ad hoc* bodies and became **compendious** authorities. Since 1945, however, there has been a return to the idea of creating *ad hoc* bodies as the best means of administering certain functions (e.g. gas, electricity, hospitals) on a national or regional basis, by using the concept of the public corporation, agencies of Ministries, or by the Ministries taking over the functions themselves.

Changes. Apart altogether from changes which any Government may initiate there are social and economic forces operating on local authorities continuously. There are increases in population, for example. In 1871 the population of England and Wales was 23 million; in 1901, 31 million; in 1931, 40 million, and in 1961 there were 46 million people. Moreover, people have tended to move from the country to the towns. As a consequence urban areas have grown and increased their revenue; rural areas have declined and correspondingly lost their revenue from the ratepayers, who left for the larger towns. The cities and larger towns have extended their boundaries into the counties.

The advent of the motor-car during the past fifty years has increased the ease of transport, communications and quicker supervision by central authorities of outlying authorities. It has also meant more pollution (a pressing problem) and road accidents on an increasing scale (7,000 killed per annum, and 400,000 injured).

Post-war measures of reform have included the establishment of the Local Boundary Commission set up in 1945; Local Government Commissions for England and Wales, set up in 1958; and the Royal Commission on Local Government in the Greater London Area, set up in 1957, which resulted in the *London Government Act, 1963*, and the setting up of new authorities.

Principal Types of Local Authority: 1972

The main pattern of local government organisation in England and Wales continued in existence until 1 April 1974.

Fig. 24. Local government structure (up to 1974)

The Greater London Area will be discussed later (see below) The rest of the country is divided into: (i) **county boroughs;** and (ii) **administrative counties.**

The above diagram may appear to indicate a fairly straightforward and rational organisation. However, in 1966 a Royal Commission was set up (see p. 327), and reported in 1969. Eventually the *Local Government Act, 1972* (running to some 450 pages), was passed which brought about far-reaching reforms. We shall consider in the following pages the structure and functions of local government as it applies today following the important changes which took place in 1974 and more recently. The effective date for the change-over from the former authorities to the present was 1 April 1974, a landmark in the history of the country.

London Government

The administration of local government in London has always differed from other parts of England and Wales, partly for historic reasons, but mainly because London is the capital city, the centre of trade and commerce and is such a large unit.

Briefly the London County Council (which ceased to exist on 1 April 1965) was established, with other county councils, by the *Local Government Act, 1888.* Its constitution, powers and duties were consolidated in the *London Government Act, 1939.* A Royal Commission was set up to review the system and working of local government in London and its Report (*Cmnd. 1164*) was issued in October 1960. A White Paper (London Government Proposals for Reorganisation (*Cmnd. 1562*)) was published in 1961, which endorsed the Commission's overall design and subsequently the *London Government Act, 1963,* established a new structure.

The Greater London Council and thirty-two London Borough Councils were constituted under the Act of 1963. In 1965 they replaced the London County Council, the Middlesex County Council, the County Borough Councils of Croydon, East Ham and West Ham, twenty-eight metropolitan boroughs, thirty-nine non-county boroughs and fifteen urban district councils. The boundaries and constitution of the Corporation of the City of London were not affected.

Under the Act, Greater London became for the first time a clearly defined local government area. Greater London had a population estimated in 1969 at 7,703,410, and an area of 610 square miles, including, in addition to the former counties of London and the greater part of Middlesex, parts of Metropolitan Essex, Kent, Surrey and Hertfordshire.

The Greater London Council consisted of one hundred councillors and sixteen aldermen. Elections were held every third year and for the first three elections in April 1964, 1967, and 1970, the electoral areas were the thirty-two London boroughs, each returning two, three or four councillors, according to the size of the electorate.

Aldermen existed up to 1976. They were chosen by the councillors and held office for six years, half their number retiring every third year. The Chairman, Vice-Chairman, and Deputy Chairman were elected annually by the councillors (and aldermen). The political head of the administration was the Leader of the Council, elected by the majority party. The GLC was responsible for:

(*a*) Ambulance service
(*b*) Traffic control
(*c*) Fire service
(*d*) Vehicle licensing
(*e*) Housing (major projects and estates inherited from LCC)
(*f*) Main highways (metropolitan roads)
(*g*) Main sewers and disposal works
(*h*) Planning (overall development plan)
(*i*) Certain parks, later to be transferred to Boroughs

Each of the thirty-two **London Borough Councils** consists of a mayor and a (differing) number of councillors. In 1965 they were given the following responsibilities:

(*a*) Housing
(*b*) Highways (other than metropolitan roads)
(*c*) Libraries
(*d*) Education
(*e*) Parks
(*f*) Lighting
(*g*) Local health and welfare and child care
(*h*) Planning (subordinate to overall GLC planning)
(*i*) Sewers (except main sewers)
(*j*) Public health (including refuse collection and street cleaning)

Abolition of the GLC

Under the *Local Government Act, 1985*, the Great London Council (along with the six Metropolitan County Councils) was abolished in 1986, on the grounds that it lacked functions and was therefore unnecessary. It also regularly spent beyond the Government's guidelines. As a result its responsibilities were reallocated, with most of them going to the Boroughs (often, by law, under joint or co-operative arrangements e.g. for refuse disposal). Fire and civil defence functions have been transferred to statutory joint boards (consisting of Borough councillors).

While education has been a responsibility of most of the London Boroughs since 1965, for an area corresponding with the area of the twelve inner London Boroughs (and the City), a special body was created in that year to provide education. This was the Inner London Education Authority (or ILEA). It consisted of nominees drawn from each of the inner London Borough councils together with members of the GLC who came from those Boroughs. The latter representation has now ceased (with the abolition of the GLC) and members of the ILEA are now separately elected, every four years (though the continued existence of the ILEA is now in doubt as some Boroughs may opt out).

The City Corporation

Lying at the very heart of the metropolis occupying one square mile is the

City of London (the centre of the financial world, banking interests, Fleet St., St. Paul's, the Law Courts). It has a unique place in the constitution, mainly due to its history and is unlike any other local authority in England and Wales. The full title of the City Corporation is **Mayor and Commonalty and Citizens of the City of London.**

The City Corporation acts through three courts: (i) The Court of Common Hall, consisting of the Lord Mayor, the sheriffs, the aldermen, and such of the liverymen of the City Companies (of which there are seventy) as are freemen of the City; (ii) the Court of Aldermen, consisting of the twenty-five aldermen, and (iii) the Court of Common Council, which is a legislative and deliberative assembly, consists of the Lord Mayor, the aldermen, and the common councilmen.

The Lord Mayor is nominated by the liverymen of the City Companies and is elected by the Court of Aldermen to hold office for one year. During his term of office, he is, ex officio, a member of the Privy Council. He presides over the meetings of the Corporation, attends to the civic and ceremonial duties and dispenses hospitality on behalf of the City Corporation. The Lord Mayor receives a salary to help towards his substantial expenses.

The aldermen are elected for life by the ratepayers and inhabitants of the twenty-five wards in the City. The common councilmen are elected annually by the same voters who elect the aldermen, in different proportions for each ward. There are now 139 councilmen.

The City Corporation was not affected by the reorganisation of the GLC and the London Boroughs or by abolition of the GLC.

Local Government Reform: 1969–72

Introduction

In 1966 a Royal Commission on Local Government Reform was set up under the Chairmanship of Lord Redcliffe-Maud. The Commission comprised eleven members and its terms of reference were:

> To consider the structure of local government in England, outside Greater London, in relation to its existing functions; and to make recommendations for authorities and boundaries, and for functions and their division, having regard to the size and character of areas in which these can be most effectively exercised and the need to sustain a viable system of local democracy; and to report.

The Commission presented its report to Parliament in June 1969. The Commission took written and oral evidence from over 2,000 witnesses and its published report ran to two volumes and contained 650 pages.

In February 1970 the Labour Government having accepted and studied it then made its proposals in a White Paper *Reform of Local Government in England (Cmnd. 4276)*. This broadly accepted the conclusions of the Royal Commission's Report, subject to a number of minor exceptions. The Labour Government reserved its position on the idea of Provincial Councils until the Report of the **Royal Commission on the Constitution** (i.e.

regional devolution) had been received. The Chairman of this Commission was the late Lord Crowther.

In June 1970 the Conservative Government came to power having pledged itself to 'a sensible measure of local government reform, which will involve a genuine devolution of power from the central Government and will provide for the existence of a two-tier structure'.

In February 1971 the Conservative Government presented its White Paper *Local Government in England* (*Cmnd. 4584*). In October 1971 the Conservative Government introduced a Local Government Bill which found expression in the *Local Government Act, 1972*, the main provisions of which will be considered later at page 334.

The Redcliffe-Maud Proposals

Only the briefest outline can be given here of the Report:

(*1*) *Main Recommendations*

The Royal Commission recommended replacing the present structure of local government. Its main proposals were:

(*a*) There should be sixty-one new local government areas.

(*b*) Fifty-eight of these areas should be governed by single-tier authorities, called unitary authorities.

(*c*) In the three areas surrounding (1) Birmingham, (2) Liverpool, and (3) Manchester, there should be a two-tier system, divided between major or metropolitan authorities, and second-tier metropolitan districts. There should be twenty metropolitan districts: seven for Birmingham, four for Liverpool, and nine for Manchester.

(*d*) The sixty-one new areas (see (*a*) above), together with Greater London, should be formed into eight provinces, each with a provincial council. These provincial councils would be in part elected by the unitary and metropolitan authorities (and in the SE province by the Greater London Council) and in part co-opted. The functions of provincial councils would be concerned with provincial strategy, economic planning, and economic and social development in co-operation with the central Government. They would replace the existing regional economic planning councils.

(*e*) Within the unitary areas, local councils should be elected to represent the areas of the existing county and non-county borough, urban district and parish councils (in metropolitan districts local councils would be elected where the inhabitants wanted them). Their duty would be to represent local opinion; they would have the right to be consulted on matters of special and local interest; and they would have powers to do a number of things best done locally. Subject to agreement of the major authorities, it should be possible for local councils to play some part in major services.

(*2*) *Ideas Underlying Recommendations*

(a) Defects of Existing Structure

The Commission suggested there were four basic faults in the existing structure (i.e. before 1971):

(i) The failure of the existing areas to meet the present needs of the country.

(ii) The impracticability of separating town and country when planning development and transportation.

(iii) The present fragmentation of the administration of services.

(iv) The small size of many authorities, which prevents them employing the more highly qualified manpower and technical equipment which a modern world calls for.

Because of these faults the Commission were of the opinion that few people bother to vote at local elections (thirty to forty per cent on average).

(b) The Purpose of Local Government

The Commission stated that the purpose of local government is fourfold:

(i) To perform efficiently a wide range of profoundly important tasks concerned with the safety, health and well-being of people in different localities.

(ii) To attract and hold the interest of its citizens.

(iii) To deal with national government in a valid partnership.

(iv) To adapt itself continuously to changes in the way people live, work, move, shop and enjoy themselves.

(c) How New Areas Were Determined

The Commission tried to achieve a balance between a number of considerations in recommending their areas. It followed a number of general principles:

(i) The areas should be so formed that within them there is a community of interest.

(ii) There must be interdependence between town and country.

(iii) All environmental services must be the responsibility of one authority. The same applies to personal services (as recommended by the **Seebohm Committee**). Wherever possible, these authorities should be the same.

(iv) To have the resources and manpower needed to meet the requirements of modern living, authorities must be bigger. To operate satisfactory personal services a local authority would require a population of between 250,000 and 1,000,000.

(v) Where it is impracticable for environmental and personal services to be in the hands of one authority, there must be a clear division of responsibility and related matters must be dealt with by the same authority.

(d) Advantages of Proposed System

The Commission believed their proposed new system of local government would provide four main advantages:

(i) Better services would be available.

(ii) Better use of resources.

(iii) New authorities would be more adaptable to the changing needs of society.

(iv) With a shift of power from central Government to the new local authorities there would be a strengthening of democracy.

(e) Local Democracy

On this question the Commission said:

If we are not willing to face the pains involved the prospect for local government is bleak. Local governors under the present system, we are convinced, cannot grapple effectively with their problems; this indeed was generally admitted to us. Already the odds against success are heavy, but present problems are not going to stand still. Their weight gathers momentum every year. During the next decade, unless the system is reformed, local government will be increasingly discredited and will gradually be replaced by agencies of central Government.

Reorganisation of the system will make heavy demands on present local governors, both council members and their officers. Many of them, while accepting that some reorganisation is needed, will disagree with our particular proposals. Most of them will regret disturbance of their own local authority. But if they believe that local government should have a long and fruitful future, can they resist the logic of the need for drastic and immediate change? Will not such change give them a better chance of serving effectively as local governors in years to come? There is room, of course, for endless argument about **what** change; no one knows that better than we do. But we believe that our analysis points conclusively to the new system we propose.

Throughout the course of our enquiry we have become steadily more convinced that a powerful system of local government can in some crucial ways enhance the quality of English national life. The whole Commission is unanimous in its conviction that, if the present local government system is drastically reformed, its scope extended to include functions now in the hands of nominated bodies, and the grip of central Government relaxed, England can become a more efficient, democratic and humane society.

The Commission then made recommendations on (*a*) the functions of major authorities (metropolitan authorities and metropolitan district councils); (*b*) the administration of the major authorities, and their relationship to local councils and provincial councils, whose powers were also described; (*c*) finance; (*d*) electoral system; (*e*) the mechanics of reorganisation.

One member of the Commission, Derek Senior, disagreed with the recommendations in certain major respects, and his report with his counter-proposals appeared at the end of the main report. Its details cannot be examined here.

The foregoing comments apply only to England. But Wales and Northern Ireland were similar to England in respect of local government. And it was the opinion of many (including the Government of the day) that each of these countries should broadly follow suit if any real reform of local government was to take place.

Scotland was subject to a separate Royal Commission inquiry. When it reported in 1969 it too recommended fewer and larger local authorities. Its proposals were implemented in the *Local Government (Scotland) Act, 1973* (see p. 337).

The Government White Paper: Government Proposals for Reorganisation. (Cmnd. 4584), 1971

In 1971 the structure of local government in England was largely that which was bequeathed to us by the legislation of 1888 and 1894. Then there were no motor-cars on our roads; no electricity in our homes; and the population of England was less than 28 millions. Reorganisation of local government has been under discussion for the past twenty-five years and its reorganisation was now felt to be urgent.

We have already referred to the reform of London Government and to the Royal Commission under Lord Redcliffe-Maud. The Government (and the other two major parties) pledged themselves to reform. The Conservative Party pledged themselves to introduce a system of two-tier government rationalising the operation of the various functions. Local government provides vital services on which the quality of social and economic life depends. It is an essential part of the whole democratic framework of Government. Naturally the findings of the Redcliffe-Maud Commission's Report were carefully considered together with Mr Senior's dissenting memorandum.

The pace of change and the scale of technological control over that change is such that men and women in local government can influence the environment in which they and their children will live in a way that has never been open to previous generations. The Conservative Government were determined to return power to those people who should exercise decisions locally, and to ensure that local government is given every opportunity to take that initiative and responsibility effectively, speedily and with vigour.

The Government recognised that the areas of many of the existing authorities were outdated. The division between counties and county boroughs had prolonged an artificial separation of big towns from surrounding hinterlands for functions whose planning and administration need to embrace both town and country. It recognised:

(i) There were too many authorities.
(ii) Many were too small in area and too small in resources to support the operation of services to the standards which people expect today.
(iii) The division of responsibilities between authorities is, in some fields, confusing and illogical.

The Government recognised that 'local democracy' meant that authorities must be given real functions—with powers of decision and the ability to take action without being subjected to excessive regulation by central Government through financial and other controls.

Local authority areas should be related to areas within which people had a common interest—through living in a recognisable community, through the links of employment, shopping or social activities, or through history and tradition.

The Government recognised there were advantages in simplicity and intelligibility in making the structure of local government uniform throughout the country. No one structure can be suitable equally for the densely and sparsely populated areas.

Concentrating authority for all services in the hands of one authority in each area has similar advantages and makes for coherence of administration. But it carries the grave penalty that if such areas are to be large enough for some services they will be too large for others. The theoretical

New counties for England and Wales
(as from 1st April 1974)

County	——————
Metropolitan County	�
Region	— — — — —
Island authority	—·—·—·—·

Fig. 25. Local authority areas in Great Britain (*Crown Copyright*)
Note: Though the Metropolitan County Councils were abolished in 1986, the county areas and names remain in existence.

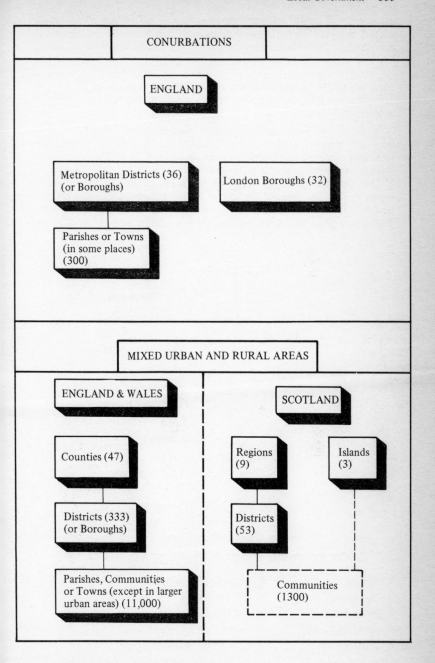

Fig. 26. Structure of local authorities since 1986

advantages of radical restructuring must be weighed against the advantages of building on the existing well-established organisations and minimising the disorganisation of services during the period of transition.

Structure of the Local Authorities in England and Wales from 1974

1. Principal Councils

(*a*) Following the Local Government Act, 1972, from April 1974, England and Wales (outside Greater London, see p. 326) was divided into local government areas known as **counties**. Within these counties there are local government areas known as **districts**.

The counties are largely based on the areas of the 1972 counties, but they absorbed the areas of the former county boroughs. The new counties bound together all of the urban and rural districts within their boundaries and, where possible, the former county boundaries were retained to pre-

Greater Manchester Metropolitan County
Greater Manchester Metropolitan District Councils: 1–10

1 Wigan MDC	6 Manchester MDC
2 Bolton MDC	7 Oldham MDC
3 Bury MDC	8 Trafford MDC
4 Rochdale MDC	9 Tameside MDC
5 Salford MDC	10 Stockport MDC

Fig. 27. Structure of a metropolitan county showing metropolitan district councils

serve existing loyalties and to lessen the administrative problems of transition. Some of the former names have disappeared from the list, e.g. Westmorland, and some new ones have been added, e.g. Avon, Cleveland, Cumbria. In total there are now 39 county councils in England (plus 8 county councils in Wales) and 296 district councils (together with 37 in Wales).

Although there are two tiers—counties and districts—the Act did not intend that one shall be answerable to the other. Each is independent with its own statutory functions.

(b) In addition, from 1974 to 1986, there were, in England, 6 **metropolitan counties.** Within these metropolitan counties were 36 **metropolitan districts** (or boroughs).

Metropolitan Counties

Greater Manchester	(10)	Tyne and Wear	(5)
Merseyside	(5)	West Midlands	(7)
South Yorkshire	(4)	West Yorkshire	(5)

The figures in brackets indicate the number of Metropolitan Districts (or Metropolitan Boroughs) within each metropolitan county.

Under the *Local Government Act, 1985*, the metropolitan county councils were abolished (along with the GLC). However, the metropolitan boroughs (districts) remain and have inherited many of the counties' functions (see p. 336).

2. Parishes

Rural parishes existing immediately before 1 April 1974 remained in existence after that date. Provision was made under the Act (s. 47) for the creation of new parishes in urban areas and the abolition of former parishes. The parishes may have either parish councils or parish meetings, and may deal with local matters, maintenance of burial grounds, footpaths, and discussion of matters as they affect the parish.

3. Local Government Boundary Commission for England

A Boundary Commission is established under the Act (s. 46). It began its work in 1971, under the chairmanship of Sir Edmund Compton. The Department of Environment invited local authorities to make representations or proposals on the future pattern of districts. Guidelines for the Boundary Commission were laid down stating that district populations should preferably be in the range 75,000–100,000. However, it was accepted that in sparsely populated areas populations might fall to 40,000 or fewer. The Commission was advised that where possible the identity of large towns should be retained.

The question of boundaries almost always gives rise to controversy. The Commissioners had, therefore, to hear the evidence, assess its worth, and try to persuade local authorities to reach local agreement. If that failed the Commission would offer its advice to the Secretary of State for decision.

The Commissioners' recommendations on the new boundaries were accepted by the Government. As noted, the 296 new districts in non-metropolitan counties replace the 953 county boroughs, boroughs, and urban and rural district councils existing before 1 April 1974. Of the 296 districts there are 14 which have populations below 40,000 and 104 with populations between 75,000 and 100,000. The average population of a district now is 90,000 as compared with 28,000 before 1 April 1974.

The Boundary Commission is a permanent body whose duty it is regularly to review the areas of counties and districts and their electoral arrangements. It is empowered to make recommendations to the Secretary of State for the alteration of local government areas, for abolishing, creating, and amalgamating authorities and for granting or withdrawing metropolitan status.

4. Borough Status and Civic Dignities

The Act provided for the new Districts to apply for a Royal Charter of incorporation. The council of districts granted a charter are known as the council of the borough and the chairman and vice-chairman are entitled to the style of mayor and deputy mayor of the borough. Thus the civic dignities attached to borough status are preserved. It is important, however, to note that the granting of borough status is of ceremonial significance; it does not create a second or more privileged council at district level.

5. The Advantages of the New Structure

The main advantages of the 1974 structure were claimed to be:

(i) The reduction in the number of English local authorities from over 1200 to 411 (including Greater London and the six new metropolitan counties).

(ii) Local government areas are larger in size, resources and population. The average population of the new districts is 90,000 compared with 28,000 before 1 April 1974.

(iii) The vast conurbations (six at present outside London) have special problems. The metropolitan counties with the 36 metropolitan districts were created to meet those problems and needs.

(iv) The interdependence of town and country is acknowledged and the disadvantages of the former dual (urban and rural) system eradicated.

(v) The areas have been rationalised in the light of the realities of modern living, e.g. roads, cars, mobility.

Parishes

The *Local Government Act, 1972*, lays down that a district council *must* establish a separate parish council if either:

(a) the parish has 200 or more local government electors; or
(b) there are 150 or more but less than 200 electors and the parish meeting so resolve.

If there are less than 150 electors, the district council *may* establish a parish council following a resolution of the parish meeting.

The minimum number of parish councillors (to constitute a parish council) is five and there is no upper limit. The number is fixed 'from time to time' by the district council within which the parish lies.

A parish council or a parish meeting may make a request for boundary review direct to the Boundary Commission (see p. 335) and it may also ask for the electoral arrangements to be reviewed.

Parish councils must hold at least four meetings a year, one being the Annual Meeting. The council may authorise committees or officers to discharge their functions and may appoint committees jointly with other local authorities. Members of the public and Press are entitled to be present at both council and committee meetings, but may be excluded by resolution if their presence would prejudice the public interest. The council may no longer exclude the public by simply going 'into committee'.

General responsibilities include maintenance of burial grounds, footpaths, bridle-paths, and similar matters of local importance.

Wales and the Local Government Act, 1972

In Wales, since 1974 there are now 8 counties and 37 districts, replacing the former 181 local authorities.

The division of functions between Welsh county and district authorities is broadly the same as that which operates outside the metropolitan counties in England. The main exceptions are that: (1) Welsh district councils are responsible for refuse disposal as well as refuse collection; (2) district councils may be designated to exercise library, weights and measures, trade descriptions, and food and drugs functions.

Communities. At a more local level than the districts, 'communities' are created throughout Wales, many of which have councils with powers broadly equivalent to those of former parish councils. Community councils also have concurrent powers with the districts relating to allotments, cemeteries and crematoria, public baths, swimming baths and washhouses. They also have powers relating to museums and art galleries, parks and playing fields.

The main differences between England and Wales are in the allocation of functions and in the introduction of communities in Wales, instead of parishes.

Scotland

Under the *Local Government (Scotland) Act, 1973* (operative 1975), the old structure of local government in Scotland was swept away. It had consisted of a mixture of counties, cities, burghs and districts; 480 authorities in total. They were replaced by a simplified two-tier structure comprising Regional and District Councils and the single-tier Island Councils; 65 in all.

This reorganisation was the result of the Report of the **Royal Commission on Local Government in Scotland**, 1966–69, under the chairmanship of Lord Wheatley. The Commission's findings and principles were very similar to those of the Redcliffe-Maud Report (see p. 328), but it differed in concluding that a clear two-tier structure was appropriate for Scotland. In practice, of course, the reorganisation in England and Wales was not so very different either in terms of structure or in the distribution of functions.

One particular area of difference should be noted. Whilst **'community councils'** have been established in Scotland, they differ from parish and community councils in England and Wales in that they are not a third tier of local government as such and they have no statutory functions. They complement local government through the process of assessing and expressing local opinion. There are about 1,300 such councils.

Northern Ireland

Local government in Ulster was reformed under the *Local Government (Boundaries) Act (NI), 1971*, and the *Local Government Act (NI), 1972*, both of which were influenced by the **Report of the Review Body on Local Government in Northern Ireland, 1970** (the Macrory Report). Under the legislation the former sixty-six local authorities were replaced by a new single-tier structure of twenty-six district authorities. At the same time responsibility for administering many of the more important services, formerly provided by local authorities (e.g. education, health), was transferred to Ministries of the Northern Ireland Government at Stormont; their administration would normally be carried out either through local offices of the Ministries concerned, or through nominated area boards responsible to them. However, direct rule from Westminster since 1972 (see p. 4) has complicated this situation.

Functions of Authorities

Allocation of Functions

County councils	District councils
Education	Passenger Transport
Personal Social services	Planning (local plans and control)
Libraries	Road maintenance (urban unclassified)
Planning:	Housing (including clearance and improvement)
Structure plans	Building regulations
Acquisition and disposal of land for planning purposes	Environmental health (clean air, food, safety, nuisance, slaughterhouses, shops and offices legislation, port health, refuse collection and sewers)
Highway authorities, Traffic and Transport co-ordination	Museums and galleries [1]
Housing (certain reserve powers, e.g. for overspill)	Parks and open spaces [1]
Consumer protection:	Playing fields and swimming baths [1]
Weights and measures	Cemeteries and crematoria
Food and drugs	
Refuse disposal	
Museums and art galleries [1]	
Parks and open spaces [1]	
Playing fields and swimming baths [1]	
Police	
Fire	

Metropolitan borough/district councils
As for district councils *plus* education, libraries and personal social services. In 1986, when the Metropolitan County Councils were abolished, the Metropolitan Boroughs inherited many of their functions, viz. planning, highways and traffic management, waste disposal, consumer protection. But the responsibility for police, fire, civil defence and public transport was instead transferred to joint authorities (or boards).

Scottish regions (and islands)[2]	*Scottish districts (and islands)*[2]
Broadly as for county councils *plus* public transport, water and sewerage, *minus* libraries, refuse disposal	Broadly as for district councils *plus* libraries, refuse disposal, *minus* public transport, and (in three regions) planning and libraries

[1] Concurrent powers exercisable by county councils and district councils.
[2] Islands councils undertake most functions (except in the Highland region).

Note: in Wales districts have refuse disposal functions and may also exercise libraries, weights and measure, and food and drugs functions.

Note on the Allocation of Functions

The district councils describe areas within counties outside the conurbations. Their powers are different from the metropolitan district councils (like Birmingham or Liverpool). In the conurbations, the metropolitan districts have the major functions (apart from the joint boards'); outside the conurbations the counties have the major functions.

There is within this framework a greater flexibility for the authorities, e.g. for sharing operations differently, by mutual 'agency' agreements etc.

Education. Includes the provision of nursery, primary and secondary education; further education (including technical and art colleges); adult education; school meals; pupils' transport; award of student grants; education of handicapped children.

Education is the responsibility of county councils and metropolitan district councils. Joint committees covering facilities like polytechnics which serve adjoining local authority areas are allowed (e.g. under the *Education Act, 1944*).

Town and Country Planning. Preparation of development plans, indicating land use (for housing, industry, recreation, open spaces, agriculture, roads); control of development; applications for planning permission; tree preservation; control of outdoor advertising.

Major planning (structure plans) are undertaken by counties and metropolitan districts, local planning (including planning applications) by districts and metropolitan districts.

Housing. Includes provision and management of local authority housing, housing improvement grants and schemes for 'general improvement areas' (that is, improvement of environment as well as houses); housing for the homeless; slum clearance.

Districts and metropolitan districts will run local authority housing and take over responsibility for housing homeless people. Special housing for staff remains with the employing authority. Counties and metropolitan districts provide rent officer service and rent assessment.

Personal Social Services. Includes domiciliary services; services for mentally ill and handicapped; services for physically handicapped (including social work support, domiciliary services, employment assistance, and transport); residential homes (for children in care, at special schools and community homes); residential accommodation for the elderly; provision of housing for the homeless. Here counties and metropolitan districts take on responsibility.

Where delegation to subcommittees applies, powers may be varied (e.g. decisions on the siting of buildings may be made at subcommittee meetings). Management of gipsy caravan sites is a district and metropolitan district council responsibility, but county councils can act as agents. District councils and counties consult about housing for the infirm and disabled and provision for homeless falls to district councils.

Environmental Health. Includes food safety and hygiene; communicable diseases; refuse collection and disposal; clean air; home safety; conditions in offices, shops, and factories; diseases of animals; slaughterhouses; public lavatories. These are retained by district and metropolitan districts. Animal diseases are the responsibility of counties and metropolitan districts. Refuse functions, formerly within the districts, are now divided: districts and metropolitan districts being responsible for collection of refuse, and counties and metropolitan districts for its disposal. Any local authority may sort and bale waste paper collected separately from other refuse. Subject to consent of the appropriate highway authority, all local authorities may provide public lavatories.

Traffic, Transport, Highways. Includes new roads and improvements to existing ones; traffic regulations (e.g. waiting restrictions and pedestrian crossings); rights of way; highway maintenance; road safety; parking; street lighting.

The highway authority is the county or metropolitan district council. Non-metropolitan Districts and metropolitan districts may opt for agency functions on certain urban roads (carrying out certain responsibilities as agents of the county) or partnership arrangement (acting within an area on decisions jointly taken). All districts' basic powers are limited: maintenance of footpaths; bridleways and urban roads other than trunk or classified roads. Disposal and removal of abandoned vehicles is the responsibility in England of county and district councils, and in Wales that of district councils.

Consumer Protection. Includes weights and measures responsibilities, such as checking goods sold in shops; testing weighbridges and petrol pumps; test weighing bagged fuel such as coal; trade descriptions in respect of goods and services; provision of advice to shoppers; sampling for analysis of foods, drinks, and drugs.

County and metropolitan district authorities are responsible in England; district councils (where orders are made by the Secretary of State) or counties in Wales. Consumer advice services may be set up by the appropriate authority. Arrangements for food and drugs services are rationalised with counties and metropolitan districts responsible for questions of quality; districts and metropolitan districts for matters relating to hygiene, food, conditions in shops, etc.

Police and Fire. Includes local police and fire brigade functions. Counties and metropolitan boroughs are responsible, with an increasing tendency towards combinations with neighbours in joint forces (e.g. Thames Valley Police Force), responsible to joint committees comprising local authority representatives (two thirds) and magistrates (one third), to use manpower and technical resources more effectively. Joint boards are mandatory (since 1986) in the areas of the former Metropolitan counties.

Libraries. County councils and metropolitan districts will run libraries. Some district councils in Wales may be designated to do so.

Museums and Art Galleries. County and/or district councils are able to provide these facilities.

Youth Employment. Service taken over by local education authorities (counties and metropolitan districts). Also known as **Careers Service**.

Swimming Baths, Parks, Open Spaces and Recreational Training. Can be provided by county and district authorities as the need arises. Basically these services are the responsibility of districts and metropolitan districts.

Coast Protection. Responsibility of district councils.

Cemeteries and Crematoria. Responsibility of district councils.

Emergencies. County councils and district councils have a new general power enabling them to take immediate action to avert or cope with an emergency or disaster in their area, e.g. an aircraft crash on a town, a railway disaster, a reservoir bursting banks, severe flooding involving loss of life and homes. The Police Service is the co-ordinating service in these cases where immediate action of rescue and preservation of life and property is concerned.

The explosion at a chemical plant making caprolactam (an ingredient of nylon) at Flixborough, near Scunthorpe, on 1 June 1974, in which 29 lives were lost, emphasises the need for a general power to meet emergencies of this kind. Local authorities also have contingency plans in the event of war.

Loss of Functions

Health Services. From 1 April 1974, the local health services formerly provided by local government—for example, the general supportive services such as home nursing, home helps, health visiting, and the ambulance service—were transferred to the new Area Health Authorities. These bodies, replaced by 201 District Health Authorities in 1982, are not therefore part of local government.

The advantage of bringing together the whole of the fragmented field of health care under the responsibility of one authority is obvious to all. The health authority is now able to define priorities and organise its responsibilities in the way best suited to its particular area.

There is a close link between the social services of local government and the health services, and it is fortunate that the boundaries of the new health authorities broadly coincide with the local authority areas.

Water Services. The Government has replaced former joint water boards and sewerage boards by 10 regional water authorities. These authorities are now responsible for water conservation, water quality control, navigation and recreational functions of the former river authorities. The regional authorities are also responsible for the water supply and sewage disposal functions of local authorities in England and Wales (*Water Act, 1973*).

Constitution of Local Authorities

All local authorities are, or act on behalf of, corporate bodies; that is, they are corporations or legal persons in their own right. They may, for example, own property, enter into contracts and sue or be sued in their legal corporate name. Another distinctive feature of the corporation is that it continues to exist independently of the persons who for the time being compose it. A corporation never dies, it has been said; it must be killed—usually by the revocation of the charter which created it or by Act of Parliament.

For every county and for every district there shall be a council consisting of the chairman and councillors; and the council shall have all such functions as are vested in them by the *Local Government Act, 1972* (s. 21) and *1985*. Each council is a body corporate by the name 'The County Council' or 'The District Council' with the addition of the name of the particular county or district, e.g. The Avon County Council, The Sedgemoor District Council.

The first duty of the council on election is the election of a Chairman and a Vice-Chairman. Each may be paid sums of money enabling him to meet the expenses of his office. The amount is such allowance as the council thinks reasonable. In the event of an equality of votes in a council meeting the chairman shall give a casting vote in addition to any other vote he may have.

Who are the Councillors?

Most readers do not know the names of the local councillors representing them, such is the lack of interest in local government. Surveys into local government by two separate committees (Robinson 1976, and Widdicombe, 1986) showed that the average age of our 25,000 councillors is above that of the population generally, with 50 per cent of councillors being at least 54 and less than 10 per cent under 35. Councillors are atypical in other ways: only 1 in 5 (19 per cent) is female; 25 per cent are retired; nearly 7 out of 10 (66 per cent) are or have been involved in non-manual occupations (and may thus be regarded as non-working class); generally councillors are better educated than the average of the population and the youngest councillors have obtained most academic qualifications; 85 per cent of councillors are home-owners (c.f. 57 per cent of the population).

Further, a survey in 1964 for the Maud Committee showed that councillors tended to be relatively immobile, with nearly two thirds having lived in the area they represented for twenty-five years. Most councillors are active in community affairs and are members of political parties or other representative local bodies.

It has been fashionable in recent years to decry the calibre of councillors. This is a difficult area in which to make meaningful assessments, though it is true that in some areas as many as 1 in 4 councillors have obtained their seat without a contest (see Tony Byrne, *Local Government in Britain*, Penguin, Chapter 6).

Allowances for Members

The new Act contains a code permitting county councillors and district councillors to claim a flat rate attendance allowance as of right in the performance of council business, without proof of loss of earnings. The allowance is taxable. Travelling and subsistence allowances on a reimbursement (non-taxable) basis are available. The amounts of the allowances are decided by each local authority within maxima prescribed by the Secretary of State (currently £16.00 per attendance). Additional payments may be made to leading members (e.g. committee chairmen).

Aldermen. All members of county councils and district councils are now directly elected. Aldermen who were formerly elected by the councillors from among their number occupied a special historic position in the council; but although many aldermen had served their communities well, they were not directly elected by the people themselves and to that extent their position was undemocratic in the opinion of many. The aldermen, who were usually over 65, hung on to office, reluctant to resign despite advancing years and declining powers, and were often elected in a 'party context'.

The *Local Government Act, 1972*, states that all county councils and all district councils are entitled to elect, as an honorary alderman, anyone who has given eminent service as a member of the authority or as a member of an existing authority superseded on reorganisation. The honour of 'honorary alderman' does not give the recipient any local government responsibilities or powers.

Local Government Electoral System

By the *Representation of the People Acts, 1949 and 1969*, any person is entitled to vote at a local government election provided that he or she is over 18 years of age, is a British subject or a citizen of the Irish Republic and is registered as a local government elector for the area for which the election is being held.

An officer of the district council (usually the Chief Executive Officer) is responsible for registration of electors and the conduct of both parliamentary and district council elections.

Electors

A person qualifies for registration as a local government elector if, on the qualifying date for the register, which is compiled annually, he or she is resident in the council area.

Voting takes place at polling stations arranged by the returning officer concerned and under the supervision of a presiding officer appointed for the purpose. The procedure for local government voting in the UK is similar to that of Parliamentary elections (except in Northern Ireland, where a proportional system is used). Postal voting, however, is more restricted. Each elector has one vote for each seat contested in the electoral area. He need not record all his votes, but must not give more than one vote for each candidate.

Candidates

A candidate for election as councillor normally stands as a representative of one of the national political parties, as a member of an association representing some local interest, or as an independent. He must be of British nationality and aged 21 years or over. He must also be registered as a local government elector in the register of electors for the area of the local authority to which he seeks election, or have resided (or have his principal place of work within that area (or within three miles of it) during the whole of the twelve months preceding the day on which he is nominated as a candidate.

Local authority areas are divided into electoral areas. Counties are divided into electoral divisions in accordance with orders made by the Home Secretary, the Minister for the Environment and the Secretary of State for Scotland. District councils are divided into wards. For district council elections or parish council elections, each ward or parish (sometimes a combination of parishes) forms an electoral area, which returns one or more members.

Under the 1972 Act, county councillors are elected on the basis of single-member electoral divisions. They will retire together every fourth year. District councillors are elected on the basis of wards, each returning three, or a multiple of three, members. One third of the councillors will retire at a time and there will be district elections in three years out of four—in those years when there are no county elections. Since 1975 all local government elections in any particular year are held on the same day. This is an improvement and should enable electors to be more aware of the date. It was hoped that this simplification would encourage a higher poll, but there has been no noticeable improvement and only about 40 per cent of voters on average make use of their democratic right.

Parish/community councillors all retire every fourth year. Parish/community elections are normally held on the same day as the district elections (1979 was an exception).

Disqualifications. The *Local Government Act, 1972*, lays down certain disqualifications for election as councillor. These include:

(i) A candidate must not be a paid employee of the council.
(ii) He must not be a bankrupt.
(iii) He must not have been found guilty of corrupt or illegal practices at a previous election: e.g. bribery (gifts, loans or promises of money to a voter to influence his vote); treating (e.g. to food and drink); undue influence; impersonation of another voter; making a false declaration of election expenditure.
(iv) A candidate must not have been convicted of an offence punishable

with three months' imprisonment or more without the option of a fine, during the last five years before the election.

(v) A candidate must not, as a member of a local authority, have been found by a Court of law to have incurred or authorised expenditure which is unlawful and exceeds £2,000

Where a serving councillor incurs any of these disqualifications he can no longer serve on the council and if he fails to attend for 6 months. The vacancy is then filled by holding a by-election.

Internal Organisation of Local Authorities

Local authorities are free to a large extent to make their own internal arrangements and to choose the means and methods by which they perform their duties and responsibilities.

Committee System

All councils (except perhaps some parish councils) use the committee system. The range of services administered by a local authority is too wide for a full council to deal with the entire work. The council resorts to committees to carry out or administer the various services, e.g. highways, planning, environmental health, estates, markets, and so on. Most councils now establish a Policy and Resources Committee (or its equivalent) which operates as a management committee (see p. 364).

Most councils have adopted the concept of a number of committees responsible for groups of functions of the council or 'programme areas' as they are called in the Bains' Report on Management (see p. 363). Some committees may be purely advisory committees or co-ordinating committees.

We shall deal later with the various kinds of committees. In general there was a substantial reduction in their number as a result of the reorganisation in April 1974.

Whatever re-structuring may take place, the fact remains that committees tend to be overburdened and any committee of the council may itself form sub-committees for particular purposes. The subcommittee stands to the parent committee in a relationship similar to that of the main committee to the full council.

Powers and Duties of Committees

The powers and duties of local authority committees are usually laid down in Statutes (e.g. Education Committee under the *Education Act, 1944*) or more usually in the appointing council's standing orders. A council is free to delegate all its powers to committees, subcommittees or officers (s. 101, *Local Government Act, 1972*). Certain powers in connection with (i) raising loans, (ii) levying rates, or (iii) making financial demands on other authorities (known as raising precepts in England and Wales) are excepted; these powers are reserved to the council as a whole.

Kinds of Committees

These are various kinds of committees detailed below.

Standing Committee. This type of committee is appointed each year for a particular service. Thus a district council may choose the title of Housing Committee or Development Committee, Policy and Resources Committee, etc. Such committees are permanent (hence standing) committees. However, this is entirely within the discretion of the authority.

Special Committee. This committee is appointed *ad hoc*, i.e. to perform a special task, such as to make arrangements for a Royal visit or centenary celebrations of a borough. Once the task allocated to the committee is accomplished the committee dissolves.

Statutory Committee. Certain Statutes make the appointment of some committees obligatory. These are:

(i) The *Education Act, 1944*, requires every county council to appoint an Education Committee.

(ii) The *Local Authorities Social Services Act, 1970*, requires every County Council to appoint a Social Services Committee.

(iii) The *Police Act, 1964*, requires the appointment of a Police Committee. This applies to county councils who may be amalgamated for police purposes (e.g. Thames Valley Police Force).

Under the *Local Government Act, 1972*, local authorities may appoint such other committees as they think fit.

Optional Committees. It follows from the above that much depends on the type of local authority, the area it services and the needs of the people. Although the intention is that the structure of committees will be on Programme Areas, there is bound to be devolution of power and function to subcommittees which will deal with special matters appertaining to that authority, e.g. Parks Committee, Markets Committee, Entertainments Committee. Such are optional committees set up at the discretion of the council.

Admission of Public and Press to Committee Meetings

Under the *Local Government Act, 1972* (s. 100), and (for Scotland) *1973* the public, including the Press, have a right to attend all committee meetings and meetings of the local authorities themselves. This right was strengthened under the *Local Government (Access to Information), Act 1985*, in that it provides for public access to sub-committees and council papers and records. However, the right to attend is subject to the qualification that the local authority or the committee may exclude the public and the Press on a specific occasion, e.g. for the discussion of confidential matters, staff promotions or defaults, property transactions of a confidential nature.

The Necessity of the Committee

The committee system is one of the chief characteristics of local government. It is difficult to see how a local authority could function without such a system. Parliament itself makes increasing use of the device.

The **advantages** of the committee system are:

Saving time. The setting up of a committee saves the time of the full council and it saves the time of individual councillors.

Specialisation. Councillors prefer the work of some committees to others. They become interested in special aspects (e.g. social services, education, amenities, etc.) and then tend to specialise. This imparts a degree of professionalism and skill in administration. A councillor gets to know the duties imposed by the council and by law, the resources of the local authority, the area affected and the people living there.

Atmosphere. Full council meetings tend to be unduly formal and stiff. Committees, which usually sit in an informal atmosphere, encourage a freer exchange of views that makes for more efficient administration.

Smaller Numbers. Committees of twelve or fewer are found, in practice, to be more efficient and deal with more business than large, unwieldy groups.

Contact with Officials. A relaxed atmosphere and informality tend to make for easier relations with officials. Fruitful and beneficial administration is brought about when there is full co-operation between the councillors and the professional local government officer or specialist.

To the above advantages may be added the following which the Maud Committee considered:

(i) They lead to a better chance of the right decision being taken.
(ii) They lead to wider participation in the work of the authority.
(iii) They represent wider interests.
(iv) They safeguard against bureaucracy and unresponsive administration.
(v) They keep officers in close touch with political and public opinion.

The **disadvantages** of the committee system are summarised below.

Critics of the system point to the delays in getting people together; to the proliferation of subcommittees; to the encouragement of paper work—'red tape' and bureaucracy—all of which tend to slow down the machine. They contrast the business world where quick decisions, some vital, have to be made at once and 'red tape' eliminated. There is also the danger that the chairmanships of committees are awarded for party political reasons rather than on grounds of merit and personal ability and integrity. Co-option (i.e. selecting non-elected outsiders to be members) can be operated to the disadvantage of the local authority and the public.

Officers and Employees

The *Local Government Act, 1972*, s. 112, states that local authorities are permitted to appoint 'such officers as they think necessary' for the proper discharge of their functions.

Formerly, certain statutes laid down that local authorities had to appoint specified officers (e.g. Medical Officers of Health). Those statutes ceased to have effect from 1 April 1974, with the following exceptions, who must be appointed by law:

(i) Chief Education Officers (s. 88, *Education Act, 1944*) and the Chief Education Officer of the Inner London Authority.

(ii) Chief Officers and members of fire brigades (*Fire Services Act, 1947*).

(iii) Directors of Social Services (s. 6, *Local Authority Social Services Act, 1970*).

(iv) Public Analysts (*Food and Drugs Act, 1955*).

(v) Agricultural Analysts and Deputy Agricultural Analysts (*Agriculture Act, 1970*).

(vi) Inspectors of Weights and Measures (s. 41, *Weights and Measures Act, 1963*).

(vii) Chief Police Officers (*Police Act, 1964*).

The Minister may also be concerned with these officers' appointment and dismissal. He is concerned to ensure that in each case a suitably qualified person is appointed, and in the fields of education and the social services the central government oversees the administration of these two services, which occupy a vital part in the lives of all. The central government ensures that counties appoint statutory committees for education and social services.

The Bains Working Group argued against the compulsion of local authorities to appoint specified officers. It was felt that this militated against the introduction of the most suitable management structures. Local authorities were now encouraged to be independent and as the councils were composed of men and women of responsibility, they should be given the power to hire and fire similar to that of other independent organisations. The Bains Working Group did not see the need to obtain Ministerial approval for the appointment of certain officers, e.g. the Chief Police Officer, Director of Social Services. The local authorities were capable of selecting persons of the right qualifications and calibre and the approval of the Minister was superfluous.

The contrary view, however, is that in some authorities there had been an element of prejudice or nepotism, and it is right that central control or approval of the appointment and dismissal of certain vital officers be retained (see p. 358). In practice, the Minister rarely interferes with the appointment made locally unless there is something obviously amiss.

In 1987 there were 2.25 million full-time or equivalent local government employees in Britain. They fall into three main categories: (i) heads of department or chief officers: (ii) professional, clerical or technical; and (iii) manual workers who perform the physical work for which the council is responsible, e.g. roadsweepers, gardeners, park keepers, etc.

The appointments of senior staff are usually made by the committee particularly concerned. Junior appointments may be made by heads of departments either alone or in consultation with a personnel officer. Methods vary between councils, but control is maintained by a local authority committee and all appointments and engagements are made in conformity with the council's agreed establishment.

Rates of pay and conditions of service for local authority staff are within the jurisdiction of the employing council. The pay and conditions are based on recommendations made by **Whitley Councils**, of which the largest is the National Joint Council for Local Authorities' Administrators, Professional, Technical and Clerical Services and the National Joint Council for Local Authorities' Services (Manual Workers). Conditions of service and salary scales for senior local government officers are determined by separate joint committees for England and Wales, and for Scotland, Northern Ireland has its own joint negotiating machinery at various levels.

All local government officers are expected to maintain a high standard of conduct. As public servants they 'must be honest in fact, but must be beyond the reach of the suspicion of dishonesty'. Like the Civil Service, the local authorities' staffs are not corrupt in the main, despite the instances which were widely broadcast in relation to contracts in the North-East in 1974 the Poulson affair).. There are few criminal charges brought against officials whether of high or low rank, and the public generally has confidence in local administration.

Delegation to Officers. Under s. 101 of the *Local Government Act, 1972*, local authorities have the right to delegate: 'A local authority may arrange for the discharge of any of their functions (a) by a committee, a sub-committee or an officer of the authority; or (b) by any other authority.'

The local authority itself remains liable for any wrongs committed by the committee, officer or other authority to whom the power to act has been given. This provision merely legalises what had been the practice in the past. Clearly certain decisions, issue of licences, grant of planning approval for minor development, should be within the province of competent staff who can apply formal procedures. It is for the council itself to determine what matters should be delegated to the staff of all ranks. As the work of local authorities becomes more complex and far-reaching the delegation to officers will inevitably increase, though the responsibility remains with the council.

Personnel Management. Because local authorities are now one of the largest employers in any area it follows that the greatest use should be made of one of their major resources, namely manpower. The Bains Working Group suggested that the 'Establishment' title should give way to the more widely accepted and used 'Personnel Management'.

The working group recommended that the head of personnel should be given the status of a chief officer, and that other chief officers should accept and act on his advice in matters of personnel management, in the same way that they (other chief officers) acted upon the advice of the Treasurer in finance matters. Moreover the Personnel Officer should have direct access to the Chief Executive Officer.

Chief Executive. The Chief Officer of a Ministry of the Central Government is the Permanent Under-Secretary of State. The chief officer of a local authority is now known as the Chief Executive Officer, whether of a county or district council, and he is head of the authority's paid service. The Bains Working Group recommended that he be free of departmental responsibilities, that he lead a team of chief officers and that he secure the overall co-ordination and control at officer level.

Job specification. As chief executive officer he would

1. Have authority over all other officers so far as this is needed for the efficient management and execution of the council's functions. He is, in short, *the chief*.

2. Be *leader* of the officers' *management team*, and through the Policy and Resources Committee, be the *principal adviser* on matters of *general policy*.

3. Be responsible for securing the best advice on the *forward planning of objectives and services*, and to lead the management team in securing a *corporate approach* to the local authority's affairs generally.

4. Secure efficient and effective *implementation* of the council's *programme* and policies and secure that the *resources* of the authority are most *efficiently deployed* to those ends.

5. Keep under *review the organisation and administration* of the authority itself; *make recommendations* (through the Policy and Resources Committee) to the Council if major changes are required for *effective management*.

6. Be responsible to ensure *manpower policies* are developed and implemented in all departments of the authority in the interests of (a) the authority, and (b) the staff.

7. Be responsible for good *internal and external relations*.

It follows from the above that any such appointee should possess outstanding managerial ability, skills, and personality.

Fig. 28. Chief Officers' management team (for average non-metropolitan district)

Councillors v. Officials?

The relationship between members of a council and the staff is crucial to the working of the new authorities. The Bains Working Group stated that 'neither members nor officers can regard any area of the authority's work and administration as exclusively theirs'. The Group confirmed the view of the Maud Committee on Management, which exploded as a myth the belief that **policy** was a matter solely for elected representatives and **administration** a matter for officers. The Bains group pleaded for a **corporate** approach. It added that a 'them and us' attitude between members and officers fostered distrust and dissipated effectiveness.

The question of who runs whom, and the role of the elected member *vis-à-vis* the officers and staff is a perennial one. Mr R. G. E. Peggie, in a paper to the Local Authorities Management Services' Advisory Committee

(LAMSAC) in 1971, stated that the elected member '. . . should be concerned to ensure that the machine works, but he should not be required to operate it himself.'

The rôle of the elected member can be described as:

(i) *deliberative*. As a member of the council he should have the opportunity to discuss and decide policy and priorities.

(ii) *control*. As part of the council he should have effective control of the organisation carrying out the work of that body.

(iii) *representative*. As an elected member for an area he is concerned with the affairs of the people he represents.

Clearly the object of becoming a councillor is to achieve power, to exercise it in the interest of the community and to get things done. A councillor may be a director or manager of a company; he may run his own business skilfully and well; he may be more efficient than any local government officer could hope to be. Such a person will not readily subserve an official of a local authority by whatever name called. He may argue that either the council member is in charge (and responsible to his electors) or the official is. The same problem applies to an MP translated to a Ministry. Who runs whom?

There is no perfect system of management, and the problem of reconciling efficiency with democracy is a baffling one. The question resolves itself into a sensible compromise between members on the one hand and the officers on the other to achieve the best results for the locality and its citizenry, whose welfare and interests both should seek to promote.

Local Government Finance

In 1984 local authorities in the UK were spending £40,000 million a year. The sources of local authority income are: **government grants** (45 per cent); **local rates** (30 per cent); and **rents** from municipal houses, other **charges** (for home helps, bus fares, etc.), **dividends** and **interest** (25 per cent).

Government Grants

The first grants were made to local authorities in 1835 by the central Government on a specific and percentage basis, whereby the local authority paid one-half of the service and the central Government paid one-half. Under the *Local Government Act, 1929*, grants were made on a block (or general) basis. In order to assess the amount to be allocated to a local authority, the Government took into account (i) the size of the population of a district, weighted by the number of children under 5; (ii) a low rateable value; (iii) abnormal unemployment; and (iv) sparsity of population. *The Local Government Act, 1948*, brought back specific grants: and the *Local Government Act, 1958*, restored the general grant system (except in regard to certain special services, e.g. the police service where the percentage grant was retained).

The case for the **general** grant is that it gives a council a greater scope to make the best use of its money: a council wishing to devote more to housing than to roads or health measures may do so. The advocates of the **specific** grant argue that this system ensures that a hesitant, unimaginative and frugal council cannot cut a service too low and that this ensures the maintenance of all services at a high level of efficiency and quality. Both methods have merit, but the subject is somewhat a matter of party politics.

Capital expenditure is usually financed by borrowing (or currently by sale of assets, e.g. council houses). For some specific services, however, the Government pays capital grants to local authorities, e.g. roads and annual subsidies to local authority council housing.

Most Government grants are, however, revenue grants, which are related to local authority revenue expenditure (other than towards deficits on housing and trading accounts). These particular Government grants are payable, both in aid of revenues generally (hence they are called **rate support** grants) and for specific services such as police or rate rebates. In 1984 the Rate Support Grant to local authorities in England amounted to £9,000 million and the grants for specific services was £2,500 million (totalling a figure equivalent to 49 per cent of relevant local authority expenditure). The figures for Wales were: £876 million and £169 million (67 per cent); and for Scotland: £1,700 million and £247 million (56 per cent).

The Rate Support Grants are distributed among the various local authorities. The amount allocated to each authority is based on three points: (i) the **needs** element, which takes account of the total population and, in particular, the number of children of school age, together with supplementary payments which take account of the numbers of children under 5 and of adults over 65 years of age, the cost of various stages of education, the density of population and road mileage; (ii) the **resources** element, which is paid to authorities whose rateable resources are below the average for all authorities in relation to population; and (iii) the **domestic element** which compensates rating authorities for loss of rate income from reductions in rate poundage, which they are required to give to householders: in England 18.5p, Wales 18.5p and Scotland 7p (1987 figures). Under the *Local Government, Planning and Land Act, 1980*, the 'needs' and 'resources' elements were unified into what is now known as the **block grant**.

Rates

Rates are a local tax paid annually by the occupiers of property as a contribution towards the cost of local services provided by the local authority. (The only main class of property which is exempt from rates is agricultural land and agricultural buildings). Occasionally local authorities found it necessary to raise more money and thus levy a 'supplementary' rate, but in 1982 this power was abolished.

How, then, does one calculate the rates bill of a householder? The amount of each payment is calculated by multiplying the rate poundage (say 60p in the £), determined by the rating authority, by the rateable value of the property. The rateable value is based on or reflects the rental value of the property in the open market. It is assessed in respect of land and buildings by Valuation Officers of the Board of Inland Revenue, who are independent of the local authorities. The last valuation lists were compiled in 1973 in England and Wales, 1985 in Scotland. Where a tenant wishes to dispute the assessment of his house, building or land, he applies to have his case heard by a local valuation court. The court consists of three members of an independent local valuation panel. If he is not satisfied then a tenant may appeal to the Land Tribunal.

Rate Rebates. Where householders have small incomes, they may apply to the local authority for rate rebates, and if their application is successful they will pay less than the normal rate, whereas commercial and industrial properties are assessed higher than ordinary householders. Charities pay only half the full rate on their property which is used for charitable purposes, but further reliefs may be allowed by the rating authority. A rating authority also has the power to reduce or remit the rates for a wide range of non-profit-making bodies. Half the rates may be levied on the owners of all empty premises. Where a tenant so wishes, he may pay his rates in ten instalments a year.

Levying and Collection of Rates. In England and Wales the responsibility for levying and collecting rates lies with the district councils. In the metropolis the London Borough Councils are responsible (and in the City of London, the Common Council is the responsible authority).

The rate poundage for each county district consists mainly of a district rate and a county rate (or precept), calculated in accordance with the requirements of the two authorities (i.e. the county council and the district council). The county rate is passed on to the county council following collection by the district councils. In districts the rate levied in each parish or community takes into account precepts issued by the parish or community council or parish meeting.

The same broad principles also apply in Scotland and Northern Ireland though there are differences in the names of the assessors, courts and rating lists.

Control by Central Government

Reasons for Control

'The interests of the local areas must be subservient to the interests of the nation as a whole, and so there must be control from the centre to achieve the dominance of this interest' (Jeremy Bentham). Central control by the Government over local authorities may be justified on the following grounds:

(i) *Minimum Standards.* Certain essential services, such as health, education, police, fire service, cannot be allowed to fall below a certain minimum standard in the public interest.

(ii) *Finance.* Local services are costly, and where the central Government provides grants or financial aid it is justified in expecting the local authorities to provide satisfactory services. Moreover, the central Government bears a responsibility to the taxpayer who ultimately 'foots the bill'.

(iii) *Providing Expertise.* The central Government has greater technical resources, more knowledge and data, and a greater number of specialist and technical advisers. Local authorities are encouraged to take advantage of these resources in providing the public services for which they are responsible.

(iv) *Preventing Corruption.* Central control assists in the prevention of corruption, e.g. fraud by councillors or officials, or the misuse of powers which are vested in such officials as chief officers of police. Audit of accounts, Government inquiries and inspection by HM Inspectors assist in preventing illegal or corrupt practices by local authorities, their officials, or their members.

Forms of Control

Central control over local authorities assumes three forms: **legislative**, **administrative**, and **judicial**.

1. **Legislative Control.** All local authorities are created by statute. They owe their existence to statute (*Local Government Act, 1972*) and as corporate bodies they may act only under powers given by law, i.e. statute law made by Parliament. So where a local authority provides any of the essential services, such as housing, refuse collection, public health services, police and fire services, it must do so under authority of a statute. It must also ensure that it acts within the powers granted. Otherwise, it infringes the *ultra vires* rule. These statutes providing the services mentioned are known as *Public General Acts* which Parliament passes in the interest of the whole nation. The *Local Government Act, 1972*, is an important one in this regard.

The *Public General Acts* may (i) impose a **duty** on a local authority, or (ii) give it **permissive** power. The essential difference between these is that in (i) a local authority **must comply** with the law imposed by statute, whereas in (ii) a local authority may use its discretion, whether to adopt the power or provide the service which the particular Act permits.

Adoptive Acts is the name given to those statutes which are passed by Parliament but which permit the local authority to adopt at its discretion. In general Adoptive Acts enable progressive authorities which want to provide some extra service for their inhabitants to do so. Essential services, i.e. those which all local authorities must provide, are called **mandatory**.

Certain authorities find that existing legislation is, nevertheless, inadequate for them. Any such authority may seek to promote a **Private Local Bill** to obtain the necessary legal authority for its particular purpose. Private Bill procedure follows a special course in the legislative process and has been described on page 100. The procedure to promote a Private Bill is laid down in the *Local Government Act, 1972*. Certain preliminary steps must be taken: (i) a resolution must be passed by the whole council; (ii) the approval of the Minister for the Environment must be obtained; (iii) the Bill must be deposited at the House of Commons; (iv) in the case of a district council a public meeting of all the electors must be held to consider the promotion of the Bill. If the electors vote against the Bill it must be withdrawn. If the Bill proceeds to the Commons the procedure follows that described on page 106.

An alternative means of acquiring legislative powers for a proposal by a local authority is to apply for a **Provisional Order**. This is a simpler and less expensive method and involves an application to the Minister for an Order. The Minister holds an inquiry and, if satisfied that it is in the public interest of the locality, may make an Order, which must be confirmed by Parliament before it takes effect. Usually several Provisional Orders, from various authorities, are presented together to Parliament in a Provisional Orders Confirmation Bill which passes through Parliament in the usual way. As it has the approval of the Minister before inclusion in the Confirmation Bill its passage is normally assured without undue difficulty. A Parliamentary Committee considers the Bill, similar to the committee which adjudicates on a Private Bill.

Statutory Instruments are important means of control. Certain statutes empower a Minister to make regulations (see p. 286). These regulations are made on grounds of urgency and technicality of subject-matter to carry into effect a service, which the central Government places on local authorities. The statutory instruments are enforceable in the courts equally with statutes.

2. **Administrative Control.** Granted there is justification for central control over local authorities, the question arises how that control is carried out.

Statutory Control. Certain statutes impose a duty on a Minister. The *Education Act, 1944*, imposes a duty on the Secretary of State for Education and Science of promoting:

the education of the people of England and Wales and the progressive development of institutions devoted to that purpose, and to secure the effective execution by local authorities under his control and direction, of the national policy for providing a varied and comprehensive education service in every area.

Similar powers and duties are imposed on the Home Secretary under the *Police Act, 1964*, to ensure that the Police Committees, on which local authorities are represented, provide an adequate police force for their areas (see p. 273).

The Minister of the Department responsible for a particular service writes **circulars** of advice (e.g. explaining legislation), to local authorities indicating how the rules should be interpreted and the spirit in which they should be enforced. These circulars sometimes contain indications of policy. The Minister from time to time requires from local authorities returns, indicating e.g. the number of houses being built, the number of teachers employed in particular types of schools, the cost of school meals, the details of fire brigade equipment owned, the number of police recruits enrolled and the number of resignations, retirements, etc., from various services. These circulars keep the Government Department in touch with the local authorities who, for their part, may request information and advice from the Ministry. The general atmosphere, in which this relationship is carried on, is courteous and polite and a spirit of partnership is engendered.

Financial Control. Loans may be raised by local authorities to finance capital expenditure. They may do this under powers of a general statute or of a Private Act having local application. For expenditure in key sectors such as education, housing and roads, local authorities in England and Wales must obtain approval from the government department concerned before raising loans. For other capital expenditure, each authority receives an annual authorisation within which it determines what sums to borrow and what projects to undertake. In Scotland and Ulster the government department responsible for the service also issues the appropriate capital expenditure approvals.

Local authorities may raise long-term loans by means of private mortgages, and by issuing stock on the Stock Exchange and bonds which may or may not be quoted on the Stock Exchange. The bonds may be for any periods, though local authorities normally issue them for one year. Local authorities have a right to apply to the Public Works Loan Board, financed by the Exchequer, or, in Northern Ireland, to the Government Loans Fund, for long-term borrowing to finance a proportion of their reckonable capital payments, and may borrow temporarily for a limited proportion of their current outstanding loan debt.

A finance committee, appointed by a local authority, is charged with the function of keeping the financial policy of the council under constant review. However, following reorganisation in April 1974, local authorities in England and Wales are not required to appoint a finance committee (though some will continue to do so) but the authorities have to make proper arrangements for the administration of their financial affairs. These accounts are open for public inspection and are subject to that special form of control called audit which we consider next.

Audit. The accounts of all local authorities are made up annually, usually to 31 March. These accounts are subject to audit and checking by district auditors, appointed by the semi-independent **Audit Commission** (see p. 370). The **district auditors** are independent officers in the exercise of their powers and performance of duties conferred on them by statute.

Grants from Central Government to local authorities in the financial year 1984 amounted to nearly £16,500 million. Thus of the total amount of local government current expenditure (i.e. excluding capital) in that year the Government underwrote 45 per cent. With government aid comes government control, and one of these in the form of checking receipts and payments by local authorities is audit. District auditors were required to disallow every item of account which is contrary to the law (except for items sanctioned by the Secretary of State for the Environment), and to **surcharge** (or fine) the amount of any expenditure disallowed upon the person or persons responsible for incurring or authorising it. They could also surcharge upon the person responsible any item which had not been duly brought into account, or any item of loss or deficiency caused by negligence or misconduct (e.g. non-collection of rents). However, since 1974 the *Local Government Act, 1972*, abolished the district auditor's powers of disallowance and surcharge. He must now refer any question of the legality of payments to the Court for a ruling.

A citizen may still raise objections regarding the accounts before the district auditor, but instead of the auditor himself having the power of disallowance it will be for the Courts to decide whether or not a particular item of expenditure is legal. Thus a citizen can continue to enjoy the power of questioning the accounts, but he himself will not be burdened with the job of taking the matter to court. Important changes are occurring here (see pp. 369–71).

The power of surcharge is now therefore reserved for the Court which may make an order of restitution. The effect of this is the same as surcharge, but no order shall be made where the court is satisfied that the person concerned had acted reasonably or in the belief that the expenditure was authorised by law. The Court must also consider all the circumstances before ordering restitution, including a person's ability to pay. So members of councils and officers who have acted in good faith will not be penalised. Surcharging under the old scheme had, it was felt, an inhibiting effect on local authorities. Where there has been a failure to bring money into account or there has been loss of money, the district auditor will certify the amounts due to be repaid by the defaulting member or officer. Any appeal against the certificate of the auditor (or incidentally, any appeal by any citizen regarding the failure to issue such a certificate) will be for the Courts to decide.

Inquiry. Where a local authority proposes to take some action which may infringe the private rights of an individual or a section of the public generally, the Minister may hold a local inquiry to ascertain the facts, so that he may be able to make up his mind as to the most convenient course to take. Under the *Town and Country Planning Act, 1971*, an inquiry may be held where a Private Bill is promoted in Parliament. The Minister may wish to ascertain local feeling, for or against the measure, before coming to a decision. Where there is local disquiet over the efficiency of a particular service, such as the police, the Minister may appoint inspectors from his Department to visit the force and hold an inquiry to ascertain the facts, so that he can be assured that there is no corruption or inefficiency or maladministration. Some statutes provide for these inquiries, but where statutory powers do not exist a Minister may set up an inquiry of his own volition.

Inspection. The two services which have a notably strong inspectorate are (i) education, and (ii) the police. Inspectors of Education are 'the eyes and ears' of the Minister and visit all types of schools and colleges gathering ideas, co-ordinating schemes, advising principals, headmasters, and similar officials, and inspecting buildings and equipment to ensure that good standards are maintained. The Inspectors are, as it were, ambassadors sent out from the Ministry to ensure more efficient administration of the educational service. Formerly, these officials were looked upon with some awe and fear. Nowadays, they are regarded as helpful figures in the main, but they do have powers of control and can report adversely.

The police is a uniformed service, with rigid standards of discipline, and has a hierarchy of ranks. The powers of individual police officers have already been examined (see p. 272). The increasing number of crimes, the spread of vandalism, student riots, and similar social disturbances impose a great strain on the forces of law and order. The Inspectors of the Home Office visit each force at least once a year: again advising, co-ordinating, looking at new local experiments, inspecting the whole of the force of the area and sometimes visiting out-stations. The Inspectors make a report to the Minister, who may declare the particular force efficient and make the financial grant (one half) to the police authority.

Other Ministries have their inspectorates, and the Ministry of Agriculture and Fisheries is an important one. Essentially the same functions are carried out on behalf of the Minister, although the problems, such as

animal diseases, increasing food production, advising farmers, etc., are of
course, quite different.

Disputes between Authorities. Where a dispute arises between two local
authorities (e.g. between a district council and a county council (reference
to the Minister will settle the matter. By such means the Minister (a disinterested party) exercises a quasi-judicial control.

Approval of Schemes. Where a local authority embarks on a comprehensive scheme, e.g. slum clearance, or the construction of new roads
to ease the growing congestion in a town, a scheme is prepared which is
sent forward to the Ministry for approval. Frequently there have been
consultations before final submission so that the difficulties are ironed out
so far as possible before a final decision is made.

Default Powers. Some statutes empower a Minister to act in place of a
local authority where that authority is not fulfilling its tasks or performing
its duty. Thus, where a local education authority is not complying with the
Education Act, 1944, the Minister may declare the authority to be in default.

Early statutes empowered a Minister to make an **Order**, which was enforceable in the courts, compelling the authority to perform its duty. If the
authority failed to carry out its task the Minister could appoint some
person to do so in place of the defaulting local authority.

Where a duty in relation to public health is imposed on an authority,
which fails, in spite of an Order being made by the Minister, the members
of the defaulting local authority can be arrested. This is an extreme
measure, and rarely occurs.

The modern expedient, when a local authority is in default, is for the
Minister to transfer (by law) the functions of, say, a district council to the
county council. Where a county council defaults, the Minister may appoint members of his own Government Department to take over the
administration and carry out the task on behalf of the community. The
cost is charged to the defaulting authority.

Most local authorities are composed of sensible men and women and
prefer to negotiate their difficulties and to resolve matters amicably. Hence,
default powers are rarely used.

Appointment and Dismissal of Officers. While local authorities are free
to employ or dismiss their servants in the normal way (subject to the *Trade
Union and Labour Relations Act, 1974*) there are certain important staff
members who may only be appointed or dismissed by the local authority,
provided the Minister has given approval.

The appointment and dismissal of a Chief Constable must be approved
by the Home Secretary (the *Police Act, 1964*). This operates as a check on
the police authority. The Minister vets the names of applicants, and ensures
that a police authority does not dismiss a chief officer on frivolous or
unjust grounds. The *Local Authority Social Services Act, 1970*, empowers
the Minister to approve the appointment of Directors of Social Services.
Similarly, the *Education Act, 1944*, empowered the Minister to inspect the
list of applicants for the post of Chief Education Officer of a local education authority though this ceased in 1973.

It must not be assumed that Government Ministers operate the foregoing
list of controls autocratically. These are reserve powers: there to be used if

need be. Generally a spirit of **partnership** prevails, which involves mutual respect and a common desire to make the administrative machinery work smoothly and well, in a spirit of co-operation. This indeed is the spirit of democracy, which in the final analysis is quite as important as the letter of the law, and can be contrasted with the authoritarian control by the dictatorships.

3. **Judicial Control.** Local authorities are corporate bodies, created by statute and exercising powers conferred by statute. They are subject to the rule of law and can sue and be sued in the courts.

In the field of private law a local authority is subject particularly to the law of contract and the law of tort (e.g. nuisance, negligence, etc.).

Normally a local authority endeavours to act as a model person and complies with the law, but irregularities occur from time to time. In regard to the services or other function which a local authority is required to perform, a local authority may:

(i) Exceed the lawful powers of a statute. Where it does so it acts *ultra vires* (i.e. beyond its powers).

(ii) Fail to perform the service or functions required.

Where, therefore, any citizen or group of persons are prejudiced by the action, or inaction, of a local authority he or they have recourse to the Courts of Law to seek redress. Action is begun by taking out a writ against the local authority.

The various forms of control which exist are as follows:

(i) **Injunction.** An application may be made to the courts for an injunction restraining the local authority from proceeding on the course it proposes. The grounds for a successful application are usually that the local authority is acting *ultra vires* the statute under which it purports to be acting.

(ii) **Mandamus.** An application may similarly be made to the courts for an order of mandamus where it is averred that the local authority is not doing what it is required to do by law. Mandamus means 'we command' and the order is sufficient to secure compliance.

(iii) **Prohibition.** This order may be sought where a local authority threatens to perform some act which it has no legal power to do, or threatens or proposes to do some lawful act in an **unlawful manner.**

These three special forms exist in addition to the ordinary right to sue or prosecute a local authority. It is necessary to bear in mind that recourse to law indicates that the usual channels of negotiation have broken down. However, circumstances may arise where judicial action is the only way out, for example, where the action complained of has already been taken by the local authority, e.g. a house pulled down or a fence removed.

Judicial control is a final safeguard. Ministers of the Crown, local authority members and officers sometimes take wrong decisions. Where a private person seeks a judicial remedy he knows that his case will be heard by an impartial judge who, from his independence, is above the local feeling, personalities and pressure groups and is able to adjudicate without fear or favour, affection or ill-will. The most notable recent case occurred in 1981 when the House of Lords, following a judgement in the High

Court by Lord Denning, declared the GLC subsidy for London Transport's cheap fares to be unreasonable and unlawful. (The action had been started by Bromley Council.)

In 1986/7, a number of councillors for Hackney borough and Liverpool councils were surcharged and subsequently disqualified from office on the grounds that they had authorised the delay in setting a rate.

Party Politics in Local Government

Until 1918 most local authorities were composed of independent council-lors and aldermen. 'Party politics' were not widespread in local govern-ment. Most members were independents, local public-spirited persons, who used their skills and abilities in the interests of the local community and the common good.

Since 1918, there has been an increasing tendency for local government to be dominated by party politics. This growth has coincided with the rise of the Labour Party and its political activities. The Labour Party regarded the local councils as one of the main instruments through which their policies could be fulfilled. In 1945 the Labour administration under Mr Attlee stimulated further interest in the local councils, which were the necessary agencies or institutions through which many of their social measures were implemented. Not unnaturally the Labour Government wanted Labour-controlled councils (i.e. those with a majority of Labour councillors and aldermen). The Conservative Party was, therefore, compel-led to look to its machinery and party organisation to stimulate its own candidates to seek election. Today, therefore, most councils comprise (i) Labour members, (ii) Conservative members, (iii) Liberal SDP (Alliance) members, and (iv) Independents. The main division is between Conser-vative and Labour and the independent councillor, with limited resources, is being squeezed out of the arena. In 1985, only 15 per cent of councillors described themselves as independent (see Widdicombe Report, HMSO, 1986).

Opposition to Local Parties

Many thinking people regard this development as unfortunate. Party poli-tics is regarded as discreditable by some. The main arguments of those who oppose local political parties in local government are:

(i) Local matters should attract the best men and women, who are prim-arily interested in the localities and in rendering public service for its own sake.

(ii) Councillors who are subjected to the 'party whip', similar to that operating in Parliament, must frequently sacrifice their own judgement for that of the leaders of the local party or national leaders.

(iii) Many local issues should be settled or decided by disinterested citi-zens independently of party loyalties.

(iv) The majority party in local councils sometimes arranges chair-manships and membership of committees along party lines.

(v) Pre-council party meetings, i.e. meetings of councillors before the main monthly or quarterly meeting of the council, prevent discussion of matters in the full council meeting where they are reported in the Press.

The Case for Local Parties

The main arguments for local parties in local government are the following:

(i) Parties ensure greater unity and purpose among council members. Individual members know they have a common bond of basic political beliefs.

(ii) Decision making in the full council is quicker. A leader of a party group may speak with authority on a particular matter in the council.

(iii) Party politics rouses interest in local government elections and matters affecting the community.

(iv) Political parties give support to individual candidates, e.g. by advice literature, information and encouragement.

(v) Where a council is composed of exclusively independent members there is a tendency to indecision and delay. Independents tend to have independent policies.

(vi) Parties have declared policies. The electorate know their votes will ensure continuance of a declared and known policy. (A vote for an independent is virtually a vote for a person, not a policy or political doctrine.)

(vii) If parties are essential for Parliament (see p. 72ff.) it is illogical to argue that they are harmful to local government. The same problems in essence exist locally as nationally at Westminster.

(viii) Councillors who intend to become MPs get valuable experience in local councils as party members. This assists them in the more difficult work at Westminster.

(ix) Party members (councillors) sometimes meet before the full council meeting, exchange views and formulate policy. They thus save time in the full council meetings. Spokesmen are appointed whose views are authoritative, and business in the council is expedited.

(x) Party politics educate new councillors. Many are amateurs and have scant knowledge of the basic principles of the British Constitution, in which local government acts in partnership with the central Government.

(xi) A Government whose party members are also councillors will be assured that its policies will be implemented and not obstructed or delayed.

Summing Up

The general attitude in most local councils is that party politics plays a less important and crucial role than it does in Parliament. The whip system is less stringent and the local issues are not so controversial. Planning, markets, amenities, and leisure, highways, refuse collection, and such matters are not politically 'charged'. It matters little to what party one adheres in dealing with these routine matters in the various committees. The sensitive areas are education and housing. Common sense and a readiness to grasp the realities of the ordinary situations in life are far more useful than doctrinaire ideas and generalities in the council chamber or the committee meetings.

Managing a Local Authority

In Central Government a Minister has, as we have noted, a Permanent Under-Secretary of State as his chief adviser and chief executive of the department. Formerly a county council had its clerk and an urban district council had its town clerk. These two figures were the chief administrative officers of the respective local authorities.

The chief officers were paid a higher salary than any other employee of the council. Hitherto the chief officer was almost invariably a lawyer, usually a solicitor. The advantage of this was that as local authorities were (as they still are) created by statute and derived all their powers from statutes, it was wise to appoint an official learned and skilled in law to advise the council. Many of the problems in local government—e.g. purchase, sale, letting of land; the making of highways; control of nuisances; compulsory purchase orders and the like—could only be resolved if the chief adviser had a sure grasp of the legal technicalities involved. However, lawyers are not necessarily good managers, and some attention was paid to the question of management, not only of the staff but of the affairs of the local authority as a whole.

The City Manager

There are many ways in which a local authority may be run. The 'City Manager' form of local government was first used at Staunton, Virginia, USA. Since then many American cities have adoped the system. Broadly speaking, the elected council is empowered to make city ordinances and to decide general matters of planning. The council is empowered to hire, as head of the city organisation, a professional administrator who is specially qualified by experience and training for that kind of work. The council picks the best person, whether he lives in the city or not. The City Manager appoints the heads of departments and some of the other officers. The Manager is responsible for the enforcement of the ordinances passed by the council. He reports to the council on the needs of the city and suggests plans as to how the city's money shall be spent and how improvements shall be made, and he holds his post for as long as the council is satisfied with his work.

In the United Kingdom, Newcastle-upon-Tyne decided in 1965 to appoint a City Manager and offered a good salary (£10,000). The appointee was formerly a Production Planning Manager with the Ford Motor Company. He became the senior officer of the City Corporation and was made responsible to a special Management Committee of the Council. This practice has certain dangers in that younger ambitious officers in local government would move out to other fields of work if the top jobs were given to persons unfamiliar with the tasks facing local authorities. However, it does re-emphasise that forward-looking authorities are free to appoint those with proved managerial ability.

Reports on Management

Various official reports have been issued on the subject, and we name:

(1) The Mallaby Report on '*The Staffing of Local Government*' (Chairman Sir George Mallaby)—1967);

(2) The Maud Report on '*The Management of Local Government*' (Chairman Sir John Maud, later Lord Redcliffe-Maud)—(1967);

(3) The Bains Report on '*The New Local Authorities: Management and Structure*' (Chairman M. A. Bains, Clerk of Kent County Council)—(1972).

(4) The Widdicombe Report on '*The Conduct of Local Authority Business*' (Chairman David Widdicombe QC)—(1986).

Each committee was set up at the instance of the Minister.

The Mallaby Report recommended, *inter alia*, that:

(i) The clerk to the authority should be recognised as head of the local service.

(ii) a Central Staffing Organisation should be created.

(iii) There should be a reduction in the number of departments in local authorities,

(iv) Local government should attract more graduates in its service.

The Maud Report recommended, *inter alia*, that:

(i) There should be one Chief Executive Officer of local authorities. He should have general managerial ability and should use this to supervise and co-ordinate the activities of all other chief officers.

(ii) There should be a Management Board of Councillors co-ordinating functions, comparable to that exercised by the Cabinet in central Government.

(iii) In large authorities there should be paid councillors.

(iv) There should be substantial delegation of minor decisions from committees to the permanent officials.

The Bains Report recommended, *inter alia*, that:

(i) The **corporate approach** was vital. This is the opposite of departmentalism, under which each department (education, surveyors, planning, housing, amenities, taxation, etc.) operated under a committee and was staffed by a chief officer with subordinates. This made for fragmentation, unco-ordinated effort, confusion and the usual personal frictions operating in most human groups, such as a college or factory. The corporate approach looks at an authority's affairs as a whole rather than as a series of isolated services. An overall plan can be formulated, carried through with resources most effectively deployed. 'Departmentalism' should be discouraged.

(ii) A **Chief Executive Officer** should be appointed (see p. 349).

(iii) **A Policy and Resources Committee** should be appointed (The Maud

Committee Report similarly recommended a Management Board, as did the Royal Commission on Local Government in England, 1969). The functions of the Policy and Resources Committee should be:

(a) To aid the council in setting its **objectives** and **priorities** by providing it with a comprehensive and co-ordinated service.

(b) To co-ordinate and control the implementation of the major policy decisions reached by the Council in the light of the Policy and Resources Committee's advice.

(c) To have ultimate responsibility, under the council, for the major resources of the authority (finance, manpower, land, buildings).

(iv) **Committees based on Programme Areas.** There were too many committees before 1972; consequently (although some are still compulsory) a reduction could be made if the authority divided its work into **spheres of activity**, each having its own objectives and programme for meeting these objectives. Thus in a Metropolitan District 'Recreation and Amenities' could be a programme area, and in this field the following would be dealt with: recreation and tourism; entertainments; commons; allotments; country parks; caravan sites; gipsy sites.

In a district council let us suppose housing is a programme area. The committee would be charged with: letting of houses; assessing future needs; acquiring land and new dwellings; slum clearance; improving private dwellings: caravan sites; accommodation for aged and infirm and disabled people; assistance in providing private dwellings through housing associations and housing societies; advances for purchase; operation of a Rent Rebate Scheme, etc.; enforcement of Rent Acts, etc.; dealing with homelessness; advisory services for those in need of housing.

You will know that each local authority has discretion to frame its own committee structure.

(v) **Community Approach.** The Bains committee used this phrase to imply and urge close co-operation between county councils and district councils within their areas; between new local authorities and the voluntary agencies (Red Cross, housing associations, civic societies etc.) and other public bodies and in particular with the new area health and regional water authorities.

District joint committees should be set up consisting of members of a county council and a district council within its area. The joint committees would be deliberative and advisory. This sort of committee could be used where, for example, a district council is exercising planning functions on behalf of a county council. Joint committees provide a forum for the exchange of valuable information to both authorities.

The community approach would most usefully meet the needs of the area it serves.

The Widdicombe Report recommended, *inter alia*, that:

(i) The composition of committees should reflect the composition of the council as a whole.

(ii) Committees should be allowed, by law, to delegate urgent decisions between meetings to their chairmen.

(iii) Employees of local authorities should no longer be allowed to become councillors in other authorities when they hold the rank of principal officer or above (and vice versa).

(iv) All councillors should be entitled to a basic flat-rate allowance (of between £1,500 and £4,000, depending on the size of the authority).

(v) Local authorities should be statutorily required to appoint a chief executive, who should be the head of the authority's paid staff with overall managerial responsibility for the discharge of functions by officers.

(vi) All statutory functions relating to the propriety of council business should be vested in the chief executive rather than any other officer. This would require him to determine such matters as the application of the rules for party balance on committees (see (i) above); to determine whether matters are urgent for chairmen's decisions (see (ii) above); to provide advice as to the legality of any proposed action or inaction by the council; to be responsible for the apointment, discipline and dismissal of staff below the rank of principal officer.

(vii) Authorities should be able to appoint officers as advisers to party groups.

All local authorities have taken steps to implement certain of the recommendations contained in the above reports, especially since reorganisation in 1974/75. The result, therefore, is rationalisation and streamlining of administrative procedures. Certain authorities have invoked the aid of management consultants to examine the work and objectives of the particular authorities and the methods adopted to secure their attainment. Management is a continuous process and must adapt itself to the changes and challenges which are an inevitable accompaniment of modern life.

Fig. 29. Committee structure of non-metropolitan district. (*Note:* committees and numbers are suggested only. Each authority will determine the committees and constitution itself.)

Co-ordination in Local Government

The committee system is the accepted form in which local administration is carried on. Committees and Departments are parts of the whole, and local government works well, therefore, only when their efforts are well co-ordinated to produce the desired objectives of effective and convenient local government. Co-ordination is achieved by various means, as follows:

Through Officers. The Chief Executive Officer (and often the treasurer) attends all important committees. Any inconsistencies arising in the various committees will be pointed out by one of these officers. Thus the Planning Committee may adopt one policy which inevitably affects a Highways Committee (or sub-committee) or the Estates' Committee (or sub-committee) or vice versa. The Chief Executive Officer keeps the records and will note the points of difficulty.

Through the Council. All committees report to the Policy and Resources Committee or to the full Council. Councillors note the decisions of those committees of which they are not members and should ensure that the policies or decisions made are consistent with the general or strategic policy of the council as a whole.

Through the Policy and Resources Committee. The object of this committee is co-ordinative. It is made up of a number of councillors who form a sort of 'cabinet' with managerial functions somewhat similar to the Cabinet of the Central Government. These functions have already been discussed (see p. 364).

Through Joint Committee Meetings. Where a matter is of common interest to two or more committees of a local authority they meet together to discuss and resolve the matter. We have mentioned that joint committees exist; the county council and the district council may appoint a joint committee to ensure both councils act in concert.

Through Finance. Formerly a separate Finance Committee was common. Now finance will fall within the province of the Policy and Resources Committee. Where a Finance Committee exists independently (some authorities may feel this matter is so important as to justify separation) the committee must arrange priorities in the spending of money and arrange for its collection through rates, etc.

Through Members. Councillors will find themselves on three or four constituent committees. Each member should know what is done in at least two other committees and he or she can, by knowledge and experience, ensure that each committee's activities are consistent and co-ordinated.

Through Definition of Powers. Where a clear definition of powers and responsibilities is laid down—e.g. in Standing Orders (which are the Council's rules of procedure) or other documents—each committee will know its function and should not exceed its powers. Where overlapping occurs this leads to confusion and friction unless efforts are sensibly co-ordinated to ensure smooth administration.

Through Chairmen. Meetings of chairmen of committees or sub-committees can smooth over difficulties and co-ordinate the work of the respective committees and thus the council as a whole.

Through Party Meetings. When one political party has a clear majority it follows that power lies in that party's hands. Agreed policies are laid down and members usually act in accordance with the decisions reached.

Complaints of Maladministration

The *Local Government Act, 1974*, establishes machinery for the investigation of complaints of maladministration by local and other authorities, except parish or community councils (unless they are acting as agents for another local authority). It provides for the appointment of

(i) a Commission for Local Administration for England,
(ii) a Commission for Local Administration for Wales, and
(iii) a Commission for Local Administration for Scotland (*Local Government (Scotland) Act, 1975*).

Local Commissioners (CLAs) are appointed with responsibility for particular **areas** and with a **duty** to investigate any claim by a member of the public that he has suffered injustice through maladministration resulting from an administrative action or decision. The Commissioners work on the lines of the Parliamentary Commissioner for Administration (see p. 305): in fact the PCA is a member of the Commission for Local Administration.

How the Commissioners Work

The Commissioners will act on a complaint made in writing and:

(i) received within 12 months of the time when the aggrieved person first had notice of the matter of complaint;
(ii) received through a member of the authority concerned or with evidence that a member has been asked to refer it but has not done so.

The object of (ii) is clearly to enable a councillor when approached by the aggrieved person to take the matter up with his own local authority to enable the authority to put matters right.

The Commissioner for the area will not proceed to investigate until the authority has had a reasonable chance to look into the matter and to reply to it. However, a local Commissioner may deal with a matter directly if satisfied that a member of the authority concerned has been requested to refer the complaint to him and this has not been done.

Reports. Where a complaint is investigated, the Commissioner will send a report of his findings to: (a) the complainant; (b) to the member (i.e. councillor) concerned; (c) to any person complained of; and (d) to the authority complained of. Copies of the report are available for public inspection, and public notice of this fact is notified in the press. It is the responsibility of the local authority to tell the Commissioner what action has been taken, and if nothing happens the Commissioner may make a further report and the process of publication is repeated.

An annual general report must be made by the *local* Commissioners to the Commissioners (the central authority) and each year the commissions are required to review the operation of the complaints system of machinery. Local Commissioners are empowered to convey to local authorities, through the local authority associations, or to government departments, any recommendations or conclusions reached in the course of their reviews. For the year 1984, the CLA for England received 3,034 complaints, fully investigated 322 and found 235 cases of maladministration (mainly housing and planning).

Matters precluded from Investigation. The CLA is precluded from investigating the following matters:

(a) Any action in respect of which the complainant has a right of appeal to a statutory tribunal.

(b) Any action in respect of which the complainant has or had a right of appeal to a Minister.

(c) Any action in respect of which the person aggrieved has or had a remedy in law.

Nevertheless a CLA may conduct **any** investigation into any of these situations if he is satisfied that in the circumstances it was not reasonable to expect the complainant to have taken advantage of the remedies open to him. And since 1980, he has the right of access to relevant information and documents.

Further, he may not look into cases where the complainant claims to have suffered from a decision affecting the public at large, or into legal proceedings, the investigation of crime, certain commercial transactions, and issues relating to appointments, pay, discipline and other personnel matters.

The following organisations are subject to investigation: local authorities (excluding parishes); joint boards, consisting of local authorities; police authorities; and water authorities.

Local Authorities and the Public

We have already mentioned the lack of public interest in the work of local government shown by the poor turn-out for local government elections. There are many in the divisions and wards who do not know the names of those holding the keys of power as councillors and many more who understand little of the structure and function of the local authorities in the total scheme of government.

Public Relations. The Bains Working Group observed that the public have a positive right to information about what their elected representatives do and they should have access to committee meetings as well as to the full council meetings. Local authorities for their part had also a positive duty to inform the electorate about the council's activities and to communicate to the public its views on subjects which were of concern to the community.

The Bains Report suggested that public-relations officers be appointed. These officers should be skilled in the presentation of local news and could be most useful in highlighting those matters in which the public ought to be interested and informed. Some authorities have established information centres, and some have habitually issued news-sheets about the council's activities. These were usually drab documents, ill-presented and inefficiently distributed. Many local authorities had taken no positive action at all to improve their relationship to the public.

The Bains report advocates that in the largest authorities a public-relations unit under a suitably qualified public-relations officer be established. In the smaller authorities there might well be one officer specially deputed to do this work, but in all there ought to be some machinery for the proper dissemination of information which the public should know or be interested in.

In any event some positive action should be taken by local authorities generally to improve the relationship between themselves and the public, if vital democracy is to be achieved. To some extent this action has been forced upon local authorities as a result of the *Local Government, Planning and Land Act, 1980*. Under this and subsequent requirements, authorities are obliged to publish more information about their activities and performances to enable electors to make more balanced assessments and judgements.

Recent Developments

We have already examined some of the recent changes affecting local government. It may be convenient here to reiterate some of these and indicate further developments—such is the pace of change in local government in recent years.

Many of the changes flowed from the *Local Government, Planning and Land Act, 1980*. This had two separate but related thrusts:

(i) In respect of **central government control**, local authorities were given more freedom by the removal or relaxation of a large number of ministerial controls or constraints over them (e.g. fewer circulars, less prescription of fees, allowing local authorities to charge for planning applications, etc.). It should be noted that other recent legislation has given local authorities new freedoms, e.g. under the *Education Act, 1980*, to choose the form of secondary schooling they provide. But these have been matched by other, restrictive, requirements e.g. such that local authorities must offer their council houses for (discounted) sale, and must 'privatise' certain services by putting them out to competitive tender (known as 'contracting out') instead of providing them direct themselves (through DLOs—direct labour organisations).

(ii) In respect of local government **finance** a number of significant changes were made by the 1980 Act. On the capital side, local authorities in England and Wales became subject (as in Scotland) to capital expenditure approvals (i.e. not loan sanctions): there are thus controls over what they may *spend* rather than what they may *borrow*. On the revenue side within the Rate Support Grant, the needs and resources elements are fused to form the **block grant** which is distributed to local authorities on a similar basis to the old Rate Support Grant but with an important variation: if a local authority appears to be spending more than it should (bearing in mind its size, obligations, population structure, etc.) then beyond a certain figure (known as the Grant Related Expenditure Assessment—or GREA) its grant aid from the Government will be 'tapered' or curtailed and the local authority will have to rely more on its own rate resources. (In addition, during the years 1982–6, the Government also set spending 'targets' (or ceilings of expenditure) for each local authority: where this figure was exceeded, grant was again withheld, such that some authorities e.g. the GLC, lost all entitlement to Rate Support Grant.

Finance has become a kind of battleground for relationships between the central and local authorities: some see finance as having become the anvil upon which the Government has sought to hammer, or control, local government. Thus under the *Local Government Finance Act, 1982*, local authorities lost their power to levy supplementary rates i.e. additional to the normal annual rate demand (though the Minister may make exceptions). The same Act also established an Audit Commission (comprising some 12 members appointed by the Secretary of State) which became responsible for local audit. It draws auditors from the private sector (i.e. private firms of accountants) or from the old public sector District Audit service and has the role (apart from straight forward audit, or 'checking the books') of seeking greater efficiency and value-for-money. But some see it as a further step to centralisation, with auditors being 'politicised' and used as instruments of central government control and financial squeeze.

More drastic, especially for certain local authorities, has been the introduction of 'rate-capping', in the *Rates Act, 1984*. Under this legislation, the Minister is empowered to place an upper limit on the rate level of those councils he considers to be spending (and therefore rating) excessively. Each year about twenty authorities have been restricted in this way. But all local authorities have been affected by the Government's general reduction in grants, for, since 1981, the proportion of central grant support for local expenditure has fallen from 61 per cent to 46 per cent (68 to 56 in Scotland) with the result that councils have had to raise rates or (especially where they are 'capped') cut services.

The Government is currently introducing a radical reform of the rating system. Domestic rates are to be abolished and replaced by a **'community charge'** (or poll tax) which every adult will pay (with reductions for those on low incomes) i.e. not just rate-payers or heads of household as happens now. Non-domestic (i.e. business) rates will remain, but will be determined by the central government.

In general it would appear that the Government has lost faith in local government. For in addition to what has been said above, the Government has removed parts of local government responsibility to other bodies. This has happened in the case of some of the former functions of the GLC and the metropolitan counties (see p. 339). It has occurred in six dockland or inner city areas, where the Government has created Urban Development Corporations to take over responsibility for development from the local authority. It is about to happen further in the housing field for council tenants are to be allowed to transfer their tenancy to another landlord (housing association or trust) if they wish. Above all, it has happened in the field of education, where the Government has, since 1980, provided grants to enable pupils to transfer to private schools (the 'assisted places scheme') and has transferred much responsibility for further education from LEAs to the centralised Manpower Services Commission. At the present time (July 1987), the Government is in the process of by-passing LEAs in certain areas by introducing directly-funded 'city technology colleges'. The *Education Act, 1987*, removes from LEAs the power to negotiate teachers' pay and places it in the hands of the Minister. And, finally there are plans to draw up a national curriculum for schools (instead of allowing local determination as at present) and to allow schools not only to manage their own budgets, but also, if they wish, to transfer out of LEA control (e.g. to an independent trust).

There are a number of reasons why the Government has taken these measures. It seeks to raise standards and efficiency in local government and to reduce the wasteful use of scarce resources. Above all it wants to reduce local (and therefore overall state) expenditure (particularly among what it considers the wasteful or 'loony' authorities) with a view to reducing public-sector borrowing (the PSBR), reducing inflation and reducing general taxation. However, since it is usually Labour councils which are worst hit, many see the Government as having a party political motive. And many others are worried about these developments and interpret them as the beginning of the end for local self-government in Britain, with the central authorities using the financial device in particular to increase its scrutiny and grip over vital areas of local decision making.

Exercises

1. What are the arguments for and against the principle of co-option?
2. Describe the Greater London Council. How are the functions distributed between the GLC and the London Borough Councils?
3. Describe the qualifications of (*a*) an elector, and (*b*) a candidate for the office of councillor. What are the disqualifications for election as councillor?
4. List those council services described as 'Protective', 'Environmental', and 'Personal'.
5. What is the 'committee system' when applied to local government?
6. How is local government financed?
7. How is the work of a local authority co-ordinated?
8. Why and how was local government reorganised in 1974/5?
9. How are complaints of maladministration in local government dealt with?
10. Obtain an information leaflet from your local authority. What are the major items of expenditure? What proportions of income are received in rates, grants and other sources?
11. What is 'rate-capping'? Discover two councils which have had this experience.

12
Modern Developments

Devolution

The devolution of power from Parliament to assemblies in Scotland and Wales has been in question for some time, especially with the nationalist parties (Plaid Cymru and the Scottish Nationalist Party) pressing for more political power and independence from Westminster.

Successive governments have published reports and, following the Royal Commission, 1969–73 and the 1975 White Paper *Our Changing Democracy: Devolution to Scotland and Wales*, legislation was passed in 1978 setting up a single-chamber Scottish Assembly with 142 members and a Welsh Assembly with 72 members. Each Assembly was to have a Chief Executive (the leader of the majority party in each Assembly) who was to form an Executive which would command the support of the Assembly.

The Scottish Assembly would have legislative powers whilst in Wales the Assembly would act more like local government in exercising administrative power only. The matters to be devolved included social work, health, local government, social security, education, housing, planning, roads, natural resources and tourism. However, the sovereignty of the Westminster Parliament and the duties of HM Government would not be fundamentally affected. Reserve powers were to be retained at Westminster and disputes arising over the exercise of devolved powers were to be decided by the Government or by the Courts.

The proposals were criticised by some as far too limited and feeble, lacking in particular sufficient independence for the new authorities. Others feared that it would be the first step to the break-up of the United Kingdom and pointed out that it would also have implications for England and its regions. Some critics saw the scheme as creating yet another tier of government and they cried 'over-government'.

During the passage of the legislation through Parliament an amendment was introduced dealing with referendums to approve the scheme. As a result, to be successful, the 'yes' vote had to receive not only a majority of support, but it also had to achieve a minimum of 40 per cent of the total possible poll. In the event (the referendums occurred on 1 March 1979) the results were:

	Scotland	Wales
Voting Yes	33%	12%
Voting No	31%	47%
Total vote	64%	59%

Thus there was a clear rejection in Wales, but in Scotland it was defeated on the technical failure to achieve the minimum 40 per cent support.

In 1979 therefore the devolution legislation (in the form of the *Scotland Act* and the *Wales Act*) was repealed and the question of devolution has gone cold. However, the issue is not dead and buried, especially where Scotland is concerned. The Labour party has renewed its commitment to devolution for Scotland, and the popularity of the SNP has revived somewhat in recent years. Indeed, despite the depletion of North Sea oil (which helped to fuel the demand for devolution) there appears to be a ground swell in support for Scottish devolution (or even independence) owing to the high levels of unemployment and the perceived indifference of the (Conservative) central Government in London—exacerbated by the fact that there are very few Conservative MPs in Scotland (down in 1987 from 21 to 11 out of a total of 72 Scottish MPs).

In the meantime there is the question of Northern Ireland for which the Government is trying to find an acceptable settlement.

Referendums

The referendum is one method by which the wishes of electors may be expressed with regard to proposed legislation. It has been developed in its highest form in Switzerland, though other countries have sometimes used it and President de Gaulle used it a number of times to gain the consent of the French nation for his policies. In a democracy a referendum should be preceded by a programme of education and public debate.

In early 1975 the issue of Britain's continued membership of the EEC had arisen. The *European Communities Act, 1972*, secured membership of the EEC which was expressed to be 'of unlimited duration'. Despite a renegotiation of the terms, the Labour Party remained divided over the issue, and at a special meeting in April 1975 the Party approved (by 3.7 million votes to 1.9 million) the recommendation that the UK should leave the EEC.

To help preserve party unity, Prime Minister Wilson decided to order a referendum. Under the *Referendum Act, 1975*, Parliament voted £125,000 to each side for campaigning (more funds came from industry and the trade unions) and balloting was based on counties (not parliamentary constituencies). The result of the poll, held on 5 June 1975, was a majority for staying in the EEC of 17.3 million to 8.4 million, with a substantial turnout of 70 per cent. In contrast, when Britain went to the polls again in June 1979 to elect their 81 European MPs only 32 per cent turned out to vote. The results were: Conservatives 60, Labour 18, Independents (Ulster) 3. In 1984 turnout was the same (with results 45, 32, 4).

Thus the device of the referendum is creeping into the British Constitution, and indeed its use has been mooted by Margaret Thatcher in relation to trade union strikes. On the general principle of the referendum, the following points may be noted:

1. The referendum is a device which has consequences affecting: (*a*) Parliamentary sovereignty; (*b*) collective responsibility; (*c*) representative Par-

liament; (*d*) treaty obligations already entered into (e.g. the *European Communities Act, 1972*) and (*e*) subjecting laws to popular vote.

2. The use of the referendum is a major constitutional change which should be used, if at all, only after due deliberation.

3. If the result of a referendum is *binding* on a Government this derogates from Parliamentary sovereignty.

4. The task of Government on major matters is *decision*. If a Minister could not accept the decision of his colleagues in Cabinet he should resign (see below). The referendum may be looked upon as merely 'passing the buck' to the people. That was not 'decision by Government'.

5. If there were a low poll at a referendum it could not be argued that the people had been decisive. Uncertainty would increase.

6. If the referendum were used as a tactical device by one Minister today, it could be used by another Minister tomorrow on a different issue.

7. The people had not asked for a referendum on the EEC issue. (The *European Communities Act, 1972*, had already been passed.) The original member countries of the EEC had not used the referendum to form the EEC initially.

8. As the UK had already passed the *European Communities Act, 1972*, and were bound by the Treaty of Rome (expressed to be of 'unlimited duration'), the holding of a referendum could only damage our standing and cause in the World and in the eyes of EEC co-members. They might query whether we may repeat the exercise of the referendum at a later date, especially as British attitudes to the EEC have deteriorated since the referendum in 1975 (and voting turnout in each of our EEC Parliamentary elections, in 1979 and 1984, was only 32 per cent).

In the meantime, there have been several unofficial or 'mini' referendums. The first occurred in 1985 when a number of (Labour) councillors in the Great London Council resigned their seats and re-fought them at the subsequent by-elections. They were protesting at Government plans to abolish the GLC, and sought to show what they believed to be a similar degree of antipathy to the policy by the general public. (In the event, some seats were not actually contested; and in those which were, the turnout was low.) The second occurred in 1986 when all 12 Ulster Unionist MPs resigned and re-fought their seats in protest at the Anglo-Irish Agreement. (The result here was a somewhat lower turnout than expected, and the loss of one seat to the SDLP.)

Secrecy, Open Government and Leaks

It is often claimed that British government is the most secretive of the democratic nations, with Ministers and civil servants being far too ready to classify all papers as 'secret', 'confidential' or 'restricted' so that in general only what is not prohibited is permitted public information.

The paradox is that foreigners may often know more than we do, as when countries importing British goods may require information about those commodities (such as safety records) which is not available to the British public. Even in the area of defence, details of our weapons systems may become exposed when foreign firms become responsible for 'privatised' contract management (as with our naval dockyards).

However, for the British official, the risk of any unauthorised disclosure is prosecution under the Official Secrets Act (see pp. 168, 362) as well as internal disciplinary action.

The 1970s saw a considerable (verbal) commitment by the Government to the concept of 'open government'. There has been action as well as words: apart from the setting up of the 'Ombudsman' and Parliamentary Select Committees the Government has been more willing to publish Green Papers (or consultative documents) and official background papers to policy-making. Some critics are sceptical about the usefulness of these developments and what they urge is a fundamental reform of the *Official Secrets Act, 1911* (especially its catch-all Section 2) or the introduction of a Freedom of Information Act (such as that operating in the USA) so that the onus should be transferred to governments to justify their withholding of information.

It has been wisely said that 'information is the currency of power'. The Government promised action on the *Official Secrets Act* (see pp. 168, 362) which was investigated by the Franks Committee in 1972. But despite a White Paper on the subject in 1978 the Government has been a long time devising a system giving a suitable balance between the claims for democracy and reasonable openness of government on the one hand and the need for national security and effective government on the other.

It is Section 2 of the Official Secrets Act which is subject to most criticism. This Section makes it an offence to disclose or receive any official information without authorisation, whether or not there is intent to damage the State. Critics say it is too wide ranging, too indiscriminate. (It also places a heavy burden on the Government's law officers in deciding whether to bring cases against offenders, especially leakers or 'moles'.). The Franks Committee (1972) declared that, 'A government which operates in greater secrecy than the effective conduct of its proper function requires . . . will lose the trust of the people . . . Its critics will try to break down all barriers erected to preserve secrecy and they will disclose all that they can, by whatever means, discover. As a result, matters will be revealed when they ought to remain secret'.

We have certainly seen plenty of evidence of this in recent years. Apart from the notable Ponting and Tisdall cases (see p. 169) there have been some 40 serious leaks since 1979. Indeed, it is alleged that we are developing a system of 'government by leak' since not all premature disclosures are unwelcome to governments—indeed, they may themselves initiate them e.g. in order to test or prepare public opinion. Individual Ministers or civil servants may leak in order to sabotage or thwart proposed policies or actions. (The unprecedented disclosure of a letter from the Solicitor General in January 1986 by Leon Brittan, the Secretary of State for Trade and Industry, sought to undermine the position of a Cabinet colleague, Michael Heseltine, the Secretary of State for Defence, over the Westland affair. Subsequently, both Ministers resigned.)

It is clear that less secrecy would result in fewer leaks. The Franks Committee recommended the replacement of Section 2 by a narrower, more precise statement, since it seems unreasonable that all unauthorised disclosures of government activities should be dealt with under the same broad statute. Other critics (including the Campaign for the Freedom of Information) seek a Freedom of Information Act, where government information is presumed open unless judged otherwise, instead of presumed secret unless judged otherwise as at present. This would provide more public information, and so more public power. It would also provide a better guarantee against corruption.

However, such a change does raise the question of Ministerial accountability to Parliament. Might it also cause officials to become over cautious? And it would require a consensus between the State and the citizen as to what, in the public interest, should be kept secret and what the public has the right to know.

Political memoirs

An important element in effective government in Britain is seen as the principle of Collective Responsibility (see p. 131). 'Achievement of collective responsibility implies that there should be complete frankness between the members, who would not feel free to surrender their departmental and personal preferences for the object of their common policy unless they were confident that the stand they had taken and the points they had conceded would not become public knowledge and be used to their embarrassment.' (*The Cabinet Office to 1945*, by S. S. Wilson, HMSO.)

Underpinning this convention is the law, namely the *Official Secrets Act* and the *Public Records Act, 1950* (which permits the opening to the public of official documents after thirty years)*. But just how far the principle operates was raised by the publication of the *Crossman Diaries*.

The late Richard Crossman (Cabinet Minister 1964–70), kept a diary during his time as a Minister. This gave details of Cabinet matters and of conversations and relationships within the Cabinet and with senior civil servants. Mr Crossman's literary executors proposed to publish the diaries. The Attorney-General sought an injunction in 1975 to prohibit the publication, and the Courts dismissed his application. Its subsequent publication caused some embarrassment and led to counter-claims on the events portrayed.

The Prime Minister then appointed a Committee of Privy Counsellors to inquire into the operation of the convention of Cabinet secrecy and the writing of memoirs by Ministers even if these writings were published after death. Lord Radcliffe headed the committee, which reported in 1976. Its principal recommendation was that ministerial authors should be precluded for fifteen, instead of thirty years, from publishing information falling into three categories:

1. The author must not reveal anything that contravenes the requirements of national security operative at the time of his proposed publication.

2. He must not make disclosures that would be injurious to his country's relations with other nations.

3. He must not publish information destructive of the confidential rela-

* In 1967 the Lord Chancellor put a blanket ban on all security material (MI5, security and MI6, secret intelligence) so it is not available under the 30 year rule.

tionships upon which the system of government is based; that is, relationships between Ministers and colleagues or advisers in the civil service or outside bodies and private persons.

The committee thought the law did not provide satisfactory machinery for enforcement, and legislation creating a series of new offences was not recommended. Instead reliance was placed on a Minister's acceptance of an obligation of honour, reinforced by a rule that on taking or leaving office he should have his attention drawn to his obligations in relation to memoirs. A former Minister will also continue to submit any manuscript about his ministerial experience to the secretary of the Cabinet, with the right of appeal to the Prime Minister. Thus ministers are now expected to sign an appropriate declaration so that a transgressor would be known to be breaking an official obligation he had undertaken. (All serving and former military officers are required under section 12 of Queen's regulations to submit manuscripts for security vetting.)

The Lobby System

Most of our information about governmental activities takes the form of White Papers and Government reports, answers to Parliamentary Questions, debates and Ministerial statements in Parliament. Much is also released by Ministers or their officials through 'lobby briefings'—these are usually 'unattributable', 'off the record' or from 'sources close to the Prime Minister' i.e the convention is that lobby correspondents (some 150 from the press and other media) do not disclose the source of their information given to them privately. This is to encourage a greater willingness to speak freely. It is often a one-to-one meeting with the Minister; but for the Prime Minister, or rather, her Press Secretary, there is a twice daily meeting with the lobby as a whole.

The principle underlying this system is that Ministers have a constitutional duty to inform Parliament first about their plans and actions.

Critics of the system claim that it allows the Government to present information on its terms, and there is a suspicion that journalists are hand-in-glove with the Government, thus casting doubt on the credibility of the lobby system—indeed two national newspapers have recently opted out of the system. But most persist and claim that close observers can read between the lines so as to distinguish between 'fact' and 'slant', and perhaps distinguish the source of the stories.

Quangos

In Chapter Five attention was drawn to the existence of an intermediate level or form of government known as Public Corporations. These comprise a fairly coherent group within the wider and less clear territory of semi-governmental bodies popularly known as 'quangos'—quasi-autonomous non (or national) government organisations (or offices). Their composition, powers and roles vary greatly: they may be advisory (e.g. the Schools Council), regulatory (e.g. the Milk Marketing Board, the Monopolies and Mergers commission), executive (e.g. the Manpower Services Commission) or pursue research (e.g. the Economic and Social Research

Council). Philip Holland, MP has estimated that over 3,000 such bodies exist in Britain giving a membership exceeding 40,000 people. He believes: 'Ministers have discovered that the system can be used for shedding personal responsibility, rewarding friends, expanding the corporate state, diminishing the authority of Parliament, and enabling them to retain a measure of control over the interpretation of their own statutes.'

It is the evidently recent (post-war) profusion of these bodies which has caused the present Government to call a halt. In the pursuit of lower public expenditure, reduced patronage and greater accountability to Parliament, it has announced the dissolution of a great many of these bodies, including the Supplementary Benefits Commission, the Youth Service Forum, the Price Commission, the Personal Social Services Council, the Location of Offices Bureau, the Centre for Environmental Studies and the Advisory Council on the Penal System. The Department of the Environment alone is shedding half (sixty) of those for which it has responsibility.

Running parallel with this is the Government's policy of 'privatisation', i.e. hiving off government activities to private enterprise (see p. 186).

Clearly quangos as such are not bad; indeed, the Government itself has created some new ones (e.g. a National Advisory Body for higher education, the Local Government Audit Commission, the National Council on Vocational Qualifications and six urban development corporations).

But there is perhaps some merit in reviewing their operation, and perhaps this will be a fruitful area of inquiry by Parliament's Select Committees, and perhaps by the National Audit Office.

A Written Constitution and a Bill of Rights

We conclude this survey of Britain's system of government where we began: by looking at the Constitution in broad terms. The increasing scope of government; devolution; electoral reform; the use of the referendum; reform of the House of Lords; official secrecy; the growth of data-banks and methods of surveillance; talk of secret armies and of the corporate state; the doctrine of the Rule of Law in relation to trade unions and other groups—these are but some of the matters which give cause for concern. Lord Justice Scarman in his Hamlyn Law Lectures 1974 considered the need for a Bill of Rights; Lord Hailsham has put foward a case for a written constitution; and a Bill of Rights was introduced into the House of Lords in 1980 (by Lord Wade) and in 1985 (by Lord Broxbourne).

The advantage of Britain's having a written constitution would be to clarify the rules of our system of government (if something 'goes without saying', it is still better for being said!). A written constitution would also seek to prevent the possibility of a Government riding roughshod over the present unwritten rules (conventions). But this presupposes that such a Government is prepared to ignore the views of the Opposition, the media, pressure groups and the general public; and also that it *would* be respectful of the written law. Written constitutions in themselves may not provide a strong defence to a determined Government. Indeed, it has been said that constitutions often hide more than they reveal.

A Bill of Rights. A written constitution can exist independently of a Bill of Rights. The US Constitution was drafted in broad terms, but was then followed by amendments, the first ten of which constitute a Bill of Rights, which are the bedrock of the individual liberties that have been jealously guarded in the USA for two centuries. The First Amendment guarantees freedom of religious worship, of speech and of the press, and the rights of peaceable assembly, and of petitioning the Government.

Almost every country with a written constitution attempts to safeguard certain rights. Where such rights are so framed that they cannot be overridden by ordinary statute, they are said to be 'entrenched'. Where any subsequent statute conflicts with the entrenched rights (e.g. nationality or trade unions) disputes will arise and the Courts have to adjudge. We are then faced with the prospect of judges pronouncing on the *validity* (or constitutionality) of Acts of Parliament. Once judges have this power we are faced with the prospect of a *political* judiciary. Conflict could thus arise between the judiciary and Parliament, Thus MPs may seek to permit abortion, but this may clash with the (judge-protected) right to life; they may seek to ban the 'closed shop' (i.e. trade union only employees) which would clash with the right to collective bargaining; they may seek to prohibit corporal punishment in schools, which conflicts with teachers' rights to exercise discipline etc. In the end, these reflect values and involve **political** choices. Consequently, a Prime Minister may be tempted to fill judicial appointments with nominees of particular political views. (There is no evidence that this has occurred, but it may be noted that, for example, all members of the current Court of Appeal have been appointed since 1979 i.e. by the present government.)

Apart from this, the enactment of a Bill of Rights presupposes that the (non-elected) judges will be the guardians of the constitution and that they are fitted so to act: as Lord McCluskey (a former solicitor general) has said, 'Why it should be supposed that elderly lawyers with cautious and backward-looking habits of thought are qualified to overrule the judgements of democratically elected legislators as to what . . . is justified I do not profess to understand'. (See also p. 246.) In effect, Parliamentary sovereignty will be lost and power will have shifted to unaccountable judges.

Equally, as Chief Justice Marshall said in 1819, a constitution written to cover all eventualities 'would partake of a prolixity of a legal code and could scarcely be embraced by the human mind . . . Its nature therefore requires that only its great outlines be marked.' He added that the US Constitution was 'intended to endure . . . and to be adapted'. Any constitution must necessarily be drafted in broad terms; so too a Bill of Rights. But if they are broad, they may be vague and leave scope for argument and interpretation. Yet a Bill of Rights may also be objected to on the grounds that it would enable a particular coalition of interests, who managed to win a sufficient majority at the time the Bill is enacted, to ensure their special interest is entrenched as a right (e.g. as happened in the USA in the 1920s with the prohibition of alcohol in Amendment 18). In effect, the charter would reflect the dominant values of that particular time and could prove an obstacle to social change (e.g. the status of homosexuals or of those born out of wedlock).

Nevertheless, recent events and developments have given cause for concern over the safety of our civil liberties, including legislation limiting trade unions, enhanced police powers under Public Order and other Acts, the limitations placed on jury challenge and on access to trial by jury itself, revelations concerning the allegedly Machiavellian activities of the Security Services, an unprecedented police search and seizure at the BBC, and the increased central control of local government. In addition, a number of individuals have gone to the European Court at Strasbourg and won their case against the UK government (see p. 25). It was in the light of this that Sir Edward Gardner (unsuccessfully) introduced the Human Rights Bill into Parliament (in February 1987), to incorporate the European Convention on Human Rights into British law: thus we could appeal to our own courts for breaches of civil freedoms contained in the European Convention. It would have provided an enforceable statement or Bill of Rights for Britain, defining where State power ends and personal freedom begins.

Apart from fears of likely clashes between the judiciary and Parliament and the politicisation of judges (mentioned above) opponents of the Bill said it would result in a flood of applications to the courts which British judges could have difficulty dealing with because they are used to interpreting tightly-drawn statutes rather than interpreting vague concepts such as the 'rights of family life' or the 'peaceful enjoyment of possessions.'

More generally, there are other problems associated with 'writing up' (or 'codifying') our constitution. Firstly, there would have to be agreement about its contents. This would raise some fundamental issues: for example, what is the proper place and role of Parliament? We would have to decide between what Professor Johnson has called the 'majority model' (where the House of Commons is seen as a legitimiser of the actions of governments which have a majority and so develop policies with relatively little regard for the Parliament) and the 'bargaining model' (in which Parliament takes decisions itself, alters significantly government legislation and genuinely holds governments to account). The problem of finding agreement was well illustrated in the debacle over devolution in the 1970s. Other areas of actual or political dis-sensus are the House of Lords, the role and Finance of local government, the control mechanisms for the security services and perhaps the electoral system.

Secondly, would the contents of the new written format have to be approved by a referendum? And thirdly, we would have to provide a satisfactory mechanism of amendment to allow for change and some form of court for appeals on constitutional matters.

Recent Governments appear to have been too busy governing to reflect on such issues in any comprehensive fashion.

Appendix 1
Specimen Legislative Documents

(a) Parliamentary Bill

A
B I L L
T O

Make fresh provision about citizenship and nationality, A.D. 1981. and to amend the Immigration Act 1971 as regards the right of abode in the United Kingdom.

B E IT ENACTED by the Queen's most Excellent Majesty, by and with the advice and consent of the Lords Spiritual and Temporal, and Commons, in this present Parliament assembled, and by the authority of the same, as follows:—

5

PART I

BRITISH CITIZENSHIP

Acquisition after commencement

1.—(1) A person born in the United Kingdom after com- Acquisition mencement shall be a British citizen if at the time of the birth by birth or adoption.
10 his father or mother is—

  (a) a British citizen ; or
  (b) 'settled' in the United Kingdom.

  (2) A new-born infant who, after commencement, is found abandoned in the United Kingdom shall, unless the contrary
15 is shown, be deemed for the purposes of subsection (1)—

  (a) to have been born in the United Kingdom after com-
      mencement ; and
  (b) to have been born to a parent who at the time of
      the birth was a British citizen or settled in the United
20   Kingdom.

[Bill 20]   A 3   48/2

(b) Act of Parliament

ELIZABETH II

Education Act 1981

1981 CHAPTER 60

An Act to make provision with respect to children with special educational needs.   [30th October 1981]

BE IT ENACTED by the Queen's most Excellent Majesty, by and with the advice and consent of the Lords Spiritual and Temporal, and Commons, in this present Parliament assembled, and by the authority of the same, as follows:—

Preliminary

1.—(1) For the purposes of this Act a child has "special educational needs" if he has a learning difficulty which calls for special educational provision to be made for him.

(2) Subject to subsection (4) below, a child has a "learning difficulty" if—

    (*a*) he has a significantly greater difficulty in learning than the majority of children of his age; or

    (*b*) he has a disability which either prevents or hinders him from making use of educational facilities of a kind generally provided in schools, within the area of the local authority concerned, for children of his age; or

    (*c*) he is under the age of five years and is, or would be if special educational provision were not made for him, likely to fall within paragraph (*a*) or (*b*) when over that age.

(3) "Special educational provision" means—

    (*a*) in relation to a child who has attained the age of two years, educational provision which is additional to, or otherwise different from, the educational provision made generally for children of his age in schools maintained by the local education authority concerned; and

Meaning of "special educational needs" and "special educational provision".

(c) Statutory Instrument

S T A T U T O R Y   I N S T R U M E N T S

1981 No. 1847

NATIONAL HEALTH SERVICE, ENGLAND AND WALES

**The National Health Service (Transfer of Officers)
Regulations 1981**

Made - - - -	*22nd December* 1981
Laid before Parliament	*15th January* 1982
Coming into Operation	*5th February* 1982

The Secretary of State for Social Services, as respects England, and the Secretary of State for Wales, as respects Wales, in exercise of powers conferred upon them by section 12 of, and paragraph 10(2) of Schedule 5(**a**) to, the National Health Service Act 1977(**b**), and of all other powers enabling them in that behalf, after consulting such bodies as they have recognised as representing persons who in their opinion are likely to be affected by the regulations, hereby make the following regulations:—

Citation, commencement and interpretation

1.—(1) These regulations may be cited as the National Health Service (Transfer of Officers) Regulations 1981 and shall come into operation on 5th February 1982.

(2) In these regulations unless the context otherwise requires—

"Authority" means a health authority or a preserved Board;

"preserved Board" has the meaning given by the National Health Service Reorganisation Act 1973(**c**).

Transfer of Officers

2.—(1) Where, before 1st April 1985, it is agreed between an officer of an Authority, that Authority (in this regulation referred to as "the employing Authority") and another Authority that the officer should be transferred to the employment of that other Authority, the employing Authority shall give notice to the officer that he will be transferred to the employment of that other Authority on the date specified in the notice and such transfer shall take effect on the date specified in the notice.

(2) Where, before 1st April 1985, the employing Authority, after consultation with an officer whom it employs and another Authority, considers that it would be in the interests of the health service that the officer should be transferred to the employment of that other Authority, the employing

---

(**a**) Section 12 and paragraph 10(2) of Schedule 5 were applied to preserved Boards of teaching hospitals by the National Health Service (Preservation of Boards of Governors) Amendment Order 1981, S.I.1981/1548.
(**b**) 1977 c.49.
(**c**) 1973 c.32.

[H81/950]

Appendix 2
Study and Examination Technique

Studying British Constitution

The student of British Constitution is dealing with a 'living' subject in which he does not only study past events but observes the objects of the study in action and in the process of change. This is, at once, the attraction of the subject and a major problem of its study. Its attractiveness lies in the sheer dynamism of the political world in which things are not always what they seem and where institutions do not always carry the functions that they originally held—the student has to be prepared to probe beneath the surface to evaluate the actual working of the political system. The problem of the subject is that it *is* so fast-moving and the student is hard pressed to keep up with the changes that are continually taking place. Thus, for example, recent years have seen major reorganisation of the Civil Service, the legal system, Government Departments, and the local government structure.

The student has thus to be prepared to direct his study to achieve two major objectives:

(1) He must be able to analyse, discuss and criticise the system of government. In order to do this he must have a thorough factual knowledge of the working system on which to base his analysis. He must be aware of the practical operation of the system behind the legal or constitutional façade.

(2) His knowledge must be up to date. It is the aim of *British Constitution Made Simple* to assist the student in the achievement of these two objectives but no text book on its own is sufficient for the achievement of a successful outcome to a British constitution course. Each individual will need to consult other texts (see bibliography) and refer to a variety of newspapers and journals in order to widen, consolidate, and up-date his awareness of the workings of the system of government. In this regard the following sources are of considerable value:

Newspapers	Journals and Magazines	
The Times	The New Statesman	Public Administration
The Guardian	The Spectator	The Political Quarterly
The Daily Telegraph	The Listener	Local Government Chronicle
The Sunday Times	New Society	Municipal Journal
The Observer	The Parliamentarian	Public Law
The Independent	Parliamentary Affairs	Local Government Review

Reference
Keesing's Contemporary Archives
Whitaker's Almanac
Local Government Annotations Service

Times Index
British Humanities Index
D. Butler British Political
   Facts, Macmillan 1986

Regular consultation of these sources will keep the student up to date with current events and a further aid is now most provided by R. K. Mosley who annually publishes an admirable little booklet called *British Constitution* 1972 (year as appropriate) which is a survey of most recent events in the political system and is directed specifically at students about to take examinations in British Constitution. See also *Politics Pal* (Politics Association).

Examination Technique

Examination Preparation

Thorough preparation is essential and it is important to realise that the most successful candidate is likely to be the person who plans his work over a fairly lengthy period, studies consistently throughout this period and leaves himself some weeks before the examination for concentrated revision of what he has learned.

At the end of each chapter in this book you will find questions to enable you to test your knowledge. These questions should be used constantly throughout your course and in the concentrated revision period prior to the examination. Thorough learning and revision is an essential prerequisite to success. However able your teacher may be, in the final analysis the examination will test *your* knowledge and *your* learning. The secret of success is thorough preparation.

British Constitution Questions

The types of question set in British Constitution examinations vary according to the *level* of the examination. Thus examinations at GCSE 'O' level and similar standard tend to produce questions designed to test the factual knowledge of the candidate. For example, questions requiring a description of the process of Public and Private Bills or asking the student to show his knowledge of the functions of the Prime Minister are by no means uncommon and illustrate the type of question asked.

At 'A' level and in the intermediate examinations of various professional bodies the questions are designed not merely to test **factual** knowledge but also to test the ability of the candidate to **analyse**. Thus analytical questions ask the student for his opinions as to the effectiveness of certain parts of the political machinery, to discuss critically a particular process or to show what point of constitutional importance is demonstrated by a particular event. The general approach to answering such questions is to initially state the factual framework around which the discussion or analysis is to be built then to carry out the analysis and finally reach a conclusion to provide a neatly rounded ending to the essay.

Examination Strategy

In the previous section the importance of planning your study and revision has been stressed. It is also important that you should plan carefully your approach to examinations ensuring that you complete the technical formalities such as putting in your candidate number, etc., as well as answering the questions. In your approach to the examination bear in mind the value of having an overall strategy in dealing with the paper as a whole in addition to having a set procedure for answering individual questions.

The following simple rules will guide you in planning your overall strategy:

(i) Read the instructions printed on your **answer** sheets and be sure to write in the required details (e.g. name, candidate number, centre number, etc.).

(ii) Read the instructions at the top of the **examination** paper very carefully to ensure that you answer the requisite number of questions and that you are aware of the areas of choice available if the paper is divided into sections.

(iii) Aim to answer **all** the questions required. (If, for example, you only answer four out of five, then the maximum mark you can achieve is eighty per cent and your chances of success are diminished by that much.) This will involve planning your approximate time allocation to each question very carefully.

(iv) Read the question paper through and decide which questions you will answer.

(v) When you have completed your paper read it through for errors and omissions, ensure that the sheets (and any continuation sheets) are in their correct order and make a final check to ensure that you have written in the required information on the answer sheets.

(vi) Hand your paper in.

Individual Questions

It may seem to be statement of the obvious but the aim of the candidate must be to *answer the question*, yet we so frequently see examiners' reports in which the main criticism is the failure of so many students to answer the set question or a tendency to ignore completely certain parts of a question. Thus the objective is to answer the set question as fully as possible and in seeking this objective you will find that a fixed procedure will help you as follows:

(i) Read the question **carefully**.
(ii) Read the question again underlining the key words.
(iii) Make **rough** notes of your answer.
(iv) Arrange your points in logical order with 'a beginning, a middle, and an end'.
(v) Write your answer from your plan.

In writing your answer endeavour to excel in three areas:

1. Style

Examiners want clear and concise answers to the point of the question. Do not introduce irrelevant material and avoid facetious comments. Remember the 'ABC Rule'.

A = Accurate
B = Brief
C = Clear
D = Direct (i.e. no irrelevance)

2. Examples

It is important in British Constitution to use examples to illustrate the points that you are making. This will demonstrate that you can relate your knowledge to the actual operation of the system of government. Also use recent examples wherever possible, preferably those culled from a variety of sources thus indicating to the examiner that you have been prepared to extend your reading beyond a single textbook.

3. Presentation

A paper will commend itself to the examiner if it is grammatically correct, well paragraphed and neatly and legibly written, the latter being particularly important since the examiner cannot mark work which he cannot read. Untidy, blotched, and scribbled efforts will create a bad impression and may not justify good marks.

Example 1

Question: Examine critically the procedure for the consideration of (*a*) Private Members' Bills, and (*b*) Private Bills.

Rough Notes: (*a*) Private Members' Bills—definition: methods of introduction (i) Ballot; (ii) Ten minute rule: Process of bills. Difficulties and criticisms. Examples.

(*b*) Private Bills and definition, examples. Process in Parliament. Discussion of advantages and criticisms.

Model Answer:

(*a*) Private Members' Bills are public Bills which are introduced into the House of Commons and piloted through their procedure by an individual MP. Members of Parliament get the opportunity to introduce such Bills in two ways. Under the first method a ballot is held at the beginning of each session to determine the priority list of Bills to be considered on private members' legislation days. Since 1970 twelve Fridays have been allocated to the passage of such Bills which effectively limits the likelihood of a successful passage to the first eight or so MPs and their Bills.

Once the MP has been successful in the ballot he must then set about drafting his Bill which can be an expensive process though frequently a pressure group will bear the cost, and since 1971 the Government contribute £200 to the drafting costs of the first ten Bills on the list. After this has been completed the Bill will go through the normal stages of a public Bill. The Bill will have a formal First Reading which serves to introduce its purpose to the House, after which comes the Second Reading in which the main principles of the Bill are debated followed by the Committee Stage in which a Standing Committee will go through the Bill clause by clause accepting, amending, or rejecting each. After this the Bill goes back to the House for its Report Stage and purely formal Third Reading and then the Bill will go to the House of Lords where it will go through the same procedure but piloted now by a supporter of the Bill in that House. Finally the Bill will go for the Royal Assent.

The second method by which a Private Member's Bill may be introduced is under the Ten-Minute Rule whereby an MP may put forward in a ten-minute speech a motion requesting leave to introduce a Bill after Question Time on Tuesdays and Wednesdays. If the Bill is unopposed, which is rare, the Bill can proceed through its various stages as unopposed business after 10 p.m.

The main problem with Private Members' Bills is that so few of them get through with consequent wastage of time, money and effort. Ten-minute rule Bills, in particular, stand little chance of success since discussion must take place on opposed Bills and the time for such discussion must come out of the Government's allocation, which it is most unlikely to be prepared to give. However, there are occasions when a Bill is so worthy (*Oil Burners* (*Standards*) *Act, 1960, Tattooing of Minors Act, 1969*) that it evokes no opposition. Only about two or three such Bills will be successful in each session.

The chances of success of Bills introduced on Fridays are greater though even here there are obstacles. Much depends on the ability of the MP to get sufficient support in the House on Fridays which is not always easy to do since MPs are eager to get away to their constituencies. Also the MP will rarely be able to rally enough MPs to get a closure motion accepted which means that a small group of opponents can 'talk out' a Bill. Thus a Bill to abolish Hare Coursing has been introduced each year since 1966 and has not yet been passed. Much also depends on the attitude of the Government who will ensure the defeat of a Bill if it conflicts with their policy.

Despite these difficulties eight to ten such Bills are passed each year and while they are mainly concerned with fairly minor matters the period between 1964 and 1970 saw the passage of important social reforms, e.g. *Murder* (*Abolition of the Death Penalty*) *Act, 1965, Termination of Pregnancy Act, 1967,* The *Divorce Act, 1970*.

(*b*) Private Bills are of more limited scope than public Bills and are promoted by public and private authorities in search of additional powers. Most Private Bills are promoted these days by local authorities (e.g. *Somerset County Council Act, 1967*) and rarely excite national controversy though two Bills in recent years promoted by the Greater London Council and Manchester Corporation to introduce lotteries to assist their finances did evoke national interest and concern—they both failed.

The initial part of the process of Private Bills takes place outside Parliament. After the promoters have petitioned Parliament for permission to introduce the Bill they have to advertise its purposes twice in local newspapers and the *London Gazette* and anybody affected by compulsory purchase under the Bill must be notified. Once these formalities are completed the petitions are examined to see that the promoters have complied with standing orders. Opponents of the Bills are then required to submit petitions indicating the basis of their objections.

The Parliamentary process of a Private Bill is the same as for a public Bill but the emphasis is different in that most of the work is not done on the floor of the two Houses but in committee. If a Bill is unopposed by outside interests it will have an easy passage through Parliament where the main aim of the process is to ensure that standing orders have been complied with and that public rights have not been infringed. If the Bill is opposed the passage will be more difficult in that the opponents may ask an MP to object at Second Reading, thus leading to a debate, and at the committee stage in the Opposed Bills Committee the promoters will have to justify their Bill on grounds of public interest in the face of opposition from the various petitioners against the legislation. The proceedings of the committee are semi-judicial in character, the promoters and opponents of the Bill may employ counsel to represent them, evidence is given on oath and cross examination is allowed. If the Bill survives this hurdle it will usually be successful though opposition may be maintained in its process through the Lords (or Commons if the Bill begins in the Lords).

The Private Bill process has the advantage of bringing flexibility into legislation since it enables local peculiarities and needs to be catered for in addition to the general needs dealt with by public legislation. However, the procedure is rather cumbersome and slow. The whole process is very expensive especially if there is opposition to the Bill and it does seem ridiculous that opposition should be allowed to continue in the second House after the promoters have 'proved their case' in the House of introduction. Finally there is no guarantee that the Bill will ultimately be successful after all the expenditure. In view of the expense and uncertainty authorities tend to rely on Special Orders rather than Private Bills wherever possible.

Example 2

Question: Analyse and illustrate the different kinds of interest groups active in British political life. How do they exert their influence and with what success?

Rough Notes: Define interest groups. Classification—

   (i) sectional-examples, (ii) promotional-examples.

   Methods of influence (*a*) Departments, (*b*) Parliament, (*c*) Public—effectiveness of groups.

Model Answer:

Interest groups are organised groups of people who are linked by some common characteristic of occupation, class, opinion, race, language, or religion. An essential part of the activities of such groups is the bringing of pressure or influence to bear on Governmental authorities to achieve changes in public policy for the benefit of the members of the group. Such 'benefit' may be material (e.g. National Union of Teachers seeking improvements in the conditions of service of teachers) or spiritual (e.g. Activities of members of the RSPCA). Interest groups do not seek to govern, like the political party, but to influence those who do govern. Such groups can also be distinguished from political parties in that their aims may not be wholly political (e.g. Automobile Association mainly provides a service to motorists but also exerts influence on the Government in its area of concern).

There are many interest groups and broadly speaking they can be divided into two classes. On the one hand there are the sectional interest groups which represent certain sections of society and which are based on the common economic or vocational interests of their members. The function of such groups is to advance and defend the common interests of their members. Thus the employers associations (Confederation of British Industry, Society of Motor Manufacturers and Traders) employees associations (TUC, National Union of Mineworkers) professional associations (Law Society, British Medical Assocation) and civic associations (such as the Association of Municipal Authorities) are the main groups in this class.

On the other hand there are promotional groups which are concerned with particular causes or principles arising out of beliefs and attitudes held by members and these groups endeavour to persuade public authorities to accept the cause which they are urging. A number of such groups seek a major change in policy, e.g. Campaign for Nuclear Disarmament, while the majority are concerned with watching over administration of policy in particular spheres and achieving slight modifications, e.g. Howard League for Penal Reform, NSPCC, League against Cruel Sports, RSPCA.

Interest groups exert their influence through three main channels. In the first place they operate through consultation with Government Departments and the achievement of consultative status is much sought by the interest groups. The importance that the groups attach to being on the 'to be consulted' list merely reflects the fact that in the British political system the main source of power lies with the Government and the Departments that service the senior Ministers. Once the Government has made a decision it is accepted that the Government's supporters in the Commons will vote for it.

The relationship between Government Departments and the groups is reciprocal. The groups know that they will be consulted on any matters or changes in policy likely to affect them and will, therefore, be in a position to try to influence the proposals at an early stage. Thus the National Farmers' Union will usually be consulted on the annual agricultural price review and the National Union of Teachers on any changes in national education policy. On the other hand the Government Departments regard it as proper and necessary in a complex modern democracy to consult the 'affected interests' in the process of administration and gain expertise and information on the advantages and difficulties of Government proposals as a product of the consultative process. Consultation also has the advantage for the departments of securing agreement and reducing criticism of Government policy.

The second channel of influence is through Parliament. A number of trade union interest groups sponsor Labour candidates at general elections and many MPs will agree to be spokesmen for particular groups in Parliament, sometimes being paid a retainer for their services. These MPs will back up previous consultations with departments by various activities in the House of Commons, e.g. by putting forward amendments to legislation.

On occasions promotional groups seeking major objectives will launch a campaign designed on a short- or long-term basis to get the support of MPs on their proposals. Sometimes they are successful, as with the abolition of capital punishment and the law relating to the termination of pregnancy, but if the Government opposes the group's objectives, then it has little chance of success as was the case with the Campaign for Nuclear Disarmament.

Finally interest groups seek the favour of the public in order to gain support in the promotion of their case at either Departmental or Parliamentary level. Public favour may be sought either by publicity through radio, Press, and television, as a result of demonstrations and mass lobbying of MPs, or in a more subtle way by the use of public relations techniques to build up a favourable public image for the group in the long term, e.g. Aims of Industry seeks to build up a favourable image for 'private enterprise'.

However, group campaigns designed to appeal to the general public are the exception rather than the rule in British politics, particularly in the case of those groups normally in contact with Government Departments. Such groups are more likely to achieve their objectives through consultation. Promotional groups which are not recognised by the Government are the most likely to resort to a public opinion campaign but such a campaign has its dangers in that it may antagonise public opinion rather than gain its support, in which case the group's chances of success are remote.

It is thus generally accepted that the most effective way to achieve their objectives is to seek consultative status so that the group is consulted whenever the Government is contemplating measures which may affect the group. The other channels of influence through pressure on Parliament and public opinion, are resorted to either in order to reinforce or supplement consultations or because the groups concerned are not consulted by the Departments.

Appendix 3
Test Papers

The following questions are taken mainly from examination papers set by the Associated Examining Board (AEB), and the School Examinations Dept., University of London (UL) at Ordinary and Advanced Level for the General Certificate of Education. The author acknowledges gratefully the kindness of the examining authorities for permission to reproduce them here. The remaining questions are the author's.

Chapter 1: The Nature of the Constitution

1. How far is it true to say that the British Constitution is unwritten? 'O' (AEB).
2. What part do conventions play in the British Constitution? Illustrate your answer with examples of particular conventions. 'A' (AEB).
3. What is meant by the 'separation of powers'? How far is it a characteristic of the modern British Constitution? 'A' (UL).
4. What is meant by the phrase 'The supremacy of Parliament'? 'O' (AEB).
4. Critically examine the view that the Rule of Law has been dangerously eroded in this country. 'A' (AEB).
6. The legal Sovereign is Parliament; the political Sovereign is the people. Explain the meanings of these two statements. How far are they contradictory? 'O' (UL).

Chapter 2: Elections and the Party System

1. Describe the main changes in the franchise since 1900. 'O' (AEB).
2. Political parties give cohesion to Parliament. Discuss. 'A' (AEB).
3. Discuss the extent to which party political conferences influence the actions of (a) HM Government, and (b) HM Opposition. 'A' (AEB).
4. What anomalies and what advantages arise from the British 'simple majority' voting system? Discuss the value of other systems which might be substituted. 'A' (UL).
5. 'The party Whips are a help, not a hindrance to good and efficient government.'
6. 'The party system subordinates individual opinion to organised pressures.' Critically examine this statement. 'A' (AEB).

7. What qualifications and qualities are likely to enable a would-be Member of Parliament to secure (*a*) adoption as a candidate of one of the main political parties, and (*b*) election to the House of Commons? 'A' (UL).

Chapter 3: The Legislature

1. Give an account of the composition and functions of the House of Lords. 'O' (AEB).
2. Describe the procedure for dealing with Private Members' Bills. Why are such Bills considered desirable? 'A' (AEB).
3. Describe the main functions of the House of Commons.
4. 'The efficient secret of the English Constitution may be described as the close union, the nearly complete fusion, of the executive and legislative powers' (Bagehot). Criticise this statement, and evaluate its truth.
5. 'The House of Lords is a relic from a bygone age, but it still has its uses.' Consider this statement.
6. Write notes on any *three* of the following:

   (*a*) A Private Bill.
   (*b*) The Queen's Speech.
   (*c*) The Report Stage.
   (*d*) A 'Guillotine' motion. 'O' (AEB).

7. Write short accounts of *three* of the following:

   (*a*) The Speaker;
   (*b*) The Lord Chancellor.
   (*c*) Prorogation of Parliament.
   (*d*) The Queen's Speech.
   (*e*) Standing Committees of the House of Commons.

8. Describe the composition and functions of the various committees of the House of Commons. 'A' (AEB).
9. Describe the role that Select Committees play in the House of Commons. 'A' (AEB).
10. 'Matters affecting national security and Parliamentary privilege should be decided by the courts and not by a committee of Parliament.' Discuss 'A' (AEB).
11. Discuss the necessity of the privileges of the House of Commons. Should these privileges be enlarged or reduced? Give reasons for your answers. 'A' (AEB).
12. Describe what happens at Question Time in the House of Commons. What is the purpose of this procedure?
13. Describe a Parliamentary session in the House of Commons.

Chapter 4: The Executive

1. Describe the role of the Queen in the British Constitution today. 'O' (UL).

2. Describe the composition and work of the Privy Council. 'O' (UL).

3. What is meant by the 'Royal Prerogative'? How is it exercised in modern Britain? 'O' (AEB).

4. What factors does a British Prime Minister have to bear in mind when he chooses his Cabinet?

5. Give an account of the composition and functions of the Cabinet. 'O' (AEB).

6. Examine the reasons for the growth in the power of the Executive during this century. 'A' (AEB).

7. 'A British Prime Minister's powers are varied and enormous, but not without limits.' Discuss. 'A' (UL).

8. How is the Prime Minister of Great Britain chosen? What are his main functions? 'O' (AEB).

9. What powers are still possessed by a British Monarch in the Constitution of this country? 'A' (AEB).

10. 'Few Ministers have administrative ability, but they don't need it because they have the Civil Service to administer for them.' Discuss. 'A' (UL).

11. Describe and assess the importance of the conventions relating to the Cabinet. 'A' (AEB).

12. 'Cabinet government has been replaced by government by the Prime Minister.' 'Parliamentary sovereignty is supreme.' 'Sovereignty is vested in the electorate.' How far can these statements be reconciled? 'A' (AEB).

13. Describe the work of **either** the Treasury **or** the Foreign Office. 'O' (UL).

14. Describe the system of recruitment to the Civil Service.

15. What precisely is meant by the 'expertise' of the civil servants? In what are they expert?

16. 'Despite all the criticism we can still be proud of our Civil Service.' Discuss. 'A' (UL).

17. 'There is not enough contact between the Civil Service and the community it is there to serve.' How far do you consider this statement justified? 'A' (AEB).

18. Describe the means whereby the House of Commons controls public expenditure. How effective is House of Commons control? 'A' (AEB).

19. 'The Home Civil Service is still fundamentally the product of the nineteenth-century philosophy of the Northcote–Trevelyan Report.' Discuss. 'A' (AEB).

20. What do you consider to have been the most important changes in the British Constitution in the last ten years; 'A' (AEB).

21. Write notes on three of the following:

(*a*) The Cabinet Secretariat.
(*b*) Ministerial responsibility.
(*c*) Collective responsibility.
(*d*) The Attorney-General.

Chapter 5: The Public Corporations

1. What financial controls do Government Departments impose upon

public corporations? To what extent are these controls justified? 'A' (AEB).

2. How does a public corporation differ from a Government Department. 'A' (UL).

3. 'Public corporations are not public. We learn more about them from the Press than through Parliament.' Discuss.

4. Why did the major public corporations develop in their present form? How successful have been the arrangements made for their control by Parliament? 'A' (UL).

Chapter 6: Public Opinion, Pressure Groups, and the Mass Media

1. What importance may be attached to (*a*) public opinion polls; and (*b*) by-elections in Britain? 'A' (UL).

2. What 'interest groups' are active in British political life? By what means and with what success do they operate? 'A' (UL).

3. By what means can public opinion express itself on political issues? To what extent can it influence the Government? 'A' (UL).

4. How would you distinguish between a political party and a pressure group? How do pressure groups operate in the British system of Government? (LGTB).

5. What public control is there of (*a*) an LEA Comprehensive school, (*b*) a university, (*c*) the British Broadcasting Corporation, and (*d*) *The Times*? 'A' (UL).

6. 'We take pride in having a 'free'' Press which is an essential feature of the British Constitution.' Discuss.

7. 'Parliament ought to pass a statute abolishing social classes.' Discuss.

8. Describe what is meant by (*a*) a floating voter, (*b*) a deferential voter, and (*c*) a secular voter.

9. 'The greatest influences on voting behaviour are (*a*) social class, (*b*) workplace, and (*c*) religion.' How far do you agree with this assessment?

Chapters 7 and 8: The Law and the Courts: Judicial Officers and the Legal Profession

1. Give an account of the structure and composition of the High Court of Justice. 'O' (AEB).

2. Compare and contrast the composition and functions of a Crown Court with those of a county court.

3. Describe and comment on the organisation of the civil courts in England. 'A' (UL).

4. Give an account of the part played by laymen in the administration of justice in England today. How does the English legal system benefit from this use of laymen?

5. Give an account of the courts which administer the criminal law. 'O' (AEB).

6. Write notes on any three of the following:

(*a*) The Attorney-General.

(*b*) A puisne judge.

(*c*) The Chancery Division.

(*d*) The Lord President of the Council. 'O' (AEB).

7. 'The office of the unpaid, lay magistrate should be replaced by a system of paid, legally qualified magistrates.' Discuss. 'A' (AEB).

8. Give an account of those criminal offences which are described as 'crimes against the State'. 'A' (AEB).

9. Compare and contrast statute law with common law. 'O' (AEB).

10. What functions are performed by the Law Officers of the Crown? 'A' (AEB).

11. 'Justice must be seen to be done.' By what means is this dictum realised in this country? 'A' (AEB).

12. Explain the difference between a crime and a civil wrong. Illustrate your answer with examples. 'A' (AEB).

13. Describe the method of appointment of (*a*) Justices of the Peace, and (*b*) jurors. What are the rules regarding majority verdicts in criminal cases tried in Crown Courts?

14. Discuss the main agencies and committees specially concerned with law reform.

15. Describe the main provisions of the *Legal Aid Act, 1974*.

16. Describe the composition and jurisdiction of Crown Courts established under the *Courts Act, 1971*.

17. Write notes on **three** of the following:

1. Lord of Appeal in Ordinary.
2. Stipendiary Magistrate.
3. Circuit judge.
4. Recorder.

Chapter 9: Liberties of the Subject

1. What limitations are placed upon freedom of speech in Britain? 'O' (AEB).

2. Write notes on any **three** of the following:

(*a*) Writ of *Habeas Corpus*.

(*b*) Bail.

(*c*) The doctrine of *ultra vires*.

(*d*) The law of defamation. 'O' (AEB).

3. In what ways are the rights of the accused safeguarded in British courts? 'O' (AEB).

4. What limitations are placed by law upon the right to hold public meetings? To what extent are such limitations justifiable? 'A' (AEB).

5. What is meant by saying that there is freedom of association in Britain? To what extent, if at all, should this freedom be modified? 'A' (AEB).

6. What limitations are imposed upon freedom of expression in Britain at the present day? To what extent, in your opinion, are such limitations necessary? 'A' (AEB).

7. What safeguards does the British citizen have against tyranny? 'A' (UL).

8. 'The liberty of the individual can best be measured by the safeguard he enjoys in relation to the police and the magistrates.' What are these safeguards in Britain?

9. 'The organisation of the police is a difficult problem for any democratic society and one which in Britain has not yet been satisfactorily solved.' Discuss. 'A' (UL).

10. Discuss the merits and demerits of the present organisation of police forces in England and Wales.

11. What are the Judges' Rules? Of what importance are they in relation to the traditional freedoms of British subjects?

12. Discuss the rights which a private citizen has against the misuse of power by a police officer? How are complaints against the police dealt with by the authorities?

Chapter 10: Administrative Law and Justice

1. Define and illustrate what is meant by delegated legislation. What are the advantages of this method of law making? 'A' (UL).

2. 'Delegated legislation is essential for speedy and efficient government.' Discuss. 'A' (AEB).

3. For what purposes are Royal Commissions and Committees of Inquiry appointed? To what degree have such Commissions and Inquiries influenced government action? 'A' (AEB).

4. Why was the office of Parliamentary Commissioner for Administration created in 1966? To what extent, if at all, has he altered the role of the MP in relation to his constituents? 'A' (AEB).

5. What is meant by the phrase 'administrative tribunals'? Give varied examples and discuss their contribution to the public welfare. 'A' (UL).

6. Distinguish between (*a*) a bye-law; (*b*) an Order in Council; and (*c*) a Statutory Instrument. Give examples of the use of each type of legislation.

7. John comes to you with a complaint against a Government Department which has bungled an application of his. Advise him of the steps to be taken to bring the case before the Parliamentary Commissioner for Administration.

Chapter 11: Local Government

1. 'Local government in Britain is essentially government by committee, with all the advantages and defects inherent in committees.' Discuss.

2. Examine the part played by permanent officials in local government in England. 'A' (UL).

3. Describe and assess the relative importance of the various sources of income of the local authorities in England. 'A' (UL).

4. How are local councils financed? 'O' (AEB).

5. In what ways are local councils controlled by the central government? 'O' (AEB).

6. Write notes on any three of the following:

(*a*) the Chief Executive Officer.
(*b*) the Director of Social Services.
(*c*) District Auditor.
(*d*) Chief Education Officer.

7. Why was the *Local Government Act, 1888*, an important landmark in the history of local government in England and Wales? 'O' (AEB).

8. How are Councillors elected? What functions do they perform in local government? 'O' (AEB).

9. 'Judicial control of public authorities is inadequate.' Discuss. 'A' (AEB).

10. 'Party politics educate the public and make local government understandable to the electorate.' Discuss. 'A' (AEB).

11. Explain the significance of the doctrine of *ultra vires* as applied to local government. 'A' (AEB).

12. The Redcliffe-Maud Commission's Report (1966–9) noted four basic faults in the local government structure existing in 1969. What were they?

13. The purposes of local government, according to the Redcliffe-Maud Report (1969) were fourfold. Name the purposes.

14. What advantages did the Redcliffe-Maud Commission (1966–9) claim for its proposed system?

15. List the main functions of county councils and district councils under the *Local Government Act, 1972.*

16. 'Local-central relations should be seen as *the* constitutional issue of the 1980s'. Discuss.

Table of Statutes

Index

social factors, 208ff.
swing, 205–6
tactical, 34

Wales, 4
 devolution, 272
 local government of, 337
 Secretary of State for, 154
Walpole, Sir Robert, 21, 36, 137
Wallas, Graham, 210
Wapping, 313
Ward, Dame Irene, 67
Warrant (search), 256
Wasted votes, 43
Webb, Sidney and Beatrice, 38
Wedgwood Benn, Anthony, 53
Wells, H. G. 38
Welsh Nationalist Party, the, 39
Welsh Office, the, 154
Wesley, John and Charles, 317
Westlands, 105, 132, 375
'Wets', vi

Wharton, Lord, 35
Wheatley, Lord, 337
Whigs (*see also* Liberal Party), 35
Whips, 72–4, 360
Whitelaw, Lord, 57, 117
Whitley Council, 162, 249, 275
Whyatt Report, the, 286
Widdicombe, 342, 360, 363
William I, 19
William III (and Mary), 21
Wilson, Harold, xiv, 81, 163
Witan, the, 7
Women MPs, 94
Woolton, Lord, 135
Working class, vi, 203–8
Wright, Peter, 163, 283
Written constitution, 5, 218, 378
Writ (by-election), 71

Yonge, Sir William, 95

'Zircon', 169, 194, 278